Reading Street

Program Authors

Peter Afflerbach
Camille Blachowicz
Candy Dawson Boyd
Elena Izquierdo
Connie Juel
Edward Kame'enui
Donald Leu
Jeanne R. Paratore
P. David Pearson
Sam Sebesta
Deborah Simmons
Alfred Tatum
Sharon Vaughn
Susan Watts Taffe
Karen Kring Wixson

PEARSON

Glenview, Illinois • Boston, Massachusetts
Chandler, Arizona • Upper Saddle River, New Jersey

We dedicate Reading Street to
Peter Jovanovich.

His wisdom, courage,
and passion for education
are an inspiration to us all.

Accelerated Reader®

PEARSON

ISBN-13: 978-0-328-47025-9
ISBN-10: 0-328-47025-2
2 3 4 5 6 7 8 9 10 V064 14 13 12 11 10
CC1

Any Path, Any Pace

Reading STREET

CALLE de la Lectura

PEARSON

Who said so?

The Leading Researchers,

Program Authors

Peter Afflerbach, Ph.D.
Professor
Department of Curriculum and Instruction
University of Maryland at College Park

Camille L. Z. Blachowicz, Ph.D.
Professor of Education
National-Louis University

Candy Dawson Boyd, Ph.D.
Professor
School of Education
Saint Mary's College of California

Elena Izquierdo, Ph.D.
Associate Professor
University of Texas at El Paso

Connie Juel, Ph.D.
Professor of Education
School of Education
Stanford University

Edward J. Kame'enui, Ph.D.
Dean-Knight Professor of Education and Director
Institute for the Development of Educational Achievement and the Center on Teaching and Learning
College of Education
University of Oregon

Donald J. Leu, Ph.D.
John and Maria Neag Endowed Chair in Literacy and Technology
Director, The New Literacies Research Lab
University of Connecticut

Jeanne R. Paratore, Ed.D.
Associate Professor of Education
Department of Literacy and Language Development
Boston University

P. David Pearson, Ph.D.
Professor and Dean
Graduate School of Education
University of California, Berkeley

Sam L. Sebesta, Ed.D.
Professor Emeritus
College of Education
University of Washington, Seattle

Deborah Simmons, Ph.D.
Professor
College of Education and Human Development
Texas A&M University

Alfred W. Tatum, Ph.D.
Associate Professor and Director of the UIC Reading Clinic
University of Illinois at Chicago

Sharon Vaughn, Ph.D.
H. E. Hartfelder/Southland Corporation Regents Professor
Director, Meadows Center for Preventing Educational Risk
University of Texas

Susan Watts Taffe, Ph.D.
Associate Professor in Literacy
Division of Teacher Education
University of Cincinnati

Karen Kring Wixson, Ph.D.
Professor of Education
University of Michigan

Consulting Authors

Jeff Anderson, M.Ed.
Author and Consultant
San Antonio, Texas

Jim Cummins, Ph.D.
Professor
Department of Curriculum, Teaching and Learning
University of Toronto

Lily Wong Fillmore, Ph.D.
Professor Emerita
Graduate School of Education
University of California, Berkeley

Georgia Earnest García, Ph.D.
Professor
Language and Literacy Division
Department of Curriculum and Instruction
University of Illinois at Urbana-Champaign

George A. González, Ph.D.
Professor (Retired)
School of Education
University of Texas-Pan American, Edinburg

Valerie Ooka Pang, Ph.D.
Professor
School of Teacher Education
San Diego State University

Sally M. Reis, Ph.D.
Board of Trustees Distinguished Professor
Department of Educational Psychology
University of Connecticut

Jon Scieszka, M.F.A.
Children's Book Author
Founder of GUYS READ
Named First National Ambassador for Young People's Literature 2008

Grant Wiggins, Ed.D.
Educational Consultant
Authentic Education
Concept Development

Lee Wright, M.Ed.
Pearland, Texas

Practitioners, and Authors.

Consultant

Sharroky Hollie, Ph.D.
Assistant Professor
California State University
Dominguez Hills, CA

Teacher Reviewers

Dr. Bettyann Brugger
Educational Support Coordinator—Reading Office
Milwaukee Public Schools
Milwaukee, WI

Kathleen Burke
K–12 Reading Coordinator
Peoria Public Schools, Peoria, IL

Darci Burns, M.S.Ed.
University of Oregon

Bridget Cantrell
District Intervention Specialist
Blackburn Elementary School
Independence, MO

Tahira DuPree Chase, M.A., M.S.Ed.
Administrator of Elementary English Language Arts
Mount Vernon City School District
Mount Vernon, NY

Michele Conner
Director, Elementary Education
Aiken County School District
Aiken, SC

Georgia Coulombe
K–6 Regional Trainer/ Literacy Specialist
Regional Center for Training and Learning (RCTL), Reno, NV

Kelly Dalmas
Third Grade Teacher
Avery's Creek Elementary, Arden, NC

Seely Dillard
First Grade Teacher
Laurel Hill Primary School
Mt. Pleasant, SC

Jodi Dodds-Kinner
Director of Elementary Reading
Chicago Public Schools, Chicago, IL

Dr. Ann Wild Evenson
District Instructional Coach
Osseo Area Schools, Maple Grove, MN

Stephanie Fascitelli
Principal
Apache Elementary, Albuquerque Public Schools, Albuquerque, NM

Alice Franklin
Elementary Coordinator, Language Arts & Reading
Spokane Public Schools, Spokane, WA

Laureen Fromberg
Assistant Principal
PS 100 Queens, NY

Kimberly Gibson
First Grade Teacher
Edgar B. Davis Community School
Brockton, MA

Kristen Gray
Lead Teacher
A.T. Allen Elementary School
Concord, NC

Mary Ellen Hazen
State Pre-K Teacher
Rockford Public Schools #205
Rockford, IL

Patrick M. Johnson
Elementary Instructional Director
Seattle Public Schools, Seattle, WA

Theresa Jaramillo Jones
Principal
Highland Elementary School
Las Cruces, NM

Sophie Kowzun
Program Supervisor, Reading/ Language Arts, PreK–5
Montgomery County Public Schools
Rockville, MD

David W. Matthews
Sixth Grade Teacher
Easton Area Middle School
Easton, PA

Ana Nuncio
Editor and Independent Publisher
Salem, MA

Joseph Peila
Principal
Chappell Elementary School
Chicago, IL

Ivana Reimer
Literacy Coordinator
PS 100 Queens, NY

Sally Riley
Curriculum Coordinator
Rochester Public Schools
Rochester, NH

Dyan M. Smiley
Independent Educational Consultant

Michael J. Swiatowiec
Lead Literacy Teacher
Graham Elementary School
Chicago, IL

Dr. Helen Taylor
Director of English Education
Portsmouth City Public Schools
Portsmouth, VA

Carol Thompson
Teaching and Learning Coach
Independence School District
Independence, MO

Erinn Zeitlin
Kindergarten Teacher
Carderock Springs Elementary School
Bethesda, MD

UNIT 4

One of a Kind

In this Teacher's Edition Unit 4, Volume 1

Key

- SI Strategic Intervention
- OL On-Level
- A Advanced
- ELL ELL

In the First Stop on Reading Street

GO Digital!

See It!

- Big Question Video
- Concept Talk Video
- Interactive Sound-Spelling Cards
- Envision It! Animations

Hear It!

- eSelections
- Grammar Jammer
- Leveled Reader Database

Do It!

- Vocabulary Activities
- Story Sort
- 21st Century Skills Activities
- Online Assessment
- Letter Tile Drag and Drop

UNIT 1

Living and Learning

Key
SI Strategic Intervention
OL On-Level
A Advanced
ELL ELL

UNIT 2

Smart Solutions

Key
SI Strategic Intervention
OL On-Level
A Advanced
ELL ELL

Volume 1

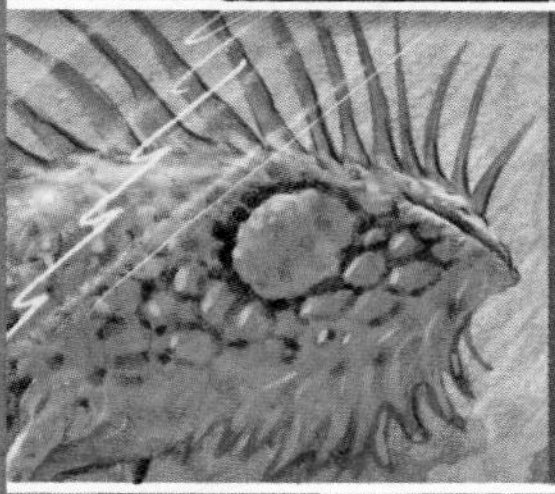

Volume 2

UNIT 3

People and Nature

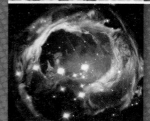

Key
- SI Strategic Intervention
- OL On-Level
- A Advanced
- ELL ELL

UNIT 4

One of a Kind

Key
SI Strategic Intervention
OL On-Level
A Advanced
ELL ELL

UNIT 5

Cultures

Key

- SI Strategic Intervention
- OL On-Level
- A Advanced
- ELL ELL

UNIT 6

Freedom

Key
- SI Strategic Intervention
- OL On-Level
- A Advanced
- ELL ELL

UNIT 4

Skills Overview

Key
T Tested Skill
Target Skill

		WEEK 1	WEEK 2
		 **The Man Who Invented Basketball** Biography, pp. 28–41 **My Turn at Bat: The Story of My Life** Autobiography, pp. 46–51	 **Hottest, Coldest, Highest, Deepest** Expository Text, pp. 62–75 **Paul Bunyan and the Great Lakes** Legend, pp. 80–83
Get Ready to Read	**Question of the Week**	How do talents make someone unique?	What makes nature's record holders unique?
	Amazing Words	*potential, mock, idle, audition, thrill, ecstatic, necessary, result, rise, succeed, verge*	*plunged, competitors, evergreens, lumber, valuable, champ, sprinter, acrobat, weaken, ranger*
	Phonics	T Irregular Plurals	T Vowels: *r*-Controlled /ėr/ spelled *ir, er, ur, ear, or,* and *ar, or, ore, oar*
	Literary Terms	Point of View	Author's Craft
	Story Structure/ Text Features	Time Line/Map	Bold Print/Key Words
Read and Comprehend	**Comprehension**	T **Skill** Generalize **Strategy** Summarize Review **Skill** Graphic Sources	T **Skill** Graphic Sources **Strategy** Important Ideas Review **Skill** Main Idea and Details
	Vocabulary	T **Skill** Unfamiliar Words	T **Skill** Unknown Words
	Fluency	Accuracy	Appropriate Phrasing/Punctuation Cues
Language Arts	**Writing**	Persuasive Text Trait: Conventions	Imaginative Story Trait: Conventions
	Conventions	Singular and Plural Nouns	Subject and Object Pronouns
	Spelling	Irregular Plurals	Vowels: *r*-Controlled
	Speaking/Listening	Presentation	Media Literacy: Weather Forecast
	Research Skills	Dictionary	Bar Graphs

The Big Question
What does it mean to be unique?

WEEK 3	WEEK 4	WEEK 5	WEEK 6

Rocks in His Head Biography, pp. 94–105 **Marvelous Marble Mania** Persuasive Text, pp. 110–113	**America's Champion Swimmer: Gertrude Ederle** Biography, pp. 124–139 **Women Athletes** Online Directories, pp. 144–147	**Fly, Eagle, Fly!** Folk Tale, pp. 158–171 **Purple Coyote** Trickster Tale, pp. 176–181	**Interactive Review**
Why is it valuable to have unique interests?	What unique traits does it take to be the first to do something?	What behaviors are unique to different animals?	Connect the Question of the Week to the Big Question
hobby, project, leftover, murmur, ancestor, ornament, descendant, forge, compartment	*imagination, magnificent, spectacle, ordinary, suspend, assemble, erect, organize, accompany, provision*	*coil, protrude, agile, armor, snout, scenery, extraordinary, intersection, pesky, unfurl*	Review Amazing Words for Unit 4
T Prefixes *pre-, mid-, over-, out-, bi-, de-*	T Suffixes *-er, -or, -ess, -ist*	T Syllables VCCCV	
Idioms	Word Choice	Sensory Details	
Problem and Solution	Chronological/ Sequence	Rising Action	
T **Skill** Fact and Opinion **Strategy** Inferring Review **Skill** Cause and Effect	T **Skill** Fact and Opinion **Strategy** Questioning Review **Skill** Generalize	T **Skill** Cause and Effect **Strategy** Monitor and Clarify Review **Skill** Draw Conclusions	Review Unit 4 Target Comprehension Skills
T **Skill** Multiple-Meaning Words	T **Skill** Multiple-Meaning Words	T **Skill** Unknown Words	Review Unit 4 Target Vocabulary Skills
Expression	Appropriate Phrasing	Rate	Review Unit 4 Fluency Skills
Biography Trait: Sentences	Autobiography Trait: Organization	Writing for Tests: Summary Trait: Word Choice	Quick Write for Fluency
Possessive Pronouns	Contractions	Prepositions	Review Conventions
Prefixes *pre-, mid-, over-, out-*	Suffixes *-er, -or, -ess, -ist*	Syllables VCCCV	Review Spelling patterns
Interview	Sportcast	Book Review	
Online Information	Bar Graphs	Outlining/ Summarizing	

UNIT 4

Monitor Progress

Don't Wait Until Friday

SUCCESS PREDICTOR	WEEK 1	WEEK 2	WEEK 3	WEEK 4
Word Reading **Phonics**	T Irregular Plurals	T Vowels: *r*-Controlled	T Prefixes *pre-, mid-, over-, out-, bi-, de-*	T Suffixes *-er, -or, -ess, -ist*
WCPM **Fluency**	Accuracy 95–105 WCPM	Appropriate Phrasing/ Punctuation Cues 95–105 WCPM	Expression 95–105 WCPM	Appropriate Phrasing 95–105 WCPM
Vocabulary **Oral Vocabulary/ Concept Development** (assessed informally)	potential mock idle audition thrill ecstatic necessary result rise succeed verge	plunged competitors evergreens lumber valuable champ sprinter acrobat weaken ranger	hobby project leftover murmur ancestor ornament descendant forge compartment	imagination magnificent spectacle ordinary suspend assemble erect organize accompany provision
Lesson Vocabulary	T disease T guard T freeze T terrible T study T popular T sports T basketball	T outrun T tides T deserts T waterfalls T peak T average T depth T erupted	T stamps T spare T chores T attic T labeled T customer T board	T drowned T strokes T medals T current T continued T stirred T celebrate
Retelling **Text Comprehension**	T **Skill** Generalize **Strategy** Summarize	T **Skill** Graphic Sources **Strategy** Important Ideas	T **Skill** Fact and Opinion **Strategy** Inferring	T **Skill** Fact and Opinion **Strategy** Questioning

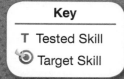

Key
- T Tested Skill
- ◎ Target Skill

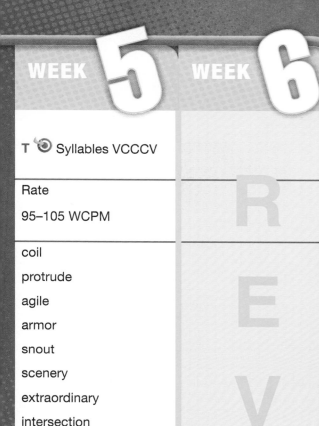

WEEK 5	WEEK 6
T ◎ Syllables VCCCV	
Rate 95–105 WCPM	R
coil protrude agile armor snout scenery extraordinary intersection pesky unfurl	E V I
T scrambled T gully T echoed T valley T reeds T clutched T thatch	E
T ◎ **Skill** Cause and Effect ◎ **Strategy** Monitor and Clarify	W

Online
ASSESSMENT
ReadingStreet.com

Online Classroom

Manage Data

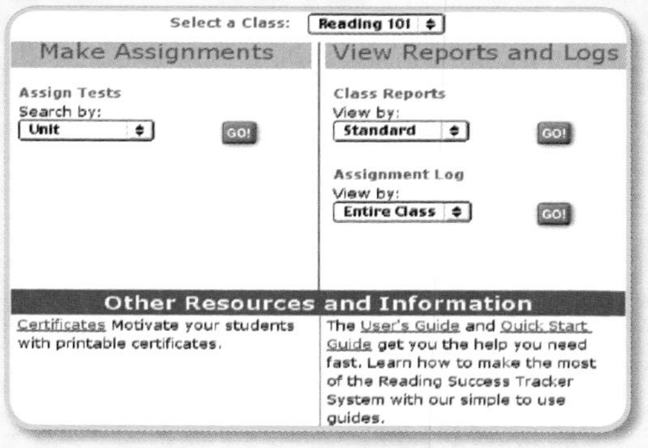

- Assign the Unit 4 Benchmark Test for students to take online.
- Online Assessment records results and generates reports by school, grade, classroom, or student.
- Use reports to disaggregate and aggregate Unit 4 skills and standards data to monitor progress.
- Based on class lists created to support the categories important for AYP (gender, ethnicity, migrant education, English proficiency, disabilities, economic status), reports let you track adequate yearly progress every six weeks.

Group

- Use results from Unit 4 Benchmark Tests taken online through Online Assessment to measure whether students have mastered the English-Language Arts Content Standards taught in this unit.
- Reports in Online Assessment suggest whether students need Extra Support or Intervention.

Individualized Instruction

- Tests are correlated to Unit 4 tested skills and standards so that prescriptions for individual teaching and learning plans can be created.
- Individualized prescriptions target instruction and accelerate student progress toward learning outcome goals.
- Prescriptions include remediation activities and resources to reteach Unit 4 skills and standards.

UNIT 4

Assessment and Grouping

for Data-Driven Instruction

4-Step Plan for Assessment

1 Diagnose and Differentiate
2 Monitor Progress
3 Assess and Regroup
4 Summative Assessment

STEP 1 Diagnose and Differentiate

Baseline Group Tests

Diagnose

To make initial grouping decisions, use the Baseline Group Tests, the *Texas Primary Reading Instruction (TPRI),* or another initial placement test. Depending on student's ability levels, you may have more than one of each group.

Differentiate

If... student performance is SI **then...** use the regular instruction and the daily **Strategic Intervention** small group lessons.

If... student performance is OL **then...** use the regular instruction and the daily **On-Level** small group lessons.

If... student performance is A **then...** use the regular instruction and the daily **Advanced** small group lessons.

Small Group Time

SI Strategic Intervention

- Daily small group lessons provide more intensive instruction, more scaffolding, more practice, and more opportunities to respond.
- Reteach lessons in the *First Stop on Reading Street* provide more instruction with target skills.
- Leveled readers build background and provide practice for target skills and vocabulary.

OL On-Level

- Explicit instructional routines teach core skills and strategies.
- Daily On-Level lessons provide more practice and more opportunities to respond.
- Independent activities provide practice for core skills and extension and enrichment options.
- Leveled readers provide additional reading and practice for core skills and vocabulary.

A Advanced

- Daily Advanced lessons provide instruction for accelerated learning.
- Leveled readers provide additional reading tied to lesson concepts and skills.

Additional Differentiated Learning Options

Reading Street Response to Intervention Kit

- Focused intervention lessons on the five critical areas of reading: phonemic awareness, phonics, vocabulary, comprehension, and fluency

My Sidewalks on Reading Street

- Intensive intervention for struggling readers

STEP 2 Monitor Progress

Don't Wait Until Friday

Weekly Tests

Fresh Reads for Fluency and Comprehension

Use these tools during lesson teaching to **monitor student progress.**

- **Skill and Strategy** instruction during reading
- **Don't Wait Until Friday** boxes to check word reading, retelling, fluency, and oral vocabulary
- **Weekly Assessment** on Day 5 checks comprehension and fluency
- **Reader's and Writer's Notebook** pages at point of use
- **Weekly Tests** assess target skills for the week
- **Fresh Reads** for Fluency and Comprehension

STEP 3 Assess and Regroup

Unit Assessment Charts in First Stop

Use these tools during lesson teaching to **assess and regroup.**

- **Weekly Assessments** Record results of weekly assessments in retelling, comprehension, and fluency to track student progress.
- **Unit Benchmark Tests** Administer this assessment to check mastery of unit skills.
- **Regroup** We recommend the first regrouping to be at the end of Unit 2. Use weekly assessment information and Unit Benchmark Test performance to inform regrouping decisions. Then regroup at the end of each subsequent unit.

Group Baseline Group Test →	Regroup Units 1 and 2 →	Regroup Unit 3 →	Regroup Unit 4 →	Regroup Unit 5 →	End of Year
Weeks 1-6	Weeks 7-12	Weeks 13-18	Weeks 19-24	Weeks 25-30	Weeks 31-36

Outside assessments, such as *TPRI, DRA,* and *DIBELS*, may recommend regrouping at other times during the year.

STEP 4 Summative Assessment

Unit and End-of-Year Benchmark Tests

Use these tools after lesson teaching to **assess students.**

- **Unit Benchmark Tests** Use to measure a student's mastery of each unit's skills.
- **End-of-Year Benchmark Test** Use to measure a student's mastery of program skills covered in all six units.

UNIT 4

Concept Launch

Understanding By Design

Grant Wiggins, Ed. D.
Reading Street Author

“A big idea is a concept, theme, or issue that gives meaning and connection to discrete facts and skills…In an education for understanding, a vital challenge is to highlight the big ideas, show how they prioritize the learning, and help students understand their value for making sense of all the ‘stuff’ of content.”

One of a Kind

Reading Street Online

www.ReadingStreet.com

- Big Question Video
- eSelections
- Envision It! Animations
- Story Sort

THE BIG ?

What does it mean to be unique?

Let's **Think** About Reading!

The Man Who Invented Basketball: James Naismith and His Amazing Game
BIOGRAPHY

connect to Social Studies

How do talents make someone unique?

Paired Selection
My Turn at Bat: The Story of My Life AUTOBIOGRAPHY

Hottest, Coldest, Highest, Deepest
EXPOSITORY TEXT

connect to Science

What makes nature's record holders unique?

Paired Selection
Paul Bunyan and the Great Lakes LEGEND

Rocks in His Head
BIOGRAPHY

connect to Science

Why is it valuable to have unique interests?

Paired Selection
Marvelous Marble Mania PERSUASIVE TEXT

America's Champion Swimmer: Gertrude Ederle
BIOGRAPHY

connect to Social Studies

What unique traits does it take to be the first to do something?

Paired Selection
Women Athletes ONLINE DIRECTORIES

Fly, Eagle, Fly!
FOLK TALE

connect to Science

What behaviors are unique to different animals?

Paired Selection
Purple Coyote TRICKSTER TALE

UNIT 4

Small Group Time

Flexible Pacing Plans

Key

- SI Strategic Intervention
- OL On-Level
- A Advanced
- ELL ELL

SI OL A

5 Day Plan

DAY 1	• Reinforce the Concept • Read Leveled Readers Concept Literacy Below-Level
DAY 2	• Comprehension Skill • Comprehension Strategy • Revisit Main Selection
DAY 3	• Vocabulary Skill • Revisit Main Selection
DAY 4	• Practice Retelling • Read/Revisit Paired Selection
DAY 5	• Reread for Fluency • Reread Leveled Readers

4 Day Plan

DAY 1	• Reinforce the Concept • Read Leveled Readers Concept Literacy Below-Level
DAY 2	• Comprehension Skill • Comprehension Strategy • Revisit Main Selection
DAY 3	• Vocabulary Skill • Revisit Main Selection
DAY 4	• Practice Retelling • Read/Revisit Paired Selection • Reread for Fluency • Reread Leveled Readers

3 Day Plan

DAY 1	• Reinforce the Concept • Read Leveled Readers Concept Literacy Below-Level
DAY 2	• Comprehension Skill • Comprehension Strategy • Revisit Main Selection
DAY 3	• Practice Retelling • Read/Revisit Paired Selection • Reread for Fluency • Reread Leveled Readers

ELL

5 Day Plan

DAY 1	• Frontload Concept • Preteach Skills • Conventions/Writing
DAY 2	• Review Concept/Skills • Frontload and Read Main Selection • Conventions/Writing
DAY 3	• Review Concept/Skills • Reread Main Selection • Conventions/Writing
DAY 4	• Review Concept/Skills • Read ELL or ELD Reader • Conventions/Writing
DAY 5	• Review Concept/Skills • Reread ELL or ELD Reader • Conventions/Writing

4 Day Plan

DAY 1	• Frontload Concept • Preteach Skills • Conventions/Writing
DAY 2	• Review Concept/Skills • Frontload and Read Main Selection • Conventions/Writing
DAY 3	• Review Concept/Skills • Reread Main Selection • Conventions/Writing
DAY 4	• Review Concept/Skills • Read ELL or ELD Reader • Conventions/Writing

3 Day Plan

DAY 1	• Frontload Concept • Preteach Skills • Conventions/Writing
DAY 2	• Review Concept/Skills • Frontload and Read Main Selection • Conventions/Writing
DAY 3	• Review Concept/Skills • Read ELL or ELD Reader • Conventions/Writing

This Week's ELL Overview

Grade 3 • Unit 4 • Week 1
The Man Who Invented Basketball
20a–53r
and DI•16–DI•25

ELL Handbook

- Maximize Literacy and Cognitive Engagement
- Research Into Practice
- Full Weekly Support for Every Selection

  The Man Who Invented Basketball
  - Multi-Lingual Summaries in Five Languages
  - Selection-Specific Vocabulary Word Cards
  - Frontloading/Reteaching for Comprehension Skill Lessons
  - ELD and ELL Reader Study Guides
- Transfer Activities
- Professional Development

Daily Leveled ELL Notes

ELL notes appear throughout this week's instruction and ELL Support is on the DI pages of your Teacher's Edition. The following is a sample of an ELL note from this week.

English Language Learners

Beginning Write several irregular plural words from the Decodable Reader on the board, such as *men, geese, children,* and *leaves.* Point to each word as you say it aloud. Then have students explain the rule for forming each plural word.

Intermediate After reading, have students make a T-chart. On the left side of the chart have them list all of the irregular plural words in the Decodable Reader. On the right side of the chart have students write the singular form of each word.

Advanced After reading, have students choose five irregular plural words and use them in complete sentences about the story.

Advanced High After reading the story, have students write a short paragraph that uses three or four irregular plural words.

ELL by Strand

The ELL lessons on this week's Support for English Language Learners pages are organized by strand. They offer additional scaffolding for the core curriculum. Leveled support notes on these pages address the different proficiency levels in your class. See pages DI•16–DI•25.

ELL Guy
Dr. Jim Cummins

The Three Pillars of ELL Instruction

ELL Strands	Activate Prior Knowledge	Access Content	Extend Language
Vocabulary pp. DI•17–DI•18	Preteach	Reteach	Leveled Writing Activities
Reading Comprehension p. DI•22	Frontloading	Sheltered Reading	After Reading
Phonics, Spelling, and Word Analysis p. DI•20	Preteach and Model	Practice	Leveled Practice Activities
Listening Comprehension p. DI•19	Prepare for the Read Aloud	First Listening	Second Listening
Conventions and Writing pp. DI•24–DI•25	Preteach/Introduce	Practice	Leveled Practice Activities/ Leveled Writing Activities
Concept Development p. DI•16	Prior Knowledge	Discuss Concept	Daily Concept and Vocabulary Development

This Week's Practice Stations Overview

Six Weekly Practice Stations with Leveled Activities can be found at the beginning of each week of instruction. For this week's Practice Stations, see pp. 20h–20i.

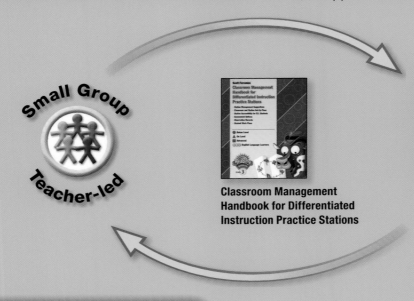

Classroom Management Handbook for Differentiated Instruction Practice Stations

Practice Stations

Daily Leveled Center Activities

- ● Below
- ■ Advanced
- ▲ On-Level
- ELL

Practice Stations Flip Charts

Word Wise

Word Work

Words to Know

Let's Write

Read For Meaning

Get Fluent

	Word Wise	Word Work	Words to Know	Let's Write	Read For Meaning	Get Fluent
Objectives	• Spell words with consonant patterns *wr, kn, gn, st,* and *mb.*	• Identify and pronounce words with consonant patterns *wr, kn, gn, st,* and *mb.*	• Identify and define words with prefixes and suffixes.	• Compare and contrast two animals.	• Identify cause and effect in nonfiction.	• Read aloud with expression.
Materials	• *Word Wise* Flip Chart Activity 16 • Teacher-made word cards • paper • pencil	• *Word Work* Flip Chart Activity 16 • Teacher-made word cards • paper • pencil	• *Words to Know* Flip Chart Activity 16 • Teacher-made word cards • dictionary • paper • pencil	• *Let's Write* Flip Chart Activity 16 • Leveled Readers • paper • pencil	• *Read for Meaning* Flip Chart Activity 16 • Leveled Readers • paper • pencil	• *Get Fluent* Flip Chart Activity 16 • Leveled Readers

This Week on Reading Street!

Question of the Week
How do talents make someone unique?

Daily Plan

Whole Group
- Generalize
- Unfamiliar Words
- Fluency/Accuracy
- Writing/Conventions
- Research and Inquiry

Don't Wait Until Friday

MONITOR PROGRESS — **Success Predictor**

Day 1	Day 2	Day 3	Day 4	Day 5
Check Oral Vocabulary	Check Word Reading	Check Retelling	Check Fluency	Check Oral Vocabulary

Small Group

Teacher Led
- Reading Support
- Skill Support
- Fluency Practice

Practice Stations

Independent Activities

Customize Literacy More support for a balanced literacy appoach, see pp. CL•1–CL•47.

Customize Writing More support for a customized writing approach, see pp. CW•1–CW•10.

Whole Group
- Writing: Persuasive Text
- Conventions: Singular and Plural Pronouns
- Spelling: Irregular Plurals

Assessment
- Weekly Tests
- Day 5 Assessment
- Fresh Reads

This Week's Reading Selections

Main Selection
Genre: **Biography**

Paired Selection
Genre: **Autobiography**

Decodable Readers

Leveled Readers

ELL and ELD Readers

Resources on Reading Street!

	Build Concepts	Phonics	Comprehension
Whole Group	 Let's Talk About pp. 20–21	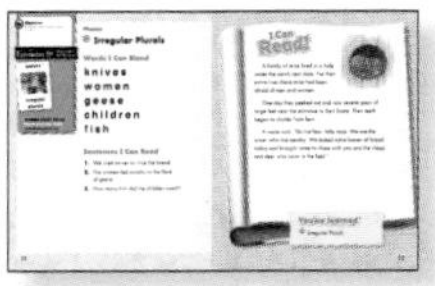 Phonics Skill Lesson pp. 22–23  Decodable Readers  Sound–Spelling Cards	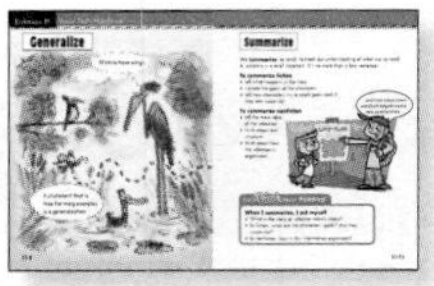 Envision It! Skills/ Strategies 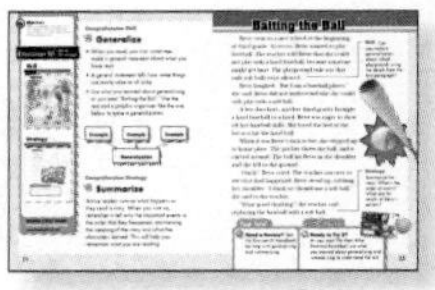 Comprehension Skill Lesson pp. 24–25
Go Digital	• Concept Talk Video	• Interactive Sound-Spelling Cards • Decodable eReaders	• Envision It! Animations • eSelections
Small Group and Independent Practice	 The Man Who Invented Basketball pp. 28–41  ELL and ELD Readers  Leveled Readers  Decodable Readers	 Decodable Readers  Practice Station Flip Chart	 The Man Who Invented Basketball pp. 28–41  ELL and ELD Readers  Leveled Readers 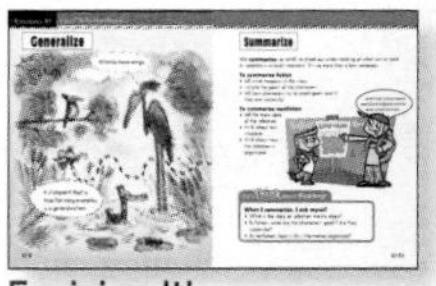 Envision It! Skills/ Strategies 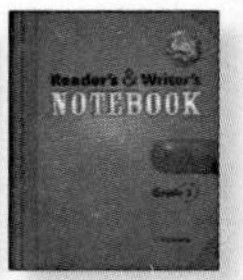 Reader's and Writer's Notebook  Practice Station Flip Chart
Go Digital	• eReaders • eSelections • Decodable eReaders	• Letter Tile Drag and Drop • Decodable eReaders	• Envision It! Animations • eSelections • eReaders
Customize Literacy	• Leveled Readers • Decodable Readers	• Decodable Readers	• Envision It! Skills and Strategies Handbook • Leveled Readers
Go Digital	• Concept Talk Video • Decodable eReaders • eReaders	• Decodable eReaders	• Envision It! Animations • eReaders • Decodable eReaders

Question of the Week
How do talents make someone unique?

Vocabulary	Fluency	Conventions and Writing
Envision It! Vocabulary Cards; Vocabulary Skill Lesson pp. 26–27	Let's Learn It! pp. 52–53; Decodable and Leveled Readers	Let's Write It! pp. 44–45; Decodable Readers
• Envision It! Vocabulary Cards • Vocabulary Activities	• eSelection • Decodable eReaders • eReaders	• Grammar Jammer
Envision It! Vocabulary Cards; The Man Who Invented Basketball pp. 28–41; Practice Station Flip Chart; Words!; Reader's and Writer's Notebook	The Man Who Invented Basketball pp. 28–41; Practice Station Flip Chart; Leveled Readers; ELL and ELD Readers	Reader's and Writer's Notebook; The Man Who Invented Basketball pp. 28–41; Practice Station Flip Chart
• Envision It! Vocabulary Cards • Vocabulary Activities • eSelection	• eSelection • eReaders	• Grammar Jammer
• Envision It! Vocabulary Cards	• Leveled Readers • Decodable Readers	• Reader's and Writer's Notebook
• Vocabulary Activities	• eReaders • Decodable eReaders	• Grammar Jammer

Week 1

My 5-Day Planner for Reading Street!

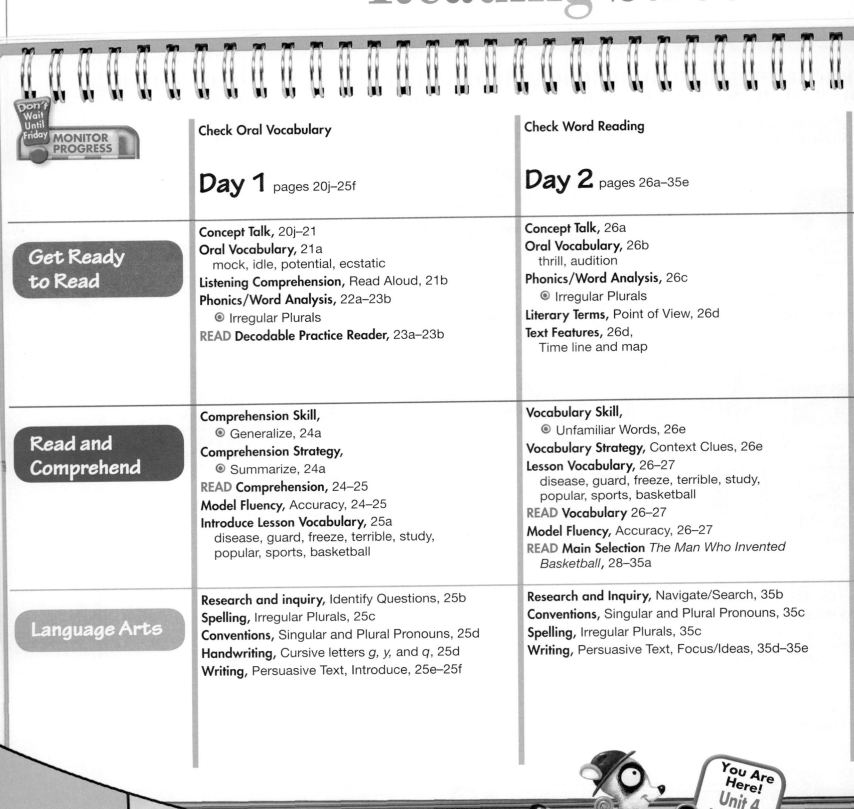

Don't Wait Until Friday MONITOR PROGRESS

	Check Oral Vocabulary **Day 1** pages 20j–25f	Check Word Reading **Day 2** pages 26a–35e
Get Ready to Read	**Concept Talk,** 20j–21 **Oral Vocabulary,** 21a mock, idle, potential, ecstatic **Listening Comprehension,** Read Aloud, 21b **Phonics/Word Analysis,** 22a–23b ◎ Irregular Plurals READ **Decodable Practice Reader,** 23a–23b	**Concept Talk,** 26a **Oral Vocabulary,** 26b thrill, audition **Phonics/Word Analysis,** 26c ◎ Irregular Plurals **Literary Terms,** Point of View, 26d **Text Features,** 26d, Time line and map
Read and Comprehend	**Comprehension Skill,** ◎ Generalize, 24a **Comprehension Strategy,** ◎ Summarize, 24a READ **Comprehension,** 24–25 **Model Fluency,** Accuracy, 24–25 **Introduce Lesson Vocabulary,** 25a disease, guard, freeze, terrible, study, popular, sports, basketball	**Vocabulary Skill,** ◎ Unfamiliar Words, 26e **Vocabulary Strategy,** Context Clues, 26e **Lesson Vocabulary,** 26–27 disease, guard, freeze, terrible, study, popular, sports, basketball READ **Vocabulary** 26–27 **Model Fluency,** Accuracy, 26–27 READ **Main Selection** *The Man Who Invented Basketball*, 28–35a
Language Arts	**Research and inquiry,** Identify Questions, 25b **Spelling,** Irregular Plurals, 25c **Conventions,** Singular and Plural Pronouns, 25d **Handwriting,** Cursive letters *g, y,* and *q*, 25d **Writing,** Persuasive Text, Introduce, 25e–25f	**Research and Inquiry,** Navigate/Search, 35b **Conventions,** Singular and Plural Pronouns, 35c **Spelling,** Irregular Plurals, 35c **Writing,** Persuasive Text, Focus/Ideas, 35d–35e

Question of the Week

How do talents make someone unique?

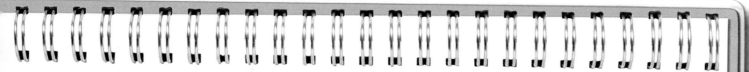

Check Retelling **Day 3** pages 36a–45c	Check Fluency **Day 4** pages 46a–53e	Check Oral Vocabulary **Day 5** pages 53f–53q
Concept Talk, 36a **Oral Vocabulary,** 36b necessary, result **Phonics/Word Analysis,** 36c–36d ◎ Irregular Plurals **Decodable Story,** 36d **Comprehension Check,** 36e **Check Retelling,** 36f	**Concept Talk,** 46a **Oral Vocabulary,** 46b succeed, rise, verge **Phonics/Word Analysis,** 46c–46f Review Consonant Patterns *wr, kn, st, mb, gn* **Decodable Story,** 46f **Genre,** Autobiography, 46g	**Concept Wrap Up,** 53f **Check Oral Vocabulary,** 53g mock, idle, potential, ecstatic, thrill, audition, necessary, result, succeed, rise, verge **Amazing Ideas,** 53g Review ◎ Generalize, 53h Review ◎ Unfamiliar Words, 53h Review ◎ Irregular Plurals, 53i Review **Literary Terms** 53i
READ **Main selection,** *The Man Who Invented Basketball*, 36–41a **Retelling,** 42–43 **Think Critically,** 43a **Model Frequency,** Accuracy, 43b **Research and Study Skills,** 43c Dictionary	READ **Paired Selection,** 46–51a "My Turn at Bat" **Let's Learn It!,** 52a–53a Fluency: Accuracy Vocabulary: ◎ Unfamiliar Words Listening and Speaking: Presentation	**Fluency Assessment,** WCPM, 53j–53k **Comprehension Assessment,** ◎ Generalize, 53l–53m
Research and Inquiry, Analyze, 43d **Conventions,** Singular and Plural Pronouns, 43e **Spelling,** Irregular Plurals, 43e **Let's Write It!,** Persuasive Text, 44–45 **Writing,** Persuasive Text, Persuasive Elements, 45a–45c	**Research and Inquiry,** Synthesize, 53b **Conventions,** Singular and Plural Pronouns, 53c **Spelling,** Irregular Plurals, 53c **Writing,** Persuasive Text, Revising, 53d–53e	**Research and Inquiry,** Communicate, 53n **Conventions,** Singular and Plural Pronouns, 53o **Spelling Test,** Irregular Plurals, 53o **Writing,** Persuasive Text, Singular and Plural Pronouns, 53p **Quick Write for Fluency,** 53q

Week 1

Grouping Options for Differentiated Instruction
Turn the page for the small group time lesson plan.

Planning Small Group Time on Reading Street!

SMALL GROUP TIME RESOURCES

Look for this Small Group Time box each day to help meet the individual needs of all your children. Differentiated Instruction lessons appear on the DI pages at the end of each week.

DAY 1

Teacher Led

SI Strategic Intervention	OL On-Level	A Advanced
Teacher Led • Reinforce the Concept • **Read** Concept Literacy Reader or Below-Level Reader	**Teacher Led** • Explain the Concept • **Read** On-Level Reader	**Teacher Led** • Explain the Concept • **Read** Advanced Reader

ELL Place English language learners in the groups that correspond to their reading abilities in English.

Practice Stations
- Read for Meaning
- Get Fluent
- Word Work

Independent Activities
- Concept Talk Video
- *Reader's and Writer's Notebook*
- Research and Inquiry

ELL

ELL Reader Advanced Advanced High

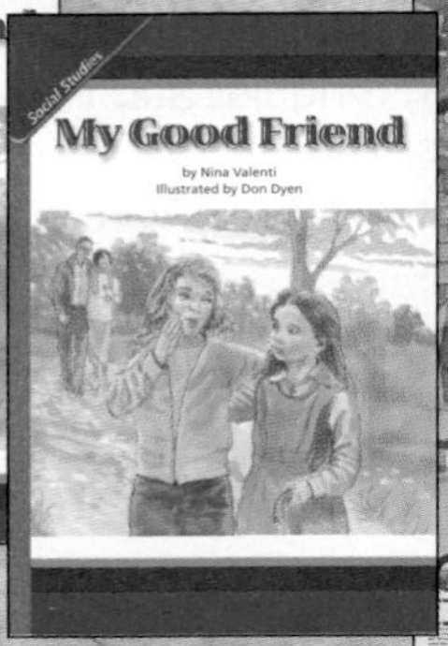

ELD Reader Beginning Intermediate

ELL Poster

	Day 1
SI Strategic Intervention	**Reinforce the Concept,** DI•1–DI•2 Read **Decodable Reader,** and **Concept Literacy Reader** or **Below-Level Reader**
OL On-Level	**Expand the Concept,** DI•7 Read **On-Level Reader**
A Advanced	**Extend the Concept,** DI•12 Read **Advanced Reader**
ELL English Language Learners	DI•16–DI•25 **Frontload Concept** **Preteach Skills** **Writing**

Reading Street Response to Intervention Kit

Reading Street Practice Stations Kit

Question of the Week

How do talents make someone unique?

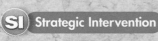

SI Strategic Intervention

Below-Level Reader

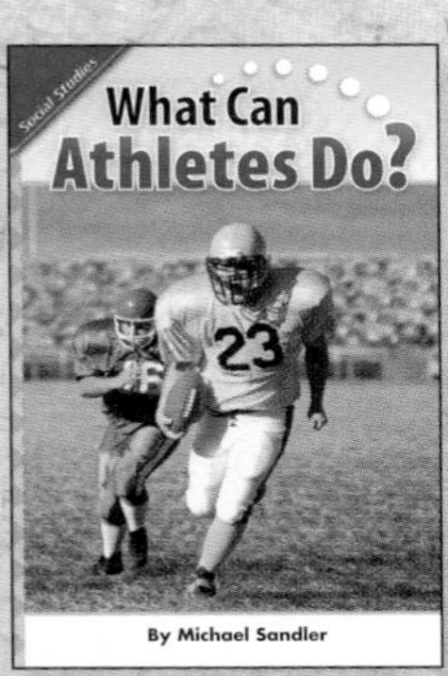

Concept Literacy Reader

OL On-Level

On-Level Reader

A Advanced

Advanced Reader

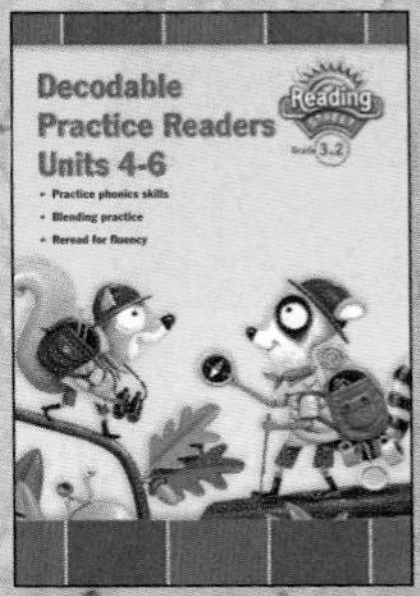

Decodable Practice Readers

The Man Who Invented Basketball pp. 28–41

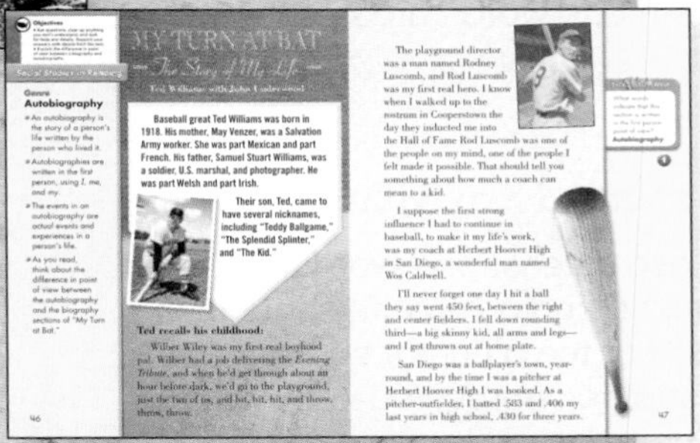

My Turn at Bat pp. 46–51

Small Group Weekly Plan

Day 2	Day 3	Day 4	Day 5
Reinforce Comprehension, DI•3 Revisit **Main Selection,** p. 28	**Reinforce Vocabulary,** DI•4 Read/Revisit **Main Selection**	**Reinforce Comprehension,** Practice Retelling, DI•5 Genre Focus Read/Revisit **Paired Selection**	**Practice Fluency,** DI•6 Reread **Concept Literacy Reader** or **Below-Level Reader**
Expand Comprehension, DI•8 Revisit **Main Selection**	**Expand Vocabulary,** DI•9 Read/Revisit **Main Selection**	**Expand Comprehension,** Practice Retelling, DI•10 Genre Focus Read/Revisit **Paired Selection**	**Practice Fluency,** DI•11 Reread **On-Level Reader**
Extend Comprehension, DI•13 Revisit **Main Selection**	**Extend Vocabulary,** DI•14 Read/Revisit **Main Selection**	**Extend Comprehension,** Genre Focus, DI•15 Read/Revisit **Paired Selection**	**Practice Fluency,** DI•15 Reread **Advanced Reader**
DI•16–DI•25 **Review Concept/Skills** **Frontload Main Selection** **Practice**	DI•16–DI•25 **Review Concept/Skills** Reread **Main Selection** **Practice**	DI•16–DI•25 **Review Concept** Read **ELL/ELD Readers** **Practice**	DI•16–DI•25 **Review Concept/Skills** Reread **ELL/ELD Reader** **Writing**

Week 1

Practice Stations for Everyone on Reading Street!

Word Wise

Consonant patterns *wr, kn, gn, st,* and *mb*

Objectives

- Spell words with consonant patterns *wr, kn, gn, st,* and *mb*.

Materials

- *Word Wise* Flip Chart Activity 16
- Teacher-made word cards
- paper
- pencil

Differentiated Activities

● Choose at least one word card, with *wr, kn, gn, st,* and *mb*. Write sentences using each of the different spelling patterns. List other words you know with spelling patterns *wr, kn, gn, st,* and *mb*.

▲ Choose at least two word cards, with *wr, kn, gn, st,* and *mb*. Write two sentences for using words with each different spelling pattern. List other words you know with these spellings.

■ Choose at least three word cards, with *wr, kn, gn, st,* and *mb*. Write three sentences using each spelling pattern. List other words with these spellings.

Technology

- Online Dictionary

Word Work

Consonant patterns *wr, kn, gn, st,* and *mb*

Objectives

- Identify and pronounce words with consonant patterns *wr, kn, gn, st,* and *mb*.

Materials

- *Word Work* Flip Chart Activity 16
- Teacher-made word cards
- paper
- pencil

Differentiated Activities

● Choose word cards until you have at least one of each with *wr, kn, gn, st,* and *mb*. Write your words in a list. Quietly say each word aloud. Write a rhyming word for each of your words.

▲ Choose word cards until you have at least two of each with *wr, kn, gn, st,* and *mb*. Write your words in a list, and quietly say each word aloud. Write a rhyming word for each of your words.

■ Choose word cards until you have at least three of each with consonant patterns *wr, kn, gn, st,* and *mb*. Quietly say each word aloud. Write a short poem using some of your words.

Technology

- Modeled Pronunciation Audio CD

Words to Know

Prefixes and suffixes

Objectives

- Identify and define words with prefixes and suffixes.

Materials

- *Words to Know* Flip Chart Activity 16
- Teacher-made word cards
- dictionary
- paper
- pencil

Differentiated Activities

● Choose four word cards. Write your words in a list. Use a dictionary to check each word's meaning. Write a sentence for each of your words. Circle the prefix or suffix in each word.

▲ Choose six word cards. Write your words in a list, and check each word's meaning in a dictionary. Write a sentence for each word. Circle the prefix or suffix in each word.

■ Choose eight word cards, and write each word in a list. Write each word's meaning, and check it in a dictionary. Write a sentence for each word.

Technology

- Online Dictionary

Use this week's materials from the Reading Street Leveled Practice Stations Kit to organize this week's stations.

Key

- ● Below-Level Activities
- ▲ On-Level Activities
- ■ Advanced Activities

Practice Station Flip Chart

Let's Write!

Compare and contrast

Objectives

- Compare and contrast two animals.

Materials

- *Let's Write!* Flip Chart Activity 16
- Leveled Readers
- paper
- pencil

Differentiated Activities

● Choose two animals. Think about how the animals are alike and different. Write one sentence telling about how the animals are alike. Write one sentence telling about how they are different.

▲ Choose two animals, and think about how the animals are alike and different. Write two sentences that compare the animals. Write two sentences that contrast the animals.

■ Think about comparisons and contrasts between two of the animals. Write a paragraph that compares and contrasts the animals. Proofread your paragraph, and focus on word choice.

Technology

- Leveled Reader Database

Read for Meaning

Cause and effect

Objectives

- Identify cause and effect in nonfiction.

Materials

- *Read for Meaning* Flip Chart Activity 16
- Leveled Readers
- paper
- pencil

Differentiated Activities

● Read one of the books your teacher provides and think about what happens. What caused this to happen? Write one sentence telling about an effect. Write one sentence telling what caused the effect.

▲ Read one of the books your teacher provides, and think about what happens in the selection. Draw a two-column chart labeled Cause and Effect. Tell what happened in the Effect column. Tell the reasons in the Cause column.

■ As you read the book you chose, think about causes and effects. Choose one effect, and write a short paragraph telling what happened. Include sentences telling what caused this to happen.

Technology

- Leveled Reader Database

Get Fluent

Practice fluent reading

Objectives

- Read aloud with expression.

Materials

- *Get Fluent* Flip Chart Activity 16
- Leveled Readers

Differentiated Activities

● Work with a partner. Choose a Concept Literacy Reader or Below-Level Reader. Take turns reading a page from the book. Use the readers to practice correct expression. Provide feedback as needed.

▲ Work with a partner. Choose an On-Level Reader. Take turns reading a page from the book. Use the reader to practice correct expression. Provide feedback as needed.

■ Work with a partner. Choose an Advanced Reader. Take turns reading a page from the book. Use the reader to practice correct expression. Provide feedback as needed.

Technology

- Leveled Reader Database
- Reading street Readers CD-ROM

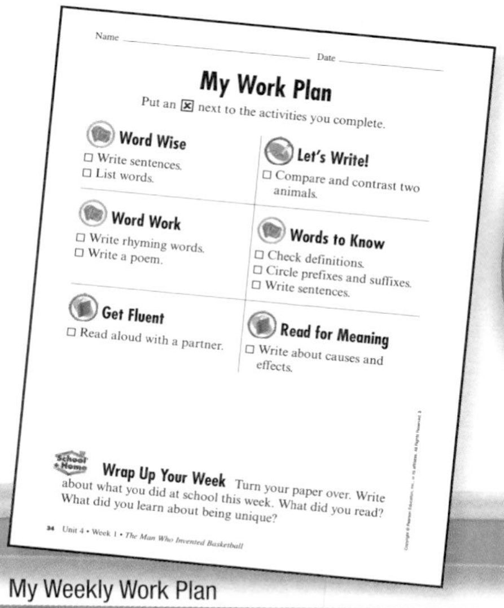

Name ______________ Date ______________

My Work Plan

Put an ☒ next to the activities you complete.

Word Wise
- ☐ Write sentences.
- ☐ List words.

Let's Write!
- ☐ Compare and contrast two animals.

Word Work
- ☐ Write rhyming words.
- ☐ Write a poem.

Words to Know
- ☐ Check definitions.
- ☐ Circle prefixes and suffixes.
- ☐ Write sentences.

Get Fluent
- ☐ Read aloud with a partner.

Read for Meaning
- ☐ Write about causes and effects.

School + Home **Wrap Up Your Week** Turn your paper over. Write about what you did at school this week. What did you read? What did you learn about being unique?

34 Unit 4 • Week 1 • *The Man Who Invented Basketball*

My Weekly Work Plan

Week 1

Objectives
- Introduce the weekly concept.
- Develop oral vocabulary.

Today at a Glance

Oral Vocabulary
mock, idle, potential, ecstatic

Phonics/Word Analysis
◎ Irregular plurals

Comprehension
◎ Generalize
◎ Summarize

Reading
"Batting the Ball"

Fluency
Accuracy

Lesson Vocabulary
Tested vocabulary

Research and Inquiry
Identify questions

Spelling
Irregular plurals

Conventions
Singular and plural pronouns

Handwriting
Cursive letters *g, y, q*

Writing
Persuasive text

Concept Talk

Question of the Week
How do talents make someone unique?

Introduce the concept

To further explore the unit concept of One of a Kind, this week students will read, write, and talk about what makes each person unique. Write the Question of the Week on the board.

ROUTINE Activate Prior Knowledge Team Talk

1. **Think** Have students think about how a person's talents make him or her unique.
2. **Pair** Have pairs of students discuss the Question of the Week.
3. **Share** Call on a few students to share their ideas with the group. Guide the discussion and encourage elaboration with prompts such as:
   - What are some talents a person could have?
   - Who is the most talented singer or athlete you can think of?
   - How does that person's talent make him or her unique?

Routines Flip Chart

Anchored Talk

Develop oral vocabulary

Have students turn to pp. 20–21 in their Student Editions. Look at each of the photos. Then, use the prompts to guide discussion and create the *How talents make people someone unique* concept map. Remind students to ask and answer questions with appropriate detail, and to build on the ideas of others.

- What kind of talent do you think the girl holding the flowers has? (dancing) Let's add *Dancing* to our concept map.
- Could these soccer players have special talents? (Yes, they might run fast or kick really far.) They won't be *idle* for long. Soon they will be running. Let's add *Running* and *Kicking* to our concept map.

Objectives
• Listen closely when someone speaks, ask questions about the topic he or she is talking about, and comment about the topic. • Take part in discussions and offer ideas that build on the ideas of others.
Oral Vocabulary
Let's Talk About
Being Unique
Share ideas about how special skills and talents make people unique.
Make and listen to comments about ways people are unique.
Pose and answer questions about what we can learn from the talents of others.
READING STREET ONLINE
CONCEPT TALK VIDEO
www.ReadingStreet.com
You've learned 147 Amazing Words so far this year!
20
21

Student Edition pp. 20–21

Amazing Words

You've learned 1 4 7 words so far.

You'll learn 0 1 1 words this week!

mock	necessary
idle	result
potential	succeed
ecstatic	rise
thrill	verge
audition	

Writing on Demand

Writing Fluency
Ask students to respond to the photos on pp. 20–21 by writing as well as they can and as much as they can about how talents can make someone unique.

- Point out the children playing the instruments. What is their talent? (playing an instrument) Let's add *Music* to our map.
- After discussing the photos, ask: How do talents make someone unique?

How talents make someone unique

- Dancing
- Running
- Kicking
- Music

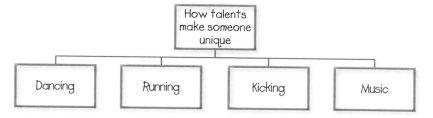

Connect to reading

Tell students that this week they will be reading about people with special talents. Encourage students to add concept-related words to this week's concept map.

ELL Preteach Concepts Use the Day 1 instruction on ELL Poster 16 to assess and build background knowledge, develop concepts, and build oral vocabulary.

ELL Poster 16

ELL

English Language Learners

ELL Support Additional ELL support and modified instruction are provided in the *ELL Handbook* and in the ELL Support lessons on pp. DI•16–DI•25.

Listening Comprehension English learners will benefit from additional visual support to understand the key terms in the concept map. Use the pictures on pp. 20–21 to scaffold understanding.

Frontload for Read Aloud Use the modified Read Aloud on p. DI•19 of the ELL Support lessons to prepare students to listen to "The Myth of Icarus" (p. 21b).

Objectives
- Develop listening comprehension.
- Develop oral vocabulary.

Check Oral Vocabulary
SUCCESS PREDICTOR

Oral Vocabulary
Amazing Words

Introduce Amazing Words "The Myth of Icarus" on p. 21b is about a boy who flies too high. Tell students to listen for this week's Amazing Words—*mock, idle, potential, ecstatic*—as you read.

Model fluency As you read "The Myth of Icarus," model accuracy with smooth, fluent reading.

Teach Amazing Words

Amazing Words Oral Vocabulary Routine

mock
idle
potential
ecstatic

1. **Introduce** Write the word *ecstatic* on the board. Have students say the word aloud with you. In "The Myth of Icarus," Icarus is *ecstatic* about being able to fly. Does the author include any context clues that tell me the meaning of this word? Supply a student-friendly definition. *Ecstatic* means "feeling very happy or excited."
2. **Demonstrate** Have students answer questions to demonstrate understanding. Would winning first prize in a contest make you *ecstatic*?
3. **Apply** Ask students to give a personal example of a time when they felt *ecstatic.*

See pp. OV•1 to teach *idle, mock,* and *potential.*

Routines Flip Chart

Apply Amazing Words To build oral vocabulary, lead the class in a discussion about the Amazing Words' meanings. Remind students to ask and answer questions with appropriate detail.

Don't Wait Until Friday

MONITOR PROGRESS Check Oral Vocabulary

During discussion, listen for students' use of Amazing Words.

If... students are unable to use the Amazing Words to discuss the concept,
then... use the Oral Vocabulary Routine on the Routines Flip Chart to demonstrate words in different contexts.

Day 1	Day 2	Day 3	Day 4	Day 5
Check Oral Vocabulary	Check Word Reading	Check Retelling	Check Fluency	Check Oral Vocabulary

Success Predictor

Read Aloud

The Myth of Icarus

Long ago in Greece, there lived a great architect, inventor, and craftsman named Daedalus. One day, the king got angry with Daedalus and banished him and his son, Icarus, to the island of Crete.

The only way to escape from the island was by sea. The sea was so vast and rough that it seemed to mock their attempts to swim across it. Daedalus and Icarus knew that if they tried to use a boat, they would be arrested.

Daedalus did not want to stay idle forever on Crete. He knew that he had the potential to find a way off the island. Daedalus thought hard about what to do. Finally, he came up with an incredible idea. If he and Icarus could not escape by swimming or using a boat, then they would fly!

Daedalus spent months designing two sets of wings. The wings had to be strong enough to support him and his son on their journey. He collected feathers and sewed them together with string. He held the feathers together on a frame with wax. He added leather straps that would secure the wings on their arms.

Finally, he finished his invention. Daedalus fitted two wings onto his son's strong arms. Then he gave him careful instructions.

He warned, "Icarus, do not fly too low. You must fly high enough so the feathers will not get wet from the sea mist. Damp wings will pull you down, and your arms will tire."

Icarus turned away, ready to fly, but his father stopped him. Daedalus added, "Son, do not fly too high either. The heat of the sun will melt the wax, and the wings will not hold together."

And so, Daedalus and Icarus jumped off a cliff, each wearing a set of wings. They flew miles and miles over the sea. They headed toward the mainland, and their wings drifted on air currents. Their arms did not tire.

The incredible flight thrilled young Icarus. He was ecstatic about his new ability. Before long, he began to ignore his father's warnings. He soared higher and higher. The soft wind blew gently on his face, and the sun warmed his skin. Icarus did not realize that the sun's rays were melting the wax that held his wings together. His wings began to fall apart, and Icarus fell into the sea.

The sea swallowed him, and soon Icarus drowned. Daedalus had lost sight of his son and he reached land alone. Days later, Icarus's wings washed up on the shore. Daedalus realized what had happened, and he cried bitterly, lamenting that his invention had killed his son.

The sea where Icarus died was later named the Icarian Sea. The sea has kept that name to this day, and you can find it near the island of Crete.

Objectives

- ◎ Blend words that contain *-ves;* irregular plurals.
- ◎ Use word analysis to recognize irregular plurals *f* to *-ves.*
- ◎ Know the irregular plurals of some common words.

Skills Trace

◎ **Irregular Plurals**

Introduce U4W1D1
Practice U4W1D3; U4W1D4
Reteach/Review U4W1D5; U4W2D4
Assess/Test Weekly Test U4W1 Benchmark Test U4
Key: U = Unit, W = Week, D = Day

Word Analysis

◎ Irregular Plurals

ROUTINE Word Parts Strategy

1. **Connect** Write *friends* and *foxes.* Many times you just add *-s* or *-es* to a word to form the plural. *Friends* and *foxes* are two examples. Read these words. Explain that today students will learn to spell and read words that do not fit the regular plural form.
2. **Model** Write *leaves* and *children.* I know that *-ves* is a plural ending for words that end with *-f* or *-fe.* When I see this ending, I work backward to check whether this is a plural word. I cover *-ves* on *leaves* and replace it with *-f* or *-fe.* Cover the *-ves* in *leaves* and replace it with *-f.* If I recognize the new word, I know the first word is the plural of that word. Other words, like *child,* have plurals that don't follow these rules. I just have to learn them: The plural of *child* is *children.*
3. **Guide practice** Write the words below. Read them together. Identify the singular form of each word and how it changes in the plural form.

children	**women**	**wives**	**men**	**mice**	**geese**
halves	**elves**	**calves**	**hooves**	**knives**	**shelves**

4. **Review** What do you know about reading irregular plurals? When you recognize an irregular plural, identify the irregular ending *(-ves)* and think of which letters the ending replaces *(-f* or *-fe),* or remember that it is an irregular plural that does not follow a pattern.

Routines Flip Chart

Model Have students turn to p. 22 in their Student Editions. Each word is an irregular plural. The first word is *knives.* I know that *-ves* is a plural ending of a word that ends with *-f* or *-fe. Knives* is the plural of *knife.*

Guide practice For each word in Words I Can Blend, ask for the sound of each letter or word part. Make sure that students identify the correct plural endings. Then have them read the words.

Corrective feedback **If...** students have difficulty reading a word,
then... model reading the parts and then the whole word. Then ask students to read it with you.

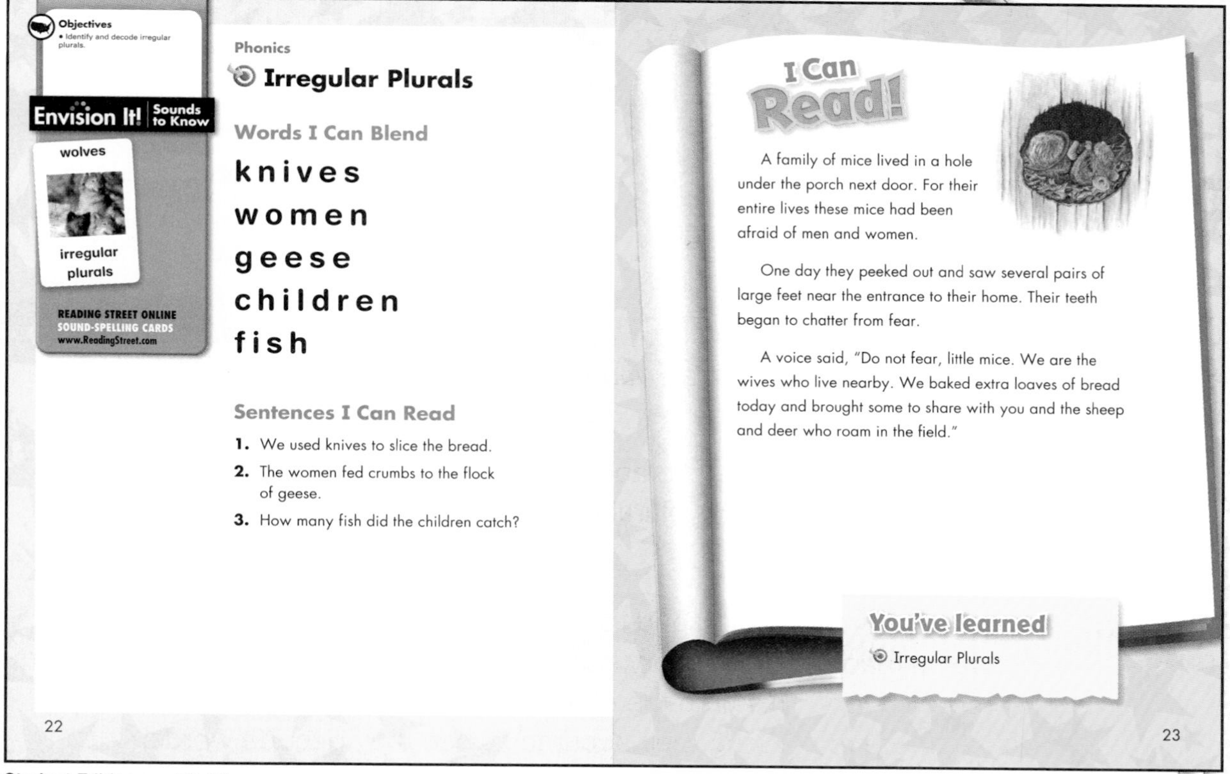

Objectives
• Identify and decode irregular plurals.

Envision It! Sounds to Know

wolves

irregular plurals

READING STREET ONLINE
SOUND-SPELLING CARDS
www.ReadingStreet.com

Phonics

Irregular Plurals

Words I Can Blend

knives
women
geese
children
fish

Sentences I Can Read

1. We used knives to slice the bread.
2. The women fed crumbs to the flock of geese.
3. How many fish did the children catch?

22

I Can Read!

A family of mice lived in a hole under the porch next door. For their entire lives these mice had been afraid of men and women.

One day they peeked out and saw several pairs of large feet near the entrance to their home. Their teeth began to chatter from fear.

A voice said, "Do not fear, little mice. We are the wives who live nearby. We baked extra loaves of bread today and brought some to share with you and the sheep and deer who roam in the field."

You've learned
Irregular Plurals

23

Student Edition pp. 22–23

Decode and Read

Read words independent of context
After students can successfully combine word parts to read the words on p. 22 in their Student Editions, point to words in random order and ask students to read them naturally.

Read words in context
Have students read each of the sentences on p. 22. Have them identify irregular plural words in the sentences.

Team Talk Pair students and have them take turns reading each of the sentences aloud.

Chorally read the "I Can Read!" passage on p. 23 with the students. Then have them read the passage aloud to themselves.

On their own
For additional practice, use the *Reader's and Writer's Notebook* p. 247.

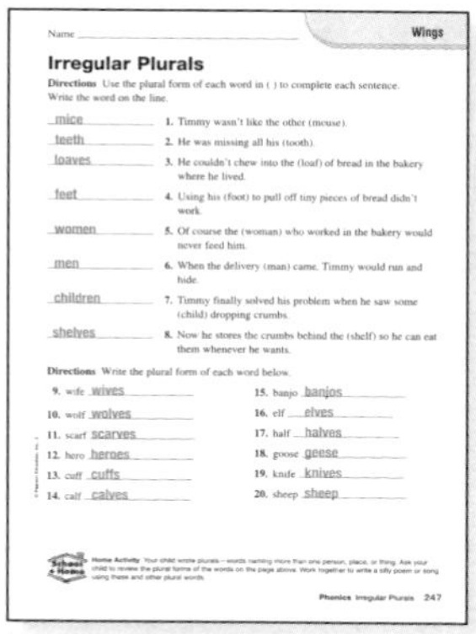

Irregular Plurals

Reader's and Writer's Notebook p. 247

Differentiated Instruction

SI Strategic Intervention

Irregular plurals To assist students having difficulty forming the irregular plural of a base word that ends in *-f* or *-fe,* have them make two sets of cards. On one set of cards write the base words *knife, wife, hoof, shelf,* and *elf.* On the other set of cards write the plural words *knives, wives, hooves, shelves,* and *elves.* Have students match each base word to its plural form and practice reading all of the words with a partner.

Vocabulary Support

You may wish to explain the meaning of these words.

hooves the hard part of the foot of horses, cows, sheep, pigs, and some other animals

geese tame or wild birds that look like a duck, except have longer necks and are usually larger

elves small lively creatures resembling humans

ELL

English Language Learners

Pronunciation Assist students with the articulation of phonemes as they blend sounds. Focus on tongue and lip positions when saying words such as *shelves* and *leaves.*

Contrastive Analysis Chart See also the Contrastive Analysis Chart in the *First Stop* book.

Objectives

- Apply knowledge of sound-spellings to decode unknown multisyllabic words when reading.
- ◎ Decode and read words with irregular plurals.
- Practice fluency with oral rereading.

Decodable Practice Reader 16A

◎ Irregular Plurals

Read words independent of context

Have students turn to page 1 in *Decodable Practice Readers 3.2.* Have students read each word.

Read high-frequency words

Have students read the high-frequency words *the, a, to, water, of, people, two, said, one, what, where, laughed, was, they, have, their,* and *watched* on the first page.

Preview Decodable Practice Reader

Have students read the title and preview the story. Tell them that they will read words with irregular plurals.

Read words in context

Pair students for reading and listen as they read. One student begins. Students read the entire story, switching readers after each page. Partners reread the story. This time the other student begins. Make sure that students are monitoring their accuracy when they decode words.

A Party for the Geese

Written by Kenneth Freid

Decodable Practice Reader 16A

Irregular Plurals

men	women	knives
children	leaves	geese
people	loaves	wolves

High-Frequency Words

the	a	to
water	of	people
two	said	one
what	where	laughed
was	they	have
their	watched	

1

Each summer the Glendale Street families held a big party. On a bright June day, everybody gladly marched to Blake Pond. Men carried large boxes filled with cold drinks. Women carried big baskets and bags filled with lunch, plates, cups, forks, and knives. Children carried gear for playing games.

The pond looked peaceful. Soft breezes ruffled leaves. Ducks floated on the pond. Big, loud geese waded in the water.

2

Decodable Practice Reader 16A

"Let's play a game," Jeff Sanders suggested. "We've got plenty of people for two teams."

"We can leave lunch on the tables," Mrs. Perez said.

"I'm not playing," Mrs. Wong said, "so I will set up the tables."

3

The neighbors played a lively game. One team scored six runs. The other team scored seven runs.

"I'm starved!" Kelly Wong finally yelled. "It's lunchtime!"

Men, women, and children quickly went back to the tables. Then everybody saw a strange sight.

4

Mrs. Wong stood near the tables looking unhappy. Crackers and loaves of bread lay nearby. Seven geese honked loudly.

Everybody spoke at the same time. "What happened? What's going on? Where's lunch?"

Mrs. Wong laughed. "It looks as if wild wolves chased me. But it was really just these geese," she said.

5

"But let me tell you what happened. I was just taking bags of crackers and loaves of bread to the tables. Seven geese came running, honking loudly. More followed them. I tripped over geese. I waved bags to make them leave, but then a bag broke. Crackers and bread tumbled out. I got upset, but those silly geese seemed really happy!"

Everybody laughed. Mrs. Wong felt fine. They still had plenty of lunch for everybody.

6

"I think Mrs. Wong has been really helpful," Mr. Perez said. "Now those geese can have their own meal. They will let us enjoy our party!"

The families ate salads, chicken, potatoes, pickles, peaches, and apples. Everybody enjoyed lunch.

7

After eating, the neighbors watched the geese. They seemed to enjoy parties too!

8

Corrective feedback

If... students have difficulty reading a word,
then... refer them to the Sound-Spelling Cards to identify the word parts. Have them read the word parts individually and then together to say the word.

- What is the new word?
- Is the new word a word you know?
- Does it make sense in the story?

Check decoding and comprehension

Have students retell the story to include characters, setting, and events. Then have students find words in the story that are irregular plurals. Students should supply *men, women, knives, children, leaves, geese, people, loaves,* and *wolves.*

Reread for Fluency

Have students reread Decodable Practice Reader 16A to develop automaticity in decoding words that are irregular plurals.

ROUTINE Oral Rereading

1. **Read** Have students read the entire book orally.
2. **Reread** To achieve optimal fluency, students should reread the text three or four times.
3. **Corrective Feedback** Listen as students read. Provide corrective feedback regarding their fluency and decoding.

Routines Flip Chart

ELL

English Language Learners

Irregular Plurals

Beginning Write several irregular plural words from the Decodable Reader on the board, such as *men, geese, children,* and *leaves.* Point to each word as you say it aloud. Then have students explain the rule for forming each plural word.

Intermediate After reading, have students make a T-chart. On the left side of the chart have them list all of the irregular plural words in the Decodable Reader. On the right side of the chart have students write the singular form of each word.

Advanced/Advanced High After reading the story, have students write a short paragraph that uses 3–4 irregular plural words.

Objectives

- ◎ Generalize to aid comprehension.
- ◎ Summarize to aid comprehension.
- Read grade-level text with accuracy.

Skills Trace

◎ Generalize

Introduce U3W4D1; U4W1D1; U6W5D1

Practice U3W4D2; U3W4D3; U3W5D2; U4W1D2; U4W1D3; U4W1D2; U6W5D2; U6W5D3

Reteach/Review U3W4D5; U4W1D5; U6W5D5

Assess/Test

Weekly Tests U3W4; U4W1; U6W5
Benchmark Tests U4

Key: U = Unit, W = Week, D = Day

Skill ↔ Strategy

◎ Generalize

◎ Summarize

Envision It! Visual Skills Handbook
Generalize
All birds have wings.
A statement that is true for many examples is a generalization.
Student Edition p. EI•8

Introduce generalize

Envision It!

When I read, I can sometimes make a statement that is true for many examples. That is called generalizing. When I generalize, I say how things are mostly alike or all alike. How can I generalize about third graders? (Possible response: Most third graders like to read.) Have students turn to p. EI•8 in the Student Edition to review generalizing. Then read "Batting the Ball" with students.

Model the skill

Think Aloud Today we're going to read about a girl who loves baseball. Have students follow along as you read the first two paragraphs of "Batting the Ball." Can we make a generalization about what we have read so far? One thing we can say is that most third graders have recess. We know this generalization is true because we have recess and so do the third graders in the story.

Guide practice

Have students finish reading "Batting the Ball" on their own. After they read, have them use a graphic organizer like the one on p. 24 and make generalizations about the passage.

Strategy check

Summarize Remind students that summarizing means briefly retelling the important events in the order that they happened. If you can tell the important events in order, it will help you remember what you have read. Model summarizing for students.

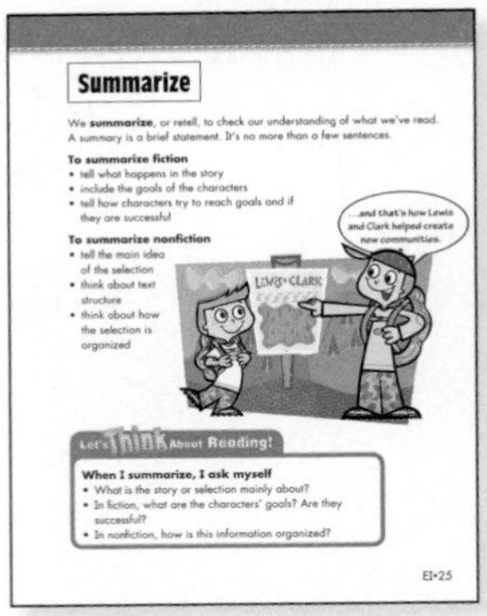
Summarize
Let's Think About Reading!
Student Edition p. EI•25

Model the strategy

Think Aloud I can sum up the beginning of "Batting the Ball." It is about a girl who loves baseball. She goes to a new school. At the new school she is not allowed to use a hard baseball.

Envision It!

Have students review the strategy of summarizing on p. EI•25 of the Student Edition.

On their own

Use p. 248 in the *Reader's and Writer's Notebook* for additional practice with generalizing.

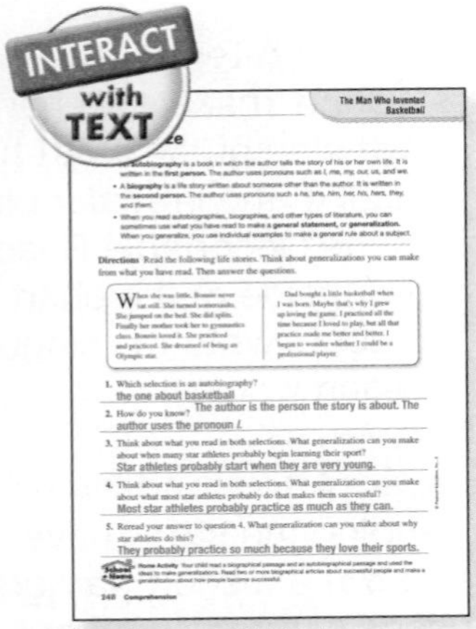
INTERACT with TEXT
The Man Who Invented Basketball
Reader's and Writer's Notebook p. 248

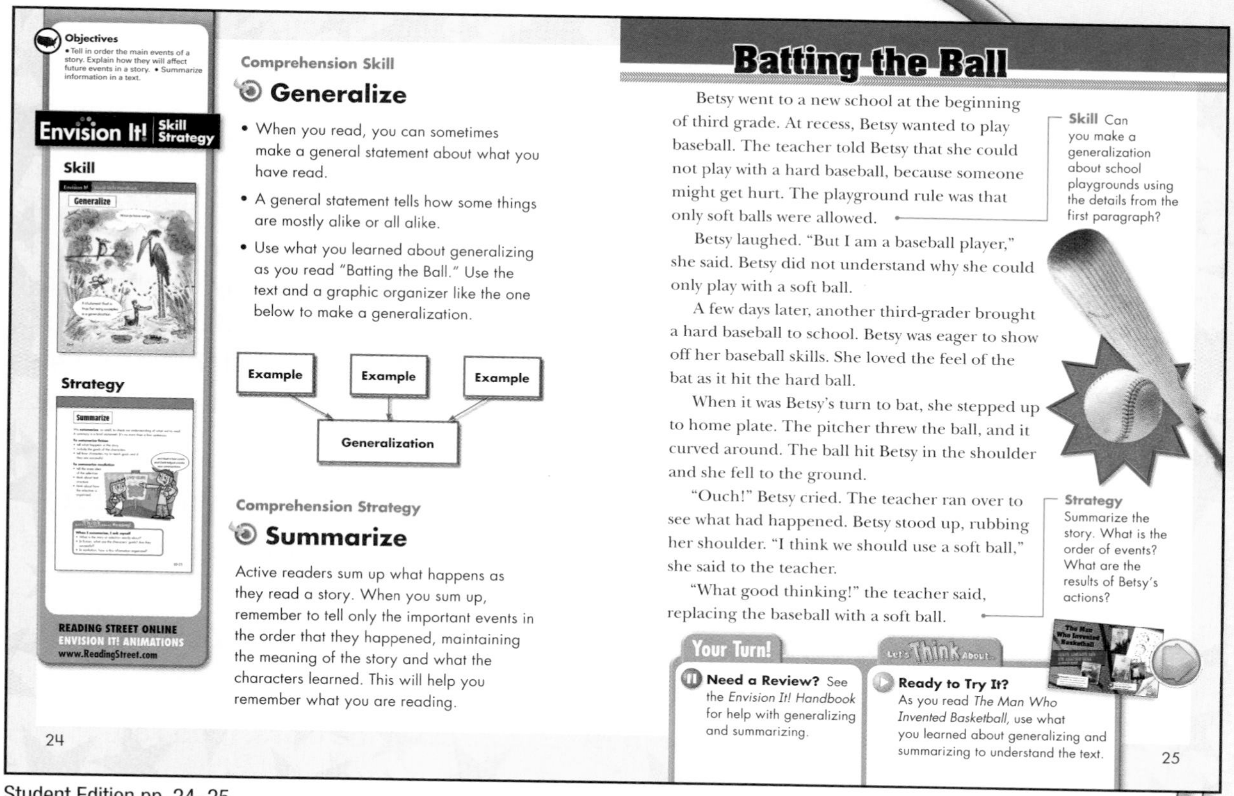
Objectives
• Tell in order the main events of a story. Explain how they will affect future events in a story. • Summarize information in a text.

Envision It! Skill Strategy

Skill

Strategy

READING STREET ONLINE
ENVISION IT! ANIMATIONS
www.ReadingStreet.com

Comprehension Skill

Generalize

- When you read, you can sometimes make a general statement about what you have read.
- A general statement tells how some things are mostly alike or all alike.
- Use what you learned about generalizing as you read "Batting the Ball." Use the text and a graphic organizer like the one below to make a generalization.

Example → Generalization
Example → Generalization
Example → Generalization

Comprehension Strategy

Summarize

Active readers sum up what happens as they read a story. When you sum up, remember to tell only the important events in the order that they happened, maintaining the meaning of the story and what the characters learned. This will help you remember what you are reading.

24

Batting the Ball

Betsy went to a new school at the beginning of third grade. At recess, Betsy wanted to play baseball. The teacher told Betsy that she could not play with a hard baseball, because someone might get hurt. The playground rule was that only soft balls were allowed.

Skill Can you make a generalization about school playgrounds using the details from the first paragraph?

Betsy laughed. "But I am a baseball player," she said. Betsy did not understand why she could only play with a soft ball.

A few days later, another third-grader brought a hard baseball to school. Betsy was eager to show off her baseball skills. She loved the feel of the bat as it hit the hard ball.

When it was Betsy's turn to bat, she stepped up to home plate. The pitcher threw the ball, and it curved around. The ball hit Betsy in the shoulder and she fell to the ground.

"Ouch!" Betsy cried. The teacher ran over to see what had happened. Betsy stood up, rubbing her shoulder. "I think we should use a soft ball," she said to the teacher.

"What good thinking!" the teacher said, replacing the baseball with a soft ball.

Strategy Summarize the story. What is the order of events? What are the results of Betsy's actions?

Your Turn!

Need a Review? See the *Envision It! Handbook* for help with generalizing and summarizing.

Let's Think About...

Ready to Try It? As you read *The Man Who Invented Basketball,* use what you learned about generalizing and summarizing to understand the text.

25

Student Edition pp. 24–25

Skill School playgrounds have rules to keep children safe.

Strategy When Betsy started going to a new school, she found that she was not allowed to play with a baseball. She did not understand why she had to play with a softball. She played with a baseball anyway, and she got hurt by the hard ball. Then she understood why the teacher only wanted them to use softballs. She got hurt as a result of her actions, but she also understood the rule better.

Model Fluency
Accuracy

Model fluent reading

Have students listen as you read paragraphs 3 and 4 of "Batting the Ball" with appropriate accuracy. Explain that reading with accuracy means reading every word on the page, and pronouncing every word correctly.

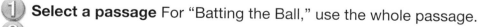

ROUTINE Paired Reading

1. **Select a passage** For "Batting the Ball," use the whole passage.
2. **Reading 1** Students read the entire passage, switching readers at the end of each paragraph.
3. **Reading 2** Partners reread the "Batting the Ball." This time the other student begins.
4. Reread For optimal fluency, have partners continue to read three or four times.
5. **Corrective Feedback** Listen as students read. Provide feedback about their accuracy and encourage them to ask questions about unfamiliar words.

Routines Flip Chart

ELL

English Language Learners

Compound words Have students find a compound word on p. 25. *(baseball, softball, hardball)* Write the words on the board. Underline the second part of each word and have students tell you what it means. Point to the first part of each word and have students tell you what it means. Explain or have students explain how the two words go together. Have students suggest more words with the word *ball* in them. Work together as a class to figure out how the two words come together to make a new word.

Objectives
- Activate prior knowledge of words.
- Identify questions for research.

Vocabulary
Tested Vocabulary

Lesson vocabulary Have students complete sentences by filling in the blanks with lesson words.

Activate prior knowledge Display the lesson words and discuss what students already know about these words. Then write incomplete sentences on the board, such as those shown below. Have students identify the lesson word that completes each sentence and makes sense in context. Students may need to check the glossary.

- We waited for the pond to _______ before we went ice skating. (freeze)
- The class stood under the hoop while the coach explained the game of _______. (basketball)
- Fred has a test tomorrow, so he needs to _______ tonight. (study)
- Basketball, baseball, and football are all different kinds of _______. (sports)
- Everyone likes Misha, the most _______ girl in the class. (popular)
- The _______ protected the queen from danger. (guard)
- Mary used salt instead of sugar in her lemon pie, and it tasted _______. (terrible)
- Sam was very sick until the doctor cured his _______. (disease)

Write the words *student* and *study* on the board and have students say them aloud. Ask how they are related in meaning.

At the end of the week, students can review these fill-in-the-blank sentences or create their own with a partner.

ELL **Academic Vocabulary** Write the following terms on the board:

pronoun	**irregular plurals**
presentation	**autobiography**
time line	**text features**

Preteach Academic Vocabulary Have students share what they know about this week's Academic Vocabulary. Use the students' responses to assess their prior knowledge. Preteach the Academic Vocabulary by providing a student-friendly description, explanation, or example that clarifies the meaning of each term. Then ask students to restate the meaning of the Academic Vocabulary term in their own words.

Research and Inquiry
Identify Questions

Teach

Discuss the Question of the Week: *How do talents make someone unique?* Tell students they will research a talented person. They will present that person's biography to the class on Day 5.

Model

Think Aloud

I'll start by brainstorming a list of questions about people who have special talents. First I will have to decide on a kind of talent. I love soccer, so I will try to find a person who has a talent for soccer. Some questions could be *Who is the best soccer player in history? Who is the most talented soccer player I can think of? Does that player have a special talent that makes him or her a great player?* and *What is that talent?*

Guide practice

After students have brainstormed and formulated open-ended inquiry questions, explain that tomorrow they will conduct library research using their questions. To generate a research plan, help students identify words or phrases that will guide their search for relevant information.

On their own

Have students work individually, in pairs, or in small groups to write an inquiry question.

Small Group Time

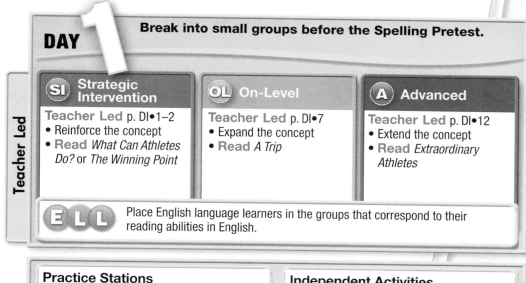

DAY 1 Break into small groups before the Spelling Pretest.

Teacher Led

SI Strategic Intervention	OL On-Level	A Advanced
Teacher Led p. DI•1–2 • Reinforce the concept • Read *What Can Athletes Do?* or *The Winning Point*	Teacher Led p. DI•7 • Expand the concept • Read *A Trip*	Teacher Led p. DI•12 • Extend the concept • Read *Extraordinary Athletes*

ELL Place English language learners in the groups that correspond to their reading abilities in English.

Practice Stations
- Read for Meaning
- Get Fluent
- Word Work

Independent Activities
- Concept Talk Video
- *Reader's and Writer's Notebook*
- Vocabulary Activities

INTERNET GUY
Don Leu

21st Century Skills

Weekly Inquiry Project

Day 1 Identify Questions
Day 2 Navigate/Search
Day 3 Analyze
Day 4 Synthesize
Day 5 Communicate

Academic Vocabulary

presentation An individual or group presents information about a particular subject. The information can be given orally or visually.

Differentiated Instruction

A Advanced

Set purpose Have students brainstorm a list of keywords for their research and set a purpose for what they expect to find.

ELL

English Language Learners

Multilingual Vocabulary
Students can apply knowledge of their home languages to acquire new English vocabulary by using the Multilingual Vocabulary Lists (*ELL Handbook*, pp. 433–446).

DAY 1 Language Arts

30–35 min

Objectives

- Spell irregular plurals.
- Use and understand singular and plural pronouns.
- Write cursive upper- and lower-case *g, y,* and *q.*

Spelling Pretest
Irregular Plurals

Introduce Remind students that many nouns form the plural by adding *s* or *es,* but some do not. Words that do not are called irregular plurals. Also, remind students to use their knowledge of letter sounds, word parts, segmentation, and syllables as they spell the words.

Pretest Use these sentences to administer the spelling pretest. Say each word, read the sentence, and repeat the word.

1. wolves	Listen to the **wolves** howl in the distance.
2. knives	Cut the sandwiches with **knives**.
3. feet	Those shoes hurt my **feet**.
4. men	The **men** on the rowing team wear uniforms.
5. children	There are ten **children** on the team.
6. women	Mom works with five other **women**.
7. sheep	Did you know that wool comes from **sheep**?
8. heroes	What would it take for us to be **heroes**?
9. scarves	Ron lost a hat and two **scarves** this winter.
10. mice	**Mice**, hamsters, and gerbils make good pets.
11. geese	The honks of the **geese** were very loud.
12. wives	How many husbands and **wives** went to the meeting?
13. elves	The **elves** made shoes for the shoemaker.
14. banjos	Like fiddles, **banjos** are four-stringed instruments.
15. halves	All the plates had **halves** of oranges on them.
16. loaves	I can smell the **loaves** of bread baking in the oven.
17. beliefs	He has strong **beliefs** about adopting pets.
18. tomatoes	The sauce is made from **tomatoes**.
19. potatoes	**Potatoes** grow in the ground.
20. tornadoes	Several **tornadoes** touched down last night.

Challenge words (16–20)

Self-correct After the pretest, you can either display the correctly spelled words or spell them orally. Have students self-correct their pretests by writing misspelled words.

On their own For additional practice, use *Let's Practice It!* page 217 on the *Teacher Resources DVD-ROM.*

Name ____________ Invented Basketball

Irregular Plurals

Generalization Sometimes plurals are formed in irregular ways: **heroes, wolves**.

Word Sort Sort the list words according to the type of plural.

-f or -fe to -ves	other plurals
1. wolves	7. feet
2. knives	8. men
3. scarves	9. children
4. elves	10. women
5. halves	11. sheep
6. wives	12. heroes
	13. mice
	14. geese
	15. banjos

Spelling Words
1. wolves
2. knives
3. feet
4. men
5. children
6. women
7. sheep
8. heroes
9. scarves
10. mice
11. geese
12. wives
13. elves
14. banjos
15. halves

School + Home **Home Activity** Your child is learning to spell irregular plurals. To practice at home, say the singular form of each list word and have your child say the plural form of the word.

Irregular Plurals DVD•217

Let's Practice It!
TR DVD•217

Conventions
Singular and Plural Pronouns

Teach Display Grammar Transparency 16, and read aloud the explanation and examples in the box.

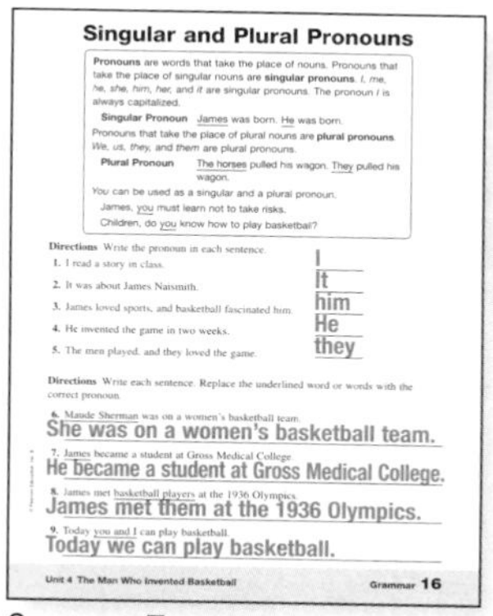

Singular and Plural Pronouns

Pronouns are words that take the place of nouns. Pronouns that take the place of singular nouns are **singular pronouns**. *I, me, he, she, him, her,* and *it* are singular pronouns. The pronoun *I* is always capitalized.

Singular Pronoun James was born. He was born.

Pronouns that take the place of plural nouns are **plural pronouns**. *We, us, they,* and *them* are plural pronouns.

Plural Pronoun The horses pulled his wagon. They pulled his wagon.

You can be used as a singular and a plural pronoun.

James, you must learn not to take risks.

Children, do you know how to play basketball?

Directions Write the pronoun in each sentence.

1. I read a story in class. I
2. It was about James Naismith. It
3. James loved sports, and basketball fascinated him. him
4. He invented the game in two weeks. He
5. The men played, and they loved the game. they

Directions Write each sentence. Replace the underlined word or words with the correct pronoun.

6. Maude Sherman was on a women's basketball team.
She was on a women's basketball team.
7. James became a student at Gross Medical College.
He became a student at Gross Medical College.
8. James met basketball players at the 1936 Olympics.
James met them at the 1936 Olympics.
9. Today you and I can play basketball.
Today we can play basketball.

Unit 4 The Man Who Invented Basketball Grammar 16

Grammar Transparency 16, TR DVD

Model Model with item 1. *I read a story in class.* The pronoun in the sentence is *I.* The pronoun *I* tells about one person, so it is a singular pronoun. Look at item 2. *It was about James Naismith.* The pronoun is *it.* The pronoun *it* refers to the word *story* in the first item. It is a singular pronoun.

Guide practice Guide students in completing items 3–5. In each item, have students identify the pronoun, tell whether the pronoun is singular or plural, and tell how they know. Record the correct responses on the transparency.

Daily Fix-It Use Daily Fix-It numbers 1 and 2 in the right margin.

Connect to oral language Have students rewrite sentences 7–10 by replacing the underlined word or words with the appropriate pronoun.

Handwriting
Cursive Letters *g, y,* and *q*

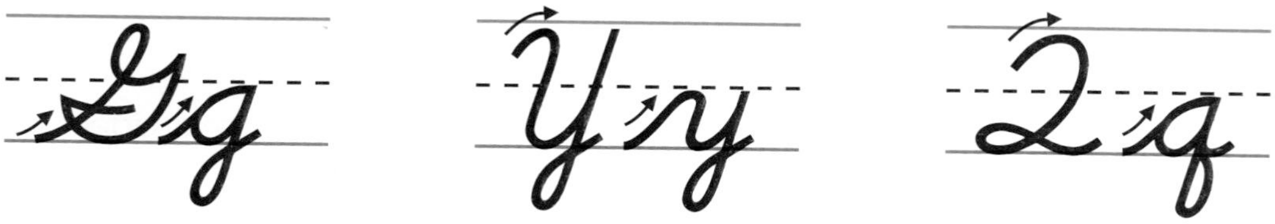

Model letter formation Display the capital and lowercase cursive letters *g, y,* and *q.* Follow the stroke instructions pictured to model letter formation.

Model letter slant and joining strokes Explain that writing legibly means letters are the correct size, form, and slant. Letters are connected with joining strokes. Model writing this sentence with correct slant and joining strokes: *Go quietly to my room.*

Guide practice Have students write these sentences: *Great heroes go on quests. You grew an inch! What was your question?* Circulate around the room, guiding students.

Academic Vocabulary

A **pronoun** is a word that takes the place of a noun, such as *she* or *he.*

Daily Fix-It

1. He flyed safly. *(flew; safely)*
2. The world look different from up in the sky. *(looks)*

ELL

English Language Learners

Irregular plurals Tell students that we form some plurals in unexpected ways. Help students memorize the most common irregular plurals.

Singular and plural pronouns Have students name several singular nouns and several plural nouns. Then have them use each noun orally in a sentence. Ask another student to repeat the sentences, substituting a pronoun for the noun.

Objectives

- Understand and identify the features of persuasive text.

MINI-LESSON

5-Day Planner
Guide to Mini-Lessons

DAY 1	Read Like a Writer
DAY 2	Write with Purpose
DAY 3	Logical and Emotional Appeals
DAY 4	Consolidating with Conjunctions
DAY 5	Proofread for Pronouns and Double Negatives

Writing—Persuasive Text
Introduce

MINI-LESSON

Read Like a Writer

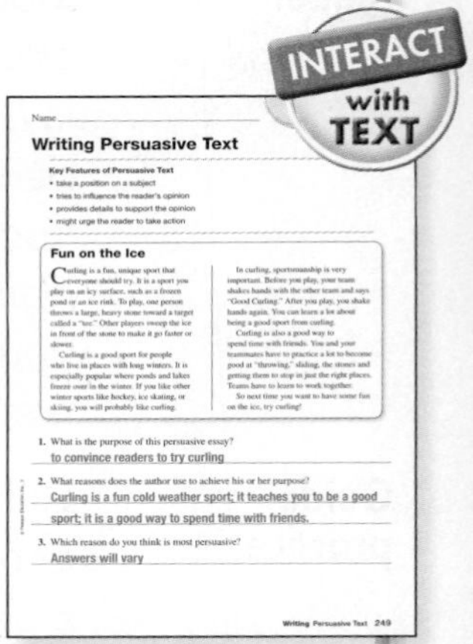
INTERACT with TEXT

Name ____________

Writing Persuasive Text

Key Features of Persuasive Text
- take a position on a subject
- tries to influence the reader's opinion
- provides details to support the opinion
- might urge the reader to take action

Fun on the Ice

Curling is a fun, unique sport that everyone should try. It is a sport you play on an icy surface, such as a frozen pond or an ice rink. To play, one person throws a large, heavy stone toward a target called a "tee." Other players sweep the ice in front of the stone to make it go faster or slower.

Curling is a good sport for people who live in places with long winters. It is especially popular where ponds and lakes freeze over in the winter. If you like other winter sports like hockey, ice skating, or skiing, you will probably like curling.

In curling, sportsmanship is very important. Before you play, your team shakes hands with the other team and says "Good Curling." After you play, you shake hands again. You can learn a lot about being a good sport from curling.

Curling is also a good way to spend time with friends. You and your teammates have to practice a lot to become good at "throwing," sliding, the stones and getting them to stop in just the right places. Teams have to learn to work together.

So next time you want to have some fun on the ice, try curling!

1. What is the purpose of this persuasive essay?
to convince readers to try curling
2. What reasons does the author use to achieve his or her purpose?
Curling is a fun cold weather sport; it teaches you to be a good sport; it is a good way to spend time with friends.
3. Which reason do you think is most persuasive?
Answers will vary

Writing Persuasive Text 249

Reader's and Writer's Notebook p. 249

■ **Introduce** This week you will write a persuasive text. A persuasive text is writing that is intended to convince or persuade the reader.

Prompt	Write an essay about your favorite sport or game, persuading someone to play it.
Trait	Conventions
Mode	Persuasive

■ **Examine Model Text** Let's read an example of a persuasive text about a sport called curling. Have students turn to "Fun on the Ice" on p. 249 of their *Reader's and Writer's Notebook*.

■ **Key Features** A persuasive text takes a position. The writer's opinion is called a position. Find the writer's position in the first paragraph and circle it. Discuss how that statement helps the reader focus on the text.

The purpose of a persuasive text **is to influence the reader's opinion.** In each paragraph of this text there is a main idea. The main idea is a reason that you should learn to curl. For each paragraph in the model, have students underline the main idea.

The writer provides details that support each main idea. For each paragraph have students double underline details that support the main idea.

The writer probably will urge the reader to do something. Which sentences urge the reader to try curling? Have the students underline them.

Review
Key features

Review the key features of a persuasive text. You might want to post the key features in the classroom for students to reference as they work on their compositions.

Key Features of Persuasive Text

- takes a position on a subject
- tries to influence the reader's opinion
- provides details to support the opinion
- might urge the reader to take action

ROUTINE **Quick Write for Fluency** Team Talk

1. **Talk** Have pairs discuss the features of persuasive text.
2. **Write** Each person writes a sentence defining persuasive text.
3. **Share** Partners share their definitions with each other.

Routines Flip Chart

Write Guy
Jeff Anderson

What Do You Notice?

When students are examining the model text, ask, "What do you notice?" By giving students the responsibility of commenting on what they find effective in the text, they build self-confidence and often begin to notice features of the writing they might not have otherwise. Eventually they will start trying them in their writing. Relish students' movement toward correctness and beauty.

Wrap Up Your Day

- ✔ **Build Concepts** What did you learn about how talents make someone unique?
- ✔ **Oral Vocabulary** Have students use the Amazing Words they learned in context sentences.
- ✔ **Homework** Send home this week's Family Times Newsletter, *Let's Practice It!* pages 218–219 on the *Teacher Resources DVD-ROM.*

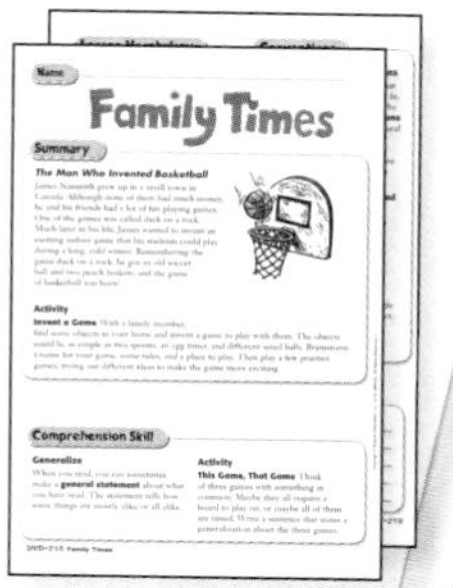

Let's Practice It!
TR DVD•218–219

ELL

English Language Learners

Writing model Help students understand the writing model by reading it aloud and defining any unfamiliar terms, such as *unique, target,* and *sportsmanship.* Ask students about sports they have played and what they like about those sports.

Preview DAY 2

Tell students that tomorrow they will read about the early life of the man who invented basketball.

Objectives
- Expand the weekly concept.
- Develop oral vocabulary.

Today at a Glance

Oral Vocabulary
thrill, audition

Phonics/Word Analysis
◉ Irregular plurals

Literary Terms
Point of view

Text Feature
Time line and map

Lesson Vocabulary
◉ Unfamiliar words

Fluency
Accuracy

Reading
"Carlos Catches Sports Fever"
The Man Who Invented Basketball

Research and Inquiry
Navigate/Search

Spelling
Irregular plurals

Conventions
Singular and plural pronouns

Writing
Persuasive text

Concept Talk

Question of the Week

How do talents make someone unique?

Expand the concept

Remind students of the weekly concept question. Tell students that today they will begin reading *The Man Who Invented Basketball: James Naismith and His Amazing Game.* As they read, encourage students to think about how talent can make someone unique.

Anchored Talk

Develop oral vocabulary

Use the photos on pp. 20–21 and the Read Aloud, "The Myth of Icarus," to talk about the Amazing Words: *mock, idle, potential,* and *ecstatic.* Add these and other concept-related words to the concept map to develop students' knowledge of the topic. Discuss the following questions. Remind students to ask and answer questions with appropriate detail, and to provide suggestions that build upon the ideas of others.

- Do you think Daedalus was *ecstatic* about his invention? Why? (Yes, with the wings he could fly off the island.)
- Why would you describe a beginner at something as someone who has *potential?* (Because they have not had time to practice yet, but they still might be good.)
- Why will you never discover your talents if you are *idle?* (If you are idle you don't do anything.)
- Imagine a girl is trying something for the first time. She makes some mistakes because she has never done it before. How could *mocking* her stop her from finding her talent? (The girl might feel bad about what she is doing and never try it again. Then she would never know if she had talent.)

Oral Vocabulary
Amazing Words

Amazing Words Oral Vocabulary Routine

Teach Amazing Words

1. **Introduce** Write the Amazing Word *thrill* on the board. Have students say it aloud with you. Relate *thrill* to the photographs on pp. 20–21 and "The Myth of Icarus." The boy and girl playing the clarinet and violin might be *thrilled* to play for their relatives. Icarus was *thrilled* by his incredible flight. Have students provide the definition of the word. To *thrill* is "to fill with a shivering, exciting feeling."
2. **Demonstrate** Have students answer questions to demonstrate understanding. In the picture of the dancers, does the girl on the right looked *thrilled?* How can you tell? (No, her head is down and she does not look happy or excited.)
3. **Apply** Have students apply their understanding. What are some antonyms, or words that mean the opposite, of *thrilled?* (sad, disappointed, bored)

See p. OV•1 to teach *audition.*

Routines Flip Chart

Apply Amazing Words

As students read "Carlos Catches Sports Fever" on p. 27, have them think about what gives Carlos a *thrill.*

Connect to reading

Explain that today students will read about the man who invented basketball. As they read, they should think about how the Question of the Week *How do talents make someone unique?* and the Amazing Words *thrill* and *audition* apply to the story of James Naismith.

ELL Reinforce Vocabulary Use the Day 2 instruction on ELL Poster 16 to teach lesson vocabulary and the lesson concept.

ELL Poster 16

Amazing Words

mock	necessary
idle	result
potential	succeed
ecstatic	rise
thrill	verge
audition	

Differentiated Instruction

A Advanced
"The Myth of Icarus" is a Greek myth. Have students look for other Greek myths in the library. Ask them to try to find different versions of the story of Icarus. Have them read and compare the versions, and then discuss the similarities and differences with their classmates.

ELL English Language Learners
Cognates Point out that one of today's Amazing Words has a Spanish cognate. The cognate for *audition* is *audición.*

Objectives

- Apply knowledge of letter-sound correspondences and irregular plurals to decode words in context and independent of context.

Check Word Reading
SUCCESS PREDICTOR

Word Analysis
Irregular Plurals

Review Review irregular plurals, pointing out that some words that end in *-f* or *-fe* form the plural by changing those letters to *-ves.*

Read words independent of context Display these words. Have the class read the words. Then point to the words in random order and ask students to read them quickly.

fish	**calves**	**deer**	**loaves**
teeth	**people**	**halves**	**sheep**

Corrective feedback Model reading the word or word parts and then have students read the words with you.

Read words in context Display these sentences. Have the class read the sentences.

Team Talk Have pairs take turns reading the sentences naturally.

The **wives** put candles on the **shelves.**
The fall **leaves** crunched under our **feet.**
Children in the play were dressed as **mice** and **geese.**

Don't Wait Until Friday

MONITOR PROGRESS **Check Word Reading**

Write the following words and have the class read them. Notice which words students miss during the group reading. Call on individuals to read some of the words.

half	**life**	**strife**	**hoof**	**shelf**	Spiral Review
hives	**fences**	**curtains**	**beaches**	**libraries**	Row 2 reviews words with regular plurals.
ices	**thieves**	**scarves**	**geese**	**horses**	Row 3 contrasts words with irregular plurals and regular plurals.

If… students cannot read words with irregular plurals at this point,
then… use the Day 1 Word Parts Strategy routine on p. 22a to reteach irregular plurals. Use words from the Decodable Practice Reader. Continue to monitor students' progress using other instructional opportunities during the week. See the Skills Trace on p. 22a.

Day 1	Day 2	Day 3	Day 4	Day 5
Check Oral Vocabulary	Check Word Reading	Check Retelling	Check Fluency	Check Oral Vocabulary

Success Predictor

Literary Terms
Point of View

Teach point of view

Tell students that *point of view* is a term that describes who is telling a story, or who the narrator is. Explain that there are clues that readers can use to help them figure out the point of view of a story or text. In the first-person point of view, which is used in texts such as autobiographies, a person is telling the story of his or her own life. The narrator uses the pronouns *I* and *we.* In the third-person point of view, which is used in texts such as biographies, someone else is telling the story of a person's life. The narrator uses the pronouns *he, she, it,* and *they.*

Model point of view

Think Aloud Let's look at "Batting the Ball" on page 25. What is the first pronoun in the story? (she) This tells us that this story is told in the third-person point of view. Do you see an *I* anywhere in the story? (Yes, but it is when Betsy is talking. She is not the narrator of the story.)

Guide practice

Have students use the first few paragraphs of *The Man Who Invented Basketball* to identify the point of view of the selection. Have students explain how they know whether the selection is a biography or an autobiography.

On their own

Have students look for examples of first- and third-person point of view in other selections of their Student Edition.

Text Features
Time Line and Map

Teach time line and map

Explain that genres such as biography and history often use text features such as maps and time lines to help readers understand information addressed in the text.

Model the strategy

Think Aloud A time line is a way to show the big events that happened in the order that they happened. Maps can show the place where something happened. I can see a map on page 31. There is a time line on page 41.

Guide practice

Discuss with students the time line at the end of *The Man Who Invented Basketball.*

On their own

Have students preview the map on p. 31 and tell how this text feature could increase their understanding of the selection.

Academic Vocabulary

text features elements in written material that help the reader locate and understand information, including titles, headings, subheadings, graphics, pictures/illustrations, boldface type, italics, and lists

time line a chart listing important events for successive years within a particular historical period

Objectives

- ◎ Use context clues to determine the meanings of unfamiliar words.
- Read grade level text with accuracy.

Vocabulary Strategy for ◎ Unfamiliar Words

Teach unfamiliar words

Envision It!

Tell students that they can use the strategy of context clues to determine the meanings of unfamiliar words. When they encounter an unfamiliar word, they can look at the words and sentences around that word for context clues to help them figure out the meaning of the unfamiliar word. Refer students to *Words!* on p. W•7 in the Student Edition for additional practice. Then read "Carlos Catches Sports Fever" on p. 27 with students.

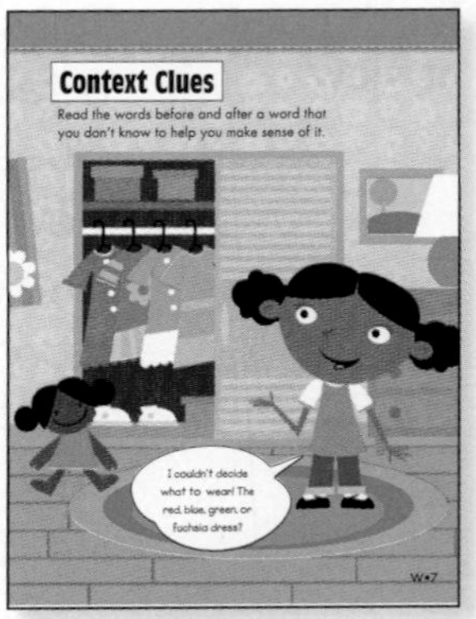

Student Edition p. W•7

Model the strategy

Think Aloud Write on the board: *Molly studies hard. Every day I see her in the library reading her school books and doing her homework.* In the first sentence, I don't know what the word *studies* means. However, if I keep reading and look for context clues, I can guess. Some context clues I see are *reading her school books* and *doing her homework.* I think that *studying* means "reading and doing schoolwork."

Guide practice

Write this sentence on the board: *Like Michael Jordan, Carlos had the basketball "disease," but he didn't want a cure!* Have students figure out the meaning of the word *disease* using context clues. If they are having difficulty, explain the meaning of the word *cure.* For additional support, use *Envision It! Pictured Vocabulary Cards* or *Tested Vocabulary Cards.*

On their own

Read "Carlos Catches Sports Fever" on p. 27. Have students use context clues to determine the meaning of the lesson vocabulary. For additional practice use the *Reader's and Writer's Notebook* p. 250.

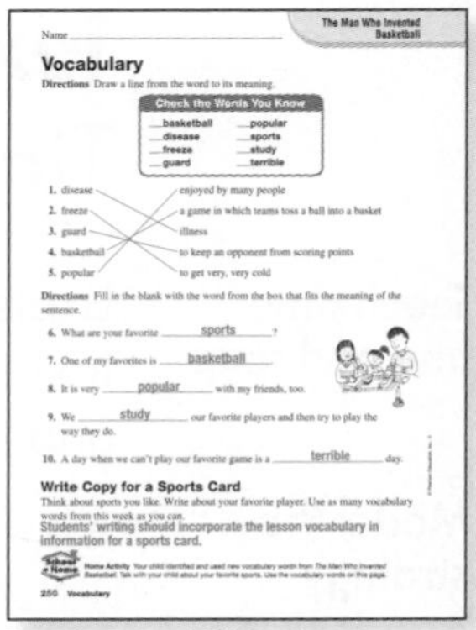

Reader's and Writer's Notebook p. 250

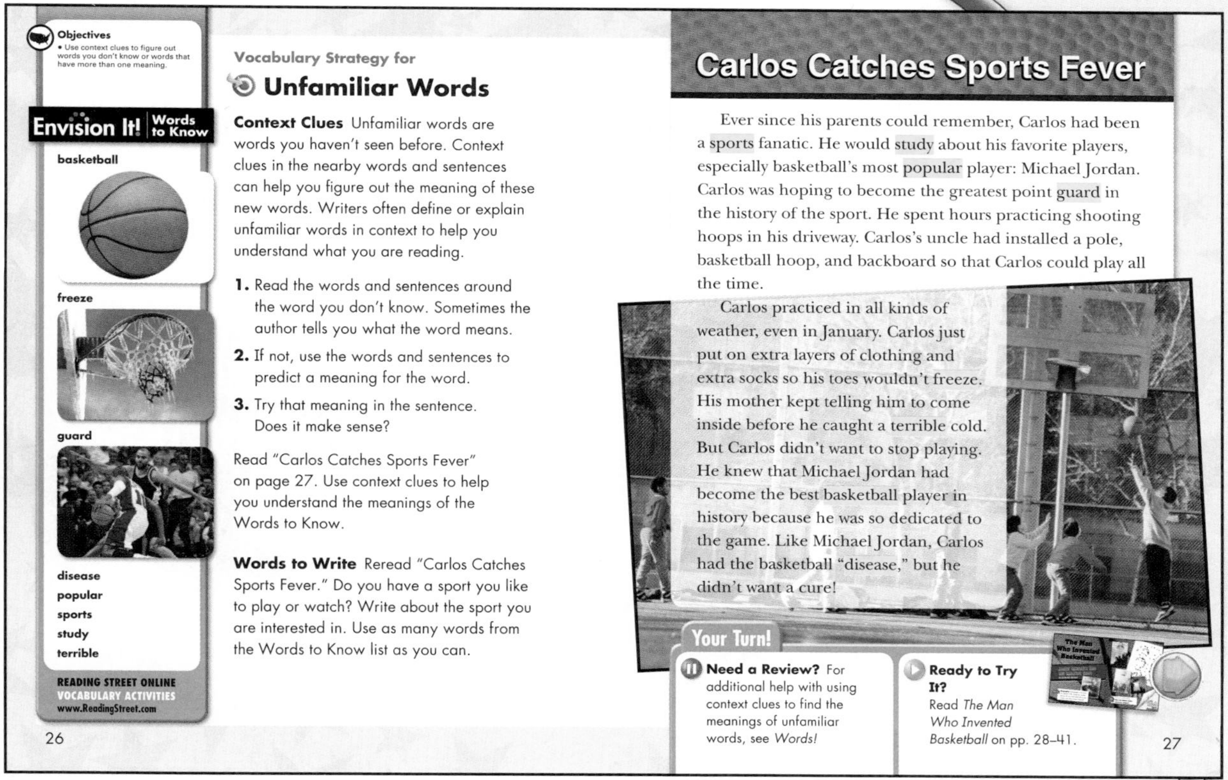

Objectives
- Use context clues to figure out words you don't know or words that have more than one meaning.

Envision It! Words to Know

basketball

freeze

guard

disease
popular
sports
study
terrible

READING STREET ONLINE
VOCABULARY ACTIVITIES
www.ReadingStreet.com

Vocabulary Strategy for

Unfamiliar Words

Context Clues Unfamiliar words are words you haven't seen before. Context clues in the nearby words and sentences can help you figure out the meaning of these new words. Writers often define or explain unfamiliar words in context to help you understand what you are reading.

1. Read the words and sentences around the word you don't know. Sometimes the author tells you what the word means.
2. If not, use the words and sentences to predict a meaning for the word.
3. Try that meaning in the sentence. Does it make sense?

Read "Carlos Catches Sports Fever" on page 27. Use context clues to help you understand the meanings of the Words to Know.

Words to Write Reread "Carlos Catches Sports Fever." Do you have a sport you like to play or watch? Write about the sport you are interested in. Use as many words from the Words to Know list as you can.

26

Carlos Catches Sports Fever

Ever since his parents could remember, Carlos had been a sports fanatic. He would study about his favorite players, especially basketball's most popular player: Michael Jordan. Carlos was hoping to become the greatest point guard in the history of the sport. He spent hours practicing shooting hoops in his driveway. Carlos's uncle had installed a pole, basketball hoop, and backboard so that Carlos could play all the time.

Carlos practiced in all kinds of weather, even in January. Carlos just put on extra layers of clothing and extra socks so his toes wouldn't freeze. His mother kept telling him to come inside before he caught a terrible cold. But Carlos didn't want to stop playing. He knew that Michael Jordan had become the best basketball player in history because he was so dedicated to the game. Like Michael Jordan, Carlos had the basketball "disease," but he didn't want a cure!

Your Turn!

Need a Review? For additional help with using context clues to find the meanings of unfamiliar words, see *Words!*

Ready to Try It? Read *The Man Who Invented Basketball* on pp. 28–41.

27

Student Edition pp. 26–27

Reread for Fluency
Accuracy

Model fluent reading

Read the first paragraph of "Carlos Catches Sports Fever" aloud. Tell students that you are going to read carefully, making sure you include all the words on the page.

ROUTINE Paired Reading

1. **Select a passage** For "Carlos Catches Sports Fever," use the whole passage.
2. **Reading 1** Students read the entire passage, switching readers at the end of each paragraph.
3. **Reading 2** Partners reread the passage. This time the other student begins.
4. **Reread** For optimal fluency, have partners continue to read three or four times.
5. **Corrective Feedback** Listen as students read. Provide feedback about their accuracy and encourage them to ask questions about unfamiliar words.

Lesson Vocabulary

basketball a game played on a court where two teams try to throw a ball through a raised hoop

disease a problem in the body; sickness

freeze turn into ice

guard a person who watches over or protects something

popular liked by many people

sports games in which people use their bodies

study to spend time learning, usually by reading

terrible really bad

Differentiated Instruction

SI Strategic Intervention

Unfamiliar Words For students who need extra help with the lesson vocabulary, go over the words and meanings with the students individually.

ELL

English Language Learners

Cognates Point out the Spanish cognates in this week's lesson vocabulary: *study/estudiar, terrible/terrible,* and *popular/popular.*

Build academic vocabulary Use the lesson vocabulary pictured on p. 26 to teach the meanings of *basketball, freeze,* and *guard.* Call on pairs to write the words on sticky notes and use them to label images of the words on the ELL Poster.

Objectives

- Understand the elements of biography.
- Use text features to preview and predict.
- Set a purpose for listening.

Student Edition pp. 28–29

Build Background

Discuss basketball

Team Talk Have students turn to a partner and discuss the Question of the Week and these questions about basketball. Remind students to ask and answer questions with appropriate detail and to give suggestions that build upon the ideas of others.

- What equipment is needed to play basketball?
- How is basketball played, and what are some of its rules?
- What are some talents a good basketball player might have?

Connect to selection

Have students discuss their answers with the class. Remind students to listen attentively to speakers and to make pertinent comments. (Possible responses: You need a ball, a court, and two nets. Players score points by throwing the ball through the basket. They can pass the ball to each other but can't run while carrying the ball. Basketball players have to be good at throwing and jumping.) For additional opportunities to build background, use the Background Building Audio.

Prereading Strategies

Genre Explain that a **biography** is a true story about a real person written by another person. A biography is told in third person (using *he* or *she*). A biography can be the story of a person's entire life, part of a person's life, or of one event. It is usually told in time order. Many biographies use text features such as maps, time lines, headings, photographs, and captions.

Preview and predict Have students preview the title, photographs, and illustrations in *The Man Who Invented Basketball: James Naismith and His Amazing Game.* Have them predict what they think they will find out as they read.

Set purpose Prior to reading, have students set their own purposes for reading this selection. To help students set a purpose, ask them to think about what they would do if they had to invent a new game.

Strategy Response Log

INTERACT with TEXT

Have students use p. 22 in the *Reader's and Writer's Notebook* to review and use the strategy of summarizing.

Small Group Time

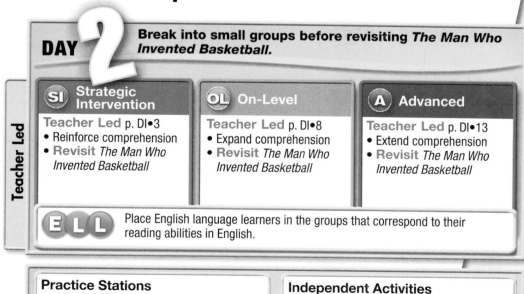

DAY 2 **Break into small groups before revisiting *The Man Who Invented Basketball.***

Teacher Led

SI Strategic Intervention	OL On-Level	A Advanced
Teacher Led p. DI•3 • Reinforce comprehension • Revisit *The Man Who Invented Basketball*	Teacher Led p. DI•8 • Expand comprehension • Revisit *The Man Who Invented Basketball*	Teacher Led p. DI•13 • Extend comprehension • Revisit *The Man Who Invented Basketball*

ELL Place English language learners in the groups that correspond to their reading abilities in English.

Practice Stations
- Words to Know
- Get Fluent
- Word Wise

Independent Activities
- Background Building Audio
- *Reader's and Writer's Notebook*
- Research and Inquiry

Differentiated Instruction

A Advanced
Have students create a diagram of a basketball court and a list of the rules of the game.

Double Day Read! Multidraft Reading

For **Whole Group** instruction, choose one of the reading options below. For each reading, have students set the purpose indicated.

Option 1
Day 2 Read the selection. Use Guide Comprehension to monitor and clarify understanding.
Day 3 Reread the selection. Use Extend Thinking to develop higher-order thinking skills.

Option 2
Day 2 Read the first half of the selection, using both Guide Comprehension and Extend Thinking instruction.
Day 3 Read the second half of the selection, using both Guide Comprehension and Extend Thinking instruction.

ELL

English Language Learners
Build background To build background, review the selection summary in English (*ELL Handbook,* p. 121). Use the Retelling Cards to provide visual support for the summary.

Objectives

- Use context to determine the relevant meaning of unfamiliar words.

OPTION 1 Guide Comprehension Skills and Strategies

Teach Unfamiliar Words

Unfamiliar Words Have students find where the word *freeze* appears on p. 30. Ask students to look at the sentence in which this word is used and the sentences around it for context clues as to the meaning of this word. ("turn into ice")

Corrective Feedback

If... students are unable to define *freeze,*
then... use the model to guide students in identifying and using context clues to figure out the meaning of an unfamiliar word.

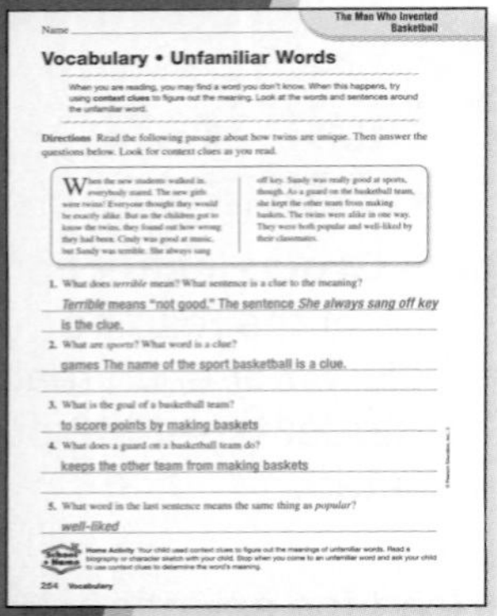
Name
The Man Who Invented Basketball

Vocabulary • Unfamiliar Words

When you are reading, you may find a word you don't know. When this happens, try using **context clues** to figure out the meaning. Look at the words and sentences around the unfamiliar word.

Directions Read the following passage about how twins are unique. Then answer the questions below. Look for context clues as you read.

When the new students walked in, everybody stared. The new girls were twins! Everyone thought they would be exactly alike. But as the children got to know the twins, they found out how wrong they had been. Cindy was good at music, but Sandy was terrible. She always sang off key. Sandy was really good at sports, though. As a guard on the basketball team, she kept the other team from making baskets. The twins were alike in one way. They were both popular and well-liked by their classmates.

1. What does *terrible* mean? What sentence is a clue to the meaning?
Terrible means "not good." The sentence *She always sang off key* is the clue.
2. What are *sports*? What word is a clue?
games The name of the sport basketball is a clue.
3. What is the goal of a basketball team?
to score points by making baskets
4. What does a guard on a basketball team do?
keeps the other team from making baskets
5. What word in the last sentence means the same thing as *popular*?
well-liked

Home Activity Your child used context clues to figure out the meanings of unfamiliar words. Read a biography or character sketch with your child. Stop when you come to an unfamiliar word and ask your child to use context clues to determine the word's meaning.

254 Vocabulary

Reader's and Writer's Notebook p. 254

Model the Skill

Think Aloud If I didn't know what the word *freeze* meant, I could get an idea about its meaning by looking at some of the words around it. I think about how a river can be solid. The only time water is solid is when it is ice.

TOUGH LOVE AND A TOUGH LIFE

Winter in Canada can be very hard. Icy wind sweeps down from the north. Rivers freeze solid. Crossing them can be scary and dangerous.

James Naismith turned eleven in 1872. He was old enough to know where the river near his home became safe, solid ice. But he took a shortcut he had never tried before. His team of horses pulled his wagon onto the frozen river. Their feet pounded the ice. Then one heavy hoof slammed through the sheet of ice. James jumped off the wagon and landed in the water. Grabbing the horses by their reins, he pulled hard. Slowly he forced them to the other side of the river.

James looked around. He saw his uncle Peter Young watching him from behind some trees. But his uncle had not helped him. Uncle Peter wanted James to learn to solve problems by himself and not to take foolish chances. It was a tough lesson.

Let's Think About...

Read the second paragraph. What do you think the biography will be about? Support your prediction with evidence from the text. **Predict** 1

30

Student Edition pp. 30–31

Let's Think About...

1. I think the biography will be about the life of James Naismith because it names important dates in his life and it tells about something that happened to him as a young boy.
2. James had a hard early childhood. His father and mother both died of typhoid fever. His grandmother died a short time later.

OPTION 2 Extend Thinking Think Critically

Higher-Order Thinking Skills

Unfamiliar Words • Synthesis If I didn't know what the word *village* on page 31 meant, how could I figure out the word's meaning? What context clues might help me? Possible response: Some context clues are *schoolhouse, blacksmith shop,* and *store.* These places might all be found in a small town, so a *village* is probably a small town.

What are some other clues? *(icy wind* and *ice skates)* That makes me think *freeze* means "turn into ice." Does that make sense in the sentence? (It does.)

On Their Own

Have students reread pp. 30–31 and use context clues to define other unfamiliar words, such as *disease.* For additional practice, use *Reader's and Writer's Notebook* p. 254.

James grew up near Almonte, Ontario, in Canada.

James was born on November 6, 1861, near Almonte, Ontario, which is in Canada. When he was almost nine, his father, John Naismith, came down with deadly typhoid fever. So they would not catch the disease, James, his sister, Annie, and brother, Robbie, were taken to their grandmother's home. A few days later, their father died. Two weeks later, their mother, Margaret, died of the same disease. A short time later, their grandmother Annie Young died of old age.

That left Uncle Peter to take care of the children in Bennie's Corners, near Almonte. The village had a schoolhouse, a blacksmith shop, a store, and lots of other kids to play with.

The children had lots of fun with very little money. When James needed ice skates, he made them. Then he raced out onto the frozen swimming hole like a champion skater.

Let's Think About...

How would you describe the early part of James Naismith's childhood? Use information from the text and maintain a logical order.
Summarize

2 31

Point of View • Synthesis What is the point of view of this biography and how can you tell? Possible response: It is told in third person. I can tell because it uses the pronoun *he.*

Predict and Set Purpose • Evaluation One thing the author does to help you make a prediction is to put clues into the selection about what is going to happen later. Examine the information on page 30, identify some clues of this kind, and use them to make a prediction about something that might happen in James's future. Possible response: The author says that Uncle Peter wanted James to learn to solve problems by himself. I know from the title that James will invent basketball, so I predict that knowing how to solve problems will help him figure out how to make up the rules for basketball. I can continue to read to confirm my prediction.

Differentiated Instruction

SI Strategic Intervention

Author's craft Point out that the first thing mentioned in the text is a birth. Tell students that this is one sign that they are reading a biography. It starts at the very beginning of a person's life.

A Advanced

Critical thinking Have students discuss reasons that a biography might begin with an event other than the birth of the subject.

ELL English Language Learners

Activate prior knowledge Have students work together to make a list of all the words they know that have to do with basketball, such as *court, ball, hoop,* and *dunk.* Have students teach each other any new words.

Objectives

◎ Make generalizations to aid comprehension.

OPTION 1 Skills and Strategies, continued

Teach Generalize

◎ **Generalize** Remind students that a generalization is a statement that applies to many examples. Write the words *most, many,* and *all* on the board. Explain that these are some of the clue words used in general statements. Have students identify a generalization in the last paragraph on page 33.

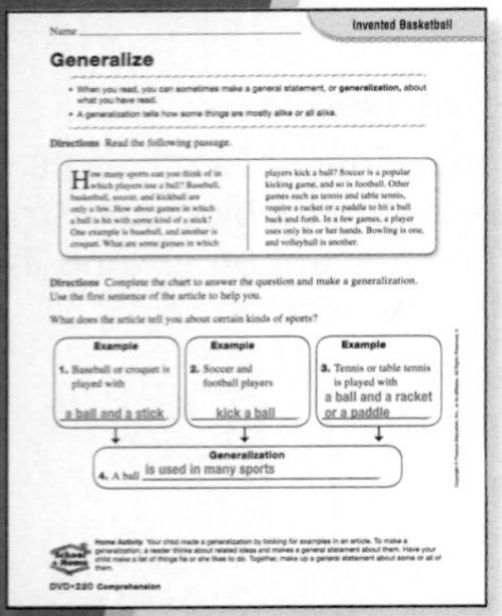
Name ____________ Invented Basketball

Generalize

- When you read, you can sometimes make a general statement, or **generalization**, about what you have read.
- A generalization tells how some things are mostly alike or all alike.

Directions Read the following passage.

How many sports can you think of in which players use a ball? Baseball, basketball, soccer, and kickball are only a few. How about games in which a ball is hit with some kind of a stick? One example is baseball, and another is croquet. What are some games in which players kick a ball? Soccer is a popular kicking game, and so is football. Other games such as tennis and table tennis, require a racket or a paddle to hit a ball back and forth. In a few games, a player uses only his or her hands. Bowling is one, and volleyball is another.

Directions Complete the chart to answer the question and make a generalization. Use the first sentence of the article to help you.

What does the article tell you about certain kinds of sports?

Example	Example	Example
1. Baseball or croquet is played with a ball and a stick	2. Soccer and football players kick a ball	3. Tennis or table tennis is played with a ball and a racket or a paddle

Generalization

4. A ball is used in many sports

Home Activity Your child made a generalization by looking for examples in an article. To make a generalization, a reader thinks about related ideas and makes a general statement about them. Have your child make a list of things he or she likes to do. Together, make up a general statement about some or all of them.

DVD•220 Comprehension

Let's Practice It!
TR DVD•220

Corrective Feedback

If... students can't find the generalization,
then... use the model to guide students in identifying generalizations.

Model the Skill

Think Aloud When I look through the paragraph, can I find one of the clue words? (yes, the word *many*) Then I read the sentence: *Hebrew is an ancient language that many ministers study.*

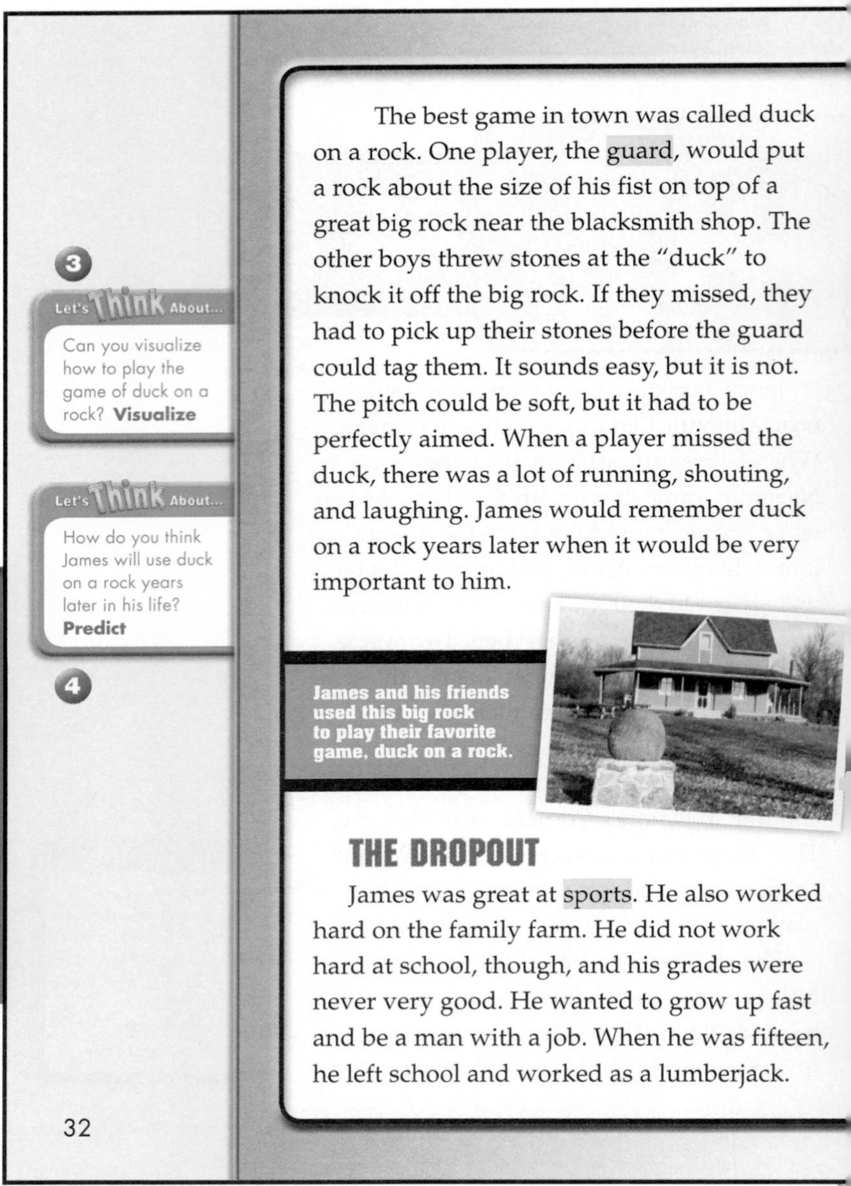
The best game in town was called duck on a rock. One player, the guard, would put a rock about the size of his fist on top of a great big rock near the blacksmith shop. The other boys threw stones at the "duck" to knock it off the big rock. If they missed, they had to pick up their stones before the guard could tag them. It sounds easy, but it is not. The pitch could be soft, but it had to be perfectly aimed. When a player missed the duck, there was a lot of running, shouting, and laughing. James would remember duck on a rock years later when it would be very important to him.

3 Let's Think About... Can you visualize how to play the game of duck on a rock? **Visualize**

Let's Think About... How do you think James will use duck on a rock years later in his life? **Predict** 4

James and his friends used this big rock to play their favorite game, duck on a rock.

THE DROPOUT

James was great at sports. He also worked hard on the family farm. He did not work hard at school, though, and his grades were never very good. He wanted to grow up fast and be a man with a job. When he was fifteen, he left school and worked as a lumberjack.

32

Student Edition pp. 32–33

Let's Think About...

3. Yes, I can imagine trying to pick up the stone before the guard can tag me.
4. James might try to use some of the rules of duck on a rock when he invents basketball.
5. James had to think about helping people. Knowing that his brother Robbie could have been saved stayed in James's mind. He also had to think about what to do with his life.

OPTION 2 Think Critically, continued

Higher-Order Thinking Skills

◎ **Generalize • Synthesis** Use your own knowledge and what you learned from reading page 33 to make a generalization about James Naismith's brother and his illness. Possible response: James's brother died because he did not have a doctor nearby. I can make a generalization based on my own knowledge and the information I have just read. When a person gets very sick, it is always important to have a doctor nearby.

Is there a general statement in that sentence? (Yes, "Many ministers study Hebrew" is a general statement.) How are many ministers alike? Many ministers study Hebrew.

On Their Own

Have students work in pairs to identify another generalization in the text on pp. 32–33. For additional practice, use *Let's Practice It!* page 220 on the *Teacher Resources DVD-ROM.*

He cut down trees for almost five years. Then he decided to change his life.

James had a plan. He wanted to go back to high school and finish fast. His next step would be college. In 1883, James entered McGill University in Montreal, Canada.

When James was home for a visit, his brother, Robbie, had a terrible pain in his side. They all thought it was just a stomachache. It was actually a very bad infection. Robbie died a few hours later. A doctor could have helped him. Knowing Robbie might have been saved stayed in James's mind every day of his life.

In 1887, James graduated from McGill University after studying Hebrew and philosophy. Hebrew is an ancient language that many ministers study. Philosophy teaches people to think about life. James had a lot to think about.

Let's Think About...

How would you summarize some of the things James had to think about? Support your answer with information from the text.
Summarize

5

33

English Language Learners

Summarize Help students learn to summarize. Read the last paragraph on p. 32 aloud. Ask: What are the most important things to remember from this paragraph? (James was a hard worker but not a good student.) Explain to students that they have just summarized the paragraph.

Unfamiliar words Go through pp. 32–33 with students and have them identify unfamiliar words that were not mentioned in the class activity. If possible, have fluent speakers explain the meaning of the words. Ask students to use each word in a sentence.

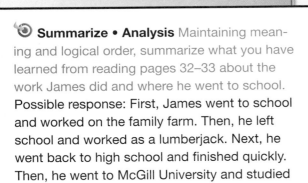

Summarize • Analysis Maintaining meaning and logical order, summarize what you have learned from reading pages 32–33 about the work James did and where he went to school. Possible response: First, James went to school and worked on the family farm. Then, he left school and worked as a lumberjack. Next, he went back to high school and finished quickly. Then, he went to McGill University and studied Hebrew and philosophy.

Unfamiliar Words • Synthesis If I didn't know what the word *terrible* on page 33 meant, how could I figure out the word's meaning? What context clues might help me? Possible response: Some context clues are *pain* and *bad infection.* I can tell from its position in the sentence that *terrible* is being used to describe the kind of pain Robbie had. Since he had a bad infection and ended up dying from it, I can tell that the word *terrible* means "really bad."

Objectives

- Summarize information in text to aid comprehension.

OPTION 1 Skills and Strategies, continued

Teach Summarize

Summarize Review how summarizing is retelling the main ideas or events and leaving out unimportant details. Ask students to summarize the information in the first two paragraphs on p. 34 while maintaining the meaning and logical order. (Possible response: James went to college. He focused on studying even though his friends wanted him to play sports. When he finally tried playing sports, he learned that he could study and have fun.)

Corrective Feedback

If... students have difficulty summarizing p. 34,
then... use the model to guide students in summarizing.

Model the Strategy

Think Aloud This section is about how James learned that he could combine studying with fun when he was a student. Some important information to remember is that at first James studied night and day.

THE MINISTER PLAYS HARDBALL

For James, the next step was studying to become a minister at McGill's Presbyterian College. There was much to learn, and he studied day and night. His friends tried to get him to play sports. They told him it would sharpen his mind and toughen up his body. He said no and kept on studying.

One day his strong friends dragged him out to the football field. James had so much fun that from then on he found time to study hard and play hard too. He was smaller than the other players, but he was powerful and smart. He learned rugby, which is a very rough game. He loved lacrosse, which can be even rougher.

One Saturday James got two black eyes in a wild game of lacrosse. The next day was Sunday, and he had to give a sermon in the church. James, the student minister, looked out from behind those two black eyes. He may have looked kind of funny, but he finished the sermon he had written.

Let's Think About... What words and phrases create a graphic visual image on this page? **Visualize** 6

34

Student Edition pp. 34–35

OPTION 2 Think Critically, continued

Higher-Order Thinking Skills

Summarize • Synthesis Summarize why James was a good choice to invent a new game. Possible response: He was good at playing games, and he was also good at teaching others how to play games.

Generalize • Analysis What generalization can you make about baseball, field hockey, football, and rugby from the information provided in the story? Possible response: Many outdoor games can't be played in cold climates.

Let's Think About...

6. sharpen, toughen, rough, dragged, two black eyes
7. As a student minister, James learns the value of sports. When he later becomes a minister, he believes he can help teens live better lives if he talks to them while teaching them sports. James teaches his students baseball, field hockey, football, and rugby. Since winter is a problem, he is asked to invent a new game that can be played indoors.

I can also talk about why his friends said sports had value and what happened when they dragged James onto the football field.

On Their Own

Have small groups summarize the last paragraph on p. 34.

In 1890, James became a Presbyterian minister. But he did not want to give sermons in a church. He thought he could help teens live better lives if he talked to them while teaching them sports. His first sports job was at the International YMCA Training School, which is now Springfield College. So he moved from Canada to Springfield, Massachusetts, in the United States.

James Naismith believed that the fun and action of sports could improve the lives of young people.

As a student teacher, James was very good at the job of teaching baseball, field hockey, football, and rugby, which are great games during spring, summer, and fall. Winter was a problem. The men had to come indoors and exercise, which was not much fun. They were so bored that some of them wanted to quit the YMCA training school. James was told to invent an exciting indoor game. It had to be ready in two weeks. That was the deadline.

Let's Think About...

Summarize the section "The Minister Plays Hardball." Be sure to maintain the meaning of the section title in your summary.
Summarize

7

35

Background Knowledge • Evaluation • Text to Self On page 35 James's friends tried to get him to play sports, but James said no and kept on studying. Later he discovered he liked playing sports. Have you ever said you didn't want to something and then like it when you tried it? Possible response: Yes, I thought swimming would not be any fun, but then I tried it and really like it.

Check Predictions Have students look back at the predictions they made earlier and discuss whether they were accurate. Then have students preview the rest of the selection and either adjust their predictions accordingly or make new predictions.

Differentiated Instruction

SI Strategic Intervention

Generalize Have students work in groups to come up with generalizations about different kinds of sports.

A Advanced

Generalize Have students work individually to write two generalizations based upon what they have read so far.

Six Pillars of Character

Fairness We show fairness when we play by the rules, share, and listen to others. How did James show fairness while playing football? (He was a rough and tough player but never mean. Therefore, he must have followed the rules.)

ELL

English Language Learners

Summarize Help students take notes about the most important parts of the first paragraph on p. 35. Ask them to use these notes to summarize the paragraph.

If you want to teach this selection in two sessions, stop here.

Objectives

- Find pertinent sources with the help of a reference librarian.
- Recognize and correctly use singular and plural pronouns.
- Practice correctly spelling irregular plurals.

Research and Inquiry
Navigate/Search

Teach Have students generate a research plan for gathering information about their research topic. Encourage them to collect information from multiple sources of written information, including reference texts such as encyclopedias and short biographies. Have them improve the focus of their research as a result of consulting expert sources such as the reference librarian. Tell students to use skimming and scanning techniques to identify important information by looking at text features within reference texts. Headings and bold words might be clues to what kind of information the text will provide. Have students look for other features such as italics, illustrations, captions, or highlighting. Remind students to take notes as they gather information.

Model Think Aloud I told the librarian that I wanted to find out about a talented soccer player. We looked in the library catalogue under "soccer" and saw the name "David Beckham." Then the librarian helped me find an encyclopedia entry about David Beckham. She also helped me find a short biography about him.

Guide practice Have students continue their review of the text sources they identified. If they are having difficulty finding information about their chosen person, then help them either choose a different subject or use the Internet to broaden their search. Make sure students understand the importance of using valid and reliable sources so that their information is accurate.

On their own Remind students that they will be presenting a biography of their subject. Have them make notes about important events in the life of their subject. Remind them to create a Works Cited page as they research, including the author, title, publisher, and publication year for each source used.

Conventions
Singular and Plural Pronouns

Teach What is the purpose of pronouns? (They take the place of nouns.) Remind students that the singular pronouns are *I, me, you, he, she, him, her,* and *it*. The plural pronouns are *we, us, you, they,* and *them*. The pronoun *you* can be used as either a singular or a plural pronoun.

Guide practice Have students write sentences that use singular pronouns, plural pronouns, or both. If they write a sentence with the pronoun *you*, have them give context clues to identify it as a singular or a plural pronoun.

Daily Fix-It Use Daily Fix-It numbers 3 and 4 in the right margin.

Connect to oral language Have students find and read aloud sentences from *The Man Who Invented Basketball*. (*When he was almost nine...* p. 31; *So they would not catch...* p. 31) Ask students to identify each pronoun as singular or plural.

On their own For more practice, use the *Reader's and Writer's Notebook* p. 251.

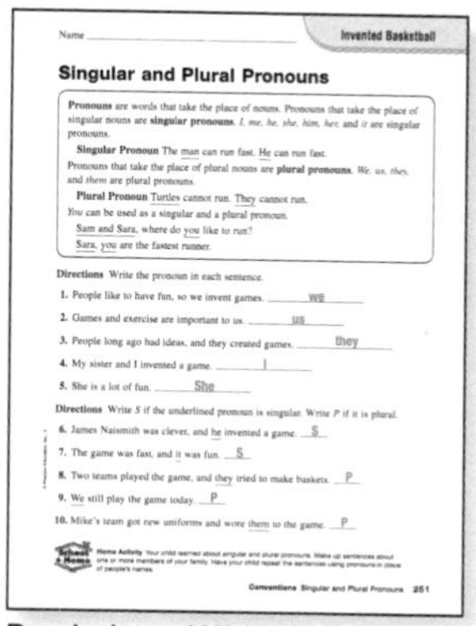
Name ______ Invented Basketball

Singular and Plural Pronouns

Pronouns are words that take the place of nouns. Pronouns that take the place of singular nouns are **singular pronouns**. *I, me, he, she, him, her,* and *it* are singular pronouns.

Singular Pronoun The man can run fast. He can run fast.

Pronouns that take the place of plural nouns are **plural pronouns**. *We, us, they,* and *them* are plural pronouns.

Plural Pronoun Turtles cannot run. They cannot run.

You can be used as a singular and a plural pronoun.

Sam and Sara, where do you like to run?

Sara, you are the fastest runner.

Directions Write the pronoun in each sentence.

1. People like to have fun, so we invent games. we
2. Games and exercise are important to us. us
3. People long ago had ideas, and they created games. they
4. My sister and I invented a game. I
5. She is a lot of fun. She

Directions Write *S* if the underlined pronoun is singular. Write *P* if it is plural.

6. James Naismith was clever, and he invented a game. S
7. The game was fast, and it was fun. S
8. Two teams played the game, and they tried to make baskets. P
9. We still play the game today. P
10. Mike's team got new uniforms and wore them to the game. P

Conventions Singular and Plural Pronouns 251

Reader's and Writer's Notebook, p. 251

Spelling
Irregular Plurals

Teach Remind students that many of their spelling words form plurals by changing *f* or *fe* to *ves*. Model how to spell words with these plurals using segmentation and letter sounds. The word *knives* is the plural form of *knife*. When a word ends in *f* or *fe*, we change the *f* or *fe* to *ves* to form the plural.

Guide practice Have students write each spelling word and say its singular form. Tell them to underline the plural of the words where *f* or *fe* was changed to *ves* (*wolves, knives, scarves, halves*).

On their own For more practice, use *Reader's and Writer's Notebook* p. 252.

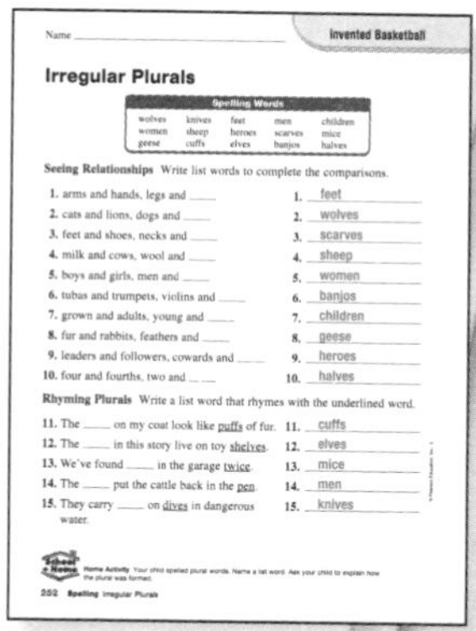
Name ______ Invented Basketball

Irregular Plurals

Spelling Words				
wolves	knives	feet	men	children
women	sheep	heroes	scarves	mice
geese	cuffs	elves	banjos	halves

Seeing Relationships Write list words to complete the comparisons.

1. arms and hands, legs and ____ feet
2. cats and lions, dogs and ____ wolves
3. feet and shoes, necks and ____ scarves
4. milk and cows, wool and ____ sheep
5. boys and girls, men and ____ women
6. tubas and trumpets, violins and ____ banjos
7. grown and adults, young and ____ children
8. fur and rabbits, feathers and ____ geese
9. leaders and followers, cowards and ____ heroes
10. four and fourths, two and ____ halves

Rhyming Plurals Write a list word that rhymes with the underlined word.

11. The ____ on my coat look like puffs of fur. cuffs
12. The ____ in this story live on toy shelves. elves
13. We've found ____ in the garage twice. mice
14. The ____ put the cattle back in the pen. men
15. They carry ____ on dives in dangerous water. knives

252 Spelling Irregular Plurals

Reader's and Writer's Notebook p. 252

Daily Fix-It

3. The boy flew high in the sky, and they got in truble for it. *(he; trouble)*
4. Did the boy learn a lessen. *(lesson; ?)*

ELL

English Language Learners

Conventions To provide students with practice on common and plural nouns, use the modified grammar lessons in the *ELL Handbook* and the Grammar Jammer at: www.ReadingStreet.com

Language transfer: Singular and plural pronouns Students might find it confusing that when a pronoun replaces a common noun, the definite article (the) is omitted. Have them practice replacing the nouns in the following sentences:

- The boy walks. (He walks.)
- The kittens are fuzzy. (They are fuzzy.)
- The road is long. (It is long.)

DAY 2 Language Arts

Objectives

- Select a topic for a persuasive text.
- Develop main ideas and details that support those ideas.

Writing—Persuasive Text
Writing Trait: Focus/Ideas

Introduce the prompt

Remind students that the selection they are reading this week, *The Man Who Invented Basketball,* is about a sport. Then explain that they will begin the writing process for a persuasive text about a sport today. Read aloud the writing prompt.

> **Writing Prompt**
> Write an essay about your favorite sport or game, persuading someone to play it.

Select a topic

Think Aloud

The purpose of a persuasive text is to persuade, or convince. You will try to convince others to try your favorite game or sport. You will give reasons a person would want to play. Let's begin by thinking of a variety of sports and reasons to play them. That information will help you decide what topic you will write about.

Draw a T-chart on the board, and have students name sports and games. List them in the left column. Have students copy this T-chart and work together in pairs to list reasons someone would play the game or sport.

Remind students that they can use the Internet and print resources, as well as their personal experiences, to find information about their sport.

Gather information

Game or Sport	Reasons to Play
curling	fun; takes concentration; unusual
chess	
soccer	

Corrective feedback

Circulate around the room as students complete their T-charts. Conference briefly with students who seem to be having trouble. Ask them to talk about how each game is played or the skills needed to play.

MINI-LESSON

Write with Purpose

- When you know your purpose for writing, you can identify a main idea and details that will support your purpose. A main idea and details graphic organizer can help you organize your writing. Display the graphic organizer. Show students that the main idea is related to their purpose for writing. The supporting details are why a person should play the game or sport.
- I'm going to write a persuasive text about playing chess. My main idea is that chess is a game everyone should learn. I'll write that in the main idea space. Then I'll write reasons chess is a game everyone should learn in the supporting details spaces.

Have students use the graphic organizer on p. 253 of their *Reader's and Writer's Notebook* to record the main idea and supporting details they will use in their persuasive texts.

ROUTINE

Quick Write for Fluency

Team Talk

1. **Talk** Have pairs discuss how their topics are similar and different.
2. **Write** Have students write one sentence about how the two topics are similar, and another about how they are different.
3. **Share** Have students share what they wrote with the class.

Routines Flip Chart

Wrap Up Your Day

- ✔ **Build Concepts** Have students discuss what they learned about how basketball was invented.
- ✔ **Generalize** What generalizations have you made about James Naismith?
- ✔ **Summarize** How did summarizing bits of information help you understand the text?

Differentiated Instruction

SI Strategic Intervention

Support purpose Have students use the following sentence frames to develop ideas for their writing.

My favorite sport is ________.

It is fun because ________.

People should try ________ because ________.

One benefit of ________ is ________.

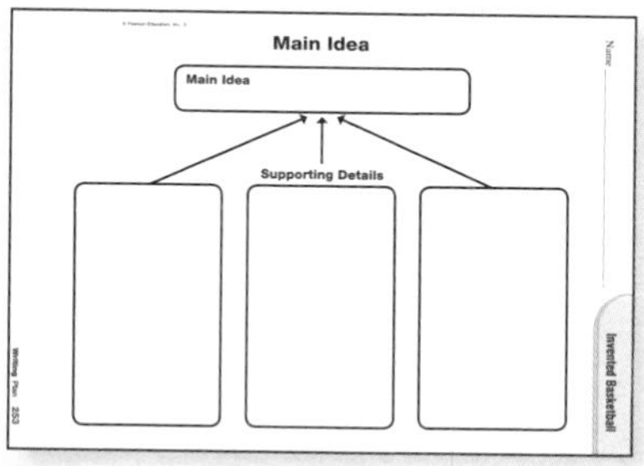

Reader's and Writer's Notebook p. 253

Teacher Tip

If students are having difficulty developing supporting details, have them first explain their reasons orally in small groups.

Preview DAY 3

Tell students that tomorrow they will read about how basketball became popular.

Objectives
- Expand the weekly concept.
- Develop oral vocabulary.

Today at a Glance

Oral Vocabulary
necessary, result

Phonics/Word Analysis
◎ Irregular plurals

Comprehension Check/Retelling
Discuss questions

Reading
The Man Who Invented Basketball

Thinking Critically
Retelling

Fluency
Accuracy

Research and Study Skills
Dictionary

Research and Inquiry
Analyze

Spelling
Irregular plurals

Conventions
Singular and plural pronouns

Writing
Persuasive text

Concept Talk

Question of the Week
How do talents make someone unique?

Expand the concept

Remind students of the weekly concept question. Discuss how the question relates to the invention of basketball. Tell students that today they will continue to read about the man who invented the game of basketball. Encourage students to think about how *thrilling* it would be to think up an entirely new sport.

Anchored Talk

Develop oral vocabulary

Use text features—time line and map—to review pp. 28–35 of *The Man Who Invented Basketball.* Discuss the Amazing Words *thrill* and *audition.* Add these and other concept-related words to the concept map. Use the following questions to develop students' understanding of the concept. Remind students to ask and answer questions with appropriate detail, and to provide suggestions that build upon the ideas of others.

- James Naismith was *thrilled* when he saw that people liked the game of basketball. When is a time when you were *thrilled*?
- You try out for sports teams and *audition* for plays. What are some other kinds of activities for which a person would have to *audition*?

Oral Vocabulary
Amazing Words

Amazing Words Oral Vocabulary Routine

Teach Amazing Words

1. **Introduce** Write the word *necessary* on the board. Have students say it with you. Yesterday we learned about James Naismith. He wanted to be a minister, so it was *necessary* for him to go to college. Have students determine a definition of *necessary*. (*Necessary* means "required.")
2. **Demonstrate** Have students answer questions to demonstrate understanding. What is one thing that is *necessary* to be able to play a game of basketball? (a ball)
3. **Apply** Have students apply their understanding. What is one thing it is *necessary* for you to have at school? (a pencil)

See p. OV•1 to teach *result*.

Routines Flip Chart

Apply Amazing Words

As students read pp. 36–41 of *The Man Who Invented Basketball,* have them consider what happened to James as a *result* of inventing the game of basketball. Ask them to think about what was *necessary* for James to do because he had to work while he went to school to be a doctor.

Connect to reading

Explain that today students will be reading the rest of James Naismith's story. As they read, students should think about how the Question of the Week and the Amazing Words *necessary* and *result* apply to the story.

Amazing Words

mock	necessary
idle	result
potential	succeed
ecstatic	rise
thrill	verge
audition	

ELL Expand Vocabulary Use the Day 3 instruction on ELL Poster 16 to help students expand vocabulary.

ELL Poster 16

Objectives

- Read words with irregular plurals.
- Apply knowledge of sound-spellings and syllable patterns to decode unknown words when reading.
- Decode and read words in context and independent of context.

Word Analysis
Sort Words

Model sorting words

Write *-f, -fe,* and *other* as heads in a three-column chart. Now we are going to sort words. We'll put words with the plural ending *-ves* and the singular ending *-f* in the first column. Words with the plural ending *-ves* and the singular ending *-fe* will go in the second column. Irregular plurals that don't fit into either of these groups will go in the third column. I will start. Write *shelves* and model how to read it, using the Word Parts Strategy Routine on p. 22a. *Shelves* in the singular form is *shelf,* which ends in *f,* so I will write *shelves* in the first column. Model reading *geese* and *knives* in the same way and writing the words in the correct columns of the chart.

Guide practice

Use practice words from the activity on p. 26c for the word sort. Point to a word. Have students read the word, identify its parts, and tell where it should be written on the chart.

Corrective feedback

For corrective feedback, model reading each word and then telling the singular form of each word.

-f	-fe	other
shelves	knives	geese
elves	wives	children
hooves		men
calves		women
halves		mice

Fluent Word Reading

Model

Write *feet.* I recognize this as a plural word I know. *Feet* is the plural of the word *foot.*

Guide practice

Write the words below. Look for word parts you know. When I point to the word, we'll read it together. Allow one second per word part previewing time for the first reading.

calves	**teeth**	**thieves**	**knives**	**people**	**heroes**

On their own

Have students read the list above three or four times, until they can read one word per second.

Decode and Read

Read words independent of context

Have students turn to p. 9 in *Decodable Practice Readers 3.2* and find the first list of words. Each word in this list is an irregular plural. Let's read these words. Be sure that students pronounce each plural word correctly.

Read high-frequency words

Next, have students read the high-frequency words.

Preview Decodable Practice Passage

Have students read the title and preview the story. Tell them that they will read words that are irregular plurals.

Read words in context

Chorally read the story along with the students. Have students identify words in the story that are irregular plurals. Make sure that students are monitoring their accuracy when they decode words.

Team Talk Pair students and have them take turns reading the story aloud to each other. Monitor students as they read to check for proper pronunciation and appropriate pacing.

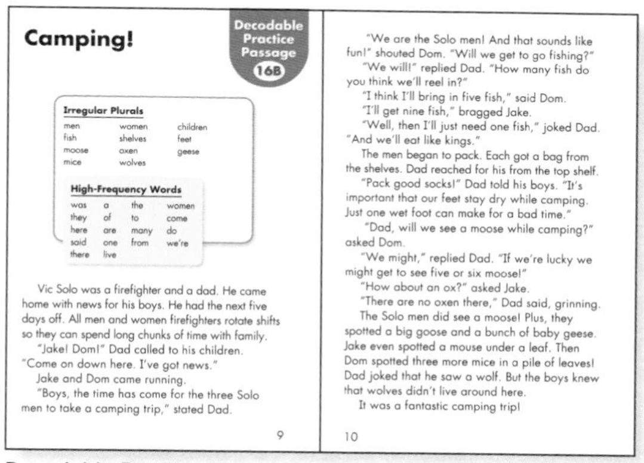

Camping!

Decodable Practice Passage 16B

Irregular Plurals

men	women	children
fish	shelves	feet
moose	oxen	geese
mice	wolves	

High-Frequency Words

was	a	the	women
they	of	to	come
here	are	many	do
said	one	from	we're
there	live		

Vic Solo was a firefighter and a dad. He came home with news for his boys. He had the next five days off. All men and women firefighters rotate shifts so they can spend long chunks of time with family.

"Jake! Dom!" Dad called to his children. "Come on down here. I've got news."

Jake and Dom came running.

"Boys, the time has come for the three Solo men to take a camping trip," stated Dad.

9

"We are the Solo men! And that sounds like fun!" shouted Dom. "Will we get to go fishing?"

"We will!" replied Dad. "How many fish do you think we'll reel in?"

"I think I'll bring in five fish," said Dom.

"I'll get nine fish," bragged Jake.

"Well, then I'll just need one fish," joked Dad. "And we'll eat like kings."

The men began to pack. Each got a bag from the shelves. Dad reached for his from the top shelf.

"Pack good socks!" Dad told his boys. "It's important that our feet stay dry while camping. Just one wet foot can make for a bad time."

"Dad, will we see a moose while camping?" asked Dom.

"We might," replied Dad. "If we're lucky we might get to see five or six moose!"

"How about an ox?" asked Jake.

"There are no oxen there," Dad said, grinning.

The Solo men did see a moose! Plus, they spotted a big goose and a bunch of baby geese. Jake even spotted a mouse under a leaf. Then Dom spotted three more mice in a pile of leaves! Dad joked that he saw a wolf. But the boys knew that wolves didn't live around here.

It was a fantastic camping trip!

10

Decodable Practice Passage 16B

Differentiated Instruction

SI Strategic Intervention

Sort words Have students make flash cards for the plural words listed on the chart in the "other" column. Have students practice reading the words until they become fluent.

A Advanced

Sort words Have students add more plural words to the three-column chart. They may use a dictionary or glossary to check spellings.

Objectives

- Identify and make generalizations to aid comprehension.
- Summarize information to aid comprehension.
- Use context clues to define unfamiliar words.

Comprehension Check

Have students discuss each question with a partner. Ask several pairs to share their responses.

☑ **Genre • Analysis**
How can you tell that *The Man Who Invented Basketball* is not an autobiography? Possible response: The story of James's life is told by another person, not by him, and the text uses pronouns such as *he* and *his* instead of *I* and *me.*

☑ **Generalize • Evaluation**
Using the information on page 34, what generalization could you make about James's friends? Possible response: They all liked sports and wanted to get James involved in sports, too.

☑ **Summarize • Synthesis**
How could you summarize James Naismith's time at college? Possible response: James studied very hard, but he learned how to play hard, too.

☑ **Unfamiliar words • Analysis**
Using context clues, figure out the meaning of the word *lumberjack* on page 32. Possible response: The next sentence says that James spent five years cutting down trees. A *lumberjack* is someone whose job is to cut down trees.

☑ **Connect text to self**
James had to work hard to do well in school. Tell about a time when you had to work hard to get something you wanted. Possible response: When I wanted to learn how to swim, I had to practice a lot and work really hard, but I finally learned how to do it.

Strategy Response Log

INTERACT with TEXT

Have students revisit the text and use p. 22 in the *Reader's and Writer's Notebook* to summarize the first half of *The Man Who Invented Basketball.*

Check Retelling

Have students retell the first part of *The Man Who Invented Basketball,* summarizing information in the text in a logical order.

Corrective feedback

If... students leave out important details,
then... have students do a Picture Walk and look back through the illustrations in the selection.

Small Group Time

DAY 3 **Break into small groups before revisiting *The Man Who Invented Basketball.***

Teacher Led

SI Strategic Intervention	OL On-Level	A Advanced
Teacher Led p. DI•4 • Reinforce vocabulary • **Read/Revisit** *The Man Who Invented Basketball*	**Teacher Led** p. DI•9 • Expand vocabulary • **Read/Revisit** *The Man Who Invented Basketball*	**Teacher Led** p. DI•14 • Extend vocabulary • **Read/Revisit** *The Man Who Invented Basketball*

ELL Place English language learners in the groups that correspond to their reading abilities in English.

Practice Stations
- Let's Write
- Get Fluent
- Word Work

Independent Activities
- AudioText: *The Man Who Invented Basketball*
- *Reader's and Writer's Notebook*
- Research and Inquiry

ELL

English Language Learners

Check retelling To support retelling, review the multilingual summary for *The Man Who Invented Basketball* with the appropriate Retelling Card/s to scaffold understanding.

Objectives

- Make and identify generalizations to aid comprehension.

OPTION 1 Skills and Strategies, continued

Teach Generalize

Generalize Have students reread the last sentence of the first paragraph and the first sentence of the second paragraph on p. 37. Which of these sentences is a generalization? (the first one)

Corrective Feedback

If... students have difficulty determining which statement is a generalization,
then... use the model to guide students in determining whether a statement is a generalization or not.

Model the Skill

Think Aloud I look at these two sentences and try to see which tells how several things are alike in one way. The first sentence tells about what many women did.

INVENTING FUN

James struggled with the problem for twelve days. The game had to be fast and fun. It could not be risky, like football or rugby, with teams of men banging into the gym walls.

That good old game from his childhood, duck on a rock, flashed into his head. He remembered how using a soft pitch was the best way to aim for the "duck." James's eyes lit up. He shouted out loud, "I've got it!"

There was no time to invent new gear. Two peach baskets were used as goals. James explained the strange rules. Two teams of men dragged themselves onto the gym floor, grumbling. They took a soccer ball and started playing. The grumbling soon stopped. Cheers and shouts filled the gym. The date was December 21, 1891. Basketball was born. Soon teams formed in gyms all around town.

Let's Think About...
What parts of the games and sports James knew well went into basketball?
Summarize

8

Peach baskets were used as basketball goals before nets.

36

Student Edition pp. 36–37

Double Day Read! Multidraft Reading

If you chose . . .

Option 1 Return to the Extend Thinking instruction starting on p. 30–31.

Option 2 Read pp. 36–41. Use the Guide Comprehension and Extend Thinking instruction.

OPTION 2 Think Critically, continued

Higher-Order Thinking Skills

Generalize • Synthesis Use the information on page 36 about football and rugby to make a generalization about outdoor games. Possible response: Outdoor games can be dangerous.

Let's Think About...

8. James used the game of duck on a rock and a soccer ball to help invent the game of basketball.

9. In his earlier games, James used peach baskets. In the later games, he used rope baskets with backboards. Players were also allowed to dribble in the later games.

The second tells about what one specific woman did. The first sentence is the generalization.

On Their Own

Ask students to identify another generalization on pp. 36–37.

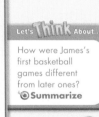

In schools across the United States, students began to play basketball. Women began playing, too.

A young woman named Maude Sherman was on one of the first women's teams. James and Maude soon became friends, and then fell in love. They married on June 20, 1894. James and Maude would have five children together.

In a few years, basketball started being played more like it is played today. The peach baskets had changed to rope baskets. Backboards were added. Dribbling became popular because players were not allowed to hold the ball very long without throwing it. When the ball bounced off the floor as a player raced down the court, it sounded like a fast drumbeat. James thought dribbling was a great idea.

Let's Think About...

How were James's first basketball games different from later ones?
Summarize

9

37

Summarize • Analysis How could you use information from the text to summarize the invention of basketball in one or two sentences? Possible response: James Naismith invented basketball when he was asked to come up with a game people could play inside in the winter.

Unfamiliar Words • Synthesis If I didn't know what the word *dribbling* on page 37 meant, how could I figure out the word's meaning? What context clues might help me? Possible response: Some context clues are that when a player is dribbling, the ball isn't held in the player's hands and the ball sounds like a drumbeat as it bounces off the floor as the player races down the court. I think *dribbling* must mean "using your hands to bounce a ball up and down on the ground very fast."

Differentiated Instruction

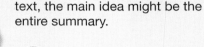

SI Strategic Intervention

Summarize To help students summarize, guide them to identify the main idea in different sections of text. Tell students that when they are summarizing shorter pieces of text, the main idea might be the entire summary.

A Advanced

Explore a topic Have students use the library or Internet to find out more about how early basketball was played and how the game developed.

ELL

English Language Learners

Compund words Help students identify compound words on pp. 36–37. *(football, basketball, backboards, drumbeat)* Discuss how to determine meaning by defining the two small words in each word.

DAY 3 Read and Comprehend

Objectives

- Summarize information in text to aid comprehension.

OPTION 1 Skills and Strategies, continued

Teach Summarize

Summarize Remind students that a summary is a retelling of information using only the most important facts and the main idea. Have students summarize the information in the last paragraph on p. 38. (After much hard work, James graduated from medical college. He later worked as a minister, a professor, and a medical doctor.)

Corrective Feedback

If... students are having difficulty summarizing,
then... use the model to guide students in summarizing.

Model the Strategy

Think Aloud I only want to include the most important details in my summary. Where James went to school is interesting, but it's more important that he graduated. It's interesting where he worked, but what he did is more important.

Let's Think About...

Were your predictions correct so far? What do you think will happen next in James's life? **Predict**

10

In 1895, James and Maude moved to Denver, Colorado. There James became director of physical education at the largest YMCA in the country.

He was always working on his plan for the future. He remembered his brother dying horribly without help from a doctor. He had seen athletes have terrible accidents. He wanted to be a doctor and help people.

There was no stopping James when he had a plan. He became a student at Gross Medical College in Denver. He would work all day at the YMCA and then study to be a doctor after work and on weekends. James graduated as a medical doctor in 1898. That year he got the job of assistant physical director at the University of Kansas. By 1909 James was working there as a minister, a professor, and a medical doctor.

38

Student Edition pp. 38–39

Let's Think About...

10 Yes. I thought James would eventually try to help sick or injured people. I think he will come up with creative ideas on how to treat people.

OPTION 2 Think Critically, continued

Higher-Order Thinking Skills

Summarize • Synthesis If you were to summarize the story so far, would you include all the dates that are mentioned? Why or why not? Possible response: No; although the dates are important details, they are not necessary in a summary.

On Their Own

Have students summarize p. 39.

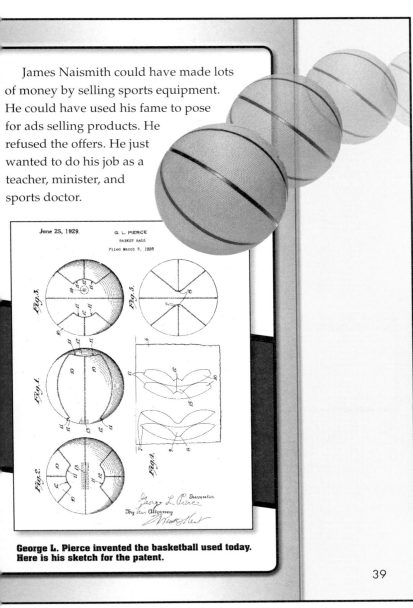

James Naismith could have made lots of money by selling sports equipment. He could have used his fame to pose for ads selling products. He refused the offers. He just wanted to do his job as a teacher, minister, and sports doctor.

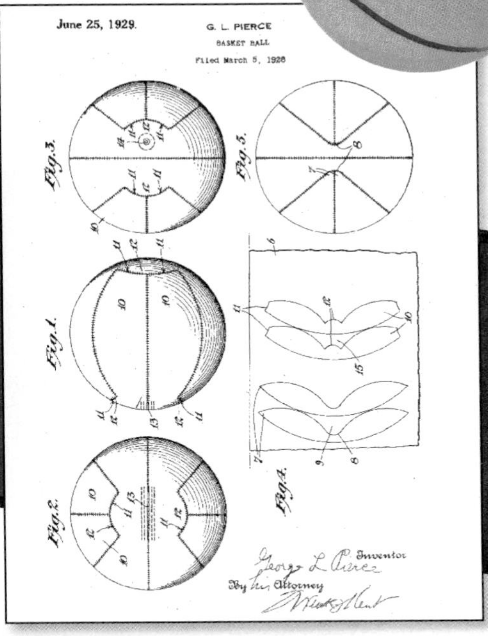

George L. Pierce invented the basketball used today. Here is his sketch for the patent.

39

Generalize • Analysis What is an example of a generalization on page 38? Possible response: Doctors help people.

Unfamiliar Words • Synthesis If I didn't know what the word *products* on page 39 meant, how could I figure out the word's meaning? What context clues might help me? Possible response: One context clue is *ads selling. Products* must be things people sell.

Differentiated Instruction

SI Strategic Intervention

Summarize Have students work in pairs to create a one-paragraph summary of James Naismith's life.

Connect to Social Studies

The Olympics were athletic contests that happened in ancient Greece. The modern Olympic games started in 1896. Basketball became an official game in the Olympics in 1936.

ELL

English Language Learners

Cognates Point out the words *professor* and *doctor* at the bottom of p. 38. There are two Spanish words for *doctor. medico* and the cognate *doctor.* The cognate for *professor* is *profesor*.

OPTION 1 Skills and Strategies, continued

Objectives

- Use graphic sources to aid in understanding information.
- Check predictions.

Teach Graphic Sources

Review **Graphic Sources** Have students read through the events included on the time line on p. 41. How does this graphic source help us learn about Naismith's life? (It lists the most important events, in order.)

Corrective Feedback

If... students are having difficulty understanding why the author included this time line,
then... use the model to guide students in understanding the purpose of a time line.

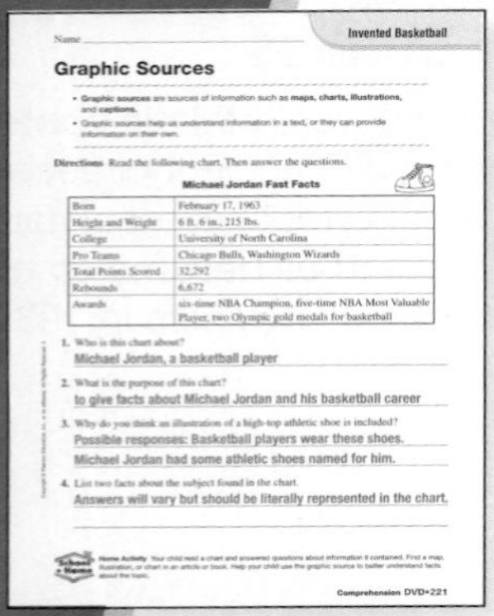
Name ______ Invented Basketball

Graphic Sources

- Graphic sources are sources of information such as maps, charts, illustrations, and captions.
- Graphic sources help us understand information in a text, or they can provide information on their own.

Directions Read the following chart. Then answer the questions.

Michael Jordan Fast Facts

Born	February 17, 1963
Height and Weight	6 ft. 6 in., 215 lbs.
College	University of North Carolina
Pro Teams	Chicago Bulls, Washington Wizards
Total Points Scored	32,292
Rebounds	6,672
Awards	six-time NBA Champion, five-time NBA Most Valuable Player, two Olympic gold medals for basketball

1. Who is this chart about?
Michael Jordan, a basketball player
2. What is the purpose of this chart?
to give facts about Michael Jordan and his basketball career
3. Why do you think an illustration of a high-top athletic shoe is included?
Possible responses: Basketball players wear these shoes. Michael Jordan had some athletic shoes named for him.
4. List two facts about the subject found in the chart.
Answers will vary but should be literally represented in the chart.

Home Activity Your child read a chart and answered questions about information it contained. Find a map, illustration, or chart in an article or book. Help your child use the graphic source to better understand facts about the topic.

Comprehension DVD•221

Let's Practice It!
TR DVD•221

Model the Skill

Think Aloud The first thing I see when I examine this time line are dates. In what kind of order are the dates placed? (time order) What information is listed next to each date? (an important event from James Naismith's life)

NAISMITH'S ORIGINAL THIRTEEN RULES OF BASKETBALL, 1891

1. The ball may be thrown in any direction.
2. It can be batted with hands, but not with the fist.
3. No running with the ball.
4. Hold the ball only with the hands.
5. No holding, pushing, hitting, or tripping the other team's players.
6. Follow the rules or a foul will be declared.
7. Make three fouls and the other team is given a goal.
8. A goal is made when the ball goes into the basket.
9. When the ball goes out of bounds, the first person to touch it, or the umpire, will throw it onto the court.
10. The umpire is the judge of the players. He can call fouls.
11. The referee is the judge of the ball. He decides on goals.
12. Game time is two fifteen-minute halves.
13. The team with the most goals in that time is the winner.

Let's Think About...

Use the rules to imagine how the game was played in 1891. How was the game different then? **Visualize**

11

40

Student Edition pp. 40–41

Let's Think About...

11 The game lasted a much shorter time back then.

12 All events from 1861–1909.

OPTION 2 Think Critically, continued

Higher-Order Thinking Skills

Review **Graphic Sources • Analysis** Why might playing duck on a rock not be one of the events included on the time line on page 41? Possible response: It is only a small detail in James's life, not one of the most important events.

Summarize • Synthesis Summarize the purpose of the list provided on page 40. Possible response: Rules for basketball include how players should handle the ball, what will happen if the rules are not followed, how long the game will last, and how one team can win the game.

This time line is visually summarizing the most important events, in order, from the biography we just read.

TIME LINE

- **1861** Born on November 6, Almonte, Ontario, Canada.
- **1870** Parents die; moves to Bennie's Corners, Ontario.
- **1887** Graduates from McGill University in Montreal, Quebec, Canada.
- **1890** Becomes a Presbyterian minister.
- **1891** Invents basketball; first game is played December 21.
- **1894** Marries Maude Sherman on June 20.
- **1895** Becomes director of physical education at YMCA in Denver, Colorado.
- **1898** Graduates as a medical doctor
- **1909** Is professor, minister, and doctor at the University of Kansas.
- **1917** Helps American soldiers in World War I as a military chaplain.
- **1925** Becomes United States citizen.
- **1936** Is honored at Olympic Games in Berlin, Germany.
- **1939** Dies on November 28 in Lawrence, Kansas.

Let's Think About...

Which of the events in the time line are supported by facts and details in the biography?
Summarize

12

41

On Their Own

Have students use the time line to identify the years in which Naismith was born, got married, and died. For additional practice, use *Let's Practice It!* page 221 on the *Teacher Resources DVD-ROM.*

Comprehension Check

Spiral Review

Cause and Effect • Synthesis What effect did his brother's death have on James Naismith? Possible response: It made him want to become a doctor.

Predict and Set a Purpose • Evaluation If your purpose for reading this story was to find out about basketball, what would be more important: the section about Naismith's early life or the section about how he invented the game? (the section about how he invented the game) If your purpose for reading the story was to find out how people overcome challenges, then which section would be more important? (the section about Naismith's early life)

Check Predictions Have students return to the predictions they made earlier and confirm whether they were accurate.

Differentiated Instruction

SI Strategic Intervention

Graphic sources Work with students to create a class time line for the year on the board. Include events such as vacations, birthdays, and field trips.

A Advanced

Graphic sources Have students work individually to create a time line of their own lives, starting with their birth and including events they consider the most important.

ELL English Language Learners

Language production Explain to students that a time line is a series of events listed in time order. Tell students that to talk or write about the time line, they will need to be familiar with the following sequence words: *before, after, next, later, first, second,* and *finally.* Explain the meaning of each word and give students an example of how it might be used in relation to the time line. For example: James was a minister before he invented basketball. Help students use each word in a sentence.

DAY 3 Read and Comprehend

Objectives

- ◎ Generalize to aid in comprehension.
- ◎ Summarize to aid comprehension.

Check Retelling
SUCCESS PREDICTOR

Plan to Assess Retelling

- ☑ **This week assess Strategic Intervention students.**
- ☐ **Week 2** Assess Advanced students.
- ☐ **Week 3** Assess Strategic Intervention students.
- ☐ **Week 4** Assess On-Level students.
- ☐ **Week 5** Assess any students you have not yet checked during this unit.

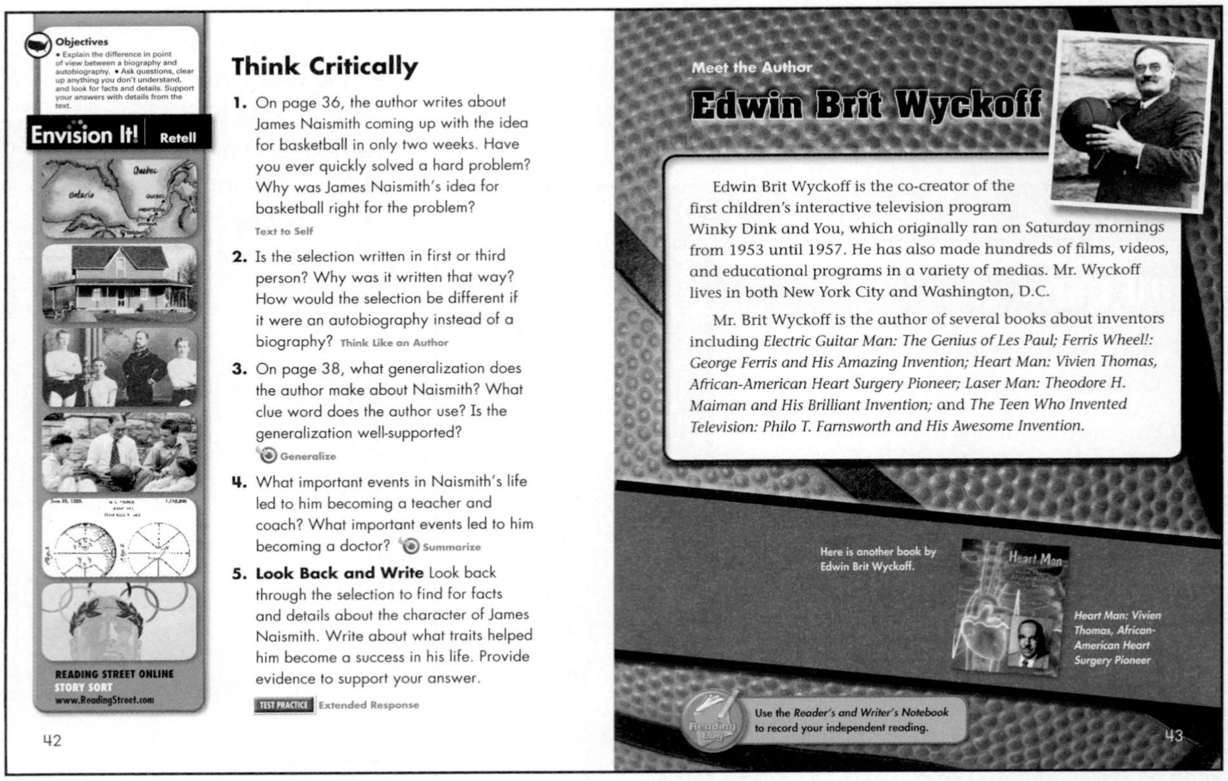

Objectives
• Explain the difference in point of view between a biography and autobiography. • Ask questions, clear up anything you don't understand, and look for facts and details. Support your answers with details from the text.

Envision It! | Retell

READING STREET ONLINE
STORY SORT
www.ReadingStreet.com

Think Critically

1. On page 36, the author writes about James Naismith coming up with the idea for basketball in only two weeks. Have you ever quickly solved a hard problem? Why was James Naismith's idea for basketball right for the problem? Text to Self
2. Is the selection written in first or third person? Why was it written that way? How would the selection be different if it were an autobiography instead of a biography? Think Like an Author
3. On page 38, what generalization does the author make about Naismith? What clue word does the author use? Is the generalization well-supported? Generalize
4. What important events in Naismith's life led to him becoming a teacher and coach? What important events led to him becoming a doctor? Summarize
5. **Look Back and Write** Look back through the selection to find for facts and details about the character of James Naismith. Write about what traits helped him become a success in his life. Provide evidence to support your answer. TEST PRACTICE Extended Response

42

Meet the Author

Edwin Brit Wyckoff

Edwin Brit Wyckoff is the co-creator of the first children's interactive television program Winky Dink and You, which originally ran on Saturday mornings from 1953 until 1957. He has also made hundreds of films, videos, and educational programs in a variety of medias. Mr. Wyckoff lives in both New York City and Washington, D.C.

Mr. Brit Wyckoff is the author of several books about inventors including *Electric Guitar Man: The Genius of Les Paul; Ferris Wheel!: George Ferris and His Amazing Invention; Heart Man: Vivien Thomas, African-American Heart Surgery Pioneer; Laser Man: Theodore H. Maiman and His Brilliant Invention;* and *The Teen Who Invented Television: Philo T. Farnsworth and His Awesome Invention.*

Here is another book by Edwin Brit Wyckoff.

Heart Man: Vivien Thomas, African-American Heart Surgery Pioneer

Use the *Reader's and Writer's Notebook* to record your independent reading.

43

Student Edition pp. 42–43

Retelling

Envision It! Have students work in pairs to retell the selection, using the Envision It! Retelling Cards as prompts. Remind students that they should accurately describe the main topic and important ideas and use key vocabulary as they retell. Monitor students' retellings.

Scoring rubric

> **Top-Score Response** A top-score response makes connections beyond the text, describes the main topic and important ideas using accurate information, evaluates generalizations, and draws conclusions from the text.

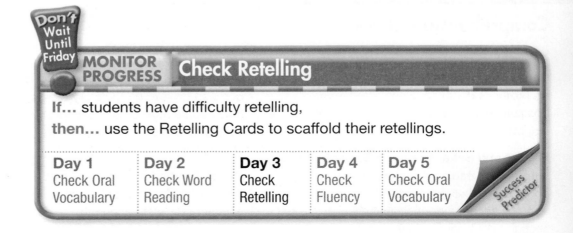

Don't Wait Until Friday MONITOR PROGRESS **Check Retelling**

If... students have difficulty retelling,
then... use the Retelling Cards to scaffold their retellings.

Day 1	Day 2	Day 3	Day 4	Day 5
Check Oral Vocabulary	Check Word Reading	Check Retelling	Check Fluency	Check Oral Vocabulary

Success Predictor

Think Critically

Text to self

1. I helped my friend build a snow fort. The fort kept caving in. I told my friend to make the walls of the fort thicker. Then the fort stopped caving in. James Naismith's idea was right because it was for a game that could be played inside. It was exciting and fun. It was good exercise, but no one would hurt themselves.

Think like an author

2. The selection is written in the third person. It was written in the third person because someone other than James Naismith wrote it. If this selection were an autobiography, it would have been written in the first person and it would have used the pronouns *I* and *me.*

Generalize

3. The generalization is *He was always working on his plan for the future.* The clue word is *always.* This is a well-supported generalization because the author shows how Naismith worked hard to become a doctor.

Summarize

4. Naismith was good at sports when he was young. Then in college his friends dragged him out to play football. He realized that it was important to do sports and exercise. This made Naismith want to be a teacher and a coach. When Naismith was little his brother needed a doctor, but there was no doctor nearby and his brother died. This made Naismith want to be a doctor when he grew up.

Writing on Demand

5. **Look Back and Write** To build writing fluency, assign a 10–15 minute time limit.

Suggest that students use a prewriting strategy, such as brainstorming or using a graphic organizer, to organize their ideas. Remind them to establish a topic sentence and support it with facts, details, or explanations. As students finish, encourage them to reread their responses, revise for organization and support, and proofread for errors in grammar and conventions.

Scoring rubric

Top-Score Response A top-score response uses details from the text to tell about the traits that made James Naismith become a success.

A top-score response should include:

- He worked hard all his life.
- He knew how to play hard but fairly.
- He never gave up.

Differentiated Instruction

SI Strategic Intervention

Help students find information by asking the following questions: What helped James succeed in college? (He studied day and night.) What helped James succeed at football? (He was powerful and smart.) What helped James succeed at inventing basketball? (He thought of "duck on a rock," a game from his childhood.)

Meet the Author

Have students read about author Edwin Brit Wyckoff on p. 43. Ask them how his other books are like *The Man Who Invented Basketball.*

Independent Reading

After students enter their independent reading information into their Reading Logs, have them paraphrase a portion of the text they have just read. Remind students that when we paraphrase we express the meaning of a passage using other words and maintaining logical order.

ELL

English Language Learners

Retelling Use the Retelling Cards to discuss the selection with students. Place the cards in an incorrect order and have volunteers correct the mistake. Then have students explain where each card should go as they explain the sequence of the selection.

Check Retelling

Success Predictor

Objectives

- Read grade-level text with accuracy.
- Reread for fluency.
- Use text features to find words in a dictionary.

Model Fluency

Accuracy

Model fluent reading Have students turn to p. 30 in *The Man Who Invented Basketball.* Have students follow along as you read this page. Point out that as you read you are including all the words on the page. Tell students to listen for difficult or unfamiliar words. Remind them that part of reading with accuracy is understanding the meaning of and reading fluently any unfamiliar words.

Guide practice Have students follow along as you read the page again. Ask questions to be sure students comprehend the text. Have students reread the page as a group without you until they read with accuracy and make no mistakes. Continue in the same way on p. 31.

Reread for Fluency

Corrective feedback

If... students are having difficulty reading with accuracy,
then... prompt:

- Did you read every word? Where do you see difficult words?
- How can you read with better accuracy?
- Read the sentence again. Make sure you read carefully and do not miss any words.

ROUTINE Paired Reading Team Talk

1. **Select a passage** For *The Man Who Invented Basketball,* use p. 36.
2. **Reading 1** Students read the entire page, switching readers at the end of the second paragraph.
3. **Reading 2** Partners reread p. 36 of *The Man Who Invented Basketball.* This time the other student begins.
4. **Reread** For optimal fluency, have partners continue to read three or four times.
5. **Corrective Feedback** Listen as students read. Provide feedback about their accuracy and encourage them to ask questions about unfamiliar words.

Routines Flip Chart

Research and Study Skills
Dictionary

Teach

Ask students what kinds of information they might look up in a dictionary. Students may mention word meanings, syllabication, or pronunciation. Explain to students that they can find print dictionaries in libraries and electronic dictionaries on the Internet or on CD-ROMs in classroom computers. Display a print dictionary and use it to review these terms:

- Each word defined in a dictionary is called an entry word.
- The **entry words** in a dictionary are organized in alphabetical order so you can quickly and easily find each one.
- The **guide words,** or the two words at the top of every dictionary page, tell the first and last words on that page. You can use your knowledge of alphabetical order to tell which guide words occur before and after the word you are seeking.
- A **pronunciation key** on every spread shows how to say words.
- The parts of an entry might include the word's syllabication and pronunciation, its part of speech or how to use it in a sentence, its definition, and a phrase or sentence showing how to use it in context.

Provide groups with dictionaries. Have groups use the dictionaries to locate the entry words, guide words, and pronunciation key.

Guide practice

Discuss these questions:

How do you know on which page the word you are looking for will fall? (Look at the guide words at the top of each page and find the two that occur before and after the word for which you are looking.)

Why might the entry words be boldfaced? (to make it easier to tell them apart from their definitions and the other information contained in each entry)

Have students model how they would look up the meaning, syllabication, and pronunciation of an unknown word in the dictionary.

On their own

Have students review the instructions and complete p. 255 of the *Reader's and Writer's Notebook.*

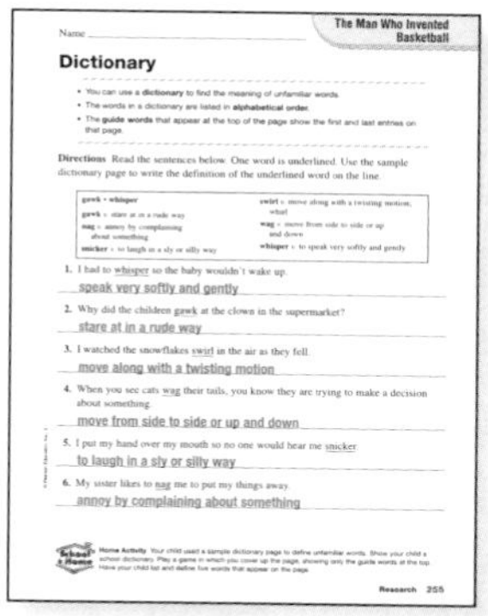
Name ______

The Man Who Invented Basketball

Dictionary

- You can use a **dictionary** to find the meaning of unfamiliar words.
- The words in a dictionary are listed in **alphabetical order.**
- The **guide words** that appear at the top of the page show the first and last entries on that page.

Directions Read the sentences below. One word is underlined. Use the sample dictionary page to write the definition of the underlined word on the line.

gawk • whisper
gawk = stare at in a rude way
nag = annoy by complaining about something
snicker = to laugh in a sly or silly way
swirl = move along with a twisting motion; whirl
wag = move from side to side or up and down
whisper = to speak very softly and gently

1. I had to whisper so the baby wouldn't wake up.
speak very softly and gently
2. Why did the children gawk at the clown in the supermarket?
stare at in a rude way
3. I watched the snowflakes swirl in the air as they fell.
move along with a twisting motion
4. When you see cats wag their tails, you know they are trying to make a decision about something.
move from side to side or up and down
5. I put my hand over my mouth so no one would hear me snicker.
to laugh in a sly or silly way
6. My sister likes to nag me to put my things away.
annoy by complaining about something

Home Activity Your child used a sample dictionary page to define unfamiliar words. Show your child a school dictionary. Play a game in which you cover up the page, showing only the guide words at the top. Have your child list and define five words that appear on the page.

Research 255

Reader's and Writer's Notebook p. 255

ELL

English Language Learners

Professional Development: What ELL experts say about think-alouds "Think-alouds can be particularly informative when used with second-language students. Through this type of dialogue, the teacher can discover not only the types of challenges that students encounter with the text, but also how they deal with such challenges." —Dr. Georgia Earnest Garcia

Objectives

- Analyze data for usefulness.
- Identify and correctly use singular and plural pronouns.

Research and Inquiry
Analyze

Teach Have students follow their research plans to collect information from multiple sources of written information, including reference texts. Tell students that today they will analyze their findings and may have to get more information or change the focus of their original inquiry question.

Model Think Aloud I thought that I had all the information I needed about David Beckham. But when I look at my notes I see that I can't answer my inquiry question *Does that player have a special talent that makes him or her a great player?* I will ask the librarian to help me find out more about David Beckham's talent.

Guide practice Remind students that if they have difficulty improving their focus they can ask their reference librarian for guidance. Remind students what they have just learned about time lines. Have students begin a time line about the subject of their biography.

On their own Have students evaluate the research they have done so far. Have them determine whether they have enough information to write their biography, and whether they have found enough information to answer their inquiry questions.

Conventions
Singular and Plural Pronouns

Review Remember, pronouns take the place of nouns. Singular pronouns take the place of singular nouns, and plural pronouns take the place of plural nouns. *You* can be used as either a singular or a plural pronoun. We can use pronouns to avoid repeating a noun. This is one way to make our writing and speaking less wordy.

Daily Fix-It Use Daily Fix-It numbers 5 and 6 in the right margin.

Connect to oral language Have the class complete these sentence frames orally.

The boys can fly. ________ can fly. (They)

The plane got ready for takeoff. ________ got ready for takeoff. (It)

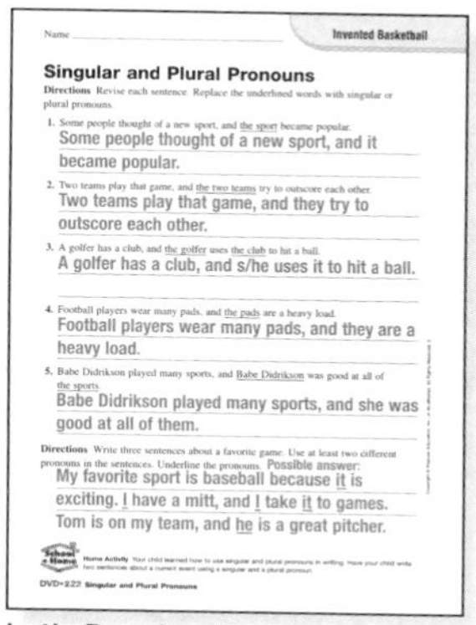
Name ________ Invented Basketball

Singular and Plural Pronouns

Directions Revise each sentence. Replace the underlined words with singular or plural pronouns.

1. Some people thought of a new sport, and the sport became popular.
Some people thought of a new sport, and it became popular.
2. Two teams play that game, and the two teams try to outscore each other.
Two teams play that game, and they try to outscore each other.
3. A golfer has a club, and the golfer uses the club to hit a ball.
A golfer has a club, and s/he uses it to hit a ball.
4. Football players wear many pads, and the pads are a heavy load.
Football players wear many pads, and they are a heavy load.
5. Babe Didrikson played many sports, and Babe Didrikson was good at all of the sports.
Babe Didrikson played many sports, and she was good at all of them.

Directions Write three sentences about a favorite game. Use at least two different pronouns in the sentences. Underline the pronouns. Possible answer:
My favorite sport is baseball because it is exciting. I have a mitt, and I take it to games. Tom is on my team, and he is a great pitcher.

DVD•222 Singular and Plural Pronouns

Let's Practice It!
TR DVD•222

On their own For additional support, use *Let's Practice It!* page 222 on the *Teacher Resources DVD-ROM.*

Spelling
Irregular Plurals

Frequently misspelled words The words *clothes* and *want* are often misspelled, because the spelling and pronunciation don't quite match. You must memorize these spellings. Have students practice writing the words *clothes* and *want* by completing the following sentences.

1. **I ________ a new dress.** (want)
2. **His ________ were blue.** (clothes)
3. **I have to put on my ________.** (clothes)
4. **She does not ________ to go for a walk.** (want)

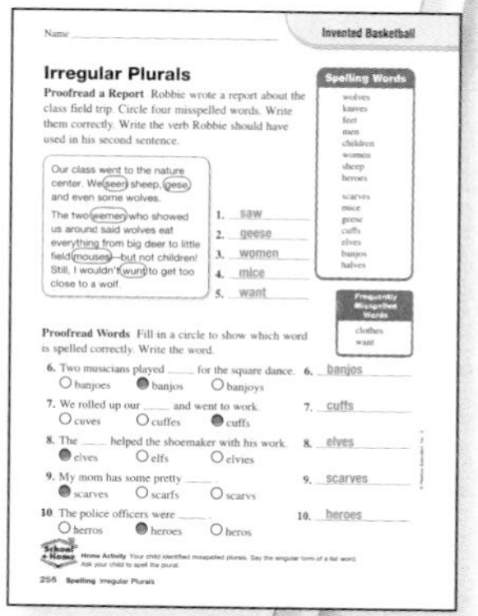
Name ________ Invented Basketball

Irregular Plurals

Proofread a Report Robbie wrote a report about the class field trip. Circle four misspelled words. Write them correctly. Write the verb Robbie should have used in his second sentence.

Our class went to the nature center. We seen sheep, gese and even some wolves. The two wemen who showed us around said wolves eat everything from big deer to little field mouses—but not children! Still, I wouldn't wunt to get too close to a wolf.

1. saw
2. geese
3. women
4. mice
5. want

Spelling Words: wolves, knives, feet, men, children, women, sheep, heroes, scarves, mice, geese, cuffs, elves, banjos, halves

Frequently Misspelled Words: clothes, want

Proofread Words Fill in a circle to show which word is spelled correctly. Write the word.

6. Two musicians played ____ for the square dance. ○ banjoes ● banjos ○ banjoys — 6. banjos
7. We rolled up our ____ and went to work. ○ cuves ○ cuffes ● cuffs — 7. cuffs
8. The ____ helped the shoemaker with his work. ● elves ○ elfs ○ elvies — 8. elves
9. My mom has some pretty ____. ● scarves ○ scarfs ○ scarvs — 9. scarves
10. The police officers were ____. ○ herros ● heroes ○ heros — 10. heroes

256 Spelling Irregular Plurals

Reader's and Writer's Notebook p. 256

On their own For additional support, use the *Reader's and Writer's Notebook* p. 256.

Differentiated Instruction

SI Strategic Intervention

Singular and plural pronouns Have students write ten nouns on index cards, including at least three spelling words. On the other side of each card, have students write the pronouns that can replace the nouns in sentences. Have students work in pairs to quiz each other using the cards.

Daily Fix-It

5. childen doesn't have wings, but birds do. (Children; don't)
6. Peaple move around with their feets. (People; feet)

Objectives

- Understand the criteria for writing an effective persuasive text.

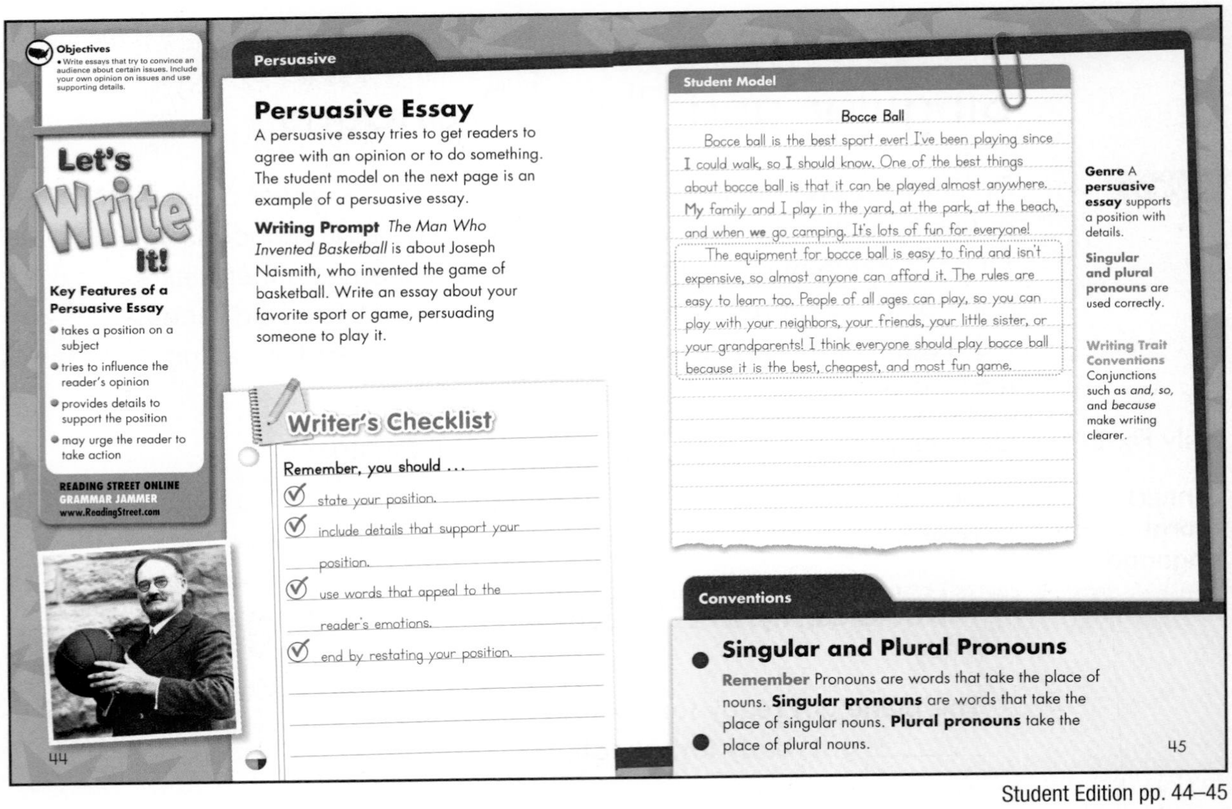
Objectives
- Write essays that try to convince an audience about certain issues. Include your own opinion on issues and use supporting details.

Let's Write It!

Key Features of a Persuasive Essay
- takes a position on a subject
- tries to influence the reader's opinion
- provides details to support the position
- may urge the reader to take action

READING STREET ONLINE
GRAMMAR JAMMER
www.ReadingStreet.com

Persuasive

Persuasive Essay

A persuasive essay tries to get readers to agree with an opinion or to do something. The student model on the next page is an example of a persuasive essay.

Writing Prompt *The Man Who Invented Basketball* is about Joseph Naismith, who invented the game of basketball. Write an essay about your favorite sport or game, persuading someone to play it.

Writer's Checklist

Remember, you should ...
- state your position.
- include details that support your position.
- use words that appeal to the reader's emotions.
- end by restating your position.

44

Student Model

Bocce Ball

Bocce ball is the best sport ever! I've been playing since I could walk, so I should know. One of the best things about bocce ball is that it can be played almost anywhere. My family and I play in the yard, at the park, at the beach, and when **we** go camping. It's lots of fun for everyone!

The equipment for bocce ball is easy to find and isn't expensive, so almost anyone can afford it. The rules are easy to learn too. People of all ages can play, so you can play with your neighbors, your friends, your little sister, or your grandparents! I think everyone should play bocce ball because it is the best, cheapest, and most fun game.

Genre A **persuasive essay** supports a position with details.

Singular and plural pronouns are used correctly.

Writing Trait Conventions Conjunctions such as *and*, *so*, and *because* make writing clearer.

Conventions

Singular and Plural Pronouns

Remember Pronouns are words that take the place of nouns. **Singular pronouns** are words that take the place of singular nouns. **Plural pronouns** take the place of plural nouns.

45

Student Edition pp. 44–45

Let's Write It!
Persuasive Text

Teach Use pp. 44–45 in the Student Edition. Direct students to read the key features of a persuasive text, which appear on p. 44. Remind students that they can refer to the information in the Writer's Checklist as they write their own persuasive essays.

Read the student model on p. 45. Point out the key features of a persuasive text in the model.

Connect to conventions Remind students that singular nouns refer to only one person, place, or thing, so they are replaced with singular pronouns. Plural nouns refer to more than one person, place, or thing, so they are replaced by plural pronouns. Point out the correct use of singular and plural pronouns in the model.

Writing—Persuasive Text
Writer's Craft: Persuasive Elements

Display rubric

Display Scoring Rubric 16 from the *Teacher Resources DVD-ROM* and go over the criteria for each trait below each score. Then, using the model in the Student Edition, have student volunteers explain why the model should score a 4 for one of the traits. If a student says that the model should score below 4 for a particular trait, the student should offer support for that response. Remind students that this is the rubric that will be used to evaluate the persuasive text they write.

Scoring Rubric: Persuasive Text

	4	3	2	1
Focus/Ideas	Clear statement and support of author's purpose	Mostly clear statement and support of author's purpose	Somewhat clear statement and support of author's purpose	Unclear statement and support of author's purpose
Organization	Contains clear main idea and details	Contains mostly clear main idea and some details	Main idea somewhat unclear; few details	Unclear main idea; no supporting details
Voice	Persuasive and knowledgeable	Somewhat persuasive; somewhat knowledgeable	Tries to be persuasive; rarely knowledgeable	Not persuasive; not knowledgeable
Word Choice	Uses persuasive language	Uses some persuasive language	Uses little persuasive language	Uses no persuasive language
Sentences	Clear and complete	Mostly clear and complete	Somewhat clear and complete	Unclear and incomplete
Conventions	Few to no errors in use of singular and plural pronouns	Moderate errors in use of singular and plural pronouns	Several errors in use of singular and plural pronouns	Consistently incorrect use of singular and plural pronouns

T-chart

Have students get out the T-charts they created. If their charts are not complete, allow additional time for students to finish. Have students work in pairs if they are struggling to complete their charts.

Write

You will be using your charts to write a first draft of your text. While you are writing this draft, don't worry about spelling or grammar. Just put your ideas on paper. You will have a chance later to revise your text.

Differentiated Instruction

SI Strategic Intervention

Use the model Have students use a main idea and details chart to analyze the student model.

ELL English Language Learners

Connect to conventions Give students extra practice with pronouns by having them list nouns they might use in their persuasive texts, such as *team(s), player(s), rules, ball,* or *bat.* Then have them practice replacing these nouns with pronouns in simple sentences. If students use the singular pronoun *he* or *she* to replace a singular noun that names an inanimate object, then say the sentence with the pronoun *it* and have students repeat the sentence after you several times.

Objectives

- Write a first draft of a persuasive essay.
- Use logical and emotional appeals to persuade.

Writing, continued
Writer's Craft: Persuasive Elements

MINI-LESSON

Logical and Emotional Appeals

- **Introduce** Today students will focus on writing details that include logical and emotional appeals. Discuss the difference between logical and emotional appeals. A logical appeal gives readers logical reasons they should try the game or sport. For example, playing tennis will help you learn to react quickly. An emotional appeal gives readers emotional reasons to try the game or sport. You'll love hearing people cheer for you. The details you choose to support your main idea should help persuade readers to try your favorite sport or game.

A Game of Strategy

Chess is a game that everyone should learn. It takes skill and strategy. If you are patient enough to learn the rules, you will find it can be exciting and fun.

Chess is good exercise for your brain. Chess is challenging. Each piece on a chessboard can only move a certain way. You have to remember how each piece moves. Also, you have to think about what the other player might do with his or her pieces.

You feel good when you win a game of chess. To win, you play until your opponent's king can't make no moves without being captured. This is called checkmate. You feel prowd when you win after a difficult game.

Chess is never boring. Chess can be a quiet game, or it can be a fast game. Some people play a kind of chess called "fast chess, where each player has a short amount of time to make its moves.

Unit 4 The Man Who Invented Basketball   Writing: Model 16A

Writing Transparency 16A, TR DVD

- Explain to students that they will refer to their main idea and details charts and other information they have gathered to provide material for their drafts. Students can use their main idea or purpose as the first sentence of their essay. Details should include logical and emotional appeals.

- Display the Drafting Tips.

Drafting Tips

- ✔ Start by looking at your T-chart.
- ✔ Make sure your draft includes a clear statement of purpose.
- ✔ Make sure the supporting details include both logical and emotional appeals.
- ✔ Don't worry about grammar and mechanics when drafting. You will concentrate on these things during the editing stage.

Logical and Emotional Appeals, continued

Think Aloud I am going to look at my first draft to see whether I have main ideas and supporting details. I will underline each main idea once and the supporting details twice.

Display Transparency 16A. Help students identify the main idea and details of each paragraph of *A Game of Strategy.* Then have students begin their drafts.

Differentiated Instruction

A Advanced

Emotional appeals Have students make a list of adjectives that describe their sport or game. Then have them rank each adjective according to emotional appeal using a scale of 1 to 10.

ROUTINE Quick Write for Fluency

Team Talk

1. **Talk** Have pairs talk about a time they tried a new game or sport.
2. **Write** Have students write a short paragraph about the experience.
3. **Share** Have each student share his or her paragraph with another student.

Routines Flip Chart

Wrap Up Your Day

- **Build Concepts** Have students discuss what they learned about the talents James Naismith used to invent basketball.
- **Generalize** What generalizations have you made about why basketball became popular?
- **Summarize** How do you know which parts of the text to include in a summary?

Preview DAY 4

Tell students that tomorrow they will read about the life of a famous baseball player.

Objectives
- Develop the weekly concept.
- Develop oral vocabulary.

Today at a Glance

Oral Vocabulary
succeed, rise, verge

Phonics
Consonant Patterns *wr, kn, st, mb, gn*

Genre
Autobiography

Reading
"My Turn at Bat"

Let's Learn It!
Fluency: Accuracy
Vocabulary: ◉ Unfamiliar words
Listening and Speaking: Presentation

Research and Inquiry
Synthesize

Spelling
Irregular plurals

Conventions
Singular and plural pronouns

Writing
Persuasive text

Concept Talk

Question of the Week

How do talents make someone unique?

Expand the concept Remind students that this week they have read stories about people with special talents. Tell students that today they will read a true story about a baseball player named Ted Williams.

Anchored Talk

Develop oral vocabulary Use text features—timelines, illustrations, captions, and heads—to review pp. 36–41 of *The Man Who Invented Basketball.* Discuss the Amazing Words *necessary* and *result.* Add these and other concept-related words to the concept map. Use the following questions to develop students' understanding of the concept. Remind students to ask and answer questions with appropriate detail, and to provide suggestions that build upon others' ideas.

- It was *necessary* for James Naismith to have a good imagination to invent basketball. When is it *necessary* for you to use your imagination?
- James Naismith used his imagination, and the *result* was that he thought up a new sport. If you work hard at a talent that you possess, what might be the *result*?

INTERACT with TEXT

Strategy Response Log

Have students complete p. 22 in the *Reader's and Writer's Notebook.* Then have students work in pairs to summarize *The Man Who Invented Basketball.*

Oral Vocabulary
Amazing Words

Amazing Words Oral Vocabulary Routine

Teach Amazing Words

1. **Introduce** Write the word *succeed* on the board. Have students say it with you. James Naismith *succeeded* in inventing a new sport. He also *succeeded* in becoming a doctor. Have students determine a definition of *succeed.* (*Succeed* means "to turn out well or to reach a goal.")
2. **Demonstrate** Have students answer questions to demonstrate understanding. Did James Naismith *succeed* at school when he was young? (no) Did James Naismith *succeed* in finding a wife? (yes) How does a team *succeed* in a game of basketball? (It scores the most points.)
3. **Apply** Have students apply their understanding. When a person *succeeds* in finishing high school, what happens? (He or she graduates.) When a person *succeeds* in winning a race, what does that mean? (The person came in first.) When someone *succeeds* in third grade, into which grade does he or she go next? (He or she goes into fourth grade.)

See p. OV•1 to teach *rise* and *verge.*

Routines Flip Chart

Apply Amazing Words

As students read "My Turn at Bat " on pp. 46–51, have them think about the word *succeed.* Ask them to decide if Ted Williams *succeeded.* Discuss how a baseball can *rise* in the air, and a player's stats can *rise* as he or she gets better. Explain the meaning of the word *verge,* and point out that in 1938, Williams was on the *verge* of joining the big leagues.

Connect to reading

As students read today's selection about a great baseball player, have them think about how the Question of the Week and the Amazing Words *succeed, rise,* and *verge* relate to Ted Williams's story.

ELL **Produce Oral Language** Use the Day 4 instruction on ELL Poster 16 to extend and enrich language.

ELL Poster 16

Amazing Words

mock	necessary
idle	result
potential	succeed
ecstatic	rise
thrill	verge
audition	

Objectives

- Read and identify words with consonant patterns *wr, kn, st, mb,* and *gn.*
- Read words fluently independent of context.

Phonics Review
Consonant Patterns *wr, kn, st, mb, gn*

Review sound-spellings

Review last week's phonics skill: consonant patterns *wr, kn, st, mb,* and *gn.* Write these words: *write, knight, listen, thumb, gnaw, know, comb, gnats, wrote, gnu, knock,* and *lamb.* We studied the silent consonants in *wr, kn, st, mb, gn.* Let's review by looking at these words. Have students identify the word with the sound /s/. *(listened)* Which consonants stand for /s/ in *listen*? *(st)* Continue in the same way for the consonants that stand for the following sounds: /n/ *(knight, gnaw, know, gnats, gnu, knock);* /r/ *(wrote);* /m/ *(thumb, comb, lamb).* Tell students that the silent consonants *k* and *g* stand for /n/ when they precede the letter *n.*

Corrective feedback

If students are unable to answer the questions about consonant patterns *wr, kn, st, mb,* and *gn,* refer them to Sound-Spelling Cards 40, 42, 43, 48, and 53.

Guide practice

Draw a five-column chart with the headings *wr, kn, st, mb,* and *gn.* Write the following words and help students sort them into the correct columns on the chart: *know, castle, numb, sign, gnats, wrap, knit, glisten, climb, wrist.* Then have students read the words. Ask volunteers to underline the silent consonant in each word.

wr	kn	st	mb	gn
wrap	know	castle	numb	sign
wrist	knit	glisten	climb	gnats

On their own

For additional practice, use *Let's Practice It!* page 223 on the *Teacher Resources DVD-ROM.*

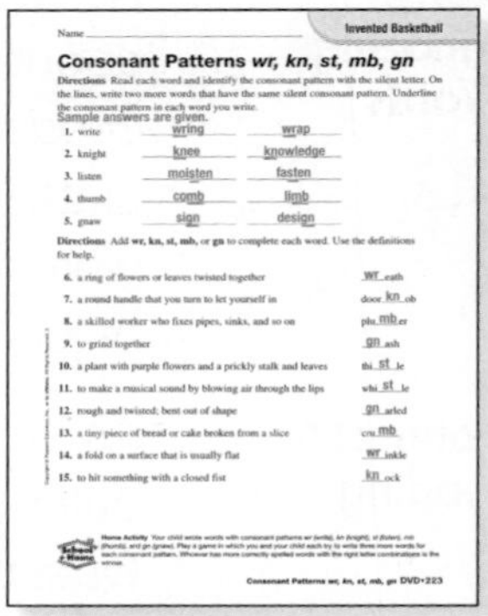
Consonant Patterns wr, kn, st, mb, gn

Let's Practice It!
TR DVD•223

Fluent Word Reading

Spiral Review

Read words independent of context

Display these words. Tell students that they can already decode some words on this list. Explain that they should know other words because they appear often in reading.

Have students read the list three or four times until they can read at the rate of two to three seconds per word.

Word Reading

untrue	replace	dependable	fearless	door
sadly	stuck	mistake	disagree	one
city	cheerful	echoed	bridge	your
the	sensible	have	what	darkness

Corrective feedback

If... students have difficulty reading whole words,
then... have them use sound-by-sound blending for decodable words or chunking for words that have word parts, or have them say and spell high-frequency words.

If... students cannot read fluently at a rate of two to three seconds per word,
then... have pairs practice the list until they can read it fluently.

Differentiated Instruction

SI Strategic Intervention

Consonant patterns *wr, kn, st, mb, gn* To assist students having difficulty with silent consonant patterns, have students use crayons to write the words from the review chart on paper. Have students write all letters in each word in black, except for the silent consonant. Have students write the silent consonant in white. Then have students practice reading the words to actually see which consonant in each word should not be pronounced.

Spiral Review

Review these activities:

- previously taught high-frequency words *the, have, what, door, one, your.*
- prefixes *un-, re-, mis-, dis-;* spellings of *c* /s/, *ck* /k/, *ch* /k/, *dge* /j/; suffixes *-ly, -ful, -ness, -less, -able, -ible.*

ELL

English Language Learners

Fluent word reading Have students listen to a more fluent reader say the words. Then have them repeat the words.

Objectives

- Read words fluently in context.
- Apply knowledge of sound-spellings to decode unknown words when reading.
- Practice fluency with oral rereading.

Read words in context

Display these sentences. Call on individuals to read a sentence. Then randomly point to review words and have students read them. To help you monitor word reading, high-frequency words are underlined and decodable words are italicized.

MONITOR PROGRESS **Sentence Reading**

Your *cheerful* voice *echoed* through the *darkness* and over the *bridge.*

I have a friend who is *dependable, sensible,* and *fearless.*

The door is *stuck,* so dad will *replace* the hinges.

What one *mistake* did Sara make driving in the *city*?

I *sadly disagree* with saying things that are *untrue.*

If... students are unable to read an underlined high-frequency word,
then... read the word for them and spell it, having them echo you.

If... students have difficulty reading an italicized decodable word,
then... guide them in using sound-by-sound blending or chunking.

Reread for Fluency

Have students reread the sentences to develop automaticity decoding words.

ROUTINE **Oral Rereading**

1. **Read** Have students read all the sentences orally.
2. **Reread** To achieve optimal fluency, students should reread the sentences three or four times.
3. **Corrective Feedback** Listen as students read. Provide corrective feedback regarding their fluency and decoding.

Routines Flip Chart

Decode and Read

Read words independent of context

Have students turn to p. 11 in *Decodable Practice Readers 3.2* and find the first list of words. Each word in this list is an irregular plural. Let's read these words. Be sure that students pronounce each plural word correctly.

Read high-frequency words

Next, have students read the high-frequency words.

Preview Decodable Practice Passage

Have students read the title and preview the story. Tell them that they will read words that are irregular plurals. Make sure that students are monitoring their accuracy when they decode words.

Read words in context

Chorally read the story along with the students. Have students identify words in the story that are irregular plurals.

Team Talk Pair students and have them take turns reading the story aloud to each other. Monitor students as they read to check for proper pronunciation and appropriate pacing.

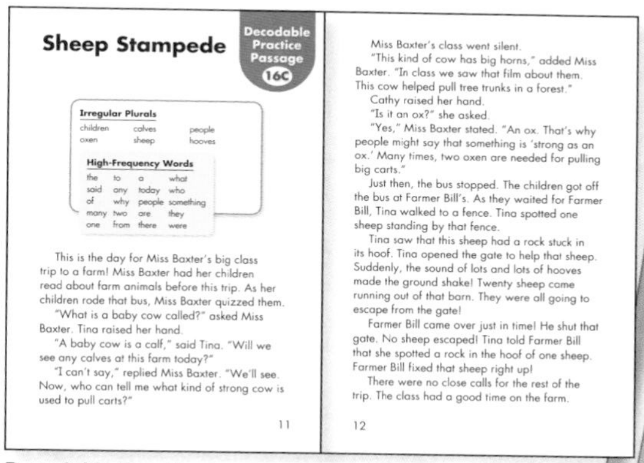

Sheep Stampede

Decodable Practice Passage 16C

Irregular Plurals

children	calves	people
oxen	sheep	hooves

High-Frequency Words

the	to	a	what
said	any	today	who
of	why	people	something
many	two	are	they
one	from	there	were

This is the day for Miss Baxter's big class trip to a farm! Miss Baxter had her children read about farm animals before this trip. As her children rode that bus, Miss Baxter quizzed them.

"What is a baby cow called?" asked Miss Baxter. Tina raised her hand.

"A baby cow is a calf," said Tina. "Will we see any calves at this farm today?"

"I can't say," replied Miss Baxter. "We'll see. Now, who can tell me what kind of strong cow is used to pull carts?"

11

Miss Baxter's class went silent.

"This kind of cow has big horns," added Miss Baxter. "In class we saw that film about them. This cow helped pull tree trunks in a forest."

Cathy raised her hand.

"Is it an ox?" she asked.

"Yes," Miss Baxter stated. "An ox. That's why people might say that something is 'strong as an ox.' Many times, two oxen are needed for pulling big carts."

Just then, the bus stopped. The children got off the bus at Farmer Bill's. As they waited for Farmer Bill, Tina walked to a fence. Tina spotted one sheep standing by that fence.

Tina saw that this sheep had a rock stuck in its hoof. Tina opened the gate to help that sheep. Suddenly, the sound of lots and lots of hooves made the ground shake! Twenty sheep came running out of that barn. They were all going to escape from the gate!

Farmer Bill came over just in time! He shut that gate. No sheep escaped! Tina told Farmer Bill that she spotted a rock in the hoof of one sheep. Farmer Bill fixed that sheep right up!

There were no close calls for the rest of the trip. The class had a good time on the farm.

12

Decodable Practice Passage 16C

Differentiated Instruction

A Advanced

Prefixes and suffixes Have students make a list of the prefixes and suffixes used in the sentences at the top of p. 46e. Have students work with a partner to brainstorm other words that use those same prefixes and suffixes.

Objectives
- Introduce autobiography.

Let's Think About Genre
Literary Nonfiction: Autobiography

Introduce autobiography

Literary Nonfiction: Autobiography Explain to students that what we read is structured differently, depending on the author's reasons for writing and what kind of information he/she wishes to convey. Different types of texts are called genres. Tell them that autobiography is one type of genre.

Discuss autobiography

Discuss with students the difference between biography and autobiography. For example, ask: If I wrote a book about my mother's life, would it be a biography or an autobiography? Why? (biography because you wrote about her life for her) If you wrote a story about what you did on your summer vacation, would it be a biography or an autobiography? Why? (autobiography because you wrote about your own life)

On the board, draw a Venn diagram like the one below. Label one side *Biography* and the other *Autobiography.* Have students answer the following questions as you fill in the diagram:

- What do both biographies and autobiographies have in common? Possible response: They are both true stories. They are both about real people. They are both stories about a person's life or a special event in a person's life.
- What is the point of view of a biography? of an autobiography? third person; first person
- How can you tell if something is written in the third person or in the first person? the pronouns *he, she, it, they;* the pronouns *I, we*

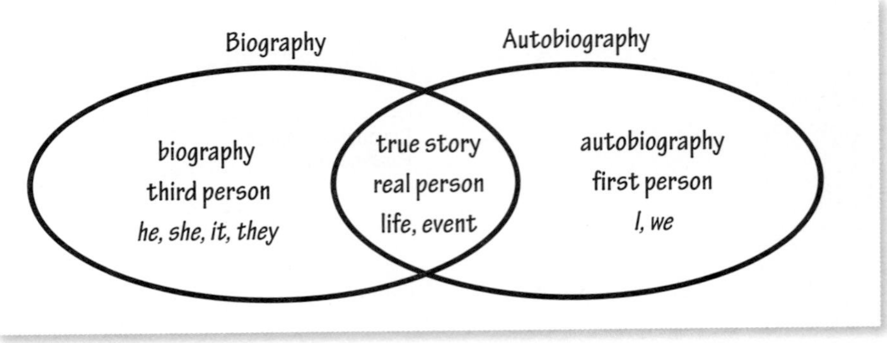

Guide practice

Have students work in pairs to create a T chart to list the pronouns that they would see in an autobiography and a biography. Ask them to share their lists with the class.

Connect to reading

Tell students that they will now read about a story about a famous baseball player that is both a biography and an autobiography. Have the class think about how they will be able to tell which is which.

Small Group Time

DAY 4 **Break into small groups before reading or revisiting "My Turn at Bat."**

Teacher Led

SI Strategic Intervention	OL On-Level	A Advanced
Teacher Led p. DI•5 • Practice retelling • Genre focus • **Read/Revisit** "My Turn at Bat"	**Teacher Led** p. DI•10 • Practice retelling • Genre focus • **Read/Revisit** "My Turn at Bat"	**Teacher Led** p. DI•15 • Genre focus • **Read/Revisit** "My Turn at Bat"

ELL Place English Language learners in the groups that correspond to their reading abilities in English.

Practice Stations
- Read for Meaning
- Get Fluent
- Words to Know

Independent Activities
- AudioText: "My Turn at Bat"
- *Reader's and Writer's Notebook*
- Research and Inquiry

ELL

English Language Learners

Cognates Point out that both of the genre words have Spanish cognates. The cognate for *biography* is *biografía* and the one for *autobiography* is *autobiografía.*

DAY 4 Read and Comprehend

40–50 min

Objectives

- Identify the difference between a biography and an autobiography.
- Distinguish between first- and third-person points of view.

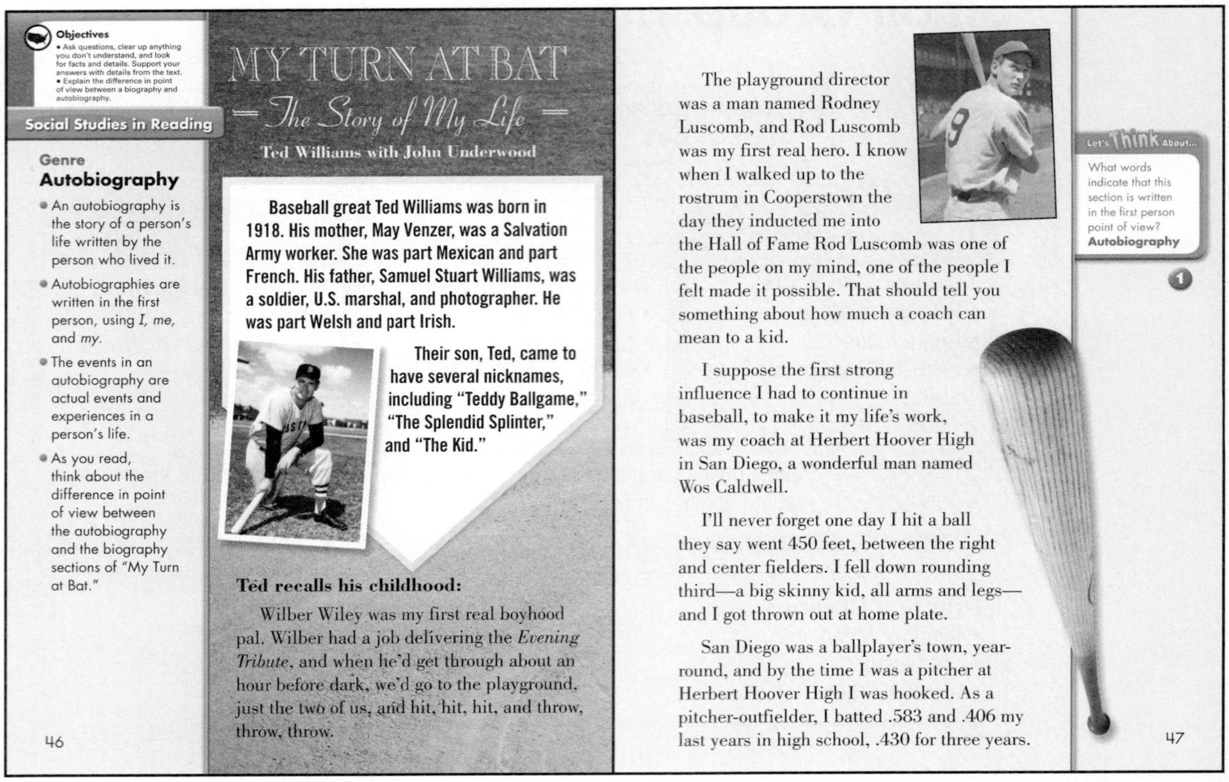

Objectives
- Ask questions, clear up anything you don't understand, and look for facts and details. Support your answers with details from the text.
- Explain the difference in point of view between a biography and autobiography.

Social Studies in Reading

Genre
Autobiography
- An autobiography is the story of a person's life written by the person who lived it.
- Autobiographies are written in the first person, using *I*, *me*, and *my*.
- The events in an autobiography are actual events and experiences in a person's life.
- As you read, think about the difference in point of view between the autobiography and the biography sections of "My Turn at Bat."

MY TURN AT BAT
The Story of My Life
Ted Williams with John Underwood

Baseball great Ted Williams was born in 1918. His mother, May Venzer, was a Salvation Army worker. She was part Mexican and part French. His father, Samuel Stuart Williams, was a soldier, U.S. marshal, and photographer. He was part Welsh and part Irish.

Their son, Ted, came to have several nicknames, including "Teddy Ballgame," "The Splendid Splinter," and "The Kid."

Ted recalls his childhood:

Wilber Wiley was my first real boyhood pal. Wilber had a job delivering the *Evening Tribute*, and when he'd get through about an hour before dark, we'd go to the playground, just the two of us, and hit, hit, hit, and throw, throw, throw.

46

The playground director was a man named Rodney Luscomb, and Rod Luscomb was my first real hero. I know when I walked up to the rostrum in Cooperstown the day they inducted me into the Hall of Fame Rod Luscomb was one of the people on my mind, one of the people I felt made it possible. That should tell you something about how much a coach can mean to a kid.

I suppose the first strong influence I had to continue in baseball, to make it my life's work, was my coach at Herbert Hoover High in San Diego, a wonderful man named Wos Caldwell.

I'll never forget one day I hit a ball they say went 450 feet, between the right and center fielders. I fell down rounding third—a big skinny kid, all arms and legs—and I got thrown out at home plate.

San Diego was a ballplayer's town, year-round, and by the time I was a pitcher at Herbert Hoover High I was hooked. As a pitcher-outfielder, I batted .583 and .406 my last years in high school, .430 for three years.

Let's Think About...
What words indicate that this section is written in the first person point of view? **Autobiography**
1

47

Student Edition pp. 46–47

Guide Comprehension
Skills and Strategies

Teach autobiography

Genre: Autobiography Explain that students will be learning the difference between a biography and an autobiography. Have them preview pp. 46–47 of "My Turn at Bat." Remind students that the story they are reading is *both* a biography and an autobiography. Ask: How can you tell when the story is a biography and when it is an autobiography? (The word *I* indicates when it is an autobiography. The words *he* and *his* hint that it may be a biography.)

Corrective feedback

If... students are unable to distinguish between the different points of view in the selection,
then... use the Model to help students recognize the difference.

Model the skill

Think Aloud: The box at the beginning of the story has someone explaining about Ted Williams's life. It uses the pronouns *he* and *his.* These are not Ted Williams's own words. The next paragraph uses the pronoun *my.* This paragraph is in Ted Williams's own words.

On their own

Have student pairs write sentences in the first and third person. One sentence should be about the student and the other about the student's partner.

Extend Thinking
Think Critically

Higher-order thinking skills

Summarize • Analysis How would you describe what parts of his childhood Ted thinks are most important to recall to tell about his life? Possible response: He seems to be talking about the people who had the biggest effect on him and how these people contributed to his later success at baseball.

Generalize • Evaluation After reading page 47, what is a generalization you can make about the effect his coaches had on Ted? Possible response: All of his coaches had a positive influence on Ted and helped him achieve great things by inspiring him to work hard and play baseball well.

Let's Think About...

1 Possible responses: *I, my,* and *me*

ELL

English Language Learners

Language production Review baseball terminology with students to help them understand the selection. Words taught could include *diamond, field, center, plate, home, first, second,* and *third,* among others. Draw a baseball diamond on the board and name the positions for students.

Objectives

- Identify first-person point of view.
- Write in the first person.

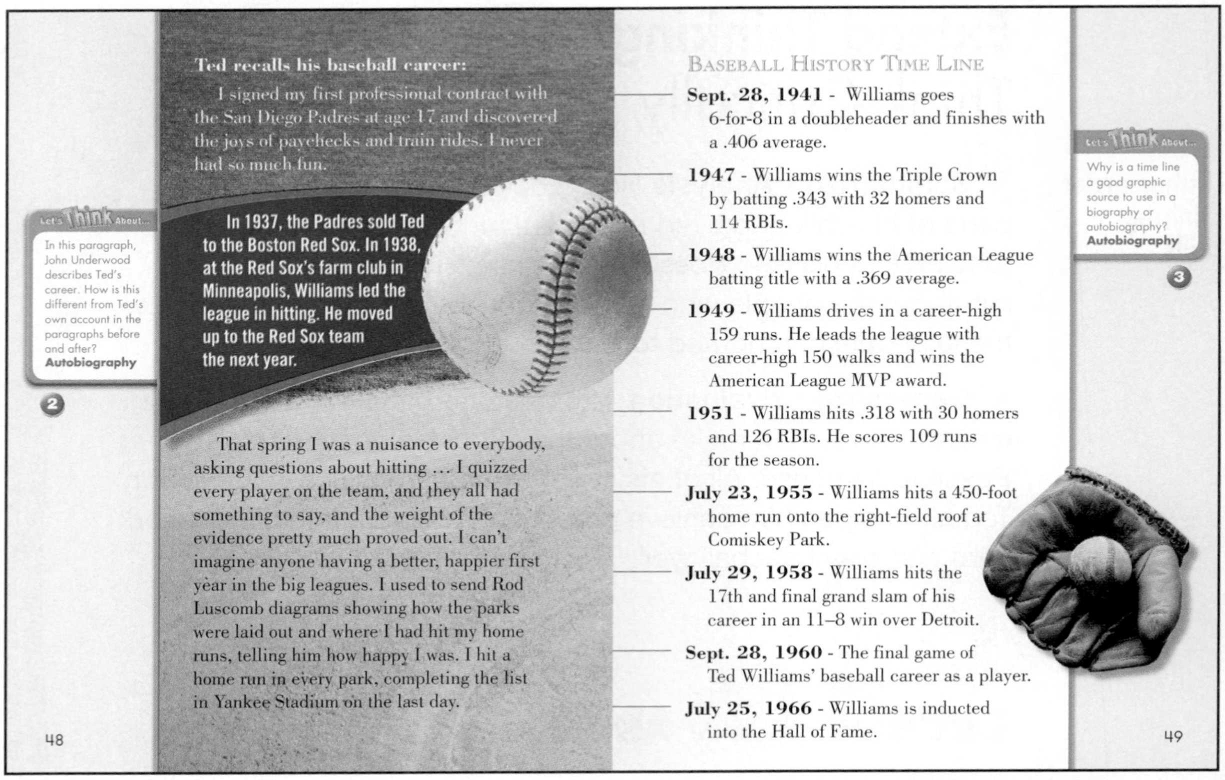

Ted recalls his baseball career:

I signed my first professional contract with the San Diego Padres at age 17 and discovered the joys of paychecks and train rides. I never had so much fun.

In 1937, the Padres sold Ted to the Boston Red Sox. In 1938, at the Red Sox's farm club in Minneapolis, Williams led the league in hitting. He moved up to the Red Sox team the next year.

That spring I was a nuisance to everybody, asking questions about hitting … I quizzed every player on the team, and they all had something to say, and the weight of the evidence pretty much proved out. I can't imagine anyone having a better, happier first year in the big leagues. I used to send Rod Luscomb diagrams showing how the parks were laid out and where I had hit my home runs, telling him how happy I was. I hit a home run in every park, completing the list in Yankee Stadium on the last day.

Let's Think About…

In this paragraph, John Underwood describes Ted's career. How is this different from Ted's own account in the paragraphs before and after?
Autobiography

2

48

Baseball History Time Line

Sept. 28, 1941 - Williams goes 6-for-8 in a doubleheader and finishes with a .406 average.

1947 - Williams wins the Triple Crown by batting .343 with 32 homers and 114 RBIs.

1948 - Williams wins the American League batting title with a .369 average.

1949 - Williams drives in a career-high 159 runs. He leads the league with career-high 150 walks and wins the American League MVP award.

1951 - Williams hits .318 with 30 homers and 126 RBIs. He scores 109 runs for the season.

July 23, 1955 - Williams hits a 450-foot home run onto the right-field roof at Comiskey Park.

July 29, 1958 - Williams hits the 17th and final grand slam of his career in an 11–8 win over Detroit.

Sept. 28, 1960 - The final game of Ted Williams' baseball career as a player.

July 25, 1966 - Williams is inducted into the Hall of Fame.

Let's Think About…

Why is a time line a good graphic source to use in a biography or autobiography?
Autobiography

3

49

Student Edition pp. 48–49

Guide Comprehension
Skills and Strategies

Teach autobiography

Genre: Autobiography Have students preview pp. 48–49. Ask: What is the point of view in the first paragraph of page 48? (It is first-person point of view.) Who is the author of a text that is told in the first-person point of view? (The author is the subject, or the person who is described as *I* in the text.)

Corrective feedback

If… students are unable to identify and explain first-person point of view, **then…** use the Model to help explain it.

Model the skill

Think Aloud: When I tell you about something that has happened to me, I use the first-person point of view. "When I was little I flew in a hot air balloon. It was the most fun I ever had." That is me talking about me. If you told the same story, you might say, "When my teacher was little she rode in a hot air balloon. She really liked it." That is third-person point of view.

On their own

Have students begin their own autobiography by writing two sentences about their own childhood.

Extend Thinking
Think Critically

Higher-order thinking skills

Unfamiliar words • Synthesis Look through pages 48 and 49 and identify any unfamiliar words. Then see if there are any context clues in the sentence in which a word appears or in the sentences nearby. If not, look up the words in a dictionary. Possible responses: Students may identify the words *nuisance* (p. 48; means "an annoyance or inconvenience") or *doubleheader* (p. 49; means "a sporting event with two games or contests").

Review **Graphic Sources • Evaluation** Does the time line cover all of the events in Ted's life from his birth to his death? If not, which events does it cover, and why might it cover only these? Possible response: It covers only events from a doubleheader game Ted played in 1941 to his induction into the Baseball Hall of Fame in 1966. The title of the time line is "Baseball History Time Line," so the events included on it cover only important events in Ted's baseball career, not all the important events in his life.

Let's Think About...

2. Possible response: John Underwood writes in the third person and uses the pronoun *he.* Also, this paragraph gives only facts about Ted's life, while the parts Ted writes himself also mention his feelings and opinions about the things that were happening in his life at each moment he discusses.

3. Possible response: Biographies and autobiographies talk about the most important events in a person's life, and a time line is a good way to show the main things that happened in a person's life in a visual way.

Differentiated Instruction

SI Strategic Intervention

Point of view If students are having difficulty understanding the different points of view, have them act out sentences written in the different points of view, pointing away from themselves when they are reading a sentence in third-person point of view and toward themselves when they are reading a sentence in first-person point of view.

A Advanced

Point of view Introduce students to the concept of wide knowledge (omniscience) in third-person point of view, or the idea that the narrator knows what all of the characters are thinking and feeling, not just the thoughts and feelings of the main character.

ELL

English Language Learners

Practice pronunciation Write proper nouns and city names from the story on the board and say them slowly. Have students repeat after you. Then, have students suggest names of other U.S. cities. Write those on the board and have students practice saying them.

Objectives

- Identify third-person point of view.
- Write in the third person.

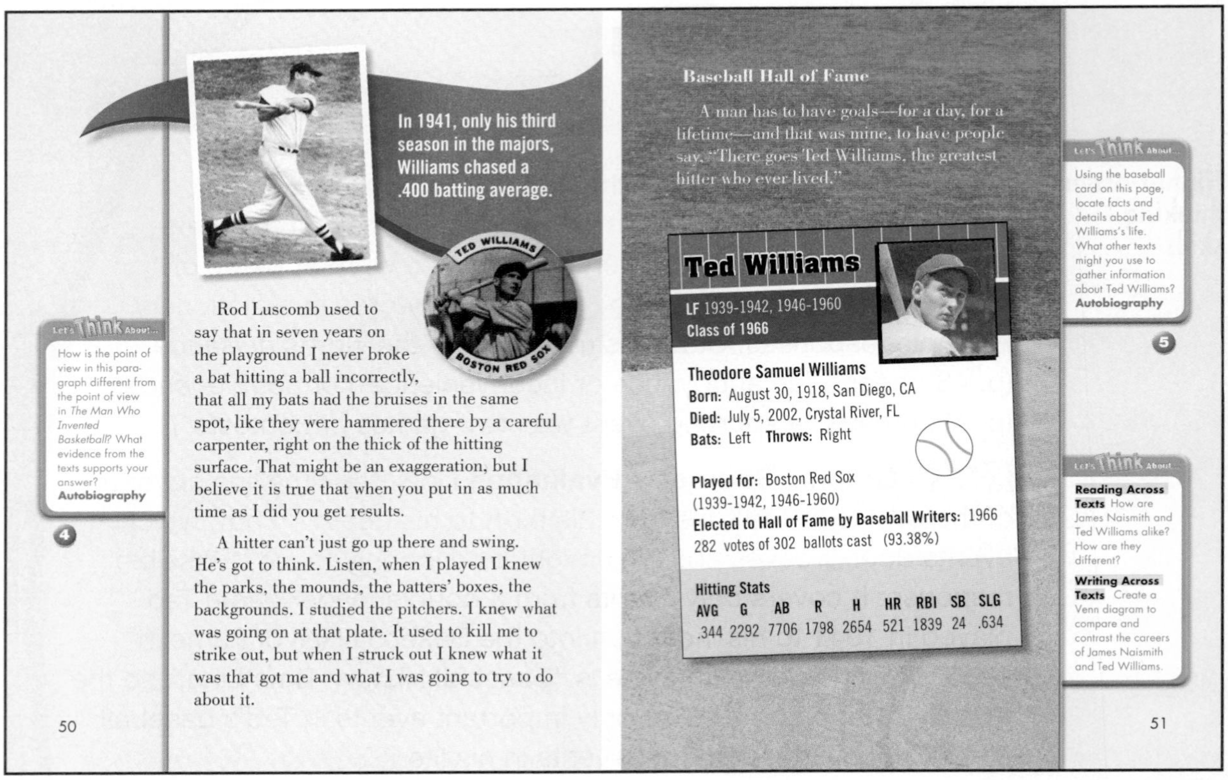

Let's Think About...

How is the point of view in this paragraph different from the point of view in *The Man Who Invented Basketball*? What evidence from the texts supports your answer? **Autobiography**

4

In 1941, only his third season in the majors, Williams chased a .400 batting average.

TED WILLIAMS

BOSTON RED SOX

Rod Luscomb used to say that in seven years on the playground I never broke a bat hitting a ball incorrectly, that all my bats had the bruises in the same spot, like they were hammered there by a careful carpenter, right on the thick of the hitting surface. That might be an exaggeration, but I believe it is true that when you put in as much time as I did you get results.

A hitter can't just go up there and swing. He's got to think. Listen, when I played I knew the parks, the mounds, the batters' boxes, the backgrounds. I studied the pitchers. I knew what was going on at that plate. It used to kill me to strike out, but when I struck out I knew what it was that got me and what I was going to try to do about it.

50

Baseball Hall of Fame

A man has to have goals—for a day, for a lifetime—and that was mine, to have people say, "There goes Ted Williams, the greatest hitter who ever lived."

Ted Williams

LF 1939-1942, 1946-1960

Class of 1966

Theodore Samuel Williams

Born: August 30, 1918, San Diego, CA

Died: July 5, 2002, Crystal River, FL

Bats: Left **Throws:** Right

Played for: Boston Red Sox (1939-1942, 1946-1960)

Elected to Hall of Fame by Baseball Writers: 1966

282 votes of 302 ballots cast (93.38%)

Hitting Stats

AVG	G	AB	R	H	HR	RBI	SB	SLG
.344	2292	7706	1798	2654	521	1839	24	.634

Let's Think About...

Using the baseball card on this page, locate facts and details about Ted Williams's life. What other texts might you use to gather information about Ted Williams? **Autobiography**

5

Let's Think About...

Reading Across Texts How are James Naismith and Ted Williams alike? How are they different?

Writing Across Texts Create a Venn diagram to compare and contrast the careers of James Naismith and Ted Williams.

51

Student Edition pp. 50–51

Guide Comprehension

Skills and Strategies

Teach autobiography

Genre: Autobiography Have students look at the baseball card on p. 51. Ask: In which point of view is the baseball card written? (It is written in third-person point of view.) Who is the author of a text that is written in the third-person point of view? (Someone other than the subject of the text.)

Corrective feedback

If... students are unable to explain third-person point of view,
then... use the Model to help explain it.

Model the skill

Think Aloud: I think about who is telling the story. I know Ted Williams is not "telling" the baseball card because the pronoun *I* is not used. That means that someone other than Ted Williams wrote the baseball card. So, it is written in the third-person point of view.

On their own

Have students begin a biography of someone they know by writing two sentences about this person, using the third-person point of view.

Extend Thinking
Think Critically

Higher-order thinking skills

Fact and Opinion • Analysis Is the text to the right of the photo on page 50 a statement of fact or opinion? How can you tell? Possible response: It is a statement of fact because it can be looked up and proved true that Williams chased a .400 batting average in 1941.

Summarize • Synthesis Summarize the information on Ted Williams' baseball card. Possible response: Ted Williams played for the Boston Red Sox. He got voted into the Hall of Fame in 1966.

Let's Think About...

4 Possible response: The point of view in this paragraph is the first-person point of view. The point of view of *The Man Who Invented Basketball* is the third person. This story uses pronouns like *I* and *my. The Man Who Invented Basketball* uses pronouns like *he* and *his.*

5 Possible responses: Web sites, encyclopedias, biographies

Reading Across Texts

Have students make a T-chart listing details about both James Naismith and Ted Williams. Tell them to use the chart to answer the question.

Writing Across Texts

Have students brainstorm how the careers of James Naismith and Ted Williams were alike and different. Encourage students to use the time lines on p. 41 and p. 49 to answer the question.

Connect to Social Studies

The first recorded official baseball game was played in Hoboken, New Jersey, in 1846. The two teams were the Knickerbocker Base Ball Club of New York and the New York Nine. The first professional team played in 1869. The first professional baseball league was founded in 1871.

DAY 4 Read and Comprehend

Objectives

- Read with fluency and comprehension.
- ◎ Use context clues to figure out the meanings of unfamiliar words.
- Give a presentation.

Fluency: WCPM
SUCCESS PREDICTOR

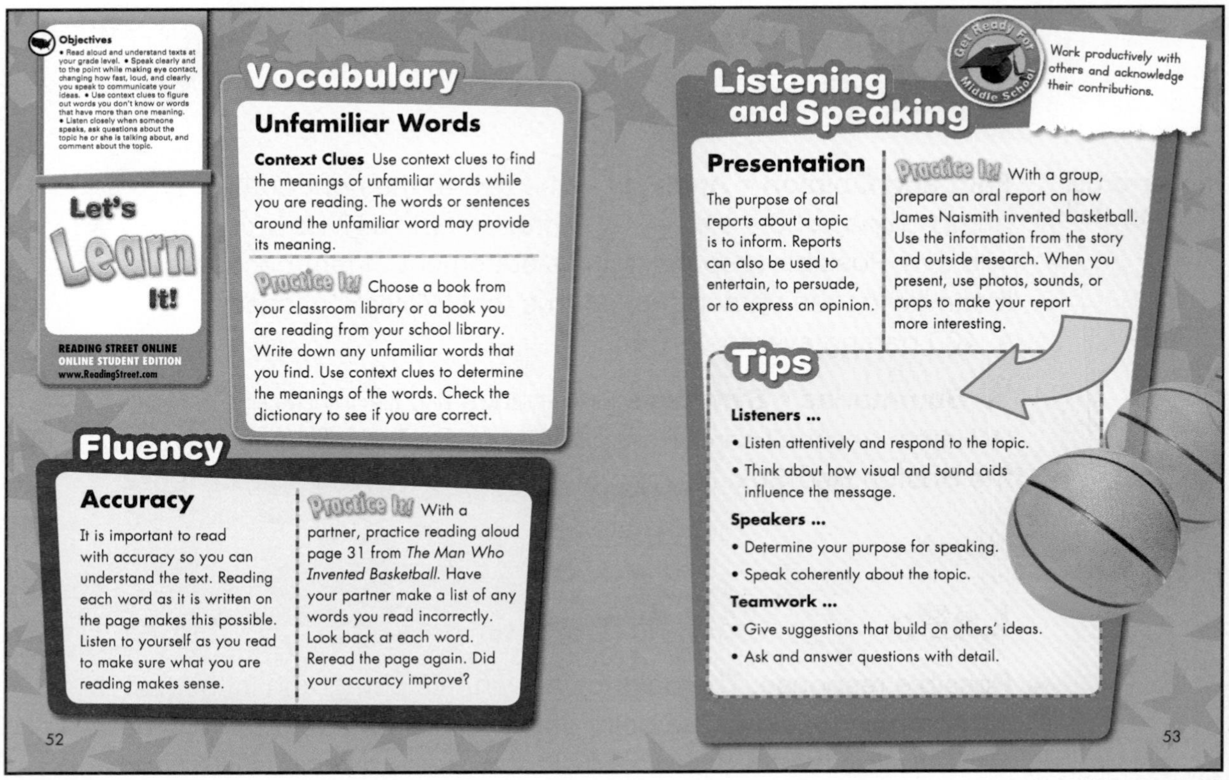

Objectives
• Read aloud and understand texts at your grade level. • Speak clearly and to the point while making eye contact, changing how fast, loud, and clearly you speak to communicate your ideas. • Use context clues to figure out words you don't know or words that have more than one meaning. • Listen closely when someone speaks, ask questions about the topic he or she is talking about, and comment about the topic.

Let's Learn It!

READING STREET ONLINE
ONLINE STUDENT EDITION
www.ReadingStreet.com

Vocabulary

Unfamiliar Words

Context Clues Use context clues to find the meanings of unfamiliar words while you are reading. The words or sentences around the unfamiliar word may provide its meaning.

Practice It! Choose a book from your classroom library or a book you are reading from your school library. Write down any unfamiliar words that you find. Use context clues to determine the meanings of the words. Check the dictionary to see if you are correct.

Fluency

Accuracy

It is important to read with accuracy so you can understand the text. Reading each word as it is written on the page makes this possible. Listen to yourself as you read to make sure what you are reading makes sense.

Practice It! With a partner, practice reading aloud page 31 from *The Man Who Invented Basketball*. Have your partner make a list of any words you read incorrectly. Look back at each word. Reread the page again. Did your accuracy improve?

52

Listening and Speaking

Get Ready For Middle School

Work productively with others and acknowledge their contributions.

Presentation

The purpose of oral reports about a topic is to inform. Reports can also be used to entertain, to persuade, or to express an opinion.

Practice It! With a group, prepare an oral report on how James Naismith invented basketball. Use the information from the story and outside research. When you present, use photos, sounds, or props to make your report more interesting.

Tips

Listeners ...
- Listen attentively and respond to the topic.
- Think about how visual and sound aids influence the message.

Speakers ...
- Determine your purpose for speaking.
- Speak coherently about the topic.

Teamwork ...
- Give suggestions that build on others' ideas.
- Ask and answer questions with detail.

53

Student Edition pp. 52–53

Fluency
Accuracy

Guide practice Use the Student Edition activity as an assessment tool. Make sure the reading passage is at least 200 words in length. As students read aloud with partners, walk around to make sure that they are reading the text accurately and pausing at the end of sentences.

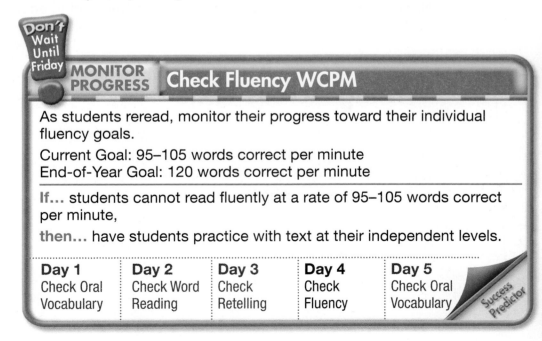

Don't Wait Until Friday

MONITOR PROGRESS **Check Fluency WCPM**

As students reread, monitor their progress toward their individual fluency goals.

Current Goal: 95–105 words correct per minute
End-of-Year Goal: 120 words correct per minute

If... students cannot read fluently at a rate of 95–105 words correct per minute,

then... have students practice with text at their independent levels.

Day 1	Day 2	Day 3	Day 4	Day 5
Check Oral Vocabulary	Check Word Reading	Check Retelling	Check Fluency	Check Oral Vocabulary

Success Predictor

Vocabulary
Unfamiliar Words

Teach unfamiliar words

Context clues Write the following sentences containing unfamiliar words on the board:

> **Juanita fumbled the basketball, and it slipped out of her fingers and fell to the ground.**
>
> **Harry had to retrieve the basketball when it bounced out of the court.**
>
> **Ginny defended the basketball when a player from the other team tried to steal it from her.**

Guide practice

Ask students to use the context clues in each sentence to figure out the meaning of each unfamiliar word.

On their own

Walk around the room as students are reading on their own and check to make sure that they can understand the context clues in their books.

Listening and Speaking
Presentation

Teach

Tell students that in order for a presentation to be effective, they must speak coherently about the topic under discussion. Tell them that when they do a presentation, they are trying to communicate specific information, that they want their audience to understand and remember. Have students use outside research, photos, sounds, or props to make the reports more interesting.

Guide practice

Remind students to use good eye contact, speaking rate, volume, enunciation, and the conventions of language to communicate the ideas in their reports. Remind students in the audience to listen attentively to speakers and ask relevant questions and make pertinent comments once speakers are done.

On their own

Have students give their presentations to the class.

Get Ready For Middle School

Presentation

Remind students to use grammatically correct sentences. Tell students that having good posture and using hand gestures and the appropriate facial expressions can also help them communicate during a presentation.

ELL

English Language Learners

Practice pronunciation Assist students by modeling the correct pronunciation of the unfamiliar words, having students repeat after you. Pair students with mixed language proficiencies together to practice pronunciation and employ self-correction techniques.

Objectives

- Synthesize research material.
- Review singular and plural pronouns.
- Spell irregular plurals.

Research and Inquiry
Synthesize

Teach Have students synthesize their research findings and results. Review how to choose relevant details from a number of sources and organize them logically. Remind students to include the answers to their inquiry questions in their biographies.

Guide practice Have students use a word processing program or index cards to prepare for their presentations on Day 5. If students are using index cards, remind them to number the cards so that they can tell what order the cards should be in. If students are using a word processing program, remind them to use a large enough font so that they can read it while standing in front of the class.

On their own Have students organize and combine the information they have gathered into a biography. Remind them to complete their presentation notes and any time lines they have started.

Conventions
Singular and Plural Pronouns

Test practice Tell students that important assessments often include questions about singular and plural pronouns. Remind students that a singular pronoun takes the place of a singular noun, while a plural pronoun takes the place of a plural noun.

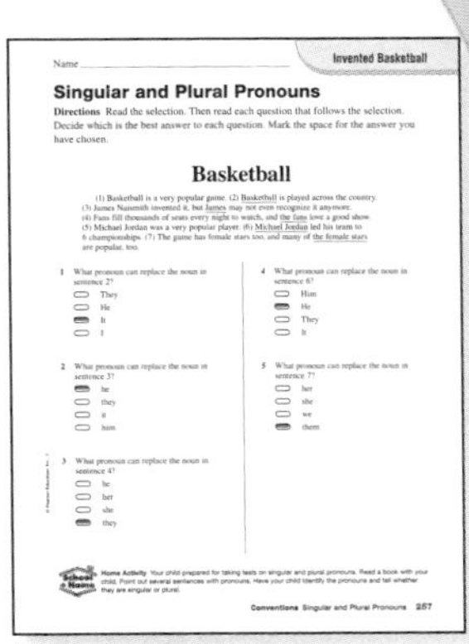
Invented Basketball

Singular and Plural Pronouns

Basketball

Reader's and Writer's Notebook p. 257

Daily Fix-It Use Daily Fix-It numbers 7 and 8 in the right margin.

On their own For additional practice, use the *Reader's and Writer's Notebook* p. 257.

Spelling
Irregular Plurals

Practice spelling strategy Remind students of the common spelling strategies to spell new words, such as segmenting words by letter sound, syllables, and word parts. Have them apply these strategies during the following activity. Supply pairs of students with index cards on which the spelling words have been written. Have one student read a word while the other writes it. Then have students switch roles. Have them use the cards to check their spelling and correct any misspelled words.

On their own For additional practice, use *Let's Practice It!* page 224 on the *Teacher Resources DVD-ROM.*

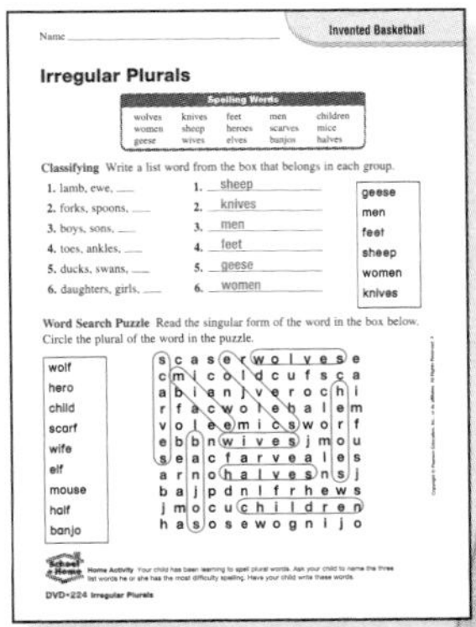
Invented Basketball

Irregular Plurals

Let's Practice It!
TR DVD•224

Daily Fix-It

7. Do the boys classmates diss-like him? (*boy's, dislike*)

8. The kids think he is diferent, and he like him. (*different; they*)

Objectives

- Revise draft of persuasive essay using conjunctions to combine sentences.
- Apply reversing strategy of consolidating.

Writing—Persuasive Text
Revising Strategy: Consolidating

MINI-LESSON

Consolidating with Conjunctions

- Yesterday we wrote a persuasive text about a sport or game. Today we will revise our drafts. The goal is to make your writing clearer, more interesting, and more informative.

- Display Writing Transparency 16B. Remind students that revising does not include corrections of grammar and mechanics. Then introduce the revising strategy of consolidating.

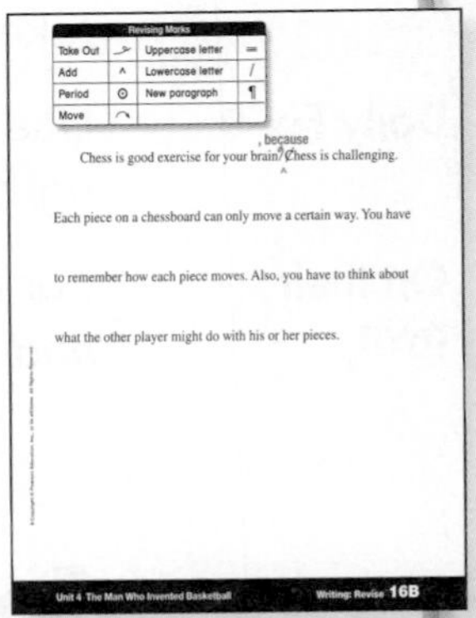

Revising Marks			
Take Out		Uppercase letter	=
Add	^	Lowercase letter	/
Period	⊙	New paragraph	¶
Move			

Chess is good exercise for your brain, because chess is challenging.

Each piece on a chessboard can only move a certain way. You have to remember how each piece moves. Also, you have to think about what the other player might do with his or her pieces.

Unit 4 The Man Who Invented Basketball — Writing: Revise 16B

Writing Transparency 16B, TR DVD

- I can see that the first two sentences say, "Chess is good exercise for your brain. Chess is challenging." These two sentences show a cause-and-effect relationship. The cause is "chess is challenging." The effect is "chess is good exercise for your brain." So, I can use the conjunction *because* to combine these two sentences. "Chess is good exercise for your brain because it is challenging."

Explain to students that as they revise, they should ask themselves if there are sentences that could be combined with conjunctions such as *because, since, yet,* or *until.*

Revising Tips

- ✓ Make sure that your purpose is clearly stated.
- ✓ Be sure that you give reasons someone should play the game or sport you chose.
- ✓ Use conjunctions to combine sentences.

Peer conferencing

Peer Revision Have students switch papers with a partner. As partners read, they should try to complete the sentence *The purpose of this essay is_____.* Then they should list the details that support the purpose. Refer to the *Readers and Writers Notebook* for more information about peer conferencing.

Have students revise their drafts using the revising strategy and feedback from their partner. Remind students to reread the key features of a persuasive text before they revise.

Corrective feedback Circulate around the room to monitor students and confer with students as they revise. Remind students who are correcting spelling and capitalization errors that they will have time to edit tomorrow. They should be working on content and flow today.

ROUTINE Quick Write for Fluency — Team Talk

1. **Talk** Students talk about what makes their sport or game unique.
2. **Write** Students write two or three sentences about what makes their sport or game unique.
3. **Share** Students share what they wrote with a partner.

Routines Flip Chart

Wrap Up Your Day

- ✔ **Build Concepts** What did you learn about Ted Williams's talents?
- ✔ **Oral Vocabulary** Monitor students' oral vocabulary as they respond: How can talents help a person achieve great things?
- ✔ **Text Features** Ask students how the time line and sidebars help them understand the selection.

Write Guy
Jeff Anderson

Adding Without Leaving Readers Hanging

A student might add worthwhile information to his or her writing, but often write sentence fragments. I like to encourage the writer by welcoming the idea and, at the same time, helping students form solid sentences or add dependent parts in order to communicate.

Differentiated Instruction

SI Strategic Intervention

Conjunctions If students are having trouble using conjunctions, give them examples of sentences that use *and* and *but* as well as *because, since, yet,* and *until.*

ELL English Language Learners

Support revising Have students write conjunctions on self-stick notes and place them at points in their text where they will help with consolidation. Once students have decided which conjunctions to use and where to use them, have them read their texts aloud again.

Preview DAY 5

Remind students to think about how people can use their talents to do unique things.

Objectives
- Review the weekly concept.
- Review oral vocabulary.

Today at a Glance

Oral Vocabulary

Comprehension
◎ Generalize

Lesson Vocabulary
◎ Unfamiliar words

Phonics/Word Analysis
◎ Irregular plurals

Literary Terms
Point of view

Assessment
Fluency
Comprehension

Research and Inquiry
Communicate

Spelling
Irregular plurals

Conventions
Singular and plural pronouns

Writing
Persuasive text

Check Oral Vocabulary
SUCCESS PREDICTOR

Concept Wrap Up

Question of the Week

How do talents make someone unique?

Review the concept Have students look back at the reading selections to find examples that best demonstrate how talents make people unique.

Review Amazing Words Display and review this week's concept map. Remind students that this week they have learned eleven Amazing Words related to talent. Have students use the Amazing Words and the concept map to answer the Question of the Week, *How do talents make someone unique?*

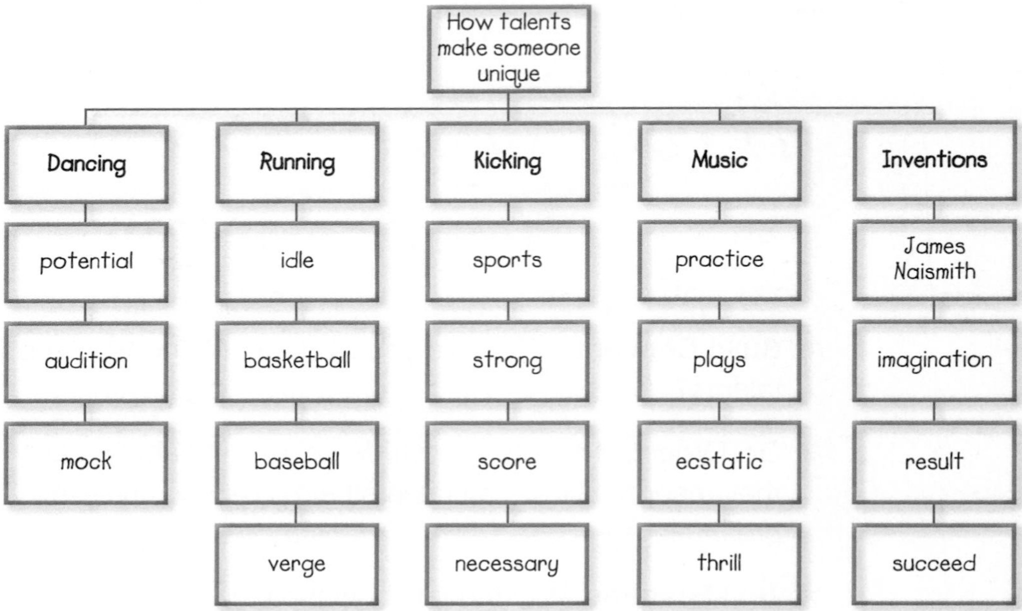

ELL Check Concepts and Language Use the Day 5 instructions on ELL Poster 16 to monitor students' understanding of the lesson concept.

Amazing Ideas

Connect to the Big Question Have pairs of students discuss how the Question of the Week connects to the Big Question: *What does it mean to be unique?* Tell students to use the concept map and what they have learned from this week's Anchored Talks and reading selections to form an Amazing Idea—a realization or "big idea" about being One of a Kind. Remind Partners to ask and answer questions with appropriate details, and to give suggestions that build on each other's Ideas. Then ask each pair to share its Amazing Idea with the class.

Amazing Ideas might include these key concepts:

- There are different kinds of talent.
- People's talents help make them one of a kind.
- People have to practice to develop their talents.
- Everyone should be allowed to develop his or her talents.

Write about it Have students write a few sentences about their Amazing Idea, beginning with "This week I learned..." Encourage students to include simple facts, details, and explanations in their compositions.

It's Friday

MONITOR PROGRESS **Check Oral Vocabulary**

Have individuals use this week's Amazing Words to describe ways people can be one of a kind. Monitor students' abilities to use the Amazing Words and note which words you need to reteach.

If... students have difficulty using the Amazing Words,
then... reteach using the Oral Vocabulary Routine, pages 21a, 26b, 36b, 46b, OV•1.

Day 1	Day 2	Day 3	Day 4	Day 5
Check Oral Vocabulary	Check Word Reading	Check Retelling	Check Fluency	Check Oral Vocabulary

Success Predictor

Amazing Words

mock	necessary
idle	result
potential	succeed
ecstatic	rise
thrill	verge
audition	

ELL

English Language Learners
Concept Map Work with students to add new words to the concept map.

Objectives

- Review generalizing.
- Review unfamiliar words.
- Review irregular plurals.
- Review point of view.

Comprehension Review
Generalize

Teach generalize

Envision It!

Review the definition of generalizing on p. 24a. Remind students that general statements can have one of the general clue words added without changing the meaning of the sentence. For additional support have students review p. EI•8 on generalizing.

Envision It! Visual Skills Handbook
Generalize
All birds have wings.
A statement that is true for many examples is a generalization.
Student Edition p. EI•8

Guide practice

Have pairs find an example of generalizing in *The Man Who Invented Basketball: James Naismith and His Amazing Game.* Then have them show how one of the generalizing clue words can be inserted into the sentence.

On their own

For additional practice with generalizing, use *Let's Practice It!* page 225 on *the Teacher Resources DVD-ROM.*

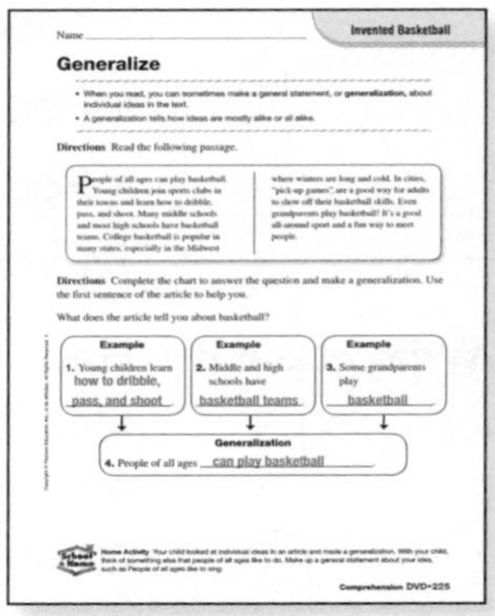

Name ______ Invented Basketball

Generalize

- When you read, you can sometimes make a general statement, or **generalization,** about individual ideas in the text.
- A generalization tells how ideas are mostly alike or all alike.

Directions Read the following passage.

People of all ages can play basketball. Young children join sports clubs in their towns and learn how to dribble, pass, and shoot. Many middle schools and most high schools have basketball teams. College basketball is popular in many states, especially in the Midwest where winters are long and cold. In cities, "pick-up games" are a good way for adults to show off their basketball skills. Even grandparents play basketball! It's a good all-around sport and a fun way to meet people.

Directions Complete the chart to answer the question and make a generalization. Use the first sentence of the article to help you.

What does the article tell you about basketball?

Example	Example	Example
1. Young children learn how to dribble, pass, and shoot	2. Middle and high schools have basketball teams	3. Some grandparents play basketball

Generalization

4. People of all ages can play basketball.

Home Activity Your child looked at individual ideas in an article and made a generalization. With your child, think of something else that people of all ages like to do. Make up a general statement about your idea, such as People of all ages like to sing.

Comprehension DVD•225

Let's Practice It!
TR DVD•225

Vocabulary Review
Unfamiliar Words

Teach unfamiliar words

Remind students that checking for context clues around an unfamiliar word can often help them figure out what that word means.

Guide practice

Review with students how to use context clues to figure out the meaning of the word *study.* Write the following sentence on the board: *When I study for a test, I read carefully and look at all my notes.* Have students identify the context clues in the sentence and determine the meaning of *study.*

On their own

Have students work in pairs to write context sentences using this week's lesson vocabulary. Partners can trade sentences and identify the context clues that help them determine each word's meaning.

Word Analysis Review
Irregular Plurals

Teach irregular plurals

Write the following sentences on the board. Have students read each one, first quietly to themselves and then aloud as you track the print.

1. **The men stamped their feet in time to the music.**
2. **You can find the toy elves on those shelves.**
3. **Wolves will eat deer, field mice, and other prey.**
4. **The women wore red scarves.**
5. **Children should not play with knives.**

Team Talk Have students discuss with a partner which words are simply irregular plurals that they have to memorize and which words form the plural by changing the final *-f* or *-fe* to *-ves.* Then call on individuals to share with the class.

Literary Terms Review
Point of View

Teach point of view

Have students reread "My Turn at Bat: The Story of My Life" on pp. 46–51. Remind students of the difference between biography and autobiography. Review with them the pronouns used in first-person and third-person points of view.

Guide practice

Remind students that the selection has *both* points of view in it. Find an example where the point of view changes within the selection. Point it out to students and explain how they can identify the different points of view.

On their own

As students reread the selection, have them indicate which sections are written in first person and which are written in third person.

Lesson Vocabulary

basketball a game played on a court where two teams try to throw a ball through a raised hoop

disease a problem in the body; sickness

freeze turn into ice

guard a person who watches over or protects something

popular liked by many people

sports games in which people use their bodies

study to spend time learning, usually by reading

terrible really bad

ELL

English Language Learners

Generalize If students are having difficulty finding a generalization within the selection, help them find examples. Then write a number of both general and specific statements. Have students identify which sentences are generalizations.

Articulation tip In Spanish, plurals are formed by adding *-s* to words ending in a vowel *(madre/madres)* and *-es* to words ending in a consonant *(arbol/arboles).* Spanish speakers may thus add *-es* to any words ending in a consonant. Give students additional practice writing plural endings, especially those formed by adding *-ies* and *-ves.*

DAY 5 Wrap Up your Week

15–20 min

Objectives

- Read grade-level text with fluency.

Plan to Assess Fluency

- [x] **This week assess Advanced students.**
- [ ] **Week 2** Assess Strategic Intervention students.
- [ ] **Week 3** Assess On-Level students.
- [ ] **Week 4** Assess Strategic Intervention students.
- [ ] **Week 5** Assess any students you have not yet checked during this unit.

Set individual goals for students to enable them to reach the year-end goal.

- Current Goal: 95–105 WCPM
- Year-End Goal: 120 WCPM

Assessment

Check words correct per minute

Fluency Make two copies of the fluency passage on p. 53k. As the student reads the text aloud, mark mistakes on your copy. Also mark where the student is at the end of one minute. To check the student's comprehension of the passage, have him or her retell what was read. To figure words correct per minute (WCPM), subtract the number of mistakes from the total number of words read in one minute.

WCPM

Corrective feedback

If... students cannot read fluently at a rate of 95–105 WCPM,
then... make sure they practice with text at their independent reading level. Provide additional fluency practice by pairing nonfluent readers with fluent readers.

If... students already read at 120 WCPM,
then... have them read a book of their choice independently.

Small Group Time

DAY 5 **Break into small groups before the comprehension lesson.**

Teacher Led

SI Strategic Intervention	OL On-Level	A Advanced
Teacher Led p. DI•6	**Teacher Led** p. DI•11	**Teacher Led** p. DI•15
• Practice fluency	• Practice fluency	• Practice fluency
• **Read** *What Can Athletes Do?* or *The Winning Point*	• **Read** *A Trip*	• **Read** *Extraordinary Athletes*

ELL Place English language learners in the groups that correspond to their reading abilities in English.

Practice Stations
- Words to Know
- Get Fluent
- Read for Meaning

Independent Activities
- Grammar Jammer
- Concept Talk Video
- Vocabulary Activities

Name ____

Zora the Zebra

Zora was a zebra with only one stripe. Most of the time Zora 13
struggled to hold her head up high. It wasn't easy hearing what the 26
other animals had to say. 31

"A zebra isn't a zebra unless it has at least seven stripes," the other 45
zebras would say. 48

"Zora should change her name to Zero," laughed the mice. 58

"But I would love you if you had *no* stripe," her mother would say. 72

One day, while the other zebras were drinking from the lake, Zora 84
was standing on a hill. She could see them because their stripes stood 97
out against the light ground. 102

Then Zora noticed something terrible. A pack of wolves was glaring 113
down at the zebras. 117

"Oh no, I must warn them!" Zora cried. 125

She quickly ran down the hill. 131

It was clear that the wolves couldn't see Zora because she only had 144
one stripe. Her color blended well with the ground. 153

"Quick, run for your lives!" Zora shouted. 160

At that moment, the wolves came swooping down the hill. The 171
zebras had a head start and ran to safety. 180

That night, the zebras held a party for Zora. They were sorry for the 194
way they had treated her. "Three cheers for Zora!" they yelled. 205

"Now, this is the kind of attention I like," Zora said. 216

MONITOR PROGRESS

- **Check Fluency**

Objectives
- Read grade-level text with comprehension.

Assessment

Check generalize

Generalize Use "Wanda's Bad Play" on p. 53m to check students' understanding of generalizing.

1. How does Coach Johnson help Wanda in this story? Possible response: He helps her identify a skill she is good at and gets her to start thinking about things she can do well instead of focusing on how bad she is at playing baseball.
2. Name two general statements Wanda makes in the story. Possible response: *I can't tell where a ball is going. I don't catch balls well.*
3. Identify another general statement made in the story and explain how you can tell this is a general statement. Possible response: *The kids often groaned at her bad plays* is a general statement. I can tell this because it contains the clue word *often.*

Corrective feedback

If... students are unable to answer the comprehension questions,
then... use the Reteach lesson in the *First Stop* book.

Name ______________________________

Wanda's Bad Play

Wanda raced to catch the baseball in the air. But she wasn't fast enough, and the ball bounced in front of her. When she tried to scoop it up after that, she completely missed it. Other kids on her team groaned loudly at Wanda's bad play. The kids often groaned at her bad plays.

Later, Wanda sat next to Coach Johnson. "I'm an awful baseball player. In fact, the truth is I'm an awful athlete," Wanda said.

"Why do you say that?" asked Coach Johnson.

Wanda thought for an instant and said, "I'd say that for six reasons. First, I don't run very fast. Second, I can't tell where a ball is going. Third, I don't catch balls well. Fourth, I don't throw balls well. Fifth, I don't hit well when I bat. Sixth, when I do hit something, it doesn't go far because I'm not strong. There is only one thing I'm good at. I know baseball rules."

"Hmm," said Coach Johnson. "I know something else you're good at, Wanda."

Wanda couldn't guess what it was. She asked, "Making lists?"

"Maybe," answered Coach Johnson with a laugh. "But that's not what I was thinking. You're good at analyzing things. That means you are good at thinking about things and figuring out what's right and wrong."

It was Wanda's turn to say, "Hmmm."

Then she asked, "Coach, does that mean I might make a good scientist?"

"Sure," said Coach Johnson. "Or a baseball coach."

Wanda smiled. She liked that idea!

MONITOR PROGRESS

• Generalize

Objectives
- Communicate inquiry results.
- Administer spelling test.
- Review singular and plural pronouns.

Research and Inquiry
Communicate

Present ideas

Have students share their inquiry results by presenting their biographies and giving a brief talk on their research. Have students show the class the time lines they began on Day 3.

Listening and speaking

Remind students how to be good speakers and how to communicate effectively with their audience.

- Respond to relevant questions with appropriate details.
- Speak clearly and loudly.
- Keep eye contact with audience members.

Remind students of these tips for being a good listener.

- Wait until the speaker has finished before raising your hand to ask a relevant question or make a comment.
- Be polite, even if you disagree.

Spelling Test
Irregular Plurals

Spelling test To administer the spelling test, refer to the directions, words, and sentences on p. 25c.

Conventions
Extra Practice

Teach Ask students to explain the difference between singular and plural pronouns. (Singular pronouns replace singular nouns; plural pronouns replace plural nouns.)

Guide practice Write the following sentences, with words underlined. Have the class tell you which pronouns replace the underlined words, and whether they are singular or plural.

A girl saw the boy fly. (*She, him,* singular)

Three girls watched the boy as he flew. (*They, him,* plural and singular)

James cannot fly. (*He,* singular)

Daily Fix-It Use Daily Fix-It numbers 9 and 10 in the right margin.

On their own Read the following sentences: Have students look back at *The Man Who Invented Basketball* to find the correct singular and plural pronouns to complete the sentences. Then have them identify each one as singular or plural. Students should complete *Let's Practice It!* page 226 on the *Teacher Resources DVD-ROM.*

1. **Then ___ raced out onto the frozen swimming hole like a champion skater.** *(he)*
2. **James would remember duck on a rock years later when ___ would be very important to ___.** *(it, him)*
3. **___ thought ___ could help teens live better lives if ___ talked to ___ while teaching sports.** *(He, he, he, them)*
4. **___ were so bored that some of ___ wanted to quit the YMCA training school.** *(They, them)*

Daily Fix-It

9. The girl worryed about the boy but he was all right. *(worried; boy,)*
10. What a helpfull friend she was. *(helpful, was!)*

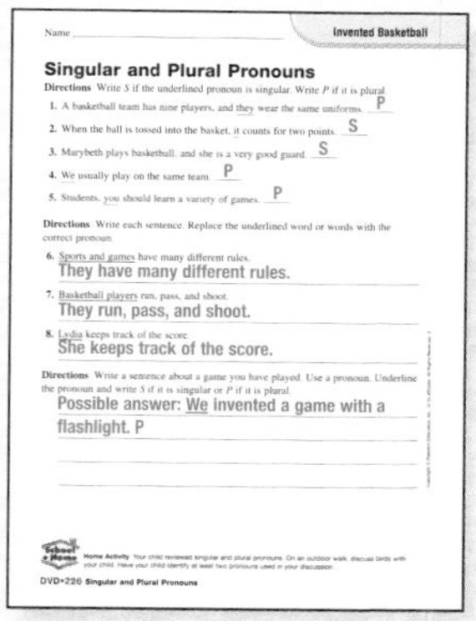

Name ______ Invented Basketball

Singular and Plural Pronouns

Directions Write *S* if the underlined pronoun is singular. Write *P* if it is plural.

1. A basketball team has nine players, and they wear the same uniforms. P
2. When the ball is tossed into the basket, it counts for two points. S
3. Marybeth plays basketball, and she is a very good guard. S
4. We usually play on the same team. P
5. Students, you should learn a variety of games. P

Directions Write each sentence. Replace the underlined word or words with the correct pronoun.

6. Sports and games have many different rules.
They have many different rules.
7. Basketball players run, pass, and shoot.
They run, pass, and shoot.
8. Lydia keeps track of the score.
She keeps track of the score.

Directions Write a sentence about a game you have played. Use a pronoun. Underline the pronoun and write *S* if it is singular or *P* if it is plural.

Possible answer: We invented a game with a flashlight. P

School + Home **Home Activity** Your child reviewed singular and plural pronouns. On an outdoor walk, discuss birds with your child. Have your child identify at least two pronouns used in your discussion.

DVD•226 Singular and Plural Pronouns

Let's Practice It!
TR DVD•226

DAY 5 Wrap Up your Week

20–25 min

Objectives

- Proofread revised compositions, paying attention to the use of pronouns.
- Understand and avoid double negatives.
- Create and present final draft.

Writing—Persuasive Text
Singular and Plural Pronouns

Review Revising Remind students that yesterday they revised their essays by combining sentences with conjunctions. Today they will proofread their essays.

MINI-LESSON

Proofread for Pronouns and Double Negatives

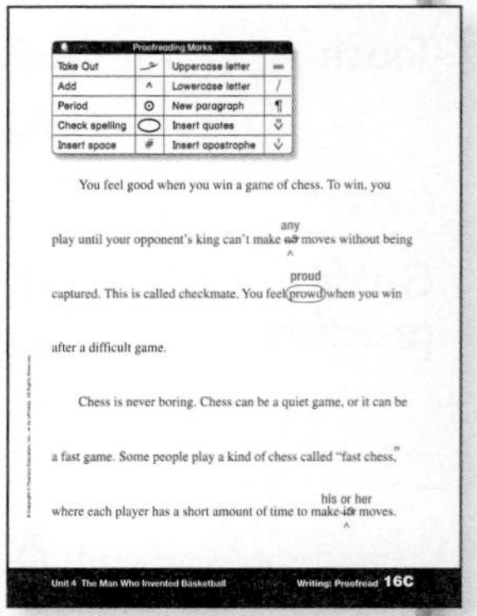

Proofreading Marks			
Take Out		Uppercase letter	≡
Add	^	Lowercase letter	/
Period	⊙	New paragraph	¶
Check spelling	◯	Insert quotes	
Insert space	#	Insert apostrophe	

You feel good when you win a game of chess. To win, you play until your opponent's king can't make ~~no~~ any moves without being captured. This is called checkmate. You feel (prowd) proud when you win after a difficult game.

Chess is never boring. Chess can be a quiet game, or it can be a fast game. Some people play a kind of chess called "fast chess," where each player has a short amount of time to make ~~its~~ his or her moves.

Unit 4 The Man Who Invented Basketball Writing: Proofread 16C

Writing Transparency 16C, TR DVD

- **Teach** When we proofread, we look for errors in spelling, capitalization, punctuation, and grammar. Today we'll make sure we've used pronouns correctly, and we'll eliminate double negatives.
- **Model** Let's look at the persuasive text we worked on yesterday. Display Transparency 16C. Explain that you will look for errors in spelling, punctuation, and capitalization; and you'll make sure pronouns are used correctly. Then you will eliminate any double negatives. Review the double negative in the sentence *I don't want nothing.* I see a problem. It says *your opponent's king can't make no moves*. I can see that the combination of *can't* and *no* makes a double negative. I'll rewrite this sentence. Continue to point out spelling, capitalization, and punctuation problems. Then have students proofread their own persuasive texts.

Proofread Display the Proofreading Tips. Ask students to proofread their compositions, using the Proofreading Tips and paying particular attention to correct use of pronouns. Circulate around the room answering students' questions. When students have finished editing their own work, have pairs proofread one another's persuasive texts.

Proofreading Tips

- ✔ Make sure you have used pronouns correctly.
- ✔ Eliminate any double negatives.
- ✔ Reread your persuasive text, checking for errors in grammar and capitalization.
- ✔ Use a dictionary to check the spelling of difficult words.

Present

Have students incorporate revisions and proofreading edits into their persuasive texts to create a final draft.

Give students a choice between presenting their persuasive texts orally to a small group or to the whole class. Students should read their persuasive texts aloud to themselves a few times before presenting them to others.

ROUTINE **Quick Write for Fluency**

1. **Talk** Pairs talk about a new sport or game they would like to try.
2. **Write** Students write two sentences giving reasons they want to try the new sport or game.
3. **Share** Students share their reasons aloud with the class.

Routines Flip Chart

Teacher Note

Writing self-evaluation Make copies of the Writing Self-Evaluation Guide on p. 39 of the *Reader's and Writer's Notebook* and hand out to students.

ELL

English Language Learners

Poster preview Prepare students for next week by using Week 2, ELL Poster 17. Read the Poster Talk-Through to introduce the concept and vocabulary. Ask students to identify and describe objects and actions in the art.

Selection summary Send home the summary of *Hottest, Coldest, Highest, Deepest* in English and the students' home languages, if available. They can read the summary with family members.

Preview NEXT WEEK

What makes nature's record holders unique? Tell students that next week they will read about things in nature that set records.

DAY 5 Assessment Checkpoints for the Week

Weekly Assessment

Use pp. 111–118 of *Weekly* Tests to check:

✔ **Phonics** Irregular Plurals

✔ **Comprehension Skill** Generalize

✔ **Lesson Vocabulary**

✔ Review **Comprehension Skill** Graphic Sources

basketball	popular
disease	sports
freeze	study
guard	terrible

Weekly Tests

A Advanced

OL On-Level

SI Strategic Intervention

Differentiated Assessment

Use pp. 91–96 of *Fresh Reads for Fluency and Comprehension* to check:

✔ **Comprehension Skill** Generalize

✔ Review **Comprehension Skill** Graphic Sources

✔ **Fluency** Words Correct Per Minute

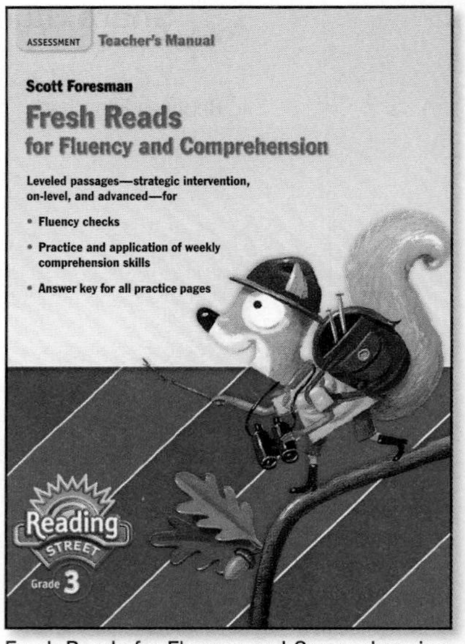

Fresh Reads for Fluency and Comprehension

Managing Assessment

Use *Assessment Handbook* for:

✔ **Weekly Assessment Blackline Masters for Monitoring Progress**

✔ **Observation Checklists**

✔ **Record-Keeping Forms**

✔ **Portfolio Assessment**

Assessment Handbook

Teacher Notes

Pacing Small Group Instruction

15–20 min

5-Day Plan

DAY 1	• Reinforce the concept • Read Leveled Readers Concept Literacy Below Level
DAY 2	• Generalize • Summarize • Revisit Student Edition pp. 28–35
DAY 3	• Unfamiliar Words • Revisit Student Edition pp. 36–41
DAY 4	• Practice Retelling • Read/Revisit Student Edition pp. 46–51
DAY 5	• Reread for fluency • Reread Leveled Readers

3- or 4-Day Plan

DAY 1	• Reinforce the concept • Read Leveled Readers
DAY 2	• Generalize • Summarize • Revisit Student Edition pp. 28–35
DAY 3	• Unfamiliar Words • Revisit Student Edition pp. 36–41
DAY 4	• Practice Retelling • Read/Revisit Student Edition pp. 46–51 • Reread for fluency • Reread Leveled Readers

3-Day Plan: Eliminate the shaded box.

SI Strategic Intervention

DAY 1

Build Background

■ **Reinforce the Concept** Reinforce the weekly question *How do talents make someone unique?* Sometimes we have to work to uncover our talents. One example is Michael Jordan, who was cut from his high school basketball team. Jordan practiced on his own and went on to become the best basketball player in the world. Add new words to the concept map. Who are some people you can think of whose talents make them one of a kind? Think about famous athletes, musicians, and inventors as well as people you know well. This week we will read about James Naismith, the inventor of basketball. He went through some difficult times but ended up succeeding at several careers.

Preview Decodable Practice Reader 16A

■ **Before Reading** Review the words on p. 1 of *Decodable Practice Readers 3.2*. Then have students blend these words from the story: *everybody, ruffled, suggested, gear, strange,* and *tumbled.* Be sure students understand the meaning of such words as *strange* and *tumbled.* Guide students through the text by performing a choral reading of it.

Objectives

• Participate in teacher-led discussions by answering questions with appropriate detail.

SI Strategic Intervention

DAY 1

For a complete literacy instructional plan and additional practice with this week's target skills and strategies, see the **Leveled Reader Teaching Guide.**

Concept Literacy Reader

- **Read** *What Can Athletes Do?*

- **Before Reading** Preview the book with students, focusing on key concepts and vocabulary. Then have them set a purpose for reading.
- **During Reading** Read the first two pages aloud while students track along with the print. Then have students finish reading the book with a partner.
- **After Reading** After students finish reading, ask: What talents do these sports require? *(jumping high; swimming fast; running fast, long, and far; leaping and spinning while on ice skates; hitting a ball; catching a ball and running with it)*

Below-Level Reader

- **Read** *The Winning Point*

- **Before Reading** Have students use the pictures to preview the book. Then have them set a purpose for reading.
- **During Reading** Read the first two pages aloud. Then do a choral reading of the next three pages. If students are able, have them read and discuss the remainder of the book with a partner. Ask: How can focusing on the ball help calm nervousness? *(It can make you focus on what you are doing rather than who is watching you.)*
- **After Reading** Ask students to look at and discuss the concept map. Connect the Below-Level Reader to the weekly question *How do talents make someone unique?* What ability does someone need in order to become a high scorer in soccer? *(an ability to pay attention to the game instead of the crowd)*

MONITOR PROGRESS

If... students have difficulty reading the selection with a partner,
then... have them follow along as they listen to the Leveled Readers DVD-ROM.

If... students have trouble understanding how a good soccer player might never get a goal,
then... reread the first few pages of the story and discuss Lucy's problem.

Objectives

- Participate in teacher-led discussions by answering questions with appropriate detail.

SI Strategic Intervention

DAY 2

Student Edition p. EI•8

More Reading

Use additional Leveled Readers or other texts at students' instructional levels to reinforce this week's skills and strategies. For text suggestions, see the Leveled Reader Database or the Leveled Readers Skills Chart on pp. CL24–CL29.

Reinforce Comprehension

Skill Generalize Review with students the *Envision It! Skill* material on Generalizing. Then use p. 24 to review the definition of generalize. To *generalize* is to make a broad statement or rule that applies to many examples. What word is part of *generalize*? *(general, which can mean "broad, not specific")* When you make a generalization, you think about a number of examples or facts and what they have in common. What generalization can you make about how hard great athletes work? *(All great athletes work hard at the sports they play.)*

Strategy Summarize Review the definition of summarize. Point out that summarizing as you read can help you remember facts. Remind students to summarize sections of the biography as they read. You might summarize the first page this way: James had an accident at age 11 that taught him an important lesson. For additional support, refer students to *Envision It!* p. EI•25.

Revisit *The Man Who Invented Basketball* on pp. 28–35. Have students begin reading aloud *The Man Who Invented Basketball* with a partner. As they read, have them apply the comprehension skill and strategy to the biography.

- What generalizations can you make about James's early life? *(He suffered through many sad events; he enjoyed playing games with other children.)*
- What generalization can you make about life in the 1860s? You may want to reread p. 31 before you answer. *(Life was dangerous because of deadly diseases.)*
- What was James's Uncle Peter like? *(He let James solve his own problems.)*

Use the During Reading Differentiated Instruction for additional support for struggling readers.

MONITOR PROGRESS

If... students have difficulty reading along with the group,
then... have them follow along as they listen to the AudioText.

Objectives
- Make and support generalizations about text.
- Summarize information in text, maintaining meaning.

SI Strategic Intervention DAY 3

Reinforce Vocabulary

- **Reread for Fluency** Use Decodable Practice Reader 16A.
- **Decoding Multisyllabic Words** Write *everybody* on the board. Then model how to use meaningful parts to read it. First, I ask myself if I see any parts I know. I see *every* at the beginning of the word, and I see *body* at the end. I know *every* means *"all,"* and I know *body* can mean "person." So I think *everybody* must mean "all people."

Use the Multisyllabic Words routine on the *Routines Flip Chart* to help students read these words from the biography: *disease, terrible, study, popular,* and *basketball.*

Unfamiliar Words/Context Clues Write the word *freeze* on the board. I know the word *freeze* can mean "turn solid from cold," as in "The water I put in the ice cube tray will freeze soon." However, it can also mean "stand still." In the biography, the sentences around the word *freeze* say "Icy wind sweeps down from the north. Rivers *freeze* solid." Those sentences make the most sense if I think of the river turning solid from cold.

- **Revisit** *The Man Who Invented Basketball* on pp. 36–41. Review *Words!* on p. W•7. Then have students finish reading the biography. Encourage them to use context clues to figure out the meaning of any unfamiliar words. Ask: Which definition of the word *guard* makes more sense on p. 32: "a position on a basketball team" or "a person who keeps watch over someone or something"? *(The guard keeps watch over a rock, so the second definition makes more sense.)*

Use the During Reading Differentiated Instruction for additional support for struggling readers.

MONITOR PROGRESS

If... students need more practice with the lesson vocabulary,
then... use *Envision It! Pictured Vocabulary Cards*.

Objectives

- Use context to determine the relevant meaning of unfamiliar words.

Student Edition p. W•7

More Reading

Use additional Leveled Readers or other texts at students' instructional levels to reinforce this week's skills and strategies. For text suggestions, see the Leveled Reader Database or the Leveled Readers Skills Chart on pp. CL24–CL29.

Strategic Intervention

DAY 4

Practice Retelling

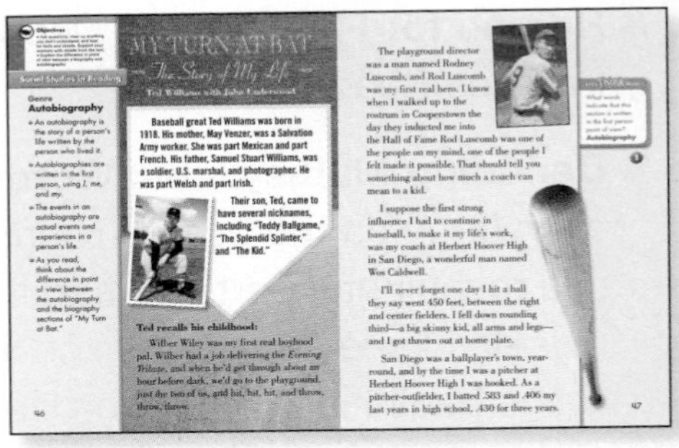

■ **Retell** Guide students in using the Retelling Cards to summarize Naismith's life.

- Who is this biography about? *(James Naismith)*
- What is he famous for? *(He invented basketball.)*

If students struggle, model a fluent retelling.

Genre Focus

■ **Before Reading or Revisiting** "My Turn at Bat: The Story of My Life" on pp. 46–51, read aloud the genre information on p. 46. An autobiography is the story of a person's life, written by the person who lived it. Autobiographies tell about actual events and experiences. This selection tells about the life of Ted Williams, a member of the baseball Hall of Fame. Read the rest of the panel. Then have students read the introduction to the selection.

■ **During Reading or Revisiting** Have students perform a choral reading of the selection. As they read, write each subhead on the board. Subheads can help you locate specific information quickly. How do the subheads organize information in this autobiography? *(They divide the autobiography into Ted Williams's childhood, his baseball career, a time line, and his Hall of Fame statistics.)*

■ **After Reading or Revisiting** Have students share their reactions to the selection. Then guide them through the Reading Across Texts and Writing Across Texts activities, prompting if necessary.

- Name the two athletes you just read about. *(James Naismith and Ted Williams)*
- What did each accomplish? *(One invented basketball; the other became one of baseball's best hitters.)*
- How were they alike? How were they different? *(Both loved sports. One invented and taught basketball; the other broke records as a hitter in baseball.)*

MONITOR PROGRESS

If... students have difficulty retelling the selection,
then... have them review the selection using the photos and text features.

Objectives

- Explain the difference in point of view between a biography and autobiography.

SI Strategic Intervention

DAY 5

For a complete literacy instructional plan and additional practice with this week's target skills and strategies, see the **Leveled Reader Teaching Guide.**

Concept Literacy Reader

What Can Athletes Do?

- **Model** Model the fluency skill of accuracy for students. Ask students to listen carefully as you read aloud the first two pages of *What Can Athletes Do?* Have them note the care you take to pronounce words accurately and observe punctuation cues.
- **Fluency Routine**
  1. Have students reread passages from *What Can Athletes Do?* with a partner.
  2. For optimal fluency, students should reread three to four times.
  3. As students read, monitor fluency and provide corrective feedback. Encourage them to pause and sound out words in order to achieve accuracy.

  See *Routines Flip Chart* for more help with fluency.
- **Retell** Have students retell *What Can Athletes Do?* Prompt as necessary.

Below-Level Reader

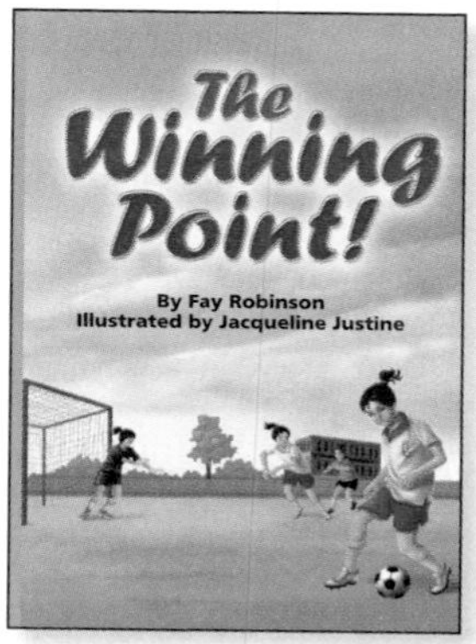

The Winning Point

- **Model** Ask students to listen carefully as you read aloud the first two pages of *The Winning Point,* emphasizing accuracy.
- **Fluency Routine**
  1. Have students reread passages from *The Winning Point* with a partner or individually.
  2. For optimal fluency, students should reread three to four times.
  3. As students read, monitor fluency and provide corrective feedback. Discuss how pausing to sound out words improves accuracy.

  For more help with fluency, see *Routines Flip Chart.*
- **Retell** For additional practice, have students retell *The Winning Point* page by page, using the pictures. Prompt students as necessary.
  - What was Lucy's talent? How did she make the most of it? *(She was good at playing soccer; she learned to focus on the ball.)*
  - What did you learn about talents from reading this book? *(Sometimes talents have to be developed.)*

MONITOR PROGRESS

If... students have difficulty reading fluently,
then... provide additional fluency practice by pairing nonfluent readers with fluent ones.

Objectives
- Read aloud grade-level appropriate text with fluency.

Pacing Small Group Instruction

15–20 min

5-Day Plan

DAY 1	• Expand the concept • Read On-Level Reader
DAY 2	• Generalize • Summarize • Revisit Student Edition pp. 28–35
DAY 3	• Unfamiliar Words • Revisit Student Edition pp. 36–41
DAY 4	• Practice Retelling • Read/Revisit Student Edition pp. 46–51
DAY 5	• Reread for fluency • Reread On-Level Reader

3- or 4-Day Plan

DAY 1	• Expand the concept • Read On-Level Reader
DAY 2	• Generalize • Summarize • Revisit Student Edition pp. 28–35
DAY 3	• Unfamiliar Words • Revisit Student Edition pp. 36–41
DAY 4	• Practice Retelling • Read/Revisit Student Edition pp. 46–51 • Reread for fluency • Reread On-Level Reader

3-Day Plan: Eliminate the shaded box.

OL On-Level

DAY 1

Build Background

- **Expand the Concept** Connect to the weekly question *How do talents make someone unique?* Then expand the concept. A person who loves an activity may work to develop his or her talent at that activity. Sometimes reading about people who have accomplished greatness can inspire a beginner to work toward greatness, too. Discuss the meaning of the words on the concept map.

On-Level Reader

For a complete literacy instructional plan and additional practice with this week's target skills and strategies, see the **Leveled Reader Teaching Guide.**

- **Before Reading** *A Trip,* have students preview it by looking at the title, cover, and pictures in the book. Ask:
  - What is the topic of this book? *(a trip to the Basketball Hall of Fame)*
  - How might a Hall of Fame visit help someone develop talents? *(It might give a person hope or inspire him or her to work hard.)*

  Have students create a two-column chart with the headings *Player* and *Accomplishment.* Explain that students will complete their charts as they read.

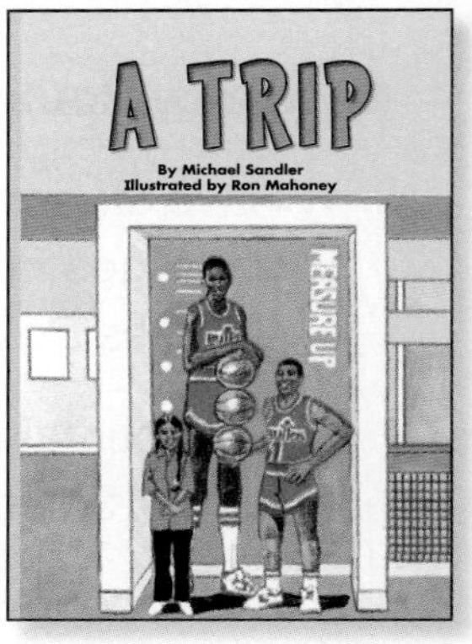

A Trip

- **During Reading** Read aloud the first three pages of the book as students follow along. Then have them finish reading the book on their own. Remind students to add names and accomplishments to their two-column charts as they read. Ask: What do all the players in the Hall of Fame have in common? *(They used their talents to break records and become the best they could be at basketball.)*
- **After Reading** Have partners compare their two-column charts.
  - Which player do you most admire? Why? *(Encourage students to support their choices by using evidence from the text.)*
  - How does the topic relate to the weekly question? *(The Hall of Famers developed their talents in order to do well in the positions they played.)*

Objectives

- Participate in teacher-led discussions by answering questions with appropriate detail.

OL On-Level DAY 2

Expand Comprehension

Skill Generalize Use p. 24 to review the definition of generalize. For additional review, see Generalize on *Envision It!* p. EI•8. I will read the biography, think about the different facts it presents, and generalize about Naismith's life. My generalization will be a broad statement or rule that applies to many examples.

Strategy Summarize Review the definition of summarize, and encourage students to summarize sections of the biography as they read. How would you summarize the second page of text in one sentence? *(Because of deaths in James's family, he went to live with his uncle.)* For additional support, use the Extend Thinking questions during reading or refer students to p. EI•25 of *Envision It!*

Revisit *The Man Who Invented Basketball* on pp. 28–35. Then have students begin reading aloud. As they read, have them make generalizations about the biography.

- What generalization can you make about Canadian winters? *(They are cold and sometimes dangerous.)*
- Describe James's work habits in one sentence. *(He worked hardest at things he found interesting.)*

Objectives
- Make and support generalizations about text.
- Summarize information in text, maintaining meaning.

Student Edition p. EI•8

More Reading

Use additional Leveled Readers or other texts at students' instructional levels to reinforce this week's skills and strategies. For text suggestions, see the Leveled Reader Database or the Leveled Readers Skills Chart on pp. CL24–CL29.

Context Clues
Read the words before and after a word that you don't know to help you make sense of it.

Student Edition p. W•7

More Reading

Use additional Leveled Readers or other texts at students' instructional levels to reinforce this week's skills and strategies. For text suggestions, see the Leveled Reader Database or the Leveled Readers Skills Chart on pp. CL24–CL29.

OL On-Level

DAY 3

Expand Vocabulary

Unfamiliar Words/Context Clues Point out the word *terrible* on p. 33.

- What are some different meanings of *terrible*? *("severe," "awful," "poorly" "performing")*
- Where does the word appear in this biography? *(in a description of Robbie's pain)*
- Based on the words and sentences around *terrible,* what does the word mean in this biography? *("severe" or "awful")* Have students refer to a dictionary if necessary. Then have them finish reading the selection, encouraging them to use context clues to decode unfamiliar words.

Revisit *The Man Who Invented Basketball* on pp. 36–41. Encourage students to use context clues as they read the entire selection and whenever they read challenging material. Point out these sentences: "James was told to invent an exciting indoor game. It had to be ready in two weeks. That was the deadline."

- What context clue might help you figure out the meaning of *deadline*? *(the phrase "in two weeks")*
- Based on that context clue, what does *deadline* mean? *("a date or time by which a project must be finished")*

If possible, allow students to consult a print or online dictionary to check their answers. Then prompt students to invent sentences of their own that contain *deadline.*

Objectives

- Use context to determine the relevant meaning of unfamiliar words.

OL On-Level DAY 4

Practice Retelling

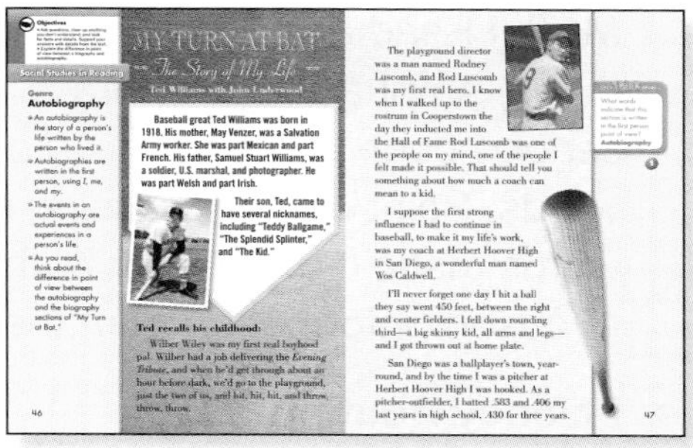

- **Retell** To assess students' comprehension, use the Retelling Cards. Monitor retelling and prompt students as needed.

Genre Focus

- **Before Reading or Revisiting** "My Turn at Bat: The Story of My Life" on pp. 46–51, read aloud the genre information about autobiography on p. 46. Explain that autobiographies can be fascinating to read and can also help students find information for research papers. Have students preview "My Turn at Bat" and set a purpose for reading.
  - How does an autobiography differ from a biography? *(An autobiography uses the words* I, me, *and* my *because the person describing events is the person who experienced them.)*
  - Who seems to be telling this story? *(Ted Williams)*
- **During Reading or Revisiting** Have students read along with you while tracking the print.
  - How is this autobiography organized? *(This one is organized in different sections, starting with Ted Williams's childhood and then describing his career in baseball.)*
  - How is this autobiography similar to and different from the biography you just read? *(Both are about the life and accomplishments of one person, and both are related to sports. The autobiography tells the story from the athlete's point of view, using words like* I *and* mine. *In contrast, the biography is written by another person and told from that person's point of view, and uses words like* he *or* she *or* her.*)*
- **After Reading or Revisiting** Have students share their reaction to "My Turn at Bat." Then have them write a conversation between James Naismith and Ted Williams about sports.

Objectives

- Use context to determine the relevant meaning of unfamiliar words.

OL On-Level

DAY 5

On-Level Reader

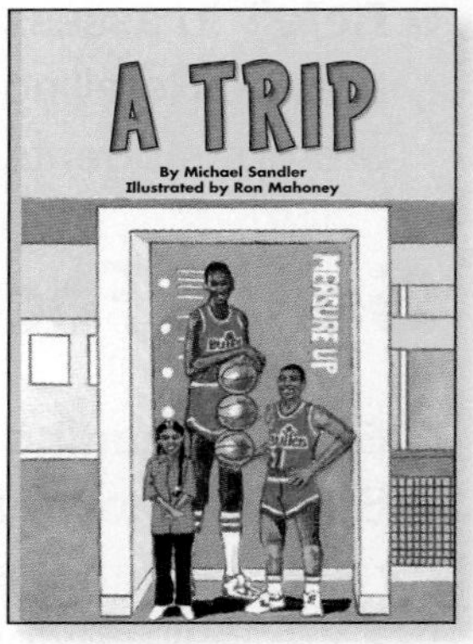

- **Model** Read aloud the first page of the On-Level Reader *A Trip,* emphasizing accuracy. If you wish, read aloud the second page and either skip or mispronounce some of the words. Point out that missing or incorrectly pronounced words make it difficult for both the reader and the listener to absorb information from the text.
- **Fluency Routine**

  1. Have students reread passages from *A Trip* with a partner.
  2. For optimal fluency, students should reread passages three to four times.
  3. As students read, monitor fluency and provide corrective feedback. Have students take care to pronounce words precisely and observe punctuation cues. Remind students to work on accurate, fluent reading in your class, in their other classes, and in their everyday lives.

  See *Routines Flip Chart* for more help with fluency.
- **Retell** For additional practice, have students use illustrations as a guide to retelling *A Trip.* Prompt as necessary.
  - How would you describe the Hall of Fame?
  - What did you learn from reading about the athletes?
  - What do you think the main character learned?

Objectives

- Read aloud grade-level appropriate text with fluency.

A Advanced DAY 1

Build Background

- **Extend the Concept** Extend the weekly question *How do talents make someone unique?* Think about your favorite athletes. What qualities and talents help them become the best at a particular sport? *(athletic skills such as strength, speed, balance, and gracefulness; also determination, hard work, and perhaps luck)*

Advanced Reader

For a complete literacy instructional plan and additional practice with this week's target skills and strategies, see the **Leveled Reader Teaching Guide.**

- **Before Reading** *Extraordinary Athletes,* tell students to look at the title and cover art. How do you think this book is related to the weekly question? *(*Extraordinary Athletes *most likely tells about people who overcame physical limits to demonstrate their athletic talents.)* Then help students set a purpose for reading.

Extraordinary Athletes

- **During Reading** Have students read the Advanced Reader independently, and encourage them to think critically. For example, ask:
  - What makes Jean Driscoll a champion? *(She holds a record in all divisions, even among people who are not disabled.)*
  - What abilities helped Erik Weihenmayer climb Mount Everest? *(his other senses; his inventiveness; his determination)*
- **After Reading** Have students review the concept map and explain how *Extraordinary Athletes* helps them answer the weekly question *How do talents make someone unique?* Prompt as necessary.
  - Of the accomplishments you read about in this book, which one impressed you the most? Why?
  - What talents made each of these athletes unique? How did limitations help each athlete develop unique talents?
- **Now Try This** Have students form small groups. Ask each group to use the Internet or library resources to research the Paralympics, a sporting event for athletes with physical disabilities. After completing their research, each group should make a short presentation about the Paralympics. Groups should work on their presentations throughout the week

Objectives

- Participate in teacher-led discussions by answering questions with appropriate detail.

Pacing Small Group Instruction

15–20 min

5-Day Plan

DAY 1	• Extend the concept • Read Advanced Reader
DAY 2	• Generalize • Summarize • Revisit Student Edition pp. 28–35
DAY 3	• Unfamiliar Words • Revisit Student Edition pp. 36–41
DAY 4	• Genre Focus • Read/Revisit Student Edition pp. 46–51
DAY 5	• Reread for fluency • Reread Advanced Reader

3- or 4-Day Plan

DAY 1	• Extend the concept • Read Advanced Reader
DAY 2	• Generalize • Summarize • Revisit Student Edition pp. 28–35
DAY 3	• Unfamiliar Words • Revisit Student Edition pp. 36–41
DAY 4	• Genre Focus • Read/Revise Student Edition pp. 46–51 • Reread for fluency • Reread Advanced Reader

3-Day Plan: Eliminate the shaded box.

More Reading

Use additional Leveled Readers or other texts at students' instructional levels to reinforce this week's skills and strategies. For text suggestions, see the Leveled Reader Database or the Leveled Readers Skills Chart on pp. CL24–CL29.

A Advanced

DAY 2

Extend Comprehension

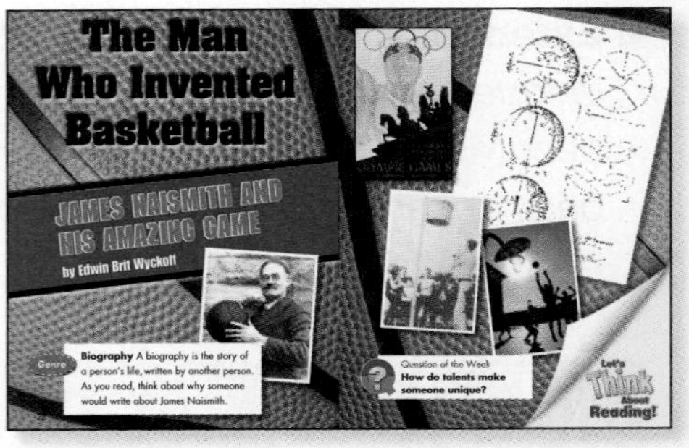

Skill Generalize Remind students that a generalization is a broad statement or rule that applies to many examples. Explain that biographies often generalize about a subject's talents. Think of the book that you just read, *Extraordinary Athletes.* If you were to generalize about the athletes featured in the book, what statement would you make? *(They did not let disabilities stand in their way.)*

Strategy Summarize Review the definition of the strategy and remind students to summarize information as they read the rest of the selection. Point out the time line and explain that it is a type of summary. During reading, use the Extend Thinking questions and the During Reading Differentiated Instruction for additional support.

Revisit *The Man Who Invented Basketball* on pp. 28–35. Encourage students to stop after each page or two and make generalizations about what they have just read. Ask: Based on the first two pages of text, what generalization would you make about James Naismith's early life? *(It had a lot of sadness but a lot of fun and friendship too.)*

Objectives
- Make and support generalizations about text.
- Summarize information in text, maintaining meaning.

A Advanced DAY 3

Extend Vocabulary

Unfamiliar Words/Context Clues Read a sentence containing an unfamiliar word, such as "Follow the rules or a foul will be declared."

- What are some meanings of the word *foul*? *("disgusting" or "dirty"; "a violation of a rule")*
- How can I figure out which meaning is correct in this selection? *(The word appears in a list of basketball rules, so the second definition must be correct.)*

■ **Revisit** *The Man Who Invented Basketball* on pp. 36–41. Challenge students to figure out the meanings of other unfamiliar words throughout the selection. For example, ask:

- Why did James Naismith name his new sport "basketball"? *(because of the peach baskets that served as goals)*
- The section titled "The Minister Plays Hardball" includes the word *sermon.* Based on the words and phrases around *sermon,* what does that word mean? *(A sermon must be a speech that a minister gives.)* How did you figure that out? *(The section mentions that James is a student minister and that he has to write something for church.)*
- What does the author mean by *bounds* on p. 40? *(The phrase is "out of bounds," so that must refer to limits rather than to leaps or jumps.)*

■ **Critical Thinking/Creative Thinking** Encourage students to reflect on what they learned from the selection.

- James Naismith had many different careers. What do you think that was—a strength or a weakness? Explain.
- What would the world be like without basketball? *(Students may say that famous basketball players might have become famous in other sports.)* Describe how you believe sports would be different. *(Students may say that other sports that may be played indoors, such as volleyball and tennis, might be more popular than they are now.)*

Objectives

- Use context to determine the relevant meaning of unfamiliar words.

More Reading

Use additional Leveled Readers or other texts at students' instructional levels to reinforce this week's skills and strategies. For text suggestions, see the Leveled Reader Database or the Leveled Readers Skills Chart on pp. CL24–CL29.

A Advanced

DAY 4

Genre Focus

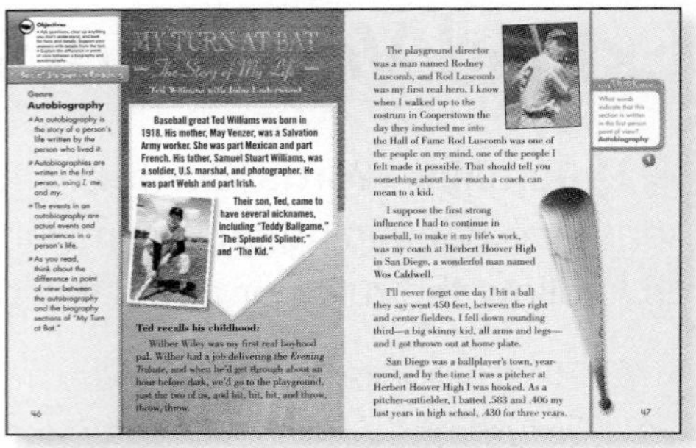

"My Turn at Bat: The Story of My Life"

- **Before Reading or Revisiting** "My Turn at Bat: The Story of My Life" on pp. 46–51, read aloud the panel information on autobiographies. Have students use the text features, including the time line and statistics, to set a purpose for reading. Then have students read "My Turn at Bat" on their own.
- **During Reading or Revisiting** Point out that an autobiography tells events from the author's point of view. How is the narrator of an autobiography different from the narrator of a biography? *(In an autobiography, the narrator and the subject are the same person.)* As they read, have students find examples of the author's point of view.
- **After Reading or Revisiting** Have students discuss Reading Across Texts. Then have them complete the Writing Across Texts activity independently.

Objectives

- Explain the difference in point of view between a biography and autobiography.

A Advanced

DAY 5

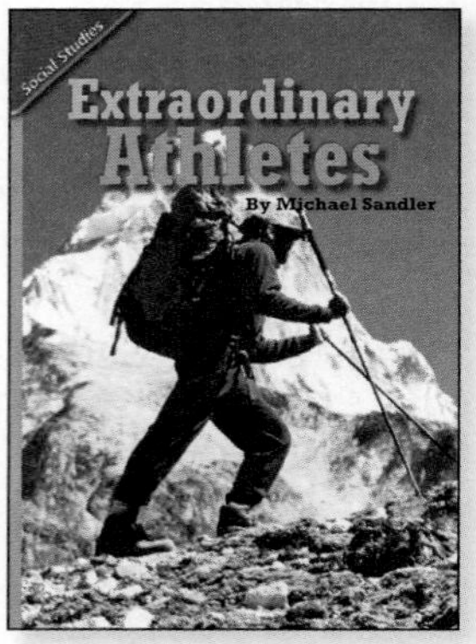

Extraordinary Athletes

- **Reread for Fluency** Have students silently reread passages from the Advanced Reader *Extraordinary Athletes.* Allow them to reread aloud with a partner or individually. As students read, monitor fluency and provide corrective feedback. If students read fluently on the first reading, they do not need to reread three to four times. Assess the fluency of students in this group using p. 53j.
- **Retell** Have students summarize the main idea and key details from the Advanced Reader *Extraordinary Athletes.*
- **Now Try This** Have groups deliver their presentations. Discuss what students learned about the Paralympics and which Paralympic sports interest them the most.

Objectives

- Read aloud grade-level appropriate text with fluency.

ELL English Language Learners

The ELL lessons are organized by strands. Use them to scaffold the weekly curriculum of lessons or during small group time instruction.

Academic Language

Students will hear or read the following academic language in this week's core instruction. As students encounter the vocabulary, provide a simple definition or concrete example. Then ask students to suggest an example or synonym of the word and identify available cognates.

Skill Words	generalize *(generalizar)* conjunction *(conjunción)* singular *(singular)*	unfamiliar words irregular plurals plural pronouns
Concept Words	talent *(talento)* unique *(único)*	team invert

**Spanish cognates in parentheses*

Concept Development

How do talents make someone unique?

■ **Preteach Concept**

- **Prior Knowledge** Have students turn to pp. 20–21 in the Student Edition. Call attention to the picture of the children playing instruments and tap into students' knowledge of special talents. What are the children doing? Do you think they are good at playing their instruments? Why do you think that girl is holding a bouquet of flowers? What do you think she was good at?
- **Discuss Concept** Have students tell about a talent that makes them or someone they know unique. Have students work in small groups to share information and express their opinions about this talent. Do you know someone who has a special talent? What is it? How does it make you or others feel special?
- **Poster Talk-Through** Read aloud the Poster Talk-Through on ELL Poster 16 and work through the Day 1 activities.

■ **Daily Concept and Vocabulary Development** Use the daily activities on ELL Poster 16 to build concept and vocabulary knowledge.

Objectives

- Use prior knowledge and experiences to understand meanings in English.

Content Objectives

- Use concept vocabulary related to how talents make someone unique.

Language Objectives

- Express ideas in response to art and discussion.
- Respond to questions and request.

Daily Planner

DAY 1	• **Frontload Concept** • **Preteach** Comprehension Skill, Vocabulary, Phonics/Spelling, Conventions • **Writing**
DAY 2	• **Review** Concept, Vocabulary, Comprehension Skill • **Frontload Main Selection** • **Practice** Phonics/Spelling, Conventions/Writing
DAY 3	• **Review** Concept, Comprehension Skill, Vocabulary, Conventions/Writing • **Reread Main Selection** • **Practice** Phonics/Spelling
DAY 4	• **Review Concept** • **Read ELL/ELD Readers** • **Practice** Phonics/Spelling, Conventions/Writing
DAY 5	• **Review** Concept, Vocabulary, Comprehension Skill, Phonics/Spelling, Conventions • **Reread ELL/ELD Readers** • **Writing**

**See the ELL Handbook for ELL Workshops with targeted instruction.*

ELL English Language Learners

Basic Vocabulary

- **High-Frequency Words** Use the ELL Vocabulary Routine on p. 471 of the *ELL Handbook* to systematically teach newcomers the first 300 sight words in English. Students who began learning ten words per week at the beginning of the year are now learning words 151–160 (*ELL Handbook,* p. 452). p. 446 of the handbook contains a bank of strategies that you can use to ensure students' mastery of high-frequency words.

Lesson Vocabulary

- **Preteach** Use the following routine to introduce the Lesson Vocabulary:

1. Distribute copies of this week's Word Cards (*ELL Handbook,* p. 119).
2. Display ELL Poster 16 and reread the Poster Talk-Through.
3. Using the poster's illustrations, model how a word's meaning can be expressed with other similar words: The girl is holding the orange, round ball that bounces, or a *basketball*.
4. Use these sentences to reveal the meaning of the other words.
   - I give medicine to my dog every day to cure his *disease*. (sickness)
   - Soccer is the most *popular* sport in Mexico. (well-liked, enjoyed)
   - We need to *freeze* the ice cream before it melts. (chill, ice up)
   - Baseball is one of my favorite *sports*. (games)
   - Dolores and I love to play *basketball* at the playground after school. (a game with a ball and a hoop)
   - You need to *study* very hard to become a doctor. (learn, read lessons)
   - The *guard* jumped to block the other player from getting his ball in the basket. (defender)
   - We had a *terrible* time at the parade after it started to rain! (awful, very bad)

Language Objectives

- Understand and use basic vocabulary.
- Learn meanings of grade-level vocabulary. Using visual ans contextual support.

ELL Workshop

Provide opportunities for students to give information using high-frequency, high-need, and concrete vocabulary. *Give a Speech* (*ELL Handbook,* pp. 412–413) supports students with speaking.

Mini-Lesson

Help students expand and internalize the high-frequency words. Read each word aloud. Then use each word to identify or describe people, places or object, such as You are a *child*. I am an adult. Then have students repeat the high-frequency word, using it in a sentence if possible.

Objectives

- Expand and internalize initial English vocabulary by learning and using high-frequency English words necessary for identifying and describing people, places, and objects, by retelling simple stories and basic information represented or supported by pictures, and by learning and using routine language needed for classroom communication.

ELL English Language Learners

- **Reteach** Distribute a copy of the Word Cards to each student. Have students write a clue on each card and explain how this can help them understand and remember the words.

  Ask questions to check understanding of word meaning and use.

  - What word is a synonym for *awful*? (terrible)
  - Which word means "a sickness"? (disease)
  - Which word means "to chill"? (freeze)
  - What sport are you playing if you try to throw a ball into a basket? (basketball)
  - What are football and soccer examples of? (sports)
  - What word means "well-liked"? (popular)
  - What word means the same as *defender*? (guard)
  - What should you do if you have a test coming up? (study)

- **Writing** Have partners create their own picture/word cards. Assign or have students pick a word. Ask them to write the word on one side of an index card and write or draw the definition on the other side of the card. Then have students quiz their partner by showing the illustrated definition and asking their partner to guess which word it represents.

Leveled Support

Beginning Have students illustrate and label their picture/word cards.

Intermediate Have students illustrate and write an example of the word on their picture/word cards.

Advanced Have students illustrate and write the word's meaning.

Advanced High Have students illustrate and write the word's meaning as well as provide a sample sentence using the word. Encourage them to check the meaning of each word in a dictionary or glossary.

Objectives

- Use strategic learning techniques to acquire basic vocabulary.

Content Objectives

- Show understanding of Lesson Vocabulary.

Language Objectives

- Produce drawings, phrases, and short sentences to show understanding of lesson vocabulary.

ELL Teacher Tip

For English learners who have developed emergent writing skills in their home language, build on these skills. Have them write in both languages. Short sentences and picture labels written in a home language and in English help children with writing and English acquisition.

ELL Workshop

Provide opportunities for students to give information using new abstract and content-based vocabulary. *Give a Speech* (*ELL Handbook,* pp. 412–413) supports students with their speaking.

ELL English Language Learners

Content Objectives

- Monitor and adjust oral comprehension.

Language Objectives

- Discuss oral passages.
- Use a graphic organizer to take notes.

Graphic Organizer

Beginning

↓

Middle

↓

End

ELL Teacher Tip

Use a familiar classroom book or story to reinforce the meaning of the words *beginning, middle,* and *end*.

ELL Workshop

Have students turn to p. El•24 in the Student Edition. Taking notes while listening to someone talk can help you to better understand what they are saying. Have students take notes while tell them what is happening in the three pictures. After reading, have students share their notes. Have them repeat this task after reading the oral passage for a third time.

Listening Comprehension

Read Aloud

Do Not Fly Too Close to the Sun

Long ago a man named Daedelus lived in Greece. He designed, invented, and built things. One day the king of Greece got angry at Daedelus. He sent Daedelus and his son, Icarus, to the island of Crete.

The only way to escape Crete was by sea. The sea was too rough to swim across and they would be arrested if they used a boat. Daedelus thought of a way to get off the island. He decided they would fly!

Daedelus made two sets of wings. He used wax to hold feathers to a frame. He added leather straps that would hold the wings to their arms. Daedelus attached two wings to Icarus. Then he told Icarus, "Don't fly too low or your wings will get wet from the sea. That will make them too heavy." Then Daedelus told Icarus not to fly too high either. "The heat of the sun will melt the wings."

Daedelus and Icarus jumped off a cliff. They flew over the sea. Icarus was so excited about flying. He did not listen to his father. He began to fly higher and higher. The heat of the sun melted the wax on his wings. The wings fell apart. Icarus fell into the sea and drowned.

Daedelus reached land alone. Then he saw the wings of Icarus on the beach. He cried for his son. The sea where Icarus drowned was named the Icarian Sea. It is still called that today.

Prepare for the Read Aloud The modified Read Aloud above prepares students for listening to the oral reading "The Myth of Icarus" on p. 21b.

- **First Listening: Listen to Understand** Write the title of the Read Aloud on the board. This is a story about a man who invents something. What does he invent? Afterward, ask the question again and have students share their answers.
- **Second Listening: Listen to Check Understanding** Using Story Map A (*ELL Handbook,* p. 483), work with students to retell the beginning, middle, and end of the story. Now listen again and take notes on what happens in the beginning, middle, and end of the story.

Objectives

- Use strategic learning techniques such as concept mapping, drawing, memorizing, comparing, contrasting, and reviewing to acquire basic and grade-level vocabulary.

ELL English Language Learners

Phonics and Spelling

- **Irregular Plurals** Use Sound-Spelling Cards 140 and 141 to teach the sounds, pronunciations, and spellings of irregular plurals.

  Display card 141. This word is *dogs*. Say it with me: dogs. For many words in English, you add *s* to the end to make it plural. *Dog* becomes *dogs*. Write the word on the board and circle the *s*.

  Some plurals in English are irregular and follow special spelling rules. Display card 141. This word is *wolves*. Say it with me: wolves. If a noun ends with *f*, you change the *f* to *v* and add *-es* to make it plural. *Wolf* becomes *wolves*. Write the word on the board and circle the *-ves*.

  For more practice pronouncing these sounds, use the Modeled Pronunciation Audio CD Routine (*ELL Handbook,* p. 478).

Vocabulary Skill: Unfamiliar Words

- **Preteach and Model** Write the following sentence: *Ice cream is a popular dessert.* Have students guess the meaning of the word *popular.* You can tell from the other words in the sentence that *popular* means "well-liked." The other words are context clues. Explain that using context clues to guess the meaning of new words is one way to learn the meanings of unfamiliar words.
- **Practice** Have students read the first two sentences of the third paragraph of p. 36 of the Student Edition. What does the word *invent* mean in the first sentence? Explain that the words *no time* and *new* may help them determine the word's meaning.

Leveled Support

Beginning/Intermediate Have partners create picture/word cards that show the word on one side with a picture on the other that gives a clue to the meaning of the unfamiliar words.

Advanced/Advanced High Have students create word cards with the unfamiliar word on one side and a sentence that gives clues to the word's meaning on the other. Partners can trade cards and use the context clues in the sentences to guess the meaning of the unfamiliar words.

Objectives

- Learn relationships between sounds and letters of the English language and decode (sound out) words using a combination of skills such as recognizing sound-letter relationships and identifying cognates, affixes, roots and base words.
- Spell familiar English words with increasing accuracy, and employ English spelling patterns and rules with increasing accuracy as more English is acquired.

Content Objectives

- Identify words with irregular plurals.
- Identify unfamiliar words using contextual support.

Language Objectives

- Apply spelling rules to irregular plurals.
- Discuss how to create irregular plurals.

Transfer Skills

Irregular Plurals English learners may add *s* to irregular nouns in sentences or to nouns for which English uses the singular for a quantity: *sheeps, mens, clothings.* Remind ELL students that irregular English nouns do not require *s* at the end.

ELL Teaching Routine

For more practice with plurals, use the Nondecodable Word Strategy Routine (*ELL Handbook,* p. 472).

Content Objectives

- Use summary statements to generalize about a story.
- Recognize generalizations in a reading

Language Objectives

- Use deductive reasoning to make generalizations.
- Write a summary that is a generalization.
- Understand main points of spoken language.

ELL Workshop

Monitor students understanding of instruction of comprehension skills by having students ask questions of each other's responses. Use *Ask Clarifying Questions* (*ELL Handbook,* pp. 404–405) for practice.

ELL English Language Learners

Comprehension
Generalize

- **Preteach** When you generalize, you say something that might be true in a lot of cases. *Cats like to drink milk* is a generalization. Have students turn to *Envision It!* on p. EI•8 in the Student Edition. Read aloud the text together. Have students explain how the statement on the page is a generalization. Ask volunteers for other examples of a generalization.
- **Reteach** Distribute copies of Picture It! (*ELL Handbook,* p. 120). Explain that good readers know how to generalize, or focus on the big picture. Once a reader understands the big picture, they can go back and reread for details. Model by reading the passage aloud, and then demonstrate a fix-up strategy: *There are many facts here about dragons, but I'm not sure what the overall idea of this passage is. I think I'll reread it and look for one or two sentences that tell what the passage is about.* Then, write the last sentence on the board. (1. They are nice, they breathe fire. 2. The dragons no longer destroy the homes in Dragonland.)

Leveled Support

Beginning Ask students to draw a picture that generalizes what this passage is about. Help them write a one sentence summary.

Intermediate Ask students to write a summary of the passage in two or three sentences.

Advanced/Advanced High Ask students to partner up. Have each write two summaries: a good one, and then an example of a poor summary. Have them switch papers, and determine which summary is the better one.

MINI-LESSON

Social Language

Tell students that people often make generalizations in daily life, such as *It is hot in August* or *Many people like ice cream.* Have students make generalizations about the following familiar topics: *animals, food, music.* Then have students offer the details of their generalizations.

Objectives

- Understand the general meaning, main points, and important details of spoken language ranging from situations in which topics, language, and contexts are familiar to unfamiliar.

ELL English Language Learners

Reading Comprehension *The Man Who Invented Basketball*

Student Edition pp. 28–41

- **Frontloading** Read aloud the title and discuss what it means to invent something. I wonder how basketball was invented. Let's look through the selection to find clues. Guide students on a picture walk through *The Man Who Invented Basketball.* Ask students to predict how James Naismith invented basketball and record their predictions. During the reading, pause and invite students to adjust their predictions. Provide students with a two-column chart to fill out as they read the selection. Supply these headings: *What I think happened; What really happened.*

Sheltered Reading Ask questions such as the following to guide students' comprehension:

- **p. 31:** Where was James born and in what year? (near Almonte, Ontario, Canada, in 1861)
- **p. 32:** What was "duck on a rock"? (a game that James and his friends played with rocks when he was a boy)
- **p. 35:** Why was James told to invent an indoor sports game at his first teaching job in Springfield? (The men were bored during the winter.)
- **p. 36:** How did James come up with the idea for basketball? (He remembered how "duck on a rock" was played.)

- **Fluency: Read with Accuracy** Remind students that reading accurately means saying the words correctly. Read the first paragraph on p. 30. Model accurate reading. Have pairs of students choose a paragraph on p. 32. Have students read the passage to their partners. Have partners follow along with the text and give feedback for improvement. For more practice, use the Fluency: Paired Reading Routine (*ELL Handbook,* p. 474).

After Reading Have students summarize the text using the Envision It! strip on p. 42 of their Student Edition. Ask questions that prompt students to summarize the important part of the story.

Objectives

- Use visual and contextual support and support from peers and teachers to read grade-appropriate content area text, enhance and confirm understanding, and develop vocabulary, grasp of language structures, and background knowledge needed to comprehend increasingly challenging language.

Content Objectives

- Monitor and adjust comprehension.
- Make and adjust predictions.

Language Objectives

- Read grade-level text with accuracy.
- Summarize text using visual support.

Graphic Organizer

What I think happened	What really happened

Audio Support

Students can prepare for reading *The Man Who Invented Basketball* by using the eSelection or the AudioText CD. See the AudioText CD Routine (*ELL Handbook,* p. 477).

ELL Workshops

Students can use the selection art to retell stories or information in selections. Support students with Retell or Summarize (*ELL Handbook,* pp. 408–409).

Students may need assistance with comprehending English language structures used in the selections. Take Notes/Create an Outline (*ELL Handbook,* pp. 410–411) supports students.

ELL Reader ELD Reader

ELL English Language Learners

For additional leveled instruction, see the **ELL/ELD Reader Teaching Guide.**

Comprehension
My Good Friend

- **Before Reading** Distribute copies of the ELL and ELD Readers, *My Good Friend,* to students at their reading level.
  - **Preview** Read the title aloud with students. This is a story about a girl who meets a new student in her class and becomes her good friend. Have them predict what made the new girl a good friend.
  - **Set a Purpose for Reading** Let's read to figure out how the new girl became a good friend.
- **During Reading** Follow the Reading Routine for both reading groups.
  1. Read the entire Reader aloud slowly.
  2. Reread pp. 1–4, pausing to build background knowledge or model comprehension. Have students put their fingers on the starting point in the text as you read. Use the questions in the chart to check students' comprehension.
  3. Have students reread pp. 1–4 in pairs, taking turns reading alternate pages.
  4. Repeat steps 2–3 above for pp. 5–8 of the Reader.
- **After Reading** Use the exercises on the inside back cover of each Reader and invite students to share their writing. In a whole-group discussion, ask students, How did Sasha and Luz become good friends? Record their answers on the board and invite them to point to pictures in the book to support their answers.

ELD Reader Beginning/Intermediate

- **p. 2:** What is the name of the girl telling the story? (Sasha)
- **p. 6:** Why was Luz sad? (She missed her old school.)
- **p. 8:** What did Sasha and Luz do during recess? (They talked and shared secrets.)

Writing How do you know Luz is a good friend? Find the sentence in the book that tells this. Copy the sentence. Then read it aloud to your partner.

ELL Reader Advanced/Advanced High

- **p. 2:** What does Sasha's teacher say is different about Luz? (She doesn't see things the same way as the other students.)
- **p. 4:** How did the special computer help Luz? (It had a special light and it made things look bigger.)
- **p. 7:** How did Luz help the other kids? (She helped them understand math.)

Study Guide Distribute copies of the ELL Reader Study Guide (*ELL Handbook,* p. 124). Have students look back through the Reader to find details about Luz. Then have them compare her to their best friends. Discuss students' responses with them. (See *ELL Handbook,* pp. 209–212.)

Objectives

- Express opinions, ideas, and feelings ranging from communicating single words and short phrases to participating in extended discussions on a variety of social and grade-appropriate academic topics.

ELL English Language Learners

Conventions
Singular and Plural Pronouns

- **Preteach** Write the following sentences:
  - *Sasha went to English class. Sasha had a test.*
  - *Sasha and Luz met at school. Sasha and Luz are best friends now.*
  - Nouns can be replaced with shorter words called pronouns. Circle *Sasha* in the second sentence. *Sasha* can be replaced with *she.* Circle *Sasha* and *Luz* in the last two sentences. *Sasha* and *Luz* can be replaced with *they.*
- **Practice** Write the following sentences on sentence strips:
  - *Juan went to the store. Juan saw his friend Gary at the store.*
  - *Juan and Gary went back to Juan's house.*
  - Have students replace repetitive subjects with subject pronouns.

Leveled Support

Beginning/Intermediate Help students point to the subject of each sentence. Help students to first identify the pronouns *he* and *they* and then to write them on sentence strips appropriately.

Advanced/Advanced High Have students arrange the sentence strips in order and replace repetitive subjects with subject pronouns. Then have them add two more sentences that contain subject pronouns.

- **Reteach** Ask students which words could be replaced with pronouns in the following sentences:
  - *Mom told Jeff to do his homework. Mom gave Jeff a cookie after that.*
  - *Then Mom saw Jack and Mary. Mom told Jack and Mary to do their homework.*
  - Guide students in replacing *Mom* in the second and fourth sentences with *she.* Tell students that in sentence #2, *Jeff* can be replaced with *him.*
- **Practice** Write the following pronouns: *he, she, him, her, they, them.*

Leveled Support

Beginning/ Intermediate Have pairs pick one pronoun and have each student use it in a sentence. identify it as singular or plural.

Advanced/Advanced High Have pairs pick a singular and a plural pronoun and have them use each pronoun in a sentence. Have students to share their sentences.

Objectives
- Edit writing for standard grammar and usage, including subject-verb agreement, pronoun agreement, and appropriate verb tenses commensurate with grade-level expectations as more English is acquired.

Content Objectives
- Decode and use singular and plural pronouns.
- Correctly write sentences with singular and plural pronouns.

Language Objectives
- Speak using singular and plural pronouns.
- Write sentences with singular and plural pronouns.

Transfer Skills
Pronouns In Spanish, the subject pronoun sometimes is omitted because the verb ending indicates it. If students say is *coming* instead of *She is coming,* provide extra practice using subject pronouns in sentences.

Grammar Jammer
For more practice with pronouns, use the Grammar Jammer for this target skill. See the Grammar Jammer Routine (*ELL Handbook,* p. 478) for suggestions on using this learning tool.

Content Objectives

- Identify conjunctions in a text.

Language Objectives

- Write sentences using conjunctions.
- Share feedback for editing and revising.

ELL Teaching Routine

For practice spelling words related to sports and games use the Spelling Routine (*ELL Handbook,* p. 476).

ELL Workshop

Students can collaborate with peers to discuss their writing. Discuss with Classmates (*ELL Handbook,* pp. 418–419) provides assistance with discussion.

ELL English Language Learners

Conjunctions

- **Introduce** Display the model and read it aloud. Remind students that writers use a variety of sentences to make their writing more interesting. Explain that conjunctions, or joining words, combine two clauses, or parts of a sentence, to form a complete sentence. Writers can use conjunctions such as *because, since, yet,* or *until* to combine two related thoughts. Circle the conjunctions in the model. Underline the two thoughts that were combined in each sentence.

Writing Model

No one had ever played basketball until James Naismith invented it. Later, dribbling became popular because players were not allowed to hold the ball very long without throwing it.

- **Practice** Write these incomplete sentences on the board. Work together to finish the sentences with the correct conjunction: *because, since, yet, until.*

I never liked baseball _______ I saw a professional baseball game.

Rudy likes to trade cards _______ he has so many of them.

Jessie has two cats,_______ she would like another one.

Kevin cannot play soccer _______ he is only three years old.

- **Write** Have students write paragraphs about their favorite sport or playground game.

Leveled Support

Beginning Have students write the name of the sport or game at the top of their paper and draw a picture of it. Then have students dictate sentences to you about the game or sport. Encourage students to use conjunctions. Write out their sentences and have students copy them.

Intermediate Have students work together in pairs to write a paragraph about their favorite sport or game, using conjunctions.

Advanced/Advanced High Have students write their paragraph independently. Then have pairs exchange papers and provide feedback for revising and editing. Have partners check for conjunctions in the paragraphs.

Objectives

- Write using a variety of grade-appropriate sentence lengths, patterns, and connecting words to combine phrases, clauses, and sentences in increasingly accurate ways as more English is acquired.

This Week's ELL Overview

Grade 3 • Unit 4 • Week 2
Hottest, Coldest, Highest, Deepest
54a–85r
and DI•41–DI•50

ELL Handbook

- Maximize Literacy and Cognitive Engagement
- Research Into Practice
- Full Weekly Support for Every Selection

Hottest, Coldest, Highest, Deepest
- Multi-Lingual Summaries in Five Languages
- Selection-Specific Vocabulary Word Cards
- Frontloading/Reteaching for Comprehension Skill Lessons
- ELD and ELL Reader Study Guides

- Transfer Activities
- Professional Development

Daily Leveled ELL Notes

ELL notes appear throughout this week's instruction and ELL Support is on the DI pages of your Teacher's Edition. The following is a sample of an ELL note from this week.

English Language Learners

Beginning Choose several words with the *r*-controlled vowel sound /er/, such as *bird, her,* and *pearls,* from the Decodable Practice Reader, and write them on the board. Point to each word as you say it aloud. Then underline the letters that spell the sound /er/ in each word. Have students repeat the words with you. Do the same for words with /är/ and /ôr/.

Intermediate Remind students that the letter *r* and the vowel it controls must be in the same syllable. Write several multisyllable words with the *r*-controlled vowel sound from the Decodable Practice Reader, such as *morning, soaring,* and *certain.* Have students divide each word into syllables and then blend them to read the entire word.

Advanced Have partners take turns scanning pages of the story for words that have *r*-controlled vowels, reading the words aloud as they find them.

Advanced High After reading the story, have students choose four or five words with the *r*-controlled vowel sound and write a sentence for each word.

ELL by Strand

The ELL lessons on this week's Support for English Language Learners pages are organized by strand. They offer additional scaffolding for the core curriculum. Leveled support notes on these pages address the different proficiency levels in your class. See pages DI•41–DI•50.

ELL Guy
Dr. Jim Cummins

The Three Pillars of ELL Instruction

ELL Strands	Activate Prior Knowledge	Access Content	Extend Language
Vocabulary pp. DI•42–DI•43	Preteach	Reteach	Leveled Writing Activities
Reading Comprehension p. DI•47	Frontloading	Sheltered Reading	After Reading
Phonics, Spelling, and Word Analysis p. DI•45	Preteach/Model	Practice	Leveled Practice Activities
Listening Comprehension p. DI•44	Prepare for the Read Aloud	First Listening	Second Listening
Conventions and Writing pp. DI•49–DI•50	Preteach/Introduce	Practice	Leveled Practice Activities/ Leveled Writing Activities
Concept Development p. DI•41	Prior Knowledge	Discuss Concept	Daily Concept and Vocabulary Development

Grade 3 • Unit 4 • Week 2
Hottest, Coldest, Highest, Deepest
54a–85r

This Week's Practice Stations Overview

Six Weekly Practice Stations with Leveled Activities can be found at the beginning of each week of instruction. For this week's Practice Stations, see pp. 54h–54i.

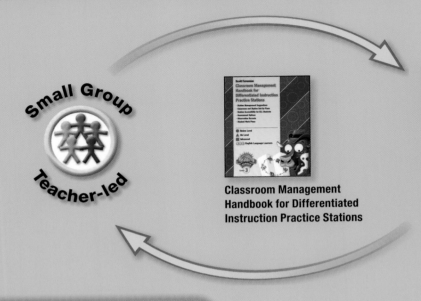

Classroom Management Handbook for Differentiated Instruction Practice Stations

Practice Stations

Daily Leveled Center Activities

- Below
- On-Level
- Advanced
- ELL

Practice Stations Flip Charts

Word Wise	**Word Work**	**Words to Know**	**Let's Write**	**Read For Meaning**	**Get Fluent**

	Word Wise	Word Work	Words to Know	Let's Write	Read For Meaning	Get Fluent
Objectives	• Spell irregular plurals.	• Identify and pronounce irregular plurals.	• Identify and define unfamiliar words.	• Write persuasive text.	• Make generalizations based on information presented in the text.	• Read aloud with accuracy.
Materials	• *Word Wise* Flip Chart Activity 17 • Teacher-made word cards • paper • pencil	• *Word Work* Flip Chart Activity 17 • Teacher-made word cards • paper • pencil	• *Words to Know* Flip Chart Activity 17 • Teacher-made word cards • magazines • pencil • paper	• *Let's Write* Flip Chart Activity 17 • paper • pencils	• *Read for Meaning* Flip Chart Activity 17 • Leveled Readers • paper • pencils	• *Get Fluent* Flip Chart Activity 17 • Leveled Readers

This Week on Reading Street!

Question of the Week
What makes nature's record holders unique?

Daily Plan

Don't Wait Until Friday

Whole Group
- Graphic Sources
- Unknown Words
- Fluency/Phrasing
- Writing/Conventions
- Research and Inquiry

MONITOR PROGRESS Success Predictor

Day 1	Day 2	Day 3	Day 4	Day 5
Check Oral Vocabulary	Check Word Reading	Check Retelling	Check Fluency	Check Oral Vocabulary

Small Group

Teacher Led
- Reading Support
- Skill Support
- Fluency Practice

Practice Stations

Independent Activities

Customize Literacy More support for a balanced literacy appoach, see pp. CL•1–CL•47.

Customize Writing More support for a customized writing approach, see pp. CW•1–CW•10.

Whole Group
- Writing: Imaginative Story
- Conventions: Subject and Object Pronouns
- Spelling: Vowels: *r*-Controlled

Assessment
- Weekly Tests
- Day 5 Assessment
- Fresh Reads

This Week's Reading Selections

Main Selection
Genre: **Expository Nonfiction**

Paired Selection
Genre: **Legend**

Decodable Readers

Leveled Readers

ELL and ELD Readers

Resources on Reading Street!

	Build Concepts	Phonics	Comprehension
Whole Group	 Let's Talk About pp. 54–55	 Phonics Skill Lesson pp. 56–57  Decodable Readers  Sound–Spelling Cards	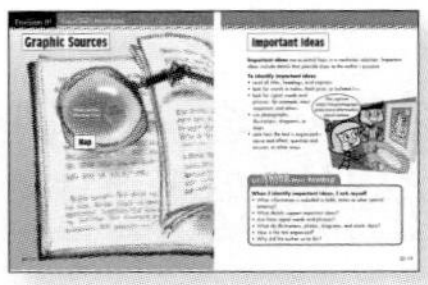 Envision It! Skills/ Strategies 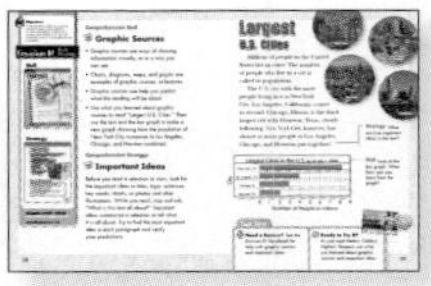 Comprehension Skill Lesson pp. 58–59
Go Digital	• Concept Talk Video	• Interactive Sound-Spelling Cards • Decodable eReaders	• Envision It! Animations • eSelections
Small Group and Independent Practice	 Hottest, Coldest, Highest, Deepest pp. 62–75  ELL and ELD Readers  Leveled Readers  Decodable Readers	 Decodable Readers  Practice Station Flip Chart	 Hottest, Coldest, Highest, Deepest pp. 62–75  ELL and ELD Readers  Leveled Readers 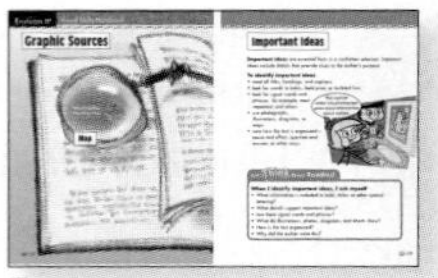 Envision It! Skills/Strategies  Reader's and Writer's Notebook  Practice Station Flip Chart
Go Digital	• eReaders • eSelections • Decodable eReaders	• Letter Tile Drag and Drop • Decodable eReaders	• Envision It! Animations • eSelections • eReaders
Customize Literacy	• Leveled Readers • Decodable Readers	• Decodable Readers	• Envision It! Skills and Strategies Handbook • Leveled Readers
Go Digital	• Concept Talk Video • Decodable eReaders • eReaders	• Decodable eReaders	• Envision It! Animations • eReaders • Decodable eReaders

Question of the Week

What makes nature's record holders unique?

Vocabulary	Fluency	Conventions and Writing
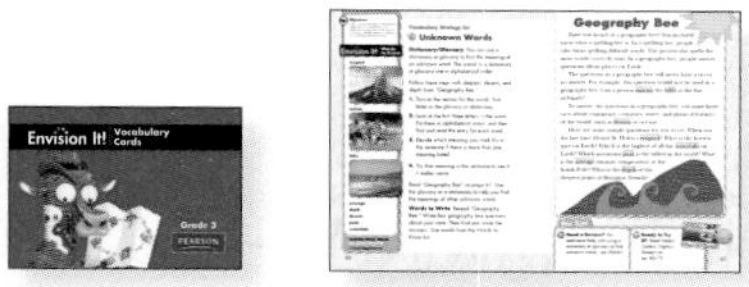 Envision It! Vocabulary Cards; Vocabulary Skill Lesson pp. 60–61	 Let's Learn It! pp. 84–85; Decodable and Leveled Readers	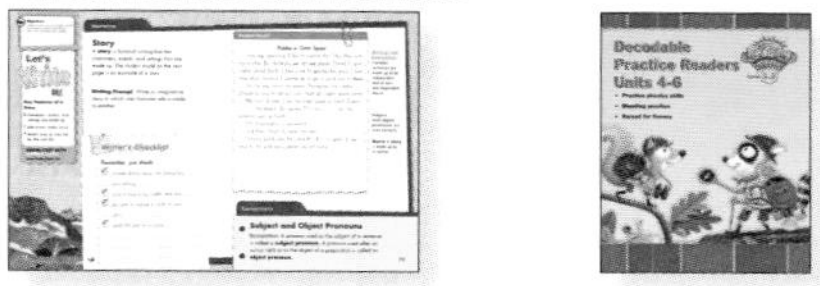 Let's Write It! pp. 78–79; Decodable Readers
• Envision It! Vocabulary Cards • Vocabulary Activities	• eSelection • Decodable eReaders • eReaders	• Grammar Jammer
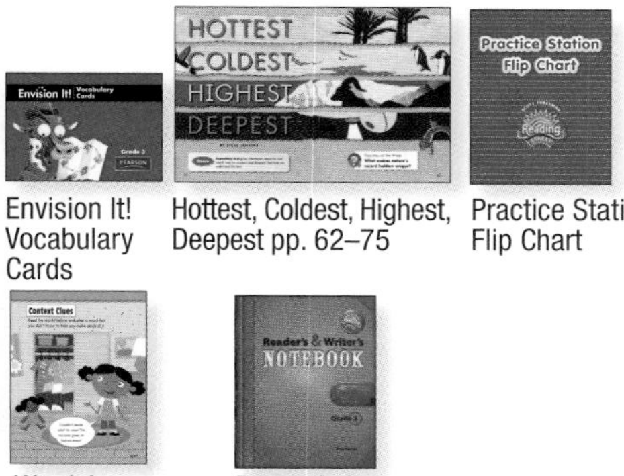 Envision It! Vocabulary Cards; Hottest, Coldest, Highest, Deepest pp. 62–75; Practice Station Flip Chart; Words!; Reader's and Writer's Notebook	 Hottest, Coldest, Highest, Deepest pp. 62–75; Practice Station Flip Chart; Leveled Readers; ELL and ELD Readers	 Reader's and Writer's Notebook; Hottest, Coldest, Highest, Deepest pp. 62–75; Practice Station Flip Chart
• Envision It! Vocabulary Cards • Vocabulary Activities • eSelection	• eSelection • eReaders	• Grammar Jammer
• Envision It! Vocabulary Cards	• Leveled Readers • Decodable Readers	• Reader's and Writer's Notebook
• Vocabulary Activities	• eReaders • Decodable eReaders	• Grammar Jammer

Week 2

My 5-Day Planner for Reading Street!

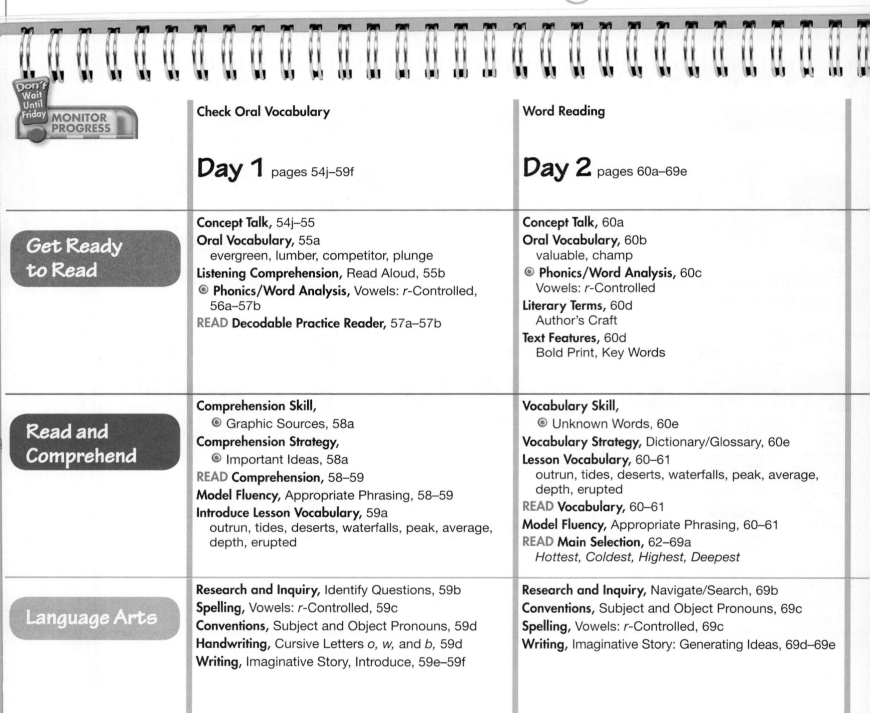

Don't Wait Until Friday MONITOR PROGRESS	Check Oral Vocabulary **Day 1** pages 54j–59f	Word Reading **Day 2** pages 60a–69e
Get Ready to Read	**Concept Talk,** 54j–55 **Oral Vocabulary,** 55a evergreen, lumber, competitor, plunge **Listening Comprehension,** Read Aloud, 55b ◎ **Phonics/Word Analysis,** Vowels: *r*-Controlled, 56a–57b READ **Decodable Practice Reader,** 57a–57b	**Concept Talk,** 60a **Oral Vocabulary,** 60b valuable, champ ◎ **Phonics/Word Analysis,** 60c Vowels: *r*-Controlled **Literary Terms,** 60d Author's Craft **Text Features,** 60d Bold Print, Key Words
Read and Comprehend	**Comprehension Skill,** ◎ Graphic Sources, 58a **Comprehension Strategy,** ◎ Important Ideas, 58a READ **Comprehension,** 58–59 **Model Fluency,** Appropriate Phrasing, 58–59 **Introduce Lesson Vocabulary,** 59a outrun, tides, deserts, waterfalls, peak, average, depth, erupted	**Vocabulary Skill,** ◎ Unknown Words, 60e **Vocabulary Strategy,** Dictionary/Glossary, 60e **Lesson Vocabulary,** 60–61 outrun, tides, deserts, waterfalls, peak, average, depth, erupted READ **Vocabulary,** 60–61 **Model Fluency,** Appropriate Phrasing, 60–61 READ **Main Selection,** 62–69a *Hottest, Coldest, Highest, Deepest*
Language Arts	**Research and Inquiry,** Identify Questions, 59b **Spelling,** Vowels: *r*-Controlled, 59c **Conventions,** Subject and Object Pronouns, 59d **Handwriting,** Cursive Letters *o, w,* and *b,* 59d **Writing,** Imaginative Story, Introduce, 59e–59f	**Research and Inquiry,** Navigate/Search, 69b **Conventions,** Subject and Object Pronouns, 69c **Spelling,** Vowels: *r*-Controlled, 69c **Writing,** Imaginative Story: Generating Ideas, 69d–69e

Question of the Week

What makes nature's record holders unique?

Check Retelling **Day 3** pages 70a–79c	Check Fluency **Day 4** pages 80a–85e	Check Oral Vocabulary **Day 5** pages 85f–85q
Concept Talk, 70a **Oral Vocabulary,** 70b sprinter, acrobat ◎ **Phonics/Word Analysis,** Vowels: *r*-Controlled, 70c–70d **Decodable Story,** 70d **Comprehension Check,** 70e **Check Retelling,** 70f	**Concept Talk,** 80a **Oral Vocabulary,** 80b weaken, ranger Review **Phonics/Word Analysis,** Irregular Plurals, 80c–80f **Decodable Story,** 80f **Genre,** Legend, 80g	**Concept Wrap Up,** 85f **Check Oral Vocabulary,** 85g evergreen, lumber, competitor, plunge, valuable, champ, sprinter, acrobat, weaken, ranger **Amazing Ideas,** 85g Review ◎ **Graphic Sources,** 85h Review ◎ **Unknown Words,** 85h Review ◎ **Vowels: *r*-Controlled,** 85i Review **Literary Terms,** 85i
READ **Main Selection,** *Hottest, Coldest, Highest, Deepest*, 70–75a **Retelling,** 76–77 **Think Critically,** 77a **Model Fluency,** Appropriate Phrasing and Punctuation Cues, 77b **Research and Study Skills,** Bar Graphs, 77c	READ **Paired Selection,** 80–83a "Paul Bunyan and the Great Lakes" **Let's Learn It!,** 84–85a Fluency: Appropriate Phrasing and Punctuation Cues Vocabulary: ◎ Unknown Words Media Literacy: Weather Forecast	**Fluency Assessment,** WCPM, 85j–85k **Comprehension Assessment,** ◎ Graphic Sources, 85l–85m
Research and Inquiry, Analyze, 77d **Conventions,** Subject and Object Pronouns, 77e **Spelling,** Vowels: *r*-Controlled, 77e **Let's Write It!,** Imaginative Story, 78–79 **Writing,** Imaginative Story: Dialogue, 79a–79c	**Research and Inquiry,** Synthesize, 85b **Conventions,** Subject and Object Pronouns, 85c **Spelling,** Vowels: *r*-Controlled, 85c **Writing,** Imaginative Story, Revising, 85d–85e	**Research and Inquiry,** Communicate, 85n **Conventions,** Subject and Object Pronouns, 85o **Spelling Test,** Vowels: *r*-Controlled, 85o **Writing,** Imaginative Story: Subject and Object Pronouns, 85p–85q **Quick Write for Fluency,** 85q

Week 2

Grouping Options for Differentiated Instruction
Turn the page for the small group time lesson plan.

Planning Small Group Time on Reading Street!

SMALL GROUP TIME RESOURCES

Look for this Small Group Time box each day to help meet the individual needs of all your children. Differentiated Instruction lessons appear on the DI pages at the end of each week.

DAY 1

Teacher Led

SI Strategic Intervention	OL On-Level	A Advanced
Teacher Led • Reinforce the Concept • Read Concept Literacy Reader or Below-Level Reader	**Teacher Led** • Explain the Concept Read On-Level Reader	**Teacher Led** • Explain the Concept • Read Advanced Reader

ELL Place English language learners in the groups that correspond to their reading abilities in English.

Practice Stations	Independent Activities
• Read for Meaning • Get Fluent • Word Work	• Concept Talk Video • *Reader's and Writer's Notebook* • Research and Inquiry

ELL

ELL Reader
Advanced
Advanced High

ELD Reader
Beginning
Intermediate

ELL Poster

	Day 1
SI Strategic Intervention	**Reinforce the Concept,** DI•26–DI•27 Read **Decodable Reader,** and **Concept Literacy Reader** or **Below-Level Reader**
OL On-Level	**Expand the Concept,** DI•32 Read **On-Level Reader**
A Advanced	**Extend the Concept,** DI•37 Read **Advanced Reader**
ELL English Language Learners	DI•41–DI•50 **Frontload Concept** **Preteach Writing** **Writing**

Reading Street Response to Intervention Kit

Reading Street Practice Stations Kit

Question of the Week

What makes nature's record holders unique?

SI Strategic Intervention

Below-Level Reader

Concept Literacy Reader

OL On-Level

On-Level Reader

A Advanced

Advanced Reader

Decodable Readers

Hottest, Coldest, Highest, Deepest, pp. 62–75

Paul Bunyan and the Great Lakes pp. 80–83

Small Group Weekly Plan

Day 2	Day 3	Day 4	Day 5
Reinforce Comprehension, DI•28 Revisit **Main Selection**	**Reinforce Vocabulary,** DI•29 Read/Revisit **Main Selection**	**Reinforce Comprehension,** Practice Retelling, DI•30 Genre Focus Read/Revisit **Paired Selection**	**Practice Fluency,** DI•31 Reread **Concept Literacy Reader** or **Below-Level Reader**
Expand Comprehension, DI•33 Revisit **Main Selection**	**Expand Vocabulary,** DI•34 Read/Revisit **Main Selection**	**Expand Comprehension,** Practice Retelling, DI•35 Genre Focus Read/Revisit **Paired Selection**	**Practice Fluency,** DI•36 Reread **On-Level Reader**
Extend Comprehension, DI•38 Revisit **Main Selection**	**Extend Vocabulary,** DI•39 Read/Revisit **Main Selection**	**Extend Comprehension,** Genre Focus, DI•40 Read/Revisit **Paired Selection**	**Practice Fluency,** DI•40 Reread **Advanced Reader**
DI•41–DI•50 **Review Concept/Skills** **Frontload Main Selection** **Practice**	DI•41–DI•50 **Review Concept/Skills** Reread **Main Selection** **Practice**	DI•41–DI•50 **Review Concept** Read **ELL/ELD Readers** **Practice**	DI•41–DI•50 **Review Concept/Skills** Reread **ELL/ELD Reader** **Writing**

Week 2

Practice Stations for Everyone on Reading Street!

Word Wise
Irregular plurals

Objectives
- Spell irregular plurals.

Materials
- *Word Wise* Flip Chart Activity 17
- Teacher-made word cards
- paper • pencil

Differentiated Activities

● Choose four word cards. Write the words. Write a sentence for each word. Next, write the singular form of each word. Add other irregular plurals you know to your list.

▲ Choose six word cards, and write the words. Write a sentence for each word. Write each word's singular form. Add other irregular plurals you know to your list.

■ Choose eight word cards. Write the words, and then write sentences for them. Write each word's singular form. Add other irregular plurals you know to your list.

Technology
- Online Dictionary

Word Work
Irregular plurals

Objectives
- Identify and pronounce irregular plurals.

Materials
- *Word Work* Flip Chart Activity 17
- Teacher-made word cards
- paper • pencil

Differentiated Activities

● Choose five word cards, and write the words. Say each word. Write sentences using each word. Read your sentences.

▲ Choose seven word cards, and write the words. Say each word. Write sentences using each word, and read each sentence.

■ Choose ten word cards, and write the words. Read each word. Write a short, fictional paragraph, and use as many of the words as you can.

Technology
- Modeled Pronunciation Audio CD

Words to Know
Unfamiliar words

Objectives
- Identify and define unfamiliar words.

Materials
- *Words to Know* Flip Chart Activity 17
- Teacher-made word cards
- magazines
- pencil • paper

Differentiated Activities

● Use a magazine to find three words that are unfamiliar to you. Write each word. Use a dictionary to find each word's meaning. Write a sentence for each word.

▲ Use a magazine to find four words that are unfamiliar to you. Write the words. Use a dictionary to find each word's meaning. Write sentences using the words.

■ Look through the magazines, and list five unfamiliar words. Use context to try to determine each word's meaning. Check definitions in a dictionary. Write sentences using each word.

Technology
- Online Dictionary

Use this week's materials from the Reading Street Leveled Practice Stations Kit to organize this week's stations.

Key

- ● Below-Level Activities
- ▲ On-Level Activities
- ■ Advanced Activities

Practice Station Flip Chart

Let's Write!
Persuasive text

Objectives
- Write persuasive text.

Materials
- *Let's Write!* Flip Chart Activity 17
- paper • pencils

Differentiated Activities

● Write a short paragraph that persuades other students to read your favorite book. Tell about what makes this book so great and why you think other students would enjoy reading it.

▲ Write a short paragraph persuading other students to read your favorite book. Explain what makes this book your favorite, and give reasons why you think other students would enjoy reading it.

■ Write two short paragraphs persuading other students to read your favorite book. State what made the book such an enjoyable read, and give reasons why you think they would enjoy reading it.

Technology
- Online Graphic Organizers

Read for Meaning
Generalize

Objectives
- Make generalizations based on information presented in the text.

Materials
- *Read for Meaning* Flip Chart Activity 17
- Leveled Readers
- paper • pencils

Differentiated Activities

● Choose a book from those your teacher provided. Think about the facts in the book. Write one sentence that tells a generalization you made. Write one sentence that gives a detail that supports your generalization.

▲ Read one of the books your teacher provided, and think about the facts the author presents. Write a short paragraph that states a generalization you made. Provide facts from the selection to support your generalization.

■ Choose and read a leveled reader. Write a paragraph stating a generalization you've made based on the facts presented in the book you read. Include sentences providing details or facts from the article to help support your generalization.

Technology
- Leveled Reader Database

Get Fluent
Practice fluent reading

Objectives
- Read aloud with accuracy.

Materials
- *Get Fluent* Flip Chart Activity 17
- Leveled Readers

Differentiated Activities

● Work with a partner. Choose a Concept Literacy Reader or Below-Level Reader. Take turns reading a page from the book. Use the readers to practice reading with accuracy. Provide feedback as needed.

▲ Work with a partner. Choose an On-Level Reader. Take turns reading a page from the book. Use the reader to practice reading with accuracy. Provide feedback as needed.

■ Work with a partner. Choose an Advanced Reader. Take turns reading a page from the book. Use the reader to practice reading with accuracy. Provide feedback as needed.

Technology
- Leveled Reader Database
- Reading Street Readers CD-ROM

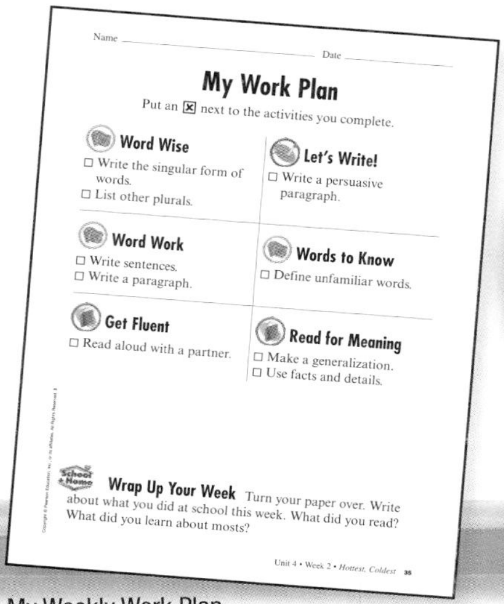
Name ______ Date ______

My Work Plan

Put an ☒ next to the activities you complete.

Word Wise
- ☐ Write the singular form of words.
- ☐ List other plurals.

Let's Write!
- ☐ Write a persuasive paragraph.

Word Work
- ☐ Write sentences.
- ☐ Write a paragraph.

Words to Know
- ☐ Define unfamiliar words.

Get Fluent
- ☐ Read aloud with a partner.

Read for Meaning
- ☐ Make a generalization.
- ☐ Use facts and details.

School + Home **Wrap Up Your Week** Turn your paper over. Write about what you did at school this week. What did you read? What did you learn about mosts?

Unit 4 • Week 2 • *Hottest, Coldest* 35

My Weekly Work Plan

Week 2

Objectives

- Introduce the weekly concept.
- Develop oral vocabulary.

Today at a Glance

Oral Vocabulary
evergreen, lumber, competitor, plunge

Phonics/Word Analysis
◎ Vowels: *r*-controlled

Comprehension
◎ Graphic sources
◎ Important ideas

Reading
"Largest U.S. Cities"

Fluency
Appropriate phrasing

Lesson Vocabulary
Tested vocabulary

Research and Inquiry
Identify questions

Spelling
Vowels: *r*-controlled

Conventions
Subject and object pronouns

Handwriting
Cursive letters *o, w,* and *b*

Writing
Imaginative story

Concept Talk

Question of the Week

What makes nature's record holders unique?

Introduce the concept

To further explore the unit concept of One of a Kind, this week students will read, write, and talk about what makes nature's record holders unique. Write the Question of the Week on the board.

ROUTINE **Activate Prior Knowledge** Team Talk

1. **Think** Have students think about what some of nature's record holders might be, such as the longest river or highest mountain.
2. **Pair** Have pairs of students discuss the Question of the Week.
3. **Share** Call on a few students to share their ideas with the group. Guide the discussion and encourage elaboration with prompts such as:
   - What are some places with extreme weather conditions?
   - What things in nature might be record holders because they are so big?

Routines Flip Chart

Anchored Talk

Develop oral vocabulary

Have students turn to pp. 54–55 in their Student Editions. Look at each of the photos. Then, use the prompts to guide discussion and create the *What makes nature's record holders unique?* concept map. Remind students to listen attentively to other students and to answer with appropriate detail. Encourage students to build on others' ideas when they answer.

- What is unusual about those trees? (They are very tall.) They are redwood trees, a kind of evergreen tree that is extremely tall. Let's add *Height* to our concept map.
- What is unusual about the rattlesnake? (It is very long.) This kind of snake is one of the longest in Texas. Something that is very long, like a river or a snake, can be an extreme in nature. Let's add *Length* to the concept map.

Amazing Words

You've learned 1 5 7 words so far.

You'll learn 0 1 0 words this week!

evergreen	champ
lumber	sprinter
competitor	acrobat
plunge	weaken
valuable	ranger

Objectives
Oral Vocabulary
You've learned
1 5 7
Amazing Words
so far this year!
Let's Talk About
Nature's Record Holders
Ask relevant questions about natures's record holders.
Comment on nature's unique environments.
Offer suggestions for how we might protect unique places in nature.
READING STREET ONLINE
CONCEPT TALK VIDEO
www.ReadingStreet.com
54
55

Student Edition pp. 54–55

Writing on Demand

Writing Fluency
Ask students to respond to the photos on pp. 54–55 by writing as well as they can and as much as they can about what makes nature's record holders unique.

- What is unusual about the iceberg? (It is in a very cold climate.) The most extreme climates are either very hot or very cold. Let's add *Being the most* to the map.

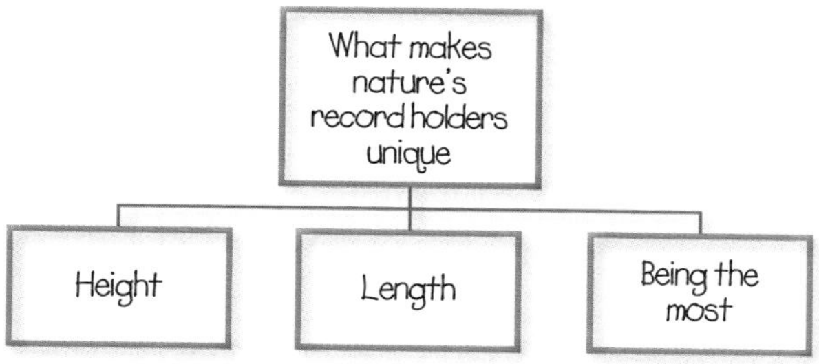

Connect to reading Tell students that this week they will be reading about extremes in nature, including real places and in a legend. Throughout the week, encourage students to add concept-related words to this week's concept map.

ELL Preteach Concepts Use the Day 1 instruction on ELL Poster 17 to assess and build background knowledge, develop concepts, and build oral vocabulary.

ELL Poster 17

ELL
English Language Learners

ELL support Additional ELL support and modeled instruction is provided in the *ELL Handbook* and in the ELL Support lessons on pp. DI•41–DI•50.

Listening comprehension
English learners will benefit from additional visual support to understand the key terms in the concept map. Use the pictures on pp. 54–55 to scaffold understanding.

Frontload for Read Aloud
Use the modified Read Aloud on p. DI•44 of the ELL Support lessons to prepare students to listen to "To Climb the Tallest Tree" (p. 55b).

Objectives

- Develop listening comprehension.
- Develop oral vocabulary.

Check Oral Vocabulary
SUCCESS PREDICTOR

Oral Vocabulary
Amazing Words

Introduce Amazing Words "To Climb the Tallest Tree" on p. 55b tells how Stephen Sillett climbed the tallest tree in the world. Tell students to listen for this week's Amazing Words—*evergreen, lumber, competitor,* and *plunge*—as you read.

Model fluency As you read "To Climb the Tallest Tree," model appropriate phrasing by grouping words in a meaningful way and paying attention to punctuation cues.

Teach Amazing Words

Amazing Words **Oral Vocabulary Routine**

evergreen
lumber
competitor
plunge

1. **Introduce** Write the word *evergreen* on the board. Have students say the word aloud with you. In "To Climb the Tallest Tree," we learn that redwood trees are *evergreens*. Does the author include any context clues that tell me the meaning of this word? Supply a student-friendly definition.
2. **Demonstrate** Have students answer questions to demonstrate understanding. Do *evergreen* trees lose their leaves? (no) Are pine trees, which keep their leaves all year, evergreens? (yes)
3. **Apply** Ask students to give a sentence using *evergreens*.

See p. OV•2 to teach *lumber, competitors,* and *plunge*.

Routines Flip Chart

Apply Amazing Words To build oral language, lead the class in a discussion about the meanings of the Amazing Words. Remind students to listen attentively and make pertinent comments.

Don't Wait Until Friday **MONITOR PROGRESS** **Check Oral Vocabulary**

During discussion, listen for students' use of the Amazing Words.

If... students are unable to use the Amazing Words to discuss the concept,

then... use Oral Vocabulary Routine on the Routines Flip Chart to demonstrate words in different contexts.

Day 1	Day 2	Day 3	Day 4	Day 5
Check Oral Vocabulary	Check Word Reading	Check Retelling	Check Fluency	Check Oral Vocabulary

Success Predictor

Read Aloud

To Climb the Tallest Tree

Stephen Sillett loves trees. He loves to study trees. He loves to climb trees. In the summer of 2006, he climbed the tallest tree in the world because he wanted to measure just how high it is.

Sillett, a university professor, lives in California, near a forest where redwood trees grow. The tallest trees in the world are redwoods. They are one of nature's giants. Some stand over 350 feet tall and are still growing.

How can these trees grow so tall? The rich soil in the redwood forest helps the trees grow. The weather helps too. Redwoods are evergreens, which means that they keep their leaves all year. In the winter, rain falls often in the redwood forest, so the trees get plenty of water. In the summer, they get water from the thick fog that covers their leaves.

A long time ago, there were many more redwoods. These giant trees usually live for thousands of years. But about 40 years ago, people started to cut down the tallest redwoods to use them for lumber. Sillett wanted to find the tallest tree that was still standing.

Sillett looked all over the redwood forest. He went to an area he had never been to before. There were plenty of tall redwoods in that part of the forest. But which one was the tallest? He found several competitors, but chose one that looked tallest to him. But to find out if that tree was really the tallest, he would have to climb to the top.

The tree wasn't easy to climb. In fact, it took longer than Sillett thought. First, he had to wait until nesting season was over. A rare bird builds its nest in the redwoods' branches. Sillett did not want to disturb the nests. So he waited until the baby birds hatched and grew strong enough to fly.

Then, Sillett had to find a way to climb the tree's giant trunk. The first branch was hundreds of feet above the ground! How would he get up there to step on it? Sillett tied a large bolt to the end of a rope and used a crossbow to shoot the rope over the branch. The rope caught on the branch. The bolt sailed over the branch and then plunged to the ground. Sillett hammered the bolt into another tree. Then, he climbed the rope up to the lowest branch.

From there, he still had a long way to go. But Sillett was determined to reach the top. When he did, he dropped down a long measuring tape. He was right! At a little over 379 feet high, that tree IS the tallest one on Earth.

That redwood was named Hyperion after a famous giant in Greek stories. Sillett wants people to know about Hyperion. He wants people to save nature's giants and help keep them growing strong.

Objectives

- Blend and read words with r-controlled vowels.
- Associate the vowel sound /ėr/ with *ir, er, ur, ear, or;* /är/ with *ar;* and /ôr/ with *or, ore, oar.*

Skills Trace

Vowels: *r*-Controlled
Vowels /ėr/ spelled *ir, er, ur, ear, or,* and *ar, or, ore, oar*
Introduce/Teach U4W2D1
Practice U4W2D3, U4W2D4
Reteach/Review U4W2D5, U4W3D4
Assess/Test Weekly Test U4W2
Benchmark Test U4
Key: U = Unit, W = Week, D = Day

Sound-Spelling Card 55

Sound-Spelling Cards 72, 92, 104

Sound-Spelling Cards 87, 91, 93

Phonics

Vowels: *r*-Controlled

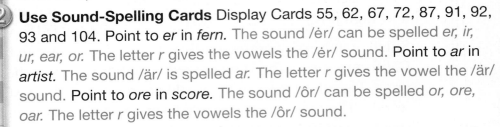

ROUTINE Blending Strategy

1. **Connect** Connect today's lesson to previously learned sound-spellings *r* and *wr*. Write *rocket* and *writing*. You can read words like these already. The both begin with the /r/ sound. Today you'll learn to spell and read words with /ėr/ spelled *ir, er, ur, ear, or;* /är/ spelled *ar;* and /ôr/ spelled *or, ore, oar.*
2. **Use Sound-Spelling Cards** Display Cards 55, 62, 67, 72, 87, 91, 92, 93 and 104. Point to *er* in *fern.* The sound /ėr/ can be spelled *er, ir, ur, ear, or.* The letter *r* gives the vowels the /ėr/ sound. Point to *ar* in *artist.* The sound /är/ is spelled *ar.* The letter *r* gives the vowel the /är/ sound. Point to *ore* in *score.* The sound /ôr/ can be spelled *or, ore, oar.* The letter *r* gives the vowels the /ôr/ sound.
3. **Model** Write *earth.* I see that this word has the letters *ear* that spell the sound /ėr/. This is how I blend this word. Point to each spelling as you say its sound. Then blend the word: /er/ /th/, *earth.* Follow this procedure to model *third, verb, market, normal,* and *soaring.*
4. **Guide Practice** Continue the process in step 3. This time have students blend with you. Remind them that the letter *r* changes the sound of a vowel or vowels in a syllable.

third	**heard**	**forth**	**large**	**store**
boar	**party**	**curtain**	**word**	**germ**

5. **Review** What do you know about reading these words? When you see the letter *r* plus a vowel or vowels, it makes one sound.

Routines Flip Chart

Model Have students turn to p. 56 in their Student Editions. Each word on this page has the vowel sound /ėr/, /är/, or /ôr/. The first word is *ferment.* I hear /ėr/ in the first syllable. In *ferment,* /ėr/ is spelled *er.*

Guide practice For each word in Words I Can Blend, ask for the sound of each letter or group of letters. Make sure that students identify the correct sounds for the *r*-controlled vowels. Then have them blend the words.

Corrective feedback
If... students have difficulty blending a word,
then... model blending the word. Then have students blend it with you.

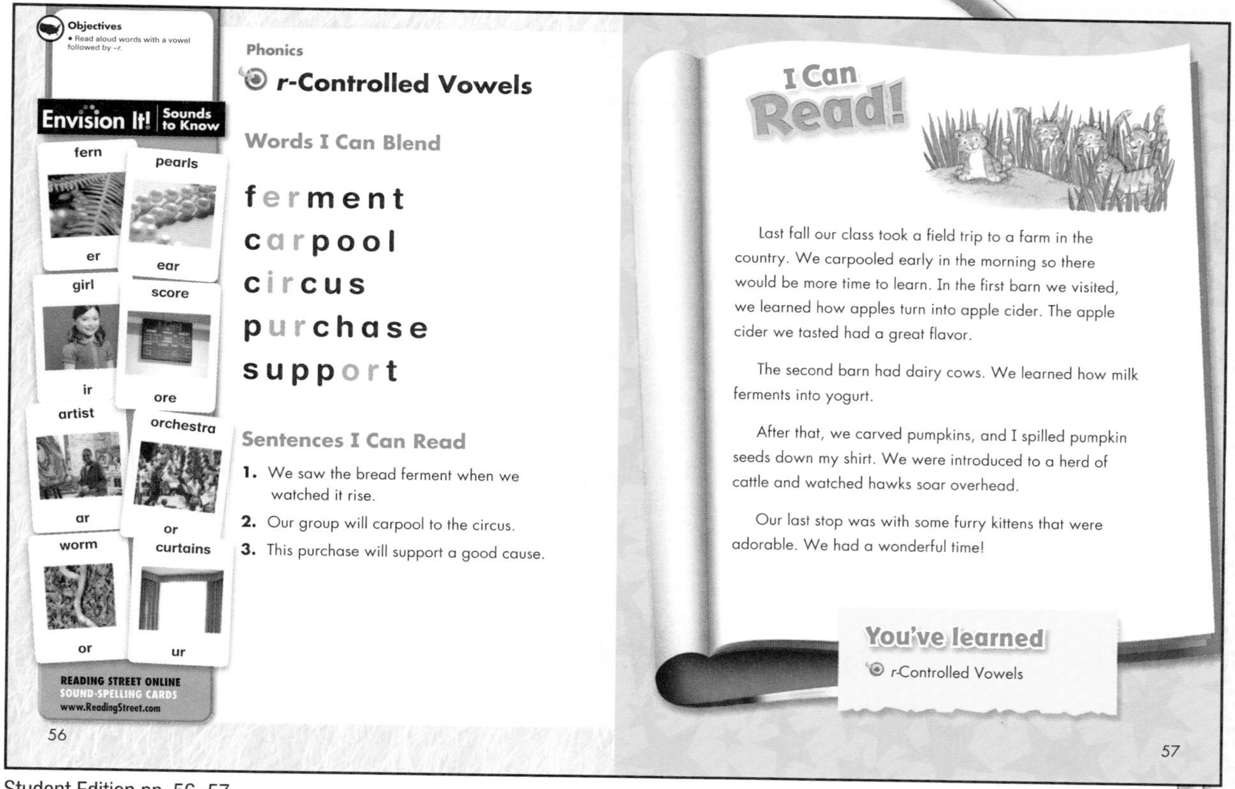
Objectives
• Read aloud words with a vowel followed by -r.

Envision It! Sounds to Know

fern er · pearls ear · girl ir · score ore · artist ar · orchestra or · worm or · curtains ur

READING STREET ONLINE SOUND-SPELLING CARDS www.ReadingStreet.com

Phonics

r-Controlled Vowels

Words I Can Blend

ferment
carpool
circus
purchase
support

Sentences I Can Read

1. We saw the bread ferment when we watched it rise.
2. Our group will carpool to the circus.
3. This purchase will support a good cause.

56

I Can Read!

Last fall our class took a field trip to a farm in the country. We carpooled early in the morning so there would be more time to learn. In the first barn we visited, we learned how apples turn into apple cider. The apple cider we tasted had a great flavor.

The second barn had dairy cows. We learned how milk ferments into yogurt.

After that, we carved pumpkins, and I spilled pumpkin seeds down my shirt. We were introduced to a herd of cattle and watched hawks soar overhead.

Our last stop was with some furry kittens that were adorable. We had a wonderful time!

You've learned
r-Controlled Vowels

57

Student Edition pp. 56–57

Blend and Read

Read words independent of context After students can successfully segment and blend the words on p. 56 in their Student Editions, point to words in random order and ask students to read them naturally.

Read words in context Have students read each of the sentences on p. 56. Have them identify words in the sentences that have the vowel sounds /ėr/, /är/, and /ôr/.

Team Talk Pair students and have them take turns reading each of the sentences aloud.

Chorally read the I Can Read! passage on p. 57 with students. Then have them read the passage aloud to themselves.

On their own For additional practice, use the *Reader's and Writer's Notebook* p. 258.

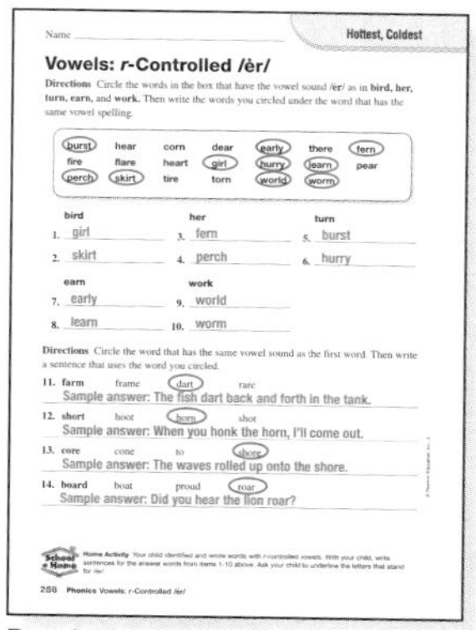
Hottest, Coldest

Vowels: r-Controlled /ėr/

Reader's and Writer's Notebook p. 258

Differentiated Instruction

SI Strategic Intervention

Blend Words with *r*-Controlled Vowels If students have difficulty blending words with *r*-controlled vowels, then have them practice saying rhyming words with each sound: *her, stir, purr; car, star, afar; for, score, soar.* Add words to each series for more practice.

Vocabulary Support

You may wish to explain the meaning of these words.

boar a male pig or hog

curtain a window covering made from fabric

ELL

English Language Learners

Pronunciation Assist students with the articulation of phonemes as they blend sounds. Focus on tongue and lip positions when saying words such as *hurt* and *perform.*

Contrastive Analysis Chart See also the Contrastive Analysis Chart in the *First Stop Book.*

Language Transfer Many languages do not have a sound like /ėr/. Therefore, many students for whom English is not the home language may have trouble pronouncing words such as *dirt* or *fern.* Help students practice saying and writing words, such as *her, bird,* and *turn.*

DAY 1 Get Ready to Read

Objectives

- Apply knowledge of sound-spellings to decode unknown multisyllabic words when reading.
- Decode and read words in context and independent of context.
- Practice fluency with oral rereading.

Decodable Practice Reader 17A

Vowels: *r*-Controlled

Read words independent of context Have students turn to p. 13 in *Decodable Practice Readers 3.2*. Have students read each word.

Read high-frequency words Have students read the high-frequency words *from, the, one, was, o, saw, what, who, of, put, could, do, into were, wanting, you, said, they, have.*

Preview Decodable Practice Reader Have students read the title and preview the story. Tell them that they will read words with the *r*-controlled vowel sounds /ėr/, /är/, and /ôr/.

Read words in context Pair students for reading and listen as they read. One student begins. Students read the entire story, switching readers after each page. Partners reread the story. This time the other student begins. Make sure that students are monitoring their accuracy when they decode words and are understanding what they read.

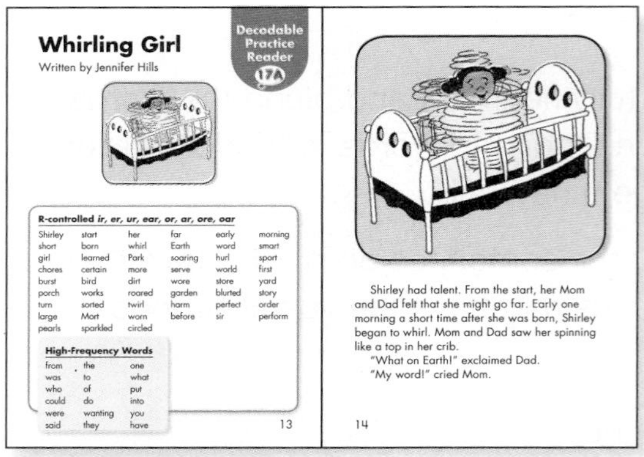

Whirling Girl

Written by Jennifer Hills

Decodable Practice Reader 17A

R-controlled *ir, er, ur, ear, or, ar, ore, oar*

Shirley	start	her	far	early	morning
short	born	whirl	Earth	word	smart
girl	learned	Park	soaring	hurl	sport
chores	certain	more	serve	world	first
burst	bird	dirt	wore	store	yard
porch	works	roared	garden	blurted	story
turn	sorted	twirl	harm	perfect	order
large	Mort	worn	before	sir	perform
pearls	sparkled	circled			

High-Frequency Words

from	the	one
was	to	what
who	of	put
could	do	into
were	wanting	you
said	they	have

13

Shirley had talent. From the start, her Mom and Dad felt that she might go far. Early one morning a short time after she was born, Shirley began to whirl. Mom and Dad saw her spinning like a top in her crib.

"What on Earth!" exclaimed Dad.

"My word!" cried Mom.

14

Decodable Practice Reader 17A

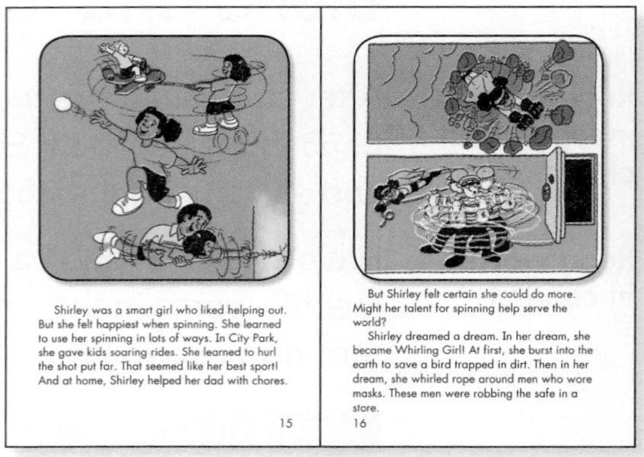

Shirley was a smart girl who liked helping out. But she felt happiest when spinning. She learned to use her spinning in lots of ways. In City Park, she gave kids soaring rides. She learned to hurl the shot put far. That seemed like her best sport! And at home, Shirley helped her dad with chores.

15

But Shirley felt certain she could do more. Might her talent for spinning help serve the world?

Shirley dreamed a dream. In her dream, she became Whirling Girl! At first, she burst into the earth to save a bird trapped in dirt. Then in her dream, she whirled rope around men who wore masks. These men were robbing the safe in a store.

16

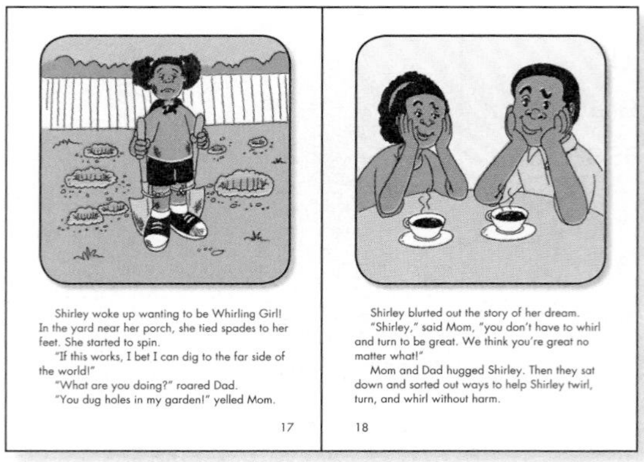

Shirley woke up wanting to be Whirling Girl! In the yard near her porch, she tied spades to her feet. She started to spin.

"If this works, I bet I can dig to the far side of the world!"

"What are you doing?" roared Dad.

"You dug holes in my garden!" yelled Mom.

17

Shirley blurted out the story of her dream.

"Shirley," said Mom, "you don't have to whirl and turn to be great. We think you're great no matter what!"

Mom and Dad hugged Shirley. Then they sat down and sorted out ways to help Shirley twirl, turn, and whirl without harm.

18

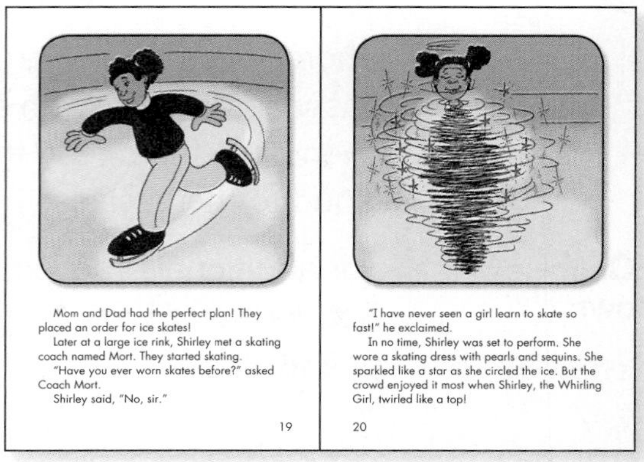

Mom and Dad had the perfect plan! They placed an order for ice skates!

Later at a large ice rink, Shirley met a skating coach named Mort. They started skating.

"Have you ever worn skates before?" asked Coach Mort.

Shirley said, "No, sir."

19

"I have never seen a girl learn to skate so fast!" he exclaimed.

In no time, Shirley was set to perform. She wore a skating dress with pearls and sequins. She sparkled like a star as she circled the ice. But the crowd enjoyed it most when Shirley, the Whirling Girl, twirled like a top!

20

Corrective feedback

If... students have difficulty decoding a word,
then... refer them to the Sound-Spelling Cards to identify the sounds in the word. Then prompt them to blend the word.

- What is the new word?
- Is the new word a word you know?
- Does it make sense in the story?

Check decoding and comprehension

Have students retell the story to include characters, setting, and events. Then have students find words in the story that have *r*-controlled vowels. Students should supply *Shirley, start, her, far, early, morning, short, born, whirl, Earth, word, smart, girl, learned, Park, soaring, hurl, sport, chores, certain, more, serve, world, first, burst, bird, dirt, wore, store, yard, porch, works, roared, garden, blurted, story, turn, sorted, twirl, harm, perfect, order, large, Mort, worn, before, sir, perform, pearls, sparkled,* and *circled.*

Reread for Fluency

Have students reread Decodable Practice Reader 17A to develop automaticity decoding words with *r*-controlled vowels.

ROUTINE **Oral Rereading**

1. **Read** Have students read the entire book orally.
2. **Reread** To achieve optimal fluency, students should reread the text three or four times.
3. **Corrective Feedback** Listen as students read. Provide corrective feedback regarding their fluency and decoding.

Routines Flip Chart

Academic Vocabulary

An ***r*-controlled vowel** is a vowel followed by the letter *r*. The *r* influences the sound of the vowel, which is neither long nor short *(bark, girl, term, fur).*

ELL

English Language Learners

***r*-Controlled vowels**

Beginning Choose several words with the *r*-controlled vowel sound /ėr/, such as *bird, her,* and *pearls,* from the Decodable Practice Reader, and write them on the board. Point to each word as you say it aloud. Then underline the letters that spell the sound /ėr/ in each word. Have students repeat the words with you. Do the same for words with /är/ and /ôr/.

Intermediate Remind students that the letter *r* and the vowel it controls must be in the same syllable. Write several multisyllable words with the *r*-controlled vowel sound from the Decodable Practice Reader, such as *morning, soaring,* and *certain.* Have students divide each word into syllables and then blend them to read the entire word.

Advanced/Advanced High After reading the story, have students choose 4 or 5 words with the *r*-controlled vowel sound and write a sentence for each word.

Objectives

- ◎ Locate and use information in graphic features to aid comprehension.
- ◎ Identify important ideas to aid comprehension.
- • Read grade-level text with appropriate phrasing.

Skills Trace

◎ Graphic Sources

Introduce U3W3D1; U4W2D1; U6W3D1

Practice U3W3D2; U3W3D3; U4W1D3; U4W2D2; U4W2D3; U6W3D2; U6W3D3

Reteach/Review U3W3D5; U4W2D5; U6W3D5

Assess/Test Weekly Tests U3W3; U4W2; U6W3

Benchmark Tests

Key: U = Unit, W = Week, D = Day

Skill ↔ Strategy

◎ Graphic Sources

◎ Important Ideas

Student Edition p. EI•10–11

Introduce graphic sources

Envision It!

Graphic sources are ways of showing information visually. Is a map a graphic source? (yes) Why should you look at graphics before you read something? (The graphics can help me know what to expect as I read.) Have students turn to pp. EI•10–11 in the Student Edition to review graphic sources. Then read "Largest U.S. Cities" with students.

Model the skill

Think Aloud Today we're going to read about the largest cities in the United States. Have students follow along as you read the first paragraph of "Largest U.S. Cities." The paragraph tells us the four largest cities in the United States in order of size. I can see that information visually in the bar graph at the bottom of the page. What do the bars that go across the graph show? (the number of people in each city, in millions) I can see at a glance that New York has the most people living in it, because the bar for New York is the longest one. The graph is a useful graphic source.

Guide practice

Have students finish reading "Largest U.S. Cities" on their own. After they read, have them make their own graphs of the information to apply their understanding of graphic sources.

Strategy check

Important Ideas Remind students that if they have difficulty understanding "Largest U.S. Cities," they can use the strategy of important ideas. Model using graphic sources to find important ideas.

Model the strategy

Envision It!

Think Aloud When I read "Largest U.S. Cities," I looked for information in the type, photos, and the bar graph to identify the important ideas. What is one important idea? (The U.S. has four large cities.) The type size and color for the title of the article, as well as the photos, captions, and graph, showed me that an important idea is that the U.S. has four very large cities.

On their own

Use p. 259 in the *Reader's and Writer's Notebook* for additional practice with graphic sources.

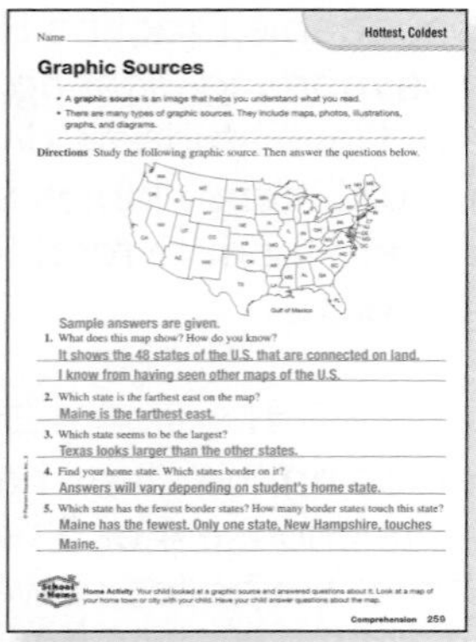

Reader's and Writer's Notebook, p. 259

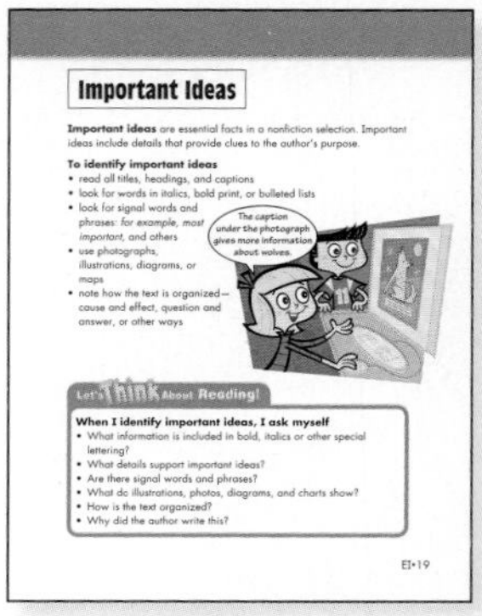

Student Edition p. EI•19

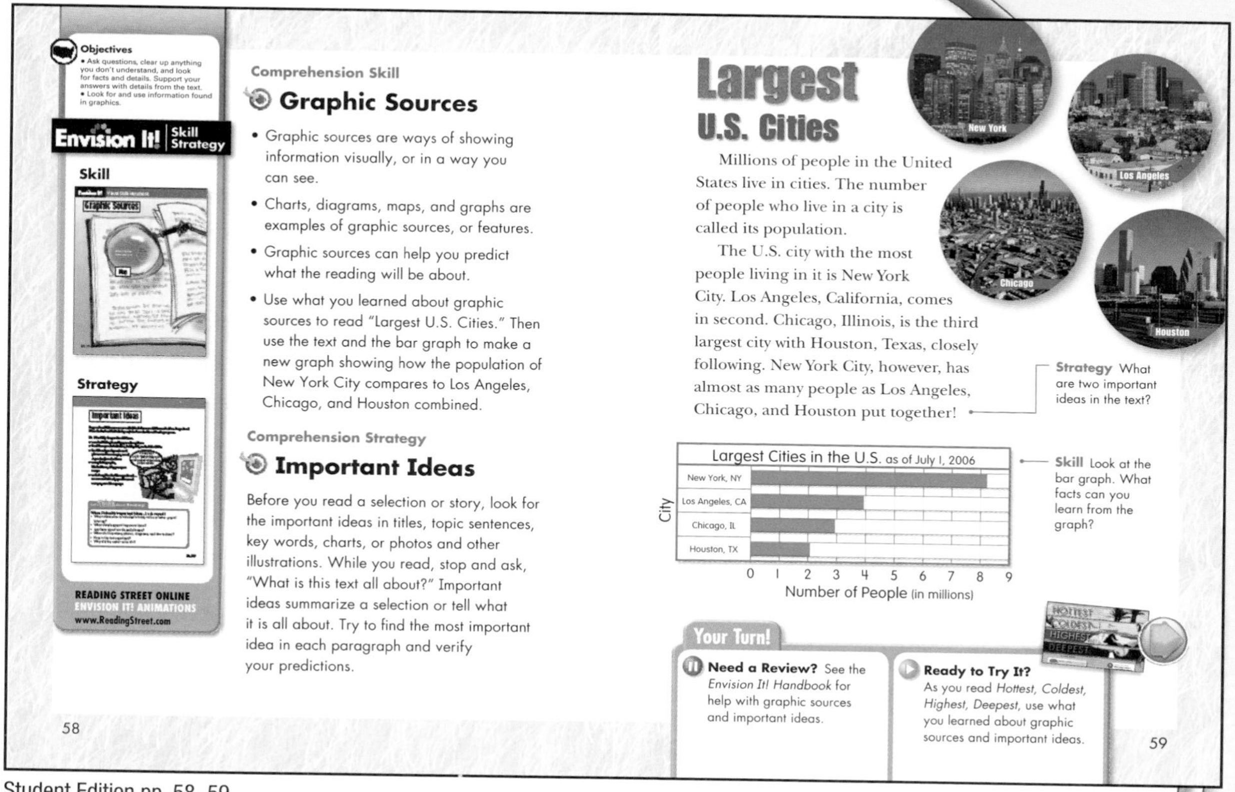
Objectives
• Ask questions, clear up anything you don't understand, and look for facts and details. Support your answers with details from the text.
• Look for and use information found in graphics.

Envision It! Skill Strategy

Skill

Strategy

READING STREET ONLINE
ENVISION IT! ANIMATIONS
www.ReadingStreet.com

Comprehension Skill

Graphic Sources

- Graphic sources are ways of showing information visually, or in a way you can see.
- Charts, diagrams, maps, and graphs are examples of graphic sources, or features.
- Graphic sources can help you predict what the reading will be about.
- Use what you learned about graphic sources to read "Largest U.S. Cities." Then use the text and the bar graph to make a new graph showing how the population of New York City compares to Los Angeles, Chicago, and Houston combined.

Comprehension Strategy

Important Ideas

Before you read a selection or story, look for the important ideas in titles, topic sentences, key words, charts, or photos and other illustrations. While you read, stop and ask, "What is this text all about?" Important ideas summarize a selection or tell what it is all about. Try to find the most important idea in each paragraph and verify your predictions.

58

Largest U.S. Cities

Millions of people in the United States live in cities. The number of people who live in a city is called its population.

The U.S. city with the most people living in it is New York City. Los Angeles, California, comes in second. Chicago, Illinois, is the third largest city with Houston, Texas, closely following. New York City, however, has almost as many people as Los Angeles, Chicago, and Houston put together!

Strategy What are two important ideas in the text?

Skill Look at the bar graph. What facts can you learn from the graph?

Your Turn!

Need a Review? See the *Envision It! Handbook* for help with graphic sources and important ideas.

Ready to Try It? As you read *Hottest, Coldest, Highest, Deepest*, use what you learned about graphic sources and important ideas.

59

Student Edition pp. 58–59

Strategy The U.S has four large cities. The names of the cities are New York, Los Angeles, Chicago, and Houston.

Skill New York City has a population much larger than any other city in the United States.

Academic Vocabulary

graph a pictorial representation of data that shows how any one piece of information compares to other pieces

Model Fluency
Appropriate Phrasing

Model fluent reading

Have students listen as you read the second paragraph of "Largest U.S. Cities" with appropriate phrasing. Explain that punctuation marks help to divide sentences into phrases, and the pause for a period is longer than the pause for a comma.

ROUTINE Oral Rereading

1. **Read** Have students read paragraph 2 of "Largest U.S. Cities" orally.
2. **Reread** To achieve optimal fluency, students should reread the text three or four times.
3. **Corrective Feedback** Have students read aloud without you. Provide feedback about their phrasing, helping students to group phrases by pausing at punctuation marks.

Routines Flip Chart

ELL

English Language Learners

Graphic sources Point to the different graphic sources on the page and name each one, having students repeat: *photographs, bar graph.* List the features on the board and have students use them to complete a sentence frame: ____ *and* ____ *are examples of graphic sources.*

Objectives

- Activate prior knowledge of words.
- Generate research topics.

Vocabulary
Tested Vocabulary

Lesson vocabulary Use the following Question and Answer activity to help students acquire word knowledge that improves reading, speaking, listening, and writing vocabularies.

Activate prior knowledge Display the lesson vocabulary words. Give students the opportunity to tell what they already know about these words. Then ask oral questions like those below. Students should respond *yes* or *no* and give reasons for their choice.

- Is the *average* temperature warm in some cities and cool in others?
- Can you measure the *depth* of an ocean with a ruler?
- Are *deserts* good places for penguins to live?
- Have any volcanoes ever *erupted* more than once?
- Can a cat *outrun* a turtle?
- Can you jump over the *peak* of a mountain?
- Do *tides* cause water to cover the sand near the ocean?
- Do *waterfalls* flow upward?

Compound words Use the word *waterfalls* to point out that some words are compound words. Have students identify the two words in *waterfalls* and ask if separating the two words helped them understand the meaning of the compound word.

By the end of the week, students should know the lesson vocabulary words. Have write *yes* and *no* questions using the words for classmates to answer.

Preteach Academic Vocabulary ELL **Academic Vocabulary** Write the following terms on the board:

***r*-controlled**	**legend**
cue	**author's craft**
punctuation	**graph**

Have students share what they know about this week's Academic Vocabulary. Use the students' responses to assess their prior knowledge. Preteach the Academic Vocabulary by providing a student friendly description, explanation, or example that clarifies the meaning of each term. Then ask students to restate the meaning of the Academic Vocabulary term in their own words.

Research and Inquiry
Identify Questions

Teach Discuss the Question of the Week: *What makes nature's record holders unique?* Tell students they will research and write an article about some record holders. They will present their findings to the class on Day 5.

Model Think Aloud I'll start by brainstorming a list of questions about people or places that hold records. I know many athletes have set records. There are also cities that have the tallest buildings or the most people. Some possible questions could be *Who are the fastest runners in the world? What are the tallest buildings?* and *Who has written the most books?*

Guide practice After students have brainstormed inquiry questions, explain that tomorrow they will conduct online research using their questions. Help students identify keywords that will guide their search.

On their own Have students work individually, in pairs, or in small groups to write an inquiry question.

INTERNET GUY
Don Leu

21st Century Skills

Weekly Inquiry Project
- **Day 1** Identify Questions
- **Day 2** Navigate/Search
- **Day 3** Analyze
- **Day 4** Synthesize
- **Day 5** Communicate

Small Group Time

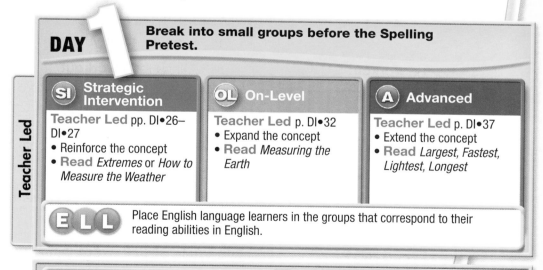

DAY 1 **Break into small groups before the Spelling Pretest.**

Teacher Led

SI Strategic Intervention	OL On-Level	A Advanced
Teacher Led pp. DI•26–DI•27 • Reinforce the concept • **Read** *Extremes* or *How to Measure the Weather*	**Teacher Led** p. DI•32 • Expand the concept • **Read** *Measuring the Earth*	**Teacher Led** p. DI•37 • Extend the concept • **Read** *Largest, Fastest, Lightest, Longest*

ELL Place English language learners in the groups that correspond to their reading abilities in English.

Practice Stations
- Read for Meaning
- Get Fluent
- Word Work

Independent Activities
- Concept Talk Video
- *Reader's and Writer's Notebook*
- Vocabulary Activities

ELL

English Language Learners

Multilingual vocabulary
Students can apply knowledge of their home languages to acquire new English vocabulary by using the Multilingual Vocabulary Lists (*ELL Handbook* pp. 433–446).

Objectives

- Spell words with the *r*-controlled vowel sound /ėr/ spelled *ir, er, ur, ear,* and *or.*
- Identify and use subject and object pronouns correctly.
- Use appropriate letter spacing to write words and phrases using cursive letters *o, w,* and *b.*

Spelling Pretest
Vowels: *r*-Controlled

Introduce Tell students to think of words with the *r*-controlled vowel sound /ėr/ spelled *ir, er, ur, ear,* and *or.* This week we will spell words with the vowel sound /ėr/ spelled *ir, er, ur, ear,* and *or.*

Pretest Use these sentences to administer the spelling pretest. Say each word, read the sentence, and repeat the word.

1. third	I am **third** in line behind Shawn and Lea.
2. early	It's better to be **early** than late.
3. world	Where in the **world** are we?
4. certain	I'm **certain** you called me.
5. dirty	The rug is **dirty** so we will clean it.
6. herself	Dana saw **herself** in the mirror.
7. earth	We planted some seeds in the **earth.**
8. word	Look up that **word** in the dictionary.
9. perfect	Dale got a **perfect** score in the game.
10. verb	Every sentence has a **verb.**
11. nerve	**Nerve** endings let us feel things.
12. worm	I found a **worm** in the garden.
13. thirsty	Drink water if you are **thirsty.**
14. workout	The gym is a place for a **workout.**
15. earn	If you work, you **earn** money.

Challenge words

16. determine	I must **determine** whether I need a coat today.
17. commercial	That **commercial** was selling cereal.
18. whirlwind	A **whirlwind** stirred up dust in the desert.
19. worthwhile	It is **worthwhile** to read that book
20. virtual	Jake and Tim finished the race in a **virtual** tie.

Self-correct After the pretest, you can either display the correctly spelled words or spell them orally. Have students self-correct their pretests by rewriting misspelled words correctly.

On their own For additional practice, use *Let's Practice It!* page 227 on the *Teacher Resources DVD-ROM.*

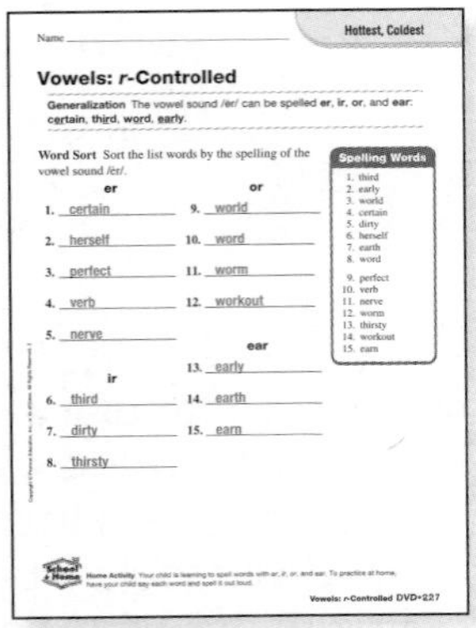
Name ______ Hottest, Coldest!

Vowels: *r*-Controlled

Generalization The vowel sound /ėr/ can be spelled **er, ir, or,** and **ear**: certain, third, word, early.

Word Sort Sort the list words by the spelling of the vowel sound /ėr/.

er: 1. certain 2. herself 3. perfect 4. verb 5. nerve
ir: 6. third 7. dirty 8. thirsty
or: 9. world 10. word 11. worm 12. workout
ear: 13. early 14. earth 15. earn

Spelling Words: 1. third 2. early 3. world 4. certain 5. dirty 6. herself 7. earth 8. word 9. perfect 10. verb 11. nerve 12. worm 13. thirsty 14. workout 15. earn

Vowels: *r*-Controlled DVD•227

Let's Practice It!
TR DVD•227

Conventions
Subject and Object Pronouns

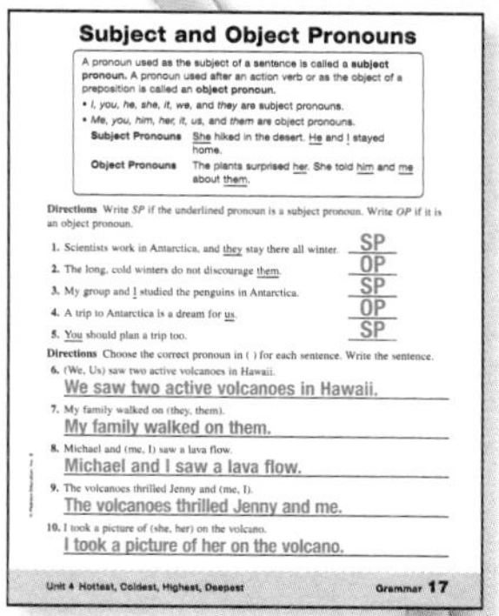
Subject and Object Pronouns

A pronoun used as the subject of a sentence is called a **subject pronoun.** A pronoun used after an action verb or as the object of a preposition is called an **object pronoun.**

- *I, you, he, she, it, we,* and *they* are subject pronouns.
- *Me, you, him, her, it, us,* and *them* are object pronouns.

Subject Pronouns She hiked in the desert. He and I stayed home.

Object Pronouns The plants surprised her. She told him and me about them.

Directions Write *SP* if the underlined pronoun is a subject pronoun. Write *OP* if it is an object pronoun.

1. Scientists work in Antarctica, and they stay there all winter. SP
2. The long, cold winters do not discourage them. OP
3. My group and I studied the penguins in Antarctica. SP
4. A trip to Antarctica is a dream for us. OP
5. You should plan a trip too. SP

Directions Choose the correct pronoun in ( ) for each sentence. Write the sentence.

6. (We, Us) saw two active volcanoes in Hawaii.
We saw two active volcanoes in Hawaii.
7. My family walked on (they, them).
My family walked on them.
8. Michael and (me, I) saw a lava flow.
Michael and I saw a lava flow.
9. The volcanoes thrilled Jenny and (me, I).
The volcanoes thrilled Jenny and me.
10. I took a picture of (she, her) on the volcano.
I took a picture of her on the volcano.

Unit 4 Hottest, Coldest, Highest, Deepest Grammar 17

Grammar Transparency 17, TR DVD

Teach Display Grammar Transparency 17, and read aloud the explanation and examples in the box. Point out the subject pronouns *I, you, me, he, she, it, we,* and *they* and the object pronouns *me, you, him, her, it, us,* and *them.*

Model Model identifying *they* as a subject pronoun in sentence 1 and *them* as an object pronoun in sentence 2. Apply the rules for using subject pronouns and object pronouns to show how you identified each one.

Guide practice Guide students to complete items 3–5. Remind them to note how the pronoun is used in each sentence. Record the correct responses on the transparency.

Daily Fix-It Use Daily Fix-It numbers 1 and 2 in the right margin.

Connect to oral language Have students read sentences 6–10 on the transparency and write the subject or object pronoun to complete each sentence correctly.

Handwriting
Cursive Letters *o, w,* and *b*

Model letter formation Display the lowercase cursive letters *o, w,* and *b.* Follow the stroke instruction pictured to model letter formation.

Model letter spacing Explain that writing legibly means that letters are evenly spaced. The sidestrokes that join letters are not too long or too short, and there is more space between words than between the letters in a word. Model writing this sentence with proper letter spacing: *The bunny borrowed a burrow.*

Guide practice Have students write this sentence: *The burro wore a bow on its brow.* Circulate around the room, guiding students.

Daily Fix-It

1. Some of the worst weather in the werld is in antarctica. *(world; Antarctica)*
2. The days is freezeing there even in summer. *(are; freezing)*

ELL

English Language Learners

Language production: Subject and object pronouns Model statements using subject and object pronouns while demonstrating their meaning. For example, say: I (point to yourself) give him (point to a boy) this pencil. He (point to the boy) gives me (point to yourself) the pencil. Have students repeat and then create their own statements.

Handwriting: Homographs To provide practice in handwriting lowercase cursive *o, w,* and *b* and to extend language opportunities with homographs, have students write two sentences using *bow* (/bō/) and *bow* (/bou/).

Objectives

- Understand and identify the features of an imaginative story.

MINI-LESSON

5 Day Planner
Guide to Mini-Lessons

DAY 1	Read Like a Writer
DAY 2	Developing a Story Sequence Chart
DAY 3	Writing Dialogue
DAY 4	Revising Strategy: Consolidating
DAY 5	Proofread for Subject and Object Pronouns

Writing—Imaginative Story

Introduce

MINI-LESSON

Read Like a Writer

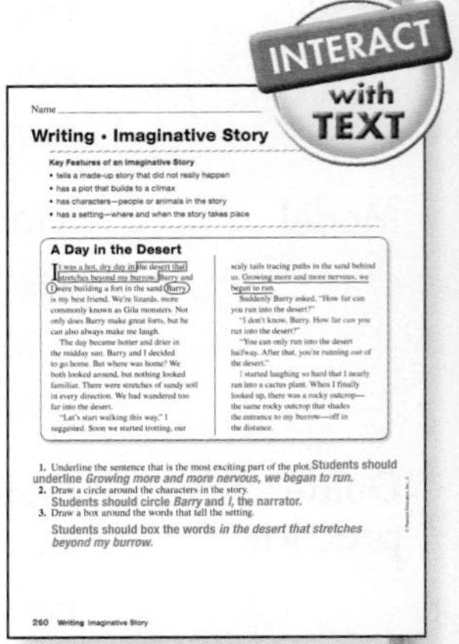

Name

Writing • Imaginative Story

Key Features of an Imaginative Story
- tells a made-up story that did not really happen
- has a plot that builds to a climax
- has characters—people or animals in the story
- has a setting—where and when the story takes place

A Day in the Desert

It was a hot, dry day in the desert that stretches beyond my burrow. Barry and I were building a fort in the sand. Barry is my best friend. We're lizards, more commonly known as Gila monsters. Not only does Barry make great forts, but he can also always make me laugh.

The day became hotter and drier in the midday sun. Barry and I decided to go home. But where was home? We both looked around, but nothing looked familiar. There were stretches of sandy soil in every direction. We had wandered too far into the desert.

"Let's start walking this way," I suggested. Soon we started trotting, our scaly tails tracing paths in the sand behind us. Growing more and more nervous, we began to run.

Suddenly Barry asked, "How far can you run into the desert?"

"I don't know, Barry. How far can you run into the desert?"

"You can only run into the desert halfway. After that, you're running out of the desert."

I started laughing so hard that I nearly ran into a cactus plant. When I finally looked up, there was a rocky outcrop—the same rocky outcrop that shades the entrance to my burrow—off in the distance.

1. Underline the sentence that is the most exciting part of the plot. Students should underline *Growing more and more nervous, we began to run.*
2. Draw a circle around the characters in the story. Students should circle *Barry* and *I*, the narrator.
3. Draw a box around the words that tell the setting. Students should box the words *in the desert that stretches beyond my burrow.*

260 Writing Imaginative Story

Reader's and Writer's Notebook p. 260

Introduce This week you will write an **imaginative story.** An imaginative story is a fictional story about events that did not really happen. You will use your imagination to write the story.

Prompt	Write an imaginative story in which one character tells a riddle to another.
Trait	Conventions
Mode	Narrative

Examine Model Text Let's read an example of an imaginative story in which one character tells a riddle to another. Have students read "A Day in the Desert" on p. 260 of their *Reader's and Writer's Notebook.*

Key Features An imaginative story has a **plot.** The action in the story builds to an exciting, sometimes tense point. That point is called the **climax.** Have students underline the sentence that is the climax of the story. *(Growing more and more nervous, we began to run.)*

An imaginative story has **characters,** or the **people or animals** in the story. Have students draw a circle around the characters in the story. (Barry and the narrator) Then have them talk about what they know about the characters in the story.

An imaginative story has a **setting,** which is the place and time where the story takes place. Have students draw a box around the words that tell the setting. *(In the desert that stretches beyond the burrow)*

Review key features

Review the key features of an imaginative story with students. You may want to post the key features in the classroom for students to reference as they work on their imaginative stories.

Key Features of an Imaginative Story

- tells a story that did not really happen
- has a plot that builds to a climax
- has characters—people or animals in the story
- has a setting—where and when the story takes place

ROUTINE Quick Write for Fluency — Team Talk

1. **Talk** Have small groups take several minutes to discuss the features of an imaginative story.
2. **Write** Each student writes a short description of an imaginative story.
3. **Share** Group members read their descriptions to each other.

Routines Flip Chart

Wrap Up Your Day

- ✔ **Build Concepts** What did you learn about record holders in nature?
- ✔ **Oral Vocabulary** Have students use the Amazing Words they learned in context sentences.
- ✔ **Homework** Send home this week's Family Times newsletter, *Let's Practice It!* pages 228–229 on the *Teacher Resources DVD-ROM.*

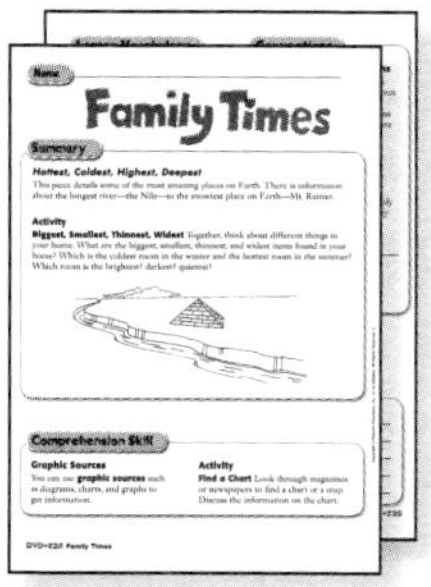

Let's Practice It!
TR DVD•228–229

Write Guy
Jeff Anderson

Two Words: Subject, Verb!

Let's help students gain confidence in composing sentences. Guide partners as they make up fun two-word sentences. *Rex howled! Kathy giggled. Lions growl.* Then let the students continue creating sentences, checking to make sure each includes a subject and verb. Another activity is to challenge students to find favorite sentences in books, and then whittle them down to the simple subject and verb. This paves the way for grammar to support students' writing.

ELL

English Language Learners

Read like a writer Read the writing model aloud and help students understand it. Point out that it is an imaginative story, which is a fictional story about events that did not really happen. Use a picture to explain the riddle if students do not understand *halfway in, then out.* Ask students what kind of setting they would like to use in a story and have them describe it.

Preview DAY 2

Tell students that tomorrow they will read about places in nature that are the hottest, coldest, deepest, and highest.

Objectives

- Expand the weekly concept.
- Develop oral vocabulary.

Today at a Glance

Oral Vocabulary
valuable, champ

Phonics/Word Analysis
◉ Vowels: *r*-controlled

Literary Terms
Author's craft

Text Features
Bold print, key words

Lesson Vocabulary
◉ Unknown words

Reading
"Geography Bee"
Hottest, Coldest, Highest, Deepest

Fluency
Appropriate phrasing

Research and Inquiry
Navigate/Search

Spelling
Vowels: *r*-controlled

Conventions
Subject and object pronouns

Writing
Imaginative story

Concept Talk

Question of the Week

What makes nature's record holders unique?

Expand the concept

Remind students of the weekly concept question. Tell students that today they will begin reading *Hottest, Coldest, Highest, Deepest.* As they read, encourage students to think about what makes nature's record holders unique.

Anchored Talk

Develop oral vocabulary

Use the photos on pp. 54–55 and the Read Aloud, "To Climb the Tallest Tree," to talk about the Amazing Words—*evergreen, lumber, competitor,* and *plunge.* Add the words to the concept map to develop students' knowledge of the topic. Discuss the following questions. Remind students to listen attentively to other students and to answer with appropriate detail. Encourage students to build on others' ideas when they answer.

- How can having the most of something, like a lake with the most water or a tree with the most *lumber,* lead to a record holder in nature?
- Why could an *evergreen* hold a record for the oldest tree?
- How might *competitors* find the hottest place in Texas?

Oral Vocabulary
Amazing Words

Amazing Words Oral Vocabulary Routine

Teach Amazing Words

1. **Introduce** Write the Amazing Word *valuable* on the board. Have students say it aloud with you. Relate *valuable* to the photographs on pp. 54–55 and "To Climb the Tallest Tree." Is a camel a *valuable* animal to have when you cross a desert? What makes it *valuable*? Have students determine the definition of the word. *Valuable* means useful or worth a great deal of money.
2. **Demonstrate** Have students answer questions to demonstrate understanding. Is climbing a tree a *valuable* way to measure it? What is something *valuable* to wear on your feet when you are in an area where rattlesnakes live?
3. **Apply** Have students apply their understanding. What is a synonym for *valuable*? (expensive, useful)

See pp. OV•2 to teach *champ*.

Routines Flip Chart

Apply Amazing Words As students read "Geography Bee" on p. 61, have them think about why it is *valuable* to know about places on Earth and whether a *champ* could outrun a fast-moving tide.

Connect to reading Explain that today students will read about the Nile, the longest river in the world. As they read, they should think about how the Question of the Week and the Amazing Words *valuable* and *champ* apply to the Nile.

ELL **Reinforce Vocabulary** Use the Day 2 instruction on ELL Poster 17 to teach lesson vocabulary and the lesson concept.

ELL Poster 17

Amazing Words

evergreen	champ
lumber	sprinter
competitor	acrobat
plunge	weaken
valuable	ranger

Connect to Science

Point out that one of the sample geography bee questions asks about the average summer temperature at the South Pole. Explain there are several reasons why it is so cold at the South Pole, even in the summertime. One reason is that the atmosphere above Antarctica is very thin, so there are few clouds to trap the heat and raise the temperature. Instead, the snow and ice reflect sunshine back into space.

Objectives

- Apply knowledge of letter-sound correspondences and syllable patterns to decode *r*-controlled words in context and independent of context.

Check Word Reading
SUCCESS PREDICTOR

Phonics

Vowels: *r*-Controlled

Review Review *r*-controlled vowels using Sound-Spelling Cards 55, 62, 67, 72, 87, 91, 92, 93, and 104.

Read words independent of context Display these words. Have the class blend the words. Then point to the words in random order and ask students to read them quickly.

shirt	**heard**	**word**	**permit**
fur	**carpool**	**confirm**	**former**

Corrective feedback Model blending decodable words and then ask students to blend them with you.

Read words in context Display these sentences. Have the class read the sentences.

Team Talk Have pairs take turns reading the sentences naturally.

The **worm burrowed** into the **earth.**
Were you **first** in line at the **carwash**?
This **morning** we talked about **current** events**.**

Don't Wait Until Friday **MONITOR PROGRESS** **Check Word Reading**

Words with *r*-Controlled Vowels

Write the following words and have the class read them. Notice which words students miss during the group reading. Call on individuals to read some of the words.

mirth	**merge**	**work**	**early**	
shrunk	**switch**	**speckled**	**spendthrift**	
purple	**birdbath**	**energy**	**herself**	**backyard**

Spiral Review
Row 2 reviews words with /a/, /e/, /i/, /o/, /u/.
Row 3 contrasts words with spellings of /ėr/ and /är/, and /a/, /e/, /i/, /o/, /u/.

If… students cannot read words with *r*-controlled vowels at this point,
then… use the Day 1 Blending Strategy routine on p. 56a to reteach *r*-controlled vowels. Use words from the Decodable Practice Passages (or Reader). Continue to monitor students' progress using other instructional opportunities during the week. See the Skills Trace on p. 56a.

Day 1	Day 2	Day 3	Day 4	Day 5
Check Oral Vocabulary	Check Word Reading	Check Retelling	Check Fluency	Check Oral Vocabulary

Success Predictor

Literary Terms
Author's Craft

Teach author's craft

Explain to students that authors make choices when they write, including choices about what words to use. Authors may use superlatives—words that show something is the best or the most in a group, such as the hottest or coldest—to help readers understand ideas. These words also help to get readers' attention.

Model author's craft

Think Aloud Let's look at "Largest U.S. Cities." What word showing that something is the most can you find in the title? (*largest*) What does it tell us about the topic of the article? (The article will be about the cities in the U.S. that have the most people.)

Guide practice

Direct students to look at pp. 64–65 of *Hottest, Coldest, Highest, Deepest.* Have students identify the superlatives the author uses to grab the reader's attention.

On their own

Have students skim the pages of *Hottest, Coldest, Highest, Deepest* and list the boldfaced words the author chose to use to show that something is the best or the most.

Text Features
Bold Print, Key Words

Teach bold print, key words

Text features are parts of a text that call attention to certain words, phrases, or ideas. Sometimes the words are bold so the reader notices them as soon as he or she looks at the page. When the words are bold, it tells the reader that they are key words that will help them understand the text.

Model the strategy

Think Aloud Text features can help us to better understand a selection. I see that each page of *Hottest, Coldest, Highest, Deepest* has boldfaced words. These key words help us understand the important ideas on each page. For instance, an important idea on page 63 is that the Nile is the longest river in the world.

Guide practice

Skim the pages of *Hottest, Coldest, Highest, Deepest* and discuss with students the other boldfaced words found in the selection.

On their own

Have students preview the chart on p. 65 and tell how the boldfaced labels make the information easier to understand.

Academic Vocabulary

author's craft an author's choice of words and language for specific purposes

Objectives

- Use a dictionary or glossary to find meanings of unknown words.
- Read grade-level text with appropriate phrasing and punctuation cues.

Vocabulary Strategy for Unknown Words

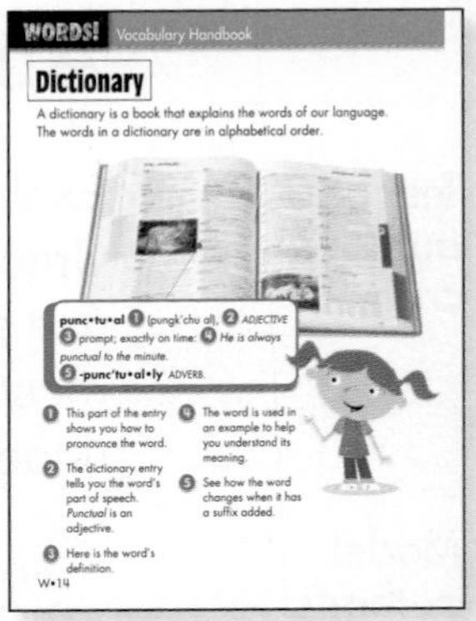
WORDS! Vocabulary Handbook

Dictionary

A dictionary is a book that explains the words of our language. The words in a dictionary are in alphabetical order.

Student Edition p. W•14

Teach unknown words

Envision It!

Tell students that when they encounter an unknown word, they can use a dictionary or glossary to look up the meaning. Explain that a dictionary or glossary provides definitions that help students understand the meanings of unknown words. Refer students to *Words!* on p. W•14 in the Student Edition for additional practice.

Model the strategy

Think Aloud

Write on the board: *Which volcano has erupted the most times?* The words in the sentence don't help me to figure out the meaning of *erupted,* so I will use a dictionary or glossary for help. A glossary is usually part of a book and has words from that book, while a dictionary is a separate book of words and definitions. When I look up *erupt* in a dictionary, I see that it means "to burst out" or "to throw forth lava, water, gases, or other material." Now I understand the question about which volcano has erupted the most times.

Guide practice

Write on the board: *We can measure the depth of the box with a ruler to see if it will fit on the shelf.* Have students determine the meaning of *depth* using context clues. If they are unable to use context clues to define *depth,* then have them look up the word in a dictionary or glossary. For additional support, use *Envision It! Pictured Vocabulary Cards* or *Tested Vocabulary Cards.*

INTERACT with TEXT

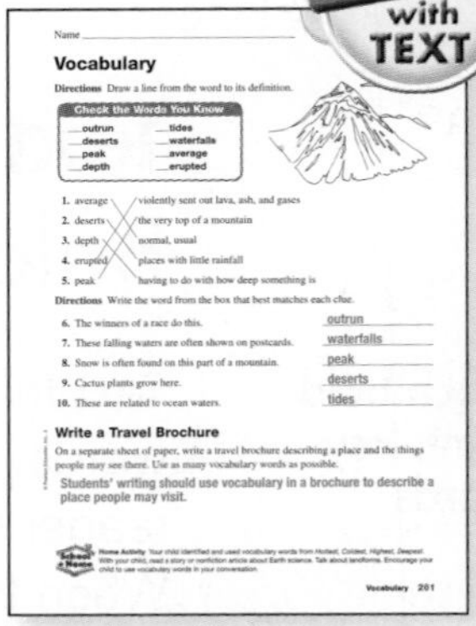
Vocabulary

Write a Travel Brochure

Reader's and Writer's Notebook p. 261

On their own

Read "Geography Bee" on p. 61. Have students use a dictionary or glossary to list the definitions for the lesson vocabulary. For additional practice use *Reader's and Writer's Notebook* p. 261.

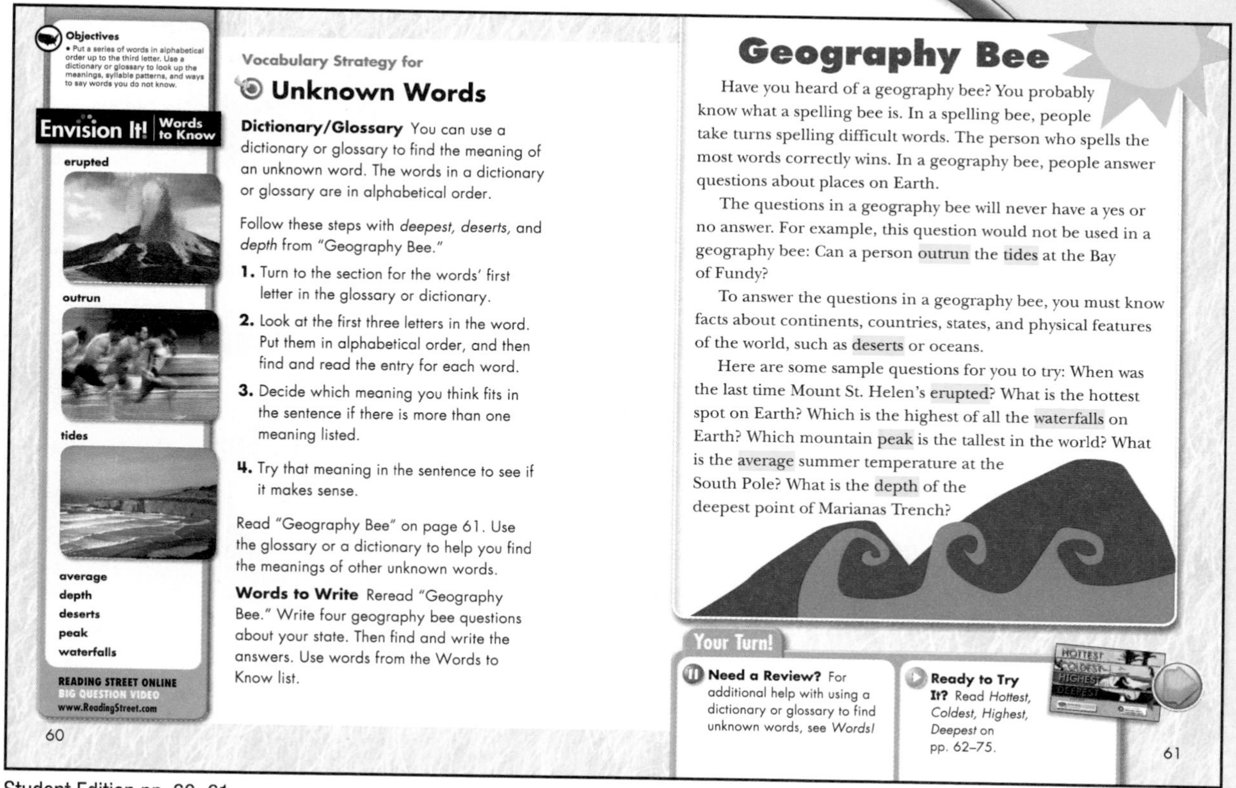

Objectives
• Put a series of words in alphabetical order up to the third letter. Use a dictionary or glossary to look up the meanings, syllable patterns, and ways to say words you do not know.

Envision It! Words to Know

erupted

outrun

tides

average
depth
deserts
peak
waterfalls

READING STREET ONLINE
BIG QUESTION VIDEO
www.ReadingStreet.com

Vocabulary Strategy for

Unknown Words

Dictionary/Glossary You can use a dictionary or glossary to find the meaning of an unknown word. The words in a dictionary or glossary are in alphabetical order.

Follow these steps with *deepest, deserts,* and *depth* from "Geography Bee."

1. Turn to the section for the words' first letter in the glossary or dictionary.
2. Look at the first three letters in the word. Put them in alphabetical order, and then find and read the entry for each word.
3. Decide which meaning you think fits in the sentence if there is more than one meaning listed.
4. Try that meaning in the sentence to see if it makes sense.

Read "Geography Bee" on page 61. Use the glossary or a dictionary to help you find the meanings of other unknown words.

Words to Write Reread "Geography Bee." Write four geography bee questions about your state. Then find and write the answers. Use words from the Words to Know list.

60

Geography Bee

Have you heard of a geography bee? You probably know what a spelling bee is. In a spelling bee, people take turns spelling difficult words. The person who spells the most words correctly wins. In a geography bee, people answer questions about places on Earth.

The questions in a geography bee will never have a yes or no answer. For example, this question would not be used in a geography bee: Can a person outrun the tides at the Bay of Fundy?

To answer the questions in a geography bee, you must know facts about continents, countries, states, and physical features of the world, such as deserts or oceans.

Here are some sample questions for you to try: When was the last time Mount St. Helen's erupted? What is the hottest spot on Earth? Which is the highest of all the waterfalls on Earth? Which mountain peak is the tallest in the world? What is the average summer temperature at the South Pole? What is the depth of the deepest point of Marianas Trench?

Your Turn!

Need a Review? For additional help with using a dictionary or glossary to find unknown words, see *Words!*

Ready to Try It? Read *Hottest, Coldest, Highest, Deepest* on pp. 62–75.

61

Student Edition pp. 60–61

Reread for Fluency
Appropriate Phrasing

Model fluent reading

Read the first paragraph of "Geography Bee" aloud, pausing after end punctuation and commas. Tell students that when they read words in groups, they should make a short pause after a comma and a longer pause after punctuation at the end of a sentence.

ROUTINE **Oral Rereading**

1. **Read** Have students read the first paragraph of "Geography Bee" orally.
2. **Reread** To achieve optimal fluency, students should reread the text three or four times.
3. **Corrective Feedback** Have students read aloud without you. Provide feedback about their phrasing, helping students to group phrases by pausing at punctuation marks.

Routines Flip Chart

Lesson Vocabulary

average the quantity found by dividing the sum of all quantities by the number of quantities
depth the distance from the top to the bottom
deserts dry, sandy regions without water and trees
erupted burst out
outrun run faster than someone or something else
peak the pointed top of a mountain or hill
tides rise and fall of the ocean's waters about every twelve hours
waterfalls streams of water that fall from a high place

Differentiated Instruction

SI Strategic Intervention

Review with students that often they will find a root word (*erupt*, not *erupted*) listed first in a dictionary entry.

ELL

English Language Learners

Cognates Point out the Spanish cognate *desert/desierto* in this week's lesson vocabulary on p. 60.

Build Academic Vocabulary Use the lesson vocabulary pictured on p. 60 to teach the meanings of *erupted*, *outrun*, and *tides*. Call on pairs to write the words on sticky notes and use them to label images of the words in the ELL Poster.

Objectives

- Understand characteristics of expository text.
- Set a purpose for reading.
- Use text features to preview and predict.

HOTTEST
COLDEST
HIGHEST
DEEPEST
BY STEVE JENKINS
Genre
Expository text gives information about the real world. Look for numbers and diagrams that help you understand the facts.
Question of the Week
What makes nature's record holders unique?
62
63
Student Edition pp. 62–63

Build Background

Discuss nature's record holders

Team Talk Have students turn to a partner and discuss the Question of the Week and these questions about nature's record-holders.

- What are some hot and cold places on Earth?
- How do we measure the temperature of the air?
- What happens when a volcano erupts?
- How can we observe how much rain falls in a place?

Connect to selection

Have students discuss their answers with the class. Possible solutions: Deserts are hot places on Earth, while the North and South Poles are cold places. We measure air temperature with a thermometer. When a volcano erupts, hot lava flows down its sides. We can observe how much rain falls in a place by catching it in a container and measuring it. For additional opportunities to build background, use the Background Building Audio.

Prereading Strategies

Genre Explain that **expository text** tells about real people or events and gives information about things. Its purpose is to explain what a person, event, or thing is like. Expository texts often include text features such as boldfaced words, subheads, charts, graphs, photos, and maps to help readers better understand the topic.

Preview and predict Prior to reading have students locate and preview the title, illustrations, boldfaced words, maps, charts, diagrams, and graphs for *Hottest, Coldest, Highest, Deepest.* Ask them to predict what they will learn about as they read. Remind them that they can check and verify their predictions when they read.

Set purpose Prior to reading, have students set their own purpose for reading this selection. To help students set a purpose, ask them to think about what it means for a geographical feature to be unique, or one of a kind.

Strategy Response Log

INTERACT with TEXT

Have students use p. 23 in the *Reader's and Writer's Notebook* to review and use the strategy of important ideas.

Small Group Time

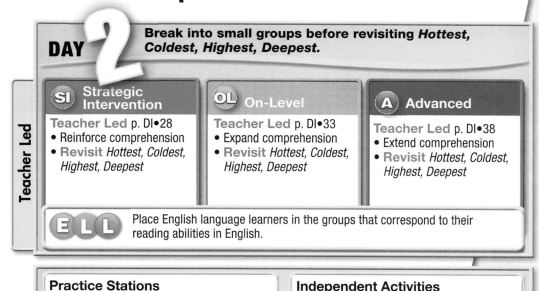

DAY 2 **Break into small groups before revisiting *Hottest, Coldest, Highest, Deepest.***

Teacher Led

SI Strategic Intervention	OL On-Level	A Advanced
Teacher Led p. DI•28 • Reinforce comprehension • Revisit *Hottest, Coldest, Highest, Deepest*	Teacher Led p. DI•33 • Expand comprehension • Revisit *Hottest, Coldest, Highest, Deepest*	Teacher Led p. DI•38 • Extend comprehension • Revisit *Hottest, Coldest, Highest, Deepest*

ELL Place English language learners in the groups that correspond to their reading abilities in English.

Practice Stations	Independent Activities
• Words to Know • Get Fluent • Word Wise	• Background Building Audio • *Reader's and Writer's Notebook* • Research and Inquiry

Differentiated Instruction

A Advanced

Have students make a list of the kinds of records that people want to know about (sports, weather, etc.).

Double Day Read! Multidraft Reading

For **Whole Group** instruction, choose one of the reading options below. For each reading, have students set the purpose indicated.

Option 1

Day 2 Read the selection. Use Guide Comprehension to monitor and clarify understanding.

Day 3 Reread the selection. Use Extend Thinking to develop higher-order thinking skills.

Option 2

Day 2 Read the first half of the selection, using both Guide Comprehension and Extend Thinking instruction.

Day 3 Read the second half of the selection, using both Guide Comprehension and Extend Thinking instruction.

ELL

English Language Learners

Build background To build background, review the summary selection in English in the *ELL Teaching Guide,* p. 127. Use the Retelling Cards to provide visual support for the summary.

Objectives

- Identify important ideas to aid comprehension.

OPTION 1 Guide Comprehension Skills and Strategies

Teach Important Ideas

Important Ideas Remind students that as they read they should stop and think about the important ideas in the text. Often important ideas will be in titles, captions, or different type. Look at the first sentence on page 65. It looks like an important idea. I notice that the word *longest* is in bold type. Let me read on to see if it is really an important idea.

Corrective Feedback

If... students cannot determine important ideas,
then... model guiding students in identifying important ideas.

Model the Strategy

Think Aloud I see that the rest of the sentences tell about other rivers that are not as long as the Nile. The fact that the Nile is the longest river in the world is an important idea in the selection.

If you could visit any spot on Earth, where would you go? What if you wanted to see some of the most amazing natural wonders in the world?

There are deserts that haven't seen rain for hundreds of years and jungles where it pours almost every day. There are places so cold that even in the summer it's below freezing and spots where it's often hot enough to cook an egg on the ground. There are mountains many miles high and ocean trenches that are even deeper. You can find rivers thousands of miles long and waterfalls thousands of feet high.

Where are the very hottest and coldest, windiest and snowiest, highest and deepest places on Earth? Travel the world and visit the planet's record holders.

64

Student Edition pp. 64–65

Background Knowledge • Evaluation • Text to Self Do you know the names or locations of any of the natural wonders the author mentions? Answers will vary.

OPTION 2 Extend Thinking Think Critically

Higher-Order Thinking Skills

Important Ideas • Analysis Read the sentence about the Amazon River on page 65. In what way is this fact as important as the fact about the Nile? Possible response: It tells us that the Amazon is mightier than the Nile. It's not the longest, but it is important, too.

On Their Own

Have students reread pp. 64–65 to find other clues that the sentence is an important idea in the book.

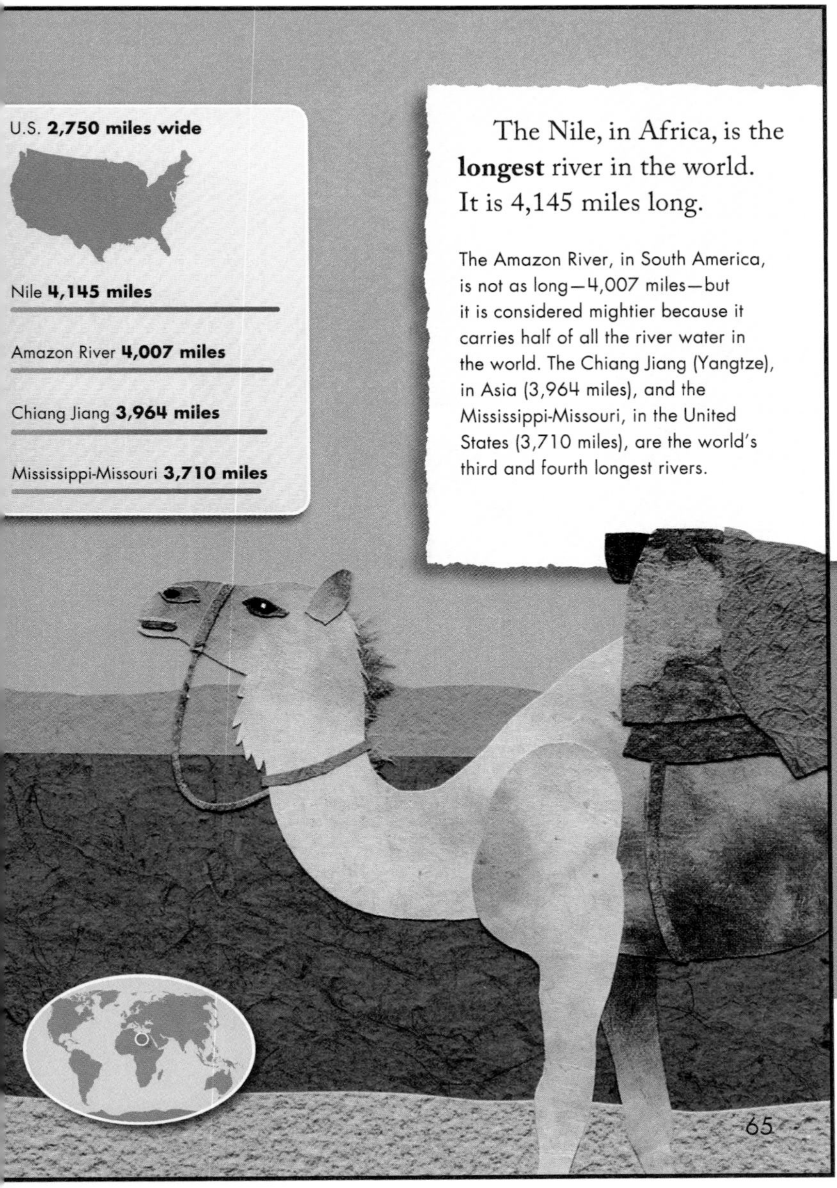

The Nile, in Africa, is the **longest** river in the world. It is 4,145 miles long.

The Amazon River, in South America, is not as long—4,007 miles—but it is considered mightier because it carries half of all the river water in the world. The Chiang Jiang (Yangtze), in Asia (3,964 miles), and the Mississippi-Missouri, in the United States (3,710 miles), are the world's third and fourth longest rivers.

Differentiated Instruction

A Advanced

Compare and contrast Ask students to find out more information about the Nile and the Amazon. Then have them make a T-chart showing how the two rivers are alike and different. Have them use the chart to explain why the Nile is the longest river, yet the Amazon is the mightiest.

ELL

English Language Learners

Activate background knowledge Define *extreme* (having or being very much of something) and explain that p. 64 tells us about many different places on Earth that are extreme, including deserts with no rain and very rainy jungles. Partner students and ask pairs to find more examples of extreme places found on p. 64. Have partners share one idea with the group.

Text features Use newspaper headlines to explain the concept of using text features such as bigger or darker type to show important ideas. Then page through the selection with students and have them find examples of bigger or darker type to show important ideas.

DAY 2 Read and Comprehend

Objectives

- Identify main idea and details to aid comprehension.

OPTION 1 Skills and Strategies, continued

Teach Main Idea and Details

Review **Main Idea and Details** Have students read about Lake Baikal and Lake Superior on p. 66. Then ask students to identify the main idea on the page.

Corrective Feedback

If... students are unable to identify the main idea,
then... use the Model to help them find the main idea.

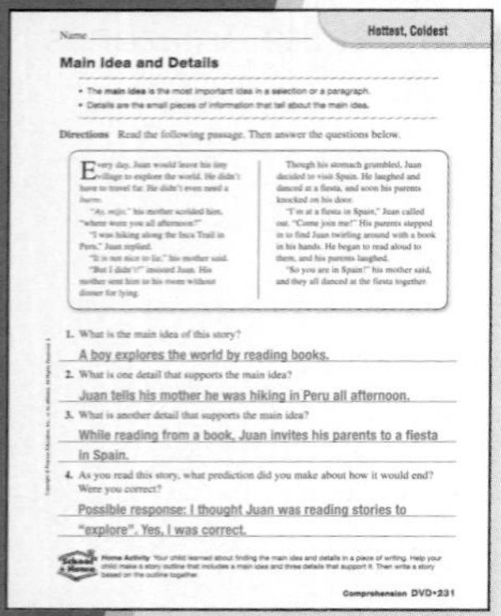
Name ______ Hottest, Coldest

Main Idea and Details

- The **main idea** is the most important idea in a selection or a paragraph.
- Details are the small pieces of information that tell about the main idea.

Directions Read the following passage. Then answer the questions below.

Every day, Juan would leave his tiny village to explore the world. He didn't have to travel far. He didn't even need a burro.

"Ay, mijo," his mother scolded him, "where were you all afternoon?"

"I was hiking along the Inca Trail in Peru," Juan replied.

"It is not nice to lie," his mother said.

"But I didn't!" insisted Juan. His mother sent him to his room without dinner for lying.

Though his stomach grumbled, Juan decided to visit Spain. He laughed and danced at a fiesta, and soon his parents knocked on his door.

"I'm at a fiesta in Spain," Juan called out. "Come join me!" His parents stepped in to find Juan twirling around with a book in his hands. He began to read aloud to them, and his parents laughed.

"So you are in Spain!" his mother said, and they all danced at the fiesta together.

1. What is the main idea of this story?
A boy explores the world by reading books.
2. What is one detail that supports the main idea?
Juan tells his mother he was hiking in Peru all afternoon.
3. What is another detail that supports the main idea?
While reading from a book, Juan invites his parents to a fiesta in Spain.
4. As you read this story, what prediction did you make about how it would end? Were you correct?
Possible response: I thought Juan was reading stories to "explore". Yes, I was correct.

Home Activity Your child learned about finding the main idea and details in a piece of writing. Help your child make a story outline that includes a main idea and three details that support it. Then write a story based on the outline together.

Comprehension DVD•231

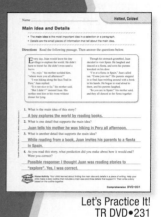

Let's Practice It!
TR DVD•231

Model the Skill

Think Aloud Remember that supporting details tell more about the main idea. I see that the topic of the page is two lakes that are record holders. Lake Baikal is the oldest and deepest lake, while Lake Superior is the largest freshwater lake.

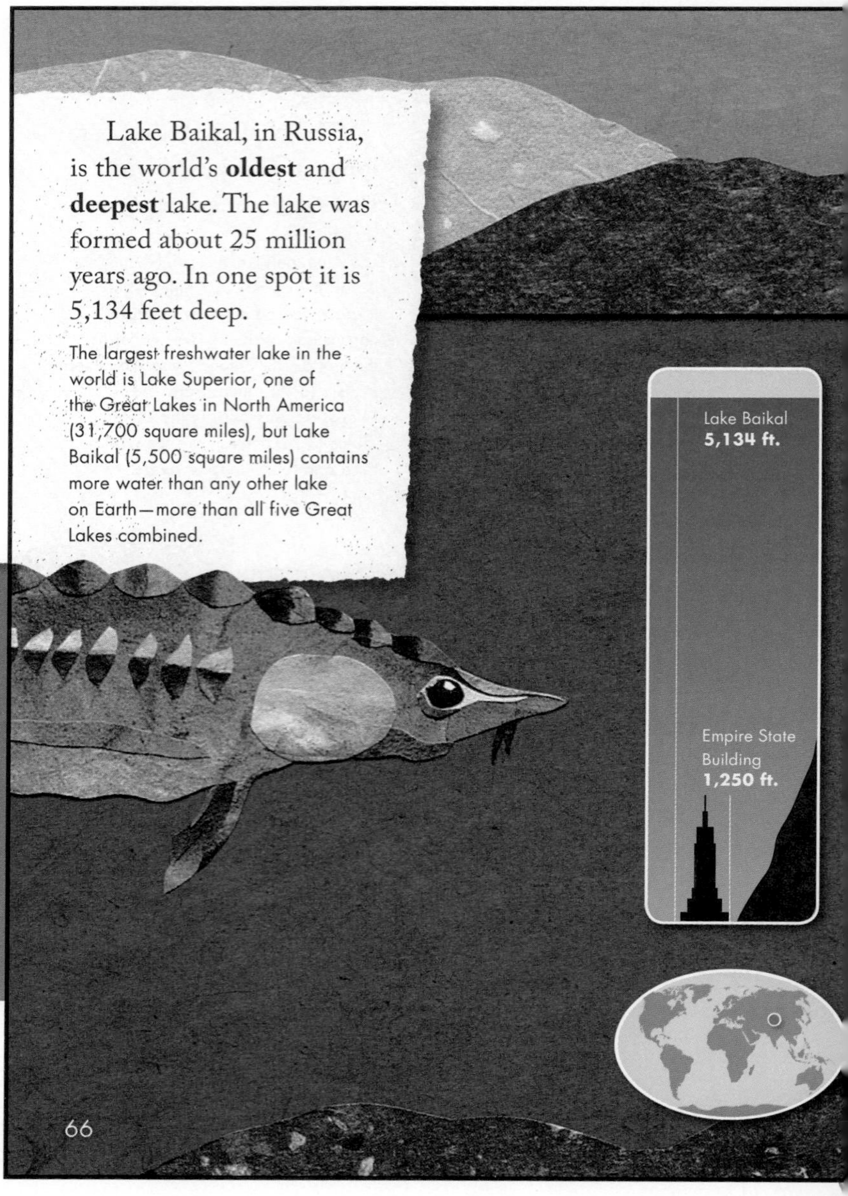
Lake Baikal, in Russia, is the world's **oldest** and **deepest** lake. The lake was formed about 25 million years ago. In one spot it is 5,134 feet deep.

The largest freshwater lake in the world is Lake Superior, one of the Great Lakes in North America (31,700 square miles), but Lake Baikal (5,500 square miles) contains more water than any other lake on Earth—more than all five Great Lakes combined.

66

Student Edition pp. 66–67

Author's Craft • Analysis Why do you think the author chose to emphasize the words oldest and deepest on page 66? Possible response: These words make the reader think of the most of something. They jump out as if to say "I'm important."

OPTION 2 Think Critically, continued

Higher-Order Thinking Skills

Review **Main Idea and Details • Synthesis** What is an important detail that supports the main idea on page 67? Possible response: An important detail is that Mauna Kea is 33,476 feet tall.

What is a supporting detail in the text that tells which lake has more water? **(Lake Baikal contains more water.)** The main idea is that even though Lake Superior is larger, Lake Baikal is the deepest lake and has more water.

On Their Own

Ask students to identify the topic of p. 67 and then use supporting details to identify the main idea. (The topic is mountains that are record holders. The main idea is that Mount Everest is the highest mountain in the world, but Mauna Kea is the tallest.) For additional practice with main idea and details, use *Let's Practice It!* page 231 on the *Teacher Resources DVD-ROM.*

Mount Everest is the **highest** mountain in the world. Its peak is 29,028 feet above sea level.

Mount Everest is considered the **highest** mountain—above sea level—in the world, but it's not really the **tallest.** Measured from its base on the floor of the ocean, Mauna Kea, in Hawaii, is 33,476 feet tall. Only the top 13,796 feet of Mauna Kea are above sea level.

67

Graphic Sources • Evaluate Look at the three oval maps of the world on pages 66 and 67. Of the three places mentioned in the text (Lake Baikal, Mount Everest, and Mauna Kea), which two are located nearest to each other? How can you tell? Lake Baikal and Mount Everest are the nearest. The dots marking their locations are on the same continent. Mauna Kea is far away from them.

Differentiated Instruction

SI Strategic Intervention

Graphic sources Make a simple graphic like the one on p. 66 to demonstrate the relative heights of Mount Everest and Mauna Kea. Show Mount Everest rising from land and Mauna Kea extending from the base of the ocean floor to its peak. Have partners work together to label each mountain and write its total height.

Connect to Science

Explain that we use investigations to learn about the natural world. Ask students to discuss what challenges scientists might have had as they measured Mauna Kea.

ELL English Language Learners

Vocabulary: Adjectives Write on the board: oldest. Explain that *oldest* is an adjective, or a word that tells more about something. Ask what small word they see in *oldest* (old). Explain that adding -est to a word shows that something is the most, so oldest means "most old." Model adding -est to deep, high, and cold and have students explain what the new word means.

Important ideas Ask students to name the boldfaced words on pp. 66 and 67 that show important ideas (oldest, deepest, highest, tallest). Then have them use each word in a sentence.

Objectives

- Use graphic sources to aid comprehension.

OPTION 1 Skills and Strategies, continued

Teach Graphic Sources

Graphic Sources Have students read about Al Aziziyah on p. 68. Then ask students to use the text and the chart on p. 68 to decide if there is anywhere in the United States that can reach a temperature nearly as hot as the hottest spot on the planet.

Corrective Feedback

If... students are unable to interpret the text and chart together,
then... use the Model to help them link graphic sources to text.

INTERACT with TEXT

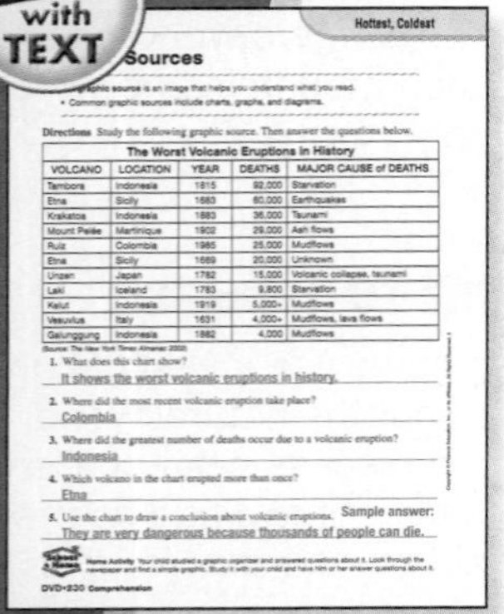

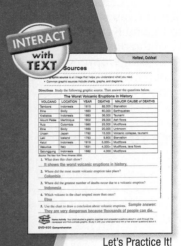

Let's Practice It!
TR DVD•230

Model the Skill

Think Aloud The first sentence tells us that Al Aziziyah can reach a temperature of 136°F. What does the second sentence tell us about the temperature in Death Valley, California? (It once reached 134.6°F.)

The **hottest** spot on the planet is Al Aziziyah, Libya, in the Sahara, where a temperature of over 136°F has been recorded.
The hottest temperature ever recorded in the United States is 134.6°F, in Death Valley, California.
136°F
134.6°F
98.6°F
Body temp.
68°F
Room temp.
32°F
Water freezes
68

Student Edition pp. 68–69

Compare and Contrast • Synthesis Choose two places mentioned in the text and compare and contrast them. Answers will vary, but both comparisons and contrasts should be included in students' answers.

OPTION 2 Think Critically, continued

Higher-Order Thinking Skills

Graphic Sources • Analysis How can you use graphic sources to find that the hottest and coldest spots in the world are on different continents? Possible response: You can look at the maps on pp. 68 and 69 and see that the dot showing where each place is located is on a different continent on each of the maps.

Review **Main Idea and Details • Analysis** What is an important detail supporting the main idea that Vostok, Antarctica is the coldest place on the planet? Possible response: An important detail is that the temperature once reached 129°F below zero there.

What do the two thermometers at the right of the chart show? (The temperatures 136°F and 134.6°F.) Are they close together? (yes) I know Death Valley is in the U.S. I can see that it can be nearly as hot as Al Aziziyah, the hottest spot on the planet.

The **coldest** place on the planet is Vostok, Antarctica. A temperature of 129°F below zero was recorded there.

It is so cold at the South Pole that the average summer temperature is –58°F. The coldest temperature ever recorded in the United States is –80°F, at Prospect Creek Camp, Alaska.

The **wettest** place on Earth is Tutunendo, Colombia, where an average of 463 inches of rain falls every year.

Mount Wai-ale-ale, on the island of Kauai in Hawaii, has the most rainy days—350 a year. On the island of La Réunion, in the Indian Ocean, more than 61 inches of rain fell in a single day.

69

On Their Own

Have students look at the other thermometers and labels in the chart. Ask why the author might have chosen to include those facts to help us understand the text. For additional practice with graphic sources, use *Let's Practice It!* page 230 on the *Teacher Resources DVD-ROM.*

Background Knowledge • Evaluation • Text to Text Skim through pages 65–69. Why might the author frequently include a fact about a place in the United States? Possible response: Since we know more about places in the United States than other countries, we can use the facts about places here to help us understand facts about nature's record holders.

Check Predictions Have students look back at the predictions they made earlier and discuss whether they were accurate. Then have students preview the rest of the selection and either adjust their predictions accordingly or make new predictions.

Differentiated Instruction

SI Strategic Intervention

Compare and contrast Display the sentence *The wettest place on Earth is Tutunendo, Colombia, but the rainiest place is Mount Wai-ale-ale.* Explain that the author shows on p. 69 that the *wettest* place on Earth is different from the *rainiest* place. Have students discuss how this might be possible.

A Advanced

Graphic sources Have students use the information at the top of p. 69 to make a graphic similar to the one on p. 68 that shows the three extremely cold temperatures mentioned on the page. Remind them that temperatures below zero are written with a minus sign.

ELL English Language Learners

Formal and informal language Explain that *recorded* is a formal way to say that information was written down to use at a later time. Provide examples: *The teacher recorded the students' grades. The nurse recorded my temperature on the chart.*

If you want to teach this selection in two sessions, stop here.

Objectives

- Find pertinent information from online sources.
- Recognize and correctly use subject and object pronouns.
- Practice correctly spelling words with *r*-controlled vowels.

Research and Inquiry
Navigate/Search

Teach Have students generate a research plan for gathering information about their topics. Suggest students conduct an Internet search using their inquiry questions and the keywords they identified. Tell them to skim and scan each site for information that helps answer their inquiry question or leads them to specific information that will be useful. Bolded or italicized words may be clues to what kind of information the Web site will provide. Have students also look for charts, graphs, and highlighted text. Have students take notes as they research.

Model Think Aloud When I conducted a search on *fastest runners,* I realized that I might want to know the fastest runner for different races. The person who runs the fastest 50-yard dash probably wouldn't win a marathon. I will look at different races to see who set records for different events. I will pay attention to captions and boldfaced words to help me find important information.

Guide practice Have students review Web sites they identified. Remind them that they should look at several sites and make sure that the information about a record holder is the same on all the sites. Explain that while this is a good process to follow whenever they do Internet research, it is especially important when they are dealing with record holders, since record holders may change over time. There also may be disagreements about who or what really holds the record.

On their own Have students continue their review of Web sites, taking notes as they find relevant information.

Conventions

Subject and Object Pronouns

Teach Write *He and I said hello to her* on the board. Ask students to identify the subjects of the sentence. *(He* and *I)* Remind students that a pronoun used as the subject of a sentence is called a subject pronoun. Have students identify the object pronoun in the sentence. *(her)* Remind them that object pronouns are used after action verbs or as objects of prepositions.

Guide practice Have students create a sentence with a proper noun as the subject and then replace it with a subject pronoun. Then have them say a sentence with a noun in the predicate and replace it with an object pronoun.

Daily Fix-It Use Daily Fix-It numbers 3 and 4 in the right margin.

Connect to oral language Have students look for and read aloud subject and object pronouns in *Hottest, Coldest, Highest, Deepest.* (*It is 3,212 feet high.*, p. 72; *It once erupted more than 400 times in a single day.*, p. 73; *The tide here comes in so fast that it can overtake a person trying to outrun it.*, p. 74)

On their own For more practice, use *Reader's and Writer's Notebook* p. 262.

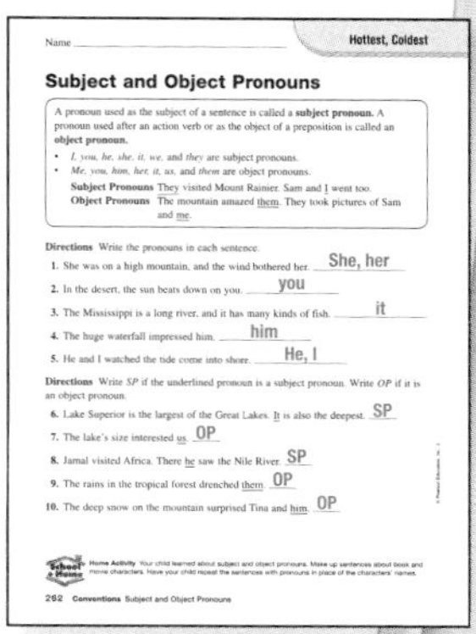

Name ______ Hottest, Coldest

Subject and Object Pronouns

A pronoun used as the subject of a sentence is called a **subject pronoun.** A pronoun used after an action verb or as the object of a preposition is called an **object pronoun.**

- *I, you, he, she, it, we,* and *they* are subject pronouns.
- *Me, you, him, her, it, us,* and *them* are object pronouns.

Subject Pronouns They visited Mount Rainier. Sam and I went too.
Object Pronouns The mountain amazed them. They took pictures of Sam and me.

Directions Write the pronouns in each sentence.

1. She was on a high mountain, and the wind bothered her. She, her
2. In the desert, the sun beats down on you. you
3. The Mississippi is a long river, and it has many kinds of fish. it
4. The huge waterfall impressed him. him
5. He and I watched the tide come into shore. He, I

Directions Write *SP* if the underlined pronoun is a subject pronoun. Write *OP* if it is an object pronoun.

6. Lake Superior is the largest of the Great Lakes. It is also the deepest. SP
7. The lake's size interested us. OP
8. Jamal visited Africa. There he saw the Nile River. SP
9. The rains in the tropical forest drenched them. OP
10. The deep snow on the mountain surprised Tina and him. OP

Home Activity Your child learned about subject and object pronouns. Make up sentences about book and movie characters. Have your child repeat the sentences with pronouns in place of the characters' names.

262 **Conventions** Subject and Object Pronouns

Reader's and Writer's Notebook p. 262

Spelling

Vowels: *r*-Controlled

Teach Remind students that the sound /ėr/ has several spellings. It may be spelled *ir, er, ur, ear,* and *or.*

Guide practice Have students write each spelling word on the board and underline the sound /ėr/ spelled *ir, er, ur, ear,* or *or.*

On their own For more practice, use *Reader's and Writer's Notebook* p. 263.

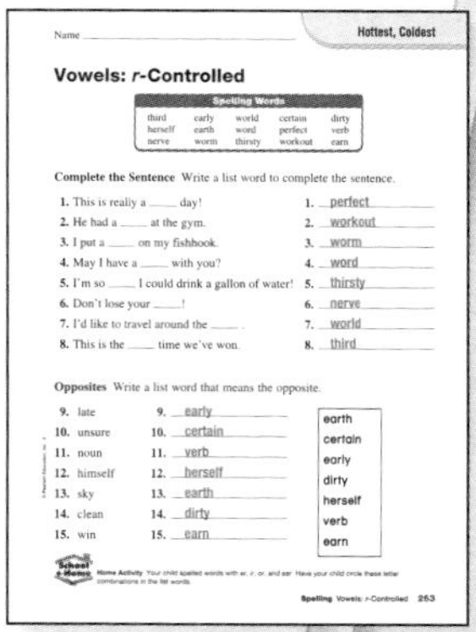

Name ______ Hottest, Coldest

Vowels: *r*-Controlled

Spelling Words				
third	early	world	certain	dirty
herself	earth	word	perfect	verb
nerve	worm	thirsty	workout	earn

Complete the Sentence Write a list word to complete the sentence.

1. This is really a ____ day! 1. perfect
2. He had a ____ at the gym. 2. workout
3. I put a ____ on my fishhook. 3. worm
4. May I have a ____ with you? 4. word
5. I'm so ____ I could drink a gallon of water! 5. thirsty
6. Don't lose your ____! 6. nerve
7. I'd like to travel around the ____. 7. world
8. This is the ____ time we've won. 8. third

Opposites Write a list word that means the opposite.

9. late 9. early
10. unsure 10. certain
11. noun 11. verb
12. himself 12. herself
13. sky 13. earth
14. clean 14. dirty
15. win 15. earn

earth, certain, early, dirty, herself, verb, earn

Home Activity Your child spelled words with er, ir, or, and ear. Have your child circle these letter combinations in the list words.

Spelling Vowels: r-Controlled 263

Reader's and Writer's Notebook p. 263

Daily Fix-It

3. Terry and me read about Mt. everest. *(I; Everest)*
4. Its the highest mountain on erth. *(It's; earth* or *Earth)*

ELL

English Language Learners

Conventions To provide students with practice using subject and object pronouns, use the modified grammar lessons in the *ELL Handbook* and Grammar Jammer online.

Language transfer: Gender-neutral pronouns English learners may use masculine or feminine personal pronouns because nouns in their home languages have genders. If this happens, say the sentence with the gender-neutral pronoun *it,* and have students repeat after you several times.

Objectives

- Select a topic and generate ideas for an imaginative story.
- Use a story sequence chart to organize ideas for writing an imaginative story.

Writing—Imaginative Story
Writer's Craft: Generating Ideas

Introduce the prompt Review the key features of an imaginative story. Remind students that they should think about these features as they plan their writing. Then explain that they will begin the writing process for an imaginative story today. Read aloud the reading prompt.

Writing Prompt
Write an imaginative story in which one character tells a riddle to another.

Select a topic Think Aloud To help choose a topic, let's make a chart and list possible settings for a story on one side and what might happen in each setting on the other side. Display a T-chart. We read about some extreme places on earth in *Hottest, Coldest, Highest, Deepest.* Yesterday we read "A Day in the Desert," about a pair of lizards in the desert. I'm going to start the chart with that. Add the information to the T-chart. Ask students to name other settings and story lines that might happen in each setting. Remind them that because this will be an imaginative story, the story line does not have to be something that could actually happen.

Setting	Story Line
desert	getting lost
highest mountain	climbing it
river	nearly going over a waterfall

Also remind students that they will need to include a riddle in their story. Explain that a riddle is a statement or question that describes something in an unusual way and therefore takes some thought to understand. People usually have to figure something out in order to understand or answer a riddle. Refer to the riddle in "A Day in the Desert."

Corrective feedback Circulate around the room as students use the chart to select a setting and story line to write about. If students are having trouble deciding, suggest they picture each setting and choose the story line they would find most exciting to write about. Then remind them to think of a riddle that they will be able to use in their story.

MINI-LESSON

Developing a Story Sequence Chart

- A story sequence chart helps you organize your story. It also helps you organize the events. I'm going to write about sailing on the Nile River. Write *the Nile River with waterfall* in the Setting box.
- For my characters, I think I'll create a family. There will be a mother, a father, and two girls. Enter this information in the Characters box.
- In the Events boxes, write the main events of the story that will lead up to a climax. First, the family will be sailing down the Nile River. Next, the girls will share riddles. Then they will realize that they are quickly approaching a waterfall. Last, they will all work together to get their boat to shore.

Have students begin their own story sequence charts using the form on p. 264 of their *Reader's and Writer's Notebook.* Tell them to draw one star next to the event where they will include their riddle and two stars next to the event that will be the climax.

ROUTINE

Quick Write for Fluency

Team Talk

1. **Talk** Have partners discuss the settings they selected.
2. **Write** Each student writes two sentences describing their setting.
3. **Share** Partners read their descriptions to each other. Then each partner asks the other a question about his or her setting.

Routines Flip Chart

Wrap Up Your Day

- ✓ **Build Concepts** What did you learn about places in nature that hold records?
- ✓ **Graphic Sources** How were you able to use graphic sources to compare places?
- ✓ **Important Ideas** How were you able to find the important idea on each page?

Differentiated Instruction

A Advanced

Develop a story Encourage students to write a more detailed and developed story. Supply an extra graphic organizer for students to list more events. Suggest they also include more detailed descriptions about their characters and setting.

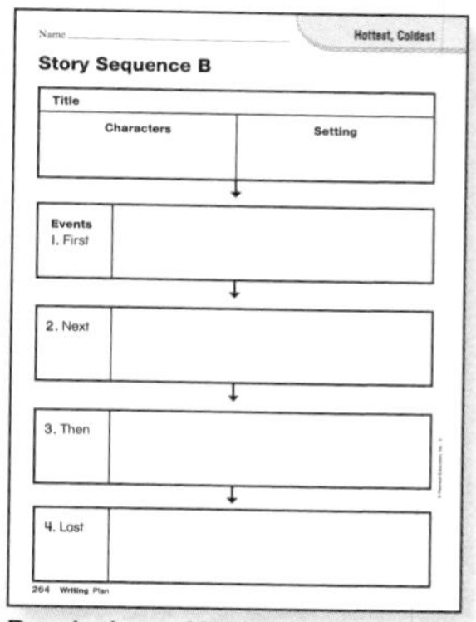
Name
Hottest, Coldest
Story Sequence B
Title
Characters
Setting
Events
1. First
2. Next
3. Then
4. Last

Reader's and Writer's Notebook p. 264

Teacher Tip

Check students' descriptions of their settings. If students are having difficulty, suggest they look at illustrations in books for descriptive details to include.

Preview DAY 3

Tell students that tomorrow they will read about other places in nature that hold records.

Objectives
- Expand the weekly concept.
- Develop oral vocabulary.

Today at a Glance

Oral Vocabulary
sprinter, acrobat

Phonics/Word Analysis
◎ Vowels: *r*-controlled

Comprehension Check/Retelling
Discuss questions

Reading
Hottest, Coldest, Highest, Deepest

Think Critically
Retelling

Fluency
Appropriate phrasing and punctuation cues

Research and Study Skills
Bar graphs

Research and Inquiry
Analyze

Spelling
Vowels: *r*-controlled

Conventions
Subject and object pronouns

Writing
Imaginative story

Concept Talk

Question of the Week

What makes nature's record holders unique?

Expand the concept

Remind students of the weekly concept question. Discuss how the question relates to places and things in nature that hold records. Remind students to make pertinent comments during the duscussion. Tell students that today they will read about some other amazing places around the world.

Anchored Talk

Develop oral vocabulary

Have students use text features, including boldfaced words, to review pp. 62–69 of *Hottest, Coldest, Highest, Deepest*. Discuss the Amazing Words *valuable* and *champ.* Add these words and other concept-related words to the concept map. Use the following questions to develop students' understanding of the concept. Have students ask and answer questions with appropriate detail and to give suggestions based on the ideas of others.

- Why can having rain be *valuable* for a farmer's crops?
- How could a *champ* help protect the wildlife along the Amazon River?
- Would very hot temperatures be *valuable* for an athlete?

Oral Vocabulary
Amazing Words

Amazing Words Oral Vocabulary Routine

Teach Amazing Words

1. **Introduce** Write the word *sprinter* on the board. Have students say it with you. Yesterday, we read about the hottest place on the planet, where a temperature of over 136°F would certainly affect a *sprinter's* speed. Have students determine a definition of *sprinter.* (A *sprinter* is a runner who is fast in short races.)
2. **Demonstrate** Have students answer questions to demonstrate understanding. What kind of animals are fast *sprinters*? (cheetahs, lions, horses, zebras, rabbits, giraffes)
3. **Apply** Have students apply their understanding. Where might you see a *sprinter* running? (at a track meet, in the Olympics)

See pp. OV•2 to teach *acrobat.*

Routines Flip Chart

Apply Amazing Words

As students read pp. 70–75 of *Hottest, Coldest, Highest, Deepest*, have them consider how the Amazing Words *sprinter* and *acrobat* might apply to extreme places in nature.

Connect to reading

Explain that today students will read about more of nature's record holders, including the world's driest and windiest places, highest waterfall, and most active volcano. As they read, students should think about how this week's concept question and the Amazing Words *sprinter* and *acrobat* apply to these places.

ELL Expand Vocabulary Use the Day 3 instruction on ELL Poster 17 to help students expand vocabulary.

ELL Poster 17

Amazing Words

evergreen	champ
lumber	sprinter
competitor	acrobat
plunge	weaken
valuable	ranger

ELL

English Language Learners

Professional Development: What ELL experts say about Shelter Instruction "English language learners benefit when teachers shelter, or make comprehensible, their literacy instruction. Sheltered techniques include using consistent, simplified, clearly enunciated, and slower-paced oral language to explain literacy concepts or activities." —Dr. Georgia Ernest García

Objectives

- ◎ Blend and read words with *r*-controlled vowels.
- Apply knowledge of sound-spellings to decode unknown words when reading.
- Decode and read words in context and independent of context.

Phonics
Sort Words

Model word sorting Write /ėr/, /är/, and /ôr/ as heads on a three-column chart. Now we are going to sort words. We'll sort words with the *r*-controlled vowel sounds /ėr/, /är/, and /ôr/ into the columns on the chart. I will start. Write *burn* and model how to read it, using the Blending Strategy on p. 56a. *Burn* has the sounds /b/ /ėr/ /n/ with /ėr/ spelled *ur*, so I will write *burn* in column under /ėr/. Model reading *park* (/är/) and *chore* (/ôr/) in the same way.

Guide practice Use the practice words from the activities on p. 56a for the word sort. Point to a word. Have students read the word, identify the *r*-controlled vowel sound in the word, and tell where it should be written on the chart.

Corrective feedback For corrective feedback, model tracking each word and reading it.

/ėr/	/är/	/ôr/
third	large	forth
heard	party	store
curtain		boar
word		
germ		

Fluent Word Reading

Model Write *birth*. I know the sounds for *b, ir,* and *th.* Blend them and read the word *birth.*

Guide practice Write the words below. Say the sounds in your head for each spelling you see. When I point to the word, we'll read it together. Allow one second per sound previewing time for the first reading.

whirl **learn** **carver** **porch** **dirty** **storm**

On their own Have students read the list above three or four times, until they can read one word per second.

Blend and Read

Read words independent of context

Have students turn to p. 21 in *Decodable Practice Readers 3.2* and find the first list of words. Each word in this list has an *r*-controlled vowel sound. Let's blend and read these words. Be sure that students identify the correct vowel sound in each word.

Next, have students read the high-frequency words.

Preview Decodable Practice Passage

Have students read the title and preview the story. Tell them that they will read words with the vowel sounds /ėr/, /är/, or /ôr/.

Read words in context

Chorally read the story along with the students. Have students identify words in the story that have the vowel sounds /ėr/, /är/, or /ôr/.

Team Talk Pair students and have them take turns reading the story aloud to each other. Monitor students as they read to check for proper pronunciation and appropriate pacing.

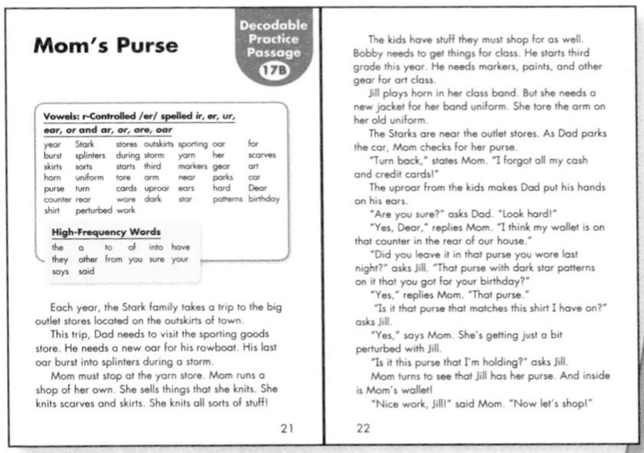

Mom's Purse

Decodable Practice Passage 17B

Vowels: r-Controlled /er/ spelled *ir, er, ur, ear, or* and *ar, or, ore, oar*

year	Stark	stores	outskirts	sporting	oar	for
burst	splinters	during	storm	yarn	her	scarves
skirts	sorts	starts	third	markers	gear	art
horn	uniform	tore	arm	near	parks	car
purse	turn	cards	uproar	ears	hard	Dear
counter	rear	wore	dark	star	patterns	birthday
shirt	perturbed	work				

High-Frequency Words

the	a	to	of	into	have
they	other	from	you	sure	your
says	said				

Each year, the Stark family takes a trip to the big outlet stores located on the outskirts of town.

This trip, Dad needs to visit the sporting goods store. He needs a new oar for his rowboat. His last oar burst into splinters during a storm.

Mom must stop at the yarn store. Mom runs a shop of her own. She sells things that she knits. She knits scarves and skirts. She knits all sorts of stuff!

21

The kids have stuff they must shop for as well. Bobby needs to get things for class. He starts third grade this year. He needs markers, paints, and other gear for art class.

Jill plays horn in her class band. But she needs a new jacket for her band uniform. She tore the arm on her old uniform.

The Starks are near the outlet stores. As Dad parks the car, Mom checks for her purse.

"Turn back," states Mom. "I forgot all my cash and credit cards!"

The uproar from the kids makes Dad put his hands on his ears.

"Are you sure?" asks Dad. "Look hard!"

"Yes, Dear," replies Mom. "I think my wallet is on that counter in the rear of our house."

"Did you leave it in that purse you wore last night?" asks Jill. "That purse with dark star patterns on it that you got for your birthday?"

"Yes," replies Mom. "That purse."

"Is it that purse that matches this shirt I have on?" asks Jill.

"Yes," says Mom. She's getting just a bit perturbed with Jill.

"Is it this purse that I'm holding?" asks Jill.

Mom turns to see that Jill has her purse. And inside is Mom's wallet!

"Nice work, Jill!" said Mom. "Now let's shop!"

22

Decodable Practice Passage 17B

Differentiated Instruction

A Advanced

Sort Words Have students choose pairs of words from the chart and write sentences using the pair of words *third, heard.* Write sentences using the pairs of words *store, boar; large, party.*

Objectives

- Identify characteristics of expository texts.
- Locate and use graphic features in text.
- Identify important ideas that support the main idea.
- Use the strategy for unknown words to define new vocabulary.

Comprehension Check

Have students discuss each question with a partner. Ask several pairs to share their responses.

Genre • Analysis
Why might expository nonfiction authors choose to organize their information with many short paragraphs? Possible response: It lets the reader easily find all the important points, one to a paragraph.

Graphic Sources • Evaluation
Why does the graph on page 68 show body and room temperatures and the temperature at which water freezes? Possible response: It lets the reader compare those temperatures to the temperatures in Al Aziziyah and Death Valley. It makes it easier to understand how hot those places are.

Important Ideas • Synthesis
How can you figure out the important ideas in the selection? Possible response: I can look at each paragraph and ask myself what is important. If I make a list of the important ideas as I go, I can look at all the important ideas and see what is most important.

Unknown Words
The word *base* has several meanings. Use a dictionary or glossary to define the word *base* as it is used on page 67. Possible response: On p. 67, the word *base* means the lowest part, or bottom.

Connect Text to Self
Which of nature's record holders presented in the text would you most like to visit? Explain your response. Answers will vary.

Strategy Response Log

INTERACT with TEXT

Have students list 2 or 3 important ideas presented in *Hottest, Coldest, Highest, Deepest* on p. 23 in the *Reader's and Writer's Notebook.*

Check Retelling

Have students retell the details of *Hottest, Coldest, Highest, Deepest* through p. 69. Encourage students to use the boldfaced words in their retellings.

Corrective feedback

If... the students leave out important details,
then... have students look back through the illustrations in the selection.

Small Group Time

DAY 3 **Break into small groups before revisiting *Hottest, Coldest, Highest, Deepest*.**

Teacher Led

SI Strategic Intervention	OL On-Level	A Advanced
Teacher Led p. DI•29 • Reinforce vocabulary • **Read/Revisit** *Hottest, Coldest, Highest, Deepest*	**Teacher Led** p. DI•34 • Expand vocabulary • **Read/Revisit** *Hottest, Coldest, Highest, Deepest*	**Teacher Led** p. DI•39 • Extend vocabulary • **Read/Revisit** *Hottest, Coldest, Highest, Deepest*

ELL Place English language learners in the groups that correspond to their reading abilities in English.

Practice Stations
- Let's Write
- Get Fluent
- Word Work

Independent Activities
- AudioText: *Hottest, Coldest, Highest, Deepest*
- *Reader's and Writers Notebook*
- Research and Inquiry

ELL

English Language Learners

Check Retelling To support retelling, review the multilingual summary for *Hottest, Coldest, Highest, Deepest* with the appropriate Retellings Cards to scaffold understanding.

DAY 3 Read and Comprehend

40–45 min

Objectives

- Use a dictionary or glossary to understand unknown words.

OPTION 1 Skills and Strategies, continued

Teach Unknown Words

Unknown Words Have students use a dictionary or glossary to determine the meaning, pronunciation, and syllabication of the word *current* at the end of p. 71, paragraph 2.

Corrective Feedback

If... students are unable to figure out the meaning of *current,*
then... model using a dictionary or glossary.

Model the Skill

Think Aloud When I look up *current* in a dictionary, I see two meanings: "a flow or stream of water, electricity, air, or any fluid" and "of or about the present time."

INTERACT with TEXT

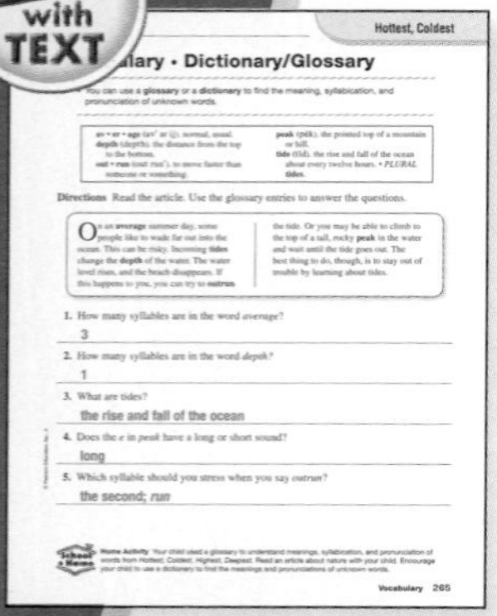

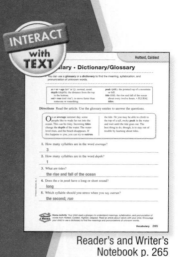

Reader's and Writer's Notebook p. 265

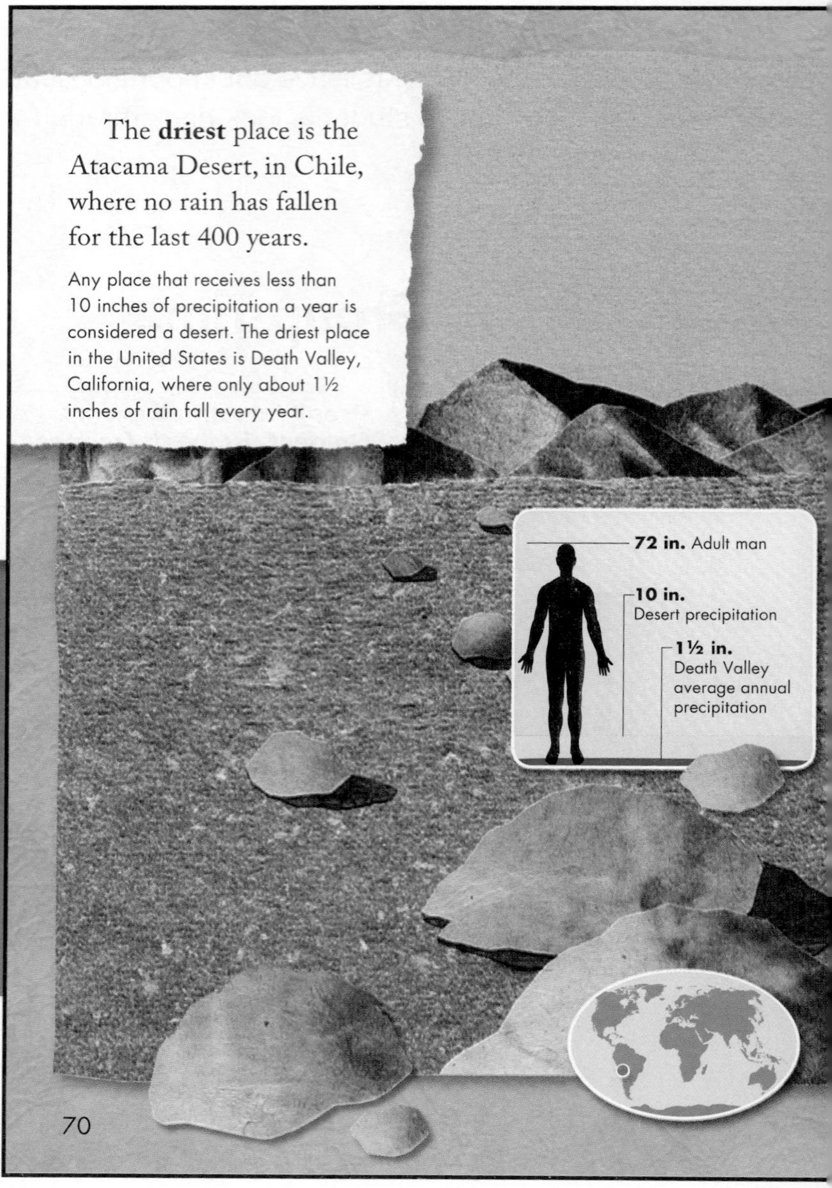

The **driest** place is the Atacama Desert, in Chile, where no rain has fallen for the last 400 years.

Any place that receives less than 10 inches of precipitation a year is considered a desert. The driest place in the United States is Death Valley, California, where only about 1½ inches of rain fall every year.

Student Edition pp. 70–71

Double Day Read! Multidraft Reading

If you chose . . .

Option 1 Return to the Extend Thinking instruction starting on p. 64–65.

Option 2 Read pp. 70–75. Use the Guide Comprehension and Extend Thinking instruction.

OPTION 2 Think Critically, continued

Higher-Order Thinking Skills

Unknown Words • Analysis Use context clues to tell the meaning of the word *annual* in the chart on page 70. Possible response: The chart shows that Death Valley receives 1 1/2 in. of average annual precipitation. In the text, I see that only about 1 1/2 inches of rain falls every year in Death Valley. *Annual* must mean "every year." When I look the word up in a dictionary, it says that *annual* means "happening every year or yearly."

Compare and Contrast • Evaluation How is the Atacama Desert in Chile both like and unlike Death Valley, California? Possible response: Like Death Valley, the Atacama Desert is a desert that receives very little precipitation. Unlike Death Valley, the Atacama Desert has received no rain at all for the last 400 years.

Since the passage says a "a narrow, strong air current," I know they mean the first definition. I see the word has two syllables, stressing the first, and it is pronounced kėr′ ənt.

The **windiest** spot on Earth is atop Mount Washington, in New Hampshire. A wind speed of 231 miles per hour has been recorded there.

It is also very windy near the tops of the world's highest mountains, the Himalayas. Many of these peaks are tall enough to reach the jet stream, a narrow, strong air current that is found above 28,000 feet.

71

Draw Conclusions • Synthesis What would be a challenge to people living in the Atacama Desert? Why? Possible response: Finding drinking water would be a challenge, because no rain falls there.

On Their Own

Have students use a dictionary to figure out the meaning, pronunciation, and syllabication of the word *peaks* on p. 71, paragraph 2. For additional practice, use *Reader's and Writer's Notebook* p. 265.

Differentiated Instruction

A Advanced

Have students look back at what they learned about Al Aziziyah, Libya, and remind them that it is located in the Sahara Desert. Have students use what they learned about deserts on p. 64 to predict the precipitation each year in Al Aziziyah. (Because it is in a desert, it receives less than 10 inches of precipitation a year.)

Connect to Science

The Atacama Desert is so dry that few things can live there. In some portions of the desert, there are not even any insects. In some areas, moisture collects from fog, allowing plants to grow.

ELL

English Language Learners

Vocabulary: Unknown words

After reviewing the meaning of precipitation, have partners ask and answer these questions using the word: *What is one kind of precipitation? What is another kind of precipitation? Does a desert have much precipitation?*

Objectives

- Identify important ideas to aid comprehension.

OPTION 1 Skills and Strategies, continued

Teach Important Ideas

Important Ideas Remind students that important ideas summarize a selection or tell what it is all about. It helps to understand what you read if you pause to find the important idea in each paragraph as you read. What is the important idea on page 72?

Corrective Feedback

If... students have difficulty determining the important idea,
then... model how to find important ideas.

Model the Skill

Think Aloud I notice the word *highest* is in bold type. That makes it stand out and look important. It says that Angel Falls is the world's highest waterfall. I need to read on, however, to be sure if that is the important idea of the page.

The world's **highest** waterfall is Angel Falls, in Venezuela. It is 3,212 feet high.
Angel Falls is more than seventeen times higher than Niagara Falls (180 feet), in New York State. Victoria Falls, in Zimbabwe, Africa, carries more water than any other waterfall. It is 355 feet high.
Angel Falls 3,212 ft.
Victoria Falls 355 ft.
Empire State Building 1,250 ft.
Niagara Falls 180 ft.
72

Student Edition pp. 72–73

Draw Conclusions • Evaluation Reread the bottom half of page 73. Have volcanic eruptions existed throughout modern times? Yes, volcanoes, including Mount Etna, have been erupting regularly since 1500 B.C.

OPTION 2 Think Critically, continued

Higher-Order Thinking Skills

Important Ideas • Synthesis Why might the author have boldfaced two words in the bottom half of page 73? Possible response: Sangay is the world's most active volcano. If the author only boldfaced *active*, the sentence would not make its point clearly.

On Their Own

Have students read the rest of the page and decide if Angel Falls being the highest waterfall is the important idea on the page. Have them explain their reasoning.

The **deepest** spot in the ocean is the Marianas Trench, in the Philippines. It is 36,202 feet deep.

The average depth of the world's oceans is about 3 miles, or 16,000 feet. The lowest spot on dry land is the shore of the Dead Sea, 1,100 feet below sea level.

The world's **most active** volcano is Sangay, in Ecuador. Since 1937 it has erupted once every 24 hours on average. It once erupted more than 400 times in a single day.

Other very active volcanoes include Colima, in Mexico (it has erupted regularly since 1560); Aso, in Japan (erupting since 533); and Mount Etna, in Italy (erupting regularly since 1500 B.C.).

73

Graphic Sources • Analysis Look at the charts on pages 66 and 72. If you were to add Angel Falls to the first chart, where would it go? In the middle between the Empire State Building and Lake Baikal.

Differentiated Instruction

SI Strategic Intervention

Use details Help students to understand the details about waterfalls on p. 72 by explaining the phrase "carries more water." (A waterfall is measured not just by how high it is, but by how much water falls from the top to the bottom of the waterfall.)

Connect to Science

Explain that some animals are uniquely adapted to living in or near waterfalls. An example is Australia's waterfall frog, whose tadpoles attach themselves by the mouth to rocks in fast-flowing streams.

ELL

English Language Learners

Vocabulary: Compound words Use the illustration p. 72 to review that *waterfall* is a compound word made of two smaller words, *water* and *fall*. Say, A waterfall is water that falls. Then provide the compound words *airplane, flashlight, bedroom,* and *mailbox.* Have students use the smaller words to explain the meaning of the compound words.

Objectives

◎ Use graphic sources to aid comprehension.

OPTION 1 Skills and Strategies, continued

Teach Graphic Sources

◎ **Graphic Sources** Have students read about Mount Rainier on p. 75. Then ask students to use the text and the graph on p. 75 to explain how showing the height of an adult man helps us to understand how much snow falls on Mount Rainier.

Corrective Feedback

If... students are unable to explain why the fact is useful,
then... use the Model to help them interpret graphic sources.

Model the Skill

Think Aloud On the graph, I see the fact that 1,200 inches of snow, which is 100 feet, fell on Mount Rainier in one year. I also see the figure of a six-foot-tall man.

The **most extreme tides** occur in the Bay of Fundy, in Nova Scotia, Canada. There the water level rises and falls more than 50 feet every 6 hours.

The tide here comes in so fast that it can overtake a person trying to outrun it.

74

Student Edition pp. 74–75

OPTION 2 Think Critically, continued

Higher-Order Thinking Skills

◎ **Graphic Sources • Analysis** Look at the picture on page 74. How can you tell that people can live near places with extreme tides? The picture shows houses.

Review **Main Idea and Details • Analysis** What is the main idea of *Hottest, Coldest, Highest, Deepest?* What details support that idea? The main idea is that there are places on Earth that hold records for being extreme. The author tells many places with extremes, such as Mount Rainier, with more than 100 feet of snow in a year and a volcano in Ecuador that once erupted 400 times in a single day.

Can everyone picture the size of a six-foot man? (yes) Is 100 feet a little taller or a lot taller than a six-foot man? (a lot taller) The author includes the fact to help us understand how high 100 feet is.

On Their Own

Have students explain another way they could use a graphic source to show an important idea on p. 74.

The **snowiest** place on Earth is Mount Rainier, in Washington State. One year, more than 1,200 inches of snow fell there.

Mount Rainier is covered in snow the whole year. Some of the snow has formed glaciers, masses of ice that slowly move down the mountain under their own weight.

75

Comprehension Check

Spiral Review

Generalize • Evaluate Do you think most people would want to visit all the places mentioned in the text? Possible response: No, people probably would not want to see some of the places, such as the hottest and coldest places on Earth.

Cause and Effect • Synthesis What do you think is the cause of the dry climate in the Atacama Desert and Death Valley? Possible response: the lack of precipitation

Check Predictions Have students return to the predictions they made earlier and confirm whether they were accurate.

Differentiated Instruction

SI Strategic Intervention

Graphic sources Have students work in pairs to explain how graphic sources help them identify the main idea and an important detail on p. 75. Have one student look for boldfaced words and another look at type sizes on the page.

A Advanced

Explain that the Mi'kmaq people of North America believed the tides in the Bay of Fundy were caused by a giant whale splashing in the water. Have students discuss how this concept could explain a place with extreme tides.

Connect to Science

Explain that the surface of the earth can be changed by glaciers like the ones at Mount Rainier. Glaciers slide over the rock on which they lie, and one of the Mount Rainier glaciers was once measured moving as fast as 29 inches per day.

ELL English Language Learners

Monitor comprehension Read aloud the first sentence on p. 74. Model using the reading strategy of monitor and clarify by saying: I wonder what most extreme tides are. The sentence doesn't give me a clue. I will read on to find the answer. Read the second and third sentences and then ask students to use the information to explain what an extreme tide is.

Objectives

- ◎ Locate and use information in graphic features.
- ◎ Identify important ideas.

Check Retelling
SUCCESS PREDICTOR

Plan to Assess Retelling

- ☑ **Week 1** Assess Strategic Intervention students.
- ☑ **This week assess Advanced students.**
- ☐ **Week 3** Assess Strategic Intervention students.
- ☐ **Week 4** Assess On-Level students.
- ☐ **Week 5** Assess any students you have not yet checked during this unit.

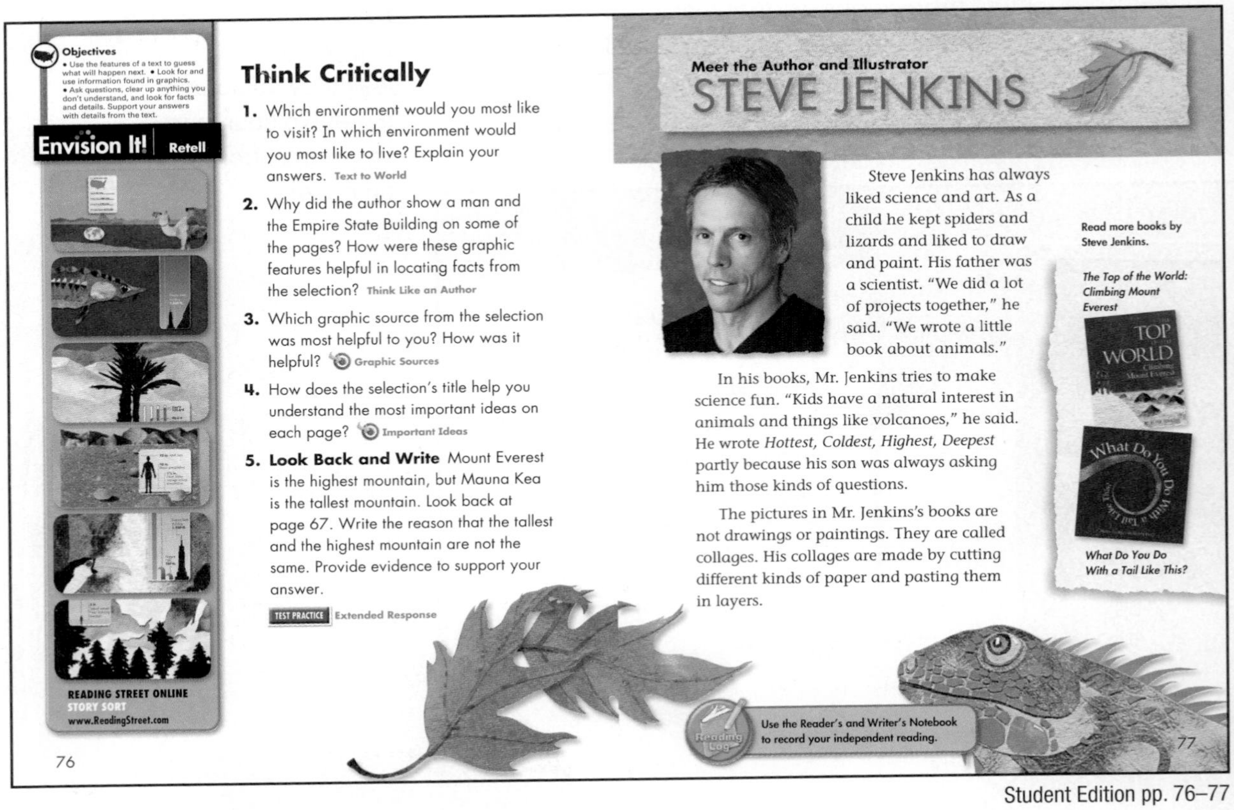

Objectives
• Use the features of a text to guess what will happen next. • Look for and use information found in graphics. • Ask questions, clear up anything you don't understand, and look for facts and details. Support your answers with details from the text.

Envision It! | **Retell**

READING STREET ONLINE
STORY SORT
www.ReadingStreet.com

Think Critically

1. Which environment would you most like to visit? In which environment would you most like to live? Explain your answers. Text to World
2. Why did the author show a man and the Empire State Building on some of the pages? How were these graphic features helpful in locating facts from the selection? Think Like an Author
3. Which graphic source from the selection was most helpful to you? How was it helpful? ◎ Graphic Sources
4. How does the selection's title help you understand the most important ideas on each page? ◎ Important Ideas
5. **Look Back and Write** Mount Everest is the highest mountain, but Mauna Kea is the tallest mountain. Look back at page 67. Write the reason that the tallest and the highest mountain are not the same. Provide evidence to support your answer.

TEST PRACTICE Extended Response

Meet the Author and Illustrator
STEVE JENKINS

Steve Jenkins has always liked science and art. As a child he kept spiders and lizards and liked to draw and paint. His father was a scientist. "We did a lot of projects together," he said. "We wrote a little book about animals."

In his books, Mr. Jenkins tries to make science fun. "Kids have a natural interest in animals and things like volcanoes," he said. He wrote *Hottest, Coldest, Highest, Deepest* partly because his son was always asking him those kinds of questions.

The pictures in Mr. Jenkins's books are not drawings or paintings. They are called collages. His collages are made by cutting different kinds of paper and pasting them in layers.

Read more books by Steve Jenkins.

The Top of the World: Climbing Mount Everest

What Do You Do With a Tail Like This?

Reading Log — Use the Reader's and Writer's Notebook to record your independent reading.

76 77

Student Edition pp. 76–77

Retelling

Envision It! Have students work in pairs to retell the selection, using the Envision It! Retelling Cards as prompts. Remind students that they should accurately describe the main topic and important ideas and use key vocabulary in their retellings. Monitor students' retellings.

Scoring rubric

Top-Score Response A top-score response makes connections beyond the text, describes the main topic and important ideas using accurate information, evaluates graphic sources, and draws conclusions from the text.

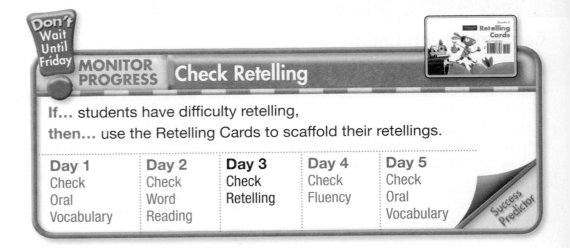

Don't Wait Until Friday **MONITOR PROGRESS** **Check Retelling**

If... students have difficulty retelling,
then... use the Retelling Cards to scaffold their retellings.

Day 1	Day 2	Day 3	Day 4	Day 5
Check Oral Vocabulary	Check Word Reading	Check Retelling	Check Fluency	Check Oral Vocabulary

Success Predictor

Think Critically

Text to world

1. Responses will vary. Possible response: I would most like to visit Mount Everest, because it is the highest mountain in the world. I would most like to live near Mauna Kea, because it is in Hawaii.

Think like an author

2. The author showed a man and the Empire State Building on some of the pages to compare the size of things he was talking about to things that we already know. These graphic features helped us locate facts because we can start with facts that we understand.

Graphic sources

3. Responses will vary. Possible response: The graphic source I found most helpful was the chart on p. 72, because it showed the height of all the waterfalls in the text and compared them to the height of the Empire State Building.

Important ideas

4. The selection's title helps me to understand the most important ideas on each page because it reminds me that the text is about places that are the most extreme in nature.

Writing on Demand

5. **Look Back and Write** To build writing fluency, assign a 10–15 minute time limit.

Suggest that students use a prewriting strategy, such as brainstorming or using a graphic organizer, to organize their ideas. Remind them to establish a topic sentence and support it with facts, details, or explanations. As students finish, encourage them to reread their responses, revise for organization and support, and proofread for errors in grammar and conventions.

Scoring rubric

Top-Score Response A top-score response uses details to tell why the highest mountain is not the same as the tallest mountain.

A top-score response should include:

- Mount Everest is the highest mountain because its peak is 29,028 feet above sea level.
- Mauna Kea is the tallest mountain because it is 33,476 feet tall when measured from its base to its top.
- Mauna Kea is taller than Mount Everest because if both mountains started at the same place, Mauna Kea would tower over Mount Everest.

Differentiated Instruction

SI Strategic Intervention

Model organizing the information about Mount Everest and Mauna Kea into a chart with columns labeled Mountain, *Record (highest, tallest), How it is measured (above sea level, base to top), Total height.* Have students use the chart to complete the writing exercise.

Meet the Author

Have students read about author Steve Jenkins on p. 77. Ask them why he decided to write *Hottest, Coldest, Highest, Deepest.*

Independent Reading

After students enter their independent reading information into their Reading Logs or a journal, have them summarize what they have read. Remind students that a summary should be no more than a few sentences about the main idea of a text.

ELL

English Language Learners

Retelling Use the Retelling Cards to discuss the selection with students. Place the cards in an incorrect order and have volunteers correct the mistake. Then have students explain where each card should go as they describe the sequence of the selection.

Objectives
- Read grade-level text with appropriate phrasing.
- Reread for fluency.
- Locate and use information from bar graphs.

Model Fluency
Appropriate Phrasing and Punctuation Cues

Model fluent reading

Have students turn to p. 68 of *Hottest, Coldest, Highest, Deepest.* Have students follow along as you read the page. Tell them to listen as you make a short pause for commas that separate place names, such as Al Aziziyah, Libya. Point out that you also pause at commas used to group words into phrases that tell where the places are, such as "in Death Valley, California." Explain that you will make a short pause at the commas and a longer pause at the periods so you can read with appropriate phrasing.

Guide practice

Have students follow along as you read the page again. Then have them reread the page as a group without you until they read with appropriate phrasing, grouping words as needed. Ask questions to be sure that they comprehend the text. Continue in the same way with p. 69.

Reread for Fluency

Corrective feedback

If... students are having difficulty reading with correct phrasing, **then...** prompt:

- Where can we break up this sentence? Which words are related?
- Read the sentence again. Pause after each group of words.
- Tell me the sentence. Now read it with pauses after each group of words.

ROUTINE Oral Reading

1. **Read** Have students read p. 70 of *Hottest, Coldest, Highest, Deepest* orally.
2. **Reread** To achieve optimal fluency, students should reread the text three or four times.
3. **Corrective Feedback** Have students read aloud without you. Provide feedback about their phrasing, helping students to group phrases by pausing at punctuation cues. Listen for appropriate phrasing.

Routines Flip Chart

Research and Study Skills
Bar Graphs

Teach

Ask students when they are likely to see bar graphs as they read. Students may mention textbooks, newspapers, or magazines. Display a bar graph and use it to review these terms:

- A graph shows data, or information, in visual form. A special kind of graph, called a bar graph, uses bars to compare numbers or amounts.
- Bar graphs usually show numbers rounded to the nearest ten or hundred, rather than exact numbers.
- Bar graphs have a title that tells what the graph is about.
- The horizontal and vertical lines of the graph are called axes. One axis has a scale of numbers or amounts.

Guide practice

Discuss these questions:

How can you compare things with a bar graph without looking at the numbers? (You can compare the lengths of the bars.)

How can you find information in a bar graph? (First, read the label to see what the bar represents. Then see what number is near the end of the bar.)

Have students tell what is being compared in the bar graph you displayed. Direct their attention to the labels on the axes. Then ask questions specific to the information in the graph.

On their own

Have students review and complete p. 266 of the *Reader's and Writer's Notebook.*

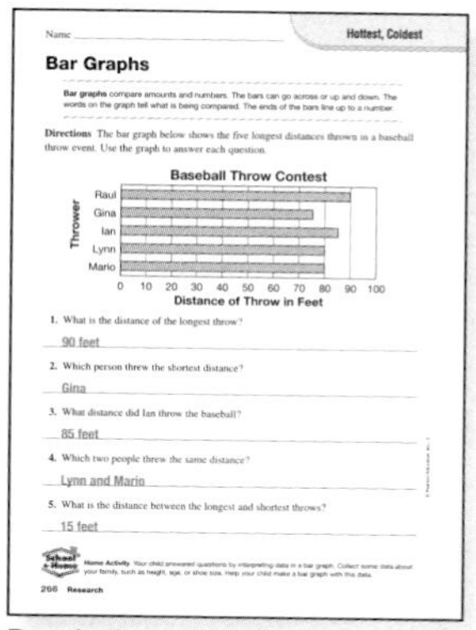
Name ____________ Hottest, Coldest

Bar Graphs

Bar graphs compare amounts and numbers. The bars can go across or up and down. The words on the graph tell what is being compared. The ends of the bars line up to a number.

Directions The bar graph below shows the five longest distances thrown in a baseball throw event. Use the graph to answer each question.

1. What is the distance of the longest throw?
   90 feet
2. Which person threw the shortest distance?
   Gina
3. What distance did Ian throw the baseball?
   85 feet
4. Which two people threw the same distance?
   Lynn and Mario
5. What is the distance between the longest and shortest throws?
   15 feet

Home Activity Your child answered questions by interpreting data in a bar graph. Collect some data about your family, such as height, age, or shoe size. Help your child make a bar graph with this data.

266 Research

Reader's and Writer's Notebook p. 266

English Language Learners

Graphs Help students create a simple bar graph. List the colors *red, yellow, blue, pink, green, purple* on the board and have students vote for their favorite of these colors. Then have students put the information into bar graph form with number of students on the vertical axis and colors on the horizontal axis. Ask students questions they can answer using the information on their graphs: *Which color is the students' favorite? How many students like the color green? Do more students like pink or purple best?*

Objectives

- Analyze data for usefulness.
- Identify and use subject and object pronouns correctly.
- Spell frequently misspelled words.

Research and Inquiry
Analyze

Teach Tell students that today they will analyze their research findings and may want to change the focus of their original inquiry question.

Model Think Aloud Originally I thought it would be easy to discover the fastest runner on Earth. However, when I researched the question, I discovered that there are many people who are the fastest. I also realized it is interesting to find out how these runners got to be so fast. I think I am going to focus on how runners who set records train. Now my inquiry question is *How do runners get fast enough to set records?* I can talk with my neighbor who runs on the track team in high school.

Guide practice Have students analyze their findings. They may need to refocus their inquiry question to better fit the information they found. Explain to students that if they have difficulty improving their focus they can ask a reference librarian or a local expert for guidance.

Remind students that they can use a graphic source, such as a bar graph to provide a visual representation of their findings.

On their own Pair students to evaluate research findings. Ask partners to consider if the research opened any new avenues of inquiry that should be addressed.

Conventions
Subject and Object Pronouns

Review Remind students that this week they learned about subject and object pronouns:

- A subject pronoun is used as the subject of a sentence. *I, you, he, she, it, we,* and *they* are subject pronouns.
- An object pronoun is used after an action verb or as the object of a preposition. *Me, you, him, her, it, us,* and *them* are object pronouns.

Daily Fix-It Use Daily Fix-It numbers 5 and 6 in the right margin.

Connect to oral language Have the class use pronouns to complete these sentence frames orally.

> **_______ used a thermometer to measure the temperature.**
> **Look at the tallest peaks. Scientists measure _______.**

On their own For additional support, use *Let's Practice It!* page 232 on the *Teacher Resources DVD-ROM.*

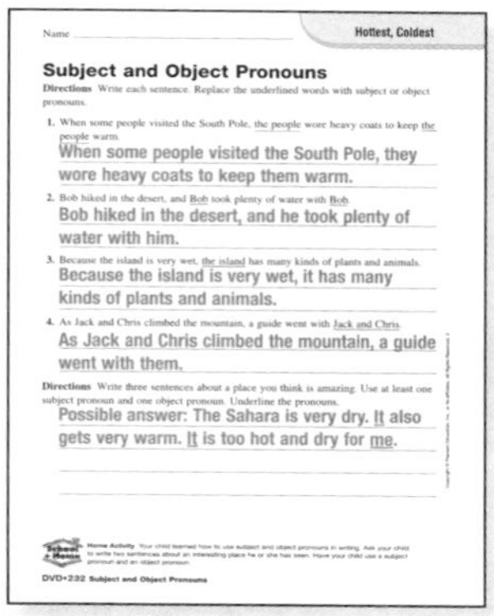
Name ______ Hottest, Coldest

Subject and Object Pronouns

Directions Write each sentence. Replace the underlined words with subject or object pronouns.

1. When some people visited the South Pole, the people wore heavy coats to keep the people warm.
When some people visited the South Pole, they wore heavy coats to keep them warm.
2. Bob hiked in the desert, and Bob took plenty of water with Bob.
Bob hiked in the desert, and he took plenty of water with him.
3. Because the island is very wet, the island has many kinds of plants and animals.
Because the island is very wet, it has many kinds of plants and animals.
4. As Jack and Chris climbed the mountain, a guide went with Jack and Chris.
As Jack and Chris climbed the mountain, a guide went with them.

Directions Write three sentences about a place you think is amazing. Use at least one subject pronoun and one object pronoun. Underline the pronouns.

Possible answer: The Sahara is very dry. It also gets very warm. It is too hot and dry for me.

DVD•232 Subject and Object Pronouns

Let's Practice It!
TR DVD•232

Spelling
Vowels: *r*-Controlled

Frequently misspelled words Students often misspell the words *another, brother,* and *heard* because they have the same sound spelled different ways. I'm going to read a sentence. Choose the correct word to complete the sentence and write it correctly.

> 1. **May I have _____ piece of pizza, please?** (another)
> 2. **I didn't see lightning, but I _______ thunder.** (heard)
> 3. **Lauren is my sister, and Sean is my _______.** (brother)

Students can practice reading and spelling these high-frequency words to develop automatic recognition.

On their own For additional support, use *Reader's and Writer's Notebook* p. 267.

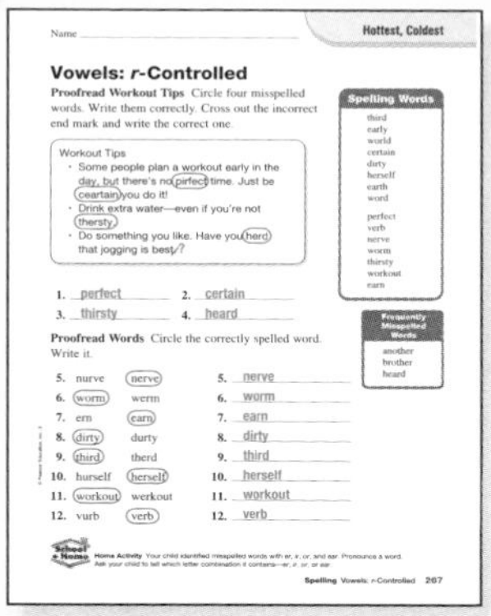
Name ______ Hottest, Coldest

Vowels: *r*-Controlled

Proofread Workout Tips Circle four misspelled words. Write them correctly. Cross out the incorrect end mark and write the correct one.

Workout Tips
- Some people plan a workout early in the day, but there's no pirfect time. Just be ceartain you do it!
- Drink extra water—even if you're not thersty.
- Do something you like. Have you herd that jogging is best?

1. perfect 2. certain
3. thirsty 4. heard

Proofread Words Circle the correctly spelled word. Write it.

5.	nurve	nerve	nerve
6.	worm	wern	worm
7.	ern	earn	earn
8.	dirty	durty	dirty
9.	third	therd	third
10.	hurself	herself	herself
11.	workout	werkout	workout
12.	vurb	verb	verb

Spelling Words: third, early, world, certain, dirty, herself, earth, word, perfect, verb, nerve, worm, thirsty, workout, earn

Frequently Misspelled Words: another, brother, heard

Spelling Vowels: *r*-Controlled 267

Reader's and Writer's
Notebook p. 267

Daily Fix-It

5. Mr. Jackson showed Tracy and I a picture of cammels in the desert. *(me; camels)*
6. Sand were blowing in the dessert like a snowstorm. *(was; desert)*

Objectives

- Understand the criteria for writing an effective imaginative story.

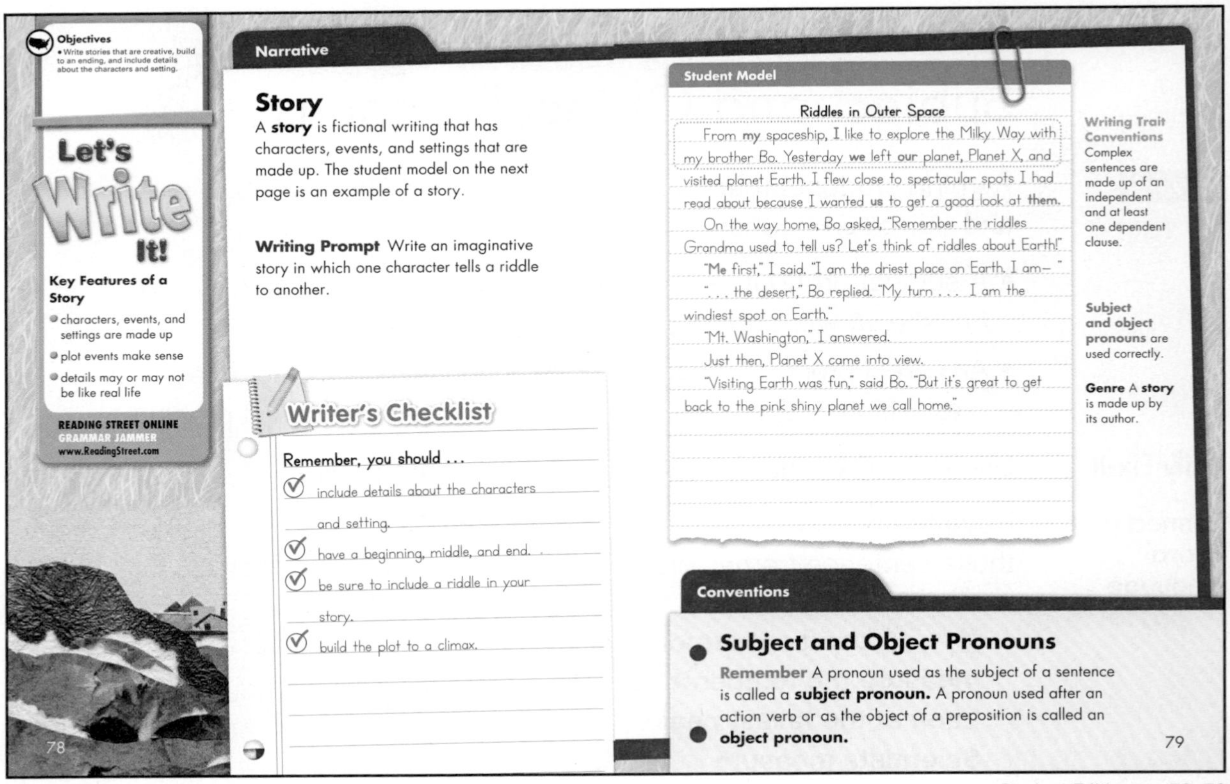

Objectives
• Write stories that are creative, build to an ending, and include details about the characters and setting.

Let's Write It!

Key Features of a Story
- characters, events, and settings are made up
- plot events make sense
- details may or may not be like real life

READING STREET ONLINE
GRAMMAR JAMMER
www.ReadingStreet.com

Narrative

Story

A **story** is fictional writing that has characters, events, and settings that are made up. The student model on the next page is an example of a story.

Writing Prompt Write an imaginative story in which one character tells a riddle to another.

Writer's Checklist

Remember, you should ...
- include details about the characters and setting.
- have a beginning, middle, and end.
- be sure to include a riddle in your story.
- build the plot to a climax.

Student Model

Riddles in Outer Space

From **my** spaceship, I like to explore the Milky Way with my brother Bo. Yesterday **we** left **our** planet, Planet X, and visited planet Earth. I flew close to spectacular spots I had read about because I wanted **us** to get a good look at **them**.

On the way home, Bo asked, "Remember the riddles Grandma used to tell us? Let's think of riddles about Earth!"

"Me first," I said. "I am the driest place on Earth. I am– "

". . . the desert," Bo replied. "My turn . . . I am the windiest spot on Earth."

"Mt. Washington," I answered.

Just then, Planet X came into view.

"Visiting Earth was fun," said Bo. "But it's great to get back to the pink shiny planet we call home."

Writing Trait Conventions Complex sentences are made up of an independent and at least one dependent clause.

Subject and object pronouns are used correctly.

Genre A **story** is made up by its author.

Conventions

Subject and Object Pronouns

Remember A pronoun used as the subject of a sentence is called a **subject pronoun.** A pronoun used after an action verb or as the object of a preposition is called an **object pronoun.**

78 79

Student Edition pp. 78–79

Let's Write It!
Imaginative Story

Teach

Use pp. 78–79 in the Student Edition. Direct students to read the key features of an imaginative story, which appear on p. 78. Remind students that they can refer to the information in the Writer's Checklist as they write their own imaginative story.

Read the student model on p. 79. Point out the characters, setting, and plot in the model.

Connect to conventions

Remind students that subject pronouns are used as subjects of sentences and object pronouns are used after action verbs or as objects of prepositions. Point out the correct use of subject and object pronouns in the model.

Writing—Imaginative Story
Writer's Craft: Dialogue

Display rubric Display Scoring Rubric 17 from the *Teacher Resources DVD–ROM* and review the criteria for each trait under each score. Then, using the student writing model in the Student Edition, choose students to explain whether the model should score a 4 for each of the traits and why. If a student offers that the model should score below 4 for a particular trait, the student should provide support for that response. Remind students that this is the rubric that will be used to evaluate the imaginative stories they will begin writing.

Scoring Rubric: Imaginative Story

	4	3	2	1
Focus/Ideas	Vivid story, well-developed characters, detailed setting, plot building to climax	Story with adequate characters, setting, and plot development	Story lacks focus, developed characters, detailed setting, and plot development	No focus or development of characters, setting, or plot
Organization	Clear beginning, middle, and end; clear sequence of events	Beginning, middle, and end; able to follow sequence of events	Unclear beginning, middle, and end; unclear sequence of events	No beginning, middle, or end; no sequence of events
Voice	Effective use of dialogue helps develop characters	Some effective use of dialogue	Dialogue often flat and ineffective	No dialogue used
Word Choice	Strong use of vivid, precise words	Some use of precise words	Few precise words	Vague, general words
Sentences	Clear sentences of various lengths and types; strong variety of beginnings	Sentences of a few lengths and types; variety of beginnings	Sentences of similar length and type; weak variety of beginnings	No attempt at sentences of various lengths and types; no variety of beginnings
Conventions	Few, if any, errors; correct use of subject and object pronouns	Several minor errors; correct use of subject and object pronouns	Many errors; a few errors in use of subject and object pronouns	Numerous errors; incorrect use of subject and object pronouns

Story sequence chart Have students get out the story sequence charts that they worked on yesterday. If their charts are not complete, allow time for them to generate ideas to complete their story lines.

Write You will be using your story sequence charts as you write the draft of your imaginative story. When you are drafting, don't worry if your composition does not sound exactly as you want it to. You will have a chance to revise it tomorrow.

Differentiated Instruction

SI Strategic Intervention

Using the model Have pairs of students complete a story sequence chart based on the student model on p. 79 of the Student Edition. Then have them compare it to their own story sequence charts. Ask them to decide if their charts will help them write a composition with the same qualities as the model. Monitor their discussion and provide feedback.

ELL English Language Learners

Understanding the rubric Read the rubric aloud and help students understand it. Then focus on the score 4. Ask students to explain in their own words what qualities a score 4 story has.

Objectives

- Write a first draft of an imaginative story.
- Write dialogue.

Writing, continued
Writer's Craft: Dialogue

MINI-LESSON

Writing Dialogue

Introduce Explain to students that dialogue between characters can make a story more interesting and lively to read. Dialogue should sound similar to natural speech, or the way people speak. Because students' stories must include a riddle that one character tells another, it's a good idea to write the riddle as dialogue. They may include other dialogue if they like.

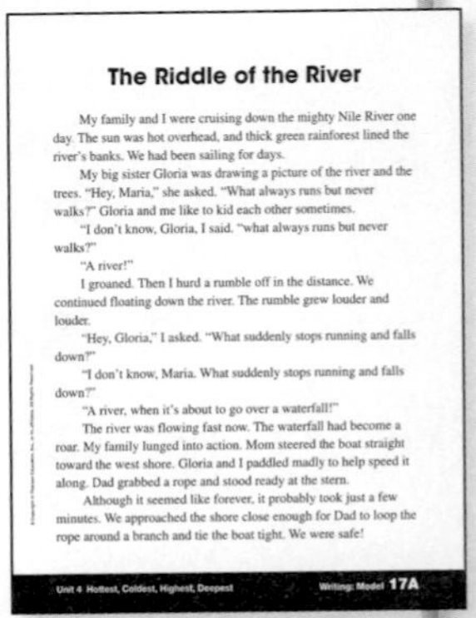
The Riddle of the River

My family and I were cruising down the mighty Nile River one day. The sun was hot overhead, and thick green rainforest lined the river's banks. We had been sailing for days.

My big sister Gloria was drawing a picture of the river and the trees. "Hey, Maria," she asked. "What always runs but never walks?" Gloria and me like to kid each other sometimes.

"I don't know, Gloria, I said. "what always runs but never walks?"

"A river!"

I groaned. Then I hurd a rumble off in the distance. We continued floating down the river. The rumble grew louder and louder.

"Hey, Gloria," I asked. "What suddenly stops running and falls down?"

"I don't know, Maria. What suddenly stops running and falls down?"

"A river, when it's about to go over a waterfall!"

The river was flowing fast now. The waterfall had become a roar. My family lunged into action. Mom steered the boat straight toward the west shore. Gloria and I paddled madly to help speed it along. Dad grabbed a rope and stood ready at the stern.

Although it seemed like forever, it probably took just a few minutes. We approached the shore close enough for Dad to loop the rope around a branch and tie the boat tight. We were safe!

Unit 4 Hottest, Coldest, Highest, Deepest Writing: Model 17A

Writing Transparency 17A, TR DVD

Display the Drafting Tips for students. Remind them that the focus of drafting is to get their ideas down in an organized way. Then display Writing Transparency 17A.

Drafting Tips

- ✔ To get started, review your story sequence chart.
- ✔ Make sure to include details about your characters and setting and to build your events up to a climax.
- ✔ Don't worry about grammar and mechanics when drafting. You'll concentrate on them during the proofreading stage.

Think Aloud I'm going to write the first paragraph of my imaginative story. It will describe the setting in detail. When I draft, I develop my story line. I don't worry about revising or proofreading because those tasks come later. I'll refer to my story sequence chart to make sure I include all the elements of a good imaginative story: characters, a setting, and events that build up to a climax.

Explain the process of drafting using the Writing Transparency. Direct students to use the Drafting Tips to guide them in writing their drafts. Remind them to include dialogue in their stories.

ROUTINE **Quick Write for Fluency** Team Talk

1. **Talk** Pairs talk about the characters in their stories.
2. **Write** Each student writes a brief paragraph describing his or her characters, using subject and object pronouns correctly.
3. **Share** Partners check each other's writing for the correct use of subject and object pronouns. Then each partner asks the other a question about his or her characters.

Routines Flip Chart

Wrap Up Your Day

- ✔ **Build Concepts** What makes the places you read about unique?
- ✔ **Graphic Sources** How did the graphic sources help you to clarify the information?
- ✔ **Important Ideas** How were you able to determine the important ideas in the text?

Differentiated Instruction

SI Strategic Intervention

Using resources If students are having difficulty thinking of a riddle to include in their stories, provide books of riddles or examples downloaded from the Internet.

Preview DAY 4

Tell students that tomorrow they will read about an American legend.

Objectives

- Expand the weekly concept.
- Develop oral vocabulary.

Today at a Glance

Oral Vocabulary
weaken, ranger

Phonics/Word Analysis
Irregular plurals

Genre
Legend

Reading
"Paul Bunyan and the Great Lakes"

Let's Learn It!
Fluency: Appropriate phrasing and punctuation clues
Vocabulary: ◉ Unknown Words
Media Literacy: Weather Forecast

Research and Inquiry
Synthesize

Spelling
Vowels: *r*-Controlled

Conventions
Subject and object pronouns

Writing
Imaginative story

Concept Talk

Question of the Week

What makes nature's record holders unique?

Expand the concept

Remind students that this week they have read about some places and things in nature that hold records because they are so extreme. Tell students that today they will read a legend that explains how America's Great Lakes came to be. These lakes are so large it would take a *sprinter* a long time to run around them.

Anchored Talk

Develop oral vocabulary

Have students use text features, including boldfaced words, charts, and maps, to review pp. 70–75 of *Hottest, Coldest, Highest, Deepest.* Discuss the Amazing Words *sprinter* and *acrobat.* Add these and other concept-related words to the concept map. Use the following questions to develop students' understanding of the concept. Remind students to ask and answer questions with appropriate detail and to build on other students' answers.

- Picture a *sprinter* trying to outrun the Bay of Fundy. Did you ever have to run away from something very quickly?
- A person who skis from the top of Mount Rainier has to be quite an *acrobat.* Do you know anyone who is a good *acrobat*?

Strategy Response Log

INTERACT with TEXT

Have students complete p. 23 in the *Reader's and Writer's Notebook.* Then have students summarize the important ideas that they found in the selection.

Oral Vocabulary
Amazing Words

Amazing Words Oral Vocabulary Routine

Teach Amazing Words

1. **Introduce** Write the word *weaken* on the board. Have students say it with you. Yesterday, we read that the snowiest place on Earth is Mount Rainier. How might all that snow *weaken* a person who tried to climb Mount Rainier? Have students determine a definition of *weaken.* (To *weaken* something means to take away some of its power.)
2. **Demonstrate** Have students answer questions to demonstrate understanding. What things might *weaken* a tree? (Possible responses: lack of water, damage from insects)
3. **Apply** Have students apply their understanding. Which of these things might *weaken* the roof of a house: high winds or a butterfly?

See p. OV•2 to teach *ranger.*

Routines Flip Chart

Apply Amazing Words As students read "Paul Bunyan and the Great Lakes" on pp. 80–83, have them think about whether walking a mile would *weaken* Paul Bunyan, and if he would make a good forest *ranger.*

Connect to reading As students read today's selection about the legendary Paul Bunyan, have them think about how the Question of the Week and the Amazing Words *weaken* and *ranger*, apply to the story of Paul Bunyan and how the Great Lakes were created.

ELL Produce Oral Language Use the Day 4 instruction on ELL Poster 17 to extend and enrich language.

ELL Poster 17

Amazing Words

evergreen	champ
lumber	sprinter
competitor	acrobat
plunge	weaken
valuable	ranger

ELL

English Language Learners

Vocabulary: Activate prior knowledge Use photos from the Internet or magazines to show images of forest or park rangers. Use them to discuss with students what a ranger does, including keeping people and animals safe, fighting fires, educating the public, and looking for people who are lost.

DAY 4 Get Ready to Read

Objectives

- Read and identify words with irregular plurals.
- Read words fluently independent of context.

Word Analysis Review
Irregular Plurals

Review irregular plurals To review last week's word analysis skill, write *children, people, teeth*, and *leaves.* You studied words like these last week. What do you know about words like these, which have irregular plural forms? (The plurals are not formed by simply adding an *-s* or *-es* to the base word.) Have students read the word *children.* What is the singular form of *children*? *(child)* Of *people*? *(person)* Continue in the same way for *teeth (tooth)* and *leaves (leaf).*

Corrective feedback If students are unable to answer the questions about irregular plurals, refer them to Sound-Spelling Card 140.

Guide practice Draw a three-column chart with the heads Singular Form; *-f, -fe* to *-ves;* and *Irregular Plural.* Write the singular forms of the words in the first column. We will work together to place irregular plurals of words in the chart. Listen as I say the singular form of each word. Then you say the plural form and tell me which column to write in. Write each word in the appropriate column. Then have students read the words.

Singular Form	*-f, -fe* to *-ves*	Irregular Plural
life	lives	
sheep		sheep
half	halves	
mouse		mice

On their own For additional practice, use *Let's Practice It!* page 233 on the *Teacher Resources DVD-ROM.*

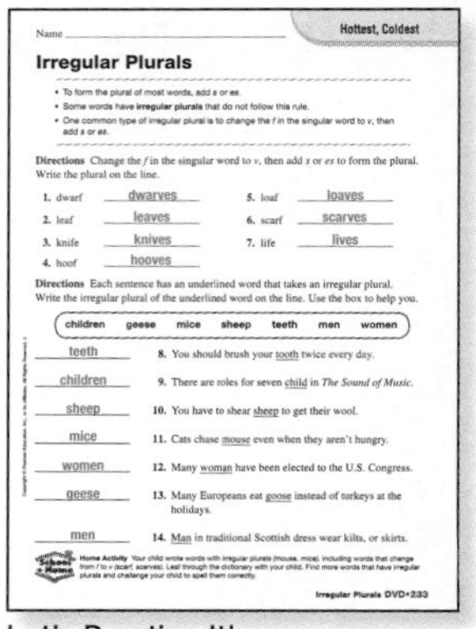
Name ____________ Hottest, Coldest

Irregular Plurals

- To form the plural of most words, add *s* or *es.*
- Some words have **irregular plurals** that do not follow this rule.
- One common type of irregular plural is to change the *f* in the singular word to *v*, then add *s* or *es.*

Directions Change the *f* in the singular word to *v*, then add *s* or *es* to form the plural. Write the plural on the line.

1. dwarf dwarves
2. leaf leaves
3. knife knives
4. hoof hooves
5. loaf loaves
6. scarf scarves
7. life lives

Directions Each sentence has an underlined word that takes an irregular plural. Write the irregular plural of the underlined word on the line. Use the box to help you.

children geese mice sheep teeth men women

teeth 8. You should brush your tooth twice every day.
children 9. There are roles for seven child in *The Sound of Music.*
sheep 10. You have to shear sheep to get their wool.
mice 11. Cats chase mouse even when they aren't hungry.
women 12. Many woman have been elected to the U.S. Congress.
geese 13. Many Europeans eat goose instead of turkeys at the holidays.
men 14. Man in traditional Scottish dress wear kilts, or skirts.

Home Activity Your child wrote words with irregular plurals (mouse, mice), including words that change from f to v (scarf, scarves). Leaf through the dictionary with your child. Find more words that have irregular plurals and challenge your child to spell them correctly.

Irregular Plurals DVD•233

Let's Practice It!
TR DVD•233

Fluent Word Reading
Spiral Review

Read words independent of context

Display these words. Tell students that they will know some of the words on this list from their reading. Explain that they can decode the unfamiliar words.

Have students read the list three or four times until they can read at the rate of two to three seconds per word.

Word Reading

illness	were	wren	cheerful	very
whistled	sadly	come	crumb	where
your	have	sensible	want	done
to	who	signs	dependable	know

Corrective feedback

If... students have difficulty reading whole words,
then... have them use sound-by-sound blending for decodable words or chunking for words that have word parts, or have them say and spell high-frequency words.

If... students cannot read fluently at a rate of two to three seconds per word,
then... have pairs practice reading the list until they can read it fluently.

Differentiated Instruction

SI Strategic Intervention

Irregular Plurals To assist students having difficulty with irregular plurals, write the following words on cards: *tooth, teeth, mouse/mice, life/lives, person/people, sheep/sheep.* Shuffle the cards and place them facedown in rows. Have students play a memory game by choosing two cards. If the singular and plural forms match, students keep them. If not, they put them back in the same place. You may wish to include additional pairs of words to make the game more challenging.

Spiral Review

These activities review:

- previously taught high-frequency words *were, very, come, where, your, have, want, done, to, who.*
- consonant patterns *(wr, kn, gn, st, mb);* suffixes *(-ly, -ful, -ness, -less, -able, -ible).*

ELL

English Language Learners

Practice Pronunciation Have students say words with silent letters until they become comfortable saying them as one sound.

Objectives

- Read words fluently in context.
- Apply knowledge of sound-spellings to decode unknown words when reading.
- Practice fluency with oral rereading.

Read words in context

Display these sentences. Call on individuals to read a sentence. Then randomly point to review words and have students read them. To help you monitor word reading, high-frequency words are underlined and decodable words are italicized.

MONITOR PROGRESS Sentence Reading

The *cheerful wren whistled* a happy song.
It is not *sensible* to <u>come</u> when you <u>have</u> an *illness.*
Do you *know* someone <u>who</u> is <u>very</u> *dependable*?
***Sadly* there wasn't a *crumb* left when we <u>were</u> <u>done</u>.**
<u>Where</u> do you <u>want</u> <u>your</u> *signs* <u>to</u> go?

If… students are unable to read an underlined high-frequency word,
then… read the word for them and spell it, having them echo you.

If… students have difficulty reading an italicized decodable word,
then… guide them in using sound-by-sound blending or chunking.

Reread for Fluency

Have students reread the sentences to develop automaticity in decoding words.

ROUTINE Oral Rereading

1. **Read** Have students read all the sentences orally.
2. **Reread** To achieve optimal fluency, students should reread the sentences three or four times.
3. **Corrective Feedback** Listen as students read. Provide corrective feedback regarding their fluency and decoding.

Routines Flip Chart

Blend and Read

Read words independent of context

Have students turn to p. 23 in *Decodable Practice Readers 3.2* and find the first list of words. Each word in this list has the *r*-controlled vowel /er/, /är/, or /ôr/. Let's blend and read these words. Be sure that students identify the correct vowel sound in each word.

Next, have students read the high-frequency words.

Preview Decodable Story

Have students read the title and preview the story. Tell them that they will read words with *r*-controlled vowels.

Read words in context

Chorally read the story along with the students. Have students identify words in the story that have the *r*-controlled vowel sounds /er/, /är/, or /ôr/. Monitor students as they read to check for proper pronunciation and appropriate pacing.

Team Talk Pair students and have them take turns reading the story aloud to each other. Make sure that students are monitoring their accuracy when they decode words.

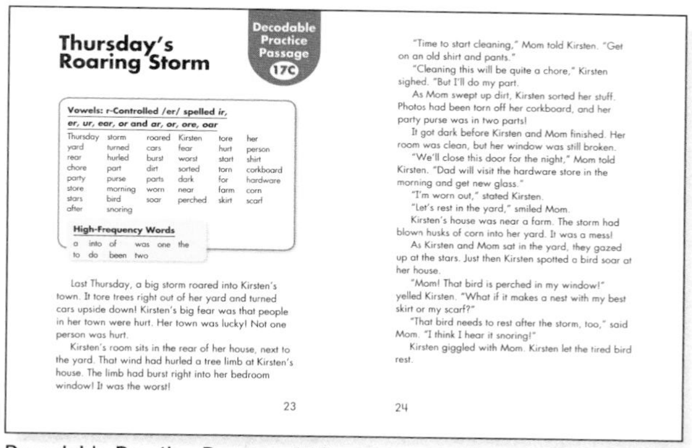

Thursday's Roaring Storm

Decodable Practice Passage 17C

Vowels: r-Controlled /er/ spelled *ir, er, ur, ear, or* and *ar, or, ore, oar*

Thursday	storm	roared	Kirsten	tore	her
yard	turned	cars	fear	hurt	person
rear	hurled	burst	worst	start	shirt
chore	part	dirt	sorted	torn	corkboard
party	purse	parts	dark	for	hardware
store	morning	worn	near	farm	corn
stars	bird	soar	perched	skirt	scarf
after	snoring				

High-Frequency Words

a	into	of	was	one	the
to	do	been	two		

Last Thursday, a big storm roared into Kirsten's town. It tore trees right out of her yard and turned cars upside down! Kirsten's big fear was that people in her town were hurt. Her town was lucky! Not one person was hurt.

Kirsten's room sits in the rear of her house, next to the yard. That wind had hurled a tree limb at Kirsten's house. The limb had burst right into her bedroom window! It was the worst!

23

"Time to start cleaning," Mom told Kirsten. "Get on an old shirt and pants."

"Cleaning this will be quite a chore," Kirsten sighed. "But I'll do my part.

As Mom swept up dirt, Kirsten sorted her stuff. Photos had been torn off her corkboard, and her party purse was in two parts!

It got dark before Kirsten and Mom finished. Her room was clean, but her window was still broken.

"We'll close this door for the night," Mom told Kirsten. "Dad will visit the hardware store in the morning and get new glass."

"I'm worn out," stated Kirsten.

"Let's rest in the yard," smiled Mom.

Kirsten's house was near a farm. The storm had blown husks of corn into her yard. It was a mess!

As Kirsten and Mom sat in the yard, they gazed up at the stars. Just then Kirsten spotted a bird soar at her house.

"Mom! That bird is perched in my window!" yelled Kirsten. "What if it makes a nest with my best skirt or my scarf?"

"That bird needs to rest after the storm, too," said Mom. "I think I hear it snoring!"

Kirsten giggled with Mom. Kirsten let the tired bird rest.

24

Decodable Practice Passage 17C

Differentiated Instruction

A Advanced

Decodable words Have students write definitions of the words with suffixes found in the sentences on p. 80e. Invite them to add some additional words with suffixes and their definitions to the list.

DAY 4 Get Ready to Read

Objectives
- Introduce legends.

Let's Think About Genre
Legend

Introduce the genre Remind students that authors structure texts differently depending on their reasons and purposes for writing. A genre is a type of writing. Explain that legends constitute a genre.

Discuss the genre Ask students what legends, such as stories about Johnny Appleseed or Robin Hood, they can recall. Explain: A legend is an old story, passed down over the years, about the great deeds of a hero. Legends are similar to myths, because they concern amazing events from the past. Unlike myths, however, legends may be based on historical facts. Like fictional stories, legends have character, a plot, a setting, and a theme. Let's look at each of these parts of a legend.

On the board, draw a chart like the one below. Ask students to think about legends they know. Ask:

- What are characters in a legend like? Possible response: They are often very brave or very strong.
- Where do legends take place? Possible response: They take place in real times in history.
- What kind of things happen in a legend? Possible responses: The character does good deeds. The character shows how strong he or she is.
- What type of theme, or Big Idea, do legends, often have? Possible response: The theme is often about doing the right thing.

Characters	Setting	Plot	Theme
very brave or strong	real time in history	Hero does good deeds or shows strength.	doing the right thing

Have students paraphrase the theme in a legend they know. Then have students work in pairs to think of the difference between a legend and a story about animal characters.

Connect to reading Tell students that they will read a legend about a hero who was very big and strong. Have the class think about why it would be interesting to read about a person who is bigger and stronger than other people.

Small Group Time

DAY 4 **Break into small groups before reading or revisiting "Paul Bunyan and the Great Lakes."**

Teacher Led

SI Strategic Intervention

Teacher Led p. DI•30
- Practice retelling
- Genre focus
- **Read/Revisit** "Paul Bunyan and the Great Lakes"

OL On-Level

Teacher Led p. DI•35
- Practice retelling
- Genre focus
- **Read/Revisit** "Paul Bunyan and the Great Lakes"

A Advanced

Teacher Led p. DI•40
- Genre focus
- **Read/Revisit** "Paul Bunyan and the Great Lakes"

ELL Place English Language learners in the groups that correspond to their reading abilities in English.

Practice Stations
- Read for Meaning
- Get Fluent
- Words to Know

Independent Activities
- AudioText: "Paul Bunyan"
- *Reader's and Writer's Notebook*
- Research and Inquiry

DAY 4 Read and Comprehend

40–45 min

Objectives

- Use ideas to make and confirm predictions.
- Identify details of a legend.

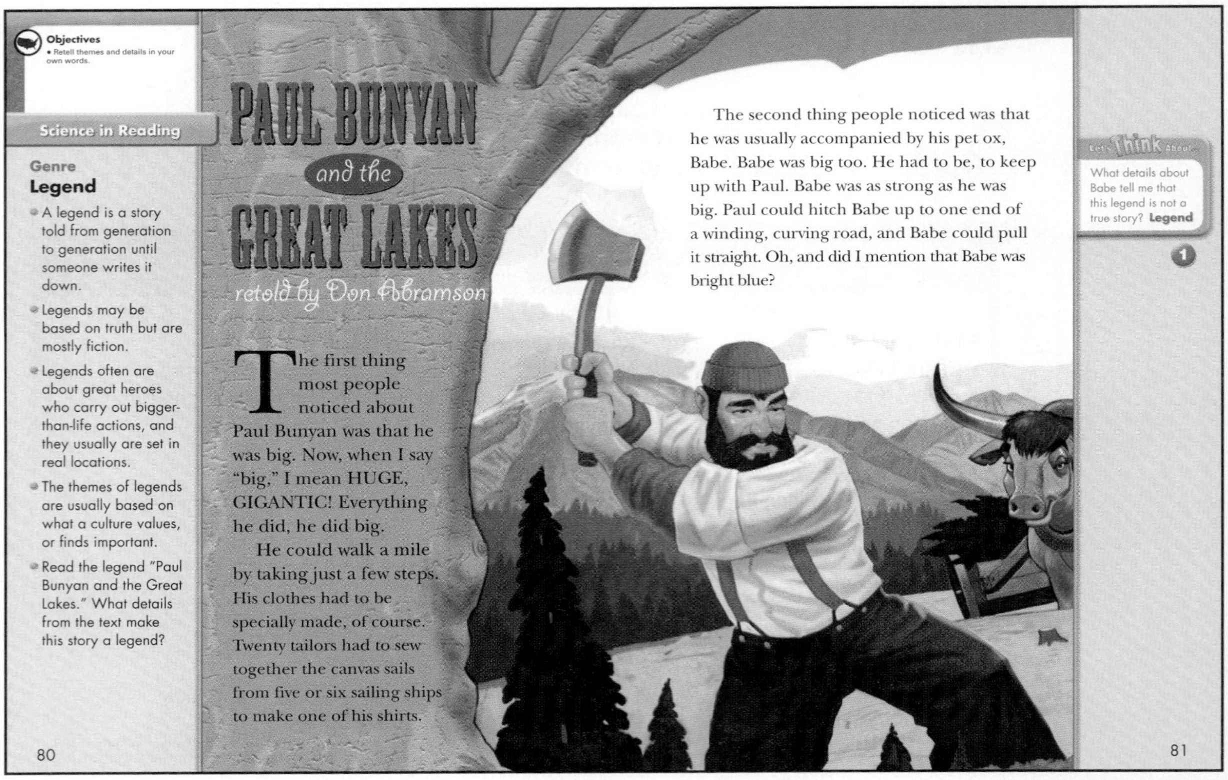

Objectives

- Retell themes and details in your own words.

Science in Reading

Genre

Legend

- A legend is a story told from generation to generation until someone writes it down.
- Legends may be based on truth but are mostly fiction.
- Legends often are about great heroes who carry out bigger-than-life actions, and they usually are set in real locations.
- The themes of legends are usually based on what a culture values, or finds important.
- Read the legend "Paul Bunyan and the Great Lakes." What details from the text make this story a legend?

80

PAUL BUNYAN and the GREAT LAKES

retold by Don Abramson

The first thing most people noticed about Paul Bunyan was that he was big. Now, when I say "big," I mean HUGE, GIGANTIC! Everything he did, he did big.

He could walk a mile by taking just a few steps. His clothes had to be specially made, of course. Twenty tailors had to sew together the canvas sails from five or six sailing ships to make one of his shirts.

The second thing people noticed was that he was usually accompanied by his pet ox, Babe. Babe was big too. He had to be, to keep up with Paul. Babe was as strong as he was big. Paul could hitch Babe up to one end of a winding, curving road, and Babe could pull it straight. Oh, and did I mention that Babe was bright blue?

Let's Think About...

What details about Babe tell me that this legend is not a true story? **Legend**

1

81

Student Edition pp. 80–81

Guide Comprehension

Teach the genre

Genre: Legends Have students preview "Paul Bunyan and the Great Lakes" on pp. 80–83. Have them look at the title, illustrations, and words written in capital letters. Then ask: How is Paul Bunyan a typical hero of a legend? Where might this story take place?

Corrective feedback

If... students are unable to explain that Paul Bunyan is a typical legendary hero because he is very big and strong, and that the setting is a real place with trees and mountains,
then... use the model to guide students in understanding legends.

Model the skill

Think Aloud: When I preview the story, I see that the title mentions a real place, the Great Lakes. The pictures show a person who is very big and who digs a big hole. I also see that the author put the words *huge, gigantic,* and *big* in capital letters. I think Paul Bunyan is a typical hero of a legend because he is very big and strong, and that the setting is the Great Lakes.

On their own

Have students look back at the chart from p. 80g and use it to predict the plot of "Paul Bunyan and the Great Lakes."

Extend Thinking
Think Critically

Higher-order thinking skills

Author's Craft • Evaluation Why might the author have chosen to use capital letters for the words *huge* and *gigantic?* Possible response: The story is about a gigantic character, so he chose to make those words bigger.

Important Ideas • Analysis Why does the author start the story by telling us the first thing most people noticed about Paul Bunyan was that he was big? Possible response: Paul Bunyan's size is an important idea in the story, so the author starts by telling us about it.

Let's Think About...

1 Possible responses: Babe is so big and strong, he can pull a road straight; Babe is bright blue.

Differentiated Instruction

SI Strategic Intervention

Scaffold legend Students may have difficulty understanding the difference between legends and other kinds of short stories. Explain that legends contain some sort of historical truth, where general short stories need not do this. The legend of Paul Bunyan probably comes from stories of the feats of real lumberjacks, who valued strength and speed at their work.

A Advanced

Explore legend Have students conduct an Internet search using the keywords *Paul Bunyan* and *origin* to learn how the legend might have begun. Explain that *origin* means *a* "place where something comes from."

ELL

English Language Learners

Monitor comprehension To check comprehension, have students respond to questions about parts of the text, such as: How did Paul Bunyan walk a mile? How did Paul and Babe make a curving road straight?

DAY 4 Read and Comprehend

Objectives

- Identify elements of a legend.
- Identify cause and effect.
- Identify main idea and details.

Babe wasn't just a pet. He was a working animal. That was useful because Paul was a lumberjack. Paul decided to hire a crew of lumberjacks. He had to build a lumber camp to give his crew a place to live. He found a nice spot and set the men to building, using lumber they had cut down themselves.

A camp needs a good supply of drinking water, so Paul dug out a huge reservoir to catch rainwater and to hold water from a number of rivers that emptied into it. People called it Lake Ontario, after some Native American words that mean "great lake." That worked fine for a while, but Babe could drink half the lake himself every morning before breakfast. So Paul dug another reservoir, and then another. They were also given Native American names: Lake Erie and Lake Huron.

Paul's lumber camp was growing too, and he had more men and more animals than ever before. So he dug Lake Michigan and then, finally, Lake Superior. Now he had a really good water supply.

As I said, Paul did everything BIG!

Let's Think About...

What is the setting of this legend? **Legend**

2

Let's Think About...

According to this legend, how were the Great Lakes made? **Legend**

3

Let's Think About...

What is the theme of the story? What details support the theme? **Legend**

4

Let's Think About...

Reading Across Texts *Hottest, Coldest, Highest, Deepest* tells interesting facts about real places on Earth. How is this legend about Paul Bunyan similar and different?

Writing Across Texts Choose one place described in *Hottest, Coldest, Highest, Deepest.* Make up a short story in which Paul Bunyan makes the amazing feature of that setting.

82

83

Student Edition pp. 82–83

Guide Comprehension

Teach elements of legends

Genre: Elements of Legends Remind students that the plot of a legend usually tells about the hero's good deeds or strength. Ask: How is the plot of "Paul Bunyan and the Great Lakes" typical of a legend?

Corrective feedback

If... students are unable to explain that the story's plot is typical of a legend because it shows Paul Bunyan using his impossibly great strength, **then...** use the model to guide students in understanding the elements of a legend.

Model the skill

Think Aloud: I know that a plot is the series of events in a story, so to think about how the plot is typical of a legend, I look at the things that happen in the story. Paul is digging reservoirs, or places to hold water, the size of some of the largest lakes in the world. This plot is typical of a legend, because it shows how Paul Bunyan uses his unusual strength.

On their own

Have students review the characteristics of a legend's theme and discuss how the theme of "Paul Bunyan and the Great Lakes" is typical of a legend.

Extend Thinking

Higher-order thinking skills

Cause and Effect • Evaluation What was the effect of Paul Bunyan's decision to dig reservoirs for drinking water? Possible response: The effect was that the Great Lakes were formed.

Main Idea and Details • Synthesis What details support the idea that Paul needed to dig more and more reservoirs? Possible response: The facts that Babe the ox could drink half the lake and that the lumber camp was growing are supporting details.

Let's Think About...

2 The setting is the Great Lakes area.

3 Possible response: According to the legend, the Great Lakes were created when Paul Bunyan wanted to dig reservoirs to catch drinking water for his crew of lumberjacks and Babe, his ox.

4 Possible response: The theme is that everything Paul Bunyan does is big. The descriptions of how each lake was dug support the theme.

Reading Across Texts

Have students create a Venn diagram listing the similarities and differences between the Paul Bunyan legend and *Hottest, Coldest, Highest, Deepest.*

Writing Across Texts

Remind students that their short story should have an imaginative plot, a description of the chosen setting, and a theme. Encourage them to work in pairs to brainstorm the different parts of their story before they begin to write. Their stories should build to a dramatic climax before the resolution.

Connect to Science

Explain that the Great Lakes were actually formed during the Ice Age. Glaciers moving over the area carved out deep basins, forming lakes when the glaciers melted.

Differentiated Instruction

SI Strategic Intervention

Graphic organizer To help students organize their writing, provide a graphic organizer with spaces to plan the beginning, middle, and end of the story before students begin to write.

A Advanced

Have students research the difference between lumberjacks from the past and modern loggers who use sophisticated equipment in their work.

ELL

English Language Learners

Discuss writing Partner students to orally rehearse their stories before they begin to write.

DAY 4 Read and Comprehend

Objectives

- Read grade-appropriate text fluently.
- ◎ Use a dictionary or glossary to find information about unknown words.
- Present a weather forecast.

Check Fluency: WCPM
SUCCESS PREDICTOR

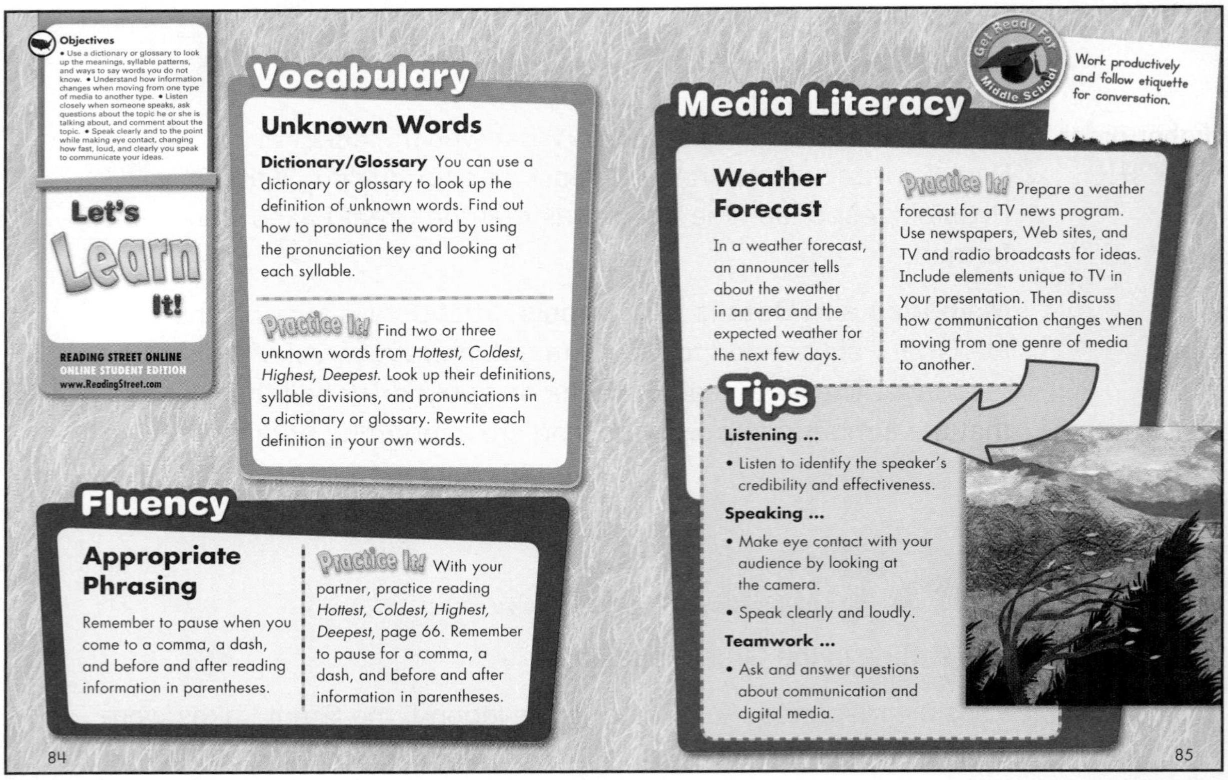

Objectives
• Use a dictionary or glossary to look up the meanings, syllable patterns, and ways to say words you do not know. • Understand how information changes when moving from one type of media to another type. • Listen closely when someone speaks, ask questions about the topic he or she is talking about, and comment about the topic. • Speak clearly and to the point while making eye contact, changing how fast, loud, and clearly you speak to communicate your ideas.

Let's Learn It!

READING STREET ONLINE
ONLINE STUDENT EDITION
www.ReadingStreet.com

Vocabulary

Unknown Words

Dictionary/Glossary You can use a dictionary or glossary to look up the definition of unknown words. Find out how to pronounce the word by using the pronunciation key and looking at each syllable.

Practice It! Find two or three unknown words from *Hottest, Coldest, Highest, Deepest*. Look up their definitions, syllable divisions, and pronunciations in a dictionary or glossary. Rewrite each definition in your own words.

Fluency

Appropriate Phrasing

Remember to pause when you come to a comma, a dash, and before and after reading information in parentheses.

Practice It! With your partner, practice reading *Hottest, Coldest, Highest, Deepest*, page 66. Remember to pause for a comma, a dash, and before and after information in parentheses.

Media Literacy

Get Ready For Middle School
Work productively and follow etiquette for conversation.

Weather Forecast

In a weather forecast, an announcer tells about the weather in an area and the expected weather for the next few days.

Practice It! Prepare a weather forecast for a TV news program. Use newspapers, Web sites, and TV and radio broadcasts for ideas. Include elements unique to TV in your presentation. Then discuss how communication changes when moving from one genre of media to another.

Tips

Listening ...
- Listen to identify the speaker's credibility and effectiveness.

Speaking ...
- Make eye contact with your audience by looking at the camera.
- Speak clearly and loudly.

Teamwork ...
- Ask and answer questions about communication and digital media.

84 85

Student Edition pp. 84–85

Fluency
Appropriate Phrasing and Punctuation Cues

Guide practice Use the Student Edition activity as an assessment tool. Make sure the reading passage is at least 200 words in length. As students read aloud with partners, walk around to make sure their phrasing is appropriate and that they use punctuation marks as guides for grouping words together.

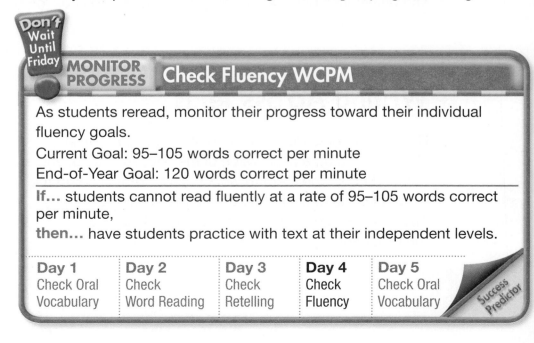

Don't Wait Until Friday

MONITOR PROGRESS **Check Fluency WCPM**

As students reread, monitor their progress toward their individual fluency goals.
Current Goal: 95–105 words correct per minute
End-of-Year Goal: 120 words correct per minute

If... students cannot read fluently at a rate of 95–105 words correct per minute,
then... have students practice with text at their independent levels.

Day 1	Day 2	Day 3	Day 4	Day 5
Check Oral Vocabulary	Check Word Reading	Check Retelling	Check Fluency	Check Oral Vocabulary

Success Predictor

Vocabulary
Unknown Words

Teach unknown words

Dictionary/Glossary Remind students that the main selection tells about the most extreme tides. Model using a dictionary or the glossary to look up the meaning, syllabication, and pronunciation of the word *extreme.* Explain: A dictionary or glossary shows how to divide a word into syllables. The pronunciation guide shows how to say each syllable and which syllable to stress when you say the word.

Guide practice

Have students select another word from the main selection with two or more syllables and look up its meaning, syllabication, and pronunciation. Point out the pronunciation key to help students with phonetic spellings.

On their own

Walk around the room as students look up the words in a dictionary or glossary. Check to make sure students understand the meaning and pronunciation of each word.

Media Literacy
Weather Forecast

Teach

Encourage classmates to think about the ways weather forecasters on television get an audience's attention. They should also think about the differences among forecasts in different genres of media such as television, the Internet, newspapers, or radio. Suggest they use current weather patterns as a guide for their forecast. Remind students to begin with a catchy or interesting statement. They can then share today's weather report, and the weather forecast for tonight and tomorrow. They may wish to include a 3-, 5-, or 7-day extended forecast.

Guide practice

Partner students to rehearse their forecasts together. Remind them to speak loudly and clearly and at a rate slow enough for their listeners to understand the words, while making eye contact with the audience.

On their own

Have students deliver the weather forecast to the class. Remind students to listen attentively and to make sure their questions or comments relate directly to the subject.

Weather Forecast

Remind students that a specialized vocabulary is used in weather forecasts. Encourage students to check the pronunciation of words such as *precipitation* before they rehearse their forecasts.

ELL

English Language Learners

Use Content-Area Vocabulary
Ask partners to work together to use content-area words in a sentence.

Check Fluency

Success Predictor

Objectives

- Use a graphic source to present information.
- Spell words with r-controlled vowels correctly.
- Identify and use subject and object pronouns correctly.

Research and Inquiry
Synthesize

Teach Have students synthesize their research findings and results. Suggest that students use a bar graph or another graphic source, such as a chart, to visually show the results of their research. Remind students that an article about a record holder should include both a main idea, stating the record, and details that include comparisons between the record holder and other athletes competing for that record or other records. These comparisons can be represented visually and labeled in a graphic source such as a graph or chart.

Guide practice Review how to choose relevant information from a number of sources and organize it logically into an article, using graphic sources in this week's readings as examples. Make sure students use captions to clearly identify factual information.

On their own Have students review and organize their notes to write their articles. Remind them that their article should include facts and details that support their main idea.

Conventions
Subject and Object Pronouns

Test practice Remind students that grammar skills, such as subject and object pronouns, are often assessed on important tests. Review that subject pronouns are used as subjects of sentences and object pronouns are used after action verbs or as objects of prepositions.

Daily Fix-It Use Daily Fix-It numbers 7 and 8 in the right margin.

On their own For additional practice, use *Reader's and Writer's Notebook* p. 268.

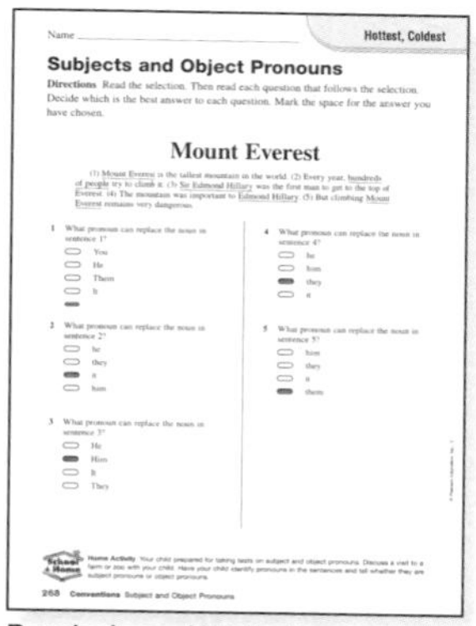
Name ______ Hottest, Coldest

Subjects and Object Pronouns

Directions Read the selection. Then read each question that follows the selection. Decide which is the best answer to each question. Mark the space for the answer you have chosen.

Mount Everest

(1) Mount Everest is the tallest mountain in the world. (2) Every year, hundreds of people try to climb it. (3) Sir Edmund Hillary was the first man to get to the top of Everest. (4) The mountain was important to Edmund Hillary. (5) But climbing Mount Everest remains very dangerous.

1 What pronoun can replace the noun in sentence 1?
- You
- He
- Them
- It

2 What pronoun can replace the noun in sentence 2?
- he
- they
- it
- him

3 What pronoun can replace the noun in sentence 3?
- He
- Him
- It
- They

4 What pronoun can replace the noun in sentence 4?
- he
- him
- they
- it

5 What pronoun can replace the noun in sentence 5?
- him
- they
- it
- them

School + Home **Home Activity** Your child prepared for taking tests on subject and object pronouns. Discuss a visit to a farm or zoo with your child. Have your child identify pronouns in the sentences and tell whether they are subject pronouns or object pronouns.

268 **Conventions** Subject and Object Pronouns

Reader's and Writer's Notebook, p. 268

Spelling
Vowels: *r*-Controlled

Practice spelling strategy Supply pairs of students with index cards on which the spelling words have been written. Have one student read a word while the other writes it. Then have students switch roles. Use the cards to check your spelling and correct any misspelled words.

On their own For additional practice, use *Let's Practice It!* page 234 on the *Teacher Resources DVD-ROM.*

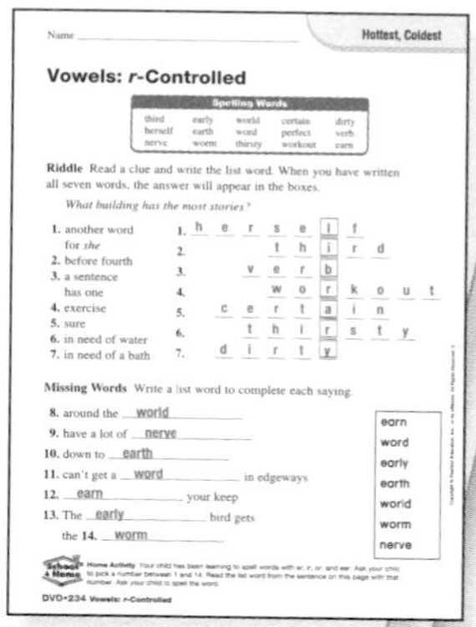
Name ______ Hottest, Coldest

Vowels: *r*-Controlled

Spelling Words				
third	early	world	certain	dirty
herself	earth	word	perfect	verb
nerve	worm	thirsty	workout	earn

Riddle Read a clue and write the list word. When you have written all seven words, the answer will appear in the boxes.

What building has the most stories?

1. another word for *she* — herself
2. before fourth — third
3. a sentence has one — verb
4. exercise — workout
5. sure — certain
6. in need of water — thirsty
7. in need of a bath — dirty

Missing Words Write a list word to complete each saying.

8. around the world
9. have a lot of nerve
10. down to earth
11. can't get a word in edgeways
12. earn your keep
13. The early bird gets the 14. worm

earn, word, early, earth, world, worm, nerve

School + Home **Home Activity** Your child has been learning to spell words with er, ir, or, and ear. Ask your child to pick a number between 1 and 14. Read the list word from the sentence on this page with that number. Ask your child to spell the word.

DVD•234 Vowels: *r*-Controlled

Let's Practice It!
TR DVD•234

Daily Fix-It

7. Is Africas river the longest in the world. *(Africa's; world?)*
8. Many unusuall animals lives there. *(unusual; live)*

Differentiated Instruction

A Advanced

Words in context Have students write the spelling words in sentences rather than in isolation.

Objectives

- Revise a draft of an imaginative story.
- Apply revising strategy of consolidating.
- Achieve sentence variety with complex and compound sentences.

Writing—Imaginative Story
Revising Strategy

MINI-LESSON

Revising Strategy: Consolidating

- Yesterday we wrote an imaginative story with one character telling a riddle to another. Today we will revise our drafts. The goal is to make your writing clearer, more interesting, and more informative.

- Display Writing Transparency 17B. Remind students that revising does not include corrections of grammar and mechanics. Tell them that this will be done during the lesson as they proofread their work. Then introduce the revising strategy of consolidating.

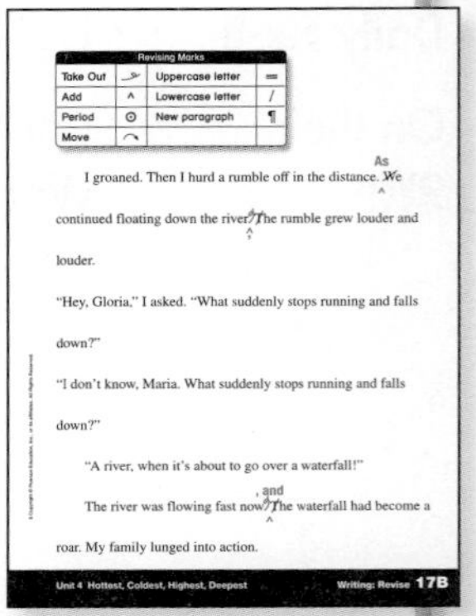

Revising Marks			
Take Out	⤳	Uppercase letter	=
Add	^	Lowercase letter	/
Period	⊙	New paragraph	¶
Move	⌒		

I groaned. Then I hurd a rumble off in the distance. As We continued floating down the river, The rumble grew louder and louder.

"Hey, Gloria," I asked. "What suddenly stops running and falls down?"

"I don't know, Maria. What suddenly stops running and falls down?"

"A river, when it's about to go over a waterfall!"

The river was flowing fast now, and The waterfall had become a roar. My family lunged into action.

Unit 4 Hottest, Coldest, Highest, Deepest — Writing: Revise 17B

Writing Transparency 17B, TR DVD

- Short, simple sentences sound choppy and dull. To make my writing more interesting to read, I'll look for places where I can combine ideas into longer sentences. These two sentences can be one complex sentence: *We continued floating down the river. The rumble grew louder and louder.* I'll combine them like this: *As we continued floating down the river, the rumble grew louder and louder.* These two sentences also sound short and choppy: *The river was flowing fast now. The waterfall had become a roar.* I'll combine them into one compound sentence: *The river was flowing fast now, and the waterfall had become a roar.* Reread your imaginative story for places where you might make simple sentences into compound complex sentences.

Display and review the Revising Tips. Tell students to use the tips as they revise their stories.

Revising Tips

- ✔ Be sure the story has details about characters and setting.
- ✔ Be sure the events are told in order and build to a climax.
- ✔ Vary sentences by combining ideas into compound or complex sentences.

Peer conferencing

Peer Revision Have pairs exchange papers for peer revision. Tell students to write compliments and suggestions for improvement directly on their partner's draft. Tell students that their questions should focus on where their partner could revise by combining simple sentences.

Have students revise their stories. They should use the comments their partners made during peer conferencing as well as the key features of an imaginative story to guide their revision. Be sure that students are using the revising strategy of consolidating.

Corrective feedback

Circulate around the room to monitor students and confer with them as they revise. Remind students who are correcting errors that they will have time to edit tomorrow. They should be working on their story line and sentence variety today.

ROUTINE **Quick Write for Fluency** Team Talk

1. **Talk** Pairs discuss their favorite places described in *Hottest, Coldest, Highest, Deepest.*
2. **Write** Each student writes a brief explanation of why he or she would like to visit the place from the selection.
3. **Share** Partners read their explanations to each other. Then each checks the partner's writing for descriptive details.

Routines Flip Chart

Wrap Up Your Day

- ✔ **Build Concepts** Have students discuss why Paul Bunyan was unique.
- ✔ **Oral Vocabulary** Monitor students' use of oral vocabulary as they respond to this question: Why do you think Paul Bunyan was a champ at chopping lumber?
- ✔ **Text Features** Discuss how focusing on words in bold print helps students understand text.

Write Guy
Jeff Anderson

Writers Write!

Student writers succeed in classrooms where they write. Simple, isn't it? Are you trying to meet some mandate or standard with such blinders on that you're forgetting daily writing? Students need to read every day and to write every day. Teachers do not need to read and assess everything that students write.

ELL

English Language Learners

Revising sentences Help students hear English sentence variety. Read aloud short, choppy sentences and then complex and compound sentences. Then have students read aloud their own sentences. Guide them to decide if the sentences need to be revised.

Preview DAY 5

Remind students to think about record holders in nature.

DAY 5 Wrap Up your Week

10–15 min

Objectives
- Review the weekly concept.
- Review oral vocabulary.

Today at a Glance

Oral Vocabulary

Comprehension
◉ Graphic sources

Lesson Vocabulary
◉ Unknown Words

Phonics/Word Analysis
◉ Vowels: *r*-controlled

Literary Terms
Author's craft

Assessment
Fluency
Comprehension

Research and Inquiry
Communicate

Spelling
Vowels: *r*-controlled

Conventions
Subject and object pronouns

Writing
Imaginative story

Check Oral Vocabulary
SUCCESS PREDICTOR

Concept Wrap Up

Question of the Week

What makes nature's record holders unique?

Review the concept

Have students look back at the reading selections to find examples that best demonstrate how different places and features in nature are unique.

Review Amazing Words

Display and review this week's concept map. Remind students that this week they have learned ten Amazing Words related to nature's record holders. Have students use the Amazing Words and the concept map to answer the question of the week, *What makes nature's record holders unique?*

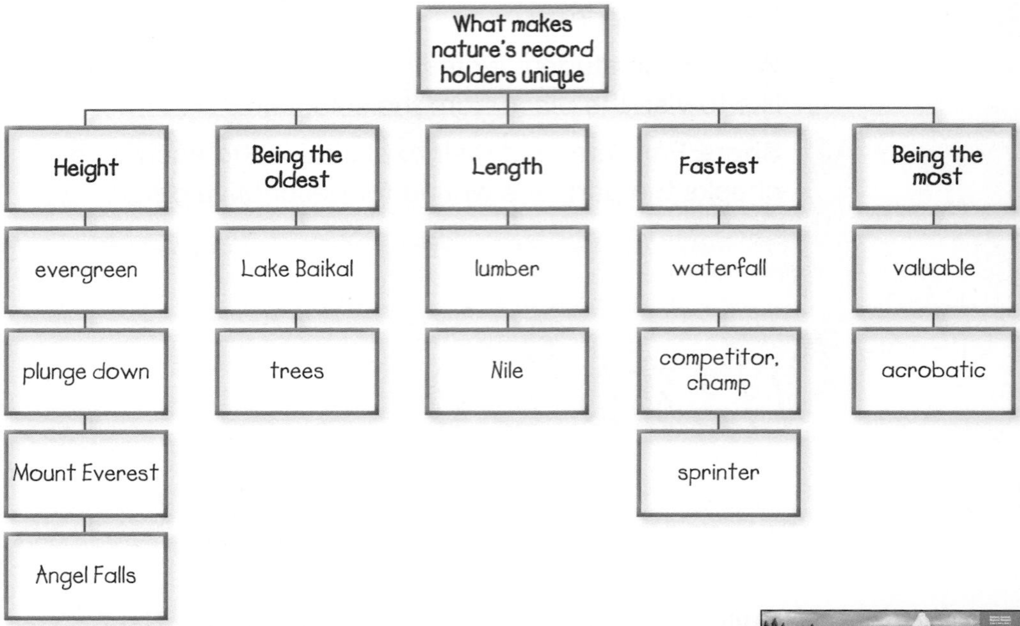

ELL **Check Concepts and Language** Use the Day 5 instructions on ELL Poster 17 to monitor students' understanding of the lesson concept.

ELL Poster 17

Amazing Ideas

Connect to the Big Question Partner students to discuss how the Question of the Week connects to the Big Question: *What does it mean to be unique?* Have students use the concept map and what they have learned from this week's Anchored Talks and reading selections to form an Amazing Idea—a realization or Big Idea about Being Unique. Remind partners to give suggestions that build on each other's ideas. Then ask each pair to share their Amazing Idea with the class.

Amazing Ideas might include these key concepts:

- Something that is unique might be the best or have the most of something.
- Length, age, and height are some ways to measure being unique in nature.

Write about it Have students write a few sentences about their Amazing Idea that begin with "This week I learned..." They should support their Amazing Idea with facts, details, or explanations.

It's Friday

MONITOR PROGRESS **Check Oral Vocabulary**

Have individuals use this week's Amazing Words to describe things that are unique. Monitor students' ability to use the Amazing Words and note which words you need to reteach.

If... students have difficulty using the Amazing Words,

then... reteach using the Oral Vocabulary Routine, pages 55a, 60b, 70b, 80b, OV•2.

Day 1	Day 2	Day 3	Day 4	Day 5
Check Oral Vocabulary	Check Word Reading	Check Retelling	Check Fluency	Check Oral Vocabulary

Success Predictor

Amazing Words

evergreen	champ
lumber	sprinter
competitor	acrobat
plunge	weaken
valuable	ranger

ELL

English Language Learners

Concept map Work with students to add new words to the concept map.

DAY 5 Wrap Up your Week

10–15 min

Objectives

- ◎ Review graphic sources.
- ◎ Review unknown words.
- ◎ Review *r*-controlled vowels.
- Review author's craft.

Comprehension Review

Graphic Sources

Student Edition p. EI•10–11

Teach graphic sources Review the definition of graphic sources on p. 58. Remind students that graphic sources show information visually and can include charts, tables, diagrams, maps, and pictures. For additional support have students review pp. EI•10–11 on graphic sources.

Envision It!

Guide practice Have student pairs find an example of two different graphic sources in *Hottest, Coldest, Highest, Deepest.* Then have pairs explain how the source helps readers to understand the information on the page.

On their own For additional practice with graphic sources, use *Let's Practice It!* page 235 on the *Teacher Resources DVD-ROM.*

Vocabulary Review

Unknown Words

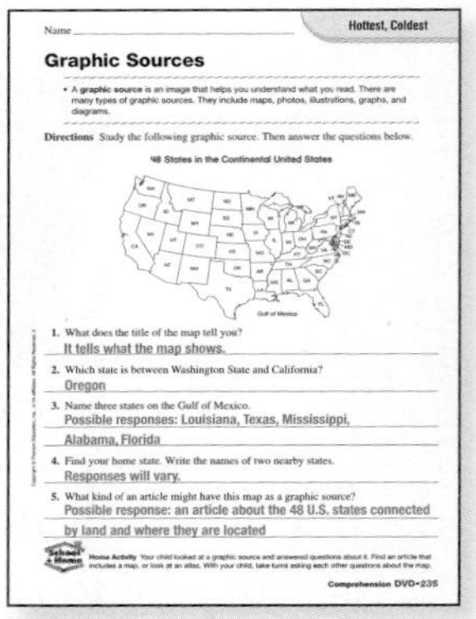

Let's Practice It!
TR DVD•235

Teach unknown words Remind students to use a dictionary or glossary to help them understand the meaning of words they do not know.

Guide practice Review with students how to find the correct meaning of *average* using a dictionary or glossary. Explain that there may be more than one definition for the word.

On their own Have students work with partners to write context sentences using this week's lesson vocabulary words. Partners can trade sentences and identify the context clues that help them determine each word's meaning.

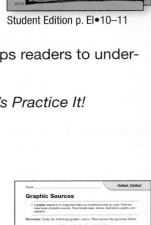

Phonics Review
Vowels: *r*-Controlled

Teach vowels: *r*-Controlled Write the following sentences on the board. Have students read each one, first quietly to themselves and then aloud as you track the print.

1. **Ben was thirsty from his workout.**
2. **Jose came in first with a perfect score.**
3. **The old curtains are dirty, but still worth saving.**
4. **The squirrel burrowed into the earth.**
5. **It took some nerve to park the big car.**

Team Talk Have pairs of students identify and circle the words with the sound /ėr/, /är/, or /ôr/. Then call on individuals to share with the class.

Literary Terms Review
Author's Craft

Teach author's craft Have students reread pp. 72–74 of *Hottest, Coldest, Deepest, Highest.* Remind students that superlatives, or words that show something is the best in a group, help readers to understand ideas.

Guided practice Direct students' attention to the text at the top of p. 73. Have students name two sentences that show something is the best or the most. Then ask students to find another sentence on the page that shows something is the best or the most. Guide a discussion of why the author chose those words to describe the *deepest* spot in the ocean, *lowest* spot on dry land, and *most active* volcano.

On their own Have students make a T-chart with the headings *superlatives with -est* and *superlatives with most.* Ask them to list examples of each from the selection.

Lesson Vocabulary

average the quantity found by dividing the sum of all quantities by the number of quantities
depth the distance from the top to the bottom
deserts dry, sandy regions without water and trees
erupted burst out
outrun run faster than someone or something else
peak the pointed top of a mountain or hill
tides rise and fall of the ocean's waters about every twelve hours
waterfalls streams of water that fall from a high place

ELL

English Language Learners
Author's craft Point out the phrase *most active volcano* and explain that we use *most* to form a superlative for a long word usually an adjective. We add *-est* to form a superlative for a short word. Provide the following words and have students give the superlative: *big (biggest), short (shortest), exciting (most exciting), expensive (most expensive).*

DAY 5 Wrap Up your Week

20–25 min

Objectives

- Read grade-level text with fluency.

Plan to Assess Fluency

- ☑ **Week 1** Assess Advanced students.
- ☑ **This week assess Strategic Intervention students.**
- ☐ **Week 3** Assess On-Level students.
- ☐ **Week 4** Assess Strategic Intervention students.
- ☐ **Week 5** Assess any students you have not yet checked during this unit.

Set individual goals for students to enable them to reach the year-end goal.

- Current Goal: 95–105 WCPM
- Year-End Goal: 120 WCPM

Assessment

Check words correct per minute

Fluency Make two copies of the fluency passage on p. 85k. As the student reads the text aloud, mark mistakes on your copy. Also mark where the student is at the end of one minute. To check the student's comprehension of the passage, have him or her retell what was read. To figure words correct per minute (WCPM), subtract the number of mistakes from the total number of words read in one minute.

WCPM

Corrective feedback

If... students cannot read fluently at a rate of 95–105 WCPM,
then... make sure they practice with text at their independent reading level. Provide additional fluency practice by pairing nonfluent readers with fluent readers.

If... students already read at 120 WCPM,
then... have them read a book of their choice independently.

Small Group Time

DAY 5 **Break into small groups before the Comprehension lesson.**

Teacher Led

SI Strategic Intervention	OL On-Level	A Advanced
Teacher Led p. DI•31 • Practice fluency • **Read** *Extremes* or *How to Measure the Weather*	**Teacher Led** p. DI•36 • Practice fluency • **Read** *Measuring the Earth*	**Teacher Led** p. DI•40 • Practice fluency • **Read** *Largest, Fastest, Lightest, Longest*

ELL Place English language learners in the groups that correspond to their reading abilities in English.

Practice Stations
- Words to Know
- Get Fluent
- Read for Meaning

Independent Activities
- Grammar Jammer
- Concept Talk Video
- Vocabulary Activities

Name ____________________

Ring of Fire

One special area of Earth is known as the Ring of Fire. It is the 15
land areas that surround the Pacific Ocean. The edges of Asia, North 27
America, Central America, and South America are a part of the Ring. 39
This area contains 75 percent of the world's volcanoes. 48

Earth's top layer is made up of plates, or layers of land. These 61
plates move. The largest plate in the world is the Pacific Plate. It is 75
located under the Pacific Ocean. When the plates collide into one 86
another, there can be trouble. The collision may cause an earthquake. 97
Ocean tides may rise very high during earthquakes too. 106

When one plate slides under another plate, melted rock called 116
magma may rise to Earth's surface. This causes volcanoes to erupt. 127
On May 18, 1980, a volcano in Washington called Mount St. Helens 139
erupted. Thousands of animals died because they could not outrun the 150
melted rock rushing from the volcano. 156

Before Mount St. Helens erupted, its peak was 9,677 feet high. 167
After the eruption, its height was 8,363 feet. The volcano lost 1,314 feet 180
when the top of the mountain blew off during the eruption. 191

Scientists are always looking for ways to warn people well ahead of 203
a volcano's eruption or an earthquake. It is important to save lives. 215

MONITOR PROGRESS

• Check Fluency

Objectives
- Read grade-level text with comprehension.

Assessment

Check graphic sources

Graphic Sources Use "The Texas 8000 Patch" on p. 85m to check students' understanding of graphic sources.

1. Which mountain did Sylvia climb first? When? (She climbed Bush Mountain first on October 12, 2007.)
2. What other mountains must Sylvia climb after she completes her climb of Mt. Livermore? (Shumard Peak, Bartlett Peak, and El Capitan)
3. How many times has she climbed with Maria Perez? (twice)

Corrective feedback

If… students are unable to answer the comprehension questions,
then… use the Reteach lesson in the *First Stop* book.

Name ______________________________

The Texas 8000 Patch

The newest members of the Texas Climbers Club were excited. This morning they were going to hike up Mt. Livermore, the fifth highest mountain in Texas. Mt. Livermore is one of Texas's seven mountains that reach more than 8,000 feet high. The club calls those mountains the Texas 8000.

"When we reach the peak of Mt. Livermore, I'll have only three more of the Texas 8000 left to climb," said Sylvia.

"When you've done that, you'll get a patch exactly like this," said Maria.

Maria pointed to a colorful patch sewn on her hiking vest. The patch had the phrase "Texas 8000" and a picture of a mountaintop on it. Maria is a leader of the club. She has climbed all the Texas 8000 mountains more than once. Like other leaders, she can sign members' cards to show that they have climbed each of the Texas 8000 mountains.

As the group started their hike, Sylvia looked at Maria's Texas 8000 patch one more time. She couldn't wait to get hers!

The Texas 8000: Sylvia's Climbs

Mountain	County	Height	Date Climbed	Leader's Name
Guadalupe Peak	Culberson	8,749 feet	Dec. 15, 2008	Maria Perez
Bush Mountain	Culberson	8,631 feet	Oct. 12, 2007	Maria Perez
Shumard Peak	Culberson	8,615 feet		
Bartlett Peak	Culberson	8,508 feet		
Mt. Livermore	Jeff Davis	8,368 feet		
Hunter Peak	Culberson	8,368 feet	April 26, 2008	David Keltner
El Capitan	Culberson	8,085 feet		

MONITOR PROGRESS
• Graphic Sources

Objectives

- Communicate inquiry results.
- Administer spelling test.
- Review subject and object pronouns.

Research and Inquiry
Communicate

Present ideas Have students share their inquiry results in small groups by presenting their articles, giving a brief talk on their research and answering discussion questions. Have students display the graphic sources they created.

Listening and speaking Remind students of the techniques they can use to be good speakers and to communicate effectively with their audience.

- Respond to relevant questions with appropriate detail.
- Speak slowly, clearly, and loudly.
- Keep eye contact with audience members.

Remind students of these tips for being a good listener:

- Pay attention.
- Think before you ask a question.
- Wait until the speaker has finished before raising your hand to ask a relevant question.
- Be polite, even if you disagree.

Spelling Test
Vowels: *r*-Controlled

Spelling test To administer the spelling test, refer to the directions, words, and sentences on p. 59c.

Conventions
Extra Practice

Teach Remind students that the subject pronouns *I, you, he, she, it, we,* and *they* are used as subjects of sentences. The object pronouns *me, you, him, her, it, us,* and *them* are used after action verbs or as objects of prepositions.

Guide practice Have students come to the front of the room and demonstrate giving books to each another while the rest of the class writes sentences using the appropriate subject and object pronouns. Include different possibilities, and challenge students to come up with different ways of expressing them. For example:

She gives the book to him.

He gives the book to her.

She and he give the books to them.

Daily Fix-It Use Daily Fix-It numbers 9 and 10 in the right margin.

On their own Write these sentences on the board. Have students copy the sentences, substituting the correct subject or object pronoun for the underlined words. Students should complete *Let's Practice It!* page 236 on the *Teacher Resources DVD-ROM.*

1. **<u>Steve Jenkins</u> wrote this book about extreme places.** *(He)*
2. **<u>Some deserts</u> have not seen rain for hundreds of years.** *(They)*
3. **The tide in the Bay of Fundy can overtake <u>a man</u>.** *(him)*
4. **<u>The Amazon River</u> contains half of the world's river water.** *(It)*
5. **These natural wonders really amaze <u>you and me</u>.** *(us)*

Differentiated Instruction

SI Strategic Intervention

Presenting spelling words Students may benefit if you make sure to pronounce the spelling words clearly and give added time for them to write.

Daily Fix-It

9. The clime up the mountain was too hard for Joe and she. *(climb; her)*
10. She sliped and hurt her self. *(slipped; herself)*

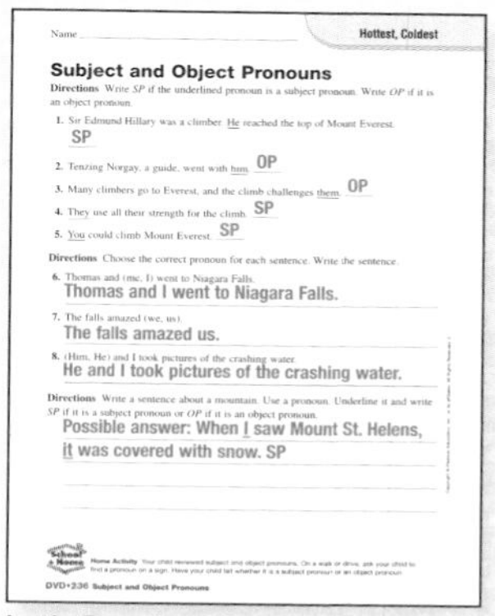
Name ______ Hottest, Coldest

Subject and Object Pronouns

Directions Write *SP* if the underlined pronoun is a subject pronoun. Write *OP* if it is an object pronoun.

1. Sir Edmund Hillary was a climber. He reached the top of Mount Everest. SP
2. Tenzing Norgay, a guide, went with him. OP
3. Many climbers go to Everest, and the climb challenges them. OP
4. They use all their strength for the climb. SP
5. You could climb Mount Everest. SP

Directions Choose the correct pronoun for each sentence. Write the sentence.

6. Thomas and (me, I) went to Niagara Falls. Thomas and I went to Niagara Falls.
7. The falls amazed (we, us). The falls amazed us.
8. (Him, He) and I took pictures of the crashing water. He and I took pictures of the crashing water.

Directions Write a sentence about a mountain. Use a pronoun. Underline it and write *SP* if it is a subject pronoun or *OP* if it is an object pronoun.

Possible answer: When I saw Mount St. Helens, it was covered with snow. SP

DVD•236 Subject and Object Pronouns

Let's Practice It!
TR DVD•236

Objectives

- Proofread a revised draft of an imaginative story, editing for correct use of subject and object pronouns.
- Create and present a final draft.

Writing—Imaginative Story
Subject and Object Pronouns

Review Revising

Remind students that yesterday they revised their imaginative stories, paying particular attention to combining ideas into compound and complex sentences. Today they will proofread their imaginative stories.

MINI-LESSON

Proofread for Subject and Object Pronouns

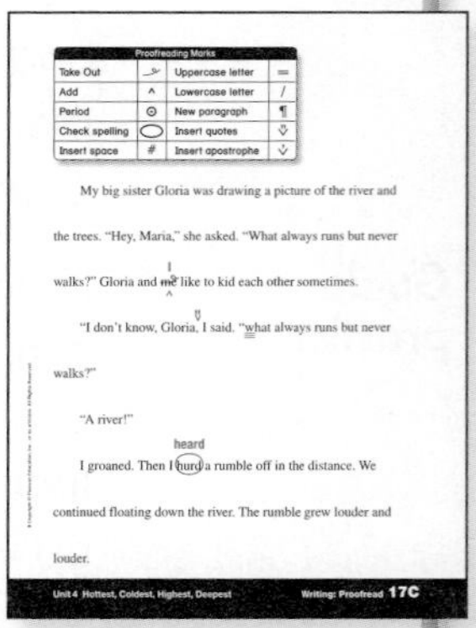

Proofreading Marks			
Take Out		Uppercase letter	≡
Add	^	Lowercase letter	/
Period	⊙	New paragraph	¶
Check spelling	◯	Insert quotes	
Insert space	#	Insert apostrophe	

My big sister Gloria was drawing a picture of the river and the trees. "Hey, Maria," she asked. "What always runs but never walks?" Gloria and me like to kid each other sometimes.

"I don't know, Gloria, I said. "what always runs but never walks?"

"A river!"

I groaned. Then I hurd a rumble off in the distance. We continued floating down the river. The rumble grew louder and louder.

Unit 4 Hottest, Coldest, Highest, Deepest Writing: Proofread 17C

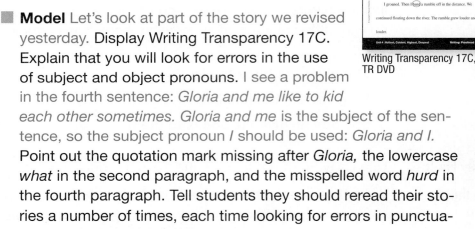

Writing Transparency 17C, TR DVD

■ **Teach** When we proofread, we look closely at our work, searching for errors in mechanics such as spelling, capitalization, punctuation, and grammar. Today we will focus on making sure subject and object pronouns are used correctly.

■ **Model** Let's look at part of the story we revised yesterday. Display Writing Transparency 17C. Explain that you will look for errors in the use of subject and object pronouns. I see a problem in the fourth sentence: *Gloria and me like to kid each other sometimes. Gloria and me* is the subject of the sentence, so the subject pronoun *I* should be used: *Gloria and I.* Point out the quotation mark missing after *Gloria,* the lowercase *what* in the second paragraph, and the misspelled word *hurd* in the fourth paragraph. Tell students they should reread their stories a number of times, each time looking for errors in punctuation, capitalization, spelling, and grammar.

Proofread

Display the Proofreading Tips. Ask students to proofread their stories, using the Proofreading Tips and paying particular attention to subject and object pronouns. Circulate around the room answering students' questions. When students have finished editing their own work, have pairs proofread one another's imaginative stories.

Proofreading Tips

- ✔ Be sure subject and object pronouns are used correctly.
- ✔ Check for punctuation and capitalization, especially with dialogue.
- ✔ Check for correct spelling.
- ✔ Check for correct grammar.

Present

Have students incorporate revisions and proofreading edits into their stories to create a final draft.

Give students two options for presenting: an oral reading or a poster. For each option, students should illustrate their stories on poster board. For an oral presentation, students should read their stories aloud to the class and explain the poster art. For a poster presentation, students should attach their stories to the poster and display it in the room. When students have finished, have each complete a Writing Self-Evaluation form.

ROUTINE **Quick Write for Fluency** Team Talk

1. **Talk** Pairs discuss what they learned about writing an imaginative story this week.
2. **Write** Each student writes a few sentences explaining what he or she learned.
3. **Share** Partners read each other's explanations and ask each other questions about what they learned.

Routines Flip Chart

Teacher Note

Writing self-evaluation Make copies of the Writing Self-Evaluation Guide on p. 39 of the *Reader's and Writer's Notebook* and hand out to students.

Academic Vocabulary

Punctuation includes marks, such as commas and periods, that are used to organize writing.

ELL

English Language Learners

Support editing Provide examples of the correct use of subject and object pronouns, to which students may refer as they edit their stories.

Poster preview Prepare students for next week by using Week 3, ELL Poster 18. Read the Poster Talk-Through to introduce the concept and vocabulary. Ask students to identify and describe objects and actions in the art.

Selection summary Send home the summary of *Rocks in His Head,* in English and in the students' home languages, if available. Students can read the summary with family members.

Preview NEXT WEEK

Why is it valuable to have unique interests? Tell students that next week they will read about a man who loved to collect rocks and find out where that interest could take him.

DAY 5 Assessment Checkpoints for the Week

Weekly Assessment

Use pp. 119–126 of *Weekly Tests* to check:

✔ **Phonics** Vowels: *r*-Controlled

✔ **Comprehension Skill** Graphic Sources

✔ **Lesson Vocabulary**

average	outrun
depth	peak
deserts	tides
erupted	waterfalls

✔ Review **Comprehension Skill** Main Idea and Details

Weekly Tests

Differentiated Assessment

A Advanced

OL On-Level

SI Strategic Intervention

Use pp. 97–102 of *Fresh Reads for Fluency and Comprehension* to check:

✔ **Comprehension Skill** Graphic Sources

✔ Review **Comprehension Skill** Main Idea and Details

✔ **Fluency** Words Correct Per Minute

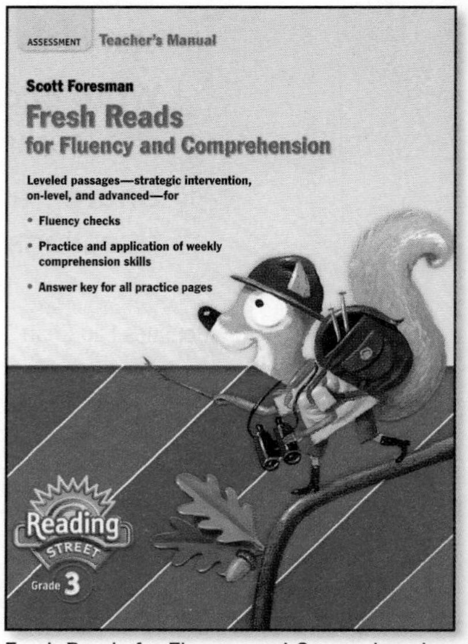

Fresh Reads for Fluency and Comprehension

Managing Assessment

Use *Assessment Handbook* for:

✔ **Weekly Assessment Blackline Masters for Monitoring Progress**

✔ **Observation Checklists**

✔ **Record-Keeping Forms**

✔ **Portfolio Assessment**

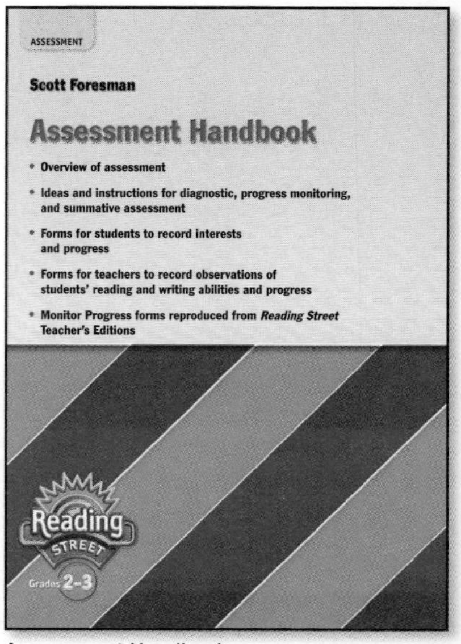

Assessment Handbook

Teacher Notes

Pacing Small Group Instruction

15–20 min

5-Day Plan

DAY 1	• Reinforce the concept • Read Leveled Readers Concept Literacy Below Level
DAY 2	• Graphic Sources • Important Ideas • Revisit Student Edition pp. 62–69
DAY 3	• Unknown Words • Revisit Student Edition pp. 70–75
DAY 4	• Practice Retelling • Read/Revisit Student Edition pp. 80–83
DAY 5	• Reread for fluency • Reread Leveled Readers

3- or 4-Day Plan

DAY 1	• Reinforce the concept • Read Leveled Readers
DAY 2	• Graphic Sources • Important Ideas • Revisit Student Edition pp. 62–69
DAY 3	• Unknown Words • Revisit Student Edition pp. 70–75
DAY 4	• Practice Retelling • Read/Revisit Student Edition pp. 80–83 • Reread for fluency • Reread Leveled Readers

3-Day Plan: Eliminate the shaded box.

SI Strategic Intervention

DAY 1

Build Background

■ **Reinforce the Concept** Reinforce the weekly question *What makes nature's record holders unique?* When we talk about nature's record holders, we mean the tallest tree or the fastest animal or the deepest ocean. Why do you think these topics interest so many people? *(These records are often surprising and amazing.)* Add new words to the concept map. Then lead a classroom discussion about the concept map. What record holders in nature do you already know about? *(Students may say that they know that Mount Everest is the world's tallest mountain.)* If you wish, talk about natural record holders in your area of the United States.

Preview Decodable Practice Reader 17A

■ **Before Reading** Review the words in Decodable Practice Reader 17A. Then have students blend these story words: *talent, bundle, tunnel, spade, bored, blurted, wormholes,* and *sequins.* Be sure students understand the meaning of words such as *talent* and *bored.* Guide students through the text by doing a picture walk.

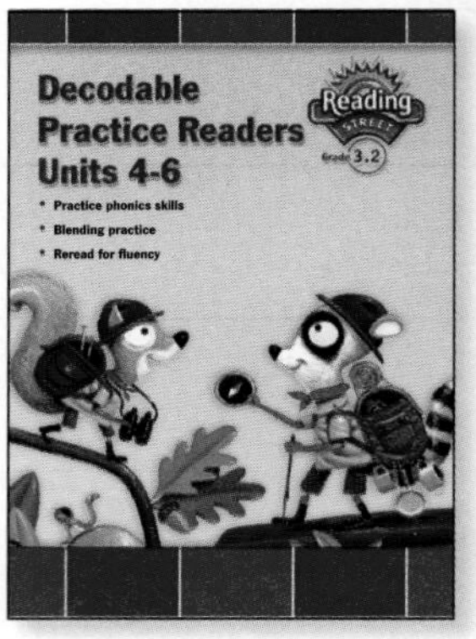

Objectives

• Participate in teacher-led discussions by answering questions with appropriate detail.

SI Strategic Intervention

DAY 1

For a complete literacy instructional plan and additional practice with this week's target skills and strategies, see the **Leveled Reader Teaching Guide.**

Concept Literacy Reader

- **Read** *Extremes*
- **Before Reading** Preview the book with students, focusing on key concepts and vocabulary. Then have them set a purpose for reading.
- **During Reading** Read the first two pages aloud while students track along with the print. Then have students finish reading the book with a partner.
- **After Reading** After students finish reading, ask: How does the place where you live compare to the extreme places in this book? *(Students should be able to support their answers with details from the selection.)*

Below-Level Reader

- **Read** *How to Measure the Weather*
- **Before Reading** Have students use the photographs to preview the book. Then have them set a purpose for reading.
- **During Reading** Read pp. 3–5 aloud. Then do a choral reading of pp. 6–9. If students are able, have them read and discuss the remainder of the book with a partner. Ask: What tools can you use to measure weather? *(thermometer, weather vane, anemometer, rain gauge, barometer)*
- **After Reading** Ask students to look at and discuss the concept map. Connect the Below-Level Reader to the weekly question. How do meteorologists' tools help us understand unique things in nature? *(They help us get facts about nature, and they help experts record measurements showing extremes.)*

MONITOR PROGRESS

If... students have difficulty reading the selection with a partner,
then... have them follow along as they listen to the Leveled Readers DVD-ROM.

If... students have trouble understanding how people measure weather,
then... reread pp. 3–5 and explain that meteorologists use thermometers to measure temperature.

Objectives

- Participate in teacher-led discussions by answering questions with appropriate detail.

Student Edition pp. EI•10–11

More Reading

Use additional Leveled Readers or other texts at students' instructional levels to reinforce this week's skills and strategies. For text suggestions, see the Leveled Reader Database or the Leveled Readers Skills Chart on pp. CL24–CL29.

SI Strategic Intervention

DAY 2

Reinforce Comprehension

Skill Graphic Sources Review with students the *Envision It!* material on Graphic Sources on pp. EI•10–EI•11. Then use p. 58 to review the definition of graphic sources. Graphic sources include photographs, illustrations, maps, graphs, charts, and diagrams, all of which help explain ideas. If you wanted to compare the amount of rain in your neighborhood and in another area, what kind of graphic source might you use? *(a graph or chart)*

Strategy Important Ideas Review the definition of important ideas. Titles, captions, and boldface type are clues to important ideas in a selection. The first sentence of a paragraph also may contain important ideas. Ask students to list the important ideas in this selection as they read. For additional support, refer students to *Envision It!* p. EI•19.

Revisit *Hottest, Coldest, Highest, Deepest* on pp. 62–68. As students read, have them apply the comprehension skill and strategy to this expository text.

- What does the chart on p. 65 show? *(the lengths of the world's longest rivers)*
- What two things does the graph on p. 66 compare? *(the height of the Empire State Building and the depth of Lake Baikal)*
- How would you show the height of Mauna Kea, in Hawaii? *(Students may recommend a chart, graph, or illustration.)*

Use the During Reading Differentiated Instruction for additional support for struggling readers.

MONITOR PROGRESS

If… students have difficulty reading along with the group,
then… have them follow along as they listen to the AudioText.

Objectives
- Locate specific information in graphic features of text.

SI Strategic Intervention

DAY 3

Reinforce Vocabulary

- **Reread for Fluency** Use Decodable Practice Reader 17A.

Decoding Multisyllabic Words Write the word *average* and model how to use nonmeaningful parts to read it. First, I divide the word into chunks: *av er age.* Does the last part mean *age,* as in "how old something or someone is"? No, I don't think so. The dictionary says *average* can mean "ordinary" or "in the middle; neither most nor least." As I read, I will think about which meaning of *average* makes sense with the other words and phrases around it.

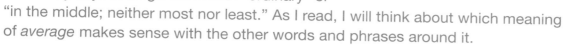

Use the Multisyllabic Words routine on the *Routines Flip Chart* to help students read these words from the text: *outrun, deserts, waterfalls,* and *erupted.*

Unknown Words/Dictionary or Glossary Write the word *tides* on the board. In the text, it says that the place with the most extreme tides is a place where the water level rises and falls the most. I don't know what *tides* are, so I'll look up the word in a dictionary. The *-s* at the end of the word is probably an ending, so I probably need to look up the word *tide.* The dictionary says a *tide* is the natural rise and fall of the ocean.

- **Revisit** *Hottest, Coldest, Highest, Deepest* on pp. 69–75. Review *Words!* on p. W•14. Encourage students to use a dictionary or glossary to figure out the meaning of any unknown words in the selection. Ask: Is a desert always hot? *(no)* What is a desert? *(a place that gets very little rain)*

Use the During Reading Differentiated Instruction for additional support for struggling readers.

MONITOR PROGRESS

If... students need more practice with the lesson vocabulary,
then... Use *Envision It! Pictured Vocabulary Cards.*

Objectives

- Use a dictionary or glossary to determine meanings of unknown words.

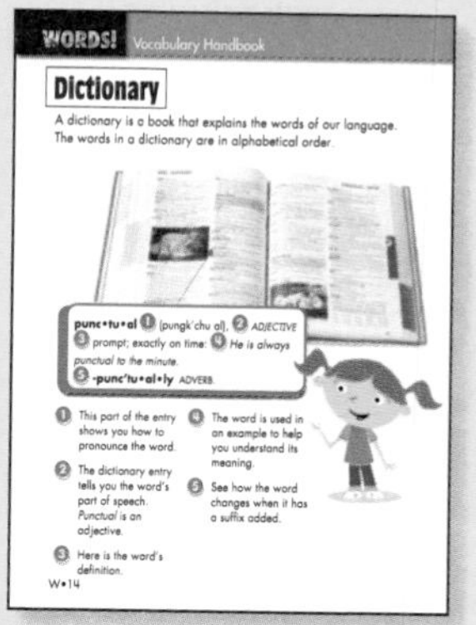

Student Edition p. W•14

More Reading

Use additional Leveled Readers or other texts at students' instructional levels to reinforce this week's skills and strategies. For text suggestions, see the Leveled Reader Database or the Leveled Readers Skills Chart on pp. CL24–CL29.

SI Strategic Intervention

DAY 4

Practice Retelling

■ **Retell** Guide students in using the Retelling Cards to recount important ideas.

- What do the places in this selection have in common? *(They all break records.)*
- What makes each one unique? *(They break records for different qualities.)*

If students struggle, model a fluent retelling.

Genre Focus

■ **Before Reading or Revisiting** "Paul Bunyan and the Great Lakes" on pp. 80–83, read aloud the genre information about legends on p. 80. A legend is a story from the past. Usually it is told from generation to generation until one person writes it down. Legends often explain something from history or culture. This legend will tell about the Great Lakes.

Read the rest of the panel. Then have students read the introduction.

■ **During Reading or Revisiting** Have students perform a choral reading of the selection. As they read, write each of the legend's exaggerations on the board. In what way are things in this legend made to seem extreme? *(Everything is made to seem big.)*

■ **After Reading or Revisiting** Have students share their reactions to the selection. Then guide them through the Reading Across Texts and Writing Across Texts activities, prompting if necessary.

- What are both selections about? *(They are both about extremes in nature.)*
- What does the main selection that you read this week tell about natural features? *(It tells how hot, cold, high, or deep they can be.)*
- What does the Paul Bunyan legend tell about natural features? *(It tells a tall tale about how the Great Lakes came to be.)*

MONITOR PROGRESS

If... students have difficulty retelling the selection,
then... have them review the selection using the illustrations.

Objectives

- Paraphrase themes of fables, legends, myths, or stories.

SI Strategic Intervention DAY 5

For a complete literacy instructional plan and additional practice with this week's target skills and strategies, see the **Leveled Reader Teaching Guide.**

Concept Literacy Reader

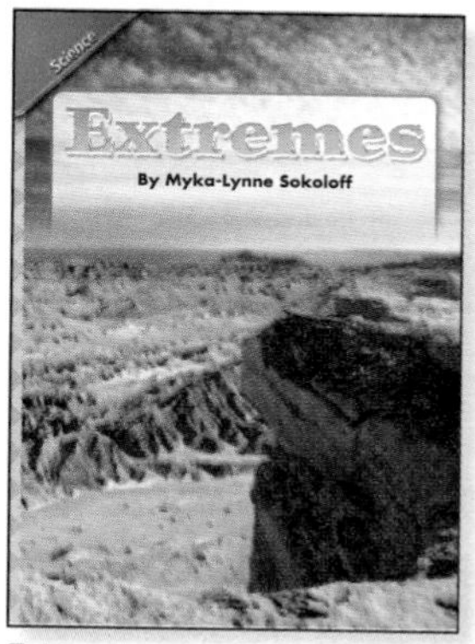

Extremes

- **Model** Model the fluency skill of appropriate phrasing and punctuation cues. Ask students to listen carefully as you read aloud the first two pages of *Extremes.* Have them note how you group words into phrases rather than reading each word haltingly and how you pause briefly at the end of each sentence.
- **Fluency Routine**
  1. Have students reread passages from *Extremes* with a partner.
  2. For optimal fluency, students should reread three to four times.
  3. As students read, monitor fluency and provide corrective feedback.

  See *Routines Flip Chart* for more help with fluency.
- **Retell** Have students retell *Extremes.* Prompt as necessary.

Below-Level Reader

How to Measure the Weather

- **Model** Ask students to listen carefully as you read aloud the first two pages of *How to Measure the Weather,* emphasizing punctuation cues and appropriate phrasing.
- **Fluency Routine**
  1. Have students reread passages from *How to Measure the Weather* with a partner or individually.
  2. For optimal fluency, students should reread three to four times.
  3. As students read, monitor fluency and provide corrective feedback.

  See *Routines Flip Chart* for more help with fluency.
- **Retell** For additional practice, have students retell *How to Measure the Weather* page by page, using the illustrations. Prompt as necessary.
  - What do meteorologists do? *(They measure and analyze changes in weather to predict how weather will change.)*
  - What elements of weather do they measure? *(changes in air temperature, wind direction, and speed; amounts of rain and snow; and air pressure)*

MONITOR PROGRESS

If... students have difficulty reading fluently,
then... provide additional fluency practice by pairing nonfluent readers with fluent ones.

Objectives

- Read aloud grade-level appropriate text with fluency.

Pacing Small Group Instruction

15–20 min

5-Day Plan

DAY 1	• Expand the concept • Read On-Level Reader
DAY 2	• Graphic Sources • Important Ideas • Revisit Student Edition pp. 62–69
DAY 3	• Unknown Words • Revisit Student Edition pp. 70–75
DAY 4	• Practice Retelling • Read/Revisit Student Edition pp. 80–83
DAY 5	• Reread for fluency • Reread On-Level Reader

3- or 4-Day Plan

DAY 1	• Expand the concept • Read On-Level Reader
DAY 2	• Graphic Sources • Important Ideas • Revisit Student Edition pp. 62–69
DAY 3	• Unknown Words • Revisit Student Edition pp. 70–75
DAY 4	• Practice Retelling • Read/Revisit Student Edition pp. 80–83 • Reread for fluency • Reread On-Level Reader

3-Day Plan: Eliminate the shaded box.

OL On-Level

DAY 1

Build Background

■ **Expand the Concept** Connect to the weekly question *What makes nature's record holders unique?* Then expand the concept. How can we explore the uniqueness of natural features? *(We can study them and measure them.)* Discuss the meaning of the words on the concept map on p. 55.

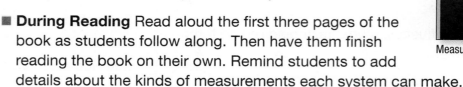

On-Level Reader

For a complete literacy instructional plan and additional practice with this week's target skills and strategies, see the **Leveled Reader Teaching Guide.**

■ **Before Reading** *Measuring the Earth,* have students preview the book by looking at the title, cover, and pictures. This book explains how experts measure different things in nature. As you read, look for different methods of measuring.

Have students create a Venn diagram with the headings *GPS Systems and Seismographs.* Explain that they will complete their Venn diagrams as they read.

Measuring the Earth

■ **During Reading** Read aloud the first three pages of the book as students follow along. Then have them finish reading the book on their own. Remind students to add details about the kinds of measurements each system can make.

- How do scientists measure distances? *(They use global positioning systems, which track distances by satellite.)*
- How do they measure earthquakes? *(They use seismographs, which measure movements in the Earth's crust.)*
- What can both GPS systems and seismographs do? *(They can both show the exact location of something.)*

■ **After Reading** Have partners compare their Venn diagrams.

- Which measuring tool do you think is used most often? Why? *(GPS systems are used the most. They can help people with everyday travel.)*
- How would life be different without GPS systems and seismographs? *(Exact measurements would be more difficult to figure out. Traveling in a desert would be more dangerous without a GPS system, and earthquakes would be more dangerous without seismographs to detect earthquake patterns.)*

Objectives

- Participate in teacher-led discussions by answering questions with appropriate detail.

OL On-Level DAY 2

Expand Comprehension

Skill Graphic Sources Use p. 58 to review the definition of graphic sources. For additional review, see the material on Graphic Sources in *Envision It!* pp. El•10–11. Ask students to preview the graphs and charts in *Hottest, Coldest, Highest, Deepest.*

Strategy Important Ideas Review the definition of important ideas, and encourage students to locate key ideas and concepts in the text as they read. For additional support, use the Extend Thinking questions during reading or refer students to p. El•19 of *Envision It!*

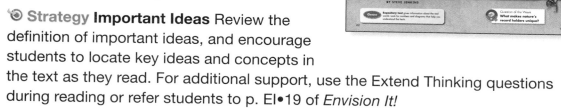

Revisit *Hottest, Coldest, Highest, Deepest* on pp. 62–68. Discuss what important ideas students have learned by studying the graphic sources.

- What kind of information do these graphic sources provide? *(very specific information that helps the reader compare extreme depths, heights, lengths, and temperatures)*
- The chart on p. 65 shows that the Mississippi-Missouri river system is longer than the United States! How do you think it fits within the country? *(It must wind back and forth across the land.)*

If possible, display a map of the United States and help students trace the length and course of this river system.

Objectives

- Locate specific information in graphic features of text.

Student Edition pp. El•10–11

More Reading

Use additional Leveled Readers or other texts at students' instructional levels to reinforce this week's skills and strategies. For text suggestions, see the Leveled Reader Database or the Leveled Readers Skills Chart on pp. CL24–CL29.

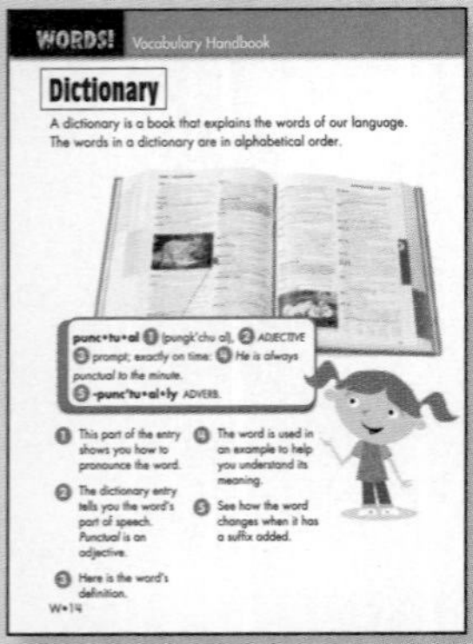

Student Edition p. W•14

More Reading

Use additional Leveled Readers or other texts at students' instructional levels to reinforce this week's skills and strategies. For text suggestions, see the Leveled Reader Database or the Leveled Readers Skills Chart on pp. CL24–CL29.

OL On-Level

DAY 3

Expand Vocabulary

Unknown Words/Dictionary or Glossary Read a sentence containing a difficult word, such as "The average *depth* of the world's oceans is about 3 miles, or 16,000 feet."

- What are some possible meanings of the word *depth* based on this sentence? In other words, what terms would make sense if you substituted them for *depth*? *(length; wideness; deepness)*
- What kind of word do you think the word *depth* is—a noun, verb, adjective, or pronoun? *(noun)*
- Check a dictionary. According to the definition, what does the word mean? *("deepness")*

Revisit *Hottest, Coldest, Highest, Deepest* on pp. 69–75. Encourage students to use a dictionary or glossary to decode unknown words they encounter at any point in the selection. Point out the label "Typical annual New York City snowfall" on p. 75.

- What are some possible meanings of the word *typical* based on this label? *(It might mean "usual"* or *"average.")*
- Check a dictionary. According to the definition, what does *typical* mean? *(It means "average, usual, or matching a certain standard.")*

Explain to students that visual dictionaries are available in print and online. These dictionaries include photographs, diagrams, and cutaway illustrations. They can show you what a certain word means instead of telling you in other words.

Objectives

- Use a dictionary or glossary to determine meanings of unknown words.

OL On-Level DAY 4

Practice Retelling

- **Retell** To assess students' comprehension, use the Retelling Cards. Monitor retelling and prompt students as needed.

Genre Focus

- **Before Reading or Revisiting** "Paul Bunyan and the Great Lakes" on pp. 80–83, read aloud the genre information about legends on p. 80. Explain that legends can offer surprising and entertaining ways to think about objects and events. Have students preview "Paul Bunyan and the Great Lakes" and set a purpose for reading. Based on the pictures, how is this legend about the Great Lakes different from the expository text you just read? *(The legend is not real. It seems to be about a giant digging a lake. The selection I just read is nonfiction. It gives interesting facts instead of telling a funny story.)*
- **During Reading or Revisiting** Have students read along with you.
  - According to this legend, how did the Great Lakes form? *(Paul Bunyan dug them out for his ox and his lumberjack crew to drink from.)*
  - What quality do Paul Bunyan, the ox, and the Great Lakes all share? *(They are all amazingly large.)*
  - How is this legend similar to and different from the expository text? *(The author of the legend imagines how amazing things might have come to be. The author of the expository text tells what amazing things are actually like.)*
- **After Reading or Revisiting** Have students share their reaction to "Paul Bunyan and the Great Lakes." Then have them work in small groups or pairs to create a legend about a natural feature in your community.

Objectives

- Paraphrase themes of fables, legends, myths, or stories.

OL On-Level

DAY 5

On-Level Reader

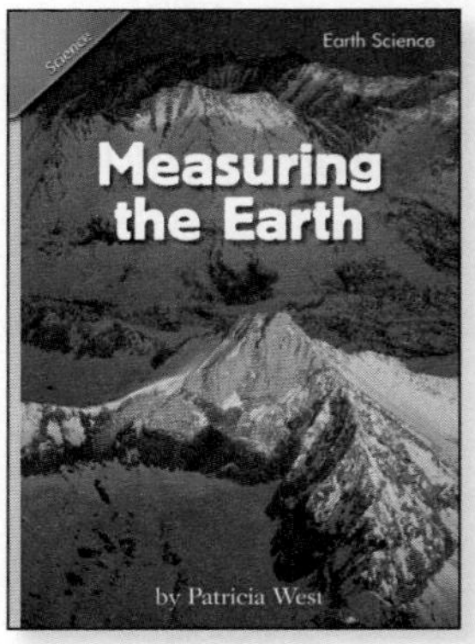

Measuring the Earth

- **Model** Read aloud p. 3 of the On-Level Reader *Measuring the Earth,* emphasizing punctuation cues and appropriate phrasing. Explain that a fluent reader pauses briefly after a comma and for a slightly longer time after a period, question mark, or exclamation point. If you wish, read a section of the On-Level Reader word by word in a monotone to show how much easier it is to understand a fluent reader.
- **Fluency Routine**

1. Have students reread passages from *Measuring the Earth* with a partner.
2. For optimal fluency, students should reread passages three to four times.
3. As students read, monitor fluency and provide corrective feedback. Have students take care to group words in a logical way and to pause at commas and at end punctuation.

See *Routines Flip Chart* for more help with fluency.

- **Retell** For additional practice, have students use illustrations as a guide to retelling *Measuring the Earth.* Prompt as necessary.
  - When would a global positioning system come in handy? *(when you're out camping, lost, or planning a trip)*
  - What is a seismograph good for? *(measuring movement in the Earth's crust)*
  - Why is it important to measure the Earth precisely? *(to avoid dangerous situations, such as getting lost in a desert or not knowing which areas of the planet have had strong earthquakes)*

Objectives

- Read aloud grade-level appropriate text with fluency.

A Advanced DAY 1

Build Background

- **Extend the Concept** Extend the weekly question *What makes nature's record holders unique?* What makes every feature in nature unique? *(Every feature is slightly different from every other feature. Unlike objects that are manufactured, every natural feature is one of a kind.)* How can you discover what is unique about a particular natural feature? *(Observe, study, and measure it. Then compare it to similar natural features.)*

Advanced Reader

For a complete literacy instructional plan and additional practice with this week's target skills and strategies, see the **Leveled Reader Teaching Guide.**

- **Before Reading** *Largest, Fastest, Lightest, Longest,* have students look at the illustrations and use them to glean details from the book. Then have them set a purpose for reading.
- **During Reading** Have students read the Advanced Reader independently, and encourage them to think critically. For example, ask:
  - What problem did Sir Hugh Beaver face, and how did he solve it?
  - What do you find interesting about the facts in this book?

Largest, Fastest, Lightest, Longest

- **After Reading** Have students review the concept map and explain how *Largest, Fastest, Lightest, Longest* helps them answer the weekly question *What makes nature's record holders unique?* Prompt students as necessary.
  - If you were going to try to break a world record, which record would you like to break? Why?
  - How would you verify your record?
  - How does the fact that any record can be broken at any time affect you? Does it motivate you to try to break a record or discourage you from trying?
- **Now Try This** Assign "Now Try This" at the end of the Advanced Reader. Students should work on their journals throughout the week.

Objectives

- Participate in teacher-led discussions by answering questions with appropriate detail.

Pacing Small Group Instruction

15–20 min

5-Day Plan

DAY 1	• Extend the concept • Read Advanced Reader
DAY 2	• Graphic Sources • Important Ideas • Revisit Student Edition pp. 62–69
DAY 3	• Unknown Words • Revisit Student Edition pp. 70–75
DAY 4	• Legend • Read/Revisit Student Edition pp. 80–83
DAY 5	• Reread for fluency • Reread Advanced Reader

3- or 4-Day Plan

DAY 1	• Extend the concept • Read Advanced Reader
DAY 2	• Graphic Sources • Important Ideas • Revisit Student Edition pp. 62–69
DAY 3	• Unknown Words • Revisit Student Edition pp. 70–75
DAY 4	• Legend • Read/Revisit Student Edition pp. 80–83 • Reread for fluency • Reread Advanced Reader

3-Day Plan: Eliminate the shaded box.

A Advanced

DAY 2

More Reading

Use additional Leveled Readers or other texts at students' instructional levels to reinforce this week's skills and strategies. For text suggestions, see the Leveled Reader Database or the Leveled Readers Skills Chart on pp. CL24–CL29.

Extend Comprehension

Skill **Graphic Sources** Explain that graphic sources can help readers analyze facts and ideas in expository text. For example, physical maps are color-coded to show where mountains and valleys lie. How would you color-code a map to show the depth of Lake Baikal and the height of Mount Everest and Mauna Kea? *(Answers should distinguish between the relative height and depth of each.)*

Strategy **Important Ideas** Review the definition of important ideas. Then remind students to note any important ideas they find as they read the rest of the selection. During reading, use the Extend Thinking questions and the During Reading Differentiated Instruction for additional support.

Revisit *Hottest, Coldest, Highest, Deepest* on pp. 62–68. As students read, they should pay close attention to the graphic sources.

- Look at the information in the chart on p. 65. Why do you think the illustrator included information on the width of the United States? *(The rivers are so long that the reader needs something familiar to understand the distance.)*
- How does the combination of text and graphic sources make the important ideas in the text easier to understand? *(The graphic sources allow the reader to understand ideas at a glance. The text explains what the graphic sources show and provides useful, interesting details.)*
- Based on what you have read so far, which of the places that the author describes would you most like to visit? Why? *(Encourage students to support their responses with evidence from the text.)*

Objectives

- Locate specific information in graphic features of text.

A Advanced DAY 3

Extend Vocabulary

Unknown Words/Dictionary or Glossary Challenge students to find information about words that are unfamiliar to them.

- The page about Mount Everest includes the word *peak.* Does *peak* mean "look briefly at something"? *(No; that doesn't make sense in the sentence.)*
- A dictionary gives several definitions of *peak.* Which one makes sense on this page? *("the highest point of a hill or mountain")*

■ **Revisit** *Hottest, Coldest, Highest, Deepest* on pp. 69–75. Encourage students to review the entire selection for confusing or unfamiliar words. Students should then check a dictionary or glossary to be sure that their understanding of the terms is correct.

- Look at the information about precipitation on p. 70. If a place got ten inches of rain and eight inches of snow in a year, would it be a desert? *(No; it would have more than 10 inches of precipitation altogether.)*
- What happens when a volcano erupts? *(Lava comes out.)*

■ **Critical Thinking** Ask students to consult a visual dictionary, either in print or online, to learn more about weather conditions, mountains, and volcanoes.

- In what ways is a visual dictionary more helpful than a regular dictionary? *(A visual dictionary shows what things look like and how they are put together. It also shows related vocabulary on the same page, such as* volcano *and* lava.*)*
- In what ways is a regular dictionary more helpful than a visual dictionary? *(A regular dictionary is better at describing things that people can't see.)*

Objectives

- Use a dictionary or glossary to determine meanings of unknown words.

More Reading

Use additional Leveled Readers or other texts at students' instructional levels to reinforce this week's skills and strategies. For text suggestions, see the Leveled Reader Database or the Leveled Readers Skills Chart on pp. CL24–CL29.

A Advanced

DAY 4

Genre Focus

Paul Bunyan and the Great Lakes

- **Before Reading or Revisiting** "Paul Bunyan and the Great Lakes" on pp. 80–83, read aloud the panel information on legends and ask students to set a purpose for reading. Then direct students to read "Paul Bunyan and the Great Lakes" on their own.
- **During Reading or Revisiting** Point out that a legendary character sometimes has the same qualities as ordinary people—but in greater quantities. How is Paul Bunyan different from an ordinary man? *(He is physically bigger and stronger in every way.)* How are his actions legendary? *(They are big and impressive like him.)*
- **After Reading or Revisiting** Lead a discussion of Reading Across Texts. Then have students do Writing Across Texts independently.

Objectives
- Paraphrase themes of fables, legends, myths, or stories.

A Advanced

DAY 5

Largest, Fastest, Lightest, Longest

- **Reread for Fluency** Have students silently reread passages from the Advanced Reader *Largest, Fastest, Lightest, Longest.* Then have them reread aloud with a partner or individually. As students read, monitor fluency and provide corrective feedback. If students read fluently on the first reading, they do not need to reread three to four times. Assess the fluency of students in this group using p. 85j.
- **Retell** Have students retell the important ideas behind the Advanced Reader *Largest, Fastest, Lightest, Longest.*
- **Now Try This** Have students complete their journals and share their results with classmates.
  - What did you learn from setting a personal record?
  - In what way are personal records important even if they never lead to a world record?

Objectives
- Read aloud grade-level appropriate text with fluency.

ELL English Language Learners

The ELL lessons are organized by strands. Use them to scaffold the weekly curriculum of lessons or during small group time instruction.

Academic Language

Students will hear or read the following academic language in this week's core instruction. As students encounter the vocabulary, provide a simple definition or concrete example. Then ask students to suggest an example or synonym of the word and identify available cognates.

Skill Words	controlled vowel graphic sources	subject *(sujeto)* object *(objeto)* pronoun *(pronombre)* complex sentence
Concept Words	natural *(naturale)* disaster *(desastre)*	volcano *(volcán)* hurricane *(huracán)* earthquake

**Spanish cognates in parentheses*

Concept Development

What makes nature's record holders unique?

■ **Preteach Concept**

- **Prior Knowledge** Have students turn to pp. 54–55 in the Student Edition. Make students cognizant of academic language by reminding them that they are tapping into their prior knowledge of amazing things in nature. How are these trees unique? Why is this snake unique? Tell about other unique things in nature.
- **Discuss Concept** Elicit students' knowledge and experience of how nature can challenge us. Let's discuss the concept. What's the biggest animal you can think of?
- **Poster Talk-Through** Read aloud the Poster Talk-Through on ELL Poster 17 and work through the Day 1 activities.

■ **Daily Concept and Vocabulary Development** Use the daily activities on ELL Poster 17 to build concept and vocabulary knowledge.

Objectives

- Learn new language structures, expressions, and basic and academic vocabulary heard during classroom instruction and interactions.
- Listen to and derive meaning from a variety of media such as audio tape, video, DVD, and CD ROM to build and reinforce concept and language attainment.

Content Objectives

- Use concept vocabulary related to record holders in nature.
- Learn academic language in context.

Language Objectives

- Express ideas in response to art and discussion.

Daily Planner

DAY 1	• **Frontload Concept** • **Preteach** Comprehension Skill, Vocabulary, Phonics/Spelling, Conventions • **Writing**
DAY 2	• **Review** Concept, Vocabulary, Comprehension Skill • **Frontload Main Selection** • **Practice** Phonics/Spelling, Conventions/Writing
DAY 3	• **Review** Concept, Comprehension Skill, Vocabulary, Conventions/Writing • **Reread Main Selection** • **Practice** Phonics/Spelling
DAY 4	• **Review Concept** • **Read ELL/ELD Readers** • **Practice** Phonics/Spelling, Conventions/Writing
DAY 5	• **Review** Concept, Vocabulary, Comprehension Skill, Phonics/Spelling, Conventions • **Reread ELL/ELD Readers** • **Writing**

**See the ELL Handbook for ELL Workshops with targeted instruction.*

Concept Talk Video

Have students listen to and view the Concept Talk Video to build and reinforce common language used when learning about nature's record holders.

Language Objectives

- Understand and use basic vocabulary.
- Learn meanings of grade-level vocabulary.

Mini-Lesson

Explain to students that learning basic vocabulary helps to create sentences. Have students write the ten high-frequency words on cards. Assign each student one word. Then have students turn to pp. 62–75 in the Student Edition and look at the illustrations in the story. Using the high-frequency word, have each student say a sentence aloud about a picture.

ELL English Language Learners

Basic Vocabulary

■ **High-Frequency Words** Use the ELL Vocabulary Routine on p. 471 of the *ELL Handbook* to systematically teach newcomers the first 300 sight words in English. Students who began learning ten words per week at the beginning of the year are now learning words 161–170 (*ELL Handbook,* p. 452). p. 446 of the handbook contains a bank of strategies that you can use to ensure students' mastery of High-Frequency words.

Lesson Vocabulary

■ **Preteach** Use the following routine to Introduce the Lesson Vocabulary:

1. Distribute copies of this week's Word Cards (*ELL Handbook,* page 125).
2. Display ELL Poster 17 and reread the Poster Talk-Through.
3. Using the poster illustrations, model how a word's meaning can be expressed with other similar words: There were three places where there was crashing water flowing from the mountains, or *waterfalls.*
4. Use these sentences to reveal the meaning of the other words.
   - The *depth* of the canyon was more than 200 feet. (how deep something is)
   - A cheetah can *outrun* all other animals. (run faster than)
   - The climber reached the *peak* in two days. (the top of a mountain)
   - Low *tide* happens when ocean water moves back from the beach. (the regular rise and fall of the ocean's surface)
   - The high *waterfalls* poured over the steep cliff. (water that flows from a high place to a low place)
   - The volcano *erupted* and sprayed rocks, ash, and lava into the air. (burst forth)
   - The wind blew the sand around the *desert.* (area of land where it is hot and dry)
   - The *average* yearly rainfall in the desert is less than six inches. (middle point of the sum of numbers)

Objectives

- Recognize elements of the English sound system in newly acquired vocabulary such as long and short vowels, silent letters, and consonant clusters.
- Use visual, contextual, and linguistic support to enhance and confirm understanding of increasingly complex and elaborated spoken language.
- Develop basic sight vocabulary, derive meaning of environmental print, and comprehend English vocabulary and language structures used routinely in written classroom materials.

ELL English Language Learners

- **Reteach** Distribute copies of the Word Cards to pairs. Have students take turns guessing the word from oral and physical word clues given by their partner.

  Have one partner pick up a card without the other seeing it. The first partner gives clues about the word's meaning without using the word itself. The clues may be gestures, pantomime, words, phrases, or sentences. The guesser tries to identify the word quickly, as the first partner adds clues. Time the play to encourage swift recognition of the word. Partners should take turns giving clues and guessing the word.

- **Writing** List the selection vocabulary words on the board: *average, depth, deserts, erupted, outrun, peak, tides, waterfalls.* Have students write or dictate individual words, phrases, or short sentences with each of the words. They may refer to the poster for ideas. Provide prompts if necessary: A desert is hot. Can you describe a desert another way? Yes, a desert can be dry too. I run fast. I can run faster than a turtle. I can outrun a turtle. What can you outrun?

Leveled Support

Beginning Have students work in pairs with more proficient students. On one side of each card, students will copy the vocabulary word. Then they will dictate a word that reminds them of the vocabulary word. The partner will write that word on the other side of the card. Students can use their set of cards to practice the meaning and spelling of each word.

Intermediate/Advanced Have pairs of students generate sentences using the Lesson Vocabulary. Suggest that they write sentences about images in the poster.

Advanced High Have students independently generate sentences and then share them with the class.

Objectives

- Use strategic learning techniques such as concept mapping, drawing, memorizing, comparing, contrasting, and reviewing to acquire basic and grade-level vocabulary.
- Speak using grade-level content area vocabulary in context to internalize new English words and build academic language proficiency.

Language Objectives

- Produce drawings, phrases, short sentences to show an understanding of Lesson Vocabulary.

ELL Teacher Tip

Beginning students may have emergent writing skills in their home language. Encourage beginners to write meanings of new vocabulary in their home language or use their home language for clues to a word's meaning until they become more proficient in English.

Content Objectives

- Monitor and adjust oral comprehension.
- Learn essential language.

Language Objectives

- Discuss oral passages.

ELL Teacher Tip

To strengthen listening comprehension, have students listen to find answers to specific questions. Write the questions on the board and have students read them chorally. Have them clarify their understanding of the questions before you begin to read aloud.

Mini-Lesson

Students may have difficulty answering your questions because they don't know the correct English word. As you read the passage aloud, use gestures to illustrate the story, such as climbing. When students respond to your follow-up question, have them use non-verbal cues to say their answers if they do not know the English word.

ELL English Language Learners

Listening Comprehension

Read Aloud

He Climbed the Tallest Tree

Stephen Sillett loves trees. He loves to study and climb trees. In 2006, he climbed the tallest tree in the world.

Sillett lives in California, where redwood trees grow. Redwoods are the tallest trees in the world. Some stand over 350 feet tall and are still growing. The rich soil and wet weather helps the trees grow. There is a lot of rain in the winter and fog in the summer.

There once were many redwood trees in the forest. But people cut them down. Sillet found the tallest tree that was still there. But he had to measure the tree to be sure. Sillet had to climb the tree to measure it. First he had to climb up to the first branch. The first branch was hundreds of feet above the ground. How could he get up there?

Sillet used a bow called a crossbow. He attached an iron bolt to the end of a long rope. Then he attached the rope to an arrow, and shot it into a high branch. It stuck! The rope with the bolt flew into the air. It flew over the branch. The rope was now attached to the tree. Sillet attached the bolt to a nearby tree.

Sillet climbed to the top of tree. Then he measured the tree with tape. It was over 379 feet. He had found and climbed the tallest tree in the world!

Prepare for the Read Aloud The modified Read Aloud above prepares students for listening to the oral reading "To Climb the Tallest Tree" on p. 55b.

- **First Listening** This true story is about a man who climbed the tallest tree in the world. How did he climb it? How did he measure it? Then have students complete the first two columns of a KWL chart (*ELL Handbook* p. 480).
- **Second Listening** Have students complete the KWL chart. Assist as needed.

Objectives

- Speak using learning strategies such as requesting assistance, employing non-verbal cues, and using synonyms and circumlocution (conveying ideas by defining or describing when exact English words are not known).

ELL English Language Learners

Phonics and Spelling

■ ***r*-Controlled Vowels: /ėr/**

Have students turn to p. 56 in the student edition.

- **Preteach** Have students point to the picture of the pearls in row 1. These are pearls. Ear has the sound /ėr/. Say it with me: pearls.
- **Decode Words** Point to *fern, girl,* and *worm.* Tell students that in addition to being spelled *ear,* the /ėr/ sound can also be spelled *er, ir,* and *or.* Have students decode the *r*-controlled words and say the words aloud.
- **Practice Decoding** Write these words on the board: *pear, clear, deer, steer, skirt, shirt, worth, mayor, alligator.* Ask students to underline the spelling of *r*-controlled vowels in each word. Have students say the word aloud. Have them monitor and self-correct their pronunciation of the words by checking to see if they have blended the /r/ sound with the vowel. Remind them to think about if the words sound correct when they say them aloud.

Vocabulary Skill: Unknown Words

■ **Preteach/Model** Have students turn to p. 67 of the Student Edition. Read the second paragraph aloud. *Measured* is a hard word. I'm not sure what it means, so I will have to look it up in the dictionary to find out. Let's find *patient* in the dictionary. Model looking up a word, then read the definition aloud. Provide an example using *measured* in a different context.

■ **Practice** Have students find other words in the selection that are unknown to them. Then have them look up the words in a dictionary.

Leveled Support

Beginning/Intermediate Have pairs of students find unknown words. Then help them find the words in a dictionary. Ask them to copy the word and draw a picture to illustrate it.

Advanced/Advanced High Have students work independently to find difficult or unknown words, and then have them find the words in a dictionary. Ask students to copy the word and its definition, and then have them write an original sentence using the word. Have students read their sentences aloud.

Objectives

- Distinguish sounds and intonation patterns of English with increasing ease.
- Practice producing sounds of newly acquired vocabulary such as long and short vowels, silent letters, and consonant clusters to pronounce English words in a manner that is increasingly comprehensible.

Content Objectives

- Review *r*-controlled vowels.
- Identify spellings of *r*-controlled vowels /ėr/.

Language Objectives

- Apply phonics and decoding skills to spelling.
- Practice spelling words.

Transfer Skills

Pronunciation of /ėr/ The /r/ sound is flapped or rolled in languages such as Spanish, Polish, Farsi, and Arabic. Therefore, speakers of these languages may have difficulty pronouncing words with *r*-controlled vowels, especially in words such as *part* and *turn.* Spanish does not have a sound equivalent to /ėr/, so Spanish speakers may need extra practice in pronouncing words with *r*-controlled vowels.

ELL Teaching Routine

For more practice with sounds, use the Sound-by-Sound Blending Strategy Routine (*ELL Handbook,* p. 472).

Content Objectives

- Identify graphic sources.
- Understand how graphics enhance information in text.

Language Objectives

- Discuss information in graphic sources.

ELL Workshop

Encourage students to ask questions to monitor their understanding of instruction of comprehension skills. Use Ask Clarifying Questions (*ELL Handbook,* pp. 404–405) for practice.

ELL English Language Learners

Comprehension
Graphic Sources

- **Preteach** Graphic sources of information are sources that help you picture information. They can be maps, charts, diagrams, graphs, or illustrations. Have students turn to *Envision It!* on p. EI•10 in the Student Edition. Read aloud the caption on the map. The caption on the map says "Where spider monkeys live." What does the red spot on the map show? (the part of South America in which spider monkeys live) Have students turn to *Envision It!* on p. EI•11. Read aloud the title of the bar graph. What does the bar graph tell you? What do monkeys eat most?

- **Reteach** Give each student a copy of Picture It! (*ELL Handbook,* p. 126). Teach the Skill Points, using the passage as an example. Have students use the illustration to predict what the passage will be about. Have them write their prediction on the line, read the paragraph, and then answer the questions.

Leveled Support

Beginning/Intermediate Reread the paragraph aloud. Monitor as students answer the questions. Then have them tell how the picture helped them make their guess.

Advanced/Advanced High Have pairs of students reread the paragraph to link the illustration and text. Then have students complete the page. (**Answers:** 1. Answers will vary; 2. Two large cities [Chicago and San Diego] with different climates; 3. beaches, water)

MINI-LESSON

Social Language

Have students look through pp. 65–66, 68, and 72 of *Hottest, Coldest, Highest, Deepest* in the Student Edition to identify the graphic sources of information. What is this graphic called? What information does it tell you? Have students write word cards with language and details in the story that are unfamiliar. Partners can practice explaining with the specificity and detail of information in the graphic sources in the selection.

Objectives

- Understand the general meaning, main points, and important details of spoken language ranging from situations in which topics, language, and contexts are familiar to unfamiliar.
- Monitor understanding of spoken language during classroom instruction and interactions and seek clarification as needed.

ELL English Language Learners

Reading Comprehension

Hottest, Coldest, Highest, Deepest

Student Edition pp. 62–75

- **Frontloading** Read aloud the title and discuss what things in nature might fit these adjectives. I wonder which places on earth are the hottest, coldest, highest, and deepest. What other things in nature might be "record holders"? Let's look through the selection to find clues. As a prereading support. Guide students on a picture walk through *Hottest, Coldest, Highest, Deepest.* Ask students to predict where these places might be. During reading, pause and invite students to adjust their predictions. Provide students with a three-column chart to fill out as they read the selection. Supply these headings: *Name of Place; Where Is It?; Why Is It Unique?*

- **Sheltered Reading** Ask questions such as the following to guide students' comprehension:
  - **p. 65:** What is the longest river in the world? (the Nile) Where is it? (in Africa) What is the second-longest river? (the Amazon) Where is it? (in South America)
  - **p. 66:** What does the diagram on this page show? (how much deeper the lake is than the Empire State Building is tall)
  - **p. 67:** What do the maps on this page show? (where the highest mountains are located) Which mountain is higher? (Mauna Kea)
  - **p. 68:** What does the diagram show? (It compares different temperatures.) Have students read the temperatures and compare them.

  Choose other pages to confirm student understanding of graphic sources.

- **Fluency: Appropriate Phrasing: Punctuation Cues** Remind students that commas in a sentence tell you when to pause, or stop briefly. Read aloud the last paragraph on p. 64. Model pausing at commas. Reread the page aloud. Have students read the paragraph chorally. For more practice, use the Fluency: Choral Reading Routine (*ELL Handbook,* p. 474).

- **After Reading** Have students show listening comprehension by guide students in summarizing the text using the Retelling Strip on p. 76 of the Student Edition. Assign each student a task based on proficiency level. Beginning students can repeat facts about each natural record holder. Intermediate and Advanced students can retell the information in the graphic source and the text.

Objectives

- Use prereading supports such as graphic organizers, illustrations, and pretaught topic-related vocabulary and other prereading activities to enhance comprehension of written text.

Content Objectives

- Monitor and clarify comprehension.
- Make and adjust predictions.

Language Objectives

- Use punctuation cues to phrase appropriately when reading aloud.
- Summarize text using visual support.

Graphic Organizer

Name of Place	Where Is It?	Why Is It Unique?

Audio Support

Have students listen to the eSelection or the AudioText CD. Reinforce language attainment and monitor comprehension by having them answer the questions in the three-column chart again.

ELL English Language Learners

For additional leveled instruction, see the **ELL/ELD Reader Teaching Guide.**

Comprehension: *How Big? How Strong?*

ELL Reader 3.4.2 ELD Reader 3.4.2

- **Before Reading** Distribute copies of the ELL and ELD Readers, *How Big? How Strong?: Hurricanes and Earthquakes,* to students at their reading level.
  - **Preview** Read the title aloud with students: This is informational text about hurricanes and earthquakes. Invite students to look through the pictures and name what they see. Have them predict what they will learn about hurricanes and earthquakes based on the picture clues and their prior knowledge.
  - **Set a Purpose for Reading** Let's read to find out how big and how strong hurricanes and earthquakes can be.
- **During Reading** For both reading groups follow this Reading Routine with a decreasing need for linguistic accomodations as students learn more English.

1. Read the entire Reader aloud slowly.
2. Reread pp. 2–4, pausing to build background knowledge or model comprehension. Have Beginning students finger-point as you read. Use the questions in the chart below to check students' comprehension.
3. Have students do a choral rereading of pp. 2–4.
4. Repeat steps 2–3 above for pp. 5–8.

- **After Reading** Use the exercises on the inside back cover of each Reader and invite students to share their writing. In a whole-group discussion, ask students, What have you seen and heard during a bad storm? Record their answers on the board and invite them to point to pictures in the book to support their answers.

ELD Reader Beginning/Intermediate

- **p. 2** What is a hurricane? What is an earthquake? Read two sentences that tell you. (p. 2, Hurricanes are big ocean storms. Earthquakes happen when the earth suddenly moves.
- **pp. 3–5** How much damage did Hurricane Andrew do in 1992? (p. 4 destroyed billions of dollars; buildings, property)

Writing Find the sentence in the book that describes the damage a hurricane can do. Copy the sentence.

ELL Reader Advanced/Advanced High

- **p. 2:** What is one way a hurricane and an earthquake are alike? (Both are natural disasters.) How are they different? (a hurricane is an ocean storm; an earthquake is a sudden movement of the earth)
- **pp. 3–5:** What does the Saffir-Simpson Scale measure? (hurricane strength) Why did Hurricane Andrew cause so much damage? (winds, high tides)

Study Guide Distribute copies of the ELL Reader Study Guide (*ELL Handbook,* p. 130). Scaffold comprehension of graphic sources by helping students review the Reader to answer questions. (See *ELL Handbook,* pp. 209–212.)

Objectives

- Understand the general meaning, main points, and important details of spoken language ranging from situations in which topics, language, and contexts are familiar to unfamiliar.
- Read linguistically accomodated context area material with a decreasing need for linguistic accomodations as more English is learned.

ELL English Language Learners

Conventions
Subject and Object Pronouns

- **Preteach** Review subject and object pronouns by displaying these sentences: *Mandy is my friend. She is funny. I see her every day.* Mandy is the subject of the first sentence. *She* is a subject pronoun that stands for *Mandy* in the second sentence. In the third sentence, *her* stands for *Mandy*. *Her* is the object of the verb see. *Her* is an object pronoun.
- **Teach/Model** Write this chart on the board: Have students create new sentences using these pronouns.

	Subject Pronouns	Object Pronouns
Singular	I, you, he, she, it	me, you, him, her, it
Plural	we, you, they	us, you, them

- **Practice**

Leveled Support

Beginning/Intermediate Write these sentence frames on the board. Have students complete the sentence frames orally, using pronouns. Ask students to identify each pronoun as a subject pronoun or an object pronoun. *Frames:* ______ brush my teeth. They see ______. ______ read with ______.

Advanced/Advanced High Have students write original sentences with subject and object pronouns and then share them with a partner.

- **Reteach** Display the chart. Review and clarify with oral examples.
- **Practice** Write these sentences on the board: *I am helping my mother clean. I am cleaning with her. My mother is making lunch. I am helping her.*

Leveled Support

Beginning/Intermediate Have students point out the subject and object pronouns in each sentence. Have students copy the sentences.

Advanced/Advanced High Divide students into two teams. One team makes a list of proper nouns including names of famous people and places. The other team is assigned pronouns. The first team calls out one of the proper nouns. The other team tells the subject and object pronouns that fit that name. Teams can then switch roles.

Objectives
- Speak using a variety of grammatical structures, sentence lengths, sentence types, and connecting words with increasing accuracy and ease as more English is acquired.

Content Objectives
- Identify subject and object pronouns.
- Understand the difference between subject and object pronouns.

Language Objectives
- Speak using a variety of grammatical structures.
- Write sentences using subject and object pronouns.

Transfer Skills

Subject Pronouns In Spanish, unlike English, speakers may omit the subject pronoun because Spanish verbs can indicate the subject. Korean speakers may add the subject pronoun after the subject word, as in *Rae, she is my friend.* Have them work with a partner to correct this error.

Object Pronouns

Spanish, Chinese, and Vietnamese speakers may use subject pronouns as objects. (*Give the food to he.*) Provide students with practice to avoid this error.

Content Objectives

- Identify complex sentence patterns.
- Identify clauses and connecting words in complex sentence patterns.
- Write using content-based grade-level vocabulary.

Language Objectives

- Write complex sentence using content-based grade-level vocabulary.
- Share feedback for editing and revising.

ELL Teaching Routine

For practice spelling words related to geography, use the Spelling Routine (*ELL Handbook*, p. 476).

ELL English Language Learners

Complex Sentences

■ **Introduce** Display the model and read it aloud. Each of these sentences is a complex sentence. It is made up of one independent clause and one dependent clause. Each clause has a subject and a verb. Point out the two clauses in the first sentence of the model. Have students identify the subject and verb in each. The two clauses are joined by a connecting word or words. In the first sentence, the connecting word is if. Repeat instruction for the other two sentences. Remind students to pay close attention to verb tenses in each sentence.

Writing Model

If I could visit any place on Earth, I would go to the Sahara Desert. I want to go there even though it is the hottest place on Earth. When I get there, I would like to ride on a camel.

■ **Practice** Write these sentence frames on the board. Work with students to fill in the blanks with appropriate words, phrases, or clauses.

If I could visit any place on Earth, I would go to ______. I want to go there because ______. When I get there, I ______.

■ **Write** Have students review pp. 62–75 in the Student Edition. Have them write a paragraph using content-based vocabulary about a place they read about in the selection. Have them explain why the place they chose is unique.

Leveled Support

Beginning Supply students with a sentence frame for a complex sentence: (*Name of place*) *is a unique place because* ______. Students may dictate to a more proficient partner and then copy the complex sentence.

Intermediate Have partners work together to write one or more complex sentences about one of the record-holding places in the selection.

Advanced/Advanced High Have students develop their paragraph independently. Require them to use at least one complex sentence in their paragraph. Then have pairs exchange papers and provide feedback for revising and editing.

Objectives

- Narrate, describe, and explain with increasing specificity and detail to fulfill content area writing needs as more English is acquired.
- Describe, and explain with increasing specificity and detail as more English is acquired.

This Week's ELL Overview

Grade 3 • Unit 4 • Week 3
Rocks in His Head
86a–115r
and DI•66–DI•75

ELL Handbook

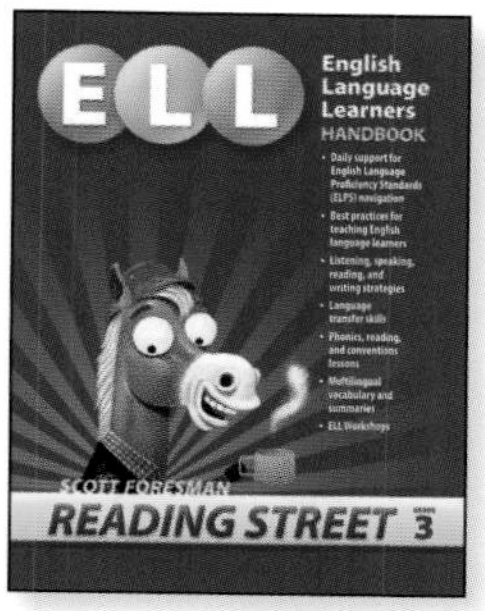

- Maximize Literacy and Cognitive Engagement
- Research Into Practice
- Full Weekly Support for Every Selection

Rocks in His Head
- Multi-Lingual Summaries in Five Languages
- Selection-Specific Vocabulary Word Cards
- Frontloading/Reteaching for Comprehension Skill Lessons
- ELD and ELL Reader Study Guides

- Transfer Activities
- Professional Development

Daily Leveled ELL Notes

ELL notes appear throughout this week's instruction and ELL Support is on the DI pages of your Teacher's Edition. The following is a sample of an ELL note from this week.

English Language Learners

Beginning Write several words with prefixes from the Decodable Reader, such as *outdoors, bicycle,* and *midsummer.* Point to each word as you say it aloud. Then cover the prefix in each word and have students read aloud the base word. Cover the base word and have students read aloud the prefix. Finally, have students read aloud the entire word with you.

Intermediate Write the prefixes *mid-, out-,* and *pre-* in one column and the words *way, soak, doors, read, point,* and *did* in a second column. Have students take turns drawing a line from a prefix to a base word to make the words *midway, presoak, outdoors, preread, midpoint,* and *outdid.*

Advanced After reading, have students choose four or five words with prefixes from the story. Have students write each word and draw a line between the prefix and the base word. Then have students pronounce each word aloud.

Advanced High Have students choose four or five words with prefixes. Have students write a sentence with the base word and another sentence with the entire word.

ELL by Strand

The ELL lessons on this week's Support for English Language Learners pages are organized by strand. They offer additional scaffolding for the core curriculum. Leveled support notes on these pages address the different proficiency levels in your class. See pages DI•66–DI•75.

ELL Guy
Dr. Jim Cummins

The Three Pillars of ELL Instruction

ELL Strands	Activate Prior Knowledge	Access Content	Extend Language
Vocabulary pp. DI•67–DI•68	Preteach	Reteach	Leveled Writing Activities
Reading Comprehension p. DI•72	Frontloading	Sheltered Reading	After Reading
Phonics, Spelling, and Word Analysis p. DI•70	Preteach/Model	Practice	Leveled Practice Activities
Listening Comprehension p. DI•69	Prepare for the Read Aloud	First Listening	Second Listening
Conventions and Writing pp. DI•74–DI•75	Preteach/Introduce	Practice	Leveled Practice Activities/ Leveled Writing Activities
Concept Development p. DI•66	Prior Knowledge	Discuss Concept	Daily Concept and Vocabulary Development

This Week's Practice Stations Overview

Six Weekly Practice Stations with Leveled Activities can be found at the beginning of each week of instruction. For this week's Practice Stations, see pp. 86h–86i.

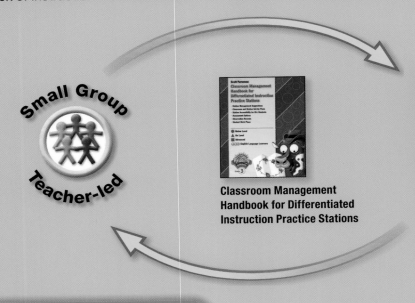

Classroom Management Handbook for Differentiated Instruction Practice Stations

Practice Stations

Daily Leveled Center Activities

- Below
- Advanced
- On-Level
- ELL

Practice Stations Flip Charts

Word Wise

Word Work

Words to Know

Let's Write

Read For Meaning

Get Fluent

	Word Wise	Word Work	Words to Know	Let's Write	Read For Meaning	Get Fluent
Objectives	• Spell words with *r*-controlled vowels (/er/ spelled *ir, er, ur, ear,* and *or; ar, or, ore,* and *oar*).	• Identify and pronounce words with *r*-controlled vowels (/er/ spelled *ir, er, ur, ear,* and *or; ar or, ore,* and *oar*).	• Identify the meaning of unknown words.	• Write an imaginative story.	• Identify graphic sources and the information they present.	• Use punctuation cues, and read aloud with appropriate phrasing.
Materials	• *Word Wise* Flip Chart Activity 18 • word cards • paper • pencil	• *Word Work* Flip Chart Activity 18 • word cards • paper • pencil	• *Words to Know* Flip Chart Activity 18 • newspapers • pencil • paper	• *Let's Write* Flip Chart Activity 18 • magazines • pencil • paper	• *Read for Meaning* Flip Chart Activity 18 • Leveled Readers • paper • pencil	• *Get Fluent* Flip Chart Activity 18 • Leveled Readers

This Week on Reading Street!

Question of the Week

Why is it valuable to have unique interests?

Daily Plan

Whole Group

- Fact and Opinion
- Multiple-Meaning Words
- Fluency/Expression
- Writing/Conventions
- Research and Inquiry

Don't Wait Until Friday

MONITOR PROGRESS **Success Predictor**

Day 1	Day 2	Day 3	Day 4	Day 5
Check Oral Vocabulary	Check Word Reading	Check Retelling	Check Fluency	Check Oral Vocabulary

Small Group

Teacher Led

- Reading Support
- Skill Support
- Fluency Practice

Practice Stations

Independent Activities

Customize Literacy More support for a balanced literacy appoach, see pp. CL•1–CL•47

Customize Writing More support for a customized writing approach, see pp. CW•1–CW•10

Whole Group

- Writing: Biography
- Conventions: Possessive Pronouns
- Spelling: Prefixes pre-, mid-, over-, out-

Assessment

- Weekly Tests
- Day 5 Assessment
- Fresh Reads

This Week's Reading Selections

Main Selection
Genre: **Biography**

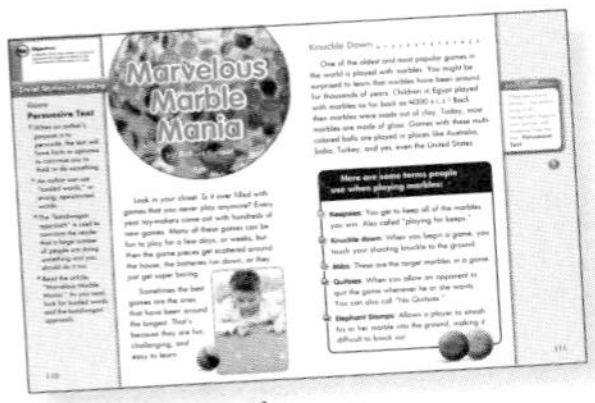

Paired Selection
Genre: **Persuasive Text**

Decodable Readers

Leveled Readers

ELL and ELD Readers

Resources on Reading Street!

	Build Concepts	Phonics	Comprehension
Whole Group	Let's Talk About pp. 86–87	Phonics Skill Lesson pp. 88–89; Decodable Readers; Sound–Spelling Cards	Envision It! Skills/ Strategies; Comprehension Skill Lesson pp. 90–91
Go Digital	• Concept Talk Video	• Interactive Sound-Spelling Cards • Decodable eReaders	• Envision It! Animations • eSelections
Small Group and Independent Practice	Rocks in his Head pp. 94–105; ELL and ELD Readers; Leveled Readers; Decodable Readers	Decodable Readers; Practice Station Flip Chart	Rocks in his Head pp. 94–105; ELL and ELD Readers; Leveled Readers; Envision It! Skills/ Strategies; Reader's and Writer's Notebook; Practice Station Flip Chart
Go Digital	• eReaders • eSelections • Decodable eReaders	• Letter Tile Drag and Drop • Decodable eReaders	• Envision It! Animations • eSelections • eReaders
Customize Literacy	• Leveled Readers • Decodable Readers	• Decodable Readers	• Envision It! Skills and Strategies Handbook • Leveled Readers
Go Digital	• Concept Talk Video • Decodable eReaders • eReaders	• Decodable eReaders	• Envision It! Animations • eReaders • Decodable eReaders

Question of the Week

Why is it valuable to have unique interests?

Vocabulary	Fluency	Conventions and Writing
 Envision It! Vocabulary Cards 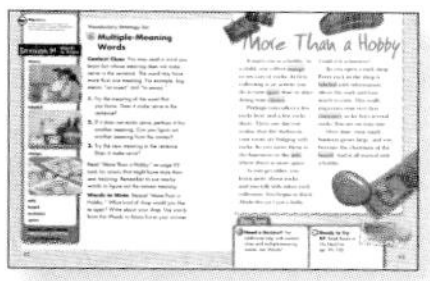 Vocabulary Skill Lesson pp. 92–93	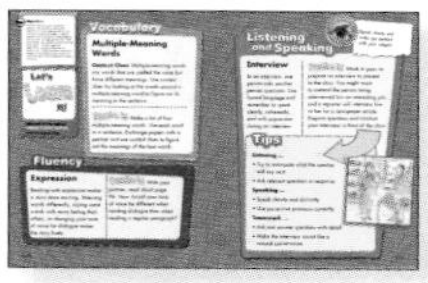 Let's Learn It! pp. 114–115  Decodable and Leveled Readers	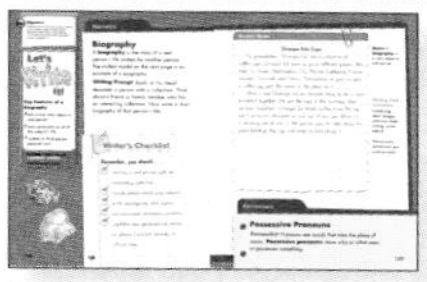 Let's Write It! pp. 108–109  Decodable Readers
• Envision It! Vocabulary Cards • Vocabulary Activities	• eSelection • Decodable eBooks • eReaders	• Grammar Jammer
 Envision It! Vocabulary Cards  Rocks in his Head pp. 94–105  Practice Station Flip Chart  Words!  Reader's and Writer's Notebook	 Rocks in his Head pp. 94–105  Practice Station Flip Chart  Leveled Readers  ELL and ELD Readers	 Reader's and Writer's Notebook  Rocks in his Head pp. 94–105  Practice Station Flip Chart
• Envision It! Vocabulary Cards • Vocabulary Activities • eSelection	• eSelection • eReaders	• Grammar Jammer
• Envision It! Vocabulary Cards	• Leveled Readers • Decodable Readers	• Reader's and Writer's Notebook
• Vocabulary Activities	• eReaders • Decodable eReaders	• Grammar Jammer

Week 3

My 5-Day Planner for Reading Street!

Don't Wait Until Friday MONITOR PROGRESS	Check Oral Vocabulary **Day 1** pages 86j–91f	Word Reading **Day 2** pages 92a–99e
Get Ready to Read	**Concept Talk,** 86j **Oral Vocabulary,** 87a hobby, project, leftover, murmur **Listening Comprehension,** Read Aloud, 87b **Phonics/Word Analysis,** 88a–89b ◎ Prefixes (*pre-, mid-, over-, out-, bi-, de-*) READ **Decodable Practice Reader,** 89a–89b	**Concept Talk,** 92a **Oral Vocabulary,** 92b ancestor **Phonics/Word Analysis,** 92c ◎ Prefixes (*pre-, mid-, over-, out-, bi-, de-*) **Literary Terms,** 92d Idioms **Text Structure,** 92d Problem and Solution
Read and Comprehend	**Comprehension Skill,** ◎ Fact and Opinion, 90a **Comprehension Strategy,** ◎ Inferring, 90a READ **Comprehension,** 90–91 **Model Fluency,** Expression, 90–91 **Introduce Lesson Vocabulary,** 91a stamps, spare, chores, attic, labeled, customer, board	**Vocabulary Skill,** ◎ Multiple-Meaning Words, 92e **Vocabulary Strategy,** Context Clues, 92e **Lesson Vocabulary,** 92–93 stamps, spare, chores, attic, labeled, customer, board READ **Vocabulary,** 92–93 **Model Fluency,** Expression, 92–93 READ **Main Selection,** *Rocks in His Head*, 94–99a
Language Arts	**Research and Inquiry,** Identify Questions, 91b **Spelling,** Prefixes *pre-, mid-, over-, out-,* 91c **Conventions,** Possessive Pronouns, 91d **Handwriting,** Cursive Letters *v* and *z,* 91d **Writing,** Biography, Introduce, 91e–91f	**Research and Inquiry,** Navigate/Search, 99b **Conventions,** Possessive Pronouns, 99c **Spelling,** Prefixes *pre-, mid-, over-, out-,* 99c **Writing,** Biography: Sequence, 99d–99e

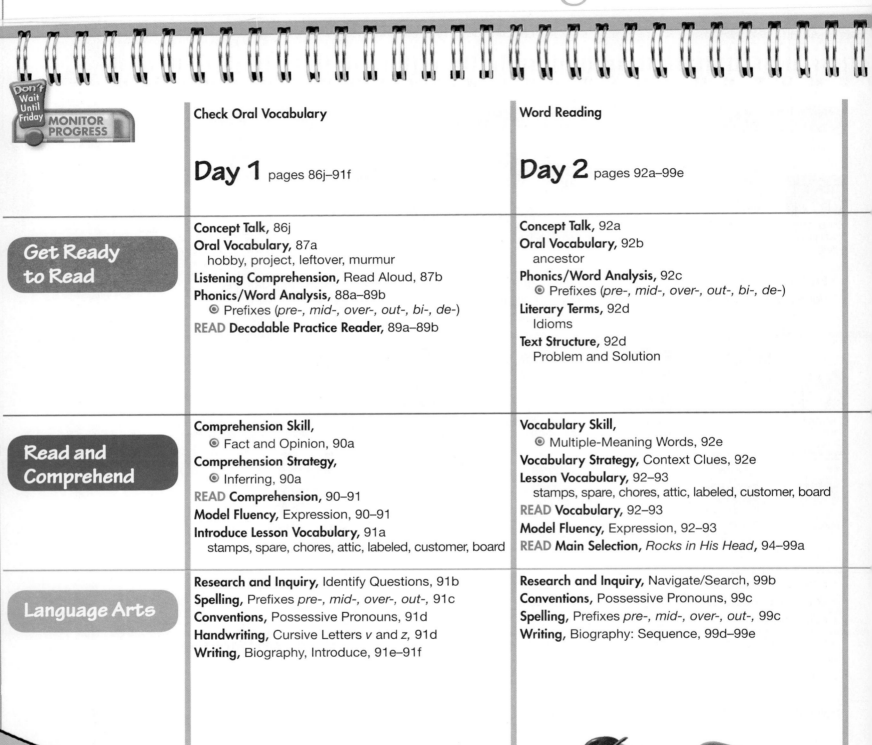

Question of the Week
Why is it valuable to have unique interests?

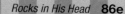

Check Retelling **Day 3** pages 100a–109c	Check Fluency **Day 4** pages 110a–115e	Check Oral Vocabulary **Day 5** pages 115f–115q
Concept Talk, 100a **Oral Vocabulary,** 100b ornament, descendant **Phonics/Word Analysis,** 100c–100d ◎ Prefixes (*pre-, mid-, over-, out-, bi-, de-*) **Decodable Story,** 100d **Comprehension Check,** 100e **Check Retelling,** 100f	**Concept Talk,** 110a **Oral Vocabulary,** 110b forge, compartment Review **Phonics/Word Analysis,** Vowels: *r*-Controlled, 110c–110f **Decodable Story,** 110f **Genre,** Persuasive Text, 110g	**Concept Wrap Up,** 115f **Check Oral Vocabulary,** 115 hobby, project, leftover, murmur, ancestor, ornament, descendant, forge, compartment **Amazing Ideas,** 115g Review ◎ **Fact and Opinion,** 115h Review ◎ **Multiple-Meaning Words,** 115h Review ◎ **Prefixes,** 115i Review **Literary Terms,** 115i
READ **Main Selection,** *Rocks in His Head,* 100–105a **Retelling,** 106–107 **Think Critically,** 107a **Model Frequency,** Expression, 107b **Research and Study Skills,** Online Information, 107c	READ **Paired Selection,** "Marvelous Marble Mania," 110–113a **Let's Learn It!,** 114–115a Fluency: Expression Vocabulary: ◎ Multiple-Meaning Words Listening and Speaking: Interview	**Fluency Assessment,** WCPM, 115j–115k **Comprehension Assessment,** ◎ Fact and Opinion, 115l–115m
Research and Inquiry, Analyze, 107d **Conventions,** Possessive Pronouns, 107e **Spelling,** 107e Prefixes *pre-, mid-, over-, out-* **Let's Write It!,** Biography, 108–109 **Writing,** Biography: Sentences, 109a–109c	**Research and Inquiry,** Synthesize, 115b **Conventions,** Possessive Pronouns, 115c **Spelling,** 115c Prefixes *pre-, mid-, over-, out-* **Writing,** Biography: Revising, 115d–115e	**Research and Inquiry,** Communicate, 115n **Conventions,** Possessive Pronouns, 115o **Spelling Test,** Prefixes, 115o **Writing,** Biography: Possessive Pronouns, 115p–115q **Quick Write for Fluency,** 115q

Grouping Options for Differentiated Instruction
Turn the page for the small group time lesson plan.

Week 3

Planning Small Group Time on Reading Street!

SMALL GROUP TIME RESOURCES

Look for this Small Group Time box each day to help meet the individual needs of all your children. Differentiated Instruction lessons appear on the DI pages at the end of each week.

DAY 1

Teacher Led

SI Strategic Intervention	OL On-Level	A Advanced
Teacher Led • Reinforce the Concept • **Read Concept** Literacy Reader or Below-Level Reader	**Teacher Led** • Explain the Concept • **Read** On-Level Reader	**Teacher Led** • Explain the Concept • **Read** Advanced Reader

ELL Place English language learners in the groups that correspond to their reading abilities in English.

Practice Stations	Independent Activities
• Read for Meaning • Get Fluent • Word Work	• Concept Talk Video • *Reader's and Writer's Notebook* • Research and Inquiry

ELL

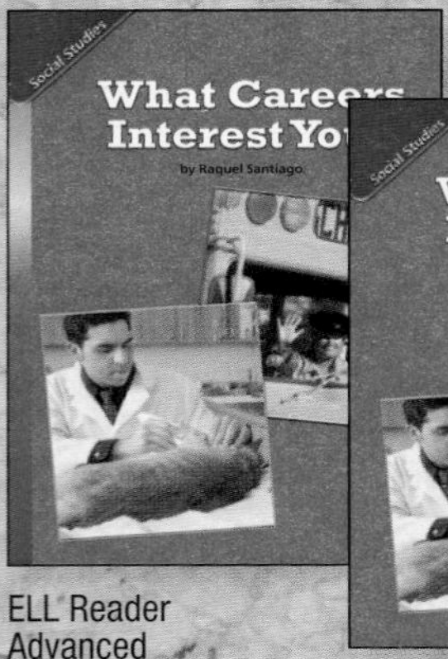

ELL Reader
Advanced
Advanced High

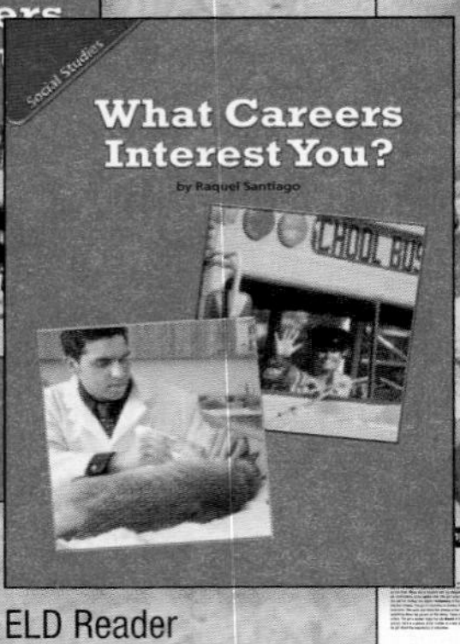

ELD Reader
Beginning
Intermediate

ELL Poster

	Day 1
SI Strategic Intervention	**Reinforce the Concept,** DI•51–DI•52 Read **Decodable Reader,** and **Concept Literacy Reader** or **Below-Level Reader**
OL On-Level	**Expand the Concept,** DI•57 Read **On-Level Reader**
A Advanced	**Extend the Concept,** DI•62 Read **Advanced Reader**
ELL English Language Learners	DI•66–DI•75 **Frontload Concept** **Preteach Writing** **Writing**

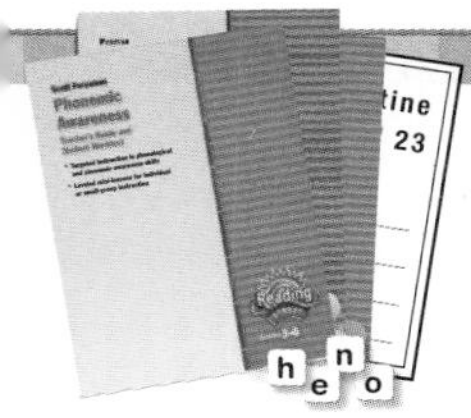

Reading Street Response to Intervention Kit

Reading Street Practice Stations Kit

Question of the Week

Why is it valuable to have unique interests?

SI Strategic Intervention

Below-Level Reader

Concept Literacy Reader

OL On-Level

On-Level Reader

A Advanced

Advanced Reader

Decodable Readers

Rocks in his Head pp. 94–105

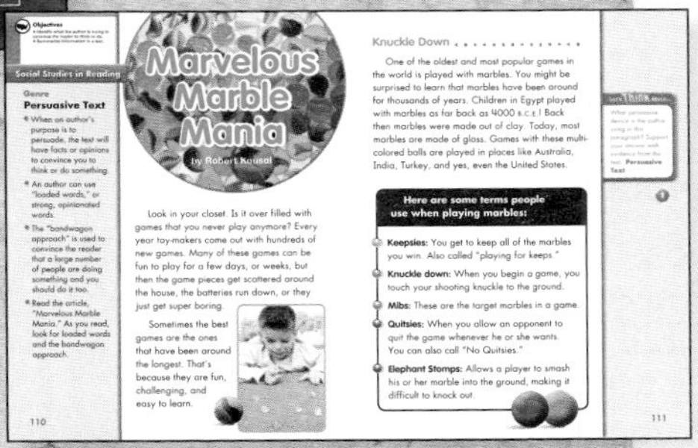

Marvelous Marble Mania pp. 110–113

Small Group Weekly Plan

Day 2	Day 3	Day 4	Day 5
Reinforce Comprehension, DI•53 Revisit **Main Selection,** p. 28	**Reinforce Vocabulary,** DI•54 Read/Revisit **Main Selection**	**Reinforce Comprehension,** Practice Retelling, DI•55 Genre Focus Read/Revisit **Paired Selection**	**Practice Fluency,** DI•56 Reread **Concept Literacy Reader** or **Below-Level Reader**
Expand Comprehension, DI•58 Revisit **Main Selection**	**Expand Vocabulary,** DI•59 Read/Revisit **Main Selection**	**Expand Comprehension,** Practice Retelling, DI•60 Genre Focus Read/Revisit **Paired Selection**	**Practice Fluency,** DI•61 Reread **On-Level Reader**
Extend Comprehension, DI•63 Revisit **Main Selection**	**Extend Vocabulary,** DI•64 Read/Revisit **Main Selection**	**Extend Comprehension,** Genre Focus, DI•65 Read/Revisit **Paired Selection**	**Practice Fluency,** DI•65 Reread **Advanced Reader**
DI•66–DI•75 **Review Concept/Skills** **Frontload Main Selection** **Practice**	DI•66–DI•75 **Review Concept/Skills** Reread **Main Selection** **Practice**	DI•66–DI•75 **Review Concept** Read **ELL/ELD Readers** **Practice**	DI•66–DI•75 **Review Concept/Skills** Reread **ELL/ELD Reader** **Writing**

Practice Stations for Everyone on Reading Street!

Word Wise
r-controlled vowels

Objectives
- Spell words with *r*-controlled vowels (/ėr/ spelled *ir, er, ur, ear,* and *or; ar, or, ore,* and *oar*).

Materials
- *Word Wise* Flip Chart Activity 18
- word cards
- paper
- pencil

Differentiated Activities
● Choose five word cards. Write your words in a list. Write sentences using each of your words. Think of other words you know with similar spellings. Add the words to your list.

▲ Choose seven word cards, and write your words in a list. Write a sentence for each of your words. Think of words you know with similar spellings, and add them to your list.

■ Choose nine word cards, and write your words in a list. Write sentences using each of your words. List two more words with similar spelling patterns for every word on your list.

Technology
- Online Dictionary

Word Work
r-controlled vowels

Objectives
- Identify and pronounce words with *r*-controlled vowels (/ėr/ spelled *ir, er, ur, ear,* and *or; ar, or, ore,* and *oar*).

Materials
- *Word Work* Flip Chart Activity 18
- word cards
- paper
- pencil

Differentiated Activities
● Choose eight word cards. Write the words. Say each word. Notice the vowel or vowels that go with the *r*-sound in each word. Circle the vowel or vowels plus *r*-.

▲ Choose ten word cards, and write the words. Say each word. Circle the vowel plus *r*-sound in each word.

■ Choose twelve word cards, and say each word. Write the words. Circle the *r*-controlled vowel sound in each word.

Technology
- Modeled Pronunciation Audio CD

Words to Know
Unknown words

Objectives
- Identify the meaning of unknown words.

Materials
- *Words to Know* Flip Chart Activity 18
- newspapers
- pencil
- paper

Differentiated Activities
● Use a newspaper to find three words you do not know. Write the words, and find each word's meaning in a dictionary. Write a sentence for each word.

▲ Use a newspaper to find five unknown words. Write the words, find each word's meaning in a dictionary. Write a sentence for each words.

■ Use a newspaper to find seven words you do not know. Write the words, and find each word's meaning and part of speech in a dictionary. Write a sentence for each word.

Technology
- Online Dictionary

Use this week's materials from the Reading Street Leveled Practice Stations Kit to organize this week's stations.

Key

- ● Below-Level Activities
- ▲ On-Level Activities
- ■ Advanced Activities

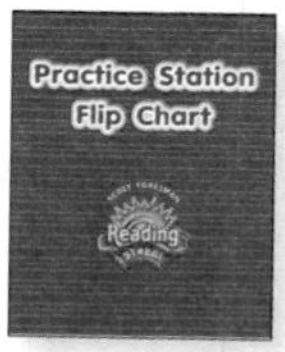

Practice Station Flip Chart

Let's Write!
Imaginative story

Objectives
- Write an imaginative story.

Materials
- *Let's Write!* Flip Chart Activity 18
- magazines • pencil • paper

Differentiated Activities
● Use the magazines to find a picture. Write a short, imaginative story to go with the picture. Use words and pictures. Cut out the picture. Display it with your story.

▲ Use the magazines to find a picture, and write an imaginative story to go with the picture. Use correct punctuation and capitalization. Cut out the picture, and display it with your story.

■ Use the magazines to find a picture, and write an imaginative story to go with the picture. Use complex sentences in your story. Cut out the picture, and display it with your story.

Technology
- Online Graphic Organizers

Read for Meaning
Graphic sources

Objectives
- Identify graphic sources and the information they present.

Materials
- *Read for Meaning* Flip Chart Activity 18
- Leveled Readers
- paper • pencil

Differentiated Activities
● Read one of the books provided by your teacher. Locate a graphic source. What type of graphic source is it? What information does it tell? Identify the graphic source. Write a sentence telling the information that it gives.

▲ Read one of the books provided by your teacher. Notice the graphic sources and the information they tell about. Write sentences about two different graphic sources. Tell the information each source gives.

■ Choose and read a leveled reader, and notice the information the graphic sources provide. Choose two graphic sources. Write a short paragraph telling about each source and the information it tells about.

Technology
- Leveled Reader Database

Get Fluent
Punctuation clues/appropriate phrasing

Objectives
- Use punctuation clues, and read aloud with appropriate phrasing.

Materials
- *Get Fluent* Flip Chart Activity 18
- Leveled Readers

Differentiated Activities
● Work with a partner. Choose a Concept Literacy Reader or Below-Level Reader. Take turns reading a page from the book. Use the readers to practice reading with appropriate phrasing. Provide feedback as needed.

▲ Work with a partner. Choose an On-Level Reader. Take turns reading a page from the book. Use the reader to practice reading with appropriate phrasing. Provide feedback as needed.

■ Work with a partner. Choose an Advanced Reader. Take turns reading a page from the book. Use the reader to practice reading with appropriate phrasing. Provide feedback as needed.

Technology
- Leveled Reader Database
- Reading Street Readers CD-ROM

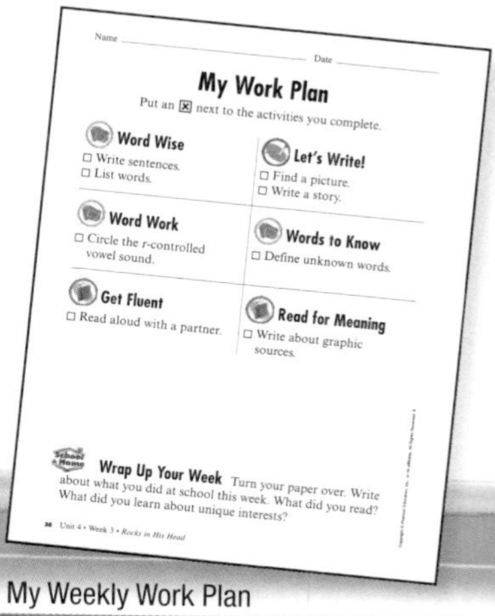

Name ______ Date ______

My Work Plan

Put an ☒ next to the activities you complete.

Word Wise
☐ Write sentences.
☐ List words.

Let's Write!
☐ Find a picture.
☐ Write a story.

Word Work
☐ Circle the *r*-controlled vowel sound.

Words to Know
☐ Define unknown words.

Get Fluent
☐ Read aloud with a partner.

Read for Meaning
☐ Write about graphic sources.

Wrap Up Your Week Turn your paper over. Write about what you did at school this week. What did you learn about unique interests?

My Weekly Work Plan

Week 3

Objectives

- Introduce the weekly concept.
- Develop oral vocabulary.

Today at a Glance

Oral Vocabulary
hobby, murmur, leftover, project

Phonics/Word Analysis
◎ Prefixes *(pre-, mid-, over-, out-, bi-, de-)*

Comprehension
◎ Fact and opinion
◎ Inferring

Reading
"Looking at Rocks"

Fluency
Expression

Lesson Vocabulary
Tested Vocabulary

Research and Inquiry
Identify questions

Spelling
Prefixes *pre-, mid-, over-, out-*

Conventions
Possessive pronouns

Handwriting
Cursive letters *v* and *z*

Writing
Biography

Concept Talk

Question of the Week

Why is it valuable to have unique interests?

Introduce the concept To further explore the weekly concept of One of a Kind, this week students will read, write, and talk about how having unique interests can enrich people's lives and benefit them in important ways.

ROUTINE Activate Prior Knowledge **Team Talk**

1. **Think** Have students think about their own unique interests or the unique interests of people they know.
2. **Pair** Have pairs of students discuss the Question of the Week.
3. **Share** Call on a few students to share their ideas with the group. Other students should listen attentively to the speakers. Guide the discussion and encourage elaboration with prompts such as the ones below. Students should answer questions with appropriate detail.
   - What do you like to do most when you have free time?
   - Do you know anyone who is an expert on something?

Routines Flip Chart

Anchored Talk

Develop oral vocabulary Have students turn to pp. 86–87 in their Student Editions. Look at each of the photos. Then, use the prompts to guide discussion and create *The value of unique interests* concept map.

- Why is the boy using a magnifying glass? (He is studying the leaf very closely.) Studying plants is a popular *hobby.* People gather details, or do research, about the things that interest them. Let's add *Research* to our concept map.
- Why are the boy and girl looking at pictures in a book? (They are identifying the shells that they have collected.) People who have unique interests gain special knowledge about their subjects. Let's add *Knowledge* to our concept map.

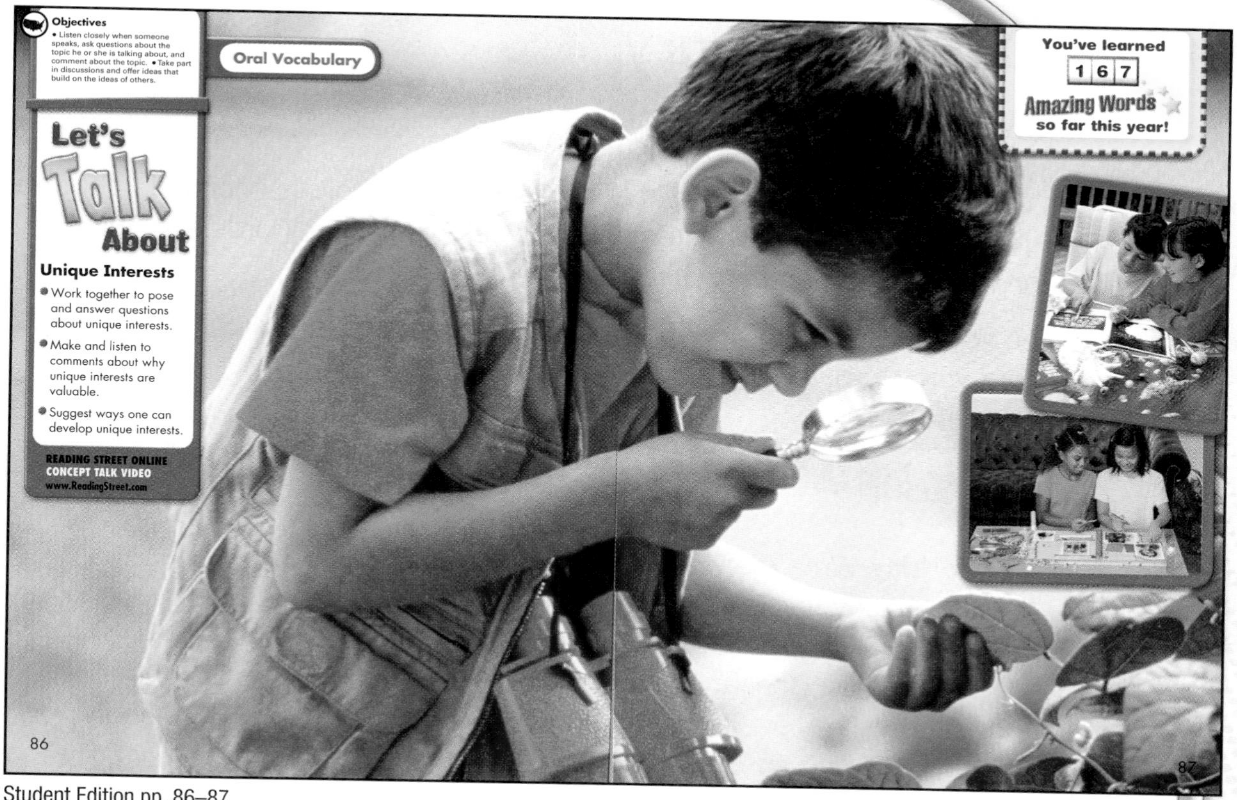
Objectives
• Listen closely when someone speaks, ask questions about the topic he or she is talking about, and comment about the topic. • Take part in discussions and offer ideas that build on the ideas of others.
Oral Vocabulary
Let's Talk About
Unique Interests
• Work together to pose and answer questions about unique interests.
• Make and listen to comments about why unique interests are valuable.
• Suggest ways one can develop unique interests.
READING STREET ONLINE
CONCEPT TALK VIDEO
www.ReadingStreet.com
You've learned 1 6 7 Amazing Words so far this year!
86
87
Student Edition pp. 86–87

Amazing Words

You've learned 1 6 7 words so far.

You'll learn 0 0 9 words this week!

hobby	ornament
project	descendant
leftover	forge
murmur	compartment
ancestor	

Writing on Demand

Writing Fluency
Ask students to respond to the photos on pp. 86–87 by writing as well as they can and as much as they can about why it is valuable to have unique interests.

- What kind of information are the girls organizing for their *project?* (They are organizing a family history.) People with unique interests often organize information about their interests. Let's add *Information* to the concept map.
- After discussing the photos, ask: Why is it valuable to have unique interests?

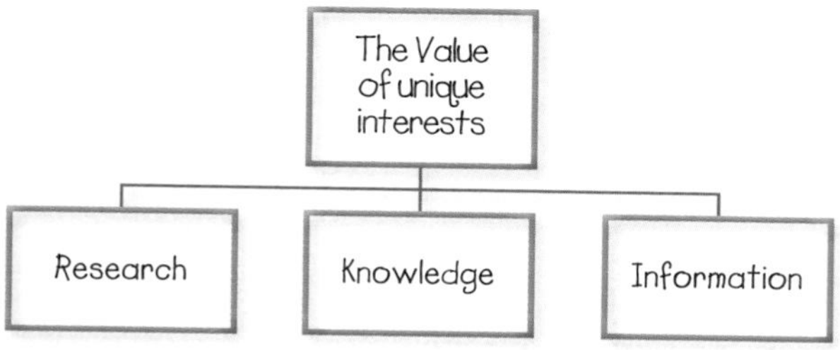
The Value of unique interests
Research
Knowledge
Information

Connect to reading Tell students that this week they will be reading about a man who has a unique interest in rocks. Encourage students to add concept-related words to this week's concept map.

ELL Preteach Concepts Use the Day 1 instructions on ELL Poster 18 to assess and build background knowledge, develop concepts, and build oral vocabulary.

ELL Poster 18

ELL

English Language Learners

ELL support Additional ELL support and modified instruction is provided in the *ELL Handbook* and in the ELL Support lessons on pp. DI•66–DI•75.

Listening comprehension English learners will benefit from additional visual support to understand the key terms in the concept map. Use the pictures on pp. 86–87 to scaffold understanding.

Frontload for Read Aloud Use the modified Read Aloud on p. DI•69 in the *ELL* Support lessons to prepare students to listen to "Picture Perfect" on p. 87b.

Objectives
- Develop listening comprehension.
- Develop oral vocabulary.

Check Oral Vocabulary
SUCCESS PREDICTOR

Oral Vocabulary
Amazing Words

Introduce Amazing Words

"Picture Perfect" on p. 87b is about a boy with a unique interest in photography. Tell students to listen for this week's Amazing Words—*hobby*, *project*, *leftover*, and *murmur*—as you read.

Model fluency

As you read "Picture Perfect," model appropriate expression by adjusting your voice to demonstrate a lively, fluent reader.

Teach Amazing Words

Amazing Words Oral Vocabulary Routine

hobby
project
leftover
murmur

1. **Introduce** Write the word *hobby* on the board. Have students say the word aloud with you. In "Picture Perfect," Sammy's *hobby* begins when he discovers that he loves to take pictures. Does the author include any context clues that help me understand the meaning of the word? Supply a student-friendly definition.
2. **Demonstrate** Have students answer questions to demonstrate understanding. Does Sammy earn money with his *hobby*? What special tools or equipment does Sammy use for his *hobby*?
3. **Apply** Ask students to give a personal example of a *hobby.*

See pp. OV•3 to teach *project, leftover,* and *murmur.*

Routines Flip Chart

Apply Amazing Words

To build oral language, lead the class in a discussion about the Amazing Words' meanings. Remind students to listen attentively, ask relevant questions, and make pertinent comments.

Don't Wait Until Friday

MONITOR PROGRESS **Check Oral Vocabulary**

During discussion, listen for students' use of the Amazing Words.

If... students are unable to use the Amazing Words to discuss the concept,

then... use Oral Vocabulary Routine in the Routine's Flip Chart to demonstrate words in different contexts.

Day 1	Day 2	Day 3	Day 4	Day 5
Check Oral Vocabulary	Check Word Reading	Check Retelling	Check Fluency	Check Oral Vocabulary

Success Predictor

Read Aloud

Picture Perfect

It was Grandpa Jay who first got Sammy hooked on taking pictures. When Sammy was barely two years old, Grandpa Jay held a digital camera up to Sammy's face and said, "Hey there, Sam my man. Push this camera button right here!" Sammy had always liked pushing things, so he happily obeyed. The camera clicked, taking a close-up picture of Grandpa Jay's fuzzy gray beard. Sammy laughed at the hilarious picture. And voila! A hobby was born.

By the time Sammy was five, his parents had given him a small disposable camera to take with him wherever he went. Sammy kept the camera in his backpack and whipped it out whenever he wanted to remember a special moment.

By age nine, Sammy owned a digital camera and a film camera. He loved taking pictures of anyone and anything: his family and friends, his dog Maxine and his hamster Chuck, his one-story house, his street with the funny cracked sidewalks, his parents' orange car, and his school—Roosevelt Elementary. Sammy took pictures up close and from far away. He printed them in color and in black and white. He even took pictures while running, jumping, and standing on his head.

Once when Sammy was at a family picnic, he heard his cousin murmur, "Why do you take so many pictures?"

"Because," said Sammy, "the camera helps me remember stuff. Photographs are like memories that stay around forever."

That evening, Sammy found out that his family would soon be hosting a huge birthday party for Grandpa Jay. Sammy knew immediately what he was going to give his grandfather as a present—a photo album of family memories. Sammy started on his new project by going through all of the photos he'd ever taken. There were so many pictures to choose from! One showed his dad and his brother eating leftover Thanksgiving turkey in some silly pajamas. Another showed his mom laughing as she tried to skateboard down the street. There were pictures from every celebration and every major event that Sammy could remember.

Finally, when Grandpa Jay's birthday arrived, Sammy eagerly brought out the album. "This is for you!" he said, giving the book to his surprised grandfather. As Grandpa Jay opened the cover, the first picture he saw was the one of his fuzzy gray beard. Grandpa Jay burst out laughing and hugged his grandson.

"I thought that this would be a way to remember the special things we've all done together as a family," Sammy said. "Just like now!" And with that, Sammy quickly pulled out his camera and snapped a photo of his smiling grandfather. "I'll save that picture for the next album! I know there are going to be a whole lot more to come!"

Objectives

- ◎ Decode and read words with prefixes *pre-*, *mid-*, *over-*, *out-*, *bi-*, and *de-*.
- ◎ Use word analysis to decode words with prefixes *pre-*, *mid-*, *over-*, *out-*, *bi-*, and *de-*.

Skills Trace

◎ **Prefixes *pre-*, *mid-*, *over-*, *out-*, *bi-*, *de-***

Introduce U4W3D1

Practice U4W3D3; U4W3D4

Reteach/Review U4W3D5; U4W4D4

Assess/Test Weekly Test U4W3

Benchmark Test U4

Key: U = Unit, W = Week, D = Day

Word Analysis

◎ Prefixes

ROUTINE Word Parts Strategy

1. **Connect** Connect today's lesson to previously learned prefixes *un-* and *re-*. Write *unfit* and *renew.* Read these words. You already know that a prefix changes the meaning of the base word. Today you'll learn to spell and read words with other prefixes.
2. **Model** Write *midpoint. Midpoint* is a two-syllable word formed from the prefix *mid-* and the base word *point.* I know that *mid-* means "middle." *Point* means "a certain position." *Midpoint* means "in the middle position."

   Write *bicycle, preview, deconstruct, overwork,* and *outfield.* Model how to read and define each word by looking for the base word and the prefix. (*bi-* means "two"; *pre-* means "before" or "in front of"; *over-* means "too much" or "above"; and *out-* can mean "to the greatest extent")
3. **Guide Practice** Continue the process in step 2. This time have students read the words with you. Identify the prefix in each word and how it changes the meaning of the base word.

pretreat	**outstanding**	**overtime**	**biped**	**midsection**	**dethrone**
preheat	**bifocals**	**overreach**	**bimonthly**	**midweek**	**outdone**

4. **Review** What do you know about reading words with prefixes? When you see a word with a prefix, identify the prefix and the base word and then read the whole word.

Routines Flip Chart

Model Have students turn to p. 88 in their Student Editions. Each word on this page has a prefix. The first word is *midway.* I see the prefix *mid-* and the base word *way.* I put them together and read the word: *midway. Midway* means "in the middle of something."

Guide practice For each word in Words I Can Blend, ask for the prefix and the base word. Make sure that students identify the correct word parts. Then have them put the parts together and read the words.

Corrective feedback **If...** students have difficulty reading a word, **then...** model reading the parts and then the whole word, and then ask students to read it with you.

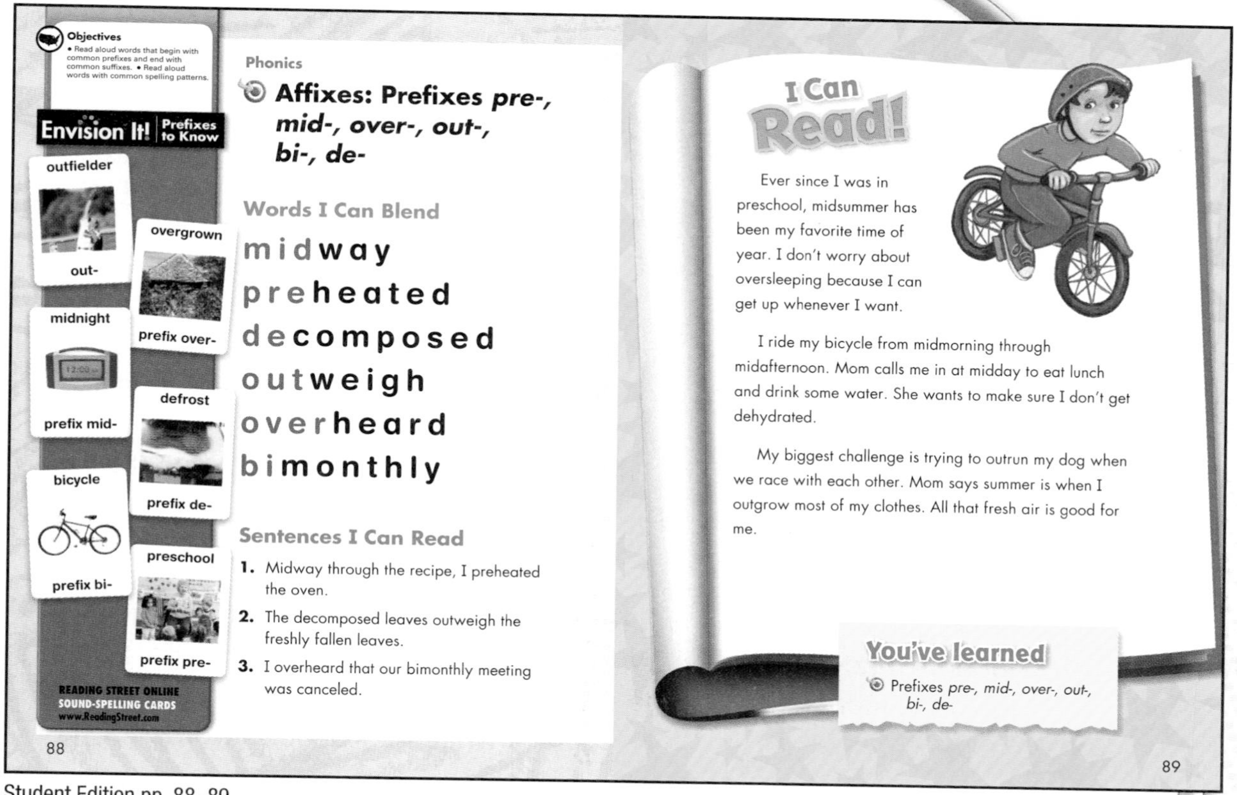

Objectives
• Read aloud words that begin with common prefixes and end with common suffixes. • Read aloud words with common spelling patterns.

Envision It! Prefixes to Know

outfielder out-
overgrown prefix over-
midnight prefix mid-
defrost prefix de-
bicycle prefix bi-
preschool prefix pre-

READING STREET ONLINE
SOUND-SPELLING CARDS
www.ReadingStreet.com

Phonics

Affixes: Prefixes *pre-, mid-, over-, out-, bi-, de-*

Words I Can Blend

midway
preheated
decomposed
outweigh
overheard
bimonthly

Sentences I Can Read

1. Midway through the recipe, I preheated the oven.
2. The decomposed leaves outweigh the freshly fallen leaves.
3. I overheard that our bimonthly meeting was canceled.

88

I Can Read!

Ever since I was in preschool, midsummer has been my favorite time of year. I don't worry about oversleeping because I can get up whenever I want.

I ride my bicycle from midmorning through midafternoon. Mom calls me in at midday to eat lunch and drink some water. She wants to make sure I don't get dehydrated.

My biggest challenge is trying to outrun my dog when we race with each other. Mom says summer is when I outgrow most of my clothes. All that fresh air is good for me.

You've learned

Prefixes *pre-, mid-, over-, out-, bi-, de-*

89

Student Edition pp. 88–89

Decode and Read

Read words independent of context

After students can successfully combine the word parts to read the words on p. 88 in their Student Editions, point to words in random order and ask students to read them naturally.

Read words in context

Have students read each of the sentences on p. 88. Have them identify words in the sentences that have prefixes.

Team Talk Pair students and have them take turns reading each of the sentences aloud.

Chorally read the I Can Read! passage on p. 89 with students. Then have them read the passage aloud to themselves.

On their own

For additional practice, use the *Reader's and Writer's Notebook* p. 269.

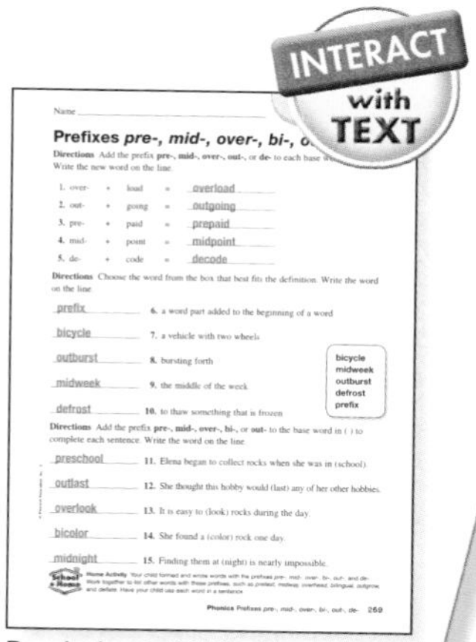

Reader's and Writer's Notebook p. 269

Differentiated Instruction

SI Strategic Intervention

Read words with prefixes If students have difficulty reading words with prefixes, have them listen as you read each word in Words I Can Blend, pausing between the prefix and the base word. Once students are familiar with the words, have them join in the reading—first with a pause and then fluently.

Vocabulary Support

You may wish to explain the meaning of these words.

biped an animal with two feet

dethrone to remove from power

ELL

English Language Learners

Formal and informal language Explain to students that all prefixes cannot be placed in front of all base words. To be sure that a prefix can be paired with a base word, tell students to check the word with the prefix in the dictionary.

Contrastive Analysis Chart See also the Contrastive Analysis Chart in the *First Stop* book.

Language transfer Prefixes are common in some European languages. Have students share words with prefixes from their home languages by writing each with its English translation, dividing it into prefix and base word, and discussing its meaning.

DAY 1 Get Ready to Read

Objectives
- Apply knowledge of sound-spellings to decode unknown multisyllabic words when reading.
- Decode and read words in context and independent of context.
- Practice fluency with oral rereading.

Decodable Practice Reader 18A
Prefixes

Read words independent of context Have students turn to p. 25 of *Decodable Practice Readers 3.2*. Have students read each word.

Read high-frequency words Have students read the high-frequency words *do, you, have, a, to, of, what, are, the, pull, into, two, water, your, ones, they,* and *want* on the first page.

Preview Decodable Practice Reader Have students read the title and preview the story. Tell them that they will read words with the prefixes *pre-, mid-, over-, out-, bi-,* and *de-.*

Read words in context Pair students for reading and listen as they read. One student begins. Students read the entire story, switching readers after each page. Partners reread the story. This time the other student begins. Make sure that students are monitoring their accuracy when they decode words.

Midsummer Fun
Written by Neil Fairbairn
Decodable Practice Reader 18A

Prefixes *pre-, mid-, over-, out-, bi-, de-*

outdoors	bicycle	outline
outside	midpoint	presoak
overcrowded	midsummer	overgrown
overhead	defrost	

High-Frequency Words

do	you	have
a	to	of
what	are	the
pull	into	two
water	your	ones
they	want	

25

Do you have a green thumb? Then try gardening for a fun way to spend time outdoors. You can get lots of fresh air—and things to eat. Think about what you can grow: peas, peppers, carrots, berries, and more.
I think beans are best. You can eat them and play with them as well. That's right, play with them. Here's how.

26

Decodable Practice Reader 18A

First, ride your bicycle to a garden shop and pick up a packet of pole bean seeds. Also get six thin poles, each at least six feet long.
Next, set up the planting space in the garden. On the ground, outline a circle three feet wide. Then pull weeds and turn over the dirt inside the circle with a garden fork.

27

Rake the ground flat. Then place six poles around the outside of the circle with their tops leaning into the midpoint. Leave a bigger space between two poles. Why? Wait and see!
Tie the pole tops with string. Now you've got a pole frame.

28

When days start getting hot in late spring, presoak your bean seeds. Plant them by placing six beans at the base of each pole and poking them an inch into the ground. Place dirt over them and water them daily.
In less than ten days, your bean plants will sprout.

29

When the bean plants are three inches high, thin them out. Take out the little ones, and leave three strong plants at each pole. The plants must not be overcrowded.
Keep sprinkling them with water, and see how fast they grow. Your plants will race up the poles.

30

By midsummer your bean plants will reach pole tops. The frame will be overgrown with big leaves and bright flowers. These flowers will turn into beans you can eat.
Now can you see why you left space between two poles? It's an opening for your pole bean tent!

31

Your bean tent is like a house with leaves and flowers growing overhead. It is a place for shade on a hot day. It is a place to play hide-and-seek or just sit inside and read.
It has plenty of green beans to pick and eat. And if you want to eat your beans during the winter, save them in the freezer. Be sure to defrost them before eating!

32

Corrective feedback

If... students have difficulty reading a word,
then... refer them to the Sound-Spelling Cards to identify the word parts. Have them read the word parts individually and then together to say the word.

- What is the new word?
- Is the new word a word you know?
- Does it make sense in the story?

Check decoding and comprehension

Have students retell the story to include characters, setting, and events. Then have students find words in the story that have the prefixes *pre-, mid-, over-, out-, bi-,* and *de-.* Students should supply *outdoors, bicycle, outline, outside, midpoint, presoak, overcrowded, midsummer, overgrown, overhead,* and *defrost.*

Reread for Fluency

Have students reread Decodable Practice Reader 18A to develop automaticity decoding words with prefixes.

ROUTINE Oral Rereading

1. **Read** Have students read the entire book orally.
2. **Reread** To achieve optimal fluency, students should reread the text three or four times.
3. **Corrective Feedback** Listen as students read. Provide corrective feedback regarding their fluency and decoding.

Routines Flip Chart

ELL

English Language Learners
Leveled support: Prefixes

Beginning Write several words with prefixes from the Decodable Reader, such as *outdoors, bicycle,* and *midsummer.* Point to each word as you say it aloud. Then cover the prefix in each word and have students read aloud the base word. Cover the base word and have students read aloud the prefix. Finally, have students read aloud all the entire word with you.

Intermediate Write the prefixes *mid-, out-,* and *pre-* in one column and the words *way, soak, doors, read, point,* and *did* in a second column. Have students take turns drawing a line from a prefix to a base word to make the words *midway, presoak, outdoors, preread, midpoint,* and *outdid.*

Advanced/Advanced High After reading the story, have students choose four or five words with prefixes from the story. Have students write each word and draw a line between the prefix and the base word. Then have students write a sentence with the base word and another sentence with the entire word.

Objectives

- ◎ Identify facts and opinions to aid comprehension.
- ◎ Use the inferring strategy to aid comprehension.
- Read aloud grade-level text with expression.

Skills Trace

◎ **Fact and Opinion**

Introduce U4W3D1; U4W4D1; U6W1D1

Practice U1W4D2; U1W4D3; U4W3D2; U4W3D3; U4W4D2; U4W4D3; U6W1D2; U6W1D3; U6W3D3

Reteach/Review U4W3D5; U4W4D5; U6W1D5

Assess/Test Weekly Tests U4W3; U4W4; U6W1

Benchmark Tests U4

Key: U = Unit, W = Week, D = Day

Skill ↔ Strategy
◎ Fact and Opinion
◎ Inferring

Student Edition p. EI•7

Introduce fact and opinion *Envision It!* A statement of fact can be proved to be true or false. How can I prove that something is true? (look in a reference book, ask an expert, or use my own knowledge and experience) The second bullet says that an opinion gives someone's thoughts or feelings. How can I identify a statement of opinion when I'm reading? (look for clue words that express feelings) Have students turn to p. 7 in the Student Edition to review fact and opinion. Then read "Looking at Rocks" with students.

Model the skill *Think Aloud* Today we're going to read about people who like to study rocks. Have students follow along as you read the first paragraph of "Looking at Rocks." The first paragraph of "Looking at Rocks" has a statement of fact in the last line. I can check in a reference book to verify that the colors in rocks come from different materials mixed together. The first sentence says that looking at rocks is fun and interesting. I know that people don't agree on what is fun or interesting, so these are clue words that this is an opinion, or judgment.

Guide practice Have students finish reading "Looking at Rocks" on their own. After they read, have them use a graphic organizer like the one on p. 90 and draw conclusions about statements of fact and opinion from the passage.

Strategy check **Inferring** Remind students that if they have difficulty understanding "Looking at Rocks," they can use the strategy of inferring.

Student Edition p. EI•20

Model the strategy *Envision It!* *Think Aloud* When I read in the text that scientists look at rocks to find out about people from long ago, I didn't understand what the author meant. But then I thought about what I know about different kinds of scientists, and I realized that the author was referring to archeologists, who dig up places where people used to live. They might find rocks that people used to make things. These rocks would teach the scientists about people long ago. Have students review the strategy of Inferring on p. EI•20 of the Student Edition.

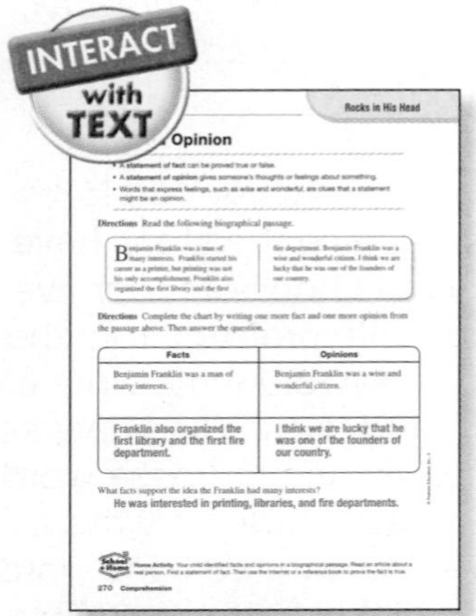

Reader's and Writer's Notebook p. 270

On their own Use p. 270 in the *Reader's and Writer's Notebook* for additional practice with fact and opinion.

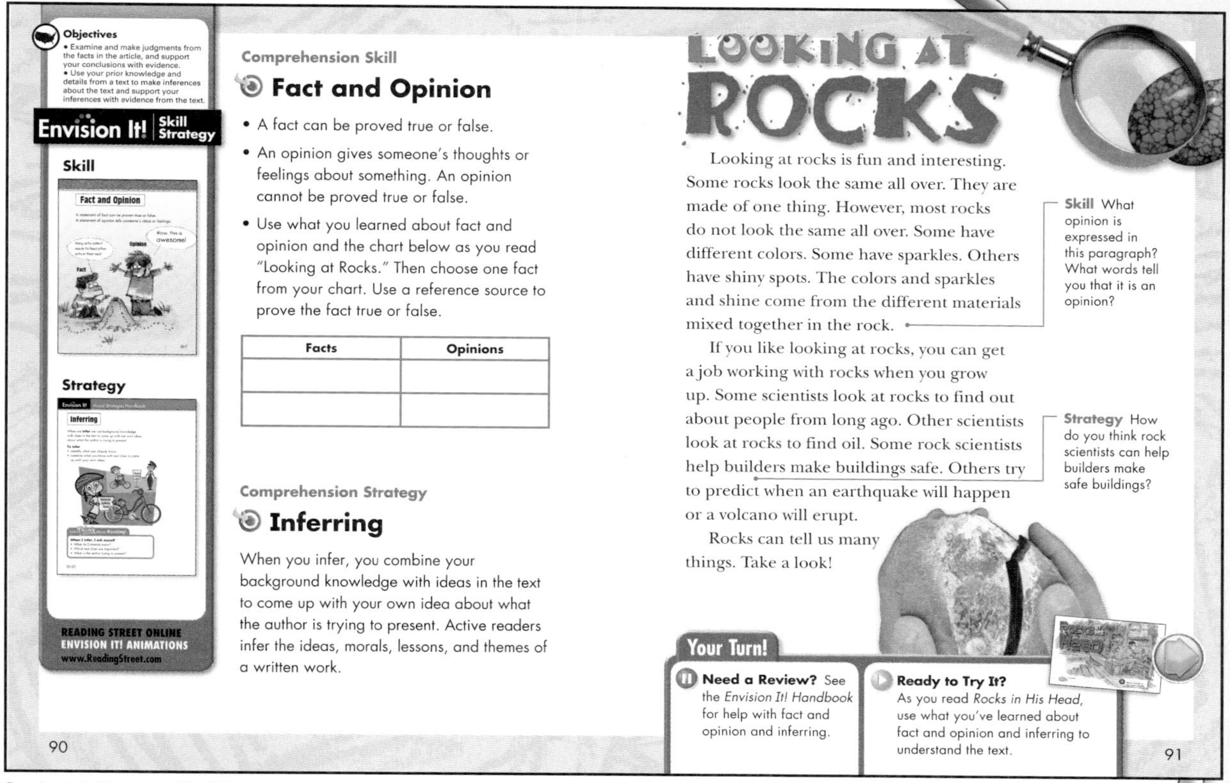
Objectives
• Examine and make judgments from the facts in the article, and support your conclusions with evidence.
• Use your prior knowledge and details from a text to make inferences about the text and support your inferences with evidence from the text.

Envision It! Skill Strategy

Skill

Strategy

READING STREET ONLINE
ENVISION IT! ANIMATIONS
www.ReadingStreet.com

Comprehension Skill

Fact and Opinion

- A fact can be proved true or false.
- An opinion gives someone's thoughts or feelings about something. An opinion cannot be proved true or false.
- Use what you learned about fact and opinion and the chart below as you read "Looking at Rocks." Then choose one fact from your chart. Use a reference source to prove the fact true or false.

Facts	Opinions

Comprehension Strategy

Inferring

When you infer, you combine your background knowledge with ideas in the text to come up with your own idea about what the author is trying to present. Active readers infer the ideas, morals, lessons, and themes of a written work.

90

LOOKING AT ROCKS

Looking at rocks is fun and interesting. Some rocks look the same all over. They are made of one thing. However, most rocks do not look the same all over. Some have different colors. Some have sparkles. Others have shiny spots. The colors and sparkles and shine come from the different materials mixed together in the rock.

If you like looking at rocks, you can get a job working with rocks when you grow up. Some scientists look at rocks to find out about people from long ago. Other scientists look at rocks to find oil. Some rock scientists help builders make buildings safe. Others try to predict when an earthquake will happen or a volcano will erupt.

Rocks can tell us many things. Take a look!

Skill What opinion is expressed in this paragraph? What words tell you that it is an opinion?

Strategy How do you think rock scientists can help builders make safe buildings?

Your Turn!

Need a Review? See the *Envision It! Handbook* for help with fact and opinion and inferring.

Ready to Try It? As you read *Rocks in His Head*, use what you've learned about fact and opinion and inferring to understand the text.

91

Student Edition pp. 90–91

Skill Looking at rocks is fun and interesting.; fun interesting

Strategy By telling them which rocks work better than others.

Academic Vocabulary

fact a statement that can be proved true or false

opinion a statement of some-one's judgment, belief, or way of thinking about something

Model Fluency
Expression

Model fluent reading Have students listen as you read paragraph 1 of "Looking at Rocks" with appropriate expression. Explain that you will adjust your voice level to stress important words and phrases.

ROUTINE Oral Rereading

1. **Read** Have students read paragraph 1 of "Looking at Rocks" orally.
2. **Reread** To achieve optimal fluency, students should reread the text three or four times.
3. **Corrective Feedback** Have students read aloud without you. Provide feedback about their expression and encourage them to adjust their voice level to stress important words and phrases. Listen for use of appropriate expression. To achieve optimal fluency, students should reread the text three to four times.

Routines Flip Chart

ELL

English Language Learners

Fact and opinion Provide oral practice by having students state facts and opinions about this week's weather. Then write these sentences on the board and read them aloud. Have students identify whether each sentence is a fact or an opinion, then ask them to support their answers.

- It was sunny every day this week. (fact)
- I think the weather is spec-tacular today. (opinion)
- It's warmer today than it was yesterday. (fact)

Objectives

- Use context to complete sentences.
- Identify questions for research.

Vocabulary
Tested Vocabulary

Lesson vocabulary Have students complete sentences by filling in the blanks with lesson words.

Activate prior knowledge Display the lesson words and discuss what students already know about these words. Then write incomplete sentences on the board, such as those below. Have students identify the lesson word that completes each sentence and makes sense in context. Students may need to check the glossary.

- The ______ of directors plans what our organization will do. (board)
- Two household ______ are laundry and making the beds. (chores)
- When I buy something at the grocery store, I am a ______. (customer)
- The librarian ______ the books and then placed them on the shelves. (labeled)
- There is a ______ tire in the trunk in case another one goes flat. (spare)
- There are stairs that lead to the ______. (attic)
- You can't mail letters without using ______. (stamps)

Related words Display the words *label* and *labeled.* Ask students how adding the *-ed* to *label* changed the meaning of the word.

At the end of the week, students can review these fill-in-the-blank sentences or create their own with a partner.

Use the Strategy for Words with Meaningful Parts to help students read and understand the lesson.

ELL **Academic Vocabulary** Write the following terms on the board:

Preteach Academic Vocabulary

biography	**idiom**
complex sentence	**possessive pronoun**
fact and opinion	**problem and solution**

Have students share what they know about this week's Academic Vocabulary. Use the students' responses to assess their prior knowledge. Preteach the Academic Vocabulary by providing a student-friendly description, explanation, or example that clarifies the meaning of each term. Then ask students to restate the meaning of the Academic Vocabulary term in their own words.

Research and Inquiry
Identify Questions

Teach Discuss the Question of the Week: *Why is it valuable to have unique interests?* Tell students they will each investigate one way that it is valuable to have unique interests and write an informational article about it. They will present their findings to the class on Day 5.

Model **Think Aloud** I'll start by brainstorming a list of questions about unique interests. I have read many biographies, or stories of people's lives that are written by other people, that feature people with many different interests. My own unique interest is playing the guitar, so I'll choose that as my topic for research. Some possible questions could be *Is learning to play a musical instrument, such as a guitar, a valuable interest for someone to pursue? Is it difficult to learn to play the guitar? What makes playing the guitar enjoyable?*

Guide practice After students have brainstormed inquiry questions, explain that tomorrow they will conduct online research using their questions. Help students identify keywords that will help their search.

On their own Have students work individually, in pairs, or in small groups to write an inquiry question.

Small Group Time

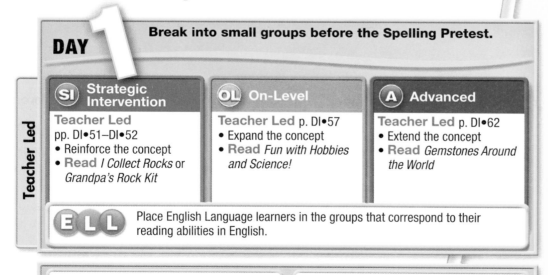

DAY 1 Break into small groups before the Spelling Pretest.

Teacher Led

SI Strategic Intervention	OL On-Level	A Advanced
Teacher Led pp. DI•51–DI•52 • Reinforce the concept • Read *I Collect Rocks* or *Grandpa's Rock Kit*	Teacher Led p. DI•57 • Expand the concept • Read *Fun with Hobbies and Science!*	Teacher Led p. DI•62 • Extend the concept • Read *Gemstones Around the World*

ELL Place English Language learners in the groups that correspond to their reading abilities in English.

Practice Stations
- Read for Meaning
- Get Fluent
- Word Work

Independent Activities
- Concept Talk Video
- *Reader's and Writer's Notebook*
- Vocabulary Activities

INTERNET GUY
Don Leu

21st Century Skills

Weekly Inquiry Project
- **Day 1** Identify Questions
- **Day 2** Navigate/Search
- **Day 3** Analyze
- **Day 4** Synthesize
- **Day 5** Communicate

Academic Vocabulary

biography a story of a real person's life, written by another person

ELL

English Language Learners
Multilingual Vocabulary
Students can apply knowledge of their home languages to acquire new English vocabulary by using the Multilingual Vocabulary Lists (*ELL Handbook, pp. 433–444*).

Objectives
- Spell words with prefixes *pre-*, *mid-*, *over-*, and *out-*.
- Identify possessive pronouns.
- Write cursive letters *v* and *z* in words.

Spelling Pretest
Prefixes *pre-, mid-, over-, out-*

Introduce Tell students to think of words with prefixes, such as *pre- (preview), over- (overthrow),* and *out- (outlast)*. This week we will spell words with prefixes *pre-, mid-, over-,* and *out-.*

Pretest Use these sentences to administer the spelling pretest. Say each word, read the sentence, and repeat the word.

1. prepaid	Avoid box office lines with **prepaid** theater tickets.
2. midnight	It's 11:58 p.m., two minutes to **midnight.**
3. overflow	Don't let the bathtub **overflow.**
4. outdoors	We go **outdoors** to ride our bikes.
5. outline	Draw the **outline** of the picture first.
6. overgrown	The garden is **overgrown** with weeds.
7. prefix	A **prefix** is part of a word.
8. Midwest	Sarah lives in the **Midwest.**
9. pretest	Use today's **pretest** to study for the test.
10. midpoint	Mark the **midpoint** of the line.
11. outgoing	My friend is very friendly and **outgoing.**
12. overtime	Dad has to work **overtime.**
13. overdue	The library books are **overdue.**
14. outside	I ride my bike **outside** in the park.
15. outfield	The player in the **outfield** caught the ball.

Challenge words

16. precaution	Hank approached the cliff's edge with **precaution.**
17. prediction	We did not believe the fortune teller's **prediction.**
18. midsection	Your belly button is at the **midsection** of your body.
19. overweight	That fat dog is **overweight.**
20. prehistoric	The scientist studied **prehistoric** dinosaur bones.

Self-correct After the pretest, you can either display the correctly spelled words or spell them orally. Have students self-correct their pretests by rewriting misspelled words correctly.

On their own For additional practice, use *Let's Practice It!* page 237 on the *Teacher Resources DVD-ROM.*

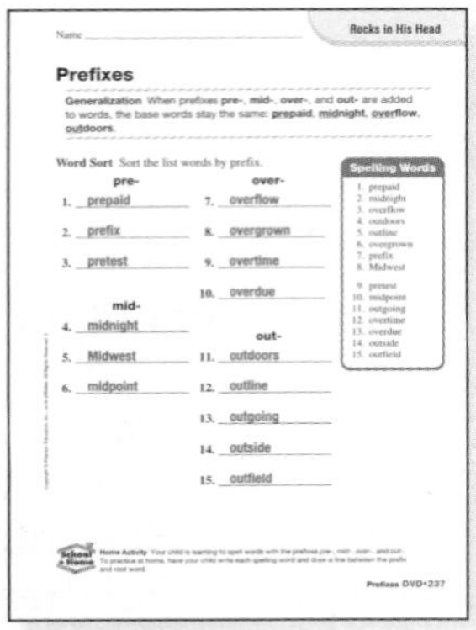
Rocks in His Head

Prefixes

Word Sort

pre-: 1. prepaid 2. prefix 3. pretest

mid-: 4. midnight 5. Midwest 6. midpoint

over-: 7. overflow 8. overgrown 9. overtime 10. overdue

out-: 11. outdoors 12. outline 13. outgoing 14. outside 15. outfield

Let's Practice It!
TR DVD•237

Conventions
Possessive Pronouns

Teach Display Grammar Transparency 18, and read aloud the explanation and examples in the box. Point out the possessive pronouns, *your* and *mine,* in the sample sentence.

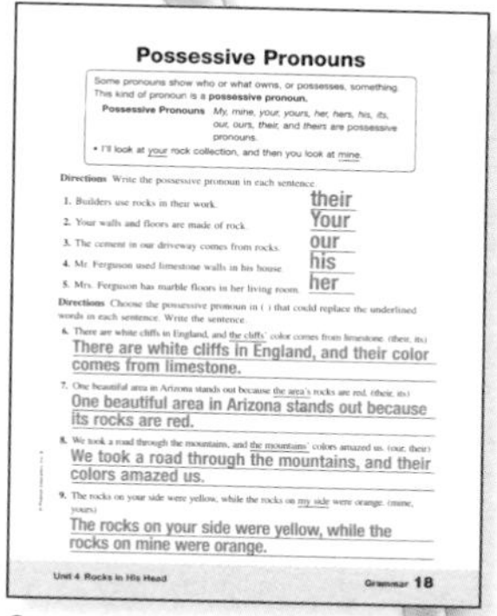
Possessive Pronouns

Some pronouns show who or what owns, or possesses, something. This kind of pronoun is a **possessive pronoun.**

Possessive Pronouns *My, mine, your, yours, her, hers, his, its, our, ours, their,* and *theirs* are possessive pronouns.

- I'll look at your rock collection, and then you look at mine.

Directions Write the possessive pronoun in each sentence.

1. Builders use rocks in their work. their
2. Your walls and floors are made of rock. Your
3. The cement in our driveway comes from rocks. our
4. Mr. Ferguson used limestone walls in his house. his
5. Mrs. Ferguson has marble floors in her living room. her

Directions Choose the possessive pronoun in ( ) that could replace the underlined words in each sentence. Write the sentence.

6. There are white cliffs in England, and the cliffs' color comes from limestone. (their, its) There are white cliffs in England, and their color comes from limestone.
7. One beautiful area in Arizona stands out because the area's rocks are red. (their, its) One beautiful area in Arizona stands out because its rocks are red.
8. We took a road through the mountains, and the mountains' colors amazed us. (our, their) We took a road through the mountains, and their colors amazed us.
9. The rocks on your side were yellow, while the rocks on my side were orange. (mine, yours) The rocks on your side were yellow, while the rocks on mine were orange.

Unit 4 Rocks in His Head Grammar 18

Grammar Transparency 18, TR DVD

Model Model writing the correct form of the possessive pronoun to complete numbers 1 and 2. Explain that you look for the word that shows ownership to identify possessive pronouns.

Guide practice Guide students to complete items 3–5. Record the correct responses on the transparency.

Daily Fix-It Use Daily Fix-It numbers 1 and 2 in the right margin.

Connect to oral language Have students read sentences 6–9 on the transparency and replace the underlined words with a possessive pronoun to correctly rewrite each sentence.

Handwriting
Cursive Letters *v* and *z*

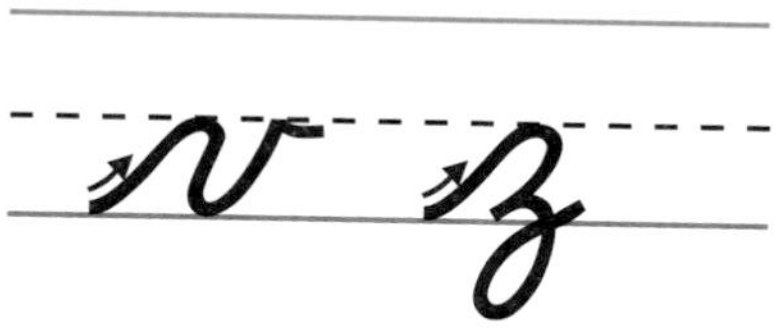

Model letter formation Display lowercase cursive letters *v* and *z.* Follow the stroke instructions pictured to model letter formation.

Model letter size and joining strokes Explain that writing legibly means letters are the correct size cursive strokes are joined together, and there is correct spacing between letters and words. The descenders touch the line below and sidestrokes are correct. Model writing this sentence with proper letter size and joining strokes: *Zach and Vera drive their van to the zoo.* Point out how sidestrokes change the beginning stroke of the following letter.

Guide practice Have students write these phrases: *invite a zebra, veer and zigzag.* Circulate around the room, guiding students.

Academic Vocabulary

A **possessive pronoun** shows who or what owns, or possesses, something.

Daily Fix-It

1. Colin and him find rocks in many places out doors. *(he; outdoors)*
2. The rocks in mine pocket has gold flecks. *(my, have)*

ELL

English Language Learners

Language production: Possessive pronouns Hold up a common classroom item, such as a pen, and identify it as *my pen.* Then pass the pen and call on students to repeat these phrases: *his pen, her pen, their pen, our pen.* Write each phrase and ask volunteers to underline the possessive pronoun and read it aloud.

Handwriting To provide practice in handwriting *v* and *z* and to extend language opportunities, have students complete the following sentence frame by naming their favorite zoo animals: *I like to visit the* ______ *when I visit the zoo.*

DAY 1 Language Arts

Objectives

- Understand and identify the features of a biography.

MINI-LESSON

5 Day Planner

Guide to Mini-Lessons

DAY 1	Read Like a Writer
DAY 2	Developing a Story Sequence Chart
DAY 3	Varying Sentence Type and Length
DAY 4	Revising Strategy: Consolidating
DAY 5	Proofread for Possessive Pronouns

Writing—Biography

Introduce

MINI-LESSON

Read Like a Writer

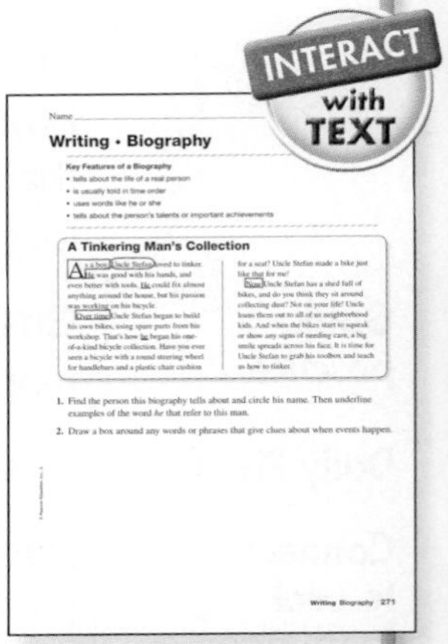

Reader's and Writer's Notebook, p. 271

Introduce This week you will write a biography. A biography is nonfiction writing that tells about the life of a real person.

Prompt Think about a friend or family member who has an interesting collection. Now write a short biography of that person's life.

Trait Sentences

Mode Expository

Examine Model Text Let's read an example of a biography that introduces us to a man who collects one-of-a-kind bicycles. Have students read "A Tinkering Man's Collection" on p. 271 of their *Reader's and Writer's Notebook.*

Key Features **Biographies give information about real people, things, or events.** Find the person this biography tells about and circle his or her name. **Point out that biographies use words like *he or she.*** Tell students to underline examples of *he* in each paragraph and tell who this pronoun represents. (Uncle Stefan)

Events in a biography are usually told in time order. Direct students to the start of each paragraph and have them draw a box around any words or phrases that give clues about time order.

Biographies tell about a person's talents or achievements. What talent does Uncle Stefan have? (He tinkers.) Have students summarize what Uncle Stefan achieved with this talent.

Review key features

Review the key features of a biography with students. You may want to post the key features in the classroom for students to reference as they work on their compositions.

Key Features of a Biography

- tells about the life of a real person
- is usually told in time order
- uses words like *he* or *she*
- tells about the person's talents or important achievements

ROUTINE **Quick Write for Fluency** **Team Talk**

1. **Talk** Have pairs discuss the key features of a biography.
2. **Write** Each student writes a few sentences defining a biography.
3. **Share** Partners read their sentences aloud to one another.

Routines Flip Chart

Wrap Up Your Day

- ✔ **Build Concepts** What did you learn about why it's valuable to have unique interests?
- ✔ **Oral Vocabulary** Have students use the Amazing Words they learned in context sentences.
- ✔ **Homework** Send home this week's Family Times Newsletter in *Let's Practice It!* pp. 238–239 on the *Teacher Resources DVD-ROM.*

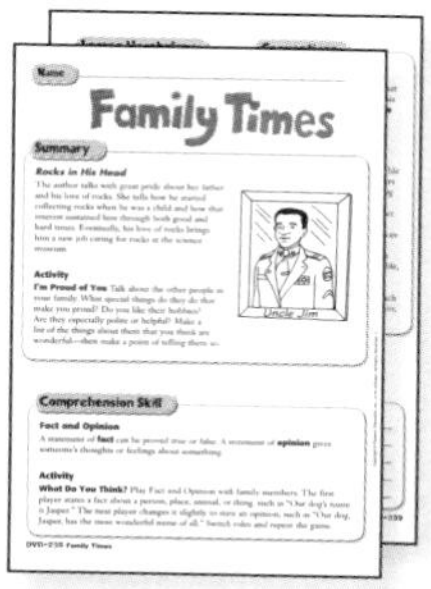

Let's Practice It!
TR DVD • 238–239

Write Guy *Jeff Anderson*

Details, Details

Ask students to notice details in mentor text—but not just any details. Rather than pointing out many details, select a detail that is beyond the obvious. With guidance, students can learn how to include *details that matter* rather than obvious details or simply longer and longer lists of details.

ELL

English Language Learners

Examine the model Read the writing model aloud and help students understand it. Point out that this model is a biography, which means it tells about the life of a real person and about events that really happened. Have students work in groups. Ask each student to name a friend or family member who collects something. Then ask the student to dictate a sentence about this person's collection. Call on group members to summarize what they have heard.

Preview DAY 2

Tell students that tomorrow they will read about a rock collector.

Objectives
- Expand the weekly concept.
- Develop oral vocabulary.

Today at a Glance

Oral Vocabulary
ancestor

Phonics/Word Analysis
◎ Prefixes *(pre-, mid-, over-, out-, bi-, de-)*

Literary Terms
Idioms

Text Structure
Problem and Solution

Lesson Vocabulary
◎ Multiple-meaning words

Reading
"More Than a Hobby"
Rocks in His Head

Fluency
Expression

Research and Inquiry
Navigate/Search

Conventions
Possessive pronouns

Spelling
Prefixes *pre-, mid-, over-, out-*

Writing
Biography

Concept Talk

Question of the Week
Why is it valuable to have unique interests?

Expand the concept

Remind students of the weekly concept question. Tell students that today they will begin reading *Rocks in His Head.* As they read, encourage students to think about why it is valuable for people to have unique interests.

Anchored Talk

Develop oral vocabulary

Use the photos on pp. 86–87 and the Read Aloud, "Picture Perfect," to talk about the Amazing Words: *hobby, murmur, project*, and *leftover.* Add these and other concept-related words to the concept map to develop students' knowledge of the topic. Discuss the following questions and encourage students to answer in detail.

- What *hobby* interests you? (Answers will vary but should mention a hobby, not a job or a one-time activity.)
- What might you *murmur* to an artist whose *project* you admire? (Possible response: I really like your painting.)
- What might be the unique interest of someone who knows how to create a wonderful dinner from *leftover* food? (Possible response: The person might love to cook.)

Oral Vocabulary
Amazing Words

Amazing Words Oral Vocabulary Routine

Teach Amazing Words

1. **Introduce** Write the Amazing Word *ancestor* on the board. Have students say it aloud with you. Relate *ancestor* to the photographs on pp. 86–87 and "Picture Perfect." The girls are putting pictures of their *ancestors* in a scrapbook. Who might some of these *ancestors* be? (grandparents, parents) Who is Sammy's *ancestor*? (his grandfather) Have students determine the definition of the word. An ancestor is a relative from a past time.
2. **Demonstrate** Have students answer questions to demonstrate understanding. Is your great-grandmother your *ancestor*? (yes) Is your father's best friend your *ancestor*? (no) Can your brother or sister be your *ancestor*? (no)
3. **Apply** Have students apply their understanding. If you and an *ancestor* were together, which of you would be older? (the ancestor)

Routines Flip Chart

Apply Amazing Words

Help students establish a purpose for reading before they read "More Than a Hobby" on p. 93. Have them think about how Sammy's hobby helps him to honor his *ancestor.*

Explain that today students will read about a man who likes to collect rocks. As they read, they should think about how this week's Question of the Week and the Amazing Word *ancestor* applies to the characters in the story.

ELL **Reinforce Vocabulary** Use the Day 2 instruction on ELL Poster 18 to teach lesson vocabulary and discuss the lesson concept.

ELL Poster 18

Amazing Words

hobby	ornament
project	descendant
leftover	forge
murmur	compartment
ancestor	

Objectives
- ◎ Apply knowledge of letter-sound correspondences and syllable patterns to decode words in context and independent of context.
- Understand common idioms.
- Identify problem and solution text structure.

Check Word Reading
SUCCESS PREDICTOR

Word Analysis
Prefixes

Review Review the prefixes *pre-, mid-, over-, out-, bi-,* and *de-,* pointing out that prefixes are added to the beginning of base words.

Read words independent of context Display these words. Have the class read the words. Then point to the words in random order and ask students to read them quickly.

outdid	**overjoyed**	**biweekly**	**derail**
preview	**midway**	**outcast**	**preheat**

Corrective feedback Model reading the prefix and then the base word, and then ask students to read the word with you.

Read words in context Display these sentences. Have the class read the sentences.

Team Talk Have pairs take turns reading the sentences naturally.

Kate played **outfield** in the **preseason** games.
Layla **departed** for school on her **bicycle.**
Chris was **overcome** by the heat at the **midpoint** of the race.

Don't Wait Until Friday

MONITOR PROGRESS **Check Word Reading**

Write the following words and have the class read them. Notice which words students miss during the group reading. Call on individuals to read some of the words.

history	**happy**	**turn**	**sense**
prehistory	**unhappy**	**return**	**nonsense**
prehistoric	**unhappily**	**returnable**	**nonsensical**

Spiral Review
Row 2 reviews words with prefixes *pre-, un-, re-, non-.*
Row 3 contrasts words with prefixes and suffixes.

If... students cannot read words with prefixes at this point,
then... use the Day 1 Word Parts Strategy routine on p. 88a to reteach prefixes. Use words from the Decodable Practice Passages (or Reader). Continue to monitor students' progress using other instructional opportunities during the week.
See the Skills Trace on p. 88a.

Day 1	Day 2	Day 3	Day 4	Day 5
Check Oral Vocabulary	Check Word Reading	Check Retelling	Check Fluency	Check Oral Vocabulary

Success Predictor

Literary Terms
Idioms

Teach idiom Tell students that an idiom is a playful use of language that is frequently found in both fiction and nonfiction. An idiom is a figure of speech that contains more than one word and that has a meaning and a use totally its own. The literal meanings of the words do not explain the meaning of the expression.

Model idioms Think Aloud Let's look at "More Than a Hobby" on page 93. The third paragraph ends with the statement *You are on your way.* What does the idiom "on your way" mean? (becoming successful) You have to learn the meaning of idioms; they usually can't be figured out by using the literal meanings of the words in the expression.

Guide practice Find an example of an idiom in *Rocks in His Head.* Explain what the idiom means.

On their own Have students look for examples of idioms in other selections in their Student Edition.

Text Structure
Problem and Solution

Teach problem and solution Authors organize their text according to patterns. One pattern is problem and solution. In this pattern, a text shows the development of a problem and one or more solutions to that problem.

Model the strategy Think Aloud Knowing what pattern the author has used to construct the text helps me understand how the important ideas are connected to one another. When I preview the title, illustrations, and text of *Rocks in His Head,* I see that people keep telling the main character he has rocks in his head. This could be a problem. As I read, I'll look for other problems and find out if there is a solution.

Guide practice Discuss with students what the illustrations suggest about problems and solutions in *Rocks in His Head.* Have them make predictions about the selection based on their preview.

On their own Have students complete a problem-solution outline as they read *Rocks in His Head.*

Academic Vocabulary

idiom An idiom is a figure of speech that has a meaning separate from the literal meaning of the expression.

problem and solution Problem and solution is a text pattern that shows the development of a problem and one or more solutions to the problem.

DAY 2 Read and Comprehend

40–45 min

Objectives

- ◎ Use context clues to find meanings of multiple-meaning words.
- Read grade-level text with expression.

Vocabulary Strategy for ◎ Multiple-Meaning Words

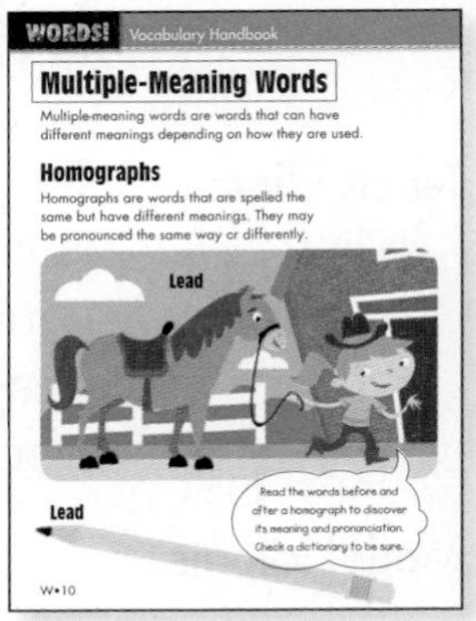

Student Edition W•10

Teach multiple-meaning words Tell students that when they encounter a multiple-meaning word, they should use context clues to determine the meaning. Explain how context clues can help students determine the correct meaning of a multiple-meaning word. Refer students to Words! on p. W•10 in the Student Edition for additional practice.

Model Think Aloud Write on the board: *My father replaced the flat tire on our car with the spare tire that he keeps in the trunk.* I know that *spare* can mean "thin," but this meaning doesn't make sense in the sentence. The meaning "extra" does make sense, though, so in this sentence, *spare* means "extra," or "ready when needed."

Guide practice Write this sentence on the board: *There are so many stamps on the envelope that there's hardly any space to write the address.* Have students determine the meaning of *stamps* using context clues.

On their own Read "More Than a Hobby" on p. 93. Have students use context clues to list the definitions for the lesson vocabulary. For additional practice, use *Reader's and Writer's Notebook* p. 272.

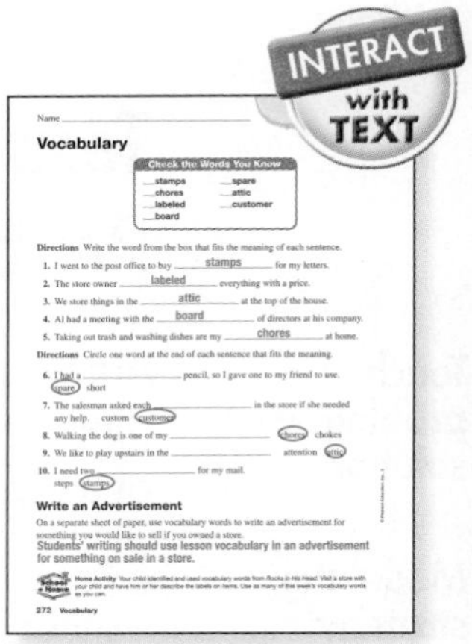

Reader's and Writer's Notebook p. 272

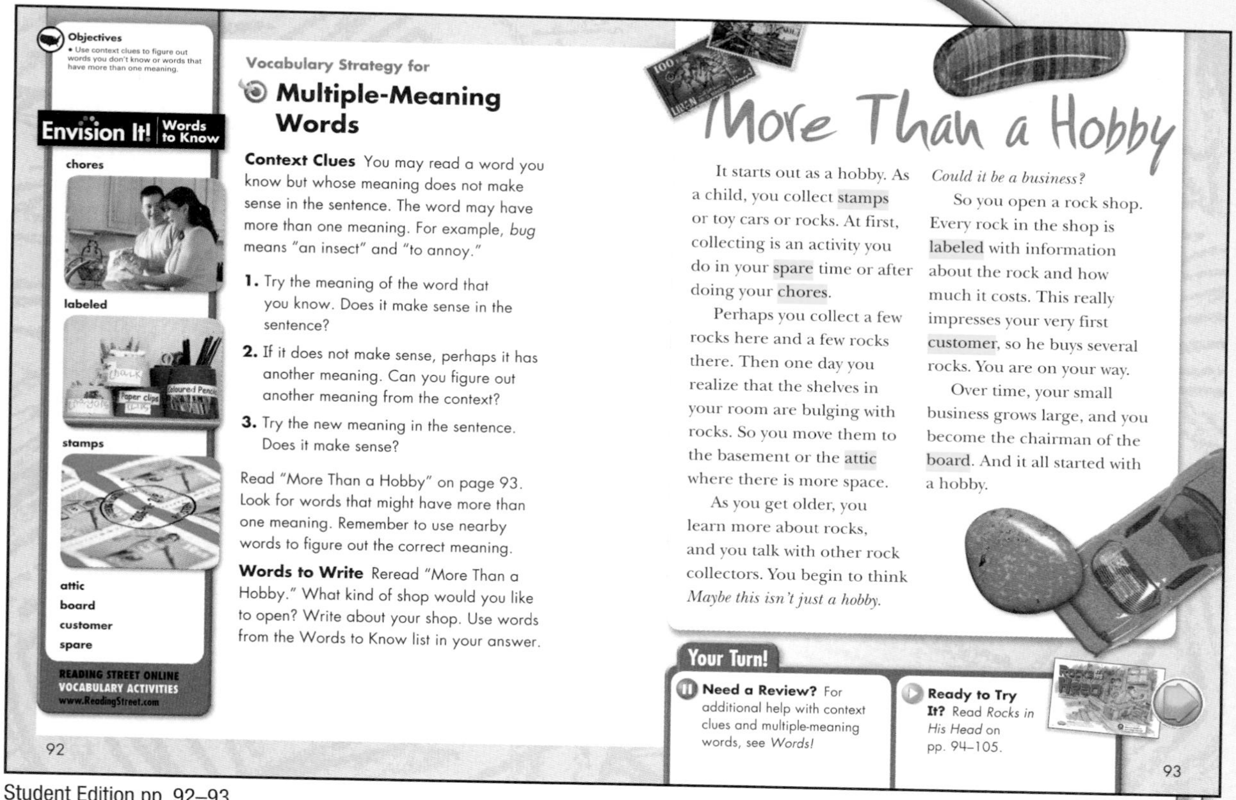
Objectives
• Use context clues to figure out words you don't know or words that have more than one meaning.

Envision It! Words to Know

chores

labeled

stamps

attic
board
customer
spare

READING STREET ONLINE
VOCABULARY ACTIVITIES
www.ReadingStreet.com

Vocabulary Strategy for

Multiple-Meaning Words

Context Clues You may read a word you know but whose meaning does not make sense in the sentence. The word may have more than one meaning. For example, *bug* means "an insect" and "to annoy."

1. Try the meaning of the word that you know. Does it make sense in the sentence?
2. If it does not make sense, perhaps it has another meaning. Can you figure out another meaning from the context?
3. Try the new meaning in the sentence. Does it make sense?

Read "More Than a Hobby" on page 93. Look for words that might have more than one meaning. Remember to use nearby words to figure out the correct meaning.

Words to Write Reread "More Than a Hobby." What kind of shop would you like to open? Write about your shop. Use words from the Words to Know list in your answer.

92

More Than a Hobby

It starts out as a hobby. As a child, you collect stamps or toy cars or rocks. At first, collecting is an activity you do in your spare time or after doing your chores.

Perhaps you collect a few rocks here and a few rocks there. Then one day you realize that the shelves in your room are bulging with rocks. So you move them to the basement or the attic where there is more space.

As you get older, you learn more about rocks, and you talk with other rock collectors. You begin to think *Maybe this isn't just a hobby. Could it be a business?*

So you open a rock shop. Every rock in the shop is labeled with information about the rock and how much it costs. This really impresses your very first customer, so he buys several rocks. You are on your way.

Over time, your small business grows large, and you become the chairman of the board. And it all started with a hobby.

Your Turn!

Need a Review? For additional help with context clues and multiple-meaning words, see *Words!*

Ready to Try It? Read *Rocks in His Head* on pp. 94–105.

93

Student Edition pp. 92–93

Lesson Vocabulary

attic the space in a house just below the roof and above the other rooms

board a group of people who manage something

chores small tasks or easy jobs that you have to do regularly

customer someone who buys goods or services

labeled put or wrote a label on something

spare extra

stamps small pieces of paper with glue on the back for mailing letters and packages

Differentiated Instruction

SI Strategic Intervention

Ask volunteers to use words from this week's lesson vocabulary in sentences of their own.

Reread for Fluency
Expression

Model fluent reading

Read paragraph 3 of "More Than a Hobby" aloud, keeping your expression slow and steady and using changes of voice level for emphasis. Use a rising pitch to emphasize the question. Tell students that you are reading the passage with expression, paying special attention to new vocabulary.

ROUTINE Oral Rereading

1. **Read** Have students read paragraph 3 of "More Than a Hobby" orally.
2. **Reread** To achieve optimal fluency, students should reread the text three or four times.
3. **Corrective Feedback** Have students read aloud without you. Provide feedback about their expression and encourage them to adjust their pitch for the appropriate expression. Have students reread three to four times.

Routines Flip Chart

ELL

English Language Learners

Build lesson vocabulary Use the lesson vocabulary pictured on p. 92 to teach the meanings of *chores, customer,* and *stamps.* Call on pairs to write the words on sticky notes and use them to label images of the words on the ELL Poster.

Objectives

- Understand the elements of biography.
- Use the title and illustrations to preview and predict.
- Set a purpose for reading.

Rocks in his Head
by Carol Otis Hurst
illustrated by James Stevenson
Genre
A **biography** is the story of a real person's life, written by another person. As you read, think about how this author is connected to the person she wrote about.
Question of the Week
Why is it valuable to have unique interests?
94
95

Student Edition pp. 94–95

Build Background

Discuss rocks

Team Talk Have students turn to a partner and discuss the question of the week and these questions about rocks. Remind students to ask and answer questions with appropriate detail, and to give suggestions that build on the ideas of others.

- What are rocks made of?
- What are some special kinds of rocks?
- What is interesting or unique about rock collecting?

Connect to selection

Have students discuss their answers with the class. Possible responses: Rocks are made of minerals. Some rocks are fossils; others are minerals that have special colors or interesting shapes. By collecting rocks, people can learn a lot about earth science. For additional opportunities to build background, use the Background Building Audio.

Prereading Strategies

Genre Explain that a **biography** tells the story of a real person's life, talents, or achievements. The story is usually told in chronological order. An autobiography is written by the person whose life is described and uses words such as *I* and *me.* A biography is written by someone else and uses words such as *he, she, him,* and *her.*

Preview and predict Have students preview the title and the illustrations in *Rocks in His Head.* Ask them to predict what they think the selection will be about.

Set purpose Prior to reading, have students set their own purposes for reading this selection. To help students set a purpose, ask them to think about why collecting rocks might be a valuable pastime.

Strategy Response Log

INTERACT with TEXT

Have students use the Strategy Response Log on p. 24 in the *Reader's and Writer's Notebook* to review the characteristics of biographies. As they read, have them look for characteristics of the genre.

Small Group Time

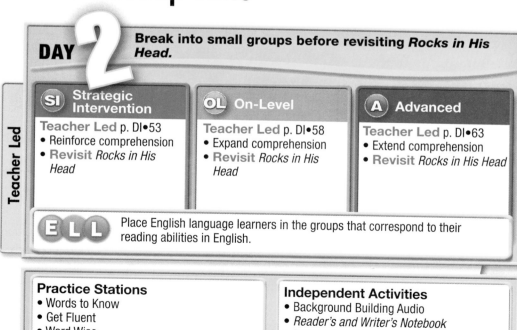

DAY 2 **Break into small groups before revisiting *Rocks in His Head.***

Teacher Led

SI Strategic Intervention	OL On-Level	A Advanced
Teacher Led p. DI•53 • Reinforce comprehension • Revisit *Rocks in His Head*	Teacher Led p. DI•58 • Expand comprehension • Revisit *Rocks in His Head*	Teacher Led p. DI•63 • Extend comprehension • Revisit *Rocks in His Head*

ELL Place English language learners in the groups that correspond to their reading abilities in English.

Practice Stations
- Words to Know
- Get Fluent
- Word Wise

Independent Activities
- Background Building Audio
- *Reader's and Writer's Notebook*
- Research and Inquiry

Differentiated Instruction

SI Strategic Intervention

Set purposes Work with students to set a purpose for reading, or if time permits, have students work with partners to set purposes.

A Advanced

Build background Have students investigate different ways people might pursue the hobby of rock collecting. Have them report their findings to the class.

Double Day Read! Multidraft Reading

For **Whole Group** instruction, choose one of the reading options below. For each reading, have students set the purpose indicated.

Option 1
Day 2 Read the selection. Use Guide Comprehension to monitor and clarify understanding.
Day 3 Reread the selection. Use Extend Thinking to develop higher-order thinking skills.

Option 2
Day 2 Read the first half of the selection, using both Guide Comprehension and Extend Thinking instruction.
Day 3 Read the second half of the selection, using both Guide Comprehension and Extend Thinking instruction.

ELL English Language Learners

Build background To build background, review the selection summary in English (*ELL Handbook,* p. 133). Use the Retelling Cards to provide visual support for the summary.

DAY 2 Read and Comprehend

Objectives

◎ Identify facts and opinions to improve comprehension.

OPTION 1 Guide Comprehension Skills and Strategies

Teach Fact and Opinion

◎ **Fact and Opinion** Write the following sentences on the board and have students determine which of the statements is a fact and which is an opinion: *They called the station the Antler Filling Station.* (Fact) *I've got rocks in my head, I guess.* (Opinion)

Corrective Feedback

If... students are unable to distinguish between statements of fact and statements of opinion,
then... model identifying statements of facts and opinions for students.

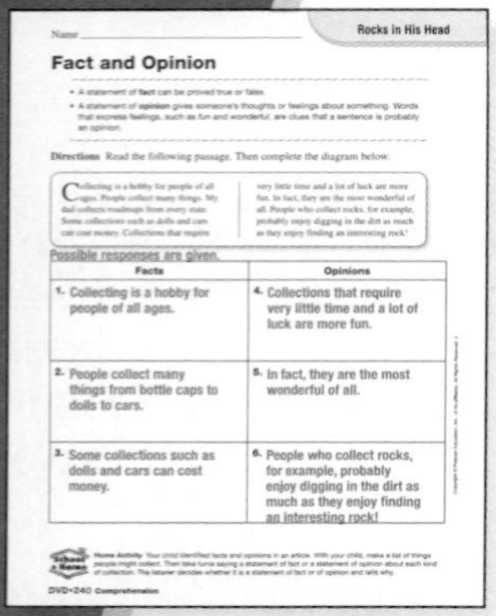
Name ______________ Rocks in His Head

Fact and Opinion

- A statement of **fact** can be proved true or false.
- A statement of **opinion** gives someone's thoughts or feelings about something. Words that express feelings, such as fun and wonderful, are clues that a sentence is probably an opinion.

Directions Read the following passage. Then complete the diagram below.

Collecting is a hobby for people of all ages. People collect many things. My dad collects roadmaps from every state. Some collections such as dolls and cars can cost money. Collections that require very little time and a lot of luck are more fun. In fact, they are the most wonderful of all. People who collect rocks, for example, probably enjoy digging in the dirt as much as they enjoy finding an interesting rock!

Possible responses are given.

Facts	Opinions
1. Collecting is a hobby for people of all ages.	4. Collections that require very little time and a lot of luck are more fun.
2. People collect many things from bottle caps to dolls to cars.	5. In fact, they are the most wonderful of all.
3. Some collections such as dolls and cars can cost money.	6. People who collect rocks, for example, probably enjoy digging in the dirt as much as they enjoy finding an interesting rock!

Home Activity Your child identified facts and opinions in an article. With your child, make a list of things people might collect. Then take turns saying a statement of fact or a statement of opinion about each kind of collection. The listener decides whether it is a statement of fact or of opinion and tells why.

DVD•240 Comprehension

Let's Practice It!
TR DVD•240

Model the Skill

Think Aloud Could I check or verify whether the first sentence is a fact? (yes, by looking it up in local records) So the first sentence is a statement of fact because it can be proved true or false.

Some people collect stamps. Some people collect coins or dolls or bottle caps. When he was a boy, my father collected rocks. When he wasn't doing chores at home or learning at school, he'd walk along stone walls and around old quarries, looking for rocks. People said he had rocks in his pockets and rocks in his head. He didn't mind. It was usually true.

When people asked what he wanted to be when he grew up, he'd say, "Something to do with rocks, I think."

"There's no money in rocks," someone said.

"Probably not," said my father.

When he grew up, my father decided to open a gas station. (People called them filling stations then.) My grandfather helped him build one on Armory Street in Springfield, Massachusetts.

They called the station the Antler Filling Station. My father carefully painted the name right over the doorway.

Inside the filling station was a desk with a cash drawer (which my father usually forgot to lock) and a table for his chess set.

96

Student Edition pp. 96–97

OPTION 2 Extend Thinking Think Critically

Higher-Order Thinking Skills

◎ **Fact and Opinion • Analysis** The sentence on page 96 says, "When he was a boy, my father collected rocks." What conclusion can you draw from this fact? Support your answer with textual evidence. Possible response: I can draw the conclusion that the father likes rocks. The sentence says that he collects rocks, and if you collect something, that probably means you like it.

Context Clues • Analysis Use context clues to figure out the meaning of the word *quarries* on page 96, paragraph 1. He walked around old quarries when he was looking for rocks. *Quarries,* then, must be places in the landscape that are filled with rocks, like mines, or pits where workers dig out valuable minerals. That definition works in the sentence.

What word in the second sentence tells me that this might be an opinion? *(guess)* A statement of opinion is someone's judgment, belief, or way of thinking about something. It cannot be proved true or false.

My father built narrow wooden shelves on the back wall and painted them white. People said, "What are those shelves for?"

He said, "I've got rocks in my head, I guess."

Then, one by one, he placed his rocks and minerals on those shelves. He carefully labeled each rock to show what kind it was and where it had come from.

In those days lots of rich people had automobiles, but then Henry Ford came out with the Model T.

That was a car many people could afford. My father had taken one apart and put it back together again and again until he knew every inch of the Model T. He thought that anyone who had spare parts for the Model T and could repair it so that it drove like new would do a good business. He bought some parts from dealers and found some parts in junkyards.

97

Inferring • Synthesis When the father was young, he wanted a job that had "something to do with rocks," but when he grew up, he opened a gas station. What does this tell you about the father and about the career choices people sometimes make? When people become adults, they sometimes make choices based on what is most practical. The father probably realized that he couldn't support a family by collecting rocks.

On Their Own

Have students reread pp. 96–97 to find more statements of fact. For additional practice, see *Let's Practice It!* page 240 on the *Teacher Resources DVD-ROM.*

Differentiated Instruction

SI Strategic Intervention

Biography Have students work in pairs to begin a timeline of the important events and decisions in the father's life.

Connect to Science

Minerals are natural substances that do not come from plants or animals. A mineral is made of the same substance throughout. Rocks are made up of two or more minerals.

ELL

English Language Learners

Idioms Explain that the expression *rocks in his head* means "he has no common sense." Ask when students might use this idiom.

DAY 2 Read and Comprehend

Objectives

- Recognize cause and effect relationships to aid comprehension.

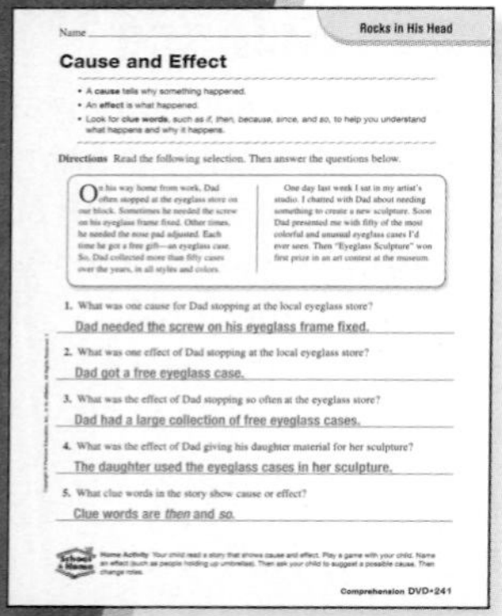

Name ______ Rocks in His Head

Cause and Effect

- A **cause** tells why something happened.
- An **effect** is what happened.
- Look for **clue words**, such as *if*, *then*, *because*, *since*, and *so*, to help you understand what happens and why it happens.

Directions Read the following selection. Then answer the questions below.

On his way home from work, Dad often stopped at the eyeglass store on our block. Sometimes he needed the screw on his eyeglass frame fixed. Other times, he needed the nose pad adjusted. Each time he got a free gift—an eyeglass case. So, Dad collected more than fifty cases over the years, in all styles and colors.

One day last week I sat in my artist's studio. I chatted with Dad about needing something to create a new sculpture. Soon Dad presented me with fifty of the most colorful and unusual eyeglass cases I'd ever seen. Then "Eyeglass Sculpture" won first prize in an art contest at the museum.

1. What was one cause for Dad stopping at the local eyeglass store?
   Dad needed the screw on his eyeglass frame fixed.
2. What was one effect of Dad stopping at the local eyeglass store?
   Dad got a free eyeglass case.
3. What was the effect of Dad stopping so often at the eyeglass store?
   Dad had a large collection of free eyeglass cases.
4. What was the effect of Dad giving his daughter material for her sculpture?
   The daughter used the eyeglass cases in her sculpture.
5. What clue words in the story show cause or effect?
   Clue words are *then* and *so*.

Home Activity Your child read a story that shows cause and effect. Play a game with your child. Name an effect (such as people holding up umbrellas). Then ask your child to suggest a possible cause. Then change roles.

Comprehension DVD•241

Let's Practice It!
TR DVD•241

OPTION 1 Skills and Strategies, continued

Teach Cause and Effect

Review Cause and Effect Point out that many people came to the filling station. Explain that this is what happened, so it is an effect. Remind students that there can be more than one cause, or reason, for something to happen. Ask students to identify *why* people came to the filling station, noting that there are several reasons, or causes. (They came to buy junk, to buy gas, to play chess, and to look at the rocks.)

Corrective Feedback

If... students are unable to identify and explain the cause-and-effect relationship,
then... model identifying facts and opinions.

Model the Skill

Think Aloud When there are no clue words to help me figure out causes, what question should I ask myself? (Why did this happen? What are the reasons this happened?)

The pile of Model T parts sat just to the left of the lift. Soon, that pile of parts was bigger than the filling station.

People said, "If you think people are going to buy that junk, you've got rocks in your head."

"Maybe I have," he said. "Maybe I have."

But people did come to buy that junk. They came to buy gas, and they came to play chess, and they came to look at the rocks.

For a while my father was too busy for the chess games. He was pumping gas, changing tires, and fixing Model Ts.

"Where did you get this one?" a customer would say, holding up a rock.

"Found it in a slag pile in New Hampshire," he'd say. Or, "Traded for it with a fella from Nevada. Gave him some garnets from Connecticut."

"People in Nevada and Connecticut collect rocks like you do?" people would ask.

"Lots of folks have rocks in their heads," said my father. He'd dig into his pocket and take out a rock. "Take a look at this one."

98

Student Edition pp. 98–99

OPTION 2 Think Critically, continued

Higher-Order Thinking Skills

Review Cause and Effect • Analysis Identify a cause-and-effect relationship on page 99 that has one cause and more than one effect. Cause: The stock market fell. Effects: bad times came; people couldn't afford to buy new cars or fix old ones; the narrator's father had time to play chess and go rock hunting.

Idioms • Analysis What is a positive meaning for the idiom "rocks in his head"? Possible response: Usually the idiom has a negative meaning, that the person is not smart, but it could also have the positive meaning that a person thinks about rocks all the time and they are very important to him.

One effect may have several causes. How can I make sure I find all the causes? (Look at the entire paragraph.)

Then the stock market fell. At first, people didn't think it would matter much to my father. After all, he had no money in the stock market.

"I may have rocks in my head," he said, "but I think bad times are coming."

And bad times did come. People couldn't afford to buy new cars or fix their old ones.

When business was slow, my father would play chess with some of his customers. When business was very slow, my grandfather would mind the filling station, and we'd pile as many of us kids as would fit into our Model T, and we'd hunt for more rocks with my father.

99

Background Knowledge • Evaluation • Text to Self The narrator's father spends a lot of time and effort on his hobby. He collects rocks, organizes them, studies them, and trades them. What hobby might you become interested in that would require such dedication? Possible responses: photography, bird watching, sports, coin collecting, music

Check Predictions Have students look back at the predictions they made earlier and discuss whether they were accurate. Then have students preview the rest of the selection and either adjust their predictions accordingly or make new predictions.

On Their Own

Have students reread pp. 98–99 to find more cause-and-effect relationships. For additional practice with cause and effect, see *Let's Practice It!* page 241 on the *Teacher Resources DVD-ROM.*

Differentiated Instruction

SI Strategic Intervention

Cause and effect Have students work in pairs to draw pictures of the causes and effects, putting the cause in one circle and the effects in another. Pairs can share their drawings.

A Advanced

Critical thinking Have students find additional effects of the stock market crash on people's everyday lives. Then have students write cause-and-effect statements based on their findings.

ELL

English Language Learners

Clarify Focus students' attention on the father's explanation of where he got the rock, on p. 98: "Found it..." This is an example of informal English in which the subject pronoun (*I,* in this case) is dropped. Restate the sentence in formal English: "I found it..." Then ask students to restate the other sentences in the paragraph in formal English, using subject pronouns.

Inferring Help students make an inference about why the rock collectors were trading rocks with each other. Suggest that they use a chart to record what they know from the text and their own knowledge. Once students have recorded their ideas, help them make an inference like, "Rocks are different from place to place, and rock collectors like to collect different kinds, so they trade with each other."

If you want to teach this selection in two sessions, stop here.

Objectives

- Find pertinent information from written and oral sources.
- Recognize and correctly use possessive pronouns.
- Practice correctly spelling words with prefixes *pre-*, *mid-*, *over-*, *out-*.

Research and Inquiry
Navigate/Search

Teach Have students generate a research plan for gathering information about their topic. Suggest that students search the Internet using their inquiry questions and keywords. Tell them to skim and scan each article entry or site for information that helps answer their inquiry question or leads them to specific information that will be useful. Bolded or italicized words may be clues to what kind of information the article or Web site will provide. Have students look for other features, such as headings, illustrations, captions, or highlighting. Encourage students to make on-site inspections to further their research, such as visiting a pertinent classroom and visiting an expert. Remind students to take notes as they gather information.

Model I used the keywords *learning to play musical instrument* to look for information about how learning to play a musical instrument is a valuable interest. I found information about learning how to play instruments, but this didn't help to answer my question. I decided to widen my search by the keywords *musical hobby* and *benefits*. This led me to more useful information such as health benefits and social benefits. To further my research, I decided to go to a music class where I could interview the musicians and inspect social benefits on-site. Everyone seemed to enjoy being at the music class and performing music together.

Guide practice Have students continue their review of Web sites and encyclopedia entries they identified, and encourage them to make on-site inspections and conduct interviews with experts. As students take notes from Web sites, advise them to be alert to additional key words that might lead them to more specific information. Explain that when such words or terms are underlined on a Web site, they can click on those words to go to a Web page that contains more detailed information.

On their own Have students create a Works-Cited page. They should write down the author, title, publisher, and publication year for each source used. For Web sites, they should record the Web addresses, authors, and the dates the Web sites were last updated.

Conventions
Possessive Pronouns

Teach Write this sentence on the board: *That dog is Madison's dog.* Point out that the possessive pronoun *hers* could replace the phrase *Madison's dog* because *hers* takes the place of a person's name and what she owns.

Guide practice Have students suggest words or phrases which are the equivalent of the following possessive pronouns.

my	**mine**	**our**	**ours**
your	**yours**	**your**	**yours**
his, her, its	**his, hers, its**	**their**	**theirs**

Daily Fix-It Use Daily Fix-It numbers 3 and 4 in the right margin.

Connect to oral language Have students look for and read aloud possessive pronouns in *Rocks in His Head.* (*his,* p. 96; *my,* p. 96; *their,* p. 99; *your,* p. 101; *mine,* p. 102; *her,* p. 103)

On their own For more practice, use the *Reader's and Writer's Notebook* p. 273.

Spelling
Prefixes *pre-, mid-, over-, out-*

Teach Remind students that their spelling words have prefixes. Model how to spell *midnight*. First I spell the prefix. Write *mid.* Then I spell the base word. Write *night*. I write both parts together to spell *midnight.* Tell students that they may also be able to divide the word by syllables to spell it, as in the case of *midnight.*

Guide practice Write the spelling words on the board. Have students write each spelling word and underline the prefix.

On their own For more practice, use the *Reader's and Writer's Notebook* p. 274.

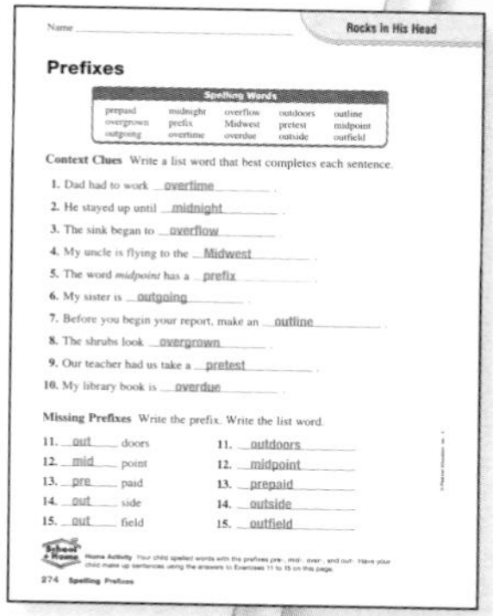
Name ______ Rocks in His Head

Prefixes

Spelling Words				
prepaid	midnight	overflow	outdoors	outline
overgrown	prefix	Midwest	pretest	midpoint
outgoing	overtime	overdue	outside	outfield

Context Clues Write a list word that best completes each sentence.

1. Dad had to work overtime.
2. He stayed up until midnight.
3. The sink began to overflow.
4. My uncle is flying to the Midwest.
5. The word *midpoint* has a prefix.
6. My sister is outgoing.
7. Before you begin your report, make an outline.
8. The shrubs look overgrown.
9. Our teacher had us take a pretest.
10. My library book is overdue.

Missing Prefixes Write the prefix. Write the list word.

11. out doors 11. outdoors
12. mid point 12. midpoint
13. pre paid 13. prepaid
14. out side 14. outside
15. out field 15. outfield

274 Spelling Prefixes

Reader's and Writer's Notebook p. 274

Daily Fix-It
3. The strangeest rocks are her's. *(strangest; hers)*
4. Didnt she find them in the Middwest? *(Didn't; Midwest)*

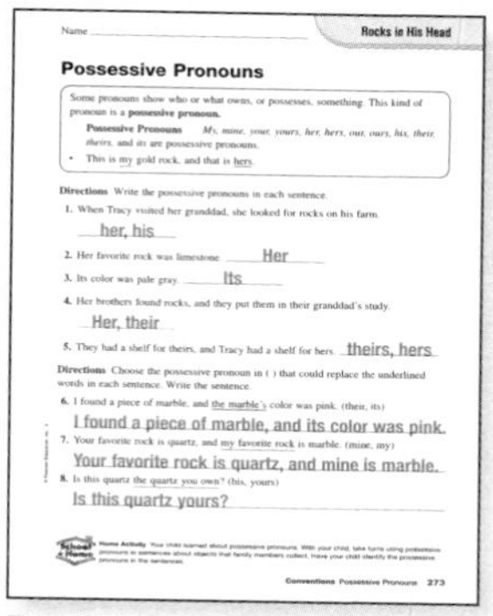
Name ______ Rocks in His Head

Possessive Pronouns

Some pronouns show who or what owns, or possesses, something. This kind of pronoun is a **possessive pronoun.**

Possessive Pronouns *My, mine, your, yours, her, hers, our, ours, his, their, theirs,* and *its* are possessive pronouns.

- This is my gold rock, and that is hers.

Directions Write the possessive pronouns in each sentence.

1. When Tracy visited her granddad, she looked for rocks on his farm. her, his
2. Her favorite rock was limestone. Her
3. Its color was pale gray. Its
4. Her brothers found rocks, and they put them in their granddad's study. Her, their
5. They had a shelf for theirs, and Tracy had a shelf for hers. theirs, hers

Directions Choose the possessive pronoun in ( ) that could replace the underlined words in each sentence. Write the sentence.

6. I found a piece of marble, and the marble's color was pink. (their, its) I found a piece of marble, and its color was pink.
7. Your favorite rock is quartz, and my favorite rock is marble. (mine, my) Your favorite rock is quartz, and mine is marble.
8. Is this quartz the quartz you own? (his, yours) Is this quartz yours?

Conventions Possessive Pronouns 273

Reader's and Writer's Notebook p. 273

ELL

English Language Learners

Conventions To provide students with practice on possessive pronouns, use the modified grammar lessons in the *ELL Handbook* and the Grammar Jammer! online at: www.ReadingStreet.com.

Objectives

- Select an appropriate topic for a biography.
- Use sequence to prepare for writing.

Writing—Biography
Writer's Craft: Sequence

Introduce the prompt

Remind students that the selection they'll be reading this week, *Rocks in His Head,* is an example of a biography. Review with students that biographies are a type of expository writing that tell about events in the life of a real person, and that these events are usually told in time order. Remind students to think about these features as they plan their writing. Then explain that they will begin the writing process for a biography today. Read aloud the writing prompt.

Writing Prompt

Think about a friend or family member who has an interesting collection. Now write a short biography of that person's life.

Select a topic

Think Aloud To help choose a topic, I will make a chart. Since I'm writing a biography of someone with an interesting collection, I'll make a list of people I know who have collections. Display a T-chart. I will write the person's name and what they collect on a list. The first person I'll list is my friend Tom. Tom has a collection of bottle caps that dates back about 40 years. Continue modeling by filling in the chart with the name of each person and what they collect, such as *Cousin Don's collection of mystery novels,* and *Great-Grandma's sock puppet collection.*

Gather information

Remind students that they can conduct personal interviews to gather more information about their friend or family member and his or her collection.

Person's Name	What They Collect
Tom	bottle cap collection
Cousin Don	mystery novels
Great-Grandma	sock puppet collection

Corrective feedback

Circulate around the room, providing assistance and corrective feedback to students as they complete their T-charts. Confer briefly with students who are having difficulty selecting a person to write about. Ask these students to recall stories they've heard about people they know who have collections. Suggest they look at home photographs to get ideas of people to write about.

MINI-LESSON

Developing a Story Sequence Chart

- A story sequence chart helps show the order in which events take place. I can use it to help me write my biography in time order.
- In the *Beginning* box I will include details about my Great-Grandma's life as a young woman.
- In the *Middle* box I will include information about how my Great-Grandma's sock puppet collection started.
- Finally, in the *End* box, I will write about my Great-Grandma's sock puppets in the present day.

Have students begin their own story sequence charts using the form on p. 275 of their *Reader's and Writer's Notebook.* Explain that they will fill in their charts with events relating to the person they chose to write about and his or her collection.

Differentiated Instruction

A **Advanced**

Elaborate Challenge students to add additional details to their charts, as well as transition words or phrases they might use when writing about each successive event.

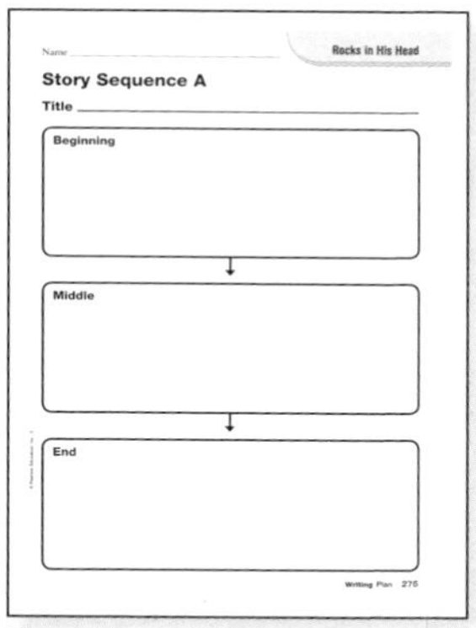

Reader's and Writer's Notebook, p. 275

ROUTINE

Quick Write for Fluency

Team Talk

1. **Talk** Have pairs discuss the person they will write about.
2. **Write** Each student writes a sentence about that person's collection.
3. **Share** Partners read their sentence to one another.

Routines Flip Chart

Teacher Tip

Help students stay focused while listening to their partner's quick write sentences. Remind students that listening is an active skill. When the speaker has finished sharing, suggest listeners ask questions to clarify information as necessary. Then have them restate the speaker's sentence in their own words.

Wrap Up Your Day

- ✔ **Build Concepts** What did you learn about collecting rocks?
- ✔ **Fact and Opinion** How were you able to determine what is a fact and what is an opinion in this section?
- ✔ **Inferring** How does inferring how the author feels about her father help you understand her purpose for writing?

Preview DAY 3

Tell students that tomorrow they will read more about how the father continues his interest in rocks.

Objectives
- Expand the weekly concept.
- Develop oral vocabulary.

Today at a Glance

Oral Vocabulary
ornament, descendant

Phonics/Word Analysis
◉ Prefixes *(pre-, mid-, over-, out-, bi-, de-)*

Comprehension Check/Retelling
Discuss questions

Reading
Rocks in His Head

Think Critically
Retelling

Fluency
Expression

Research and Study Skill
Online information

Research and Inquiry
Analyze

Conventions
Possessive pronouns

Spelling
Prefixes *pre-, mid-, over-, out-*

Writing
Biography

Concept Talk

Question of the Week

Why is it valuable to have unique interests?

Expand the concept

Remind students of the weekly concept question. Discuss how the question relates to collecting rocks. Tell students that today they will read about how collecting rocks changes the life of the narrator's father. Encourage students to think about how having a hobby can add enjoyment and satisfaction to a person's everyday life.

Anchored Talk

Develop oral vocabulary

Use illustrations to review pp. 94–99 of *Rocks in His Head.* Discuss the Amazing Word *ancestor.* Add this and other concept-related words to the concept map. Use the following questions to develop students' understanding of the concept. Students should answer the questions with appropriate detail.

- What are some ways that people honor their *ancestors?* (Possible response: People display their ancestors' pictures, and they create scrapbooks and family trees.)
- The narrator's grandfather helped to build a gas station for his son. What are some ways that people's *ancestors* affect their lives? (Possible response: Ancestors pass along important skills, values, or even money and belongings to their children and grandchildren.)

Oral Vocabulary
Amazing Words

Amazing Words Oral Vocabulary Routine

Teach Amazing Words

1. **Introduce** Write the word *ornament* on the board. Have students say it with you. Yesterday, we read that rocks can be interesting *ornaments* when they are displayed on shelves. Have students determine a definition of *ornament.* (An *ornament* is an item used for decoration.)
2. **Demonstrate** Have students answer questions to demonstrate understanding. What is an *ornament* that you might hang on your front door? (a wreath)
3. **Apply** Have students apply their understanding. What are some *ornaments* that people wear? (scarves, necklaces, bracelets, earrings)

See p. OV•3 to teach *descendant.*

Routines Flip Chart

Apply Amazing Words

Help students establish a purpose for reading before they read pp. 100–104 of *Rocks in His Head.* Have them consider how the Amazing Words *ornament* and *descendant* apply to the story of a man's special interest in collecting rocks.

Connect to reading

Explain that today students will read about how an interest in rocks changes someone's life. As they read, students should think about how this week's Question of the Week and the Amazing Words *ornament* and *descendant,* apply to this unique interest.

Amazing Words

hobby
project
leftover
murmur
ancestor
ornament
descendant
forge
compartment

ELL Expand Vocabulary Use the Day 3 instruction on ELL Poster 18 to help students expand vocabulary.

ELL Poster 18

Objectives

- ◎ Decode and read words with prefixes *pre-*, *mid-*, *over-*, *out-*, *bi-*, and *de-*.
- Apply knowledge of sound-spellings to decode unknown words when reading.
- Decode and read words in context and independent of context.

Word Analysis
Sort Words

Model word sorting Write *pre-*, *mid-*, *over-*, *out-*, *bi-*, and *de-* as heads on a six-column chart. Now we are going to sort words by prefixes. At the top of each column is a prefix. Words with the prefix *pre-* will go in that column. Words with the other prefixes will go in those columns. I will start. Write *midnight* and model how to read it, using the Word Parts Strategy Routine on page 88a. *Midnight* is made up of the base word *night* and the prefix *mid-*, so I will write *midnight* in the second column. Model reading *outside* and *pretest* in the same way.

Guide practice Use the practice words from the activity on p. 88a for the word sort. Point to a word. Have students read the word, identify its parts, and tell where it should be written on the chart.

Corrective feedback For corrective feedback, model reading the base word and then the prefix.

pre-	***mid-***	***over-***	***out-***	***bi-***	***de-***
pretreat	midsection	overtime	outstanding	biped	derail
preheat	midweek	overreach	outdone	bifocals	
				bimonthly	

Fluent Word Reading

Model Write *biplane.* I know the prefix *bi-*. I know the base word *plane.* I put them together and read the word *biplane.*

Guide practice Write the words below. Look for word parts you know. When I point to the word, we'll read it together. Allow one second per word part previewing time for the first reading.

midsection overweight outlandish prediction bisection descend

On their own Have students read the list above three or four times, until they can read one word per second.

Decode and Read

Read words independent of context

Have students turn to p. 33 in *Decodable Practice Readers 3.2* and find the first list of words. Each word in this list has a prefix. Let's decode and read these words. Be sure that students identify the prefix in each word.

Next, have students read the high-frequency words.

Preview Decodable Practice Passage

Have students read the title and preview the story. Tell them that they will read words with the prefixes *pre-, mid-, over-, out-, bi-,* and *de-.*

Read words in context

Chorally read the story along with students. Have students identify words in the story that have the prefixes *pre-, mid-, over-, out-, bi-,* and *de-.* Make sure that students are monitoring their accuracy when they decode words.

Team Talk Pair students and have them take turns reading the story aloud to each other. Monitor students as they read to check for proper pronunciation and appropriate pacing.

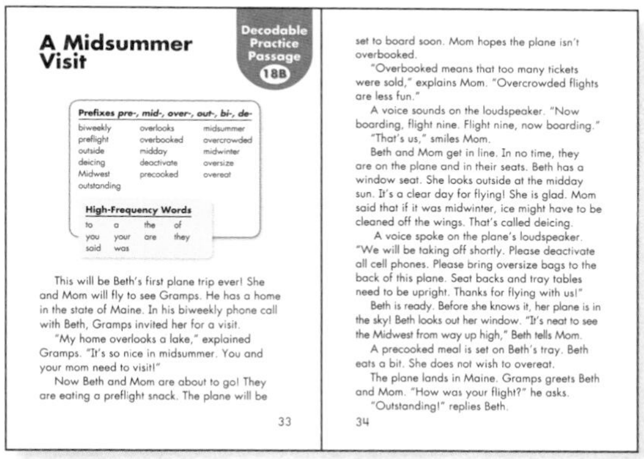

A Midsummer Visit

Decodable Practice Passage 18B

Prefixes pre-, mid-, over-, out-, bi-, de-

biweekly	overlooks	midsummer
preflight	overbooked	overcrowded
outside	midday	midwinter
deicing	deactivate	oversize
Midwest	precooked	overeat
outstanding		

High-Frequency Words

to	a	the	of
you	your	are	they
said	was		

This will be Beth's first plane trip ever! She and Mom will fly to see Gramps. He has a home in the state of Maine. In his biweekly phone call with Beth, Gramps invited her for a visit.

"My home overlooks a lake," explained Gramps. "It's so nice in midsummer. You and your mom need to visit!"

Now Beth and Mom are about to go! They are eating a preflight snack. The plane will be

33

set to board soon. Mom hopes the plane isn't overbooked.

"Overbooked means that too many tickets were sold," explains Mom. "Overcrowded flights are less fun."

A voice sounds on the loudspeaker. "Now boarding, flight nine. Flight nine, now boarding."

"That's us," smiles Mom.

Beth and Mom get in line. In no time, they are on the plane and in their seats. Beth has a window seat. She looks outside at the midday sun. It's a clear day for flying! She is glad. Mom said that if it was midwinter, ice might have to be cleaned off the wings. That's called deicing.

A voice spoke on the plane's loudspeaker. "We will be taking off shortly. Please deactivate all cell phones. Please bring oversize bags to the back of this plane. Seat backs and tray tables need to be upright. Thanks for flying with us!"

Beth is ready. Before she knows it, her plane is in the sky! Beth looks out her window. "It's neat to see the Midwest from way up high," Beth tells Mom.

A precooked meal is set on Beth's tray. Beth eats a bit. She does not wish to overeat.

The plane lands in Maine. Gramps greets Beth and Mom. "How was your flight?" he asks.

"Outstanding!" replies Beth.

34

Decodable Practice Passage 18B

Differentiated Instruction

A Advanced

Sort words Have students come up with their own words with prefixes to add to the chart.

Objectives

- Identify facts and opinions to aid comprehension.
- Use the inferring strategy to aid comprehension.
- Use context clues to determine the meanings of multiple-meaning words.

Comprehension Check

Have students discuss each question with a partner. Ask several pairs to share their responses.

☑ **Genre • Analysis**
What do we learn about Grace Johnson's character from this biography? Is this true? How do you know? Possible response: She is curious—she wants to see the father's rock collection. She's also fair. It is true. This is a biography, so it is about a real person and the real events in the person's life.

☑ **Fact and opinion • Evaluation**
Think about the narrator's relationship with the subject of this biography. Write one statement of fact and one opinion about their relationship. Possible response: Statement of Fact—the narrator is the daughter of the subject; Opinion—the narrator is proud of her father.

☑ **Inferring • Analysis**
The father takes a job as night janitor at the museum. What does this tell you about him? What does the way he performs his job tell you about him? Possible responses: He shows responsibility by taking a job to support his family. Even though he starts off as a janitor, he still takes the time to clean the rocks and correct their labels. This shows that he is knowledgeable and that he takes pride in his work.

☑ **Context clues • Analysis**
The word *board* appears on pages 103 and 104. What is the meaning of *board* in this context? The meaning is "a group of people who meet to decide something." In the context of the biography, the word refers to a group of people who act on behalf of the museum.

☑ **Connect text to self**
The narrator's father educated himself about rocks and got a job taking care of rocks in the museum. What are you interested in? What steps can you take to turn your interest into a career? Possible response: I'm interested in animals. I could go to school to learn about animals and become a veterinarian.

Strategy Response Log

INTERACT with TEXT

Have students revisit p.24 in the *Reader's and Writer's Notebook* to add additional information about biographies.

Check Retelling

Have students retell *Rocks in His Head.* Encourage students to use the text features to guide their retellings.

Corrective feedback

If... the students leave out important details,
then... have students look back through the illustrations in the selection.

Small Group Time

DAY 3 **Break into small groups before revisiting *Rocks in His Head.***

Teacher Led

SI Strategic Intervention	OL On-Level	A Advanced
Teacher Led p. DI•54 • Reinforce vocabulary • **Read/Revisit** *Rocks in His Head*	**Teacher Led** p. DI•59 • Expand vocabulary • **Read/Revisit** *Rocks in His Head*	**Teacher Led** p. DI•64 • Extend vocabulary • **Read/Revisit** *Rocks in His Head*

ELL Place English language learners in the groups that correspond to their reading abilities in English.

Practice Stations
- Let's Write
- Get Fluent
- Word Work

Independent Activities
- AudioText: *Rocks in His Head*
- *Reader's and Writer's Notebook*
- Research and Inquiry

ELL

English Language Learners
Check retelling To support retelling, review the multilingual summary for *Rocks in His Head* with the appropriate Retelling Cards to scaffold understanding.

45–50 min

Objectives

◎ Make inferences about text to aid comprehension.

OPTION 1 Skills and Strategies, continued

Teach Inferring

Inferring Point out that an author does not directly state everything in the text. Have students read p. 100. Then ask them what they can infer about the father based on the way he moved his rock collection.

Corrective Feedback

If... students are unable to make an inference to understand ideas and lessons drawn from the text,
then... model making an inference for students.

Model the Strategy

Think Aloud To make an inference, I combine text clues with my own background knowledge. What do text clues tell about moving the rock collection?

He had to build more shelves for the rocks, up the west wall of the station.

Then people stopped coming for gas. They stopped coming to play chess, and they even stopped coming to look at the rocks and minerals. They were all too busy looking for work.

One day my father picked up the chess set and carefully packed it in a big box. He took down each mineral, wrapped it in newspaper, and carefully placed it in a wooden box.

When his friends came with a truck to help us move, they said, "Watch out for those wooden boxes. He's got rocks in his boxes, now."

"Yessir," said my father. "That's just what I got in there. Take a look at this one."

The house we moved to was old and falling apart. My father said he'd have it fixed up in no time.

But before he started in on the repairs, we had to take those rocks up to the attic, where he'd already built tiny little wooden shelves.

My father did fix up the old house, and after he finished each repair, he went up to the attic with his rocks. He spent a lot of time reading about rocks, too.

100

Double Day Read! Multidraft Reading

If you chose . . .

Option 1 Return to the Extend Thinking instruction starting on p. 96–97.

Option 2 Read pp. 100–105. Use the Guide Comprehension and Extend Thinking instruction.

Student Edition pp. 100–101

OPTION 2 Think Critically, continued

Higher-Order Thinking Skills

Fact and Opinion • Analysis The narrator says that "then people stopped coming for gas." What conclusion can you draw about the father's filling station from this statement of fact? Support your answer with textual evidence. Possible response: I can conclude that the father's filling station is no longer doing well. The statement of fact says that people stopped coming for gas. In order for a filling station to do well, people need to buy gas.

Inferring • Synthesis Based on the information in the last paragraph on page 100, what can you infer about how the father's hobby made him feel? What text clue helps you understand this? The father's hobby relaxed him and made him feel good. The narrator says that after he finished doing hard work, he would go to the attic to spend time with the rocks. This suggests that studying his rocks was a treat for him.

(The father carefully wrapped and packed every rock. The first thing he did in the old house was build shelves for the rocks.) What does your background knowledge tell you about why he is so careful with the rocks? (When people are very attached to something, they treat it with great care.) I can infer, then, that the father's rock collection was very important to him.

"If you think those rocks are ever going to do you any good," said my mother, "you've got rocks in your head."

"Maybe I have," said my father. "Maybe I have." He reached into his pocket. "Take a look at this one."

My father spent a lot of time looking for any job he could find. Most jobs lasted only a day or two.

On rainy days when my father could find no other work, he'd take the bus to the science museum. They had a whole room full of glass cases containing many rocks. Sometimes he'd spend the whole day in that room.

101

Review **Cause and Effect • Analysis** When would the father go to the museum? When it was rainy and he couldn't find any work to do for the day.

On Their Own

Have students use a graphic organizer to list text clues and background knowledge for making another inference.

Differentiated Instruction

SI Strategic Intervention

Context clues Tell students that they can use text features such as illustrations to help them figure out the meaning of unknown words. Have them practice with several words from the text, such as *museum.*

A Advanced

Connect text to world Have students gather information about ways people in your community can collect, see, or study special rocks. Have them report on places and events such as local parks with rock features or museum offerings, including exhibits, lectures, and educational programs.

ELL

English Language Learners

Sequence Help students understand the sequence of events on p.100 by looking for clue words. *(then, one day, before, after)* Explain that readers can look for clue words such as *before* or *after* to better understand the order in which things happens. Have students create their own sentences using sequence words.

DAY 3 Read and Comprehend

Objectives

◎ Identify statements of fact and opinion to understand the text and improve comprehension.

OPTION 1 Skills and Strategies, continued

Teach Fact and Opinion

Fact and Opinion Have students read the last paragraph on p.103. Ask students to draw a conclusion based on the fact that the father opens the mineral cases and scrubs some of the rocks with toothbrushes.

Corrective Feedback

If... students are unable to draw a conclusion from the fact,
then... model drawing a conclusion.

Model the Skill

Think Aloud I read that the father scrubs some of the rocks with a toothbrush until they sparkle. If someone spends that much time and care cleaning something, then that must mean the person cares a lot about the work.

One afternoon he looked up to see a lady standing beside him. "I've seen you here before," she said.

"I come here a lot," he said. "I guess I've got rocks in my head."

"Tell me what you're looking for," she said.

"I'm looking for rocks that are better than mine," he said.

"How many did you find?" she asked.

"Ten," he said.

The lady looked around at the hundreds of rocks, in all those glass cases. "Only ten?"

"Maybe eleven," he said.

He smiled. She did, too.

102

Student Edition pp. 102–103

Review **Cause and Effect • Analysis** Mrs. Johnson tells the narrator's father that she can't hire him as a mineralogist. What are two reasons for, or causes of, this effect? The causes are that the father didn't study rocks at college, and the board won't allow it.

OPTION 2 Think Critically, continued

Higher-Order Thinking Skills

Fact and Opinion • Analysis Find a statement of fact from the top of page 103. How do you know that it is a statement of fact? *These rocks have come from all over the world.* This is a statement of fact. A museum keeps records about the objects it displays, so it can be proved that they come from all over the world.

I can conclude that the father cares a lot about these rocks and wants them to look their best.

On Their Own

Have students reread pp. 102–103 to look for other facts they can draw conclusions about. Have them support their assertions with textual evidence.

"You *have* got rocks in your head," she said. "I'm Grace Johnson, the director of this museum. These rocks have come from all over the world."

"So have mine," said my father. He reached into his pocket. "Take a look at this one," he said.

"Did you study rocks at college?" she asked.

"Couldn't afford to go to college," he said.

"Let me see the rest of your rocks," she said.

Mrs. Johnson got out her big Packard touring car, and my father got in. They drove to our house.

"Where are the rocks?" she asked.

"Up here," said my father, leading the way to the attic. "Watch your step."

Two hours later Mrs. Johnson said, "I can't hire you as a mineralogist. The board won't allow it. But I need a night janitor at the museum. Will you take the job?"

"Will I be cleaning rocks?" he asked.

"Sometimes," she said.

So my father took the job as night janitor at the museum. Before he went home, he'd open some of the mineral cases and scrub some of the rocks with a toothbrush until they sparkled like diamonds.

103

Genre • Evaluation What examples can you give from the selection that demonstrate the key differences between a biography and an autobiography? Possible response: It is written about the narrator's father—and it is told in chronological order using words such as *he* and *his.* An autobiography is written by the person it is about and uses words such as *I* and *me.*

Differentiated Instruction

SI Strategic Intervention

Cause and effect Tell students that to determine the causes, or reasons, something happens, they should look at the entire passage, both before and after the effect is mentioned.

A Advanced

Author's craft The author quotes her father throughout the biography, and he often repeats the same phrases. Have students use a T-chart to track the father's repetition of certain phrases such as "rocks in my head" or "Take a look at this one." Ask students to discuss how these quotations help to give an impression of the father's character.

ELL English Language Learners

Multisyllabic words Tell students that if they come to a long word they don't know, such as *mineralogist,* they can look for meaningful word parts that they recognize, such as *mineral.* Help students think of words they know that have similar word parts. For example, a *biologist* studies *biology,* so a *mineralogist* studies *minerals.* Have students determine if this meaning makes sense in the sentence.

Objectives

- Use context clues to distinguish among meanings for multiple-meaning words.

OPTION 1 Skills and Strategies, continued

Teach Multiple-Meaning Words

Multiple-Meaning Words Point out that this selection uses multiple-meaning words, tongue twisters, and idioms to demonstrate a playful use of language. Multiple-meaning words are words that have at least two different meanings. Have students use context to determine the relevant meaning of *rocks* on page 104.

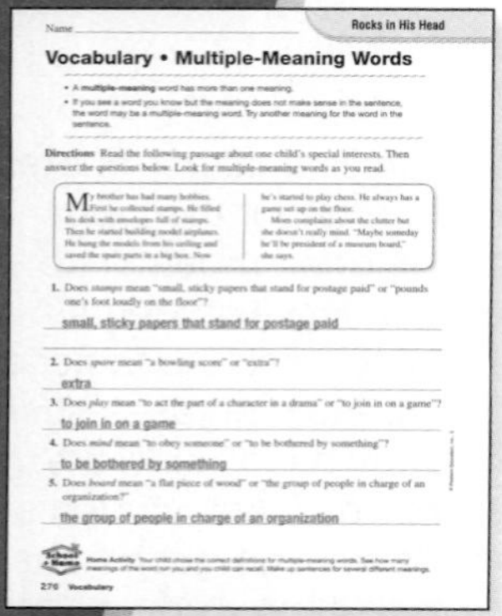
Name ______ Rocks in His Head

Vocabulary • Multiple-Meaning Words

- A **multiple-meaning** word has more than one meaning.
- If you see a word you know but the meaning does not make sense in the sentence, the word may be a multiple-meaning word. Try another meaning for the word in the sentence.

Directions Read the following passage about one child's special interests. Then answer the questions below. Look for multiple-meaning words as you read.

My brother has had many hobbies. First he collected stamps. He filled his desk with envelopes full of stamps. Then he started building model airplanes. He hung the models from his ceiling and saved the spare parts in a big box. Now he's started to play chess. He always has a game set up on the floor.

Mom complains about the clutter but she doesn't really mind. "Maybe someday he'll be president of a museum board," she says.

1. Does *stamps* mean "small, sticky papers that stand for postage paid" or "pounds one's foot loudly on the floor"?
small, sticky papers that stand for postage paid
2. Does *spare* mean "a bowling score" or "extra"?
extra
3. Does *play* mean "to act the part of a character in a drama" or "to join in on a game"?
to join in on a game
4. Does *mind* mean "to obey someone" or "to be bothered by something"?
to be bothered by something
5. Does *board* mean "a flat piece of wood" or "the group of people in charge of an organization?"
the group of people in charge of an organization

276 Vocabulary

Reader's and Writer's Notebook p. 276

Corrective Feedback

If... students have difficulty identifying the correct meaning of *rocks*, **then...** model using context clues to figure out the meaning.

Model the Skill

Think Aloud When I look up *rocks* in a dictionary, I see that it can mean "a stone" or "to move from side to side." This selection is about a father who collects stones.

Mrs. Johnson came in early for work one morning and saw him carefully writing a new label for one of the rocks.

"What are you doing?" she asked.

"One rock was labeled wrong," he said. "I fixed it."

Mrs. Johnson smiled. "I've been talking to the board of directors. They know that I need a person here who knows as much about rocks as you do."

"What about the college education?" he asked.

She said, "I told them I need somebody with rocks in his head and rocks in his pockets. Are you it?"

"Maybe I am," said my father. "Maybe I am."

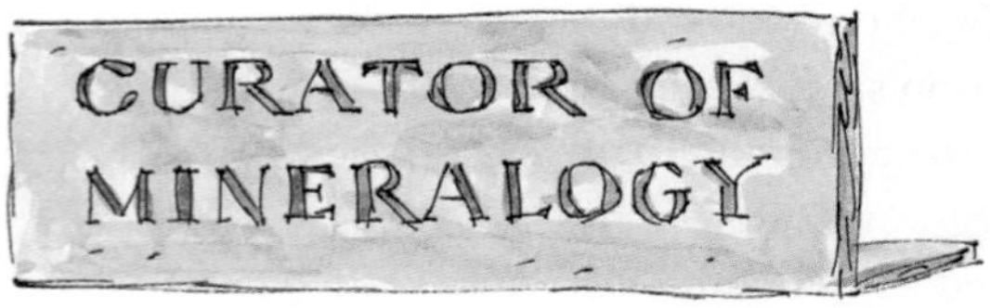

He reached into his pocket and took out a rock. "Take a look at this one," he said.

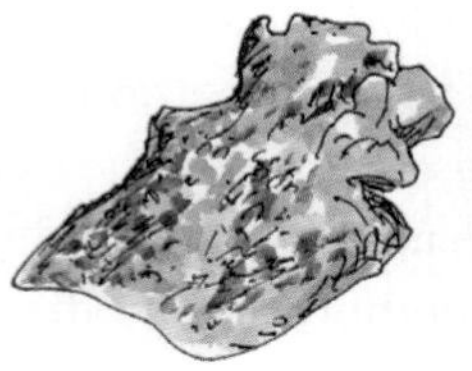

104

Student Edition pp. 104–105

Genre • Evaluation Tongue twisters are phrases or sentences that are difficult to say quickly. What are some reasons why the sayings on page 105 are hard to say? Possible response: They use alliteration, or contain many words that begin with the same sounds. They use similar consonant or vowel sounds. They also use homophones such as *wood/would.* What tongue twister can you make with the word *silly*? Possible response: Silly Sally slipped on her slippers.

OPTION 2 Think Critically, continued

Higher-Order Thinking Skills

Multiple-Meaning Words • Analysis Use context clues and a dictionary to tell the meaning of the word *pick* in the tongue twister on page 105. Possible response: In this tongue twister, Peter Piper is gathering peppers. Therefore, the meaning is "to pluck from a plant."

The idiom "rocks in his head" in this context can mean that he thinks about stones a lot. So *rocks* means "stones" in this selection.

On Their Own

Have students identify other examples of playful language in the selection, and use context clues and a dictionary to figure out the meaning of the multiple-meaning word *board* on p. 104. For additional practice, use *Reader's and Writer's Notebook* p. 276.

Differentiated Instruction

SI Strategic Intervention

Sound devices Remind students alliteration is when we use words that begin with the same sound. Work with students to identify examples of alliteration in each tongue twister on p. 105, noting that such words do not always contain the same letters to make identical sounds (for example, *shell/surely*).

A Advanced

Graphic sources Tell students that the illustration on p. 104 gives important information about the father's new job. Point out the word *curator* and have students work in pairs to examine the text for clues to the meaning of this word.

Talent with a Twist of the Tongue

The phrase "rocks in his head" is a play on words. Tongue twisters are also a type of word play. People all around the world enjoy these playful verses and they exist in every language. Below are three well-known tongue twisters. As you read, think about what makes this language playful.

Try to say these three tongue twisters as fast as you can:

She sells sea shells by the sea shore.
The shells she sells are surely seashells.
So if she sells shells on the seashore,
I'm sure she sells seashore shells.

Peter Piper picked a peck of pickled peppers.
Did Peter Piper pick a peck of pickled peppers?
If Peter Piper picked a peck of pickled peppers,
where's the peck of pickled peppers Peter Piper picked?

How much wood would a woodchuck chuck
if a woodchuck could chuck wood?
He would chuck, he would, as much as he could,
and chuck as much wood as a woodchuck would
if a woodchuck could chuck wood.

105

Comprehension Check

Spiral Review

Draw Conclusions • Analysis The narrator's father gets so much satisfaction out of his rock collecting that it keeps him happy even when times are hard. Think about other people you have read about in this unit and draw a conclusion about the role of hobbies in their lives. Possible response: Hobbies play an important role in people's lives by providing relaxation and escape from hard times.

Text Structure • Evaluation Look back at the entire selection *Rocks in His Head.* What kind of text structure does the author use in telling about her father's life, and why might she have chosen to use this particular structure? The author tells about her father's life in sequence or chronological order, which is usual for a biography, because people's lives are made up of a particular sequence of important events.

Check Predictions Have students return to the predictions they made earlier and confirm whether they were accurate.

ELL English Language Learners

Monitor understanding Reading aloud the first four paragraphs on p. 104 Ask: Why do you think Mrs. Johnson was happy? (She knew she had found someone who was very knowledgeable about rocks. She saw that the father had known a rock was mislabeled.)

Objectives

- ◎ Use the inferring strategy to aid comprehension.
- ◎ Identify facts and opinions to aid in comprehension.

Check Retelling

SUCCESS PREDICTOR

Plan to Assess Retelling

- ☑ **Week 1** Assess Strategic Intervention students.
- ☑ **Week 2** Assess Advanced students.
- ☑ **This week assess Strategic Intervention students.**
- ☐ **Week 4** Assess On-Level students.
- ☐ **Week 5** Assess any students you have not yet checked during this unit.

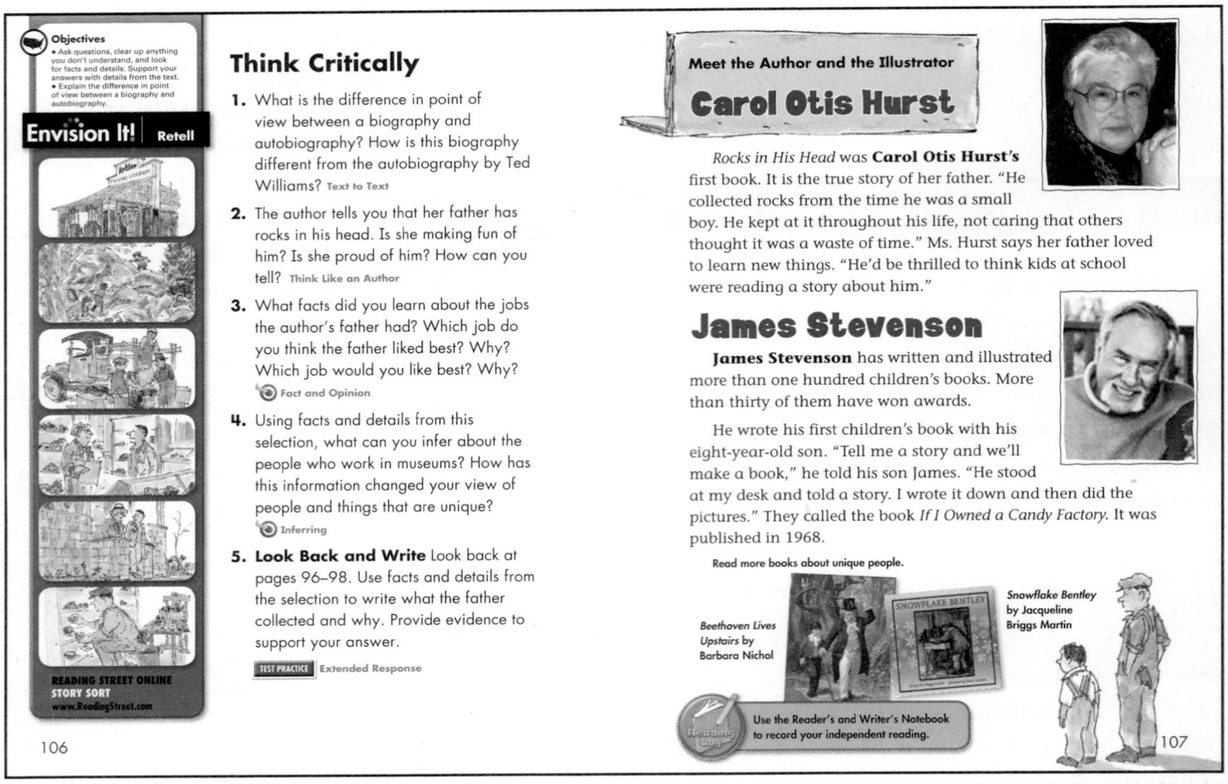

Objectives
• Ask questions, clear up anything you don't understand, and look for facts and details. Support your answers with details from the text.
• Explain the difference in point of view between a biography and autobiography.

Envision It! | **Retell**

READING STREET ONLINE STORY SORT www.ReadingStreet.com

Think Critically

1. What is the difference in point of view between a biography and autobiography? How is this biography different from the autobiography by Ted Williams? Text to Text
2. The author tells you that her father has rocks in his head. Is she making fun of him? Is she proud of him? How can you tell? Think Like an Author
3. What facts did you learn about the jobs the author's father had? Which job do you think the father liked best? Why? Which job would you like best? Why? Fact and Opinion
4. Using facts and details from this selection, what can you infer about the people who work in museums? How has this information changed your view of people and things that are unique? Inferring
5. **Look Back and Write** Look back at pages 96–98. Use facts and details from the selection to write what the father collected and why. Provide evidence to support your answer.

TEST PRACTICE Extended Response

106

Meet the Author and the Illustrator

Carol Otis Hurst

Rocks in His Head was **Carol Otis Hurst's** first book. It is the true story of her father. "He collected rocks from the time he was a small boy. He kept at it throughout his life, not caring that others thought it was a waste of time." Ms. Hurst says her father loved to learn new things. "He'd be thrilled to think kids at school were reading a story about him."

James Stevenson

James Stevenson has written and illustrated more than one hundred children's books. More than thirty of them have won awards.

He wrote his first children's book with his eight-year-old son. "Tell me a story and we'll make a book," he told his son James. "He stood at my desk and told a story. I wrote it down and then did the pictures." They called the book *If I Owned a Candy Factory.* It was published in 1968.

Read more books about unique people.

Beethoven Lives Upstairs by Barbara Nichol

Snowflake Bentley by Jacqueline Briggs Martin

Use the Reader's and Writer's Notebook to record your independent reading.

107

Student Edition pp. 106–107

Retelling

Envision It!

Have students work in pairs to retell the selection, using the Envision It! Retelling Cards as prompts. Remind students that they should accurately describe the main topic and important ideas in a logical order and use key vocabulary as they retell. Monitor students' retellings.

Scoring rubric

Top-Score Response A top-score response makes connections beyond the text, describes the main topic and important ideas using accurate information, evaluates facts and opinions, and draws conclusions from the text.

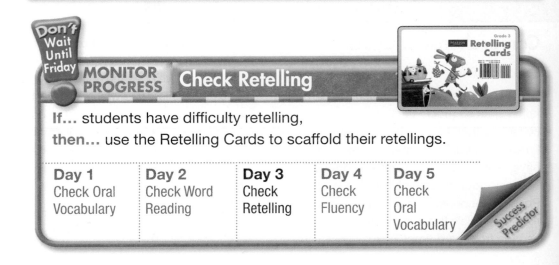

Don't Wait Until Friday **MONITOR PROGRESS** **Check Retelling**

If... students have difficulty retelling,
then... use the Retelling Cards to scaffold their retellings.

Day 1	Day 2	Day 3	Day 4	Day 5
Check Oral Vocabulary	Check Word Reading	Check Retelling	Check Fluency	Check Oral Vocabulary

Success Predictor

Think Critically

Text to world

1. This biography is written by the subject's daughter, who uses the pronoun *he* to refer to the subject of the biography. The autobiography of Ted Williams is written by the subject himself, Ted Williams, who refers to himself using the pronoun *I*.

Think like an author

2. The author is proud of her father. She admires the way he learned all about the Model T and describes how Grace Johnson was impressed by his knowledge about rocks.

Fact and opinion

3. Responses will vary; students should identify their responses as statements of facts or opinions.

Inferring

4. Responses will vary; students should back up their responses with examples from the selection.

Writing on Demand

5. **Look Back and Write** To build writing fluency, assign a 10–15 minute time limit.

Suggest that students use a prewriting strategy, such as brainstorming or using a graphic organizer, to organize their ideas. Remind them to establish a topic sentence and support it with facts, details, or explanations. As students finish, encourage them to reread their responses, revise for organization and support, and proofread for errors in grammar and conventions.

Scoring rubric

Top-Score Response A top-score response uses details from the story to tell about what the father collected and why.

A top-score response should include:

- The father collected rocks for many years.
- He liked to look at rocks, talk about them, and trade them.
- He enjoyed reading about rocks and studying them.

Differentiated Instruction

SI Strategic Intervention

Preparing to Write To help students prepare to write, have them work in pairs to create a timeline that shows the father's increasing interest in collecting rocks. Then have them brainstorm a list of words or phrases that show how he felt about his hobby.

Meet the Author

Have students read about author Carol Otis Hurst on p. 107. Ask them how she expresses her pride in her father's unique interest.

Independent Reading

After students enter their independent reading information into their Reading Logs or a journal, have them summarize what they have read. Remind students that a summary should be no more than a few sentences about the main idea of a text.

ELL

English Language Learners

Retelling Use the Retelling Cards to discuss the selection with students. Place the cards in an incorrect order and have volunteers correct the mistake. Then have students explain where each card should go as they describe the sequence of the selection.

Check Retelling
Success Predictor

Objectives
- Read aloud grade-level text with expression.
- Reread for fluency.
- Use online reference sources.

Model Fluency
Expression

Model fluent reading Have students turn to page 98 of *Rocks in His Head.* Have students follow along as you read this page. Tell them to listen to the expression of your voice as you read the words that different characters say. Adjust your voice level to stress important words and phrases.

Guide practice Have students follow along as you read the page again. Then have them reread the page as a group without you until they read with the right expression and with no mistakes. Ask questions to be sure students comprehend the text. Continue in the same way on p. 99.

Reread for Fluency

Corrective feedback

If... students are having difficulty reading with the right expression,
then... prompt:
- Which word is a problem? Let's read it together.
- Read the sentence again to be sure you understand it.
- Tell me the sentence. Now read it as if you are speaking to me.

ROUTINE **Oral Rereading**

1. **Read** Have students read p. 101 of *Rocks in His Head* orally.
2. **Reread** To achieve optimal fluency, students should reread the text three or four times.
3. **Corrective Feedback** Have students read aloud without you. Provide feedback about their expression and encourage them to adjust their voice level to stress important words and phrases. Listen for use of appropriate expression. Have students reread three to four times.

Routines Flip Chart

Research and Study Skills
Online Information

Teach

If available, have students display the results of Web research they have done. Tell students that they can use information they get from the Web in many of the same ways they would use information from reference books. Review with students how to explore Web sites.

- Enter **keywords** in a search engine to find Web sites devoted to the research topic.
- Many websites contain **online directories.** An online directory is a kind of table of contents of Web sites on a particular topic. Often this table of contents is a list of links accompanied by descriptions of what can be found on the site.
- Clicking on a **link** in an online directory brings up the new Web site.
- It's important to evaluate the reliability of a Web site for research by paying attention to the ending of the Web site's "address," or **URL.** Sites that end in *.gov* are hosted by the government. Sites ending in *.edu* are hosted by schools. Sites for museums and libraries usually end in *.org.*

Guide practice

Discuss these questions:

How do you begin an online search for information? (by entering keywords into a search engine)

Where will you find an online directory? How do you use it? (Online directories are found on Web sites. To use an online directory, click on the links provided.)

On their own

Have students review and complete p. 277 of the *Reader's and Writer's Notebook.*

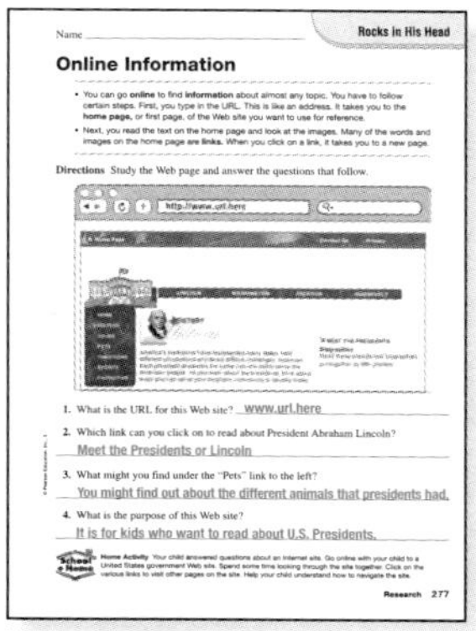
Name ____________ **Rocks in His Head**

Online Information

- You can go **online** to find **information** about almost any topic. You have to follow certain steps. First, you type in the URL. This is like an address. It takes you to the **home page,** or first page, of the Web site you want to use for reference.
- Next, you read the text on the home page and look at the images. Many of the words and images on the home page are **links.** When you click on a link, it takes you to a new page.

Directions Study the Web page and answer the questions that follow.

1. What is the URL for this Web site? www.url.here
2. Which link can you click on to read about President Abraham Lincoln? Meet the Presidents or Lincoln
3. What might you find under the "Pets" link to the left? You might find out about the different animals that presidents had.
4. What is the purpose of this Web site? It is for kids who want to read about U.S. Presidents.

Home Activity Your child answered questions about an Internet site. Go online with your child to a United States government Web site. Spend some time looking through the site together. Click on the various links to visit other pages on the site. Help your child understand how to navigate the site.

Research 277

Reader's and Writer's Notebook p. 277

ELL

English Language Learners

Professional development: What ELL experts say about reading strategies "Beginning English language learners benefit from the repeated readings of predictable texts with illustrations, especially when the teacher has provided a brief preview of each text to introduce the topic of the story and preview new vocabulary."
—Dr. Georgia Earnest Garcia

Objectives

- Analyze data for usefulness.
- Identify and correctly use possessive pronouns.
- Spell frequently mispelled words

Research and Inquiry
Analyze

Teach Tell students that today they will analyze their findings and may need to change the focus of their original inquiry question.

Model Think Aloud Originally I thought that playing a musical instrument was an interest that would be valuable mainly to the musician. But after going to a music class to hear musicians and doing online research, I learned that music is valuable to many people. It improves people's health, it relaxes people, and it can provide social interaction. I will refocus my inquiry question to include information from my research. Now my inquiry question is *Is playing a musical instrument an interest that is valuable to the community as well as to the musician?*

Guide practice Have students analyze their findings. They may need to refocus their inquiry question to better fit the information they found. Remind students that if they have difficulty improving their focus they can ask a reference librarian or a local expert for guidance.

Remind students that they can continue to consult online sources to help them refine their ideas.

On their own Have students summarize their research for a partner. Partners should discuss each other's findings and evaluate the focus of their inquiry questions.

Conventions
Possessive Pronouns

Review Remind students that this week they learned about possessive pronouns:

- Pronouns are words that take the place of nouns.
- Pronouns that show who or what owns, or possesses, something are called possessive pronouns, such as *his, hers,* and *theirs.*

Daily Fix-It Use Daily Fix-It numbers 5 and 6 in the right margin.

Connect to oral language Have the class replace the underlined word or phrase with the correct possessive pronoun and read the new sentence aloud.

> **<u>Jamal's</u> sculpture is finished.**
>
> **<u>Kaya's sculpture</u> is on view in the school library.**

On their own For additional support, use *Let's Practice It!* page 242 on the *Teacher Resources DVD-ROM.*

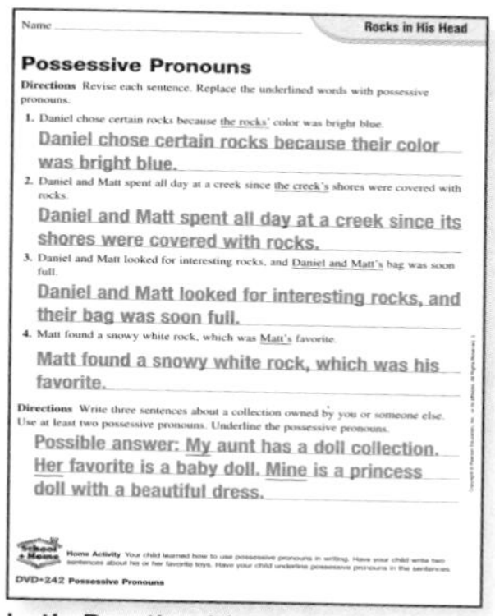
Name ______ Rocks in His Head

Possessive Pronouns

Directions Revise each sentence. Replace the underlined words with possessive pronouns.

1. Daniel chose certain rocks because <u>the rocks'</u> color was bright blue.
Daniel chose certain rocks because their color was bright blue.
2. Daniel and Matt spent all day at a creek since <u>the creek's</u> shores were covered with rocks.
Daniel and Matt spent all day at a creek since its shores were covered with rocks.
3. Daniel and Matt looked for interesting rocks, and <u>Daniel and Matt's</u> bag was soon full.
Daniel and Matt looked for interesting rocks, and their bag was soon full.
4. Matt found a snowy white rock, which was <u>Matt's</u> favorite.
Matt found a snowy white rock, which was his favorite.

Directions Write three sentences about a collection owned by you or someone else. Use at least two possessive pronouns. Underline the possessive pronouns.

Possible answer: <u>My</u> aunt has a doll collection. <u>Her</u> favorite is a baby doll. <u>Mine</u> is a princess doll with a beautiful dress.

DVD•242 Possessive Pronouns

Let's Practice It!
TR DVD•242

Spelling
Prefixes *pre-, mid-, over-, out-*

Frequently misspelled words Students often misspell the word *outside.* The words *midnight, outgoing,* and *overdue* are also difficult to spell. I'm going to read a sentence. Choose the correct word to complete the sentence and then write it correctly.

1. **Noon and _____ look the same on a clock.** (midnight)
2. **We took our sled _____ after the first snowfall.** (outside)
3. **The actor had an _____ personality.** (outgoing)
4. **Some stores charge fees for _____ payments.** (overdue)

On their own For additional support, use the *Reader's and Writer's Notebook* p. 278.

Differentiated Instruction

SI Strategic Intervention

Locate examples Provide students with a list of possessive pronouns. Have students work in pairs to find and write examples of possessive pronouns in the main selection or other grade-appropriate texts.

Daily Fix-It

5. That black rock of their's is unknow to me. *(theirs; unknown)*
6. The yellow rock was found in the camp ground by Juan and he. *(campground; him)*

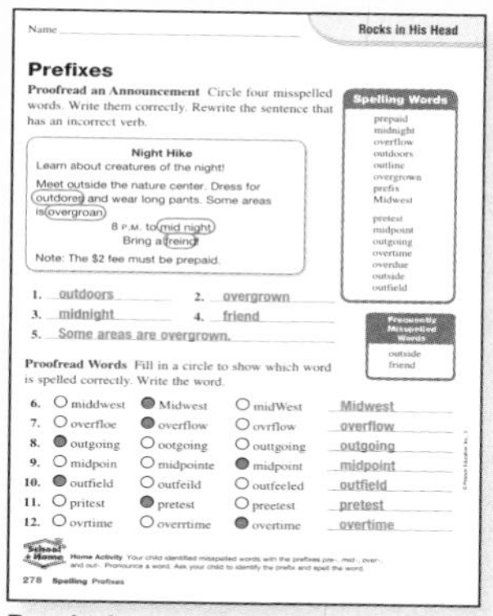
Name ______ Rocks in His Head

Prefixes

Proofread an Announcement Circle four misspelled words. Write them correctly. Rewrite the sentence that has an incorrect verb.

Night Hike
Learn about creatures of the night!
Meet outside the nature center. Dress for outdores and wear long pants. Some areas is overgroan.
8 P.M. to mid night
Bring a freind
Note: The $2 fee must be prepaid.

Spelling Words: prepaid, midnight, overflow, outdoors, outline, overgrown, prefix, Midwest, pretest, midpoint, outgoing, overtime, overdue, outside, outfield

Frequently Misspelled Words: outside, friend

1. outdoors 2. overgrown
3. midnight 4. friend
5. Some areas are overgrown.

Proofread Words Fill in a circle to show which word is spelled correctly. Write the word.

6. middwest / Midwest / midWest — Midwest
7. overfloe / overflow / ovrflow — overflow
8. outgoing / ootgoing / outtgoing — outgoing
9. midpoin / midpointe / midpoint — midpoint
10. outfield / outfeild / outfeeled — outfield
11. pritest / pretest / preetest — pretest
12. ovrtime / overrtime / overtime — overtime

278 Spelling Prefixes

Reader's and Writer's Notebook p. 278

Objectives

- Understand the criteria for an effective biography.

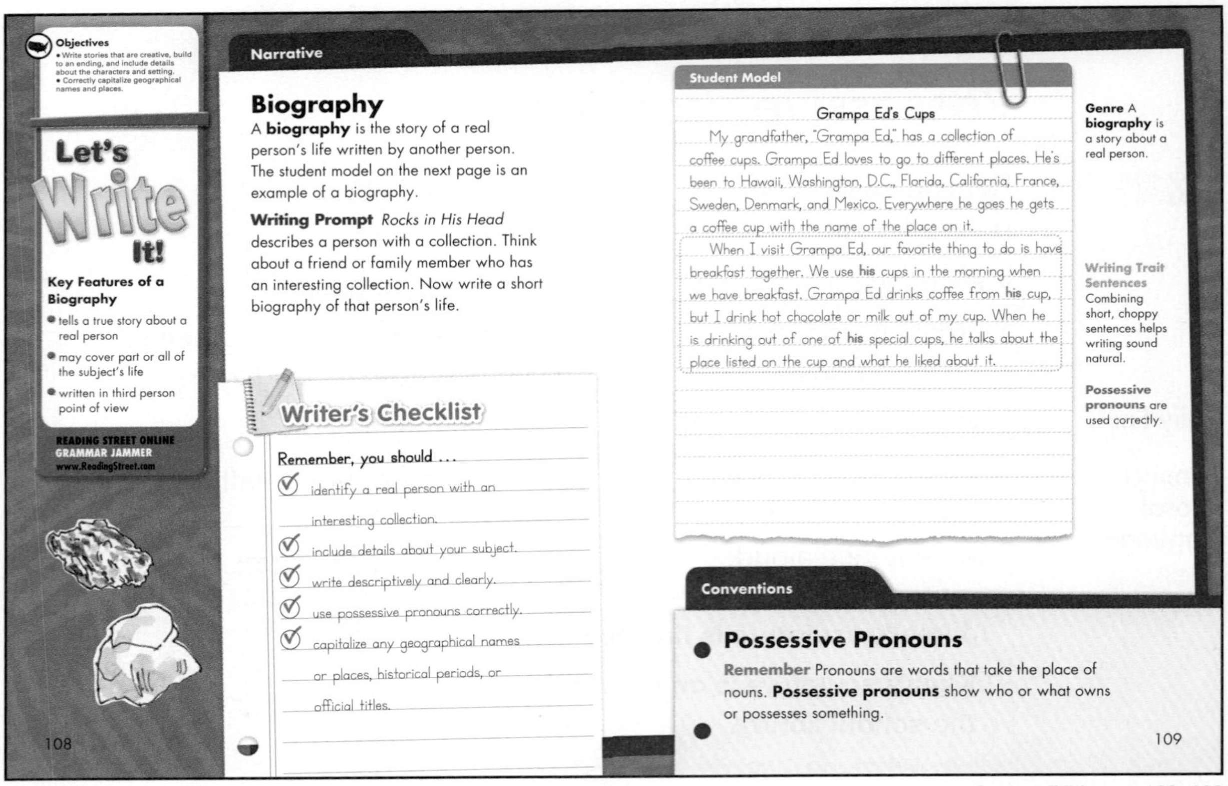

Objectives
- Write stories that are creative, build to an ending, and include details about the characters and setting.
- Correctly capitalize geographical names and places.

Let's Write It!

Key Features of a Biography
- tells a true story about a real person
- may cover part or all of the subject's life
- written in third person point of view

READING STREET ONLINE
GRAMMAR JAMMER
www.ReadingStreet.com

108

Narrative

Biography
A **biography** is the story of a real person's life written by another person. The student model on the next page is an example of a biography.

Writing Prompt *Rocks in His Head* describes a person with a collection. Think about a friend or family member who has an interesting collection. Now write a short biography of that person's life.

Writer's Checklist

Remember, you should ...
- identify a real person with an interesting collection.
- include details about your subject.
- write descriptively and clearly.
- use possessive pronouns correctly.
- capitalize any geographical names or places, historical periods, or official titles.

Student Model

Grampa Ed's Cups

My grandfather, "Grampa Ed," has a collection of coffee cups. Grampa Ed loves to go to different places. He's been to Hawaii, Washington, D.C., Florida, California, France, Sweden, Denmark, and Mexico. Everywhere he goes he gets a coffee cup with the name of the place on it.

When I visit Grampa Ed, our favorite thing to do is have breakfast together. We use **his** cups in the morning when we have breakfast. Grampa Ed drinks coffee from **his** cup, but I drink hot chocolate or milk out of my cup. When he is drinking out of one of **his** special cups, he talks about the place listed on the cup and what he liked about it.

Genre A **biography** is a story about a real person.

Writing Trait Sentences Combining short, choppy sentences helps writing sound natural.

Possessive pronouns are used correctly.

Conventions

Possessive Pronouns
Remember Pronouns are words that take the place of nouns. **Possessive pronouns** show who or what owns or possesses something.

109

Student Edition pp. 108–109

Let's Write It!
Biography

Teach Use pp. 108–109 in the Student Edition. Direct students to read the key features of a biography that appear on p. 108. Remind students that they can refer to the information in the Writer's Checklist as they write their own biographies.

Read the student model on p. 109. Point out compound and complex sentences and the possessive pronouns in the model.

Connect to conventions Remind students that a possessive pronoun shows who or what owns, or possesses something. Point out the correct use of possessive pronouns in the model.

Writing—Biography
Writing Trait: Sentences

Display rubric Display Scoring Rubric 18 from the *Teacher Resources DVD-ROM* and go over the criteria for each trait under each score. Then, using the student writing model in the Student Edition, choose students to explain why the model should score a 4 for one of the traits. If a student offers that the model should score below 4 for a particular trait, the student should offer support for that response. Remind students that this is the rubric that will be used to evaluate the biographies they will begin writing today.

Scoring Rubric: Biography

	4	3	2	1
Focus/Ideas	Well-developed characters, setting, and events	Developed characters, setting, and events	Underdeveloped characters, setting, and events	Undeveloped characters, setting, and events
Organization	Clear sequence of events	Able to follow sequence of events	Unclear sequence of events	No sequence of events
Voice	Clear interest in talents and important events in subject's life	Some interest in talents and important events in subject's life	Little interest in talents and important events in subject's life	No interest in talents and important events in subject's life
Word Choice	Strong use of vivid words	Adequate use of vivid words	Weak use of vivid words	No use of vivid words
Sentences	Clear sentences of various lengths and types; strong variety of sentence beginnings	Sentences of a few lengths and types; variety of sentence beginnings	Sentences of similar length and type; weak variety of sentence beginnings	No attempt at sentences of various lengths and types; no variety of sentence beginnings
Conventions	Few, if any, errors; strong use of possessive pronouns	Several minor errors; adequate use of possessive pronouns	Many errors; weak use of possessive pronouns	Numerous errors; no or incorrect use of possessive pronouns

Story Sequence Charts Have students get out the story sequence charts that they worked on yesterday. If their charts are not yet complete, allow students additional time to plan the beginning, middle, and end events of their biography.

Write You will be using your story sequence charts as you write the draft of your biography. When you are drafting, don't worry if your biography does not sound exactly as you would like. You will have a chance to revise it tomorrow.

A Advanced

Have students expand their Story Sequence Charts by including a list of transition words or phrases that will help them later on to connect the events listed in the chart.

ELL

English Language Learners

Story sequence charts Have students verbalize each section of information on their story sequence chart before they write. Use sentence frames to help, such as the following: *My biography is about _____. It takes place in _____. This person collects _____.*

Objectives

- Write a first draft of a biography.
- Write a variety of sentence types and lengths.

Writing, continued
Writing Trait: Sentences

MINI-LESSON

Varying Sentence Type and Length

Socks, or Puppets, or Both?

When my Great-Grandma was a young woman, she loved to knit. She was great at knitting socks. She was a fast knitter. Her designs were beautiful.

What if a sock was old? She never threw it out! "Waste not, want not" is her motto. That's how she began a sock-puppet collection—she made it herself. She would sew eyes, ears, and a nose onto hers old sock and give it new life. over time, Great-Grandma created a "family" of more than thirty sock puppetts.

My brother and me love to stage puppet shows with Great-Grandma's sock puppets whenever we visit.

Unit 4 Rocks in His Head Writing: Model 18A

Writing Transparency 18A, TR DVD

Introduce Explain to students that good writing has a natural flow. Different kinds of sentences and sentences of different lengths give writing texture and make it more interesting. Remind students of the three sentence types: declarative, interrogative, and exclamatory. Explain that students can use all three sentence types as they write their drafts. Also, they can write both short and long sentences. Display the Drafting Tips for students. Remind them that the focus of drafting is to get their ideas down in an organized way. Then display Writing Transparency 18A.

Drafting Tips

- ✔ To get started, review your story sequence chart.
- ✔ Write paragraphs that tell events in time order.
- ✔ Include sentences of varying types and lengths.

Think Aloud Now I will write my draft. I will use information I put in my story sequence chart to help me. In the *Beginning* box I might write *When my Great-Grandma was a young woman, she loved to knit* in the first box of the chart. This is how I want to start my biography. As I write, I will remember that I can include both telling and asking sentences to tell my story. I can also use short sentences and long sentences. I won't worry about revising or proofreading as I write because I will have time to do those tasks after I get my ideas down.

Direct students to use the drafting tips to guide them in writing their drafts. Remind them to write sentences that tell about their subject's talents or important achievements.

ROUTINE **Quick Write for Fluency** Team Talk

1. **Talk** Have pairs talk about the talents or important achievements of the person they chose to write about.
2. **Write** Each person writes a sentence about the person using a possessive pronoun.
3. **Share** Partners check each other's sentences for correct use of possessive pronouns.

Routines Flip Chart

Differentiated Instruction

SI Strategic Intervention
Make sure students understand the difference between a sentence and a sentence fragment. List several sentence fragments and have students complete sentences from them. When they are finished, have them tell what was needed to make the sentence complete.

Wrap Up Your Day

- ✔ **Build Concepts** Have students discuss how the father in this selection was able to stick to his interests.
- ✔ **Fact and Opinion** What statements of opinion were made about the father in this selection?
- ✔ **Inferring** How did the inferring strategy help you understand why the father was eventually hired as a mineralogist at the museum?

Preview DAY 4

Tell students that tomorrow they will read about marbles.

Objectives
- Expand the weekly concept.
- Develop oral vocabulary.

Today at a Glance

Oral Vocabulary
compartment, forge

Phonics/Word Analysis
Vowels: *r*-Controlled

Genre
Persuasive text

Reading
"Marvelous Marble Mania"

Let's Learn It!
Fluency: Expression
Vocabulary: ◉ Multiple-meaning words
Listening and Speaking: Interview

Research and Inquiry
Synthesize

Spelling
Prefixes *pre-, mid-, over-, out-*

Conventions
Possessive pronouns

Writing
Biography

Concept Talk

Question of the Week

Why is it valuable to have unique interests?

Expand the concept Remind students that this week they have read about how a man's unique hobby helped in hard times. Tell students that today they will read about the game of marbles, which has been popular for thousands of years.

Anchored Talk

Develop oral vocabulary Use text features to review pp. 100–104 of *Rocks in His Head.* Discuss the Amazing Words *ornament* and *descendant.* Add these and other concept-related words to the concept map. Use the following questions to develop students' understanding of the concept. Remind students to answer questions with appropriate detail.

- Why do you think people enjoy collecting *ornaments*? What do they do with them?
- What are some types of *ornaments* that people pass along to their children and other *descendants*?

Strategy Response Log

INTERACT with TEXT

Have students review the characteristics of a biography on p. 24 of the *Reader's and Writer's Notebook.* Then have them compare *Rocks in His Head* to another example of a biography that they have read or know about.

Oral Vocabulary
Amazing Words

Amazing Words

hobby
murmur
project
leftover
ancestor
ornament
descendant
compartment
forge

Teach Amazing Words

Amazing Words Oral Vocabulary Routine

1. **Introduce** Write the word *compartment* on the board. Have students say it aloud with you. We read about the glass cases at the science museum where rocks were stored in *compartments.* Why do you think museums store things in *compartments*? (Compartments keep things organized.) Have students supply a definition. (A *compartment* is a small section of something such as a box or drawer.)
2. **Demonstrate** Have students answer questions to demonstrate understanding. What *compartments* did the narrator's father use for storing rocks? (shelves, his pockets)
3. **Apply** Have students apply their understanding. What are some things you have that you could store in *compartments*? (socks, shoes, collections, sports equipment)

See pp. OV•3 to teach *forge.*

Routines Flip Chart

Apply Amazing Words

As students read "Marvelous Marble Mania" on pp. 110–113, have them think about what kinds of *compartments* people might use for storing marbles.

Connect to reading

Help students establish a purpose for reading. As students read today's selection about marbles, have them think about how the Question of the Week and the Amazing Words *compartments* and *forge* apply to the game of marbles.

ELL **Produce Oral Language** Use the Day 4 instruction on ELL Poster 18 to extend and enrich language.

ELL Poster 18

ELL

English Language Learners

Cognates Point out that *compartment,* one of today's Amazing Words, has a Spanish cognate, *compartimiento.*

Objectives

- Identify and read words with *r*-controlled vowels.

Phonics Review
Vowels: *r*-Controlled

Review sound-spellings

To review last week's phonics skill, write *star, purpose, birth,* and *board.* You studied words like these last week. What do you know about words like these that have *r*-controlled vowel sounds? (The *r* changes the sound of the preceding vowel.) Have students identify the letters that spell the *r*-controlled vowel sound in each word. What letters spell the *r*-controlled vowel in *star*? (*ar*) In *purpose*? (*ur*) Continue in the same way for *birth* (*ir*) and *board* (*oar*).

Corrective feedback

If students are unable to answer the questions about *r*-controlled vowels, refer them to Sound-Spelling Cards 55, 62, 67, 72, 87, 91, 92, 93 and 104.

Guide practice

Draw a three-column chart with the heads /ėr/, /är/, and /ôr/. We will work together to place words with *r*-controlled vowel sounds in the chart. Listen as I say each word. Words with the *r*-controlled vowel sound /ėr/ as in *worm* will go in the first column. Words with the *r*-controlled vowel sound /är/ as in *farm* will go in the second column. Words with the *r*-controlled vowel sound /ôr/ as in *corn* will go in the third column. Write each word in the appropriate column. Then have students read the words and ask volunteers to underline the letters that spell the *r*-controlled vowel sound in each word.

/ėr/	/är/	/ôr/
verb	carbon	former
furniture	marketplace	boredom
Thursday	shark	soaring
worthwhile	backyard	corner

On their own

For additional practice, use *Let's Practice It!* page 243 on the *Teacher Resources DVD-ROM.*

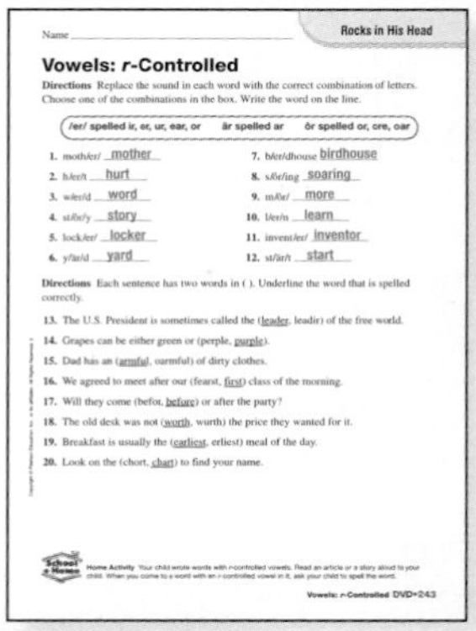
Name ____ Rocks in His Head

Vowels: *r*-Controlled

Directions Replace the sound in each word with the correct combination of letters. Choose one of the combinations in the box. Write the word on the line.

/ėr/ spelled ir, er, ur, ear, or — är spelled ar — ôr spelled or, ore, oar

1. moth/ėr/ mother
2. h/ėr/t hurt
3. w/ėr/d word
4. st/ôr/y story
5. lock/ėr/ locker
6. y/är/d yard
7. b/ėr/dhouse birdhouse
8. s/ôr/ing soaring
9. m/ôr/ more
10. l/ėr/n learn
11. invent/ėr/ inventor
12. st/är/t start

Directions Each sentence has two words in ( ). Underline the word that is spelled correctly.

13. The U.S. President is sometimes called the (leader, leadir) of the free world.
14. Grapes can be either green or (perple, purple).
15. Dad has an (armful, oarmful) of dirty clothes.
16. We agreed to meet after our (fearst, first) class of the morning.
17. Will they come (befor, before) or after the party?
18. The old desk was not (worth, wurth) the price they wanted for it.
19. Breakfast is usually the (earliest, erliest) meal of the day.
20. Look on the (chort, chart) to find your name.

Home Activity Your child wrote words with *r*-controlled vowels. Read an article or a story aloud to your child. When you come to a word with an *r*-controlled vowel in it, ask your child to spell the word.

Vowels: *r*-Controlled DVD•243

Let's Practice It!
TR DVD•243

Fluent Word Reading
Spiral Review

Read words independent of context

Display these words. Tell students that they can decode some words on this list. Explain that other words they should know because they appear often in reading.

Have students read the list three or four times until they can read at the rate of two to three seconds per word.

Word Reading

men	climbing	said	leaves	what
the	knives	listen	whistled	two
done	laughed	people	have	children
to	a	where	geese	signs

Corrective feedback

If... students have difficulty reading whole words,
then... have them use sound-by-sound blending for decodable words or chunking for words that have word parts, or have them say and spell high-frequency words.

If... students cannot read fluently at a rate of two to three seconds per word,
then... have pairs practice the list until they can read it fluently.

Differentiated Instruction

SI Strategic Intervention

***r*-Controlled vowels** To assist students having difficulty with the *r*-controlled vowels /ėr/, /är/, and /ôr/, focus on only one *r*-controlled vowel at a time. Write words with /ėr/ spelled *ir, er, ur, ear,* and *or* on separate cards. Have students sort the words by the *r*-controlled vowel spelling and then read all the words. Repeat with /är/ words spelled *ar* and /ôr/ words spelled *or, ore,* and *oar.*

Spiral Review

These activities review
- previously taught high-frequency words *said, what, the, two, done, laughed, people, have, to, a, where.*
- irregular plurals; consonant patterns *wr, kn, gn, st, mb.*

ELL English Language Learners

Pronunciation Have students say the words with consonant patterns *wr, kn, gn, st, mb.* Listen carefully to make sure that they do not pronounce the silent letters.

Objectives

- Read words fluently in context.
- Apply knowledge of sound-spellings to decode unknown words when reading.
- Practice fluency with oral rereading.

Read words in context

Display these sentences. Call on individuals to read a sentence. Then randomly point to review words and have students read them. To help you monitor word reading, high-frequency words are underlined and decodable words are italicized.

MONITOR PROGRESS **Sentence Reading**

<u>The</u> *children* <u>laughed</u> when some *geese* honked.
Jim *whistled* <u>to</u> the <u>two</u> *men climbing* the cliff.
They put *signs* <u>where</u> <u>people</u> can see them.
<u>What</u> <u>have</u> you <u>done</u> with the *knives?*
"*Listen* to the *leaves* in the trees," <u>a</u> girl <u>said</u>.

If... students are unable to read an underlined high-frequency word,
then... read the word for them and spell it, having them echo you.

If... students have difficulty reading an italicized decodable word,
then... guide them in using sound-by-sound blending or chunking.

Reread for Fluency

Have students reread the sentences to develop automaticity decoding words.

ROUTINE **Oral Rereading**

1. **Read** Have students read all the sentences orally.
2. **Reread** To achieve optimal fluency, students should reread the sentences three or four times.
3. **Corrective Feedback** Listen as students read. Provide corrective feedback regarding their fluency and decoding.

Routines Flip Chart

Decode and Read

Read words independent of context

Have students turn to p. 35 in *Decodable Practice Readers 3.2* and find the first list of words. Each word in this list has a prefix. Let's decode and read these words. Be sure that students identify the prefix in each word.

Next, have students read the high-frequency words.

Preview Decodable Practice Passage

Have students read the title and preview the story. Tell them that they will read words with the prefixes *pre-, mid-, over-, out-, bi-,* and *de-.* Make sure that students are monitoring their accuracy when they decode words.

Read words in context

Chorally read the story along with the students. Have students identify words in the story that have the prefixes *pre-, mid-, over-, out-, bi-,* and *de-.*

Team Talk Pair students and have them take turns reading the story aloud to each other. Monitor students as they read to check for proper pronunciation and appropriate pacing.

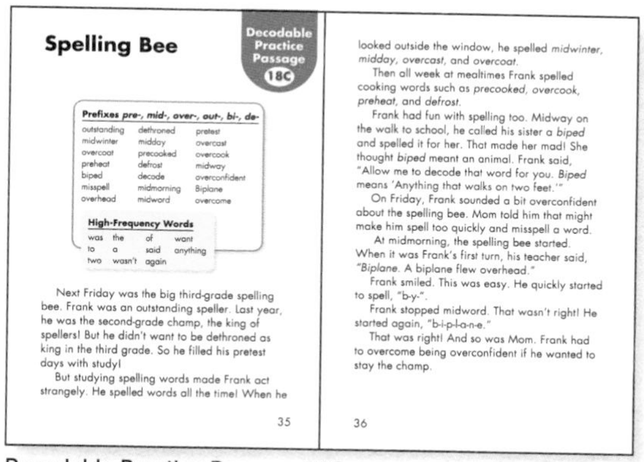

Spelling Bee

Decodable Practice Passage 18C

Prefixes *pre-, mid-, over-, out-, bi-, de-*

outstanding	dethroned	pretest
midwinter	midday	overcast
overcoat	precooked	overcook
preheat	defrost	midway
biped	decode	overconfident
misspell	midmorning	Biplane
overhead	midword	overcome

High-Frequency Words

was	the	of	want
to	a	said	anything
two	wasn't	again	

Next Friday was the big third-grade spelling bee. Frank was an outstanding speller. Last year, he was the second-grade champ, the king of spellers! But he didn't want to be dethroned as king in the third grade. So he filled his pretest days with study!

But studying spelling words made Frank act strangely. He spelled words all the time! When he

35

looked outside the window, he spelled *midwinter, midday, overcast,* and *overcoat.*

Then all week at mealtimes Frank spelled cooking words such as *precooked, overcook, preheat,* and *defrost.*

Frank had fun with spelling too. Midway on the walk to school, he called his sister a *biped* and spelled it for her. That made her mad! She thought *biped* meant an animal. Frank said, "Allow me to decode that word for you. *Biped* means 'Anything that walks on two feet.'"

On Friday, Frank sounded a bit overconfident about the spelling bee. Mom told him that might make him spell too quickly and misspell a word.

At midmorning, the spelling bee started. When it was Frank's first turn, his teacher said, "*Biplane.* A biplane flew overhead."

Frank smiled. This was easy. He quickly started to spell, "b-y-".

Frank stopped midword. That wasn't right! He started again, "b-i-p-l-a-n-e."

That was right! And so was Mom. Frank had to overcome being overconfident if he wanted to stay the champ.

36

Decodable Practice Passage 18C

Differentiated Instruction

A Advanced

Consonant Patterns Have students write their own sentences that use words with silent letters. They can use words from p. 110e or choose other words they know.

Objectives
- Introduce persuasive text.

Let's Think About Genre

Persuasive Text

Introduce the genre Explain to students that what we read is structured differently depending on the author's reasons for writing and what kind of information he or she wishes to convey. Different types of texts are called genres. Tell students that persuasive text is one type of genre.

Discuss the genre Discuss with students the different purposes authors have for writing. Explain: A movie review is written to persuade the reader to agree with the reviewer, but it might also entertain and inform the reader. Authors present facts and details to support their opinions. As a reader, you will get the most out of a text by asking yourself what the author's purpose is in presenting the facts and details. Explain that two clues that signal persuasive text are the author's use of "loaded words," or words that have strong emotional appeal, and the bandwagon approach, an appeal to the desire be part of the "in" group.

On the board, draw a T-chart like the one below. Ask the following questions. Encourage students to answer questions with appropriate detail.

- What are some negative "loaded words" that you might find in an advertisement for a cell phone? Possible responses: cheap, poor reception, flimsy
- What are some positive "loaded words" that you might find in an advertisement for a cell phone? Possible responses: affordable, excellent reception, sturdy
- "This is the movie everyone will be talking about!" Why might a movie review use this statement? Possible responses: to make readers want to be part of the group that's talking about the movie

Persuasive Text

"Loaded Words"	Bandwagon Approach
cheap, limited reception, flimsy	the movie everyone will be talking about

Guide practice Have students work in pairs to brainstorm examples of "loaded language" and the bandwagon approach that they've seen in TV ads or in persuasive text. Ask them to share their examples with the class.

Connect to reading Tell students that they will now read a persuasive text about the game of marbles. Have the class think about the author's purpose for writing the article.

Small Group Time

DAY 4 **Break into small groups before reading or revisiting "Marvelous Marble Mania."**

Teacher Led

SI Strategic Intervention

Teacher Led p. DI•55
- Practice retelling
- Genre focus
- **Read/Revisit** "Marvelous Marble Mania"

OL On-Level

Teacher Led p. DI•60
- Practice retelling
- Genre focus
- **Read/Revisit** "Marvelous Marble Mania"

A Advanced

Teacher Led p. DI•65
- Genre focus
- **Read/Revisit** "Marvelous Marble Mania"

ELL Place English language learners in the groups that correspond to their reading abilities in English.

Practice Stations
- Read for Meaning
- Get Fluent
- Words to Know

Independent Activities
- AudioText: "*Marvelous Marble Mania*"
- *Reader's and Writer's Notebook*
- Research and Inquiry

ELL

English Language Learners

Cognates The Spanish word *persuasivo* may be familiar to Spanish speakers as the cognate for *persuasive.*

Objectives

- Read persuasive text.
- ◎ Identify facts and opinions to improve comprehension.
- ◎ Make inferences.

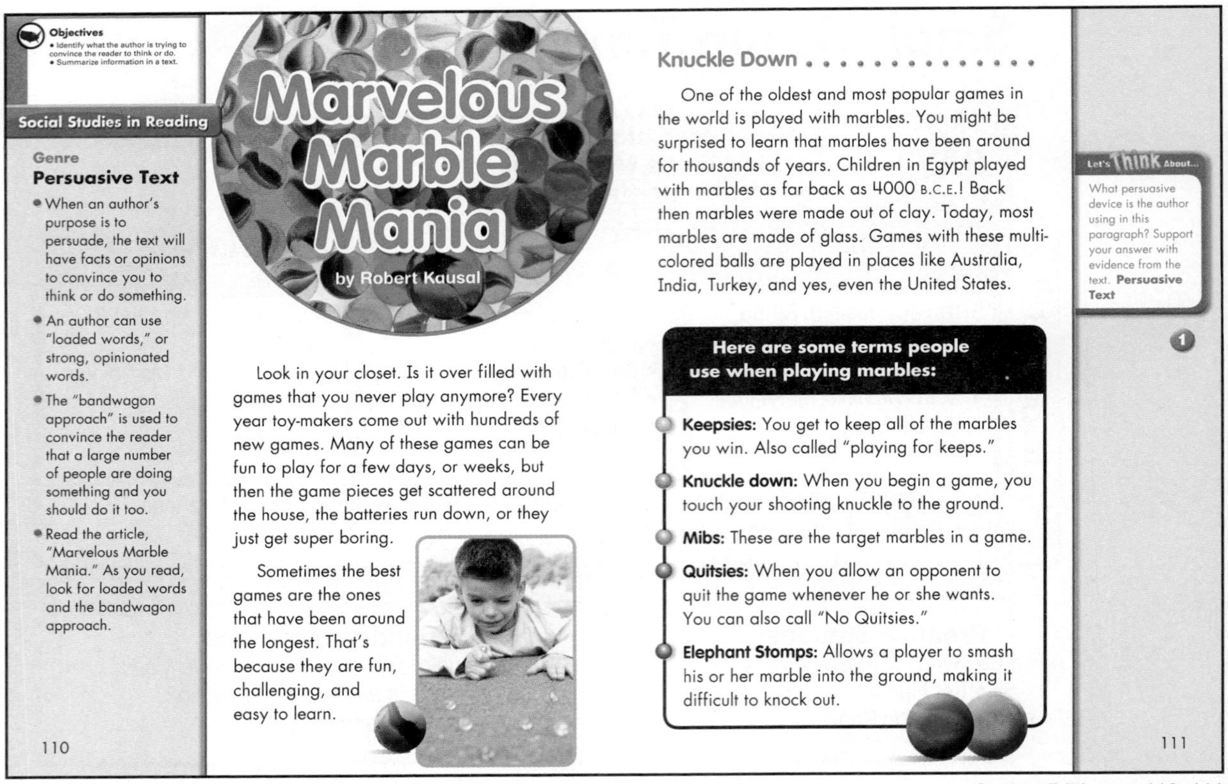

Objectives
- Identify what the author is trying to convince the reader to think or do.
- Summarize information in a text.

Social Studies in Reading

Genre
Persuasive Text
- When an author's purpose is to persuade, the text will have facts or opinions to convince you to think or do something.
- An author can use "loaded words," or strong, opinionated words.
- The "bandwagon approach" is used to convince the reader that a large number of people are doing something and you should do it too.
- Read the article, "Marvelous Marble Mania." As you read, look for loaded words and the bandwagon approach.

Marvelous Marble Mania

by Robert Kausal

Look in your closet. Is it over filled with games that you never play anymore? Every year toy-makers come out with hundreds of new games. Many of these games can be fun to play for a few days, or weeks, but then the game pieces get scattered around the house, the batteries run down, or they just get super boring.

Sometimes the best games are the ones that have been around the longest. That's because they are fun, challenging, and easy to learn.

110

Knuckle Down

One of the oldest and most popular games in the world is played with marbles. You might be surprised to learn that marbles have been around for thousands of years. Children in Egypt played with marbles as far back as 4000 B.C.E.! Back then marbles were made out of clay. Today, most marbles are made of glass. Games with these multi-colored balls are played in places like Australia, India, Turkey, and yes, even the United States.

Here are some terms people use when playing marbles:

- **Keepsies:** You get to keep all of the marbles you win. Also called "playing for keeps."
- **Knuckle down:** When you begin a game, you touch your shooting knuckle to the ground.
- **Mibs:** These are the target marbles in a game.
- **Quitsies:** When you allow an opponent to quit the game whenever he or she wants. You can also call "No Quitsies."
- **Elephant Stomps:** Allows a player to smash his or her marble into the ground, making it difficult to knock out.

Let's Think About...
What persuasive device is the author using in this paragraph? Support your answer with evidence from the text. **Persuasive Text**

1

111

Student Edition pp. 110–111

Guide Comprehension

Teach the genre

Genre: Persuasive Text Have students preview "Marvelous Marble Mania" on pp. 110–111 and ask them to look for examples of persuasive devices. Then ask: Why do you think the author uses the word *marvelous* in the title of the article?

Corrective feedback

If... students are unable to explain why the author uses the word *marvelous* in the title,
then... use the model to guide students in analyzing "loaded words."

Model the genre

Think Aloud The author could have left out the adjective *marvelous* in the title, but he had a reason for using it. What is a synonym for *marvelous*? (*wonderful*) This is a strong word. I think that the author uses this "loaded word" to persuade readers to agree with his opinion of the game of marbles.

On their own

Have students reread pp. 110–111 to look for other examples of persuasive text. Have students tell what the author is trying to persuade the reader to think.

Extend Thinking
Think Critically

Higher-order thinking skills

Fact and Opinion • Evaluation Does page 110 provide mostly statements of fact or statements of opinion? How do you know? Possible response: The page provides mostly statements of opinion. Only one statement of fact is provided: *Every year toymakers come out with hundreds of new games.* This is a statement of fact because it can be proved true or false. The other statements can't be proved.

Inferring • Synthesis On page 111, the author provides some facts about the game of marbles. What do you think is the author's purpose in providing these facts? Support your response with evidence from the text. Possible response: The author may want to convince the reader that the game of marbles is a lot of fun. He does this by saying that people around the world have been playing it for a very long time.

Let's Think About...

1 Possible response: The author is using the bandwagon approach by emphasizing that the game has been played for thousands of years and that it is still played in countries all around the world.

Differentiated Instruction

SI Strategic Intervention

Activate prior knowledge Before reading, have students preview the text features, such as the glossary box on p. 111 and the drawings and photographs on p. 113. Ask students to discuss what they know about playing the game of marbles.

ELL English Language Learners

"Loaded words" Help students understand that words with strong connotations are words that create an emotional response in the reader. Provide these examples for students and have them give a "thumbs up" or "thumbs down" sign to show their reactions: *skinny/slim, tall/looming, odd/unique.* Ask students to give other examples of "loaded words."

Objectives

- Read persuasive text.
- ◎ Make inferences.
- Identify causes and effects to improve comprehension.

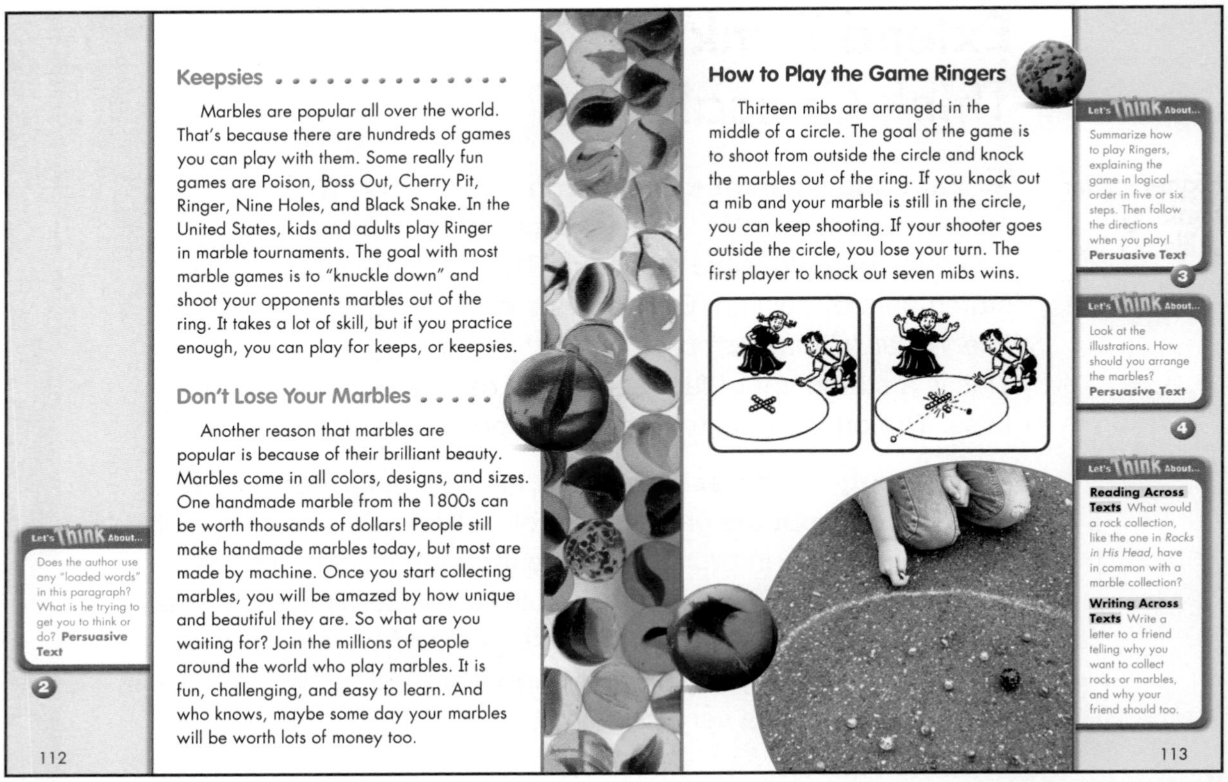

Let's Think About...

Does the author use any "loaded words" in this paragraph? What is he trying to get you to think or do? **Persuasive Text**

2

112

Keepsies

Marbles are popular all over the world. That's because there are hundreds of games you can play with them. Some really fun games are Poison, Boss Out, Cherry Pit, Ringer, Nine Holes, and Black Snake. In the United States, kids and adults play Ringer in marble tournaments. The goal with most marble games is to "knuckle down" and shoot your opponents marbles out of the ring. It takes a lot of skill, but if you practice enough, you can play for keeps, or keepsies.

Don't Lose Your Marbles

Another reason that marbles are popular is because of their brilliant beauty. Marbles come in all colors, designs, and sizes. One handmade marble from the 1800s can be worth thousands of dollars! People still make handmade marbles today, but most are made by machine. Once you start collecting marbles, you will be amazed by how unique and beautiful they are. So what are you waiting for? Join the millions of people around the world who play marbles. It is fun, challenging, and easy to learn. And who knows, maybe some day your marbles will be worth lots of money too.

How to Play the Game Ringers

Thirteen mibs are arranged in the middle of a circle. The goal of the game is to shoot from outside the circle and knock the marbles out of the ring. If you knock out a mib and your marble is still in the circle, you can keep shooting. If your shooter goes outside the circle, you lose your turn. The first player to knock out seven mibs wins.

Let's Think About...

Summarize how to play Ringers, explaining the game in logical order in five or six steps. Then follow the directions when you play! **Persuasive Text**

3

Let's Think About...

Look at the illustrations. How should you arrange the marbles? **Persuasive Text**

4

Let's Think About...

Reading Across Texts What would a rock collection, like the one in *Rocks in His Head*, have in common with a marble collection?

Writing Across Texts Write a letter to a friend telling why you want to collect rocks or marbles, and why your friend should too.

113

Student Edition pp. 112–113

Guide Comprehension

Teach the genre

Genre: Persuasive Text Have students list two examples of the bandwagon approach from p. 112. Then ask: What is the author trying to persuade the reader to think or do?

If... students have difficulty identifying examples,
then... model identifying text clues that signal the bandwagon approach.

Model the technique

Think Aloud: The first sentence on page 112 says *Marbles are popular all over the world.* Based on this information, do you think lots of people enjoy playing marbles? (yes) I think the author wants me to think that I would enjoy playing marbles because so many other people enjoy the game.

On their own

Have students reread the page and look for another example of the bandwagon approach. Ask them to explain what the author wants them to think or do.

Extend Thinking
Think Critically

Higher-order thinking skill

Inferring • Analysis Why do you think the author includes information about how beautiful and valuable marbles can be? Possible response: The author wants to appeal to readers who might be more interested in collecting marbles than in playing games with them.

Cause and Effect • Analysis The author writes that marbles are popular all over the world. Based on the text, is the popularity of marbles a cause or an effect? Possible response: It is an effect; the cause of the popularity of marbles is that there are hundreds of games people can play with them.

Let's Think About...

2. Possible response: "Loaded words" include *hundreds, popular, really fun.* He is trying to make the reader want to play marbles.
3. First, 13 mibs are arranged in the middle of a circle. Then, players try to shoot from outside the circle to knock the marbles out of the ring. If a player knocks out a mib and their marble is still in the circle, they can keep playing. If the shooter lands outside the circle, then you lose a turn. To win, a player has to be the first to knock all 7 mibs out of the circle.
4. You should arrange the marbles in the shape of an X.

Reading Across Texts

Have students create a concept web with either *Rocks* or *Marbles* in the center circle. Students can brainstorm details about each to add to the outer circles.

Writing Across Texts

Have students use their concept maps to list reasons why rocks and marbles are a good thing to collect. Then have them use the list to write their letter.

Differentiated Instruction

SI Strategic Intervention

Cause and effect Point out that the clue word *because* in the second sentence on p. 112 indicates the cause that, or reason why, marbles are so popular.

A Advanced

Cause and effect Have students look for another reason the author gives for why marbles are popular. Ask them to write a sentence that states the two causes of the popularity of marbles.

ELL English Language Learners

Graphic organizer Provide support to students when creating a concept web. Help them choose the key terms for their webs, and then work together to add details.

Objectives

- Read with fluency and comprehension.
- ◎ Use context clues to determine the meanings of multiple-meaning words.
- Conduct an interview.

Fluency: WCPM
SUCCESS PREDICTOR

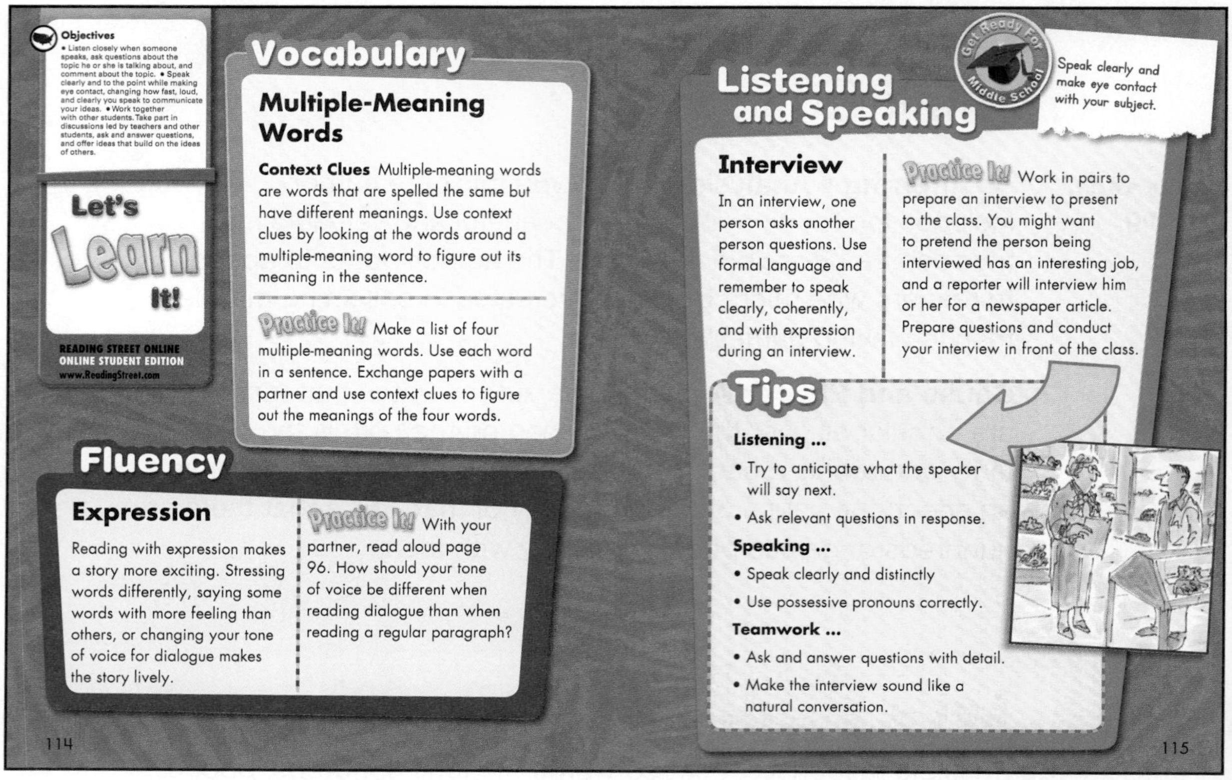

Objectives
• Listen closely when someone speaks, ask questions about the topic he or she is talking about, and comment about the topic. • Speak clearly and to the point while making eye contact, changing how fast, loud, and clearly you speak to communicate your ideas. • Work together with other students. Take part in discussions led by teachers and other students, ask and answer questions, and offer ideas that build on the ideas of others.

Let's Learn It!

READING STREET ONLINE
ONLINE STUDENT EDITION
www.ReadingStreet.com

Vocabulary

Multiple-Meaning Words

Context Clues Multiple-meaning words are words that are spelled the same but have different meanings. Use context clues by looking at the words around a multiple-meaning word to figure out its meaning in the sentence.

Practice It! Make a list of four multiple-meaning words. Use each word in a sentence. Exchange papers with a partner and use context clues to figure out the meanings of the four words.

Fluency

Expression

Reading with expression makes a story more exciting. Stressing words differently, saying some words with more feeling than others, or changing your tone of voice for dialogue makes the story lively.

Practice It! With your partner, read aloud page 96. How should your tone of voice be different when reading dialogue than when reading a regular paragraph?

Listening and Speaking

Get Ready For Middle School

Speak clearly and make eye contact with your subject.

Interview

In an interview, one person asks another person questions. Use formal language and remember to speak clearly, coherently, and with expression during an interview.

Practice It! Work in pairs to prepare an interview to present to the class. You might want to pretend the person being interviewed has an interesting job, and a reporter will interview him or her for a newspaper article. Prepare questions and conduct your interview in front of the class.

Tips

Listening ...
- Try to anticipate what the speaker will say next.
- Ask relevant questions in response.

Speaking ...
- Speak clearly and distinctly
- Use possessive pronouns correctly.

Teamwork ...
- Ask and answer questions with detail.
- Make the interview sound like a natural conversation.

114 115

Student Edition pp. 114–115

Fluency
Expression

Guide practice Use the Student Edition activity as an assessment tool. Make sure the reading passage is at least 200 words in length. As students read aloud with partners, walk around to make sure their expression is appropriate and that it changes to enhance the meaning of what they are reading.

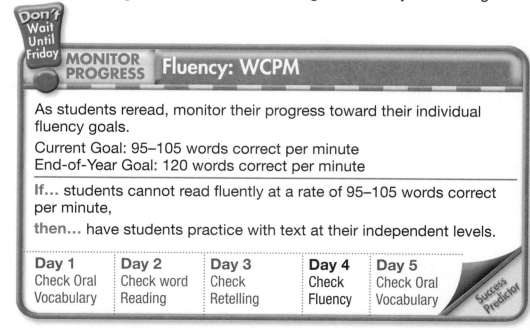

Don't Wait Until Friday — **MONITOR PROGRESS** — **Fluency: WCPM**

As students reread, monitor their progress toward their individual fluency goals.

Current Goal: 95–105 words correct per minute
End-of-Year Goal: 120 words correct per minute

If... students cannot read fluently at a rate of 95–105 words correct per minute,

then... have students practice with text at their independent levels.

Day 1	Day 2	Day 3	Day 4	Day 5
Check Oral Vocabulary	Check word Reading	Check Retelling	**Check Fluency**	Check Oral Vocabulary

Success Predictor

Vocabulary
Multiple-Meaning Words

Teach context clues

Context Clues Write the following sentence on the board.

The postal worker said I need to put more stamps on this envelope.

Point out that to students that they can determine the correct meaning of *stamps* in the sentence by looking at the words around it.

Guide practice

Tell students to be sure to use context clues in the sentences they write for their multiple-meaning words.

On their own

Walk around the room as students work with partners to check that students identify the correct meanings.

Listening and Speaking
Interview

Get Ready For Middle School

Teach

Tell students that in order for an interview to be successful, everyone must work together. Have partners brainstorm jobs and topics that might be discussed during an interview for an article. One partner can pretend to hold the job and the other can conduct the interview.

Guide practice

Remind interviewers to face the person they are interviewing, use eye contact, and speak clearly and coherently. Tell them to wait for questions to be answered before asking the next question. They should listen to the answer so that their next question follows logically. Have students restate these instructions prior to following them. If needed, have students give these instructions again to their partner.

On their own

Have students conduct the interview with their partners.

Get Ready For Middle School

Interviewing

Rehearsal Tips

- Look at the person you are interviewing.
- Ask questions in a logical order.
- Make sure each answer is completed before you ask the next question.
- Express interest in answers as they are given.

ELL

English Language Learners

Practice pronunciation Assist pairs of students by modeling the correct pronunciation of the words from the Glossary, then having students repeat after you. Pair students with mixed language proficiencies together to practice pronunciation and employ self-corrective techniques.

Objectives

- Synthesize research findings.
- Create a Web directory to organize sources.
- Review possessive pronouns.
- Spell words with prefixes *pre-*, *mid-*, *over-*, *out-* correctly.

Research and Inquiry
Synthesize

Teach Have students synthesize their research findings and results. Suggest that students create a Web directory to show the online sources they used for their research. Review how to choose relevant information from a number of sources and organize it logically. Explain to students that when writing exactly what a research source says, they must use quotation marks and cite the source in their informational article in order to avoid plagiarism, or copying someone's idea and trying to pass it off as original. If they are explaining what the research source said in their own words, or paraphrasing, then they do not need to use quotations marks, but must still cite the source.

Guide practice Have students use a word processing program or poster board to prepare for their presentations on Day 5. Remind students to include multiple sources of valid and reliable oral and written information in their informational articles. Check to see that students have prepared a works-cited page that includes the author, title, publisher, and publication year for each source they use.

On their own Have students organize their research findings in the form of an informational article. Then have them plan their presentations.

Conventions
Possessive Pronouns

Test practice Remind students that grammar skills, such as possessive pronouns, are often assessed on important tests. Recall that possessive pronouns show who or what owns, or possesses, something.

Daily Fix-It Use Daily Fix-It numbers 7 and 8 in the right margin.

On their own For additional practice, use the *Reader's and Writer's Notebook* p. 279.

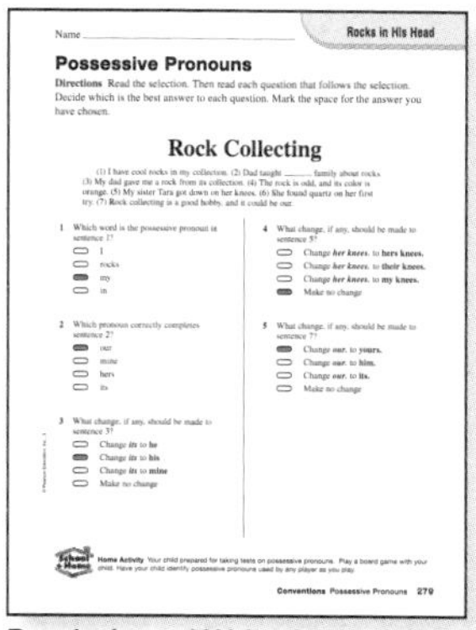
Rocks in His Head

Possessive Pronouns

Rock Collecting

Reader's and Writer's Notebook p. 279

Spelling
Prefixes *pre-, mid-, over-, out-*

Practice spelling strategy Remind students that words with prefixes in this lesson are easier to spell if the student keeps the base word in mind. Have students segment or divide each word by its prefix and base word in their mind before spelling the word. Remind them to use the letter sounds to help them spell each word part.

On their own For additional practice, use *Let's Practice It!* page 244 on the *Teacher Resources DVD-ROM.*

Rocks in His Head

Prefixes

Let's Practice It!
TR DVD•244

Daily Fix-It

7. Hers green rock was finded in South America. *(Her; found)*

8. Rob and them displayed the rocks in Ms. Shaws room. *(they; Shaw's)*

Objectives

- Revise draft of a biography.
- Apply revising strategy Consolidating.
- Combine short, choppy sentences.

Writing—Biography
Revising Strategy

MINI-LESSON

Revising Strategy: Consolidating

- Yesterday we wrote biographies about someone we know who has an interesting collection. Today we will revise our drafts. The goal is to make your writing clearer, more interesting, and more informative.

- Display Writing Transparency 18B. Remind students that revising does not include corrections of grammar and mechanics. Then introduce the revising strategy Consolidating. The two short sentences at the end of our first paragraph can be combined to make one long sentence.

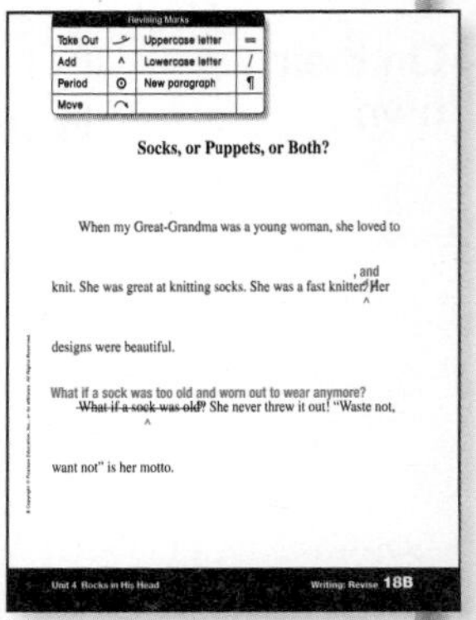

Revising Marks

Take Out	↝	Uppercase letter	≡
Add	^	Lowercase letter	/
Period	⊙	New paragraph	¶
Move	⌒		

Socks, or Puppets, or Both?

When my Great-Grandma was a young woman, she loved to knit. She was great at knitting socks. She was a fast knitter, and her designs were beautiful.

~~What if a sock was old?~~ What if a sock was too old and worn out to wear anymore? She never threw it out! "Waste not, want not" is her motto.

Unit 4 Rocks in His Head — Writing: Revise 18B

Writing Transparency 18B, TR DVD

- When you revise, ask yourself *Do my sentences sound short, choppy, or awkward*? The revising strategy Consolidating can be used to combine these types of sentences. Reread your biography for places you can combine sentences for clarity.

Display the revising tips for students. Tell students that as they revise, not only should they look for places where they can combine short and choppy sentences, they should also look for places to add transition words and phrases. The last sentence in every paragraph should offer a smooth transition to the next paragraph.

Revising Tips

- ✔ Make sure your biography is told in time order.
- ✔ Combine short and choppy sentences.
- ✔ Review writing to make sure it shows a variety of sentence types and length.

Peer conferencing

Peer Revision Have partners exchange papers and read aloud each other's biographies. Remind students to listen for sentences that sound short or choppy, as well as sentences that all begin with the same word or phrase. Have partners review their lists and discuss ways to revise language for clarity.

Have students revise their biographies. They should use the bulleted lists they wrote during Peer Revision as well as the key features of biographies to guide their revision. Check to make sure students are using the revising strategy Consolidating.

Corrective feedback

Circulate around the room to monitor and confer with students as they revise. Remind students who are correcting grammatical errors that they will have time to proofread tomorrow. They should be working on clarifying ideas and language today.

ROUTINE

Quick Write for Fluency

Team Talk

1. **Talk** Have pairs discuss how the dad in *Rocks in His Head* is one of a kind.
2. **Write** Each student writes a paragraph that gives information about the father.
3. **Share** Partners read and check each other's paragraphs for examples of the dad's talents and achievements.

Routines Flip Chart

Wrap Up Your Day

- ✔ **Build Concepts** Have students discuss what they learned through the riddles and explanations.
- ✔ **Oral Vocabulary** Monitor students' use of oral vocabulary as they respond: What hobbies are featured in the illustrations?
- ✔ **Text Features** Discuss how the illustrations help students understand text.

Write Guy
Jeff Anderson

Teaching Trait-by-Trait: Focus

In a writing conference, choose one aspect of a students' draft, not many things. This will help the student more than trying to think about multiple writing traits at once. Maybe there is one skill at this student's growing edge of knowledge that I can help him improve. I'd hate to see that lost in a swarm of my other comments.

ELL

English Language Learners

Support revising Call on a volunteer and give him or her several commands, such as: *Stand up. Raise your hands. Walk three steps forward. Turn around. Walk back.* Discuss with students how you can combine these short, choppy sentences to make a longer sentence. Call on students to combine sentences orally. Write example sentences on the board and choral read them together.

Preview DAY 5

Remind students to think about why it's important to have unique interests.

DAY 5 Wrap Up your Week

10–15 min

Objectives

- Review the weekly concept.
- Review oral vocabulary.

Today at a Glance

Oral Vocabulary

Comprehension
◎ Fact and Opinion

Lesson Vocabulary
◎ Multiple-meaning words

Phonics/Word Analysis
◎ Prefixes *(pre-, mid-, over-, out-, bi-, de-)*

Literary Terms
Idioms

Assessment
Fluency
Comprehension

Spelling
Prefixes *pre-, mid-, over-, out-*

Conventions
Possessive pronouns

Writing
Biography

Check Oral Vocabulary
SUCCESS PREDICTOR

Concept Wrap Up

Question of the Week

Why is it valuable to have unique interests?

Review the concept Have students look back at the reading selections to find examples that best demonstrate why it is valuable to have unique interests.

Review Amazing Words Display and review this week's concept map. Remind students that this week they have learned nine Amazing Words related to unique interests. Have students use the Amazing Words and the concept map to answer the question *Why is it valuable to have unique interests?*

Why it is valuable to have unique interests

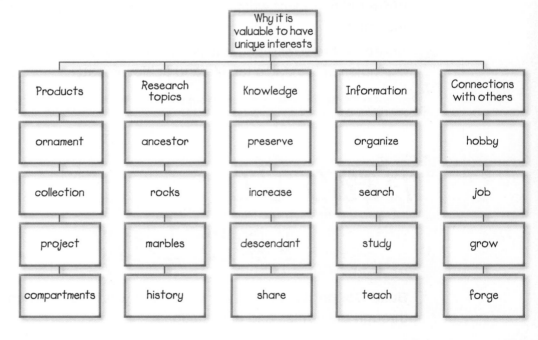

Products	Research topics	Knowledge	Information	Connections with others
ornament	ancestor	preserve	organize	hobby
collection	rocks	increase	search	job
project	marbles	descendant	study	grow
compartments	history	share	teach	forge

ELL Check Concepts and Language Use the Day 5 instruction on ELL Poster 18 to monitor students' understanding of the lesson concept.

ELL Poster 18

Amazing Ideas

Connect to the Big Question Have pairs of students discuss how the Question of the Week connects to the Big Question: *What does it mean to be unique?* Tell students to use the concept map and what they have learned from this week's Anchored Talks and reading selections to form an Amazing Idea—a realization or "big idea" about being One of a Kind. Remind students to give suggestions that build upon each other's ideas. Then ask each pair to share its Amazing Idea with the class.

Amazing Ideas might include these key concepts:

- Unique interests help you grow as a person.
- People have a variety of interests.
- People express their interests and talents in creative ways, including artwork, writing, and collecting items.

Write about it Have students write a few sentences about their Amazing Idea, beginning with "This week I learned..." They should support their Amazing Idea with facts, details, or explanations.

It's Friday

MONITOR PROGRESS Check Oral Vocabulary

Have individuals use this week's Amazing Words to describe unique interests. Monitor students' abilities to use the Amazing Words and note which words you need to reteach.

If... students have difficulty using the Amazing Words,
then... reteach using the Oral Vocabulary Routine, pp. 87a, 92b, 100b, 110b, OV•3.

Day 1	Day 2	Day 3	Day 4	Day 5
Check Oral Vocabulary	Check Word Reading	Check Retelling	Check Fluency	Check Oral Vocabulary

Success Predictor

Amazing Words

hobby	ornament
murmur	descendant
project	compartment
leftover	forge
ancestor	

ELL

English Language Learners

Concept map Work with students to add new words to the concept map.

DAY 5 Wrap Up your Week

20–25 min

Objectives

- ◎ Review fact and opinion.
- ◎ Review multiple-meaning words.
- ◎ Review prefixes.
- Review idioms.

Comprehension Review

Fact and Opinion

Student Edition EI•7

Teach fact and opinion

Envision It!

Review the definitions of statements of fact and statements of opinion on p. 90. Remind students that statements of fact can be proved true or false and that statements of opinion give someone's thoughts or feelings about something. For additional support have students review p. EI•7 on fact and opinion.

Guide practice Have partners identify the facts and opinions and evaluate whether or not they can be proved. Have student pairs find an example of a statement of fact in *Rocks in His Head.* Then have pairs tell whether their statement of fact is correct.

On their own For additional practice with fact and opinion, use *Let's Practice It!* page 245 on the *Teacher Resources DVD-ROM.*

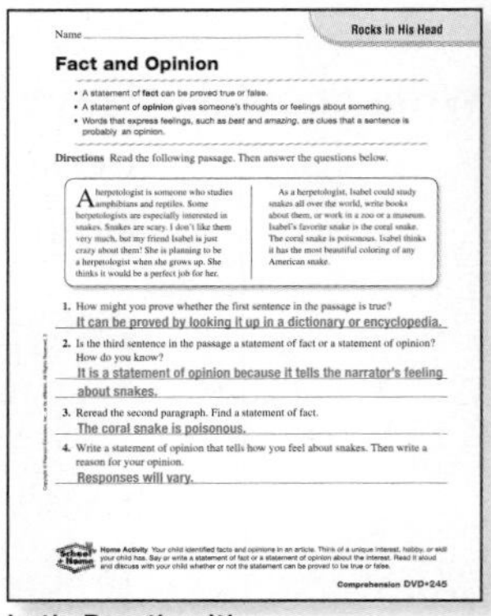

Name ______ Rocks in His Head

Fact and Opinion

- A statement of **fact** can be proved true or false.
- A statement of **opinion** gives someone's thoughts or feelings about something.
- Words that express feelings, such as *best* and *amazing*, are clues that a sentence is probably an opinion.

Directions Read the following passage. Then answer the questions below.

A herpetologist is someone who studies amphibians and reptiles. Some herpetologists are especially interested in snakes. Snakes are scary. I don't like them very much, but my friend Isabel is just crazy about them! She is planning to be a herpetologist when she grows up. She thinks it would be a perfect job for her.

As a herpetologist, Isabel could study snakes all over the world, write books about them, or work in a zoo or a museum. Isabel's favorite snake is the coral snake. The coral snake is poisonous. Isabel thinks it has the most beautiful coloring of any American snake.

1. How might you prove whether the first sentence in the passage is true?
   It can be proved by looking it up in a dictionary or encyclopedia.
2. Is the third sentence in the passage a statement of fact or a statement of opinion? How do you know?
   It is a statement of opinion because it tells the narrator's feeling about snakes.
3. Reread the second paragraph. Find a statement of fact.
   The coral snake is poisonous.
4. Write a statement of opinion that tells how you feel about snakes. Then write a reason for your opinion.
   Responses will vary.

Home Activity Your child identified facts and opinions in an article. Think of a unique interest, hobby, or skill your child has. Say or write a statement of fact or a statement of opinion about the interest. Read it aloud and discuss with your child whether or not the statement can be proved to be true or false.

Comprehension DVD•245

Let's Practice It!
TR DVD•245

Vocabulary Review

Multiple-Meaning Words

Teach multiple-meaning words Remind students that multiple-meaning words have more than one meaning. Context clues can help readers understand which meaning of the word makes sense in the sentence.

Guide practice Review with students how to find the correct meaning of *board* in this sentence: *The board of directors will meet tomorrow.* Ask students to point out the context clues that help them define the word.

On their own Have students work with partners to write context sentences using this week's lesson vocabulary words *stamps* and *spare.* Partners can trade sentences and identify the context clues that help them determine each word's meaning.

Word Analysis Review
Prefixes

Teach prefixes

Write the following sentences on the board. Have students read each one, first quietly to themselves and then aloud as you track the print.

1. **We are at the midpoint of our bicycle trip.**
2. **The view from this scenic overlook is outstanding.**
3. **Use binoculars to see the outfield.**
4. **Our midsummer vacation is overdue.**
5. **We had to prepay to depart on our trip.**

Team Talk Have students work with a partner to identify and underline the prefixes in the words. Then point to underlined words at random and have the group read them together.

Literary Terms Review
Idioms

Teach idioms

Remind students that idioms are a type of word play frequently found in both fiction and nonfiction. An idiom is a figure of speech that contains more than one word and that has a meaning and a use totally its own. The literal meanings of the words do not explain the meaning of the expression.

Guide practice

Point out the idiom *There's no money in rocks* from p. 96 of *Rocks in His Head.* Discuss the meaning of the idiom and have students find and explain other examples of idioms on pp. 97–99.

On their own

Have students make a T-chart with the headings *Idiom* and *Meaning.* Ask them to list examples of idioms from the selection in the first column and write the explanations in the second column.

ELL

English Language Learners

Fact and opinion If students have trouble distinguishing fact from opinion, advise them to consider how they could find out whether each statement is true or false. For example, they might consult a reference book or ask an expert. Tell students that if a statement can be proved true or false, it is an fact. Provide sentence frames to help students respond: *This statement is a _____ (fact/opinion) because _____.*

Articulation tip Speakers of monosyllabic languages such as Cantonese, Hmong, Khmer, Korean, and Vietnamese may have difficulty understanding that multisyllabic words are single words. Help students practice saying and writing words with prefixes as single words.

DAY 5 Wrap Up your Week 15–20 min

Objectives

- Read grade-level text with fluency.

Plan to Assess Fluency

- ☑ **Week 1** Assess Advanced students.
- ☑ **Week 2** Assess Strategic Intervention students.
- ☑ **This week assess On-Level students**
- ☐ **Week 4** Assess Strategic Intervention students.
- ☐ **Week 5** Assess any students you have not yet checked during this unit.

Set individual goals for students to enable them to reach the year-end goal.

- Current Goal: 95–105 WCPM
- Year-End Goal: 120 WCPM

Assessment

Check words correct per minute

Fluency Make two copies of the fluency passage on page 115k. As the student reads the text aloud, mark mistakes on your copy. Also mark where the student is at the end of one minute. To check the student's comprehension of the passage, have him or her retell what was read. To figure words correct per minute (WCPM), subtract the number of mistakes from the total number of words read in one minute.

wcpm

Corrective feedback

If... students cannot read fluently at a rate of 95–105 WCPM,
then... make sure they practice with text at their independent reading level. Provide additional fluency practice by pairing nonfluent readers with fluent readers.

If... students already read at 120 WCPM,
then... have them read a book of their choice independently.

Small Group Time

DAY 5 **Break into small groups before the comprehension lesson.**

Teacher Led

SI Strategic Intervention	OL On-Level	A Advanced
Teacher Led p. DI•56	**Teacher Led** p. DI•61	**Teacher Led** p. DI•65
• Practice fluency	• Practice fluency	• Practice fluency
• **Read** *I Collect Rocks* or *Grandpa's Rock Kit*	• **Read** *Fun with Hobbies and Science!*	• **Read** *Gemstones Around the World*

ELL Place English language learners in the groups that correspond to their reading ability in English.

Practice Stations

- Words to Know
- Get Fluent
- Read for Meaning

Independent Activities

- Grammar Jammer
- Concept Talk Video
- Vocabulary Activities

Name ______________________________

Mona's Stamp Collection

It was midday when Mona had finished her chores. 9
"Where are you going?" asked her friend Jules. 17
"I'm going to Stone's Stamp Store to see if I can trade this dinosaur 31
stamp for a cartoon stamp," she answered. 38
"Who are you mailing the stamp to?" Jules asked. 47
"No one. I collect stamps," Mona replied. 54
"Why?" Jules said in a puzzled voice. 61
"It's fun to collect stamps. They're small and easy to keep," Mona 73
explained. 74
"Can I come with you?" Jules asked. 81
"Sure," Mona said. 84
Mona and Jules entered the stamp store. There were racks of stamps 96
on overhead shelves. The racks were labeled with names from around 107
the world. 109
"Hi, Mr. Stone. I found this stamp in my attic," Mona started to 122
explain, "and I was wondering if I might trade it for a cartoon stamp." 136
Mr. Stone looked at the stamp carefully. "Do you know what you 148
have here?" he asked. 152
"An old prehistoric dinosaur standing in an overgrown grass field," 162
Mona answered. 164
"This is a one-of-a-kind stamp. It's worth quite a bit of money," 176
Mr. Stone explained. 179
"Does this mean I can have the cartoon stamp?" Mona asked. 190
"No, this means you can have a *hundred* cartoon stamps," 200
Mr. Stone laughed. 203

MONITOR PROGRESS

• Check Fluency

Objectives

- Read grade-level text with comprehension.

Assessment

Check fact and opinion

Fact and Opinion Use "Coyotes" on p. 115m to check students' understanding of fact and opinion.

1. Is the following sentence a fact or an opinion? *Coyotes are the most amazing animals in America!* How do you know whether it is a fact or opinion? (opinion; the speaker is making a judgment about coyotes. It cannot be proved true or false.)
2. What conclusion can you draw from the following fact? *Now coyotes roam all over the United States, except Hawaii.* (Possible response: The coyotes don't live in Hawaii because it is an island. They are unable to swim across the ocean to get there.)
3. State two facts from this passage. (Possible responses: Coyotes originally lived in the Great Plains area. Although they like to eat meat, coyotes can eat many things.)

Corrective feedback

If... students are unable to answer the comprehension questions,
then... use the Reteach lesson in the *First Stop* book.

Name ______________________________

Coyotes

What do you know about coyotes? Did you realize that they might be your neighbors? They probably are, even if you happen to live in a city.

Coyotes are the most amazing animals in America! They are wild dogs, similar to wolves. But unlike wolves, they can live near where people live.

People often think that humans moved into coyote territory. That is sometimes true, but not always. Coyotes originally lived in the Great Plains area. That includes states from North Dakota down to Texas. Now coyotes roam all over the entire United States, except Hawaii. That means coyotes moved into human territory.

In addition, coyotes have proven that they can survive almost anywhere, including in big cities and suburbs. Although they like to eat meat, coyotes can eat many things: sandwiches, grass, garbage, and more. That is why they can live just about anywhere.

If a coyote is not the most amazing animal in America, it is certainly one of the smartest! Being smart is one reason coyotes can live around people. Part of being smart means they usually stay away from humans. However, coyotes are starting to show themselves more. That may be because there are more of them. It also may be because coyotes are not as afraid of people as they used to be.

A coyote is not a pet. If you happen to see a coyote once in a while on your street and in a park, remember that it is a wild animal. Stay away!

MONITOR PROGRESS

• Fact and Opinion

Objectives

- Communicate inquiry results.
- Administer spelling test.
- Review possessive pronouns.

Research and Inquiry
Communicate

Present ideas Have students share their inquiry results by presenting their information and giving a brief talk on their research. Have students provide copies or display the web directory they created on Day 4.

Listening and Speaking Remind students how to be good speakers and how to communicate effectively with their audience.

- Respond to relevant questions with appropriate details.
- Speak clearly and loudly, with appropriate rate, volume, and enunciation.
- Keep eye contact with audience members.

Remind students of these tips for being a good listener.

- Wait until the speaker has finished before raising your hand to ask a relevant question.
- Be polite, even if you disagree.

Spelling Test
Prefixes *pre-, mid-, over-, out-*

Spelling test To administer the spelling test, refer to the directions, words, and sentences on p. 91c.

Conventions
Extra Practice

Teach Remind students that a possessive pronoun shows who or what owns, or possesses, something.

Guide practice Write the following words. Have students tell which possessive pronouns would be used with each word or phrase.

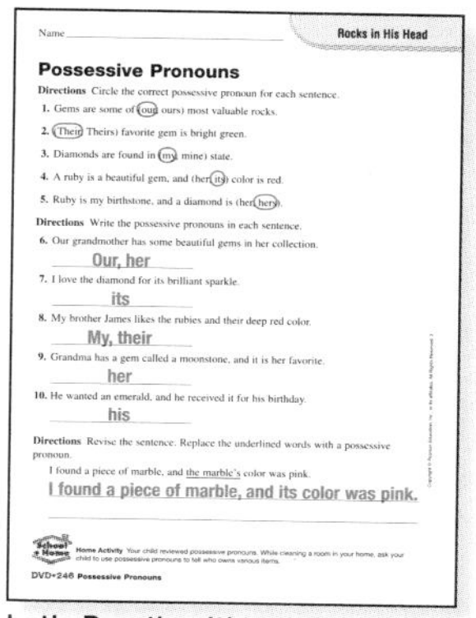
Name ______ Rocks in His Head

Possessive Pronouns

Directions Circle the correct possessive pronoun for each sentence.

1. Gems are some of (our, ours) most valuable rocks.
2. (Their, Theirs) favorite gem is bright green.
3. Diamonds are found in (my, mine) state.
4. A ruby is a beautiful gem, and (her, its) color is red.
5. Ruby is my birthstone, and a diamond is (her, hers).

Directions Write the possessive pronouns in each sentence.

6. Our grandmother has some beautiful gems in her collection. Our, her
7. I love the diamond for its brilliant sparkle. its
8. My brother James likes the rubies and their deep red color. My, their
9. Grandma has a gem called a moonstone, and it is her favorite. her
10. He wanted an emerald, and he received it for his birthday. his

Directions Revise the sentence. Replace the underlined words with a possessive pronoun.

I found a piece of marble, and the marble's color was pink.
I found a piece of marble, and its color was pink.

Home Activity Your child reviewed possessive pronouns. While cleaning a room in your home, ask your child to use possessive pronouns to tell who owns various items.

DVD•246 Possessive Pronouns

Let's Practice It!
TR DVD•246

Tanya	**my cap**	**the girl's book**	**the boy's skates**
Mr. North	**Mount Shasta**	**Sandra's room**	**Dan and Matt**

Daily Fix-It Use Daily Fix-It numbers 9 and 10 in the right margin.

On their own Write these sentences. Have students look back in Rocks in His Head to find the correct possessive pronouns to fill in the blanks. Students should complete *Let's Practice It!* page 246 on the *Teacher Resources DVD-ROM.*

1. **"You *have* got rocks in ______ head," she said.** (your)
2. **"Probably not," said ______ father.** (my)
3. **He'd dig into ______ pocket and take out a rock.** (his)
4. **People couldn't afford to buy new cars or fix ______ old ones.** (their)
5. **"I'm looking for rocks that are better than ______," he said.** (mine)

Daily Fix-It

9. The small rock is my and the big one is your. *(mine; yours)*
10. Can we put them both in the disply case. *(display; case?)*

Objectives

- Proofread revised drafts of biographies, including correct use of possessive pronouns.
- Create and present final draft.

Writing—Biography
Possessive Pronouns

Review revising Remind students that yesterday they revised their biographies, paying particular attention to combining short and choppy sentences to create smooth, flowing language. Today they will proofread their compositions.

MINI-LESSON

Proofread for Possessive Pronouns

- **Teach** When we proofread, we look closely at our work, searching for errors in mechanics. Today we will look for spelling, capitalization, and punctuation problems in the revised drafts, but first we will make sure that possessive pronouns are used correctly.

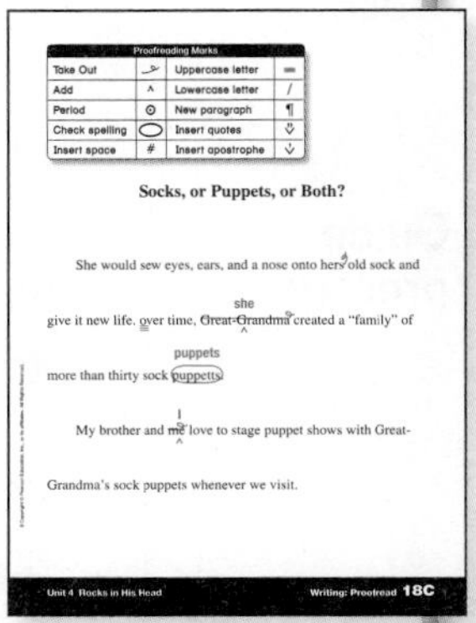

Proofreading Marks			
Take Out		Uppercase letter	
Add	^	Lowercase letter	/
Period	⊙	New paragraph	¶
Check spelling	◯	Insert quotes	
Insert space	#	Insert apostrophe	

Socks, or Puppets, or Both?

She would sew eyes, ears, and a nose onto hers old sock and give it new life. over time, Great-Grandma she created a "family" of more than thirty sock puppetts puppets

My brother and me I love to stage puppet shows with Great-Grandma's sock puppets whenever we visit.

Unit 4 Rocks in His Head Writing: Proofread 18C

Writing Transparency 18C, TR DVD

- **Model** Let's look at the last two paragraphs from our revised biographies. Display Writing Transparency 18C. Explain that you will look for errors in the use of possessive pronouns. I see a problem in the fifth sentence. We need the possessive pronoun *her* to show that Great-Grandma owns the old sock, and here we have *hers.* Since what Great-Grandma owns, an old sock, is still part of the sentence, we need to use *her instead of hers.* Explain to students that they should reread their biographies a number of times. Have them look for different types of errors with each reading: spelling, punctuation, capitalization, and grammar.

Proofread Display the Proofreading Tips. Ask students to proofread their compositions, using the Proofreading Tips and paying particular attention to possessive pronouns. Remind students to capitalize any geographical names or places as well as any historical periods. Circulate around the room answering students' questions. When students have finished editing their own work, have pairs proofread one another's biography.

Proofreading Tips

- ✔ Be sure that you use possessive pronouns correctly.
- ✔ Use a dictionary or computer spell checker to check for correct spelling of difficult words.
- ✔ Be sure that your different sentence types end with the correct punctuation.

Present Have students incorporate revisions and proofreading edits into their biographies to create a final draft.

Give students two options for presenting their work: an oral presentation or a decorative copy of their finished work to give to the person they wrote about. Have students create drawings or bring photographs to accompany their presentations. Students sharing their work orally should explain how their visuals relate to their writing. For students creating a decorative copy, suggest that they photocopy their biography and add an illustrated cover which includes their drawings or photographs. When students have finished, have each complete a Writing Self-Evaluation form.

ROUTINE **Quick Write for Fluency** Team Talk

1. **Talk** Pairs discuss what they learned about interesting collections this week.
2. **Write** Each student writes two sentences summarizing what they learned.
3. **Share** Partners read their sentences to one another.

Routines Flip Chart

Teacher Note

Writing self-evaluation Make copies of the Writing Self-Evaluation Guide on p. 39 of the *Reader's and Writer's Notebook* and hand out to students.

ELL

English Language Learners

Support editing Help students gain ease of use with possessive pronouns through modeling. Place items in a bag. Pull one out and say, for example, *Yusef, is this your hat? Is it yours?* Have students answer using the appropriate possessive pronoun.

Poster preview Prepare students for next week by using Week 4, ELL Poster 19. Read the Poster Talk-Through to introduce the concept and vocabulary. Ask students to identify and describe objects and actions in the art.

Selection summary Send home the summary of *America's Champion Swimmer: Gertrude Ederle,* in English and the students' home languages, if available, from the *ELL Handbook.* They can read the summary with family members.

Preview NEXT WEEK

What unique traits does it take to be the first to do something? Tell students that next week they will be reading a story about a champion swimmer.

DAY 5 Assessment Checkpoints for the Week

Weekly Assessment

Use pp. 127–134 of *Weekly Tests* to check:

✔ **Phonics** Prefixes *(pre-, mid-, over-, out-, bi-, de-)*

✔ **Comprehension Skill** Fact and Opinion

✔ **Lesson Vocabulary**

✔ **Review Comprehension Skill** Cause and Effect

attic	labeled
board	spare
chores	stamps
customer	

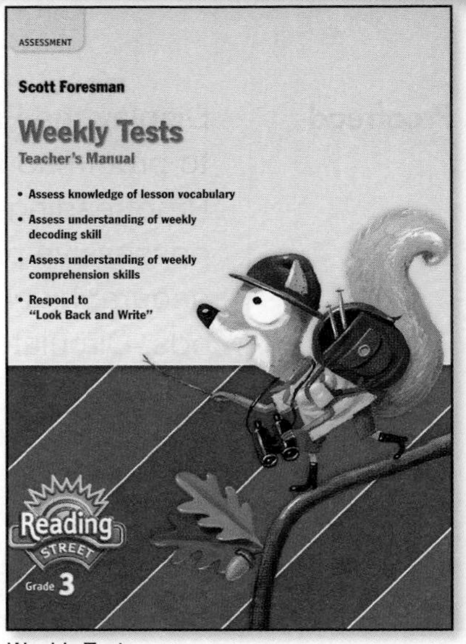

Weekly Tests

Differentiated Assessment

A Advanced

OL On-Level

SI Strategic Intervention

Use pp. 103–108 of *Fresh Reads for Fluency and Comprehension* to check:

✔ **Comprehension Skill** Fact and Opinion

✔ **Review Comprehension Skill** Cause and Effect

✔ **Fluency** Words Correct Per Minute

Fresh Reads for Fluency and Comprehension

Managing Assessment

Use *Assessment Handbook* for:

✔ **Weekly Assessment Blackline Masters for Monitoring Progress**

✔ **Observation Checklists**

✔ **Record-Keeping Forms**

✔ **Portfolio Assessment**

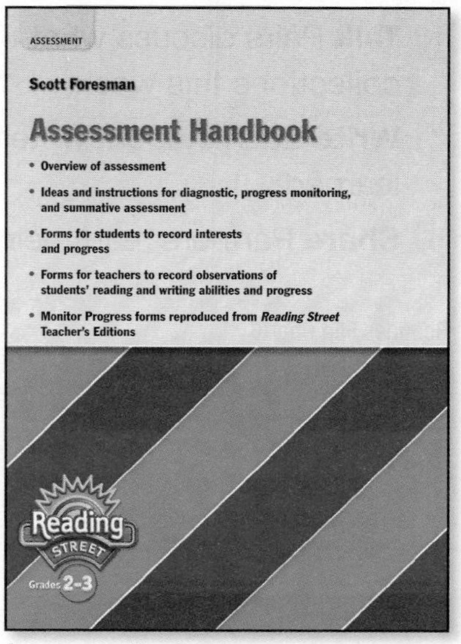

Assessment Handbook

Teacher Notes

Pacing Small Group Instruction

15–20 min

5-Day Plan

DAY 1	• Reinforce the concept • Read Leveled Readers Concept Literacy Below Level
DAY 2	• Fact and Opinion • Inferring • Revisit Student Edition pp. 94–99
DAY 3	• Multiple-Meaning Words • Revisit Student Edition pp. 100–105
DAY 4	• Practice Retelling • Read/Revisit Student Edition pp. 110–113
DAY 5	• Reread for fluency • Reread Leveled Readers

3- or 4-Day Plan

DAY 1	• Reinforce the concept • Read Leveled Readers
DAY 2	• Fact and Opinion • Inferring • Revisit Student Edition pp. 94–99
DAY 3	• Multiple-Meaning Words • Revisit Student Edition pp. 100–105
DAY 4	• Practice Retelling • Read/Revisit Student Edition pp. 110–113 • Reread for fluency • Reread Leveled Readers

3-Day Plan: Eliminate the shaded box.

SI Strategic Intervention

DAY 1

Build Background

■ **Reinforce the Concept** Reinforce the weekly question *Why is it valuable to have unique interests?* Some people like sports. Others like games or dolls. Still others collect things, such as cards, stamps, or coins. What is valuable about having a hobby? *(People can learn valuable things and make new friends. Hobbies are also fun ways to make time pass quickly.)* Add new words to the concept map. This week we are going to learn about the hobby of collecting rocks. What do you think makes rock collecting a good hobby? *(Students may say that rock collecting is inexpensive, that anyone can do it, and that it teaches about science.)* This week's question mentions "unique interests." What are the advantages to having an unusual hobby? *(Students may say that being different can be fun or that an unusual hobby can lead to positive attention from other people. If everyone had the same interests, the world would probably be a dull place.)*

Preview Decodable Practice Reader 18A

■ **Before Reading** Review the words on p. 25 of Decodable Practice Reader 18A. Then have students blend these story words: *thumb, carrots, circle, daily, sprout, sprinkling,* and *flowers.* Be sure students understand the meaning of *daily* and *sprinkling*. Guide students through the text by doing a picture walk.

Objectives

• Participate in teacher-led discussions by answering questions with appropriate detail.

SI Strategic Intervention

DAY 1

For a complete literacy instructional plan and additional practice with this week's target skills and strategies, see the **Leveled Reader Teaching Guide.**

Concept Literacy Reader

- **Read** *I Collect Rocks*
- **Before Reading** Preview the book with students, focusing on key concepts and vocabulary. Then have them set a purpose for reading.
- **During Reading** Read the first two pages aloud while students track along with the print. Then have students finish reading the book with a partner.
- **After Reading** After students finish reading, ask: In what ways is each rock one of a kind? *(Each rock has a color, shape, size, and texture that no other rock has.)*

Below-Level Reader

- **Read** *Grandpa's Rock Kit*
- **Before Reading** Have students use the illustrations to preview the book. Then have them set a purpose for reading.
- **During Reading** Read pp. 3–5 aloud. Then do a choral reading of pp. 6–9. If students are able, have them read and discuss the remainder of the book with a partner. Ask: What kind of rock is most common? *(igneous rock)* How does it form? *(from heat inside the Earth)*
- **After Reading** Ask students to look at and discuss the concept map. Connect the Below-Level Reader to the weekly question *Why is it valuable to have unique interests?* How can your unique interests be useful or of value? *(Your interests can teach you new things and help you meet new friends and see new places.)*

MONITOR PROGRESS

If... students have difficulty reading the selection with a partner,
then... have them follow along as they listen to the Leveled Readers DVD-ROM.

If... students have trouble understanding how to tell where different rocks come from,
then... reread pp. 8–11 and discuss the qualities of each featured rock.

Objectives

- Participate in teacher-led discussions by answering questions with appropriate detail.

Student Edition p. EI•7

More Reading

Use additional Leveled Readers or other texts at students' instructional levels to reinforce this week's skills and strategies. For text suggestions, see the Leveled Reader Database or the Leveled Readers Skills Chart on pp. CL24–CL29.

SI Strategic Intervention

DAY 2

Reinforce Comprehension

Skill Fact and Opinion Review the *Envision It!* p. EI•7 material on fact and opinion. Then use p. 90 to review fact and opinion. A *fact* can be proved true or false. An *opinion* tells someone's thoughts or feelings. Words that express feelings, such as *favorite* or *wonderful* or *worst,* are clues that a statement might be an opinion.

Strategy Inferring Explain that an inference is an educated guess based on information the author provides and information the reader already knows. Based on reading the title, the genre label, and the first page of text, I can infer that this is a biography about the author's father. I can also infer that her father is important to her and that she wants other people to know about him—otherwise she wouldn't have written the book. For additional support, see *Envision It!* p. EI•20.

Revisit *Rocks in His Head* on 94–99. As students read the first page, explain that a *quarry* is a place where people get certain types of rocks to build with.

- How did the father begin his rock collection? *(As a child, he walked along stone walls or old quarries looking for rocks.)* Is this statement a fact or an opinion? *(fact)*
- How was his collection important and interesting? Is the statement that you just made a fact or an opinion?
- What can you infer about the father based on what you have read so far? *(He loves rocks. He doesn't mind when others make fun of him.)*
- What is your opinion of him?

Use the During Reading Differentiated Instruction for additional support for struggling readers.

MONITOR PROGRESS

If… students have difficulty reading along with the group,
then… have them follow along as they listen to the AudioText.

Objectives

- Draw conclusions from facts presented in text.
- Make inferences about text.

SI Strategic Intervention DAY 3

Reinforce Vocabulary

- **Reread for Fluency** Use Decodable Practice Reader 18A.

- **Decoding Multisyllabic Words** Write *labeled* and model how to use meaningful parts to read it. First, I ask myself if I see any parts I know. I see *-ed* at the end of the word—that usually means "in the past." The base word seems to be *label.* A *label* is a tag that tells what something is. So *labeled* must mean "put a tag on something."

Use the strategies on the *Routines Flip Chart* to help students read these words from the biography: *junkyard, wooden,* and *customer.*

Multiple-Meaning Words/Context Clues Write the word *stamps* on the board. I know a stamp can be something that makes a mark on paper, or it can be a small sticker that pays postage fees, or it can be a verb that means "put your foot down hard." The first sentence of the biography states, "Some people collect stamps." Since postage stamps can be bought and sold, and I have heard of people collecting them, the author must mean postage stamps.

- **Revisit** *Rocks in His Head* on pp. 100–105. Then review *Words!* pp. W•7 and W•10. Encourage students to use context clues to figure out the meaning of any multiple-meaning words in the selection. Ask: Which definition of *spare* makes more sense on the second page of text: "extra, unneeded" or "small, light"? *(The father is providing parts for cars, so he must be using extra parts to replace ones that have worn out. That means the first definition makes more sense.)*

Use the During Reading Differentiated Instruction for additional support for struggling readers.

MONITOR PROGRESS

If... students need more practice with the lesson vocabulary,
then... use *Envision It! Pictured Vocabulary Cards.*

Objectives
- Use context to distinguish among multiple meaning words.
- Use context to determine the relevant meaning of unfamiliar words.

Student Edition p. W•10

Student Edition p. W•7

More Reading

Use additional Leveled Readers or other texts at students' instructional levels to reinforce this week's skills and strategies. For text suggestions, see the Leveled Reader Database or the Leveled Readers Skills Chart on pp. CL24–CL29.

SI Strategic Intervention

DAY 4

Practice Retelling

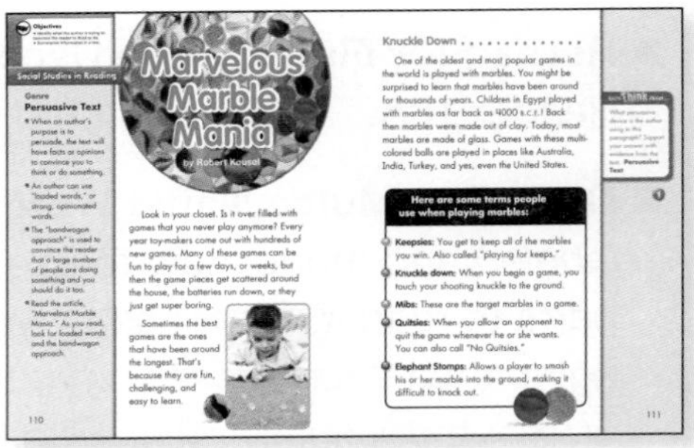

- **Retell** Guide students in using the Retelling Cards to retell the biography.
  - What kind of special interest did the father in this biography have?
  - How did he follow his special interest?
  - How was his special interest valuable to him?

If students struggle, model a fluent retelling.

Genre Focus

- **Before Reading or Revisiting** "Marvelous Marble Mania" on pp. 110–113, read aloud the genre information about persuasive text on p. 110. Persuasive texts use facts and opinions to try to convince you to think or act in a certain way. What are some persuasive texts that you see in your everyday life? *(newspaper and magazine advertisements, billboards, ads on the sides of buses)*

  Read the rest of the panel. Then have students read the introduction.

- **During Reading or Revisiting** Have students perform a choral reading of the selection. As they read, write the following words on the board: *fun, challenging, easy to learn.*
  - Where do you see these words in the text?
  - Are these words facts or opinions? How do you know?
- **After Reading or Revisiting** Have students share their reactions to the selection. Then guide students through the Reading Across Texts and Writing Across Texts activities.
  - What interests do the two texts present?
  - How are they alike and different?
  - In your opinion, which interest is more appealing? Why?

MONITOR PROGRESS

If... students have difficulty retelling the selection,
then... have them review the selection using the illustrations.

Objectives

- Identify what the author is trying to persuade the reader to think or do.

SI Strategic Intervention DAY 5

For a complete literacy instructional plan and additional practice with this week's target skills and strategies, see the **Leveled Reader Teaching Guide.**

Concept Literacy Reader

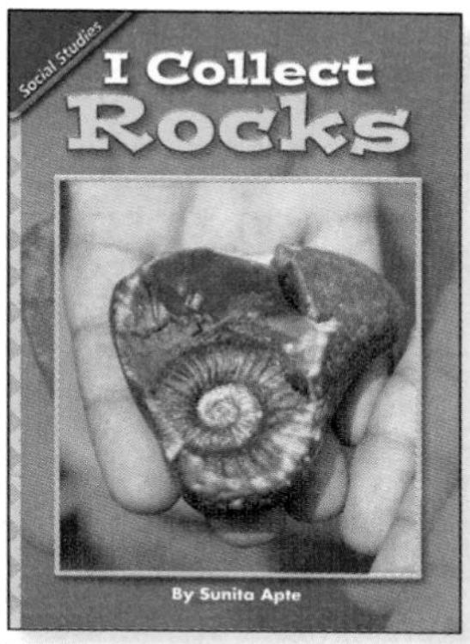

I Collect Rocks

- **Model** Model the fluency skill of expression. Ask students to listen carefully as you read aloud the first two pages of *I Collect Rocks.* Point out the care you take to group phrases and to observe punctuation cues.
- **Fluency Routine**
  1. Have students reread passages from *I Collect Rocks* with a partner.
  2. For optimal fluency, students should reread three to four times.
  3. As students read, monitor fluency and provide corrective feedback. Encourage students to stress important words and phrases in order to show expression.

  See *Routines Flip Chart* for more help with fluency.
- **Retell** Have students retell *I Collect Rocks.* Prompt students as necessary.

Below-Level Reader

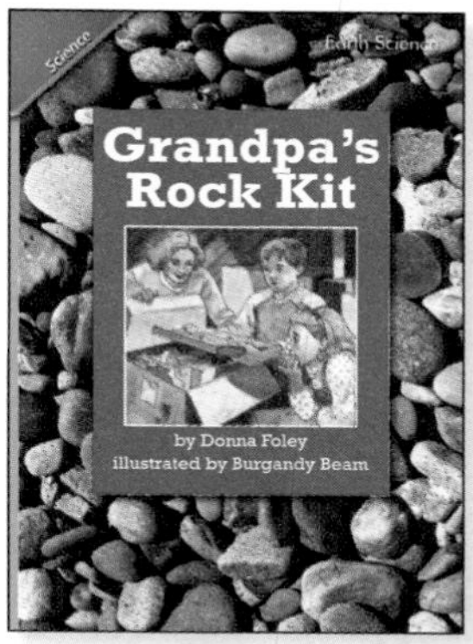

Grandpa's Rock Kit

- **Model** Ask students to listen carefully as you read aloud the first two pages of *Grandpa's Rock Kit,* emphasizing expression.
- **Fluency Routine**
  1. Have students reread passages from *Grandpa's Rock Kit* with a partner or individually.
  2. For optimal fluency, students should reread three to four times.
  3. As students read, monitor fluency and provide corrective feedback.

  See *Routines Flip Chart* for more help with fluency.
- **Retell** For additional practice, have students retell *Grandpa's Rock Kit* page by page using the illustrations. Prompt as necessary.
  - How did the children find a rock kit in the attic?
  - Why did their mother know so much about rocks?
  - What did the children learn about rocks? *(Students should share information about the three main kinds of rocks: igneous, metamorphic, and sedimentary.)*

MONITOR PROGRESS

If... students have difficulty reading fluently,
then... provide additional fluency practice by pairing nonfluent readers with fluent ones.

Objectives

- Read aloud grade-level appropriate text with fluency.

15–20 min

Pacing Small Group Instruction

5-Day Plan

DAY 1	• Expand the concept • Read On-Level Reader
DAY 2	• Fact and Opinion • Inferring • Revisit Student Edition pp. 94–99
DAY 3	• Multiple-Meaning Words • Revisit Student Edition pp. 100–105
DAY 4	• Practice Retelling • Read/Revisit Student Edition pp. 110–113
DAY 5	• Reread for fluency • Reread On-Level Reader

3- or 4-Day Plan

DAY 1	• Expand the concept • Read On-Level Reader
DAY 2	• Fact and Opinion • Inferring • Revisit Student Edition pp. 94–99
DAY 3	• Multiple-Meaning Words • Revisit Student Edition pp. 100–105
DAY 4	• Practice Retelling • Read/Revisit Student Edition pp. 110–113 • Reread for fluency • Reread On-Level Reader

3-Day Plan: Eliminate the shaded box.

OL On-Level

DAY 1

Build Background

- **Expand the Concept** Connect to the weekly question *Why is it valuable to have unique interests?* Then expand the concept. A person who has a unique interest may spend a lot of time on that activity. Sometimes people with a hobby or special interest become experts on the topic they enjoy. Some even grow up to become professionals in their area of interest. They work all day at what they love. Add new words to the concept map.

On-Level Reader

For a complete literacy instructional plan and additional practice with this week's target skills and strategies, see the **Leveled Reader Teaching Guide.**

- **Before Reading** *Fun with Hobbies and Science!,* have students preview the book by looking at the title, cover, and pictures.
  - What is the topic of this book? *(hobbies related to science)*
  - What specialties in science will the book discuss? *(zoology, archeology, astronomy)*

  Have students create a three-column chart with the headings *Zoology, Archeology,* and *Astronomy.* Explain that students will add details about each subject to their three-column charts as they read.

Fun with Hobbies and Science!

- **During Reading** Read aloud the first three pages of the book as students follow along. Then have them finish reading on their own. Remind them to add details about each category to their three-column charts. Then ask students to work with partners to create a fourth column labeled *Locations*. List some places where a person could pursue each hobby. *(Places may include categories of places, such as zoos and museums, or actual geographical sites, such as Egypt.)*

- **After Reading** Have partners compare their three-column charts. Invite students to add to their charts in response to ideas from classmates.
  - Which part of the book interested you most? Why?
  - How does the topic of this book relate to the weekly question? *(The hobbies in this book sound fun and might lead to interesting careers.)*

Objectives

- Participate in teacher-led discussions by answering questions with appropriate detail.

OL On-Level DAY 2

Expand Comprehension

Skill Fact and Opinion Use p. 90 to review the definitions of fact and opinion. For additional review, see the material on Fact and Opinion in *Envision It!* p. EI•7. *Facts* are statements that can be proved true or false. *Opinions* cannot. Opinions tell a person's thoughts and feelings.

Strategy Inferring Review the definition of inferring, and encourage students to make inferences as they read the biography. On the first page of text, the author mentions that her father often forgot to lock the cash drawer at his business. Based on that detail, I can make an inference—an educated guess—that money was not very important to him. I will keep reading and see if my inference is right. For additional support, use the Extend Thinking questions during reading or refer students to p. EI•20 of *Envision It!*

Revisit *Rocks in His Head* on pp. 94–99. Then have students begin reading aloud. Have them distinguish facts from opinions as they read the biography. Also have them watch for "loaded words" that are strongly positive or negative.

- In what way can the phrase "you've got rocks in your head" be a loaded statement? *(It can be an insult meaning that you are not making sense.)*
- In what way can it be a statement of opinion? *(It can be a way to say someone is too stubborn or thoughtless. Those are opinions, so they can't be proved.)*

Objectives

- Draw conclusions from facts presented in text.
- Make inferences about text.

Student Edition p. EI•7

More Reading

Use additional Leveled Readers or other texts at students' instructional levels to reinforce this week's skills and strategies. For text suggestions, see the Leveled Reader Database or the Leveled Readers Skills Chart on pp. CL24–CL29.

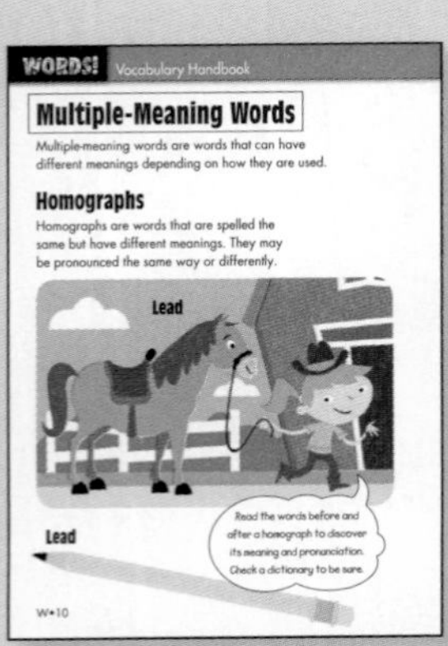

Student Edition p. W•10

Student Edition p. W•7

More Reading

Use additional Leveled Readers or other texts at students' instructional levels to reinforce this week's skills and strategies. For text suggestions, see the Leveled Reader Database or the Leveled Readers Skills Chart on pp. CL24–CL29.

OL On-Level

DAY 3

Expand Vocabulary

Multiple-Meaning Words/Context Clues Point out the word *spare* on the second page of text.

- What are some different meanings of *spare*? *(It can mean "extra", and it is also a term used in bowling. Students who check a dictionary may notice that* spare *can also mean "avoid hurting something or someone" or "lean and thin.")*
- Based on the words and sentences around *spare,* what does it mean in this biography? *("extra")*

Revisit *Rocks in His Head* on pp. 100–105. Remind students to look for multiple-meaning words throughout the text and to use context clues to understand them.

- Use what you have learned about context clues to figure out the meaning of the sentence "The stock market fell" on p. 99. If you need to, work with a partner and check a print or online dictionary. *(Help students understand that the sentence means that businesses were worth less money than they were before. Explain that when the stock market falls a lot, people may lose their jobs.)*
- Use what you have learned about context clues to figure out the meaning of *mind* on p. 99. (In that context, it means "pay attention to," not "brain or intelligence.")
- Use context clues to figure out the meaning of *cases* on p. 101. *(In that context,* cases *means "containers," not "situations.")*

Objectives

- Use context to distinguish among multiple meaning words.
- Use context to determine the relevant meaning of unfamiliar words.

OL On-Level DAY 4

Practice Retelling

- **Retell** To assess students' comprehension, use the Retelling Cards. Monitor retelling and prompt students as needed.

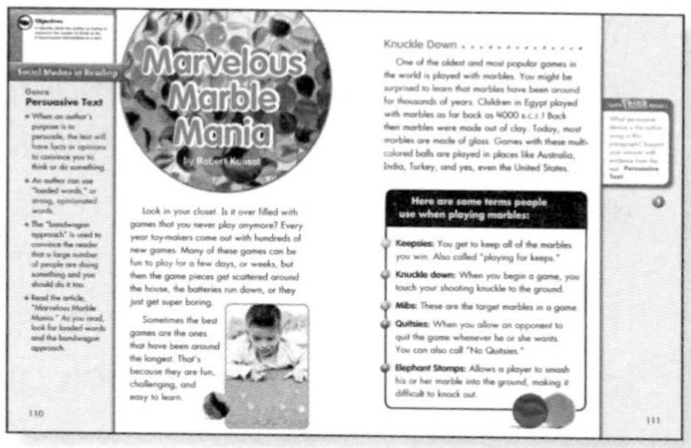

Genre Focus

- **Before Reading or Revisiting** "Marvelous Marble Mania" on pp. 110–113, read aloud the genre information about persuasive texts on p. 110. Remind the class that persuasive texts provide facts or opinions. Explain that the authors of those texts want to convince readers to have a certain opinion or to do something. Urge students to watch out for "loaded words," which can cause a strong positive or negative reaction in the reader, and the "bandwagon approach," which is a claim that, because something is popular with others, you should like it too. Have students preview "Marvelous Marble Mania" and set a purpose for reading.
  - How is a persuasive text different from a biography? *(It tries to convince you of something instead of providing information about someone.)*
  - What does this author want to persuade you to do? *(admire or play with marbles)*
- **During Reading or Revisiting** Have students read along with you.
  - How is this persuasive text organized? *(It's organized by topic.)*
  - How is this persuasive text similar to and different from a biography? *(Both may try to convince a reader. However, a biography usually tells a story.)*
- **After Reading or Revisiting** Have students share their reaction to "Marvelous Marble Mania." Then have them write and present a one- or two-minute persuasive talk from note cards about a favorite hobby of theirs.

Objectives

- Identify what the author is trying to persuade the reader to think or do.

OL On-Level

DAY 5

On-Level Reader

Fun with Hobbies and Science!

- **Model** Read aloud the first page of the On-Level Reader *Fun with Hobbies and Science!* Point out that you give more emphasis to information that is interesting or surprising. If you wish, read a few sentences of the On-Level Reader in a monotone. Help students understand that expressionless reading is boring to listen to and can cause a reader to lose track of what he or she is reading.

- **Fluency Routine**

  1. Have students work with a partner to reread passages from *Fun with Hobbies and Science!*
  2. For optimal fluency, students should reread passages three to four times.
  3. As students read, monitor fluency and provide corrective feedback. Have students take care to emphasize important words or phrases and observe punctuation cues.

  See *Routines Flip Chart* for more help with fluency.

- **Retell** For additional practice, have partners use the photographs in the text as a guide to retelling *Fun with Hobbies and Science!* Prompt students as necessary.

  - How can each hobby mentioned in the book teach science? *(Watching or playing with animals can help a person learn zoology. Finding old objects can teach about archeology. Looking at the stars can teach about astronomy.)*
  - What kind of career can come from each hobby? *(zoologist, veterinarian, archeologist, astronomer)*

Objectives

- Read aloud grade-level appropriate text with fluency.

A Advanced DAY 1

Build Background

- **Extend the Concept** Extend the weekly question *Why is it valuable to have unique interests?* How can unique interests enrich our lives? *(They give us something to do, something to be good at, and something to share with friends.)*

Advanced Reader

For a complete literacy instructional plan and additional practice with this week's target skills and strategies, see the **Leveled Reader Teaching Guide.**

- **Before Reading** *Gemstones Around the World,* ask students to read the title and look at the cover art. How do you think this book is related to the weekly question *Why is it valuable to have unique interests? (The book probably gives information about a unique interest having to do with gemstones.)* Have students look at the illustrations in the book and use them to predict what information the text will provide. Then help them set a purpose for reading.

Gemstones Around the World

- **During Reading** Direct students to read the Advanced Reader independently.
    - What makes a birthstone personal and unique? *(A person's birthstone depends on the month in which he or she was born. No two gemstones are exactly alike.)*
    - Why do you think gemstones fascinate so many people? *(They are beautiful. They are found in nature, but they have to be cut carefully so that they shine brightly. In some instances, they can be expensive.)*
    - Which gemstone did you find most interesting? Why?
- **After Reading** Have students review the concept map and explain how *Gemstones Around the World* helps them answer the weekly question *Why is it valuable to have unique interests?* Prompt students as necessary.
    - How can an interest in gemstones be valuable? *(Gemstones themselves are valuable; someone interested in gemstones can learn valuable information.)*
    - What can an interest in gemstones teach you? *(lessons in history, geography, and geology)*
- **Now Try This** Assign "Now Try This" at the end of the Advanced Reader.

Objectives
- Participate in teacher-led discussions by answering questions with appropriate detail.

Pacing Small Group Instruction

15–20 min

5-Day Plan

DAY 1	• Extend the concept • Read Advanced Reader
DAY 2	• Fact and Opinion • Inferring • Revisit Student Edition pp. 94–99
DAY 3	• Multiple-Meaning Words • Revisit Student Edition pp. 100–105
DAY 4	• Persuasive Text • Read/Revisit Student Edition pp. 110–113
DAY 5	• Reread for fluency • Reread Advanced Reader

3- or 4-Day Plan

DAY 1	• Extend the concept • Read Advanced Reader
DAY 2	• Fact and Opinion • Inferring • Revisit Student Edition pp. 94–99
DAY 3	• Multiple-Meaning Words • Revisit Student Edition pp. 100–105
DAY 4	• Persuasive Text • Read/Revisit Student Edition pp. 110–113 • Reread for fluency • Reread Advanced Reader

3-Day Plan: Eliminate the shaded box.

More Reading

Use additional Leveled Readers or other texts at students' instructional levels to reinforce this week's skills and strategies. For text suggestions, see the Leveled Reader Database or the Leveled Readers Skills Chart on pp. CL24–CL29.

A Advanced

DAY 2

Extend Comprehension

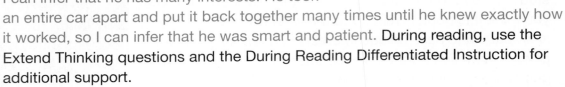

Skill Fact and Opinion Explain that opinions that are based upon facts are strong, reliable opinions. Think of the facts in the book you just read, *Gemstones Around the World.* Which gemstone do you value the most? Why?

Strategy Inferring Review the definition of the strategy of inferring. The father likes to look at rocks, play chess, and work on cars, so I can infer that he has many interests. He took an entire car apart and put it back together many times until he knew exactly how it worked, so I can infer that he was smart and patient. During reading, use the Extend Thinking questions and the During Reading Differentiated Instruction for additional support.

■ **Revisit** *Rocks in His Head* on pp. 94–99. Have students track facts and opinions as they read.

- Where in the biography is the phrase "you've got rocks in your head" spoken as a statement of fact? *(The biography shows that the father thought about rocks very frequently.)*
- Where is it spoken as a statement of opinion? *(On p. 99, the statement "I may have rocks in my head" means "I may not understand what I am talking about.")*

■ **Critical Thinking** Encourage students to reflect on what they have read so far.

- What do other people think of the father's hobby? *(They call his rocks "junk." They say he has rocks in his head—in other words, that he is foolish.)*
- Based on what he says and does, what can you infer about his reaction to others' opinions? *(He answers politely and then continues to pay attention to rocks. Therefore, he must not be too worried about what others think.)*

Objectives

- Draw conclusions from facts presented in text.
- Make inferences about text.

A Advanced DAY 3

Extend Vocabulary

Multiple-Meaning Words/Context Clues Read a section containing a multiple-meaning word, such as "I can't hire you as a mineralogist. The board won't allow it."

- What are some meanings of the word *board?* *(piece of wood; flat surface for a game; a group of people who make rules)*
- How can I use the words and phrases around *board* to figure out which meaning is correct? *(by asking how a board might give permission)*
- What is the correct definition in this context? *(a group of people who make rules)*

Revisit *Rocks in His Head* on pp. 100–105. Challenge students to note other multiple-meaning words throughout the biography.

- The father tells Mrs. Johnson, "Watch your step." Based on the context clues on p. 103, does he mean *step* as in *stair* or *step* as in "one part of a process"? *(stair)*
- The father in this biography labeled things by making signs about them. What is another way to label things? *(to call someone or something a name)*

Objectives

- Use context to distinguish among multiple meaning words.
- Use context to determine the relevant meaning of unfamiliar words.

More Reading

Use additional Leveled Readers or other texts at students' instructional levels to reinforce this week's skills and strategies. For text suggestions, see the Leveled Reader Database or the Leveled Readers Skills Chart on pp. CL24–CL29.

A Advanced

DAY 4

Genre Focus

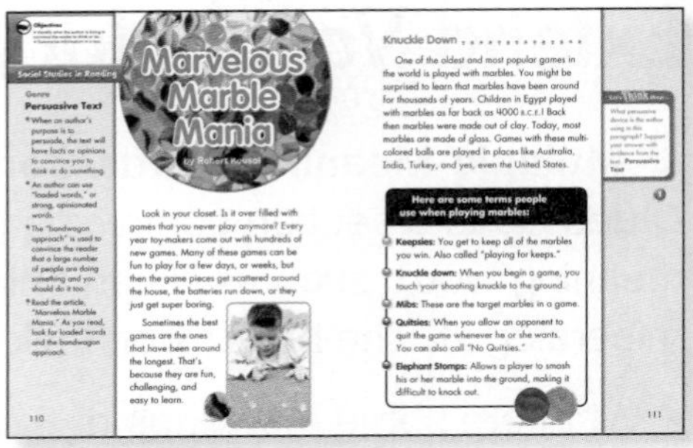

Marvelous Marble Mania

- **Before Reading or Revisiting** "Marvelous Marble Mania," read the panel information on persuasive text. Then have students use the text features—including the headings, photographs, and illustrations—to set a purpose for reading.
- **During Reading or Revisiting** Have students read the selection. Point out that a persuasive text tries to convince a reader to hold a certain opinion or to do something. How is this persuasive text organized differently from the biography you just read? *(It is organized according to ideas. The biography is organized chronologically.)* As they read, have students note elements of persuasive text.
- **After Reading or Revisiting** Have students discuss Reading Across Texts. Then have them complete the Writing Across Texts activity independently.

Objectives
- Identify what the author is trying to persuade the reader to think or do.

A Advanced

DAY 5

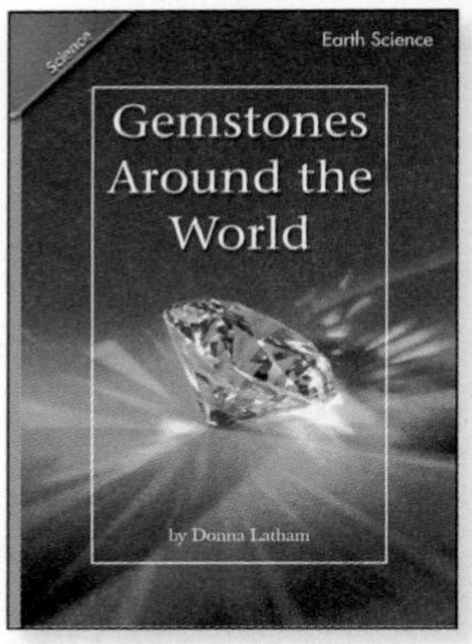

Gemstones Around the World

- **Reread for Fluency** Have students silently reread passages from the Advanced Reader *Gemstones Around the World.* Then have them reread aloud with a partner or individually. As students read, monitor fluency and provide corrective feedback. If students read fluently on the first reading, they do not need to reread three to four times. Assess the fluency of students in this group using p. 115j.
- **Retell** Have students use their prior knowledge as they discuss the main idea and key details from the Advanced Reader *Gemstones Around the World.*
- **Now Try This** Have students complete their posters and share them with classmates.

Objectives
- Read aloud grade-level appropriate text with fluency.

ELL English Language Learners

The ELL lessons are organized by strands. Use them to scaffold the weekly curriculum of lessons or during small group time instruction.

Academic Language

Students will hear or read the following academic language in this week's core instruction. As they encounter the vocabulary, provide a simple definition or concrete example. Then ask students to suggest an example or synonym of the word and identify available cognates.

Skill Words	idiom *(modismo)* prefix *(prefijo)* fact *(hecho)* opinion *(opinión)*	possessive *(posesivo)* pronoun *(pronombre)* multiple-meaning
Concept Words	unique *(único)* interest *(interés)*	career *(carrera)*

**Spanish cognates in parentheses*

Concept Development

Why is it valuable to have unique interests?

■ **Preteach Concept**

- **Prior Knowledge** Have students turn to pp. 86–87 in the Student Edition. Call attention to the picture of the girls making a scrapbook and tap into students' knowledge of scrapbooks. What are these girls doing? Have you ever made a scrapbook? Do you think it would be fun? Why or why not?
- **Discuss Concept** Elicit students' knowledge and experience of having unique interests. What are those students looking for in the book? What do you think they are interested in? Do you have any special things you like to do or learn about? What are they? Supply background information as needed.
- **Poster Talk-Through** Read aloud the Poster Talk-Through on ELL Poster 18 and work through the Day 1 activities.

■ **Daily Concept and Vocabulary Development** Use the daily activities on ELL Poster 18 to build concept and vocabulary knowledge.

Objectives
- Use accessible language and learn new and essential language in the process.

Content Objectives
- Use concept vocabulary related to having unique interests.

Language Objectives
- Express ideas in response to media, art and discussion.

Daily Planner

DAY 1	• **Frontload Concept** • **Preteach** Comprehension Skill, Vocabulary, Phonics/Spelling, Conventions • **Writing**
DAY 2	• **Review** Concept, Vocabulary, Comprehension Skill • **Frontload Main Selection** • **Practice** Phonics/Spelling, Conventions/Writing
DAY 3	• **Review** Concept, Comprehension Skill, Vocabulary, Conventions/Writing • **Reread Main Selection** • **Practice** Phonics/Spelling
DAY 4	• **Review Concept** • **Read ELL/ELD Readers** • **Practice** Phonics/Spelling, Conventions/Writing
DAY 5	• **Review** Concept, Vocabulary, Comprehension Skill, Phonics/Spelling, Conventions • **Reread ELL/ELD Readers** • **Writing**

**See the ELL Handbook for ELL Workshops with targeted instruction.*

Concept Talk Video

Have students listen to the Concept Talk Video Routine (*ELL Handbook,* p. 477) to build background knowledge about unique interests. Have them respond to one thing they learned from the video.

Language Objectives

- Understand, internalize and use basic vocabulary.
- Learn meanings of grade-level vocabulary.

Cognates

For Spanish speakers, point out the following cognates: *stamp/estampilla* (Latin America); attic/*ático.* Reinforce the concept that Spanish and English share many words that are the same or similar.

Mini-Lesson

Have students write the ten high-frequency words on cards. Help students internalize the words by having them work in pairs to write in the sentence frames with high-frequency words, such as I want to _____ the baby in my arms. Continue for all the high-frequency words. Challenge students to write their own sentences using the words.

ELL English Language Learners

Basic Vocabulary

■ **High-Frequency Words** Use the ELL Vocabulary Routine on p. 471 of the *ELL Handbook* to systematically teach newcomers the first 300 sight words in English. Students who began learning ten words per week at the beginning of the year are now learning words 171–180 (*ELL Handbook,* p. 452). p. 446 of the handbook contains a bank of strategies that you can use to ensure students' mastery of high-frequency words.

Lesson Vocabulary

■ **Preteach** Use this routine to introduce the Lesson Vocabulary:

1. Distribute copies of this week's Word Cards (*ELL Handbook,* p. 131).
2. Display ELL Poster 18 and reread the Poster Talk-Through.
3. Using the poster illustrations, model how a word's meaning can be expressed with other similar words: The girl enjoyed looking in the book filled with the sticky square pieces of paper, or *stamps.*
4. Use these sentences to reveal the meaning of the other words.
   - I have to finish my *chores* each morning before school. (jobs or duties)
   - The *customer* bought many items at the store. (person who buys things)
   - The boxes were *labeled* with our names on the top. (marked with a word or phrase that describes something)
   - There are lots of *spare* hats in our attic. (extra)
   - My sister asked Mom for two *stamps* so we could mail birthday cards to Grandpa and Uncle Jim. (stickers needed to send things through the mail)
   - The school *board* voted to hire more teachers. (group of people who run an organization or company)
   - My mother keeps my old toys in the *attic* of our house. (the space under the roof of a house)

Objectives

- Use visual, contextual, and linguistic support to enhance and confirm understanding of increasingly complex and elaborated spoken language.

ELL English Language Learners

- **Reteach** Have students work in pairs. Distribute Word Cards to each pair. Write the following sentence frames on the board. Have students pick a vocabulary word to fill in the blank. Then read the sentence and have them repeat it.
  - My sister and I like to play upstairs in my grandmother's _______. (attic)
  - The school _______ is meeting today. (board)
  - She _______ the pictures with her friends' names. (labeled)
  - I am a _______ at the grocery store. (customer)
  - I have a collection of _______ from all over the world. (stamps)
  - My _______ are to feed the dog and walk her. (chores)
  - We have a _______ tire in the trunk of the car. (spare)
- **Writing** List the selection vocabulary words on the board: *attic, board, chore, customer, labeled, spare, stamps.* Have students write or dictate individual words, phrases, or short sentences about each of the words. They may refer to the poster for ideas. Have students of mixed proficiencies work together to build background and develop challenging words. Provide prompts if necessary: Where can you find labels in a grocery store? Yes, labels are on cans and packages of food. What are some chores you do at home? Do you help clean or cook or care for brothers and sisters? Use these hints on your vocabulary cards.

Leveled Support

Beginning Have students work in pairs with more proficient students. On one side of each card, the Beginning student will copy the vocabulary word. Then beginners will dictate a word that reminds them of the vocabulary word. The partner will write that word on the other side of the card. Beginners can use their set of cards to practice the meaning and spelling of each word.

Intermediate/Advanced Have pairs of students generate sentences using the selection vocabulary. Suggest that they write sentences about their own experiences when possible.

Advanced High Have students generate sentences individually and share with the class. Remind students that *board* and *stamps* have other meanings than the one used in the sentences. Challenge students to write an additional sentence for each word using at least one of its other meanings.

Objectives

- Use visual, contextual, and linguistic support to enhance and confirm understanding of increasingly complex and elaborated spoken language.

Language Objectives

- Produce drawings, phrases, or short sentences to show understanding of Lesson Vocabulary.

ELL Teacher Tip

- Remind students that some words have more than one meaning. Write *board.* Elicit or provide these alternate meanings for *board:* a long, flat piece of wood made by a saw; a flat surface that has a special purpose, such as a chalkboard, checkerboard, bulletin board, or ironing board; a group of people who run a business, school, or museum. Have students draw pictures to illustrate the various meanings of *board.*

Language Opportunity

Have students look at p. 96 in the Student Edition and identify the environmental print "gas," "air," and "oil." Help students derive meaning from these words to understand the meaning of the phrase "filling station."

Content Objectives

- Monitor and adjust oral comprehension.

Language Objectives

- Discuss oral passages.
- Use a graphic organizer to demonstrate listening comprehension.

Graphic Organizer

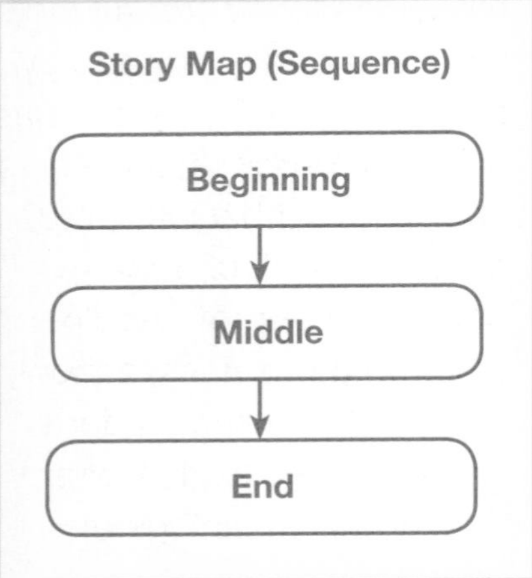

Mini-Lesson

After the second reading, read the first paragraph of the passage aloud to students. Grandpa Jay said, "Hey there, Sam, my man." Do his words sound like informal or formal language? Explain that people often use informal language when talking to family and friends.

ELL English Language Learners

Listening Comprehension

Read Aloud

Pictures In His Head

Grandpa Jay held a digital camera up to Sammy's face when he was two years old. He said, "Hey there, Sam, my man. Push this camera button right here! Sammy took a close-up picture of Grandpa Jay's gray beard. Sammy laughed. And his hobby began.

When Sammy was five years old, his parents gave him a disposable camera. He kept the camera in his backpack. He took it out when he wanted to remember a special moment.

When Sammy was nine, he owned both a digital camera and a film camera. He took pictures of his family, his dog, and his hamster. He took pictures of his street, his house, his parents' orange car, and his school. Sam took pictures when he was running, jumping, and standing on his head. People asked him why. "Pictures make memories," Sammy said.

Sammy's family had a birthday party for Grandpa Jay. Sam gave Grandpa Jay a photo album of family memories. He put the funniest pictures in the album.

Grandpa Jay opened the photo album. He saw a picture of himself with his grey beard. Sammy took a picture of his smiling grandfather. "I'll save this picture for the next album," Sam said.

Prepare for the Read Aloud The modified Read Aloud above prepares students for listening to the oral reading "Picture Perfect" on p. 87b.

- **First Listening: Listen to Understand** Write the title of the Read Aloud on the board. This story is about a young boy's hobby. Why does he like this hobby? How does he share it? Afterward, ask the questions again and have students share their answers.
- **Second Listening: Listen to Check Understanding** Using Story Map A (*ELL Handbook,* p. 483), work with students to write the events that happen in the beginning, middle, and end of the story.

Objectives

- Demonstrate listening comprehension of increasingly complex spoken English by following directions, retelling or summarizing spoken messages, responding to questions and requests, collaborating with peers, and taking notes commensurate with content and grade-level needs.

ELL English Language Learners

Phonics and Spelling

- **Prefixes *pre-, mid-, over-, out-, bi-, de-*** Have students turn to p. 88 in the Student Edition.
  - **Preteach** Point to the picture of the bicycle. Bi is the prefix. Write these word pairs on the board: *test, pretest; air, midair; grown, overgrown; side, outside; monthly, bimonthly, code, decode.* Read the words aloud and discuss their meanings. Explain that the second word in each pair has a prefix that changes the meaning of the first word.
  - **Teach/Model** Circle the prefix in the first word pair on the board. Then have students explain how the prefix changes the meaning. The prefix *pre-* means "before." It changes the word *test* to *pretest.* What is a *pretest?* (a test taken to see what you know before you study the material)
  - **Assess** Have students list words with the prefix *pre-* and discuss how the prefix changes the meaning of the base word.

To provide students additional instruction and practice for prefixes, use the lessons on p. 286 in the *ELL Handbook*.

Vocabulary Skill: Multiple-Meaning Words

- **Preteach and Model** Explain to students that many words that sound the same and are spelled the same have different meanings. You need to use context clues to figure out the meaning of the word. When you hear the word *rock* what you think it means? Listen to these sentences:
  My father built shelves for his *rock* collection. (small stones)
  She likes to *rock* the baby in the cradle and sing a lullaby. (move back and forth)
  The sentences gave clues to the meaning of the word *rock* in each one.
- **Practice** Have students use a classroom dictionary to find the different meanings of the following words: *left, open, set, play.* Have them say one sentence using the word with one meaning, and then one with the other meaning.

Leveled Support

Beginning/Intermediate Have students create a picture dictionary with labels to show the words and their different meanings.

Advanced/Advanced High Challenge students to use at least two of the words in sentences that show both of their meanings.

Objectives

- Develop basic sight vocabulary, derive meaning of environmental print, and comprehend English vocabulary and language structures used routinely in written classroom materials.

Content Objectives

- Identify prefixes *pre-, mid-, over-, out-, bi-, de-.*
- Identify and understand multiple-meaning words.

Language Objectives

- Apply phonics and decoding skills to spelling.
- Understand how the addition of a prefix changes the meaning of the word or root.

Transfer Skills

Prefixes in Spanish Point out to Spanish speakers that the prefix *mid-* is related in meaning to the Spanish word *media,* which means *half* or *middle.* Display cognates such as *midnight/medianoche* and *midday/mediadía* as examples.

Monosyllabic Languages

Speakers of monosyllabic languages such as Cantonese, Hmong, Khmer, Korean, and Vietnamese may have difficulty understanding that multisyllabic words are single words. Have these students practice saying and writing words with prefixes as single words.

Content Objectives

- Distinguish between fact and opinion.
- Recognize word clues that signal opinions.

Language Objectives

- Distinguish between formal and informal English.
- Learn when to use formal and informal English.

English Opportunity

Have students express their opinions about what they discussed in the Social Language mini-lesson. Should you use informal or formal language in school? What is your opinion. Depending on their proficiency levels, students can respond in words, short phrases or complete sentences.

ELL English Language Learners

Comprehension
Fact and Opinion

- **Preteach** Facts and opinions are different. A statement of fact can be proven to be true or false. An opinion tells someone's beliefs or feelings. It cannot be proven true or false. Have students turn to Envision It! on p. EI•7 in the Student Edition. Ask a student to read the statement made by the boy on the left. Is that a fact? How could you prove that it is true or false? (by observing ants) Ask another student to read the statement by the boy on the right. Is that a fact or an opinion? How do you know? (It shows feelings, not facts.) Could someone else express a different opinion about the ants? (yes)

- **Reteach** Distribute copies of the Picture It! (*ELL Handbook,* p. 132). Have students look at the images to develop background knowledge. Tell them to listen for facts while you read the paragraph aloud for the first time. Then, invite students to choral read, this time listening for opinions. (Fact: Many people visit Chile for fun; You can ski on the mountains. They are covered with snow. The beaches are warmer than the mountains, you can swim in the warm sea. Prove it: look up weather, or pictures of people skiing and swimming; Opinion: I think the mountains are too cold. I like to visit the beaches in Chile better. Clue word: think, like.)

Leveled Support

Beginning/Intermediate Reread the paragraph aloud. Stop between each sentence, giving students time to underline each fact, and circle each opinion. Ask for a volunteer to explain why these words might indicate an opinion.

Advanced/Advanced High Have students write three facts from the paragraph. Then, have them write three opinions.

MINI-LESSON

Social Language

Have students read the conversation between the two boys on p. EI•7 in the Student Edition. Point out that "Wow, this is awesome!" is an example of informal language, which people use when talking to friends or family. Informal language is for everyday use. Formal language is for school or in public. How do you say "How are you today?" in a casual, or informal, way?

Objectives

- Demonstrate an increasing ability to distinguish between formal and informal English and an increasing knowledge of when to use each one commensurate with grade-level learning expectations.

ELL English Language Learners

Reading Comprehension
Rocks in His Head

Student Edition pp. 94–105

- **Frontloading** Read the title aloud and discuss "rocks in his head" as an idiom, or informal saying. What does it mean when people say that someone has "rocks in his head"? This saying usually means that the person is foolish. This you do not tell your teacher a phrase like this because it is too casual. Guide students on a picture walk for visual support through *Rocks in His Head.* Ask students to predict what "He has rocks in his head" might mean in the story and record their predictions. Provide students with a two-column chart to fill in as they read the selection. Supply these headings: *What is the father's unique interest? How is it valuable to him?*
- **Sheltered Reading** Ask questions such as the following to guide students' comprehension and confirm and enhance understanding of the selection:
  - **p. 96:** Why did people say that the father had rocks in his head? (He collected rocks and minerals from the time he was a boy.)
  - **pp. 97–100:** What kind of work did the father do? (He had a filling station and fixed cars.) How did hard times affect his business? (He had to close it.)
  - **pp. 101–104:** What new job did the father get? (First he was a janitor at the science museum. Then he became a mineralogist at the museum.) How did his interest in rocks help him get the job? (He impressed the director of the museum, Mrs. Johnson, with his knowledge of rocks and minerals.)
  - **p. 108:** Do you think the father's interest in rocks was valuable? Why or why not? (Answers will vary.)
- **Fluency: Reading with Expression** Remind students that reading aloud with expression makes a story more enjoyable. Model reading the dialogue on p. 94 with expression. Then choose two proficient students to take each part and read the dialogue aloud. Then, divide students into pairs to read to each other with expression according to their level of proficiency. Have students give feedback on their partner's expressive reading. For more practice, use the Fluency: Paired Reading Routine (*ELL Handbook,* p. 474).

After Reading Guide students in summarizing the text using the Retelling Cards. Assign each student a task based on proficiency level. Beginning students can put the cards in order of events. Intermediate and Advanced students can describe events that happened in the beginning, middle, and end of the story.

Objectives
- Use visual and contextual support and support from peers and teachers to read grade-appropriate content area text, enhance and confirm understanding, and develop vocabulary, grasp of language structures, and background knowledge needed to comprehend increasingly challenging language.

Content Objectives
- Monitor and clarify comprehension.
- Make and adjust predictions.

Language Objectives
- Read aloud with appropriate expression.
- Summarize text using visual support.

Graphic Organizer

Father's Unique Interest	How is it valuable to him?

Audio Support
Students can prepare for reading *Rocks in His Head* by using the eSelection or the AudioText CD. See the AudioText CD Routine (*ELL Handbook,* p. 477) for suggestions on using these learning tools.

Mini-Lesson
Have students work in pairs to retell *Rocks in His Head.* Have one student tell what happened in the beginning, middle, and end of the story. Have the other student take notes as they listen to the retelling. Each student should exchange roles for further practice.

ELL English Language Learners

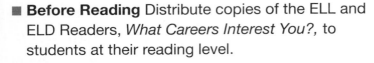

For additional leveled instruction, see the **ELL/ELD Reader Teaching Guide.**

Comprehension: *What Careers Interest You?*

ELL Reader ELD Reader

- **Before Reading** Distribute copies of the ELL and ELD Readers, *What Careers Interest You?,* to students at their reading level.
    - **Preview** Read the title aloud with students: This is informational text about different careers. Invite students to look through pictures and name the various careers they see represented. Have them predict what they will learn about these careers based on the picture clues and their prior knowledge.
    - **Set a Purpose for Reading** Let's read to find out what these careers are like and what you need to know for each job.
- **During Reading** Follow this Reading Routine for both reading groups.
    1. Read the entire Reader aloud slowly.
    2. Reread pp. 2–5, pausing to build background knowledge or model comprehension. Have Beginning students finger-point as you read. Use the questions in the chart below to check students' comprehension.
    3. Have pairs reread pp. 2–5 alternating pages as they read aloud.
    4. Repeat steps 2–3 above for pp. 6–8 of the Reader.
- **After Reading** Use the exercises on the inside back cover of each Reader and invite students to share their writing. Ask questions in a whole-class discussion. Why did you choose this career? Why does it interest you? Record their answers on the board and invite them to point to pictures and information in the book to support their answers.

ELD Reader Beginning/Intermediate

- **p. 2:** How do people pick a career? Read the sentence that tells you. (p. 2: Many people choose a career because of what they like to do.)
- **pp. 3–5** What must teachers like to do? (help children learn, speak to a group) What must astronauts study to get their job? (science and math)
- **pp. 6–8** Read aloud the sentences that tell you what gardeners do. (p. 6) Then read aloud the sentences that tell what bakers must know how to do. (p. 7)

Writing Copy a sentence from the book that tells about a career you would like. Read your sentence aloud to a partner.

ELL Reader Advanced/Advanced High

- **pp. 2–3:** What must you like to be a teacher? (helping children learn, speaking in front of a group)
- **pp. 4–5:** What are some chores that astronauts do in space? (take care of spacecrafts and computers)
- **pp. 6–8:** What does a gardener do all year? (care for plants) When does a baker begin work each day? (early in the morning)

Study Guide Distribute copies of the ELL Reader Study Guide (*ELL Handbook,* p. 136). Scaffold comprehension of distinguishing facts from opinions by helping students look back through the Reader in order to answer questions on the back cover. (See *ELL Handbook,* pp. 209–212.)

Objectives

- Understand the general meaning, main points, and important details of spoken language ranging from situations in which topics, language, and contexts are familiar to unfamiliar.

ELL English Language Learners

Conventions
Possessive Pronouns

■ **Preteach** Remind students that possessive pronouns are used to show who owns or has something. Display this list:

- Use *my, your, her, our,* and *their* before nouns.
- Use *mine, yours, hers, ours,* and *theirs* alone.
- *His* and *its* can be used before nouns and alone.

Write these examples on the board: *This is my book. It is mine.*

■ **Practice** Have students work in pairs. Ask them to listen carefully and follow directions for the activity. Give each pair seven index cards. Have students write a possessive pronoun on each card. One partner will hold up a card for his or her partner to see. The partner without the card will use the pronoun to make an oral sentence. Partners will take turns holding up the card and making sentences.

Leveled Support

Beginning Have students work in pairs to make oral sentences about objects that their classmates have. Provide this sentence frame: _________ has a backpack. It is _________.

Intermediate Have student pairs do the activity above and then add the following sentence frame: Is this backpack _________? Have students ask one another questions about various objects in the classroom using the sentence frame and using a variety of possessive pronouns to fill in the blank.

Advanced/Advanced High Have students write original questions and answers using a variety of possessive pronouns.

■ **Reteach** Review possessive pronouns with oral and written examples.

■ **Practice** Have students write two sentences in which they use one or more possessive pronouns. Invite them to share their sentences with the class. Have the class identify the possessive pronouns used in each sentence. Students should exchange papers and edit each other's work if needed.

Leveled Support

Beginning/Intermediate Have students copy the sentences and underline the possessive pronouns. Then have them say the sentences aloud to a partner.

Advanced/Advanced High Have students write the sentences with a partner.

Objectives

- Speak using a variety of grammatical structures, sentence lengths, sentence types, and connecting words with increasing accuracy and ease as more English is acquired.

Content Objectives

- Identify possessive pronouns.
- Use possessive pronouns correctly.

Language Objectives

- Practice using possessive pronouns in speaking.
- Write sentences using possessive pronouns.

Transfer Skills

Possessive Pronouns
Students who speak Asian languages may try various forms for possessive pronouns (*the hat of her*, *you hat*) or may not always state the pronoun (*Mo Yun took off hat.*). Provide these students practice with possessive pronouns.

Grammar Jammer

For more practice with pronouns, use the Grammar Jammer for this target skill. See the Grammar Jammer Routine (*ELL Handbook*, p. 478) for suggestions on using this learning tool.

Content Objectives
- Identify choppy sentences.
- Identify connecting words to combine sentences.

Language Objectives
- Write and speak by using connecting words.
- Share feedback for editing and revising.

ELL Teaching Routine
For practice spelling words related to collections use the Spelling Routine (*ELL Handbook,* p. 476).

ELL English Language Learners

Combining Short, Choppy Sentences

■ **Introduce** Display the model below and read it aloud. Most of these are short, choppy sentences. Short, choppy sentences that have the same subject can be combined. Read the first two sentences aloud. Guide students to combine them into one sentence: *My brother collects rock and minerals.* How could the third sentence be combined with the sentence we just made? (My brother and sister collect rocks and minerals.)

Writing Model
My brother collects rocks. He also collects minerals.
My sister collects rocks and minerals.

■ **Practice** Tell students that sentences that do not have the same subject or verb can be combined using connecting words like *because* or *when.* Have students rewrite the three sentences in the example text below. Instruct them to combine two of the sentences using the connecting word because. (*They need more shelves because their collection is very large.* or *My father will build shelves for them because they need more.*) Have students point out possessive pronouns (they, their, them, them, my) in the example text above. Have them edit for correct use.

Their collection is very large. They need more shelves.
My father will build shelves for them.

■ **Write** Have students look at the rock collection on p. 97 in the Student Edition. Have students think about why the father liked his collection. Then have students write a paragraph about a collection they have seen. Have them explain why they liked the collection.

Leveled Support

Beginning Supply students with a sentence frame: I saw a collection of __________. I liked it because __________. Students may dictate to a more proficient partner and then copy the sentences.

Intermediate Have partners work together to write sentences that fit the frames above. Challenge them to add other sentences on this topic.

Advanced/Advanced High Have students develop their paragraph independently. Then have pairs exchange papers and look for short, choppy sentences. Partners will help each other revise and edit.

Objectives
- Write using a variety of grade-appropriate sentence lengths, patterns, and connecting words to combine phrases, clauses, and sentences in increasingly accurate ways as more English is acquired.

Customize Your Writing

Weekly Writing Focus

Writing Forms and Patterns

- Instruction focuses on a different **product** each week.
- Mini-lessons and models help students learn key features and **organizational patterns**.

Grade 3 Products fable, friendly letter, news article, autobiography, summary, realistic fiction, and so on

Grade 3 Organization Patterns poetic forms, compare and contrast, main idea and details, narrative, letter, and so on

Daily Writing Focus

Quick Writes for Fluency

- Writing on Demand Use the Quick Write routine for **writing on demand**.
- The Quick Write **prompt and routine** extend skills and strategies from daily writing lessons.

Unit Writing Focus

Writing Process 1 2 3 4 5

- Six **writing process** lessons provide structure to move students through the steps of the writing process.
- One-week and two-week pacing allows lessons to be used in **Writing Workshop**.

Steps of the Writing Process Plan and Prewrite, Draft, Revise, Edit, Publish and Present

Grade 3 Writing Process Products personal narrative, how-to report, cause-and-effect essay, problem-solution essay, persuasive essay, research report

Writing on Reading Street

MINI-LESSON

- Daily 10-minute mini-lessons focus instruction on the **traits** and **craft** of good writing.
- Instruction focuses on one writing trait and one writer's craft skill every week.

Traits focus/ideas, organization, voice, word choice, sentences, conventions

Craft drafting strategies, revising strategies, editing strategies

Read Like a Writer

- Use **mentor text** every week as a model to exemplify the traits of good writing.
- **Interact with text** every week to learn the key features of good writing.

Mentor Text Examine literature in the Student Edition.

INTERACT with TEXT Underline, circle, and highlight model text in the *Reader's and Writer's Notebook.*

Write Guy
Jeff Anderson

Need Writing Advice?

Writing instruction is all about creating effective writers. We don't want to crush the inner writer in a child by over-correcting and over-editing. What makes effective writing instruction? Children need to write, write, write! But is that enough? Probably not. All kinds of instruction and guidance go into making an effective writer.

The Write Guy offers advice on teacher and peer conferencing, focusing on writing traits, revising strategies, editing strategies, and much, much more.

Customize Your Writing

Alternate Pacing Plan for Unit Writing Projects

Sometimes you want to spend more time on writing—perhaps you do a **Writing Workshop**. This one- or two-week plan for the unit level writing projects can help.

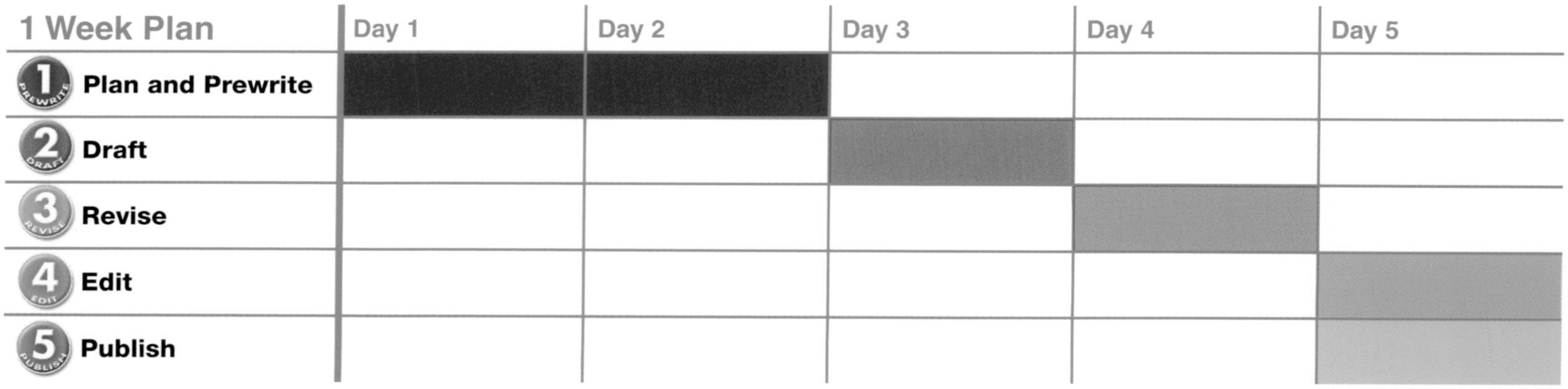
1 Week Plan
Day 1
Day 2
Day 3
Day 4
Day 5
1 PREWRITE Plan and Prewrite
2 DRAFT Draft
3 REVISE Revise
4 EDIT Edit
5 PUBLISH Publish

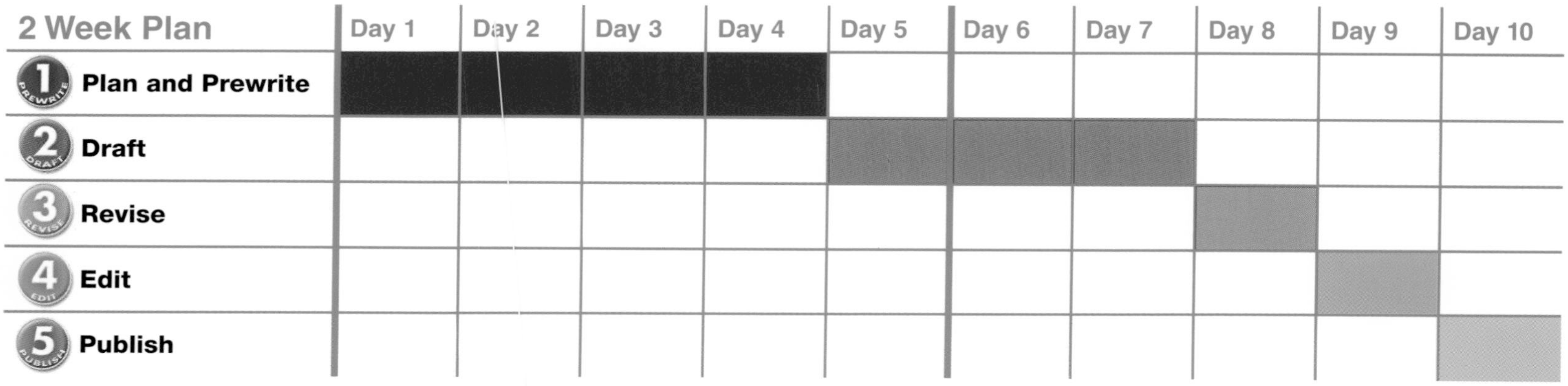

Grade 3 Unit Writing Projects

Internet Guy
Don Leu

Unit Writing Project 1–21st Century Project

Unit 1 E-Pen Pals
Unit 2 Story Exchange
Unit 3 Photo Writing
Unit 4 Classroom Profile
Unit 5 E-Newsletter
Unit 6 Discussion Forum

Unit Writing Project 2–Writing Process

Unit 1 Personal Narrative
Unit 2 How-to Report
Unit 3 Cause-and-Effect Essay
Unit 4 Problem-Solution Essay
Unit 5 Persuasive Essay
Unit 6 Research Report

Classroom Profile

Writing Project Create a classroom profile with information about the people and features that make up your classroom.

Purpose Enhance skills in interviewing and writing as well as using applications for word processing and design.

Audience Student, peers, teacher, family

Introduce genre and key features

In this workshop, we will create a classroom profile with information about what makes this classroom unique. We will write articles about the class, take photos of different activities, and then design the profile to share with our friends and family.

Key Features of a Classroom Profile

- includes lists, charts, and articles about students' interests and activities
- includes features about the classroom
- displays photographs of activities and the class
- is designed to share with other classes and family

Teacher Tip

Explore Examples Do an online search for "classroom profiles" and "classroom sharing" to find sites that provide safe and secure ways for classes to exchange information and to find models of profiles to show the class. Follow school procedures for student use of the Internet. Use an LCD projector or equivalent technology to display appropriate results.

ELL

English Language Learners

Introduce vocabulary Using examples of another classroom profile, introduce vocabulary such as *hobbies*, *interests*, *talents*, and *favorite books*. Point out that the students will be creating lists, charts, and articles for the profile. Explain each of these terms as needed.

UNIT 4 21st Century Writing

Objectives

- Understand and identify the features of a classroom profile.
- Organize ideas to prepare for writing.

1 PREWRITE Plan and Prewrite

MINI-LESSON

Read Like a Writer

- **Examine Model Text** Display other classroom profiles. Classrooms make profiles to share their interests and activities with others. Every class is unique, just like the people that make up a class. Discuss the purpose and audience of the profiles you show students. You are going to write a classroom profile. It will include lists, charts, and articles about our interests and activities and photos of our class.

- **Explore Model Text** Let's look at an example of an article that you might find in a classroom profile. This is the kind of article that you will write. Display and read aloud to students "Helping Those That Hop," 21st Century Transparency TC4. Ask them to identify key features of a classroom profile article in the student model. Make sure that students understand that all sentences in a paragraph should be about the same idea or topic.

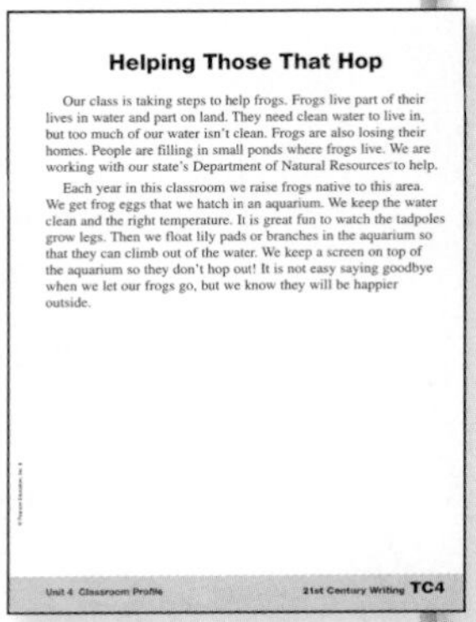
Helping Those That Hop

Our class is taking steps to help frogs. Frogs live part of their lives in water and part on land. They need clean water to live in, but too much of our water isn't clean. Frogs are also losing their homes. People are filling in small ponds where frogs live. We are working with our state's Department of Natural Resources to help.

Each year in this classroom we raise frogs native to this area. We get frog eggs that we hatch in an aquarium. We keep the water clean and the right temperature. It is great fun to watch the tadpoles grow legs. Then we float lily pads or branches in the aquarium so that they can climb out of the water. We keep a screen on top of the aquarium so they don't hop out! It is not easy saying goodbye when we let our frogs go, but we know they will be happier outside.

Unit 4 Classroom Profile 21st Century Writing TC4

21st Century Transparency TC4, TR DVD

Determine appropriate articles

We will prepare a classroom profile about our interests, activities, and favorite things. The profile will include lists, charts, and articles about our classroom. We will work in small groups on different topics about our class. First, we need to think of the kinds of information we want to include in our profile. Encourage students to brainstorm ideas for articles about the class, such as "our hobbies," "favorite books," "sports we play," and features of the classroom. Write responses on the board. When the class has generated several ideas, organize students into small groups that will write an article about one of the ideas.

Collecting information

Now that each group has an idea for an article, you will collect the information you need by interviewing classmates or using a survey. For example, the group writing about our artistic talents might prepare a survey asking questions such as *Do you like to draw? Do you play a musical instrument?* Write suggestions on the board. Encourage students to include an open-ended question on their survey, such as *What other artistic activities do you enjoy?*

Our Artistic Talents

Do you like to draw?

Do you like to paint?

Do you like to sing?

Do you play a musical instrument?

Do you like to dance?

Do you like to act?

Have you ever been in a play?

What other artistic activities do you enjoy?

Differentiated Instruction

SI Strategic Intervention

Tap into Student Interests
Place students who are reluctant to participate actively in a group that is writing about the topic that most interests them. This will encourage participation.

Teacher Tip

Interviewing or Surveying
Groups that are polling information from the entire class should prepare a survey to collect their data. Groups that need to interview a few students should write their interview questions before conducting the interviews.

ELL

English Language Learners

Build Vocabulary If students do not know some words in the model on TC4, such as *habitats* or *temperature*, read the words and use them in sentences. Offer definitions for each unfamiliar word.

UNIT 4

21st Century Writing

Objectives

- Organize ideas to prepare to write a first draft.

1 PREWRITE Plan and Prewrite

MINI-LESSON

Writing an Autobiographical Paragraph

Think Aloud In addition to your group article about the class, you will write a paragraph about yourself to include in our classroom profile. When a person writes about his or her own life, he or she is writing an autobiography. We are going to write autobiographical paragraphs about what makes each of us unique.

- **Explore Model Text** Let's look at an example of an autobiographical paragraph that you might find in a classroom profile. Notice the use of the pronoun *I* in the paragraph. The writer uses the pronoun *I* because she is talking about herself. This is the kind of paragraph that you will write about yourself. Display and read aloud "Let's Read!" on 21st Century Transparency TC5. Ask students to identify what the student tells about herself and what is unique about the student.

Let's Read!

My name is Maria and I love to read. Now most people like to read, but I love it. I enjoy it so much I help lots of younger kids read. One day a week I read to children in kindergarten and first grades at our school. Out of school I read to my younger cousins. I always try to read with lots of expression. I am good at changing my voice to sound like different characters. I think that's why people like to listen to me read.

Unit 4 Classroom Profile 21st Century Writing TC5

21st Century Transparency TC5, TR DVD

Plan and Prewrite

Classroom sharing

When we finish our classroom profile, we can post it to a classroom-sharing Web site on the Internet so that students in other third grade classrooms can read about our class. When classrooms share their activities and interests, we can learn about projects we may want to try in our classroom. Show students a classroom-sharing site where they can view other classroom profiles. Review all material prior to showing it to students. Point out interesting articles and projects from your review.

Internet safety

It is fun to share our activities and interests with others, but we do not want to share private information. Do not include your last name, birthday, address, or phone number in your autobiographical paragraph. Help students pick appropriate topics for their autobiographical paragraphs that are not too personal to share in the classroom profile. Possibly use the following questions with students:

- Will others find this information about you interesting?
- Could this information inspire others with a similar interest?
- Does this information show a unique quality about you without revealing anything too private?
- Would you enjoy reading a profile of a student with a similar interest?

Differentiated Instruction

SI Strategic Intervention

Autobiography Remind students that their autobiographical paragraph should not tell their life story, but it should describe something that makes them unique, or different from everybody else. Meet with students to discuss their ideas for their paragraphs.

Teacher Tip

Note to Parents Make parents aware of the plans for the classroom profile whether you are posting it on the Internet or not. Be sure to explain that last names and other private information will not be included in the profile.

Objectives

- Organize survey results and write a first draft of the group article.
- Write a first draft of an autobiographical paragraph.
- Revise drafts of group article and autobiographical paragraph.

2 Draft

Organize information Have each small group organize the results of their survey and decide the best way to present it. For example, groups can make a list of the class's favorite books or a bar graph of the most popular sports. Then groups will write a short article explaining their list or graph.

Getting started Have students review their survey results and write a topic sentence. Then they can write sentences that provide supporting details. Encourage them to refer to the notes from their interviews or surveys of the class for ideas to include in the article.

Examine model text Display 21st Century Transparency TC4 and review "Helping Those That Hop."

Think Aloud This group started each paragraph with a clear topic sentence. The sentences that follow support the topic sentence. In the first paragraph, the topic sentence says the class is helping frogs and the supporting sentences explain why frogs need help.

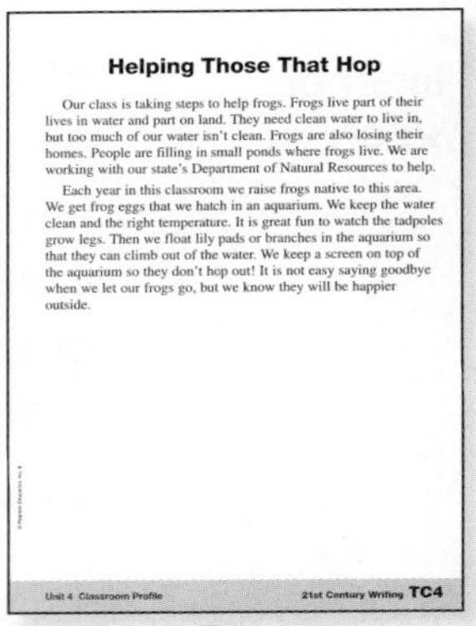

Helping Those That Hop

Our class is taking steps to help frogs. Frogs live part of their lives in water and part on land. They need clean water to live in, but too much of our water isn't clean. Frogs are also losing their homes. People are filling in small ponds where frogs live. We are working with our state's Department of Natural Resources to help.

Each year in this classroom we raise frogs native to this area. We get frog eggs that we hatch in an aquarium. We keep the water clean and the right temperature. It is great fun to watch the tadpoles grow legs. Then we float lily pads or branches in the aquarium so that they can climb out of the water. We keep a screen on top of the aquarium so they don't hop out! It is not easy saying goodbye when we let our frogs go, but we know they will be happier outside.

Unit 4 Classroom Profile 21st Century Writing TC4

21st Century Transparency TC4, TR DVD

Develop draft Remind groups that the purpose of drafting is to record their ideas. They will have a chance to revise and proofread their work to make necessary changes. Display or read Choosing a Title (below) for students. Encourage groups to work together and use ideas from each member of the group.

Choosing a Title

- ✔ If groups do not have an idea for a title to start with, that's OK. Have groups write the drafts of their articles without a title. Most likely ideas for a title will occur to them as they write their draft.
- ✔ If groups have several ideas for a title, have them make a list and vote on the one that fits the article best after the article is written.

3 Revise

MINI-LESSON

Keeping Your Focus

- One way to revise is to delete sentences that are not focused on the main idea. Read these examples:

Ideas out of focus Many students in our class play sports. Soccer is the game most students play. Jim even saw a soccer game in Spain with his family. Half of the students in class play soccer. Basketball is the next game most played. In soccer you dribble the ball with your feet, but in basketball you dribble the ball with your hands. Nine students play basketball on teams.

Ideas in focus Many students in our class play sports. Soccer is the game most students play. Half of the students in class play soccer. Basketball is the next game most played. Nine students play basketball on teams.

Discuss with students how the paragraph was improved by deleting the sentences that were not the focus of the paragraph.

Peer conferencing Have small groups exchange their drafts with other groups for peer revision. Ask each group to write at least three revision suggestions for the other group. Have groups pay particular attention to sentences that are out of focus with the rest of a paragraph.

Revise drafts Earlier we wrote drafts of our classroom profile articles. Now we will revise our drafts. When we revise, we incorporate comments from peer conferencing and try to make our writing clearer and more interesting. An interesting article has paragraphs with a topic sentence and sentences that add details. Delete or rewrite sentences that do not support the topic of the paragraph.

Corrective feedback **If...** students are reluctant to delete sentences that are not about the topic,
then... have them cut and paste the sentences at the end of the article until they decide to rewrite to include the idea or to delete it all together.

Academic Vocabulary

Topic Sentence A topic sentence tells the main idea of a paragraph.

Differentiated Instruction

A Advanced

Humble Descriptions As students revise their autobiographical paragraphs, they should look for sentences that suggest bragging or boasting. Have them delete or revise sentences that compare themselves with others.

Teacher Tip

Group Participation As groups draft and revise their work, make sure all students are participating. Although an advanced student may naturally lead a group, make sure he or she is not dominating the group or doing all the work.

ELL

English Language Learners

Supporting Details Have students make a list of details to include in their paragraph. Then have them refer to this list as they write to help generate supporting details.

Objectives

- Edit a revised draft of the classroom profile article and the autobiographical paragraph to correct errors in grammar, mechanics, and spelling.
- Use a digital camera to enhance a classroom profile article.

4 EDIT Edit

MINI-LESSON

Using Computers to Edit

- The grammar and spelling checker is a useful tool to identify errors in your writing. Read each suggestion that the checker makes carefully before you accept it to be sure that the correction is needed. Have students use the grammar and spelling checker in the word processing program that they used to write their classroom article and autobiographical paragraph.

- Although the grammar and spelling checker is very useful, it may highlight names and other proper nouns as misspellings. It is very important to check the spelling of every name in our classroom profile. We do not want anyone's name to be misspelled. Type the following sentence in a word processing program and display it on a projector:

  Mea and Luka enjoy caring for the plants in are classroom.

  Use the spelling checker to check the sentence. The spelling checker highlights Luka's name even though it is spelled correctly because it does not recognize it. However, it did not catch the misspelling of Mia's name which should be spelled *M-i-a,* and it did not catch the incorrect word *are* because it is a real word that is used incorrectly. What is the word we need? How should it be spelled? Change *are* to *our*.

- Have students practice editing the following sentences, first by using the grammar and spelling checker and then by themselves.

  Six students play base ball and too play tennis.

  Jaun took our pet hamster home over winter brake.

Edit drafts Ask groups to edit their drafts. After they use the grammar and spelling checker, have them print out their article and read it sentence by sentence to make further edits. Ask them to check their drafts for spelling, grammar, punctuation, and capitalization.

5 PUBLISH Publish and Present

MINI-LESSON

Taking Photos with a Digital Camera

- Use a school-owned digital camera to take group pictures and upload them to the computer. Photographs will make our articles more interesting for our readers. When we take photos of our classroom with a digital camera, we can easily load the photos onto the computer and put them with the articles we have written.

- I have taken several pictures of our classroom activity centers. Now I am going to load them on the computer. Show students how to dock the camera and upload images. Encourage them to give each photo a file name that describes it so that they can easily identify an image. Have them store the images in a separate folder so that the photos can be accessed easily.

Corrective feedback | **If...** students have difficulty finding an appropriate image to use, **then...** have them write a description of the image they would like so that a photo can be set up and taken.

Differentiated Instruction

A Advanced

Concepts of Print Have children who are interested in design work with the layout of the classroom profile. Encourage them to change fonts and font sizes to draw attention to headings and to use artwork to optimize space.

Technology Tip

Trimming Images Digital images taken of the classroom can be trimmed by adjusting image margins so that each image is focused on the proper subject and does not include distracting material.

ELL

English Language Learners

English Conventions Assist students in editing spelling and grammatical errors. Discuss how to correct each error and the reason for the change. Use the appropriate lessons in the *ELL Handbook* to support teaching English conventions.

Objectives

- Use a design program to lay out articles for the classroom profile.
- Publish the classroom profile for family and friends.

5 PUBLISH Publish and Present

Options for Presenting

Offer students two options for presenting their work:

Print out a hard copy of the classroom profile to take home to their families and to display in the classroom.	Convert the file to Portable Document Format (PDF) and make it available for download on a class or school Web site or educational file-sharing site.

Laying out the profile

Now that we have written and revised our articles about our class, it is time to put them together to create our Classroom Profile. We will use a design program to put the articles and pictures into a format that our audience will find interesting.

Help students decide which articles and topics should be on the front page, in the middle, and on the last page. Have students choose which articles should be grouped together. Encourage them to consider the size and color of images and the length of articles as well as the topics.

Give each student an opportunity to use a design application to lay out the articles and images. Assist students in resizing photographs and in flowing text into multiple columns, as needed. Help students combine their pages into one complete document. Print a final copy on a color printer to display in the classroom.

Customize Literacy in Your Classroom

Table of Contents
for Customize Literacy

Customize Literacy is organized into different sections, each one designed to help you organize and carry out an effective literacy program. Each section contains strategies and support for teaching comprehension skills and strategies. *Customize Literacy* also shows how to use weekly text sets of readers in your literacy program.

Weekly Text Sets
to Customize Literacy

The following readers can be used to enhance your literacy instruction.

	Decodable Readers	Concept Literacy Reader	Below-Level Reader	On-Level Reader	Advanced Reader	ELD Reader	ELL Reader
Unit 4 WEEK 1	*A Party for the Geese; Camping!; Sheep Stampede*	*What Can Athletes Do?*	*The Winning Point*	*A Trip*	*Extraordinary Athletes*	*My Good Friend*	*My Good Friend*
Unit 4 WEEK 2	*Whirling Girl; Mom's Purse; Thursday's Roaring Storm*	*Extremes*	*How to Measure the Weather*	*Measuring the Earth*	*Largest, Fastest, Lightest, Longest*	*How Big? How Strong?*	*How Big? How Strong?*
Unit 4 WEEK 3	*Midsummer Fun; A Midsummer Visit; Spelling Bee*	*I Collect Rocks*	*Grandpa's Rock Kit*	*Fun with Hobbies and Science!*	*Gemstones Around the World*	*What Careers Interest You?*	*What Careers Interest You?*

Customize Literacy in Your Classroom

Customize Instruction
to Improve Reading Behaviors

Instruction in comprehension skills and strategies provides readers with avenues to understanding a text. Through teacher modeling and guided, collaborative, and independent practice, students become independent thinkers who employ a variety of skills and strategies to help them make meaning as they read.

Mini-Lessons for Comprehension Skills and Strategies

Unit 1	Literary Elements, Sequence, Compare and Contrast, Author's Purpose, Background Knowledge, Summarize, Story Structure
Unit 2	Main Ideas and Details, Compare and Contrast, Draw Conclusions, Author's Purpose, Monitor and Clarify, Predict and Set Purpose
Unit 3	Draw Conclusions, Literary Elements, Graphic Sources, Generalize, Cause and Effect, Important Ideas, Text Structure
Unit 4	Generalize, Graphic Sources, Fact and Opinion, Cause and Effect, Inferring, Questioning
Unit 5	Draw Conclusions, Main Ideas and Details, Sequence, Compare and Contrast, Author's Purpose, Visualize, Summarize
Unit 6	Fact and Opinion, Cause and Effect, Graphic Sources, Literary Elements, Generalize, Questioning, Inferring

Envision It! A Comprehension Handbook

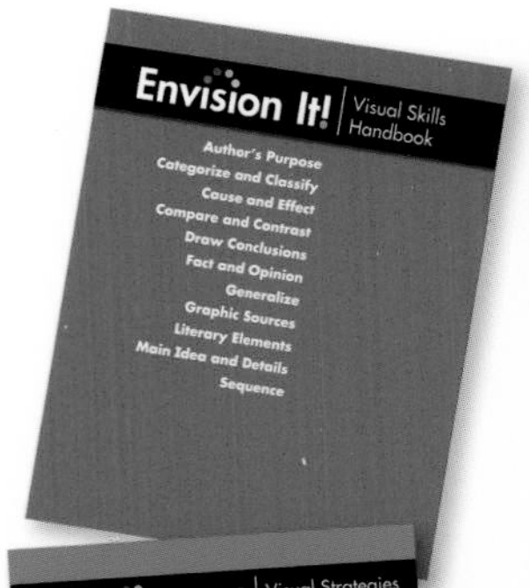

Envision It! Visual Skills Handbook
Author's Purpose
Categorize and Classify
Cause and Effect
Compare and Contrast
Draw Conclusions
Fact and Opinion
Generalize
Graphic Sources
Literary Elements
Main Idea and Details
Sequence

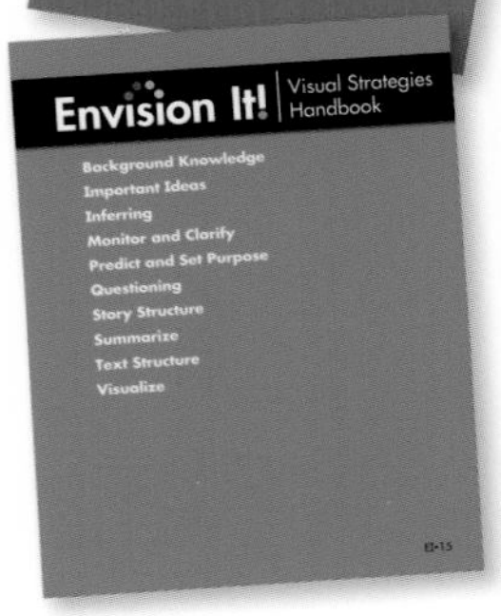

Anchor Chart Anchor charts are provided with each strategy lesson. These charts incorporate the language of strategic thinkers. They help students make their thinking visible and permanent and provide students with a means to clarify their thinking about how and when to use each strategy. As students gain more experience with a strategy, the chart may undergo revision.

See pages 107–134 in the *First Stop on Reading Street* Teacher's Edition for additional support as you customize literacy in your classroom.

Good Readers DRA2 users will find additional resources in the *First Stop on Reading Street* Teacher's Edition on pages 110–112.

Contents

Customize Literacy

Pacing Guide

This chart shows the instructional sequence from *Scott Foresman Reading Street* for Grade 3. You can use this pacing guide as is to ensure you are following a comprehensive scope and sequence. Or, you can adjust the sequence to match your calendar, curriculum map, or testing schedule.

Grade 3

READING	UNIT 1 Week 1	UNIT 1 Week 2	UNIT 1 Week 3	UNIT 1 Week 4	UNIT 1 Week 5	REVIEW WEEK	UNIT 2 Week 1	UNIT 2 Week 2
Comprehension Skill	Character, Setting, and Theme	Sequence	Sequence	Compare and Contrast	Author's Purpose		Main Idea and Details	Compare and Contrast
Comprehension Strategy	Background Knowledge	Summarize	Visualize	Background Knowledge	Story Structure		Monitor and Clarify	Visualize
Vocabulary Strategy/Skill	Context Clues/ Homonyms	Word Structure/ Compound Words	Dictionary/ Glossary/ Unknown Words	Context Clues/ Multiple-Meaning Words	Word Structure/ Prefixes and Suffixes		Context Clues/ Synonyms	Context Clues/ Unfamiliar Words
Fluency	Accuracy	Rate	Expression	Accuracy	Appropriate Phrasing		Accuracy	Expression
Phonics and Spelling	Short Vowels; Syllables VC/CV	Plurals *-s, -es, -ies*	Base Words and Endings	Vowel Digraphs	Vowel Diphthongs		Syllables V/CV, VC/V	Final Syllable *-le*

	UNIT 4 Week 1	UNIT 4 Week 2	UNIT 4 Week 3	UNIT 4 Week 4	UNIT 4 Week 5	REVIEW WEEK	UNIT 5 Week 1	UNIT 5 Week 2
Comprehension Skill	Generalize	Graphic Sources	Fact and Opinion	Fact and Opinion	Cause and Effect		Compare and Contrast	Main Idea and Details
Comprehension Strategy	Summarize	Important Ideas	Inferring	Questioning	Monitor and Clarify		Visualize	Inferring
Vocabulary Strategy/Skill	Context Clues/ Unfamiliar Words	Dictionary/ Glossary/ Unknown Words	Context Clues/ Multiple-Meaning Words	Context Clues/ Multiple-Meaning Words	Dictionary/ Glossary/ Unknown Words		Context Clues/ Synonyms	Context Clues/ Homophones
Fluency	Accuracy	Appropriate Phrasing	Expression	Appropriate Phrasing	Rate		Rate	Accuracy
Phonics and Spelling	Irregular Plurals	Vowels; *r*-Controlled	Prefixes	Suffixes *-er, -or, -ess, -ist*	Syllable Pattern VCCCV		Syllable Pattern CV/VC	Homophones

"Are you the adventurous type? Want to use some of your own ideas and materials in your teaching? But you worry you might be leaving out some critical instruction kids need? **Customize Literacy** can help."

Week 3	Week 4	Week 5 (REVIEW WEEK)
Draw Conclusions	Author's Purpose	Main Idea and Details
Questioning	Predict and Set Purpose	Text Structure
Word Structure/ Compound Words	Context Clues/ Antonyms	Context Clues/ Unfamiliar Words
Rate	Appropriate Phrasing	Rate
Compound Words	Consonant Blends *spl, thr, squ, str, scr*	Consonant Digraphs

UNIT 3

Week 1	Week 2	Week 3	Week 4	Week 5 (REVIEW WEEK)
Draw Conclusions	Character, Setting, Plot	Graphic Sources	Generalize	Cause and Effect
Important Ideas	Inferring	Text Structure	Story Structure	Predict and Set Purpose
Context Clues/ Homophones	Dictionary/ Glossary/ Unknown Words	Dictionary/ Glossary/ Unknown Words	Context Clues/ Unfamiliar Words	Word Structure/ Prefixes and Suffixes
Expression	Accuracy	Appropriate Phrasing	Rate	Expression
Contractions	Prefixes	Consonant Sounds /j/, /s/ and /k/	Suffixes *-ly, -ful, -ness, -less, -able, -ible*	Consonant Patterns *wr, kn, mb, gn, st*

Week 3	Week 4	Week 5 (REVIEW WEEK)
Sequence	Draw Conclusions	Author's Purpose
Monitor and Clarify	Summarize	Background Knowledge
Word Structure/ Compound Words	Context Clues/ Unfamiliar Words	Context Clues/ Homonyms
Expression and Punctuation Cues	Accuracy	Appropriate Phrasing
Vowel Patterns for /ô/	Vowel patterns *ei, eigh*	Suffixes *-y, -ish, -hood, -ment*

UNIT 6

Week 1	Week 2	Week 3	Week 4	Week 5 (REVIEW WEEK)
Fact and Opinion	Cause and Effect	Graphic Sources	Plot and Theme	Generalize
Questioning	Inferring	Important Ideas	Story Structure	Inferring
Word Structure/ Prefix *un-*	Context Clues/ Antonyms	Dictionary/ Glossary/ Unknown Words	Word Structure/ Prefixes and Suffixes	Context Clues/ Homographs
Rate	Appropriate Phrasing	Accuracy	Rate	Expression
Vowel Sounds /ü/ and /ů/	Schwa	Final Syllables	Prefixes; Prefixes, Suffixes, Endings	Related Words

Pacing Guide

Grade 3

LANGUAGE ARTS	UNIT 1 Week 1	Week 2	Week 3	Week 4	Week 5	REVIEW WEEK	UNIT 2 Week 1	Week 2
Speaking and Listening	News Report	Description	Tell a Story	Panel Discussion	Book Report		Speech	Persuasive Speech
Grammar	Sentences	Subjects and Predicates	Types of Sentences	Types of Sentences	Compound Sentences		Common and Proper Nouns	Singular and Plural Nouns
Weekly Writing	Narrative Poem	Fable	Thank-You Note	Description	Realistic Fiction		Poem	Fairy Tale
Trait of the Week	Word Choice	Conventions	Organization	Voice	Sentences		Word Choice	Word Choice
Writing	E-Pen Pals/Personal Narrative							

	UNIT 4 Week 1	Week 2	Week 3	Week 4	Week 5	REVIEW WEEK	UNIT 5 Week 1	Week 2
Speaking and Listening	Presentation	Weather Forecast	Interview	Sportscast	Book Review		Introduction	Drama
Grammar	Singular and Plural Pronouns	Subject and Object Pronouns	Possessive Pronouns	Contractions	Prepositions		Adjectives and Articles	Adjectives That Compare
Weekly Writing	Persuasive Text	Story	Biography	Autobiography	Summary		Letter to the Editor	Personal Narrative
Trait of the Week	Conventions	Conventions	Sentences	Organization	Word Choice		Organization	Conventions
Writing	Classroom Profile/Problem-Solution Essay							

REVIEW WEEK

Week 3	Week 4	Week 5
Presentation	Interview	Description
Irregular Plural Nouns	Singular Possessive Nouns	Plural Possessive Nouns
Persuasive Ad	Friendly Letter	Directions
Focus/Ideas	Conventions	Organization

Story Exchange/How-to Report

UNIT 3 — REVIEW WEEK

Week 1	Week 2	Week 3	Week 4	Week 5
Commercial	Drama	Voicemail	Description	Oral Report
Action and Linking Verbs	Main and Helping Verbs	Subject-Verb Agreement	Past, Present, and Future Tense	Irregular Verbs
Fiction	Drama: Play	Formal Letter	News Article	Compare/ Contrast Composition
Voice	Sentences	Conventions	Sentences	Focus/Ideas

Photo Writing/Cause-and-Effect Essay

REVIEW WEEK

Week 3	Week 4	Week 5
Song or Poem	Radio Ad	Retelling
Adverbs	Adverbs That Compare	Conjunctions
Poem	Invitation	Book Review
Word Choice	Focus/Ideas	Conventions

E-Newsletter/Persuasive Essay

UNIT 6 — REVIEW WEEK

Week 1	Week 2	Week 3	Week 4	Week 5
Announcement	Express an Opinion	Talk Show	Description	Song
Capital Letters	Abbreviations	Combining Sentences	Commas	Quotations and Parentheses
Notes	Poem	Description	Comic Book	Historical Fiction
Focus/Ideas	Organization	Word Choice	Conventions	Word Choice

Discussion Forum/Research Report

Teaching Record Chart

This chart shows the critical comprehension skills and strategies you need to cover. Check off each one as you provide instruction.

Reading/Comprehension	DATES OF INSTRUCTION		
Use ideas (e.g., illustrations, titles, topic sentences, key words, and foreshadowing clues) to make and confirm predictions.			
Ask relevant questions, seek clarification, and locate facts and details about stories and other text and support answers with evidence from text.			
Establish purpose for reading selected texts and monitor comprehension, making corrections and adjustments when that understanding breaks down (e.g., identifying clues, using background knowledge, generating questions, re-reading a portion aloud).			
Paraphrase the themes and supporting details of fables, legends, myths, or stories.			
Compare and contrast the settings in myths and traditional folktales.			
Describe the characteristics of various forms of poetry and how they create imagery (e.g., narrative poetry, lyrical poetry, humorous poetry, free verse).			
Explain the elements of plot and character as presented through dialogue in scripts that are read, viewed, written, or performed.			
Sequence and summarize the plot's main events and explain their influence on future events.			
Describe the interactions of characters including their relationships and the changes they undergo.			
Identify whether the narrator or speaker of a story is first or third person.			

"Tired of using slips of paper or stickies to make sure you teach everything you need to? Need an easier way to keep track of what you have taught, and what you still need to cover? **Customize Literacy** can help."

Reading/Comprehension	DATES OF INSTRUCTION		
Explain the difference in point of view between a biography and an autobiography.			
Identify language that creates a graphic visual experience and appeals to the senses.			
Read independently for a sustained period of time and paraphrase what the reading was about, maintaining meaning and logical order (e.g., generate a reading log or journal; participate in book talks).			
Identify the topic and locate the author's stated purposes in writing the text.			
Identify the details or facts that support the main idea.			
Draw conclusions from the facts presented in text and support those assertions with textual evidence.			
Identify explicit cause and effect relationships among ideas in texts.			
Use text features (e.g., bold print, captions, key words, italics) to locate information and make and verify predictions about contents of text.			
Identify what the author is trying to persuade the reader to think or do.			
Follow and explain a set of written multi-step directions.			
Locate and use specific information in graphic features of text.			
Establish purposes for reading selected texts based upon own or others' desired outcome to enhance comprehension.			
Ask literal, interpretive, and evaluative questions of a text.			
Monitor and adjust comprehension using a variety of strategies.			
Make inferences about a text and use evidence from the text to support understanding.			
Summarize information in a text, maintaining meaning and logical order.			
Make connections between literary and informational texts with similar ideas and provide evidence from the text.			

Envision It! Visual Skills Handbook
Generalize
All birds have wings.
A statement that is true for many examples is a generalization.
EI•8

Student Edition p. EI•8

Objectives:

- Students identify broad statements, supporting facts, and clue words such as *all, none, most, many.*
- Students make broad statements.
- Students support their broad statements using facts from the text and their own experiences.

Generalize

What is it? A **generalization** is a specific kind of conclusion. It is a broad statement or rule that applies to many examples. Clue words can signal generalizations made by authors. Students make generalizations using prior knowledge and information from the text. At Grade 3, students make generalizations based on their reading and their own experiences. They understand the concept, but do not use the term *generalization*.

How Good Readers Use the Skill Students generalize to help them comprehend and summarize texts. They need to understand generalizations to identify and evaluate an author's generalizations and to make and support their own conclusions. Generalizations need to be supported by facts and logic. Students begin making generalizations by recognizing similarities and differences about ideas, authors, or genres. Students then make judgments on the validity of generalizations. They learn that faulty generalizations may indicate bias.

Texts for Teaching

Student Edition

- *A Symphony of Whales,* 3.1, pages 476–494
- *The Man Who Invented Basketball: James Naismith and His Amazing Game,* 3.2, pages 28–41
- *Atlantis: The Legend of a Lost City,* 3.2, pages 502–519

Leveled Readers

- See pages 24–29 for a list of Leveled Readers.

Mini-Lesson 1

Teach the Skill

Use the Envision It! lesson on page EI•8 to visually review generalize.

Remind students that:

- a **broad statement** can apply to many examples that are alike or almost alike.
- **clue words** such as *all, none, most,* or *many* may appear in broad statements.

Practice

Write the following sentences.

All animals that have feathers are birds.

I saw a cardinal.

Most robins are red and brown.

Circle the clue words *all* and *most*. Discuss how these words help determine that the sentences are broad statements. Help students understand that the second sentence applies to only one person and is not a broad statement.

If... students have difficulty identifying the broad statement, **then...** provide additional example sentences and ask: *Does this statement apply to many examples, or just one or two?*

Apply

As students read the assigned text, have them look for clue words that signal broad statements.

Writing

Students can write a broad statement using this stem: *all playgrounds* __________.

Mini-Lesson 2

Teach the Skill

Use the Envision It! lesson on page EI•8 to visually review generalize.

Remind students that:
- a **broad statement** can apply to many examples that are alike or almost alike.
- **clue words** such as *usually, all, none, most,* or *many* may appear in broad statements.

Practice

Read aloud the following and have students listen for the broad statements.

Tornadoes and hurricanes are different kinds of weather that cause destruction. Tornadoes are funnel clouds that travel on the ground. Most tornadoes occur in the United States. Hurricanes begin over water. They create powerful waves, wind, and rains. They can create tornadoes! Most hurricanes form in tropical regions. There are usually more tornadoes than hurricanes in the United States each year.

Have students identify the clue words that they used to determine the broad statements.

If... students have difficulty identifying the broad statements, **then...** have students find clue words and use them to answer which sentence applies to many examples instead of just a few.

Apply

As students read the assigned text, have them look for clue words that signal broad statements.

Writing

Students can write a broad statement about their experiences using clue words.

Mini-Lesson 3

Teach the Skill

Use the Envision It! lesson on page EI•8 to visually review generalize.

Remind students that:
- a **broad statement** can apply to many examples that are alike or almost alike.
- **clue words** such as *all, none, most,* or *many* may appear in broad statements.
- broad statements should be supported by facts from the text or personal experience.
- broad statements can identify an author's ideas.

Practice

Give students two short familiar texts from the same genre, for example two fables. Identify similarities and differences between the texts. Use that information to make a broad statement about the two texts. For example, all fables teach lessons. Encourage students to use their prior knowledge as well. Use clue words in the statement to make it clear that it applies to both texts.

If... students have difficulty making generalizations, **then...** provide a group of related actions and model how to make a broad statement based on similar characteristics.

Apply

As students read the assigned text, have them note details that will help them write a broad statement.

Writing

Students can list facts about a topic, such as animals, and then complete the statement: *All* __________ *have* __________.

Objectives:

- Students interpret information in simple graphics.
- Students use graphics as a prereading tool.

Graphic Sources

Student Edition pp. EI•10–EI•11

What is it? **Graphics sources,** including charts, maps, diagrams, graphs, and timelines, provide information visually using few words, symbols, and/or numbers. Graphic sources accompany science, math, and social studies texts, as well as some fiction. At Grade 3, students use graphics to preview; they put information from reading or research into simple graphic forms.

How Good Readers Use the Skill Students see different kinds of graphics—maps, charts, diagrams, and so on—in many situations. In their reading, graphics provide lots of information in a visual way. Students first use graphics such as maps and diagrams to preview and make predictions about what a text will be about. They then understand that graphic sources aid in their comprehension of text. Students also learn to create graphics from their reading. Older readers interpret and create more sophisticated graphic aids, matching them to text. They learn to compare and evaluate how well different graphic sources communicate and synthesize information.

Texts for Teaching

Student Edition

- *Seeing Stars,* 3.1, pages 446–457
- *Hottest, Coldest, Highest, Deepest,* 3.2, pages 62–75
- *Talking Walls: Art for the People,* 3.2, pages 438–451

Leveled Readers

- See pages 24–29 for a list of Leveled Readers.

Mini-Lesson 1

Teach the Skill

Use the Envision It! lesson on pages EI•10–EI•11 to visually review graphic sources.

Remind students that:

- **graphic sources** show information visually.
- **graphic sources** include maps, charts, diagrams, pictures with captions, and graphs.

Practice

Preview a text that has graphics, pausing at each one. Model reading the title and all other words on the graphic. Decide what any symbols stand for. Ask: What kind of information does this give us? Why do you think the author included a graphic instead of describing it using words? Point out that a graphic can help readers get a lot of information quickly, for example, a map can show the route across a big area. Bar and line graphs can let readers compare information. Diagrams help readers visualize a complex process, such as the water cycle.

If... students have difficulty reading a graphic source, **then...** have them put what the graphic shows in their own words.

Apply

As students read, have them match each graphic with the text it goes with.

Writing

Students can make a mini-glossary of graphic sources, defining each one and including a sketch of it.

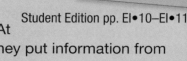

Mini-Lesson 2

Teach the Skill

Use the Envision It! lesson on pages EI•10–EI•11 to visually review graphic sources with students.

Remind students that:

- **graphic sources** show information visually.
- **graphic sources** include maps, charts, diagrams, pictures with captions, and graphs.

Practice

Provide a few selections, fiction and informational, that include graphics. Include a map, photos with captions, and a chart or graph. Show the selections to students and have them make predictions about what the selection will be about. Be sure students can name each graphic and explain what it shows. To help them, ask questions: What kind of graphics are included? What kind of information do they provide? Would you expect this graphic to tell more about a story? Or would you expect it to tell more about a topic? After students preview and make predictions, read portions of the article aloud to check their predictions.

If... students have difficulty predicting from graphics,
then... read the part of the text that the graphic explains or illustrates to help them see a connection.

Apply

As students read the assigned text, have them pay attention to the graphics and think about why the author included them.

Writing

Students can draw and label a simple map of the classroom or school.

Mini-Lesson 3

Teach the Skill

Use the Envision It! lesson on pages EI•10–EI•11 to visually review graphic sources with students.

Remind students that:

- **graphic sources** show information visually.
- **graphic sources** include maps, charts, diagrams, pictures with captions, and graphs.
- writers add graphics to illustrate their writing or tell more about their topic.

Practice

Provide a passage or two from a selection that students have read with the graphics removed. Or let students choose a piece of their own writing. Tell them to add two graphics to the passage. They can add a picture with a caption and one other graphic, such as a map, a chart, a diagram, and so on. These graphics should have a title and a few words tell what the graphic shows. Encourage students to add graphics that either tell more about the selection or illustrate some aspect of it. Let volunteers explain their graphics and tell why they included them with the passage.

If... students have difficulty matching a graphic source with text,
then... give them a choice of two, one that fits much better than the other, and have the student choose.

Apply

As students read the assigned text, have them pay attention to the graphics and think about why the author used them.

Writing

Students can cut out pictures from magazines and write captions for them.

Fact and Opinion

Student Edition p. EI•7

Objectives:

- Students define fact and opinion.
- Students use clue words to identify statements as fact or opinion.
- Students name ways to check statements of fact.

What is it? A **statement of fact** tells something that can be proved true or false. A **statement of opinion** tells a person's ideas or feelings and cannot be proved true or false. At Grade 3, students are identifying statements of fact and opinion and are naming ways to check statements of fact.

How Good Readers Use the Skill Students meet statements of facts and opinions throughout their day. We want to teach them how to distinguish the two and understand ways to check the veracity of factual statements and be able to judge statements of opinion thoughtfully. Evaluating statements of fact and statements of opinion boosts students' comprehension and helps them avoid being misled.

Texts for Teaching

Student Edition

- *Rocks in His Head,* 3.2, pages 94–104
- *America's Champion Swimmer: Gertrude Ederle,* 3.2, pages 124–139
- *The Story of the Statue of Liberty,* 3.2, pages 374–385

Leveled Readers

- See pages 24–29 for a list of Leveled Readers.

Mini-Lesson 1

Teach the Skill

Use the Envision It! lesson on page EI•7 to visually review fact and opinion with students.

Remind students that:

- a statement of **fact** tells something that can be proved true or false.
- a statement of **opinion** tells a person's ideas or feelings and cannot be proved true or false.

Practice

Write the following on the board and read them with students.

The Story of Ferdinand was written by Munro Leaf.
Everybody should read *The Story of Ferdinand.*
The Story of Ferdinand was first published in 1936.

Ask: Which statements are fact? How can you tell? Which is a statement of opinion?

Talk with students about how the facts (statements 1 and 3) could be proved to be true. (They could look at an actual book or they could check the internet or ask a librarian.) Point out the word *should* and explain that opinions often contain judgment words such as *should, I think,* and *best.*

If... students have difficulty distinguishing statements of fact, **then...** ask: *Could you check this information out? How?*

Apply

As students read, have them be alert for statements of fact and opinion.

Writing

Students can write a sentence with a statement of fact and one with a statement of opinion.

Mini-Lesson 2

Teach the Skill

Use the Envision It! lesson on page EI•7 to visually review fact and opinion with students.

Remind students that:

- a statement of **fact** tells something that can be proved true or false.
- a statement of **opinion** tells a person's ideas or feelings and cannot be proved true or false.
- Clue words and phrases such as *I think, I believe, cute, best,* and so on can signal an opinion.

Practice

Give students a familiar nonfiction selection and have partners read it together to identify statements of fact and opinion. Have them complete a chart, listing the statements they identify. Help students suggest how statements of fact can be checked.

Statement	Fact?	Opinion?
Mount Rushmore has the faces of four Presidents.	Yes. We could look in an encyclopedia.	

If... students have difficulty distinguishing opinions,
then... ask: *Can you prove this is the* [cutest] *or is that just what someone thinks?*

Apply

As students read, have them look for statements of fact and opinion.

Writing

Students can look at a photograph and write a caption that includes a statement of fact and a statement of an opinion.

Mini-Lesson 3

Teach the Skill

Use the Envision It! lesson on page EI•7 to visually review fact and opinion with students.

Remind students that:

- a statement of **fact** tells something that can be proved true or false.
- a statement of **opinion** tells a person's ideas or feelings and cannot be proved true or false. Clue words and phrases such as *best, in my opinion, I believe, I think,* and so on can signal an opinion.

Practice

Remind students that statements of opinion often have judgment words, such as *should, must,* or *best,* or phrases, such as *I think* and *in my opinion*. Let partners work together to write a paragraph that includes both statements of fact and opinion. Give pairs a topic or let them choose one of their own. Have students complete a chart like the one for Mini-Lesson 2 to show their facts and opinions. Then have students share their paragraphs.
If... students have difficulty writing statements of fact and opinion,
then... give them a topic and sentence starters to complete, such as *The weather today is... I think this kind of weather is...*

Apply

As students read, have them look for statements of fact and think about how they would check them out.

Writing

Students can write a few sentences that are statements of fact and then add a statement of opinion, underlining it.

Objectives:

- Students make inferences about characters, events, and information using clues in text and their background knowledge.

Texts for Teaching

Student Edition

- *Pushing Up the Sky,* 3.1, pages 412–423
- *Rocks in His Head,* 3.2, pages 94–105
- *I Love Saturdays y domingos,* 3.2, pages 230–245
- *Happy Birthday Mr. Kang,* 3.2, pages 402–419
- *Atlantis: The Legend of a Lost City,* 3.2, pages 502–519

Leveled Readers

- See pages 24–29 for a list of Leveled Readers.

Inferring

Mini-Lesson

Envision It! Visual Strategies Handbook

Inferring

When we **infer** we use background knowledge with clues in the text to come up with our own ideas about what the author is trying to present.

To infer

- identify what you already know
- combine what you know with text clues to come up with your own ideas

Let's Think About Reading!

When I infer, I ask myself

- What do I already know?
- Which text clues are important?
- What is the author trying to present?

EI•20

Student Edition p. EI•20

Understand the Strategy

Inferring means using what the author tells you and what you already know to explain something that is not stated in the text. Readers go beyond the literal meaning of a text and put information together to make decisions about events and ideas that are not stated in the text.

Teach

Use the Envision It! lesson on page EI•20 to visually review inferring.

Remind students that making inferences is like drawing conclusions. We use our background knowledge and clues in the text to make statements about what we are reading. Explain that we use text clues to infer word meanings, how characters are feeling, what events mean, and so on. Using a familiar story, think aloud to model how to infer from text clues. Record your thoughts on a graphic organizer.

What I Already Know	Text Clues	What I Can Infer
The family grows and preserves all its own food.	Grasshoppers come and eat all the plants.	The family will have a hard time next winter.
Losing all your food is bad.	Grasshoppers eating your crops is called a plague.	A plague is a word for something very serious.

Practice

Provide a selection for students to read and practice inferring with. They should begin a chart for recording. Be sure to remind students that everyone's background is different and so they will bring different ideas and experiences to a reading.
If... students have difficulty making an inference,
then... use a picture and have students infer emotions.

Apply

Make sure students remember to use what they know when they come across something confusing or unstated.

Anchor Chart

Anchor charts help students make their thinking visible. With an anchor chart, the group can clarify their thinking about how to use a strategy. Display anchor charts so readers can refer to them as they read. Here is a sample chart for inferring.

Inferring

1. Look over the story before you read. Try to figure out what it might be about.
2. Read a little bit to see if it will be easy or hard to read.
3. Start reading. Ask yourself:
   Does this make sense?
   Do I know who the characters are?
   Do I know what is happening?
   Do I know what this is all about?
4. Sometimes the author doesn't tell you everything. When this happens, make an inference.
5. Write down what you already know. Write down some details. Try to infer.

What I Already Know	Text Clues	What I Can Infer

6. Share your ideas.
7. Be respectful of other people's ideas.

Anchor Chart

Using Multiple Strategies

Good readers use multiple strategies as they read. You can encourage students to read strategically through good classroom questioning. Use questions such as these to help students apply strategies during reading.

Answer Questions

- Who or what is this question about?
- Where can you look to find the answer to this question?

Ask Questions

- What do you want to know about ________?
- What questions to do you have about the ________ in this selection? Use the words *who, what, when, where, why,* and *how* to ask your questions.
- Do you have any questions after reading?

Graphic Organizers

- What kind of graphic organizer could you use to help you keep track of the information in this selection?

Monitor and Clarify

- Does the story or article make sense?
- What don't you understand about what you read?
- Do you need to reread, review, read on, or check a reference source?
- Do you need to read more slowly or more quickly?
- What is a ________? Where could you look to find out?

Predict/Confirm Predictions

- What do you think this story or article will be about? Why do you think as you do?
- What do you think you will learn from this selection?
- Do the text features help you predict what will happen?
- Based on what has happened so far, what do you think will happen next?
- Is this what you thought would happen?
- How does ________ change what you thought would happen?

Preview

- What do the photographs, illustrations, or graphic sources tell about the selection?
- What do you want to find out? What do you want to learn?

Background Knowledge

- What do you already know about ________?
- Have you read stories or articles by this author before?
- How is this selection like others that you have read?
- What does this remind you of?
- How does your background knowledge help you understand ________?
- Did the text match what you already knew? What new information did you learn?

Story Structure

- Who are the characters in this story? the setting?
- What is the problem in this story? How does the problem get solved?
- What is the point of this story?

Summarize

- What two or three important ideas have you read so far?
- How do the text features relate to the important ideas?
- Is there a graphic organizer that can help you organize the information before you summarize?

Text Structure

- How has the author organized the writing?
- What clues tell you that the text is structured ________?

Visualize

- When you read this, what do you picture in your mind?
- What do you hear, see, or smell?
- What do you think ________ looks like? Why do you think as you do?

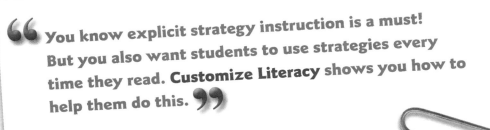

"You know explicit strategy instruction is a must! But you also want students to use strategies every time they read. **Customize Literacy** shows you how to help them do this."

Glossary of Literacy Terms

This glossary lists academic language terms that are related to literacy. They are provided for your information and professional use.

A

alliteration the repetition of a consonant sound in a group of words, especially in poetry

allusion a word or phrase that refers to something else the reader already knows from history, experience, or reading

animal fantasy a story about animals that talk and act like people

answer questions a reading strategy in which readers use the text and prior knowledge to answer questions about what they are reading

antonym a word that means the opposite of another word

ask questions a reading strategy in which readers ask themselves questions about the text to help make sense of what they read

author's point of view the author's opinion on the subject he or she is writing about

author's purpose the reason the author wrote the text

autobiography the story of a real person's life written by that person

B

background knowledge the information and experience that a reader brings to a text

biography the story of a real person's life written by another person

C

cause why something happens

character a person, an animal, or a personified object in a story

chronological order events in a selection, presented in the order in which they occurred

classify and categorize put things, such as pictures or words, into groups

climax the point in a story at which conflict is confronted

compare tell how things are the same

comprehension understanding of text being read—the ultimate goal of reading

comprehension strategy a conscious plan used by a reader to gain understanding of text. Comprehension strategies may be used before, during, or after reading.

conclusion a decision or opinion arrived at after thinking about facts and details and using prior knowledge

conflict the problem or struggle in a story

context clue the words, phrases, or sentences near an unknown word that give the reader clues to the word's meaning

contrast tell how things are different

D

details small pieces of information

dialect form of a language spoken in a certain region or by a certain group of people that differs from the standard form of that language

dialogue written conversation

diary a day-to-day record of one's activities and thoughts

draw conclusions arrive at decisions or opinions after thinking about facts and details and using prior knowledge

E

effect what happens as the result of a cause

etymology an explanation of the origin and history of a word and its meaning

exaggeration a statement that makes something seem larger or greater than it actually is

expository text text that contains facts and information. Also called *informational text.*

F

fable a story, usually with animal characters, that is written to teach a moral, or lesson

fact piece of information that can be proved to be true

fairy tale a folk story with magical characters and events

fantasy a story that could not really happen

fiction writing that tells about imaginary people, things, and events

figurative language the use of language that gives words a meaning beyond their usual definitions in order to add beauty or force

flashback an interruption in the sequence of events of a narrative to include an event that happened earlier

folk tale a story that has been passed down by word of mouth

foreshadowing the use of hints or clues about what will happen later in a story

G

generalize make a broad statement or rule after examining particular facts

graphic organizer a drawing, chart, or web that illustrates concepts or shows how ideas relate to each other. Readers use graphic organizers to help them keep track of and understand important information and ideas as they read. Story maps, word webs, Venn diagrams, and KWL charts are graphic organizers.

graphic source a chart, diagram, or map within a text that adds to readers' understanding of the text

H

historical fiction realistic fiction that takes place in the past. It is an imaginary story based on historical events and characters.

humor writing or speech that has a funny or amusing quality

hyperbole an exaggerated statement not meant to be taken literally, such as *I'm so hungry I could eat a horse.*

I

idiom a phrase whose meaning differs from the ordinary meaning of the words. *A stone's throw* is an idiom meaning "a short distance."

imagery the use of language to create beautiful or forceful pictures in the reader's mind

inference conclusion reached on the basis of evidence and reasoning

inform give knowledge, facts, or news to someone

informational text writing that contains facts and information. Also called *expository text*.

interview a face-to-face conversation in which someone responds to questions

irony a way of speaking or writing in which the ordinary meaning of the words is the opposite of what the speaker or writer is thinking; a contrast between what is expected and what actually happens

J

jargon the language of a special group or profession

L

legend a story coming down from the past about the great deeds of a hero. Although a legend may be based on historical people and events, it is not regarded as historically true.

literary elements the characters, setting, plot, and theme of a narrative text

M

main idea the big idea that tells what a paragraph or a selection is mainly about; the most important idea of a text

metacognition an awareness of one's own thinking processes and the ability to monitor and direct them to a desired goal. Good readers use metacognition to monitor their reading and adjust their reading strategies.

metaphor a comparison that does not use *like* or *as*, such as *a heart of stone*

meter the pattern of beats or accents in poetry

monitor and clarify a comprehension strategy by which readers actively think about understanding their reading and know when they understand and when they do not. Readers use appropriate strategies to make sense of difficult words, ideas, or passages.

mood the atmosphere or feeling of a written work

moral the lesson or teaching of a fable or story

motive the reason a character in a narrative does or says something

mystery a story about mysterious events that are not explained until the end, so as to keep the reader in suspense

myth a story that attempts to explain something in nature

M

narrative a story, made up or true, that someone tells or narrates

narrator the character in a selection who tells the story

nonfiction writing that tells about real things, real people, and real events

N

onomatopoeia the use of words that sound like their meanings, such as *buzz* and *hum*

opinion someone's judgment, belief, or way of thinking

oral vocabulary the words needed for speaking and listening

outcome the resolution of the conflict in a story

O

paraphrase retell the meaning of a passage in one's own words

personification a figure of speech in which human traits or actions are given to animals or inanimate objects, as in *The sunbeam danced on the waves.*

persuade convince someone to do or to believe something

photo essay a collection of photographs on one theme, accompanied by text

play a story that is written to be acted out for an audience

plot a series of related events at the beginning, middle, and end of a story; the action of a story

poem an expressive, imaginative piece of writing often arranged in lines having rhythm and rhyme. In a poem, the patterns made by the sounds of the words have special importance.

pourquoi tale a type of folk story that explains why things in nature came to be. *Pourquoi* is a French word meaning "why."

P

P

predict tell what a selection might be about or what might happen in a text. Readers use text features and information to predict. They confirm or revise their predictions as they read.

preview look over a text before reading it

prior knowledge the information and experience that a reader brings to a text. Readers use prior knowledge to help them understand what they read.

prop an item, such as an object, picture, or chart, used in a performance or presentation

R

reading vocabulary the words we recognize or use in print

realistic fiction a story about imaginary people and events that could happen in real life

repetition the repeated use of some aspect of language

resolution the point in a story where the conflict is resolved

rhyme to end in the same sound(s)

rhythm a pattern of strong beats in speech or writing, especially poetry

rising action the buildup of conflicts and complications in a story

S

science fiction a story based on science that often tells what life in the future might be like

semantic map a graphic organizer, often a web, used to display words or concepts that are meaningfully related

sensory language the use of words that help the reader understand how things look, sound, smell, taste, or feel

sequence the order of events in a selection or the order of the steps in which something is completed

sequence words clue words such as *first*, *next*, *then*, and *finally* that signal the order of events in a selection

setting where and when a story takes place

simile a comparison that uses *like* or *as*, as in *as busy as a bee*

speech a public talk to a group of people made for a specific purpose

stanza a group of lines in a poem

steps in a process the order of the steps in which something is completed

story map a graphic organizer used to record the literary elements and the sequence of events in a narrative text

story structure how the characters, setting, and events of a story are organized into a plot

summarize give the most important ideas of what was read. Readers summarize important information in the selection to keep track of what they are reading.

supporting detail piece of information that tells about the main idea

symbolism the use of one thing to suggest something else; often the use of something concrete to stand for an abstract idea

S

tall tale a humorous story that uses exaggeration to describe impossible happenings

text structure the organization of a piece of nonfiction writing. Text structures of informational text include cause-effect, chronological, compare/contrast, description, problem/solution, proposition/support, and ask/answer questions.

theme the big idea or author's message in a story

think aloud an instructional strategy in which a teacher verbalizes his or her thinking to model the process of comprehension or the application of a skill

tone author's attitude toward the subject or toward the reader

topic the subject of a discussion, conversation, or piece of text

T

visualize picture in one's mind what is happening in the text. Visualizing helps readers imagine the things they read about.

V

Leveled Readers Skills Chart

Scott Foresman Reading Street provides more than six hundred leveled readers. Each one is designed to:

- Practice critical skills and strategies
- Build fluency
- Build vocabulary and concepts
- Develop a lifelong love of reading

Grade 3

Title	Level*	DRA Level	Genre	Comprehension Strategy
The Opposite Cousins	F	10	Realistic Fiction	Background Knowledge
It's a Fair Swap!	F	10	Expository Nonfiction	Summarize
Life in the Arctic	F	10	Nonfiction	Visualize
Let's Surprise Mom	F	10	Realistic Fiction	Background Knowledge
E-mail Friends	F	10	Realistic Fiction	Story Structure
The Frozen Continent: Antarctica	F	10	Expository Nonfiction	Monitor and Clarify
Buddy Goes to School	G	12	Realistic Fiction	Visualize
The Metal Detective	G	12	Realistic Fiction	Questioning
Growing Vegetables	G	12	Narrative Nonfiction	Predict and Set Purpose
All About Birds	G	12	Nonfiction	Text Structure
Raisins	G	12	Nonfiction	Important Ideas
The Hunters and the Elk	G	12	Fiction	Inferring
Pictures in the Sky	H	14	Expository Nonfiction	Text Structure
Rescuing Whales	H	14	Expository Nonfiction	Story Structure
The Field Trip	H	14	Expository Nonfiction	Predict and Set Purpose
The Winning Point	H	14	Realistic Fiction	Summarize
How to Measure the Weather	H	14	Expository Nonfiction	Important Ideas
Grandpa's Rock Kit	H	14	Narrative Nonfiction	Inferring
Across the English Channel	H	14	Expository Nonfiction	Questioning
Swimming Like Buck	I	16	Animal Fantasy	Monitor and Clarify
A Tea Party with Obâchan	I	16	Realistic Fiction	Visualize
Independence Day/El Día de la Independencia	I	16	Nonfiction	Inferring
A Child's Life in Korea	I	16	Expository Nonfiction	Monitor and Clarify
The World of Bread!	I	16	Expository Nonfiction	Summarize
A Walk Around the City	I	16	Expository Nonfiction	Background Knowledge
The Statue of Liberty: A Gift From France	I	16	Expository Nonfiction	Questioning
Camping with Aunt Julie	J	18	Realistic Fiction	Background Knowledge
Let's Make a Trade!	J	18	Expository Nonfiction	Summarize
Ice Fishing in the Arctic	J	18	Nonfiction	Visualize
The Shopping Trip	J	18	Fiction	Background Knowledge

* Suggested Guided Reading Level. Use your knowledge of students' abilities to adjust levels as needed.

The chart here and on the next few pages lists titles of leveled readers appropriate for students in Grade 3. Use the chart to find titles that meet your students' interest and instructional needs. The books in this list were leveled using the criteria suggested in *Matching Books to Readers* and *Leveled Books for Readers, Grades 3–6* by Irene C. Fountas and Gay Su Pinnell. For more on leveling, see the *Reading Street Leveled Readers Leveling Guide.*

Target Comprehension Skill	Additional Comprehension Instruction	Vocabulary
Character, Setting, and Theme	Draw Conclusions	Context Clues/Homonyms
Sequence	Fact and Opinion	Word Structure/Compound Words
Sequence	Generalize	Dictionary/Glossary/Unfamiliar Words
Compare and Contrast	Main Idea	Context Clues/Multiple Meanings
Author's Purpose	Compare and Contrast	Word Structure/Prefixes and Suffixes
Main Idea and Details	Generalize	Context Clues/Synonyms
Compare and Contrast	Sequence	Context Clues/Unfamiliar Words
Draw Conclusions	Realism and Fantasy	Compound Words/Word Structure
Author's Purpose	Generalize	Context Clues/Antonyms
Main Idea and Details	Compare and Contrast	Context Clues/Unfamiliar Words
Draw Conclusions	Generalize	Homophones/Context Clues
Character, Setting, and Plot	Theme	Unknown Words/Dictionary/Glossary
Graphic Sources	Author's Purpose	Unknown Words/Dictionary/Glossary
Generalize	Sequence	Context Clues/Unfamiliar Words
Cause and Effect	Draw Conclusions	Prefixes/Suffixes/Word Structure
Generalize	Plot	Unfamiliar Words/Context Clues
Graphic Sources	Main Idea	Unknown Words/Dictionary/Glossary
Fact and Opinion	Fact and Opinion	Context Clues/Multiple Meanings
Fact and Opinion	Generalize	Context Clues/Multiple Meanings
Cause and Effect	Character	Unknown Words/Dictionary/Glossary
Compare and Contrast	Generalize	Context Clues/Synonyms
Main Idea and Details	Draw Conclusions	Context Clues/Antonyms
Sequence	Author's Purpose	Word Structure/Compound Words
Draw Conclusions	Main Idea	Context Clues/Unfamiliar Words
Author's Purpose	Generalize	Context Clues/Homonyms
Fact and Opinion	Fact and Opinion	Word Structure/Prefixes
Character and Setting	Theme	Context Clues/Homonyms
Sequence	Draw Conclusions	Word Structure/Compound Words
Sequence	Author's Purpose	Dictionary/Glossary/Unfamiliar Words
Compare and Contrast	Character	Context Clues/Multiple Meanings

Leveled Readers Skills Chart *Continued*

Grade 3

Title	Level*	DRA Level	Genre	Comprehension Strategy
New York's Chinatown	J	18	Expository Nonfiction	Inferring
One Forest, Different Trees	J	18	Realistic Fiction	Important Ideas
Swimming in a School	J	18	Animal Fantasy	Story Structure
Greek Myths	J	18	Nonfiction	Inferring
The Market Adventure	K	20	Realistic Fiction	Story Structure
These Birds Can't Fly!	K	20	Expository Nonfiction	Monitor and Clarify
Iguana Takes a Ride	K	20	Animal Fantasy	Visualize
The Last Minute	K	20	Realistic Fiction	Questioning
Our Garden	K	20	Realistic Fiction	Predict and Set Purpose
Bills and Beaks	L	24	Historical Fiction	Text Structure
In the Fields	L	24	Historical Fiction	Important Ideas
The Thunder and Lightning Men	L	24	Folktale	Inferring
Meet the Stars	L	24	Realistic Fiction	Text Structure
What a Day!	L	24	Realistic Fiction	Story Structure
Desert Life	L	24	Expository Nonfiction	Predict and Set Purpose
A Trip	M	28	Realistic Fiction	Summarize
Measuring the Earth	M	28	Expository Nonfiction	Important Ideas
Fun with Hobbies and Science!	M	28	Expository Nonfiction	Inferring
Great Women in U.S. History	M	28	Biography	Questioning
Buddy Ran Away	M	28	Realistic Fiction	Monitor and Clarify
Cowboy Slim's Dude Ranch	M	28	Realistic Fiction	Visualize
Celebrate Around the World	N	30	Nonfiction	Inferring
Joanie's House Becomes a Home	N	30	Realistic Fiction	Monitor and Clarify
Kapuapua's Magic Shell	N	30	Folktale	Summarize
Bobby's New Apartment	N	30	Realistic Fiction	Background Knowledge
Symbols, Signs, and Songs of America	N	30	Narrative Nonfiction	Text Structure
A Pet Bird	O	34	Expository Nonfiction	Inferring
Lily's Adventure Around the World	O	34	Realistic Fiction	Important Ideas
The Three Bears and Goldilocks	O	34	Animal Fantasy	Story Structure
Sweet Freedom!	O	34	Nonfiction	Inferring

* Suggested Guided Reading Level. Use your knowledge of students' abilities to adjust levels as needed.

"You know the theory behind leveled books: they let you match books with the interest and instructional levels of your students. You can find the right reader for every student with this chart."

Target Comprehension Skill	Additional Comprehension Instruction	Vocabulary
Cause and Effect	Generalize	Context Clues/Antonyms
Graphic Sources	Generalize	Dictionary/Glossary/Unknown Words
Plot and Theme	Realism and Fantasy	Word Structure/Prefixes and Suffixes
Generalize	Compare and Contrast	Homographs/Context Clues
Author's Purpose	Generalize	Word Structure/Prefixes and Suffixes
Main Idea and Details	Compare and Contrast	Context Clues/Synonyms
Compare and Contrast	Draw Conclusions	Context Clues/Unfamiliar Words
Draw Conclusions	Sequence	Compound Words/Word Structure
Author's Purpose	Plot	Context Clues/Antonyms
Main Idea and Details	Setting	Context Clues/Unfamiliar Words
Draw Conclusions	Author's Purpose	Homophones/Context Clues
Character, Setting, and Plot	Main Idea	Unknown Words/Dictionary/Glossary
Graphic Sources	Plot	Unknown Words/Dictionary/Glossary
Generalize	Character	Context Clues/Unfamiliar Words
Cause and Effect	Generalize	Dictionary/Glossary/Unfamiliar Words
Generalize	Author's Purpose	Unfamiliar Words/Context Clues
Graphic Sources	Fact and Opinion	Unknown Words/Dictionary/Glossary
Fact and Opinion	Draw Conclusions	Context Clues/Multiple Meanings
Fact and Opinion	Main Idea and Details	Context Clues/Multiple Meanings
Cause and Effect	Sequence	Unknown Words/Dictionary/Glossary
Compare and Contrast	Main Idea	Context Clues/Synonyms
Main Idea and Details	Compare and Contrast	Homophones/Context Clues
Sequence of Events	Draw Conclusions	Word Structure/Compound Words
Draw Conclusions	Theme	Context Clues/Unfamiliar Words
Author's Purpose	Realism and Fantasy	Context Clues/Homonyms
Main Idea	Fact and Opinion	Word Structure/Prefixes
Cause and Effect	Main Idea	Context Clues/Antonyms
Graphic Sources	Compare and Contrast	Unknown Words/Dictionary/Glossary
Plot and Theme	Character	Word Structure/Prefixes and Suffixes
Generalize	Author's Purpose	Homographs/Context Clues

Leveled Readers Skills Chart *Continued*

Grade 3

Title	Level*	DRA Level	Genre	Comprehension Strategy
Mr. Post's Project	P	38	Realistic Fiction	Background Knowledge
What's Money All About?	P	38	Expository Nonfiction	Summarize
Journey Across the Arctic	P	38	Fiction	Visualize
The Road to New York	P	38	Realistic Fiction	Background Knowledge
With a Twist	P	38	Fantasy	Story Structure
All About Penguins	P	38	Expository Nonfiction	Monitor and Clarify
Puppy Problems	Q	40	Realistic Fiction	Visualize
A Family of Collectors	Q	40	Realistic Fiction	Important Ideas
The Magic of Coyote	Q	40	Realistic Fiction	Predict and Set Purpose
Animals of the Concrete Jungle	Q	40	Expository Nonfiction	Text Structure
Grape Season	Q	40	Realistic Fiction	Important Ideas
Grandmother Spider Steals the Sun	Q	40	Folktale	Inferring
Animal Tracking: Learn More About Animals	Q	40	Expository Nonfiction	Text Structure
Whales and Other Amazing Animals	R	40	Expository Nonfiction	Story Structure
Coral Reefs	R	40	Expository Nonfiction	Predict and Set Purpose
Extraordinary Athletes	R	40	Biography	Summarize
Largest, Fastest, Lightest, Longest	R	40	Expository Nonfiction	Questioning
Gemstones Around the World	R	40	Expository Nonfiction	Inferring
Changing Times	R	40	Expository Nonfiction	Questioning
Toby the Smart Dog	R	40	Humorous Fiction	Monitor and Clarify
His Favorite Sweatshirt	S	40	Realistic Nonfiction	Visualize
Life Overseas	S	40	Expository Nonfiction	Inferring
It's a World of Time Zones	S	40	Expository Nonfiction	Monitor and Clarify
Mixing, Kneading, and Baking: The Baker's Art	S	40	Narrative Nonfiction	Summarize
Let's Go Have Fun!	S	40	Expository Nonfiction	Background Knowledge
The French Connection	S	40	Narrative Nonfiction	Questioning
China's Special Gifts to the World	T	50	Expository Nonfiction	Graphic Organizers
Thomas Hart Benton: Painter of Murals	T	50	Biography	Important Ideas
The Best Field Trip Ever!	T	50	Expository Fiction	Story Structure
Free in the Sea	T	50	Expository Nonfiction	Predict and Set Purpose

* Suggested Guided Reading Level. Use your knowledge of students' abilities to adjust levels as needed.

> "You know the theory behind leveled books: they let you match books with the interest and instructional levels of your students. You can find the right reader for every student with this chart."

Target Comprehension Skill	Additional Comprehension Instruction	Vocabulary
Character and Setting	Theme	Context Clues/Homonyms
Sequence	Draw Conclusions	Word Structure/Compound Words
Sequence	Setting	Dictionary/Glossary/Unfamiliar Words
Compare and Contrast	Character	Context Clues/Multiple Meanings
Author's Purpose	Sequence	Word Structure/Prefixes and Suffixes
Main Idea and Details	Compare and Contrast	Context Clues/Synonyms
Compare and Contrast	Cause and Effect	Context Clues/Unfamiliar Words
Graphic Sources	Realism and Fantasy	Compound Words/Word Structure
Author's Purpose	Sequence	Context Clues/Antonyms
Main Idea and Details	Fact and Opinion	Context Clues/Unfamiliar Words
Draw Conclusions	Main Idea	Homophones/Context Clues
Character, Setting, and Plot	Fact and Opinion	Dictionary/Glossary/Unfamiliar Words
Graphic Sources	Compare and Contrast	Unknown Words/Dictionary/Glossary
Generalize	Author's Purpose	Context Clues/Unfamiliar Words
Cause and Effect	Draw Conclusions	Prefixes and Suffixes/Word Structure
Generalize	Draw Conclusions	Unfamiliar Words/Context Clues
Compare and Contrast	Author's Purpose	Word Structure/Compound Words
Fact and Opinion	Cause and Effect	Context Clues/Multiple Meanings
Fact and Opinion	Generalize	Context Clues/Multiple Meanings
Cause and Effect	Character and Setting	Unknown Words/Dictionary/Glossary
Compare and Contrast	Draw Conclusions	Context Clues/Synonyms
Main Idea and Details	Cause and Effect	Homophones/Context Clues
Sequence	Draw Conclusions	Word Structure/Compound Words
Draw Conclusions	Main Idea	Context Clues/Unfamiliar Words
Author's Purpose	Compare and Contrast	Context Clues/Homonyms
Fact and Opinion	Generalize	Word Structure/Prefixes
Cause and Effect	Generalize	Context Clues/Antonyms
Graphic Sources	Author's Purpose	Unknown Words/Dictionary/Glossary
Plot and Theme	Realism and Fantasy	Word Structure/Prefixes and Suffixes
Generalize	Compare and Contrast	Context Clues/Synonyms

What Good Readers Do

You can use the characteristics and behaviors of good readers to help all your students read better. But what are these characteristics and behaviors? And how can you use them to foster good reading behaviors for all your students? Here are some helpful tips.

Good Readers enjoy reading! They have favorite books, authors, and genres. Good readers often have a preference about where and when they read. They talk about books and recommend their favorites.

Develop this behavior by giving students opportunities to respond in different ways to what they read. Get them talking about what they read, and why they like or dislike it.

This behavior is important because book sharing alerts you to students who are somewhat passive about reading or have limited literacy experiences. Book sharing also helps you when you select books for the class.

Good Readers select books they can read.

Develop this behavior by providing a range of three or four texts appropriate for the student and then letting the student choose.

This behavior is important because students gain control over reading when they can choose from books they can read. This helps them become more independent in the classroom.

Good Readers read independently for longer periods of time.

Develop this behavior by taking note of the level of support students need during guided reading. Use this information to gauge independent reading time accordingly.

This behavior is important because students become better readers when they spend time reading many texts at their independent level.

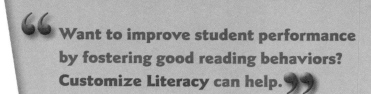

"Want to improve student performance by fostering good reading behaviors? Customize Literacy can help."

Good Readers use text features to help them preview and set purposes.

Develop this behavior by having students use the title and illustrations in fiction texts or the title, contents, headings, and other graphic features in nonfiction texts to make predictions about what they will be reading.

This behavior is important because previewing actually makes reading easier! Looking at features and sampling the text enables readers to predict and set expectations for reading.

Good Readers predict and ask questions before and while they read.

Develop this behavior by asking questions. After reading a passage, ask students what they think will happen next in a fiction text. Have them ask a question they think will be answered in a nonfiction text and read on to see if it is.

This behavior is important because when students predict and ask questions as they read, they are engaged. They have a purpose for reading and a basis for monitoring their comprehension.

Good Readers read meaningful phrases aloud with appropriate expression.

Develop this behavior by giving students lots of opportunities to read orally. As they read, note students' phrasing, intonation, and attention to punctuation and give help as needed.

This behavior is important because reading fluently in longer, meaningful phrases supports comprehension and ease in reading longer, more complex texts.

Good Readers read aloud at an appropriate reading rate with a high percent of accuracy.

Develop this behavior by timing students' oral reading to calculate their reading rates. You can also record students' miscues to determine a percent of accuracy. This will help identify problems.

This behavior is important because when students read fluently texts that are "just right," they find reading more enjoyable. A fluent reader is able to focus more on constructing meaning and is more likely to develop a positive attitude toward reading.

Section 3 Matching Books and Readers

Good Readers use effective strategies and sources of information to figure out unknown words.

CH-
QU-
ST-

Develop this behavior by teaching specific strategies for figuring out unknown words, such as sounding out clusters of letters, using context, reading on, and using references.

This behavior is important because when readers have a variety of strategies to use, they are more able to decode and self-correct quickly. Readers who do these things view themselves as good readers.

Good Readers construct meaning as they read and then share or demonstrate their understanding.

Develop this behavior by having students retell what they read or write a summary of what they read in their own words.

This behavior is important because the ability to retell or write a summary is essential for success in reading. It shows how well a student has constructed meaning.

Good Readers locate and use what is explicitly stated in a text.

Develop this behavior by asking questions that require students to go back into the text to find explicitly stated information.

This behavior is important because the ability to recall, locate, and use specific information stated in a text enables readers to respond to literal questions as well as to support opinions and justify their responses.

Good Readers make connections.

Develop this behavior by asking questions to help students make connections: *What does this remind you of? Have you ever read or experienced anything like this?*

This behavior is important because making connections helps readers understand and appreciate a text. Making connections to self, the world, and other texts supports higher-level thinking.

Good Readers interpret what they read by making inferences.

Develop this behavior by asking questions to help students tell or write about what they think was implied in the text: *Why do you think that happened? What helped you come to that conclusion?*

This behavior is important because the ability to go beyond the literal meaning of a text enables readers to gain a deeper understanding. When students make inferences, they use background knowledge, their personal knowledge, and the text to grasp the meaning of what is implied by the author.

Good Readers determine importance and evaluate what they read.

Develop this behavior by always having students identify what they think is the most important message, event, or information in a text.

This behavior is important because readers must be able to sort out important from interesting information. The ability to establish and/or use criteria and provide support when making judgments is an important critical-thinking skill.

Good Readers support their responses using information from a text and/or their own background knowledge.

Develop this behavior by always asking students to give the reason(s) they identified an event, message, or idea as most important.

This behavior is important because the ability to justify one's response is important for all learners. It enables others to know the basis for a decision and provides an opening for further discussion.

Conversation Starters

Asking Good Questions When students read interesting and thought-provoking books, they want to share! You can encourage students to think critically about what they read. Use questions such as the following to assess comprehension as well as evoke good class/group discussions.

Author's Purpose

- Why did the author write this piece?
- How does figuring out the author's purpose help you decide how to read the text?

Cause and Effect

- Why did these events happen? How might they have been different if the causes had been different?
- Are there several causes that result in a single effect?
- Is there a single cause that has several effects?

Compare and Contrast

- What clue words show the author is comparing and/or contrasting in this article?
- How are the fictional characters and events in this story like and/or different from real people and events you know of?

Draw Conclusions

- Based on what you have read, seen, or experienced, what can you conclude about this event in the selection?
- This story seems to be a fantasy. Why might you conclude this?
- What words help you draw conclusions about the relationship between the characters?

Fact and Opinion

- What clue word or words signal that this is a statement of opinion?
- How could this statement of fact be proved true or false?

Generalize

- What generalization can you make about the story or the characters in it? What examples lead to that generalization?
- What details, facts, and logic does the author use to support this generalization?

Graphic Sources

- How does the author use graphic sources (chart, maps, illustrations, time lines, and so on) to support ideas and opinions?
- This selection has many graphic sources. Which one or ones best help you understand the events or ideas in the selection? Why?

Literary Elements: Character, Setting, Plot, Theme

- Describe the main character at the beginning of the story and at the end of the story. How and why does he or she change?
- How is the setting important to the story? How might the story be different if its time or its place were different?
- What does the main character want at the beginning of the story? How does the main character go about trying to achieve this?
- In a few sentences, what is the plot of the story?
- What is the theme of the story? Use details from the story to support your statement.

Main Idea and Details

- What is the main idea of this paragraph or article? What are some details?
- The author makes this particular statement in the article. What details does the author provide to support that statement?

Sequence

- How is the sequence of events important in the text?
- Is the order of events important in this story? Why or why not?
- Based on what has already happened, what will most likely happen next?

Connecting Science and Social Studies

Get Ready For Middle School

Scott Foresman Reading Street Leveled Readers are perfect for covering, supporting, or enriching science and social studies content. Using these books ensures that all students can access important concepts.

Grade 3 Leveled Readers

Science

Earth and Space Science

Nonfiction Books

- *The Frozen Continent: Antarctica*
- *Fun with Hobbies and Science!*
- *Gemstones Around the World*
- *Grandpa's Rock Kit*
- *How to Measure the Weather*
- *Measuring the Earth*
- *Meet the Stars*
- *Pictures in the Sky*

Fiction Books

- *What a Day!*
- *Journey Across the Arctic*

Life Science

Nonfiction Books

- *A Pet Bird*
- *All About Birds*
- *All About Penguins*
- *Animal Tracking: Learn More About It*
- *Animals of the Concrete Jungle*
- *Coral Reefs*
- *Desert Life*
- *The Field Trip*
- *Free in the Sea*
- *Growing Vegetables*
- *Ice Fishing in the Arctic*
- *Largest, Fastest, Lightest, Longest*
- *Life in the Arctic*
- *Raisins*
- *Rescuing Whales*
- *These Birds Can't Fly!*
- *Whales and Other Amazing Animals*

Life Science

Fiction Books

- *The Best Field Trip Ever!*
- *Bills and Beaks*
- *Buddy Ran Away*
- *Grape Season*
- *The Hunters and the Elk*
- *In the Fields*
- *Swimming in a School*
- *Swimming Like Buck*
- *Toby the Smart Dog*

Grade 3 Leveled Readers

Social Studies

Citizenship

Nonfiction Books
- *Sweet Freedom!*
- *Symbols, Signs, and Songs of America*

Fiction Books
- *Buddy Goes to School*
- *Camping with Aunt Julie*
- *The Opposite Cousins*
- *Our Garden*
- *Puppy Problems*

Culture

Nonfiction Books
- *A Child's Life in Korea*
- *A Walk Around the City*
- *Celebrate Around the World*
- *China's Special Gifts to the World*
- *His Favorite Sweatshirt*
- *Let's Go Have Fun!*
- *Life Overseas*
- *Mixing, Kneading, and Baking*
- *New York's Chinatown*
- *The French Connection*
- *The World of Bread!*

Fiction Books
- *A Tea Party with Obâchan*
- *Bobby's New Apartment*
- *Cowboy Slim's Dude Ranch*
- *E-mail Friends*

Culture

- *Grandmother Spider Steals the Sun*
- *Iguana Takes a Ride*
- *Kapuapua's Magic Shell*
- *The Last Minute*
- *Lily's Adventure Around the World*
- *The Magic of Coyote*
- *One Forest, Different Trees*
- *The Road to New York*
- *The Three Bears and Goldilocks*
- *The Thunder and Lightning Men*

Economics

Nonfiction Books
- *It's a Fair Swap!*
- *It's a World of Time Zones*
- *Let's Make a Trade*
- *What's Money All About?*

Fiction Books
- *A Family of Collectors*
- *Joanie's House Becomes a Home*
- *Let's Surprise Mom*
- *The Market Adventure*
- *The Metal Detective*
- *Mr. Post's Project*
- *The Shopping Trip*

History

Nonfiction Books
- *Across the English Channel*
- *Celebrate Independence Day/Celebra El Día de la Independencia*
- *Changing Times: Women in the Early Twentieth Century*
- *Greek Myths*
- *The Statue of Liberty: A Gift From France*

Fiction Books
- *A Trip*
- *The Winning Point*
- *With a Twist*

More Great Titles

Biography
- *Extraordinary Athletes*
- *Great Women in U. S. History*
- *Thomas Hart Benton: Painter of Murals*

Connecting Science and Social Studies

Need more choices? Look back to Grade 2.

Grade 2 Leveled Readers

Science

Earth and Space Science	Life Science	Physical Science
Nonfiction Books • *All About Astronauts* • *An Astronaut Spacewalk* • *Desert Animals* • *Deserts* • *Hurricanes!* • *Look at Our Galaxy* **Fiction Books** • *Blizzard!* • *Maggie's New Sidekick* • *Rainbow Crow Brings Fire to Earth* • *A Slice of Mud Pie*	**Nonfiction Books** • *Arachnid or Insect?* • *Compost: Recycled Waste* • *Farming Families* • *How a Seed Grows* • *How Can Animals Help?* • *How Do Plants Grow?* • *How to Grow Tomatoes* • *Plants Grow Everywhere* • *A Vet for All Animals* **Fiction Books** • *Annie Makes a Big Change* • *Camping at Crescent Lake* • *Growing Up* • *Too Many Rabbit Holes* • *Where is Fish?*	**Nonfiction Books** • *Many Types of Energy* • *Sink or Float?* **Fiction Books** • *The Hummingbird* • *Our School Science Fair*

Grade 2 Leveled Readers

Social Studies

Citizenship

Nonfiction Books

- *America's Birthday*
- *The Barn Raising*
- *Be Ready for an Emergency*
- *Everyone Can Make a Difference!*
- *Join an Adventure Club!*
- *Keeping Our Community Safe*
- *Protect the Earth*
- *The Rescue Dogs*
- *Service Workers*
- *Special Animal Helpers*
- *Using a Net*
- *What Can You Do?*
- *Working Dogs*

Fiction Books

- *Andrew's Mistake*
- *Camping with Pup*
- *Freda the Signmaker*
- *Hubert and Frankie*
- *Let's Work Together!*
- *Marty's Summer Job*
- *Sally and the Wild Puppy*
- *Stripes and Silver*
- *Too Many Frogs!*
- *Training Peanut*

Culture

Nonfiction Books

- *Celebrations and Family Traditions*
- *Living in Seoul*
- *Showing Good Manners*
- *Special Chinese Birthdays*
- *A World of Birthdays*

Fiction Books

- *Ana Is Shy*
- *The Camping Trip*
- *Country Friends, City Friends*
- *Dotty's Art*
- *The First People to Fly*
- *Glooskap and the First Summer: An Algonquin Tale*
- *Happy New Year!*
- *The International Food Fair*
- *Just Like Grandpa*
- *Living on a Ranch*
- *The New Kid in Bali*
- *Voting Day*

Economics

Nonfiction Books

- *Services and Goods*

Fiction Books

- *Country Mouse and City Mouse*
- *A Quiet Place*
- *Snakeskin Canyon*

History

Nonfiction Books

- *A Few Nifty Inventions*
- *The Hoover Dam*
- *Living in a Democracy*
- *Making Travel Fun*
- *Saint Bernards and Other Working Dogs*
- *Starting a New Life*
- *Women Play Baseball*

Fiction Books

- *At Home in the Wilderness*
- *A Class Play*
- *A Cowboy's Life*
- *Down on the Ranch*
- *Hank's Tortilla Factory*

Government

Nonfiction Books

- *Communicating Then and Now*
- *Let's Send a Letter!*

More Great Titles

Biography

- *American Revolution Heroes*
- *Baseball Heroes Make History*
- *Thomas Adams: Chewing Gum Inventor*
- *Three Great Ballplayers*

Connecting Science and Social Studies

Need more choices? Look ahead to Grade 4.

Grade 4 Leveled Readers

Science

Earth and Space Science

Nonfiction Books

- *Danger: The World Is Getting Hot!*
- *Darkness Into Light*
- *Day for Night*
- *Earth's Closest Neighbor*
- *Let's Explore Antarctica!*
- *Looking For Changes*
- *The Mysteries of Space*
- *One Giant Leap*
- *Orbiting the Sun*
- *Putting a Stop to Wildfires*
- *Severe Weather: Storms*
- *Storm Chasers*
- *Wondrously Wild Weather*

Fiction Books

- *Exploring the Moon*
- *Flash Flood*
- *Life on Mars: The Real Story*
- *Stuart's Moon Suit*
- *Surviving Hurricane Andrew*
- *To the Moon!*

Life Science

Nonfiction Books

- *Birds Take Flight*
- *Come Learn About Dolphins*
- *Dolphins: Mammals of the Sea*
- *Florida Everglades: Its Plants and Animals*
- *The Gray Whale*
- *How Does Echolocation Work?*
- *Migration Relocation*
- *Mini Microbes*
- *Mysterious Monsters*
- *Plants and Animals in Antarctica*
- *Saving Trees Using Science*
- *Sharing Our Planet*
- *What in the World Is That?*

Life Science

Fiction Books

- *The Missing Iguana Mystery*
- *Protecting Wild Animals*
- *The Salamander Stumper*
- *Top Hat Tompkins, the Detective*

Grade 4 Leveled Readers

Social Studies

Citizenship

Nonfiction Books
- *Equality in American Schools*
- *Danger! Children at Work*
- *Dogs on The Job*

Fiction Books
- *Mountain Rescue*
- *The Super Secret Surprise Society*

Culture

Nonfiction Books
- *The Black Ensemble Theater*
- *The Diné*
- *From Spain to America*
- *What It Takes to Stage a Play*

Fiction Books
- *A Book of Their Own*
- *A New Home*
- *Birthday Surprise*
- *Cheers for the Cheetahs*
- *The Grizzly Bear Hotshots*
- *Living with Grandpa Joseph*
- *The Show Must Go On!*
- *Something to Do*
- *To Be a Star*

Economics

Nonfiction Books
- *The Alaskan Pipeline*
- *Ranches in the Southwest*
- *Ranching in the Great American Desert*
- *Two Powerful Rivers*

Fiction Books
- *The Seahaven Squids Host a Pet Wash*

History

Nonfiction Books
- *Becoming a Melting Pot*
- *The Civil Rights Movement*
- *Code Breakers: Uncovering German Messages*
- *Let's Get to Know the Incas*
- *The Long Journey West*
- *Meet the Maya*
- *The Navajo Code Talkers*
- *Pompeii, the Lost City*
- *The Rosetta Stone: The Key to Ancient Writing*
- *The Sauk and Fox Native Americans*
- *Speaking in Code*
- *The Story of Libraries*
- *Thor Heyerdahl's Incredible Raft*
- *We Shall Overcome*
- *The Women's Movement*

History

Fiction Books
- *Bessie Coleman*
- *The Incredible Alexander Graham Bell*

Geography

Nonfiction Books
- *America's National Parks*
- *Maine, Now and Then*
- *A Trip to Capitol Hill*
- *The Wonders of Western Geography*

Fiction Books
- *From Sea to Shining Sea*

Government

Nonfiction Books
- *The Power of the People*
- *The United States Government*

More Great Titles

Biography
- *Amazing Female Athletes*
- *Jim Thorpe*
- *John Muir*
- *The Legacy of César Chávez*
- *Lewis and Clark and the Corps of Discovery*

Planning Teacher Study Groups

Adventurous teachers often have good ideas for lessons. A teacher study group is a great way to share ideas and get feedback on the best way to connect content and students. Working with other teachers can provide you with the support and motivation you need to implement new teaching strategies. A teacher study group offers many opportunities to collaborate, support each other's work, share insights, and get feedback.

Think About It

A weekly or monthly teacher study group can help support you in developing your expertise in the classroom. You and a group of like-minded teachers can form your own study group. What can this group accomplish?

- Read and discuss professional articles by researchers in the field of education.
- Meet to share teaching tips, collaborate on multi-grade lessons, and share resources.
- Develop lessons to try out new teaching strategies. Meet to share experiences and discuss how to further improve your teaching approach.

Let's Meet!

Forming a study group is easy. Just follow these four steps:

1. **Decide on the size of the group.** A small group has the advantage of making each member feel accountable, but make sure that all people can make the same commitment!
2. **Choose teachers to invite to join your group.** Think about who you want to invite. Should they all teach the same grade? Can you invite teachers from other schools? Remember that the more diverse the group, the more it benefits from new perspectives.
3. **Set goals for the group.** In order to succeed, know what you want the group to do. Meet to set goals. Rank goals in order of importance and refer often to the goals to keep the group on track.
4. **Make logistical decisions.** This is often the most difficult. Decide where and when you will meet. Consider an online meeting place where group members can post discussion questions and replies if people are not able to meet.

What Will We Study? Use the goals to help determine what your group will study. Consider what materials are needed to reach your goals, and how long you think is necessary to prepare for each meeting.

How Will It Work? Think about how you structure groups in your classroom. Then use some of the same strategies.

- **Assign a group facilitator.** This person is responsible for guiding the meeting. This person comes prepared with discussion questions and leads the meeting. This could be a rotating responsibility dependent on experience with various topics. This person might be responsible for providing the materials.
- **Assign a recorder.** Have someone take notes during the meeting and record group decisions.
- **Use the jigsaw method.** Not everyone has time to be a facilitator. In this case, divide the text and assign each portion to a different person. Each person is responsible for leading the discussion on that particular part.

Meet Again Make a commitment to meet for a minimum number of times. After that, the group can reevaluate and decide whether or not to continue.

> **"Have some great teaching tips to share? Want to exchange ideas with your colleagues? Build your own professional community of teachers. Customize Literacy gets you started."**

Building Community

Trial Lessons

Use your colleagues experience to help as you think about new ways to connect content and students. Use the following plan to create a mini-lesson. It should last twenty minutes. Get the support of your colleagues as you try something new and reflect on what happened.

Be Creative!

As you develop a plan for a mini-lesson, use these four words to guide planning: *purpose, text, resources,* and *routine.*

- **Purpose:** Decide on a skill or strategy to teach. Define your purpose for teaching the lesson.
- **Text:** Develop a list of the texts you could use. Ask your colleagues for suggestions.
- **Resources:** Make a list of the available resources, and consider how to use those resources most effectively. Consider using the leveled readers listed on pages CL24–CL29 and CL36–CL41 of Customize Literacy.
- **Routine:** Choose an instructional routine to structure your mini-lesson. See the mini-lessons in the Customize Literacy Shop for suggestions.

Try It!

Try out your lesson! Consider audio- or videotaping the lesson for later review. You may wish to invite a colleague to sit in as you teach. Make notes on how the lesson went.

How Did It Go?

Use the self-evaluation checklist on page CL45 as you reflect on your trial lesson. This provides a framework for later discussion.

Discuss, Reflect, Repeat

Solicit feedback from your teacher study group. Explain the lesson and share your reflections. Ask for suggestions on ways to improve the lesson. Take some time to reflect on the feedback. Modify your lesson to reflect what you have learned. Then try teaching the lesson again.

Checklist for Teacher Self-Evaluation

How Well Did I ...	Very Well	Satisfactory	Not Very Well
Plan the lesson?			
Select the appropriate level of text?			
Introduce the lesson and explain its objectives?			
Review previously taught skills?			
Directly explain the new skills being taught?			
Model the new skills?			
Break the material down into small steps?			
Integrate guided practice into the lesson?			
Monitor guided practice for student understanding?			
Provide feedback on independent practice?			
Maintain an appropriate pace?			
Assess student understanding of the material?			
Stress the importance of applying the skill as they read?			
Maintain students' interest?			
Ask questions?			
Handle student questions and responses?			
Respond to the range of abilities?			

Books for Teachers

Students aren't the only ones who need to read to grow. Here is a brief list of books that you may find useful to fill your reading basket and learn new things.

A Professional Bibliography

Afflerbach, P. "Teaching Reading Self-Assessment Strategies." *Comprehension Instruction: Research-Based Best Practices.* The Guilford Press, 2002.

Bear, D. R., M. Invernizzi, S. Templeton, and F. Johnston. *Words Their Way.* Merrill Prentice Hall, 2004.

Beck, I. L. and M. G. McKeown. *Improving Comprehension with Questioning the Author: A Fresh and Expanded View of a Powerful Approach.* Scholastic, 2006.

Beck, I., M. G. McKeown, and L. Kucan. *Bringing Words to Life: Robust Vocabulary Instruction.* The Guilford Press, 2002.

Blachowicz, C. and P. Fisher. "Vocabulary Instruction." *Handbook of Reading Research,* vol. III. Lawrence Erlbaum Associates, 2000.

Blachowicz, C. and D. Ogle. *Reading Comprehension: Strategies for Independent Learners.* The Guilford Press, 2008.

Block, C. C. and M. Pressley "Best Practices in Comprehension Instruction." *Best Practices in Literacy Instruction.* The Guilford Press, 2003.

Daniels, H. *Literature Circles.* 2nd ed. Stenhouse Publishers, 2002.

Dickson, S. V., D. C. Simmons, and E. J. Kame'enui. "Text Organization: Instructional and Curricular Basics and Implications." *What Reading Research Tells Us About Children with Diverse Learning Needs: Bases and Basics.* Lawrence Erlbaum Associates, 1998.

Diller, D. *Making the Most of Small Groups: Differentiation for All.* Stenhouse Publishers, 2007.

Duke, N. and P. D. Pearson. "Effective Practices for Developing Reading Comprehension." *What Research Has to Say About Reading Instruction,* 3rd ed. Newark, DE: International Reading Association, 2002.

Fillmore, L. W. and C. E. Snow. *What Teachers Need to Know About Language.* Office of Educational Research and Improvement, U.S. Department of Education, 2000.

Fountas, I. C. and G. S. Pinnell. *Guiding Readers and Writers Grades 3–6: Teaching Comprehension, Genre, and Content Literacy.* Heinemann, 2001.

Guthrie, J. and E. Anderson. "Engagement in Reading: Processes of Motivated Strategic, Knowledgeable, Social Readers." *Engaged Reading: Processes, Practices, and Policy Implications.* Teachers College Press, 1999.

Harvey, S. and A. Goudvis. *Strategies That Work: Teaching Comprehension to Enhance Understanding.* 2nd ed. Stenhouse Publishers, 2007.

Keene, E. O. and S. Zimmerman. *Mosaic of Thought.* 2nd ed. Heinemann, 2007.

Leu Jr., D. J. "The New Literacies: Research on Reading Instruction with the Internet and Other Digital Technologies." *What Research Has to Say About Reading Instruction,* 3rd ed. International Reading Association, 2002.

McKeown, M. G. and I. L. Beck. "Direct and Rich Vocabulary Instruction." *Vocabulary Instruction: Research to Practice.* The Guilford Press, 2004.

McTighe, J. and K. O'Conner. "Seven Practices for Effective Learning." *Educational Leadership,* vol. 63, no. 3 (November 2005).

Nagy, W. E. *Teaching Vocabulary to Improve Reading Comprehension.* International Reading Association, 1998.

National Reading Panel. *Teaching Children to Read.* National Institute of Child Health and Human Development, 1999.

Ogle, D. and C. Blachowicz. "Beyond Literature Circles: Helping Students Comprehend Information Texts." *Comprehension Instruction: Research-Based Practices.* The Guilford Press, 2001.

Pressley, M. *Reading Instruction That Works: The Case for Balanced Teaching,* 3rd ed. The Guilford Press, 2005.

Stahl, S. A. "What Do We Know About Fluency?" *The Voice of Evidence in Reading Research.* Paul H. Brookes, 2004.

Taylor, B. M., P. D. Pearson, D. S. Peterson, and M. C. Rodriguez. "The CIERA School Change Framework: An Evidence-Based Approach to Professional Development and School Reading Improvement." *Reading Research Quarterly,* vol. 40, no. 1 (January/February/March 2005).

Valencia, S. W. and M. Y. Lipson. "Thematic Instruction: A Quest for Challenging Ideas and Meaningful Learning." *Literature-Based Instruction: Reshaping the Curriculum.* Christopher-Gordon Publishers, 1998.

WEEK 1 Oral Vocabulary for

Man Who Invented Basketball

Let's Learn Amazing Words

Amazing Words Oral Vocabulary Routine

DAY 1

idle

1. **Introduce** *Idle* means doing nothing, not busy, or not working.
2. **Demonstrate** Jack was *idle* when he should have been doing his homework.
3. **Apply** Have students describe times when they may have been *idle.*

mock

1. **Introduce** *Mock* means to laugh at or to make fun of.
2. **Demonstrate** It is unkind to *mock* another person.
3. **Apply** Discuss other meanings of *mock* with students.

potential

1. **Introduce** *Potential* means something possible.
2. **Demonstrate** Annie has the *potential* to be a great singer.
3. **Apply** Have students give other examples of *potential*.

DAY 2

audition

1. **Introduce** An *audition* is a hearing to test a person's performance.
2. **Demonstrate** Alex *auditioned* for the school play.
3. **Apply** Have students describe times when a person may need to *audition*.

DAY 3

result

1. **Introduce** A *result* is something that happens because of something else.
2. **Demonstrate** The *result* of Tony's fall from the ladder was a broken leg.
3. **Apply** Have students discuss *results* they've experienced and the causes that brought the *results.*

DAY 4

rise

1. **Introduce** We *rise* when we get out of bed in the morning or when we get up from lying, sitting, or kneeling.
2. **Demonstrate** Patty usually *rises* from bed at seven in the morning.
3. **Apply** Work with students to find synonyms for *rise.*

verge

1. **Introduce** When something is on the *verge,* it means it's about to happen.
2. **Demonstrate** Josh spent too much money and is on the *verge* of being broke.
3. **Apply** Have students think of other situations where they can use the phrase "on the *verge* of" to describe a situation.

WEEK 2 Oral Vocabulary for Let's Learn Amazing Words

Hottest, Coldest, Highest, Deepest

Amazing Words Oral Vocabulary Routine

DAY 1

lumber

1. **Introduce** *Lumber* is wood that has been cut into boards or planks to use in building.
2. **Demonstrate** The frames of many homes are built with *lumber.*
3. **Apply** Discuss with students the different uses of lumber.

competitor

1. **Introduce** A *competitor* is someone who tries hard to win or get something wanted by others.
2. **Demonstrate** There are many *competitors* in a basketball tournament.
3. **Apply** Have students discuss situations in which they compete and who the competitors are.

plunge

1. **Introduce** *Plunge* can mean to throw something (or yourself) into something with force or to fall or move downward suddenly.
2. **Demonstrate** The day was hot, and Lily *plunged* into the cool lake water.
3. **Apply** Have students use *plunge* in sentences for each meaning of the word.

DAY 2

champ

1. **Introduce** *Champ* is short for *champion.* A *champion* is someone who wins first place in a contest.
2. **Demonstrate** Our team will beat all the others, so we are the *champs!* Ray is a *champ* at chess.
3. **Apply** Have students name someone that is a *champ* at something.

DAY 3

acrobat

1. **Introduce** An *acrobat* is a performer who can do stunts like somersaults or handstands to entertain others.
2. **Demonstrate** Marcie is a good *acrobat*. She can do cartwheels and somersaults.
3. **Apply** Have students describe other stunts *acrobats* may perform.

DAY 4

ranger

1. **Introduce** A *ranger* is someone whose job is taking care of a national park or forest.
2. **Demonstrate** We met the *ranger* at the entrance to the campgrounds. The forest *ranger* explained how to prevent forest fires.
3. **Apply** Have students name another job a *ranger* might do at a national park.

Let's Learn Amazing Words

Rocks in His Head

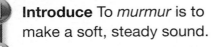

Amazing Words Oral Vocabulary Routine

DAY 1

murmur

1. **Introduce** To *murmur* is to make a soft, steady sound.
2. **Demonstrate** The mother *murmured* soothing words to the crying baby.
3. **Apply** The breeze *murmured* in the trees.

project

1. **Introduce** A *project* is a task that needs time and effort to complete.
2. **Demonstrate** I grew sunflower plants as part of a science project. Writing my family's history is a huge *project.*
3. **Apply** Ask students to describe a *project* they have recently completed.

leftover

1. **Introduce** Something that remains unused or uneaten is a *leftover.*
2. **Demonstrate** After Thanksgiving dinner, we made sandwiches from the *leftover* turkey. We took some of the *leftover* cookies and pie home from the party.
3. **Apply** Ask students to complete the sentence: We had *leftover* ________ after the ________.

DAY 3

descendant

1. **Introduce** A *descendant* is a person, animal, or plant related to one that lived in the past.
2. **Demonstrate** You are your grandfather's *descendant*. Joseph is a *descendant* of a couple who lived in this town a hundred years ago.
3. **Apply** Draw a simple family tree diagram on the chalkboard, using the terms *child, father, mother, grandfather,* and *grandmother.* Use it to explain the word *descendant.*

DAY 4

forge

1. **Introduce** *Forge* means to move ahead slowly but steadily.
2. **Demonstrate** One runner *forged* ahead of the others and won the race. Jake had mountains of homework to do, but he *forged* ahead and finished early.
3. **Apply** Discuss with students instances in which *forge* could be used to describe the situation.

NIT 4

Acknowledgments

Acknowledgments

Text

Grateful acknowledgment is made to the following for copyrighted material:

28: From *The Man Who Invented Basketball: James Naismith and His Amazing Game* by Edwin Brit Wyckoff. Copyright © 2008 by Enslow Publishers, Inc. From Enslow Publishers, Inc.

46: From *My Turn At Bat: The Story of My Life* by Ted Williams and John Underwood. Copyright © 1969, 1988 by Ted Williams and John Underwood. From Simon & Schuster, Inc.

49: "Ted Williams Timeline" from www.sportingnews.com/archives/williams/timeline.html. From *The Sporting News*.

51: "Baseball Hall of Fame Information and Baseball Card Statistics for Ted Williams" from http://www.baseballhalloffame.org/hofers/detail.jsp?playerId=124341. From National Baseball Hall of Fame (NBHOF)

62: From *Hottest, Coldest, Highest, Deepest* by Steve Jenkins. Copyright © 1998 by Steve Jenkins. Reprinted by permission of Houghton Mifflin Company. All rights reserved.

94: *Rocks in His Head* by Carol Otis Hurst. Text copyright © 2001 by Carol Otis Hurst. Illustrations © 2001 by James Stevenson. Used by permission of HarperCollins Publishers.

124: *America's Champion Swimmer: Gertrude Ederle*, text copyright © 2000 by David A. Adler, illustrations copyright © 2000 by Terry Widener, reprinted by permission of Harcourt, Inc.

126: From "Women in History: Wilma Rudolph biography." Lakewood Public Library. http://www.lkwdpl.org/wihohio/rudo-wil.htm. Reprinted by permission of Women in History, Lakewood, Ohio.

158: From *Fly, Eagle, Fly!* by Christopher Gregorowski, illustrated by Niki Daly. Text copyright © 2000 by Christopher Gregorowski, illustrations copyright © 2000 by Niki Daly. Reprinted with permission of Margaret K. McElderry Books, an imprint of Simon & Schuster Children's Publishing Division. All rights reserved.

176: *Purple Coyote* by Cornette, illustrated by Rochette. Copyright © 1997 by L'Ecole des Loisirs, Paris. First American edition 1999—Originally published in France by Pastel, 1997. English translation copyright © 1999 by Random House, Inc. Published by arrangement with Random House Children's Books, a division of Random House, Inc., New York, New York. All rights reserved.

185: "Written at the Po-Shan Monastery" by Hsin Ch'i-chi, translated by Irving Yucheng Lo, from *Sunflower Splendor: Three Thousand Years of Chinese Poetry* by Wu-Chi Liu (Author), Irving Yucheng Lo (Editor), published by Indiana University Press, 1990. Reprinted by permission of Indiana University Press.

186: "Me with apologies to Joyce Kilmer ("Trees")" from *Because I Could Not Stop My Bike* by Karen Jo Shapiro. Text copyright © 2003 Karen Jo Shapiro. Illustrations copyright © 2003 by Matt Faulkner. Used with permission by Charlesbridge Publishing, Inc. All rights reserved.

187: "By Myself" from *Honey, I Love* by Eloise Greenfield. Text copyright © 1978 by Eloise Greenfield. Used by permission of HarperCollins Publishers.

198: *Suki's Kimono*, written by Chieri Uegaki and illustrated by Stéphane Jorisch is used with the permission of Kids Can Press Ltd., Toronto. Text © 2003 Chieri Uegaki. Illustrations © 2003 Stéphane Jorisch.

230: From *I Love Saturdays y domingos* by Alma Flor Ada. Text copyright © 2002 by Alma Flor Ada. Reprinted with permission of Atheneum Books for Young Readers, an Imprint of Simon & Schuster Children's Publishing Division. All rights reserved.

250: From *Scott Foresman Social Studies Communities*, 2003. Copyright © 2003 Pearson Education, Inc. Reprinted by permission of Pearson Education, Inc.

262: Reprinted with permission of the National Geographic Society from *Good-Bye, 382 Shin Dang Dong* by Frances Park and Ginger Park. Copyright © 2002 Frances Park and Ginger Park. Illustrations © 2002 Yangsook Choi.

284: The Lois Lenski Covey Foundation, Inc., for "Sing a Song of People' from *The Life I Live* by Lois Lenski. Copyright © 1965 by The Lois Lenski Covey Foundation, Inc. Reprinted by Permission of Licensor. Copyright © Renewed 1993, no. RE 615-252.

296: From *Jalapeño Bagels* by Natasha Wing. Text copyright © 1996 by Natasha Wing. Reprinted with permission of Atheneum Books For Young Readers, an imprint of Simon &

552

Schuster Children's Publishing Division. All rights reserved.

314: Excerpts from *Viva Mexico! The Foods* by George Ancona (Benchmark Books). Copyright © 2002 by George Ancona. Reprinted with permission of Marshall Cavendish Corporation.

328: From *Me and Uncle Romie: A Story Inspired by the Life and Art of Romare Bearden* by Claire Hartfield, illustrated by Jerome Lagarrigue, copyright © 2002 by Claire Hartfield, text. Copyright © 2002 by Jerome Lagarrigue, illustrations. Used by permission of Dial Books for Young Readers, A Division of Penguin Young Readers Group, A Member of Penguin Group (USA) Inc., 345 Hudson Street, New York, NY 10014. All rights reserved.

360: "My Friend in School" from *Deshawn Days*. Text copyright © 2001 by Tony Medina. Permission arranged with Lee & Low Books, Inc., New York, NY 10016.

362: "Lunch Survey," from *Swimming Upstream: Middle Grade Poems* by Kristine O'Connell George. Text copyright © 2002 by Kristine O'Connell George. Reprinted by permission of Clarion Books, an imprint of Houghton Mifflin Company. All rights reserved.

363: "Saying Yes" by Diana Chang is reprinted by permission of the author.

374: *The Story of the Statue of Liberty* by Betsy C. Maestro, illustrations by Giulio Maestro. Text copyright © 1986 by Betsy Maestro. Illustrations copyright © 1986 by Giulio Maestro. Used by permission of HarperCollins Publishers.

390: From *Scott Foresman Social Studies:* Communities, 2003. Copyright © 2003 Pearson Education, Inc. Reprinted by permission of Pearson Education, Inc.

402: From *Happy Birthday Mr. Kang* by Susan L. Roth. Copyright © 2001 Susan L. Roth. Reprinted with permission of the National Geographic Society.

468: *Two Bad Ants* by Chris Van Allsburg. Copyright © 1988 by Chris Van Allsburg. Reprinted by permission of Houghton Mifflin Company. All rights reserved.

502: "Atlantis: The Legend of a Lost City" by Christina Balit. Atlantis copyright © 1999 by Frances Lincoln Limited. Text and illustrations copyright © 1999 by Christina Balit.

532: "Words Free as Confetti" from *Confetti: Poems for Children*. Text copyright © 1996 by Pat Mora. Permission arranged with Lee and Low Books, Inc., New York, NY.

535: "I Watched an Eagle Soar" from *Dancing Teepees: Poems of the North American Indian Youth* by Virginia Driving Hawk Sneve. Copyright © 1989 by Virginia Driving Hawk Sneve. Reprinted from *Dancing Teepees* by permission of Holiday House, Inc.

Every effort has been made to locate the copyright owner of material reproduced in this component. Omissions brought to our attention will be corrected in subsequent editions.

Illustrations

Cover: Leo Timmers
EI•1–EI•15 Mike Lester
80–82 James Madsen
113 Larry Jones
230–244 Claudia Degliuomini
284 Remy Simard
296–309 Antonio Castro
332–344 Jerome Lagarrigue
362 Laurie Keller
532 Stephen Daigle
W•2–W•15 Nomar Perez.

Photographs

Every effort has been made to secure permission and provide appropriate credit for photographic material. The publisher deeply regrets any omission and pledges to correct errors called to its attention in subsequent editions.

Unless otherwise acknowledged, all photographs are the property of Pearson Education, Inc.

Photo locators denoted as follows: Top (T), Center (C), Bottom (B), Left (L), Right (R), Background (Bkgd)

18 (C) ©Joel Sartore/Getty Images, (B) ©Rebecca Emery/Getty Images
20 (BR) ©Hans Neleman/zefa/Corbis, (BL) ©Yellow Dog Productions/Getty Images
26 (B) ©Roy Dabner/epa/Corbis, (C) ©Dennis Macdonald/PhotoLibrary Group, Ltd., (TL) Jupiter Images

553

Acknowledgments

27 (C) ©Stephen Wilkes/The Image Bank/Getty Images
30 (TC) ©Shironina Lidiya Alexandrovna/Shutterstock
46 (CL) ©Bettmann/Corbis, (B) ©Stockxpert
47 (TR) ©Bettmann/Corbis, (BR) Jupiter Images
48 (CC) Corbis
49 (BR) ©William McKellar /Jupiter Images
50 (TL) ©AP Photo, (CR) ©DK Images
54 (CR) ©Frans Lanting/Minden Pictures, (B) ©Robert Harding Picture Library Ltd/Alamy Images
55 (CC) ©Bill Draker/Rolfnp/Alamy Images
60 (C) Alamy Images, (T) ©Greg Vaughn/Alamy Images, (B) ©Nik Keevil/Alamy
86 (B,) ©Ariel Skelley/Corbis
87 (CR) ©Don Smetzer/PhotoEdit
92 (B) ©Markos Dolopikos/Alamy, (C) ©Paul Doyle/Alamy Images, (T) ©SW Productions/Getty Images
110 (T, BC) ©ZZ/Alamy, (B) Jupiter Images
111 (BR) ©ZZ/Alamy
112 (CR) ©ZZ/Alamy
113 (TR, BR, BL) ©ZZ/Alamy
116 (B) ©Pete Saloutos/Corbis
117 (BR) ©Bequest of Mrs. Benjamin Ogle Tayloe/Collection of The Corcoran Gallery of Art/Corbis, (TR) GRIN/NASA
122 (T) ©Annie Griffiths Belt/Getty Images, (C) ©David Madison/Jupiter Images, (B) ©Peter Adams/Corbis
144 (BC) ©George Silk/Time Life Pictures/Getty Images, (TR) ©Underwood & Underwood/Corbis
146 (CR) ©George Silk/Time Life Pictures/Getty Images
147 (CL) ©George Silk/Time Life Pictures/Getty Images, (CR) Bettmann/Corbis
150 (BL) ©David Shale/Nature Picture Library, (B) ©Joe McDonald/Corbis
151 (BR) ©Rick & Nora Bowers/Alamy Images
156 (C) ©Yann Arthus-Bertrand/Corbis, (B) ©Anne-Marie Weber/Getty Images, (T) ©Mireille Vautier/Alamy Images
188 (C) ©Jeremy Horner/Getty Images
190 (BC) ©Brian A. Vikander/Corbis, (B) ©Kayle M. Deioma/PhotoEdit
191 (BR) ©B&Y Photography/Alamy Images
196 (B) ©Goolia Photography/Alamy, (T) Philip Duff, (C) PhotoLibrary
216 (BC) ©Christie's Images/Peter Harholdt/Corbis, (BR) Art Resource, NY
217 (CR) ©Lynn Goldsmith/Corbis, (TR) Art Resource, NY
218 (TR) ©Historical Picture Archive/Corbis, (CR) ©Werner Forman/Corbis, (BR) Getty Images
219 (BR) ©Pavlovsky Jacques/Corbis, (TR) Corbis, (CR) Getty Images
222 (C) ©D. Hurst/Alamy Images, (BL) ©David-Young-Wolff/Alamy Images, (BC) ©Kevin Dodge/Corbis
228 (B) ©Demin Tony/PhotoLibrary Group, Ltd., (C) ©Richard Cooke/Alamy Images, (T) ©Stefan Sollfors/Alamy Images
250 (TR) Getty Images, (BR) ©Morton Beebe/Corbis
251 (BR) ©Steve Vidler/SuperStock, (TR) Getty Images
254 (BL) ©Tibor Bogner/Corbis, (B) ©Vince Streano/Corbis
255 (BR) ©Robert W. Ginn/PhotoEdit
260 (C) Corbis, (T) ©Elmari Joubert/Alamy, (B) ©Stephen Oliver/Alamy Images
288 (BC, B) Jupiter Images
289 (BR) ©foodfolio/Alamy Images
294 (B) Corbis, (T) ©Massimo Borchi/Corbis, (C) ©Vario Images GmbH & Co. KG/Alamy Images
314 (CR) George Ancona
315 (BC) George Ancona
316 (BR, B) George Ancona
317 (TR) George Ancona
320 (B) ©George Doyle/Getty Images, (TL) ©Rhoda Sidney/PhotoEdit
321 (BR) Getty Images
326 (C) ©Randy Faris/Corbis, (B) ©travelstock44/Alamy
354 (BR) ©David Zimmerman/Corbis, (TR) ©Terry W. Eggers/Corbis
355 (BR) AP/Wide World Photos
356 (BR) ©Duomo/Corbis
357 (CR) ©David Thomas/PictureArts/Corbis, (BR) ©Royalty-Free/Corbis
364 (C) ©Kevin Dodge/Corbis
366 ©Randy Faris/Corbis
372 (C) ©David Noble/Alamy Images, (B)

554

©Kai Wiechmann/Getty Images, (T) ©Taurus Taurus/PhotoLibrary Group, Ltd.
390 (CC) ©Jim Erickson/Erickson Productions, (TR) Corbis
391 (CR) ©Robert Holmes/Corbis
394 ©Canopy Photography/Veer, Inc.
400 (C) ©Foodcollection/Alamy, (T) Getty Images, (B) ©VStock/Alamy
424 (C) ©Joseph Sohm/ChromoSohm Inc./Corbis, (BC) Jupiter Images
425 (CR) ©Sandra Baker/Alamy Images
426 (BC) The Granger Collection, NY
427 (TR) ©Bill Howe/Alamy Images
430 ©David Young-Wolff/PhotoEdit, (BL) Getty Images
431 (B) ©David Young-Wolff/PhotoEdit, (BR) Jupiter Images
435 (TR) ©JM Labat/Photo Researchers, Inc.
436 (C) ©Don B. Stevenson/Alamy Images, (T) ©Ed Bock/Corbis, (BC) Getty Images, (B) ©Jim West/Alamy Images
438 (C) Meg Saligman
440 (CC) ©Ben Valenzuela
441 (B) ©Hector Ponce/Rich Puchalsky
442 (T) ©Hector Ponce/Rich Puchalsky
444 (C) *Reach High and You Will Go Far* ©2000 by Joshua Sarantitis. All Rights Reserved. Sponsored by the Philadelphia Mural Arts Program. Photograph ©2000 by Joshua Sarantitis. All rights reserved.
445 (CC) ©Paul Botello
447 (B) Getty Images
448 (B) ©Gianni Tortoli/Photo Researchers, Inc., (B) David Botello
449 (T) ©Gianni Tortoli/Photo Researchers, Inc., (BR) ©The British Museum/©DK Images, (BC) Courtesy of the U.S. Capitol Historical Society
450 (TL, B) Meg Saligman
460 (B) ©Purestock/Getty Images
461 (BR) ©Blend Images/Jupiter Images
466 (B) Alamy, (C) ©Matt Cardy/Alamy Images, (T) ©PhotosIndia LLC/Alamy
494 (B) ©David R, Frazier Photolibrary, Inc./Alamy Images
495 (TR) AP Images, (CC) Jupiter Images
499 (TR) ©Richard T. Nowitz/Corbis
500 (T) ©Franz Waldhaeusl/Alamy, (B) ©American Images Inc/Getty Images, (C) ©Pictor/Alamy
524 (T) Jupiter Images
525 (BR) Jupiter Images
527 (T) Jupiter Images
528 (CR) ©Stockxpert
529 (CR) ©Matt Carr /Jupiter Images.

555

Teacher's Edition

Text

KWL Strategy: The KWL Interactive Reading Strategy was developed and is used by permission of Donna Ogle, National-Louis University, Skokie, Illinois, co-author of *Reading Today and Tomorrow,* Holt, Rinehart & Winston Publishers, 1988. (See also the *Reading Teacher,* February 1986, pp. 564–570.)

Understanding by Design quotes: Wiggins, G. & McTighe, J. (2005). *Understanding by Design.* Alexandria, VA: Association for Supervision and Curriculum Development.

Illustrations

Cover Leo Timmers

Running Head Linda Bronson

Photographs

Every effort has been made to secure permission and provide appropriate credit for photographic material. The publisher deeply regrets any omission and pledges to correct errors called to its attention in subsequent editions.

Unless otherwise acknowledged, all photographs are the property of Pearson Education, Inc.

UNIT 4

Teacher Notes

Teacher Notes

UNIT 4

Teacher Notes

Teacher Notes

UNIT 4

Teacher Notes

Teacher Resources

Looking for Teacher Resources and other important information?

In the First Stop on Reading Street

- Dear Third Grade Teacher
- Research into Practice on Reading Street
- Guide to Reading Street
- Assessment on Reading Street
- Customize Writing on Reading Street
- Differentiate Instruction on Reading Street
- ELL on Reading Street
- Customize Literacy on Reading Street
- Digital Products on Reading Street
- Teacher Resources for Grade 3
- Index

Teacher Resources

Looking for Teacher Resources and other important information?

In the First Stop on Reading Street